Multinational Enterprise and Public Policy

NEW HORIZONS IN INTERNATIONAL BUSINESS

General Editor: Peter J. Buckley
Professor of Managerial Economics, Management Centre, University of Bradford

This important new series is aimed at the frontiers of international business research. Each volume tackles key problem areas in international political economy. The study of international business is important not least because it gives researchers the opportunity to innovate in theory, technique, empirical investigation and interpretation. The area is fruitful for interdisciplinary and comparative research. The series will rapidly become established as a lively forum for presenting new ideas in international business studies.

Published titles

New Directions in International Business
Research Priorities for the 1990s
Edited by Peter J. Buckley

Europe and the Multinationals
Issues and Responses for the 1990s
Edited by Stephen Young and James Hamill

Multinational Enterprises in the World Economy
Essays in Honour of John Dunning
Edited by Peter J. Buckley and Mark Casson

Multinational Investment in Modern Europe
Strategic Interaction in the Integrated Community
Edited by John Cantwell

The Growth and Evolution of Multinational Companies
Patterns of Geographical and Industrial Diversification
R.D. Pearce

Multinational Enterprise and Public Policy
A Study of the Industrial Countries
A.E. Safarian

Multinational Enterprise and Public Policy

A Study of the Industrial Countries

A.E. Safarian
University of Toronto

Edward Elgar

Published by
Edward Elgar Publishing Limited
Gower House
Croft Road
Aldershot
Hants GU11 3HR
England

Edward Elgar Publishing Company
Old Post Road
Brookfield
Vermont 05036
USA

A CIP catalogue record for this book is available from the British Library

Library of Congress Cataloging-in-Publication Data
Safarian, A. E.
Multinational enterprise and public policy: a study of the industrial countries/A.E. Safarian.
p. cm. — (New horizons in international business)
Includes bibliographical references and index.
1. International business enterprises—Government policy. 2. Corporations, Foreign—Government policy. 3. Investments, Foreign—Government policy. 4. International economic relations.
I. Title. II. Series.
HD2755.5.S233 1992
338.8'8—dc20 92–15820
CIP

ISBN 1 85278 714 7

Printed and Bound in Great Britain by
Hartnolls Limited; Bodmin, Cornwall.

Contents

Tables

Preface

During the 1960s and 1970s many governments developed a range of national policies to regulate multinational enterprises. This study examines the origins, operation and effectiveness of these policies. It also considers how these policies changed in form, although not always in substance, during the 1980s.

The study of multinational enterprises has been a growth industry for some time. This study brings a particular approach to the subject, concentrating on policy in the industrial countries, a topic which has received far less attention than that given elsewhere. In considering the determinants of government policy I have gone well beyond wealth maximization, and also taken into account the reactions of the firms. The major contribution of the book is to consider policy development in each of 15 countries. Some of these country studies are detailed enough to stand on their own. They are also drawn together and analysed on a cross-country basis in Part III.

My interest in public policy on multinational enterprises is long-standing, reflecting mainly the experience of Canada. Research for the present study began during an academic leave in 1981–2. The emphasis is on restricted sectors, review on entry or subsequent merger, discrimination after establishment, incentives to investment, and policy on outward investment. Other topics also receive attention in specific country studies.

I have had a great deal of help in preparing this study. The Social Sciences and Humanities Research Council of Canada made a major grant at the beginning of the project, which I could not have undertaken without the Council's generous support. In the later years of the project I was fortunate to have support from the Donner Canadian Foundation through its grant to the International Economics Program of the Department of Economics and the Institute for Policy Analysis at the University of Toronto. The Faculty of Law and Economics of the University of Nice provided a congenial and stimulating base for my European research at the beginning of the study. The Centre for International Studies and the Faculty of Management of the University of Toronto provided similar support in the last several years of the study.

I owe a very substantial debt to the many officers of companies, government officials, academics and others who gave so freely of their time and thought in the interviews and in subsequent communications. I regret that, for reasons of confidentiality, I am not able to acknowledge individually at least some of those in the first two groups who were exceptionally helpful. I do wish to acknowledge the expert help I received from members of Canadian embassies in a number of countries in arranging for some of the interviews. It is difficult to name all of the many others who helped, but a few should not go unnoted. Richard E. Caves, John H. Dunning and Raymond Vernon have, in different but important ways, stimulated my research and teaching in this area over many years. The present book is no exception. For various kinds of help over a period of time I am grateful also to C. Fred Bergsten, Gilles Y. Bertin, Jean Cartelier, Michel Delapierre, Lorraine Eden, André Farhi, Sperry Lea, Richard Lipsey, A. Micaleff, William Nicol, Alan M. Rugman, Leonard Waverman, Thomas A. Wilson and Roger Wolff.

I have also been very fortunate in the ability and enthusiasm of those who worked with me at different stages of this project. Yvonne Giordano made a valuable contribution during the critical first year of the project. In succeeding years I was ably assisted by Sheila Block, Tony Cestra, Maria Gallego, Catherine Metcalf, Nicolas Schmitt and Alison Taylor. Walid Hejazi was indispensable in the final years of the study. I was lucky also to have some expert secretarial help, notably from Lorelle Triolo, Noreen Anderson and Alexandra Grygier. I am grateful to Julie Leppard for her skilful and patient editorial work.

While acknowledging the help of all of the above, I must bear the final responsibility for what appears in this study.

A.E. Safarian
February, 1992

Acknowledgements

Several of the chapters draw on my previously published research. A brief survey of some of the material published in Part 2 appeared in my book, *Governments and Multinationals: Policies in the Developed Countries*, which was published in 1983 by the British–North American Committee, Washington, DC. The sections in Chapter 6 on Australia and Canada draw on *FIRA and FIRB: Canadian and Australian Policies on Foreign Direct Investment*, published in 1985 for the Ontario Economic Council, Toronto, and distributed by the University of Toronto Press. The section on Canada also draws on my article, 'Government Control of Foreign Business Investment', in J. Whalley (ed.), *Domestic Policies in the International Economic Environment*, published by the University of Toronto Press and prepared for The Royal Commission on the Economic Union and Development Prospects for Canada. Chapter 12 is an expanded version of 'Firm and Government Strategies', which appeared in B. Bürgenmeier and J. L. Mucchielli (eds), *Multinationals and Europe 1992: Strategies for the Future*, published in 1991 by Routledge, London and New York. I am grateful to these publishers for permission to draw on these materials.

I am also grateful for permission to reproduce material from the publications noted below. Australia, Foreign Investment Review Board, *Reports* for various years from 1977–8 to 1987–8, for material produced in Tables 6.1, 6.2, and 6.5–6.8 inclusive; Australia, Department of the Treasury, *Overseas Investment in Australia*, Treasury Economic Paper No. 1, 1972, for the quotation on p. 111; Australia, Department of the Treasury, *Australia's Foreign Investment Policy: A Guide for Investors*, 1982, for the material on p. 90; and Australia, Bureau of Investment, *Foreign Investment, 1981–2*, published in 1983, for Table 6.1. Commonwealth of Australia copyright reproduced by permission of the Australian Government Publishing Service.

John H. Dunning (ed.), *Multinational Enterprises, Economic Structure and International Competitiveness*, copyrighted in 1985 by I.R.M. Geneva. Tables 6.24, 7.1, 7.2, 7.9 and 7.12 draw on this study, and are reproduced by permission of John Wiley and Sons Limited.

John Dunning and John Cantwell, *IRM Directory of Statistics of International Investment and Production*, published in 1987 by Macmillan Publishers Ltd (Journals Division), copyright the Institute for Research and

Information on Multinationals, for material appearing in Tables 6.22, 7.9, 8.1, 8.4, 9.1 and 9.5.

Dan Fenno Henderson, *Foreign Enterprise in Japan: Laws and Policies*, published in 1973 by the University of North Carolina Press, Chapel Hill and in 1975 by Charles E. Tuttle Company, Tokyo, for the two articles of the Foreign Investment Law cited on p. 243, Table 7.7, and the quotation on p. 262.

Neil Hood and Stephen Young, *The Economics of Multinational Enterprise*, published in 1979 by the Longman Group Limited, London, for the material in Table 9.10, based in turn on US Tariff Commission, *Implications of Multinational Firms for World Trade and Investment and for U.S. Trade and Labor*, Report to the Committee on Finance, US Senate, Washington, DC: Government Printing Office, 1983, and R.G. Hawkins, 'Job Displacement and the Multinational Firm: a Methodological Review', Washington: Centre for Multinational Studies, Occasional Paper 3.

International Monetary Fund, Washington, DC, *Balance of Payments Statistics. Yearbooks Part I* (various years), for materials shown in Tables 6.24, 7.3, 8.4, 9.1 and 9.5; and Margaret Kelly *et al.*, 'Issues and Developments in International Trade Policy', Occasional Paper 63, published by the International Monetary Fund in 1988, for material appearing in Table 12.2.

Japan, Ministry of International Trade and Industry, 'Foreign Investment in Japan', *Japan Reporting*, published in April, 1980, reflecting the personal views of various government officials, for the quotation on pp. 256–8.

Organization for Economic Cooperation and Development, Paris, *National Treatment for Foreign-Controlled Enterprises*, published in 1985, on which Table 11.2 is based; *Controls and Impediments Affecting Inward Direct Investment in OECD Member Countries*, published in 1987, which is the basis for Table 11.3; *Recent Trends in International Direct Investment*, published in 1987, which is a source for Tables 7.3, 7.5, 7.6, 8.5, 9.1, 9.2, 9.4, 9.6 and 9.8; and *Industrial Policy in OECD Countries, Annual Review 1989*, published in 1989, for Table 3.3.

The Economist Newspaper Ltd., for permission to reprint Tables 7.8, copyright 1985, and 11.5, copyright 1989.

Technovation for permission to reproduce Table 3.7, from an article by J. Hagedoorn, 'Organizational Modes of Inter-Firm Co-operation and Technology Transfer', published in 1990 (10,1) by Elsevier Advanced Technology.

United Nations, Centre on Transnational Corporations, New York, *Transnational Corporations in World Development: The Third Survey*, published in 1983, and *Transnational Corporations in World Development: Trends and Prospects*, published in 1988. Table 3.5 is based on these publications, which draw in turn on data from the OECD and the International Labour Organization, and Table 9.9 is based on the 1988 publication.

Abbreviations

BNOC	British National Oil Corporation
CFIUS	Committee on Foreign Investment in the United States
DATAR	Délégation de l'Aménagement du Territoire et à l'Action Régionale (Commission on Land-Use Planning and Regional Development)
EC	European Community
EFTA	European Free Trade Association
FDI	Foreign Direct Investment
FIRA	Foreign Investment Review Agency (Canada)
FIRB	Foreign Investment Review Board (Australia)
FTC	Fair Trade Commission
GATT	General Agreement on Tariffs and Trade
ICL	International Computers Limited (United Kingdom)
IDA	Industrial Development Authority (Ireland)
ILT	Investing, Licensing and Trading Conditions Abroad (*Business International*)
IMF	International Monetary Fund
MNE	Multinational Enterprise
MITI	Ministry of International Trade and Industry (Japan)
NEP	National Energy Program (Canada)
OECD	Organization for Economic Cooperation and Development
OIC	Overseas Investment Commission (New Zealand)
OPEC	Organization of Petroleum Exporting Countries

PART I

Governments and Multinationals

1. Introduction

In 1971 Raymond Vernon's study, *Sovereignty at Bay*, examined the concerns of national governments regarding the effects of multinational enterprises. How would such enterprises affect national sovereignty and national economic strength, whether directly or through pressures on them from foreign governments? By 1981 articles had appeared with titles such as 'Multinationals at Bay', reflecting the many policies designed to control such firms. During the following decade most governments loosened or ended these policies in an effort to live with multinational firms, their own and those of other countries. National governments have not by any means given up their attempts to steer the activities of such firms, however, using policies whose welfare outcomes are as controversial as earlier more regulatory forms.

This study examines in detail the origins, nature and effectiveness of the policies adopted up to about the mid-1980s in 15 developed countries. It goes on to consider the nature and probable consequences of the so-called liberalization of policies thereafter. It relies in part on a set of interviews with officials of regulatory agencies and of multinational firms, as well as others acquainted with the policies in each country. These interviews were conducted in the early 1980s. They have been supplemented since with follow-ups in some countries as well as correspondence and public sources of information.

Most governments in the developed countries have followed a dual policy toward multinational enterprises. Such governments are likely to welcome and even to subsidize investments by such enterprises. They are also likely to ban them from some sectors of production, regulate their establishment or performance, and discriminate against them after establishment. The emphasis given to attracting rather than regulating such firms can vary even over short periods, partly because of changes in economic circumstances and in governments. Some countries also attempt, much more weakly, to regulate outward investment by their own firms.

This ambivalence in policy is partly the result of a long and complex debate about the political and economic effects of multinational enterprises (henceforth MNEs). Many writers have argued that there are economic benefits accruing to a country from the presence of MNEs, given a number of advantages they have in organizing, marketing, financing and producing goods and services. These advantages are tempered, it is also argued, by two sets of problems. First, in some sectors of activity the presence of such firms is believed to impose constraints on domestic policy making: it may cost more to implement some policies, or it may not be possible to exercise some types of policies. Second, in other cases it is the economic performance of foreign-owned firms which is of concern to governments: in such cases, government intervention is designed to increase the size or the distribution of the net national gains which are possible from MNEs.

There are also writers, especially among those who have considered the less developed countries, who would put these reservations more strongly. They would argue that substantial dependence on MNEs over long periods can weaken growth processes and create an unacceptable diminution of national independence.

Much of this criticism arises from the very nature of an MNE. It may be defined most simply as an enterprise which owns and controls operating firms in more than one country.[1] It is often argued that some minimum number of countries, or some minimum percentage of parent company assets abroad, is necessary for an MNE, but the particular number or percentage is arbitrary. What control implies is that, whatever the degree of centralization of decision making (and it can vary a good deal), there is some set of objectives towards which the officers of the subsidiaries and parent are working. This does not imply that the welfare of subsidiary companies is simply neglected – one would have to assume either persistent ignorance or a stubborn commitment to non-rationality by both sets of officers for that to occur. What worries governments of host countries is that the impact of subsidiaries on the MNEs' operations abroad are also taken into account. They are concerned, therefore, that inadequate attention will be given to the interests of the subsidiary and (what is not necessarily the same thing) of the host country as well. Thus, it is often argued, the outcome could differ from what would be the case for a national firm or a nationally-controlled MNE. Interestingly, governments of the home countries where MNE headquarters are located have also voiced concerns about the domestic impact of such firms' operations abroad.

Concern about the effects of MNEs on the economic and political welfare of the nation is only one of the possible explanations of policy in this area. Most analysts have long since agreed that there are other possible explanations for public policies regarding MNEs. Politicians must be elected at regular intervals in all of the countries covered in this study; hence they must promise or do all those things necessary to gain election. There are a host of public and private groups which are affected by MNEs, some favourably and some unfavourably, and which continually press their particular interests in the policy-making process. And each of us has a set of values, going well beyond economic concerns, that frequently colour our views on policy. MNEs have had important general and particular effects for decades. Like the large oligopolistic corporation within a country, they set the tone for much of a society's activities. It is hardly likely that all of these influences on policy will vanish when policies are made, with everyone concentrating instead on the effect of MNEs on the entire country or on the international economy.

One of the objectives of this study is to attempt to analyse the determinants of national policies towards MNEs and of the changes in such policies. Given the influences on the policy-making process just noted, it is also important to ask just how effective the policies are in practice – that is, how far they attain, or are intended to attain, their specified objectives. This leads naturally to the question of how policies can be made more effective, in the sense of attaining desired objectives while limiting any negative effects in other respects.

Governments are not free, of course, to set any policies they wish. There are two major sets of constraints. One is the policy environment each government faces; for example, what is the size of domestic market it has to offer firms and how large are the domestic problems of implementing policy? The other constraint is the strategies of the MNEs. They may, at the limit, leave countries where they are not welcome, or at least stop expanding there, but they have other means at their disposal long before such extreme choices, ranging from lobbying host-country governments to asking for the intervention of the government of the parent company. Some types of MNEs, moreover, are less susceptible to pressures from host countries than are others.

Governments, in turn, usually deal with more than one MNE in any industry, although they bring different skills and interest to the negotiations. Governments can also encourage techniques of production, marketing, finance and organization in forms other than foreign-controlled subsidiaries. They can import such techniques from abroad through licences or joint ventures, for example, and the techniques are also sometimes embodied in imports of goods. They can also develop local firms. Just how effectively each of these can substitute for MNEs is an important policy question, which will be explored in Chapter 3, where the investment decisions of MNEs are examined. In that chapter the major changes in MNE investment patterns by countries will also be noted. One of the more extreme changes was for the United States, which accounted for 66 per cent of outward direct investment flows for the developed market economies in 1961–70 and only 19 per cent in 1981–6, while the US share of inflows rose from 15 to 55 per cent over the same period.

In considering the strategies of governments towards MNEs, much of the outcome will depend on the type of policy instrument which is used. Some governments appear to be able to secure relatively painlessly what either eludes others or is achieved only at considerable cost. One question is why governments at times avoid using apparently superior instruments, including some which have already been used abroad.

The policy instruments which have been used in practice can be classified in various ways, all directed to influencing the ownership or the performance of the subsidiary. First, some sectors have been closed to MNEs, either wholly or with a requirement for a given percentage of domestic ownership in the firm. This is often accompanied by attempts to get access to foreign techniques in other ways, such as by licensing agreements or joint ventures. Second, a number of countries regulate the right of establishment by new investment or acquisition, often extending to acquisitions by established MNEs. Third, established MNEs can be treated differently from locally-owned firms, simply because they are foreign-controlled. Government purchases might be directed to locally-owned firms, for example. Fourth, a variety of fiscal and other incentives can be used to attract MNE investments, often coupled with requirements that their economic performance on foreign trade and other variables meet specified levels. Fifth, governments may prefer to use policy instruments, such as taxes or competition policies or research policies, directed to all firms wherever owned, but designed partly with an eye to the ways in which MNEs may be influenced by them. Finally, a government may attempt to reach MNEs by bilateral approaches, such as treaties with other countries, or through supporting multilateral instruments designed to influence MNE behaviour.

The focus of this study is those national policies which distinguish between enterprises controlled domestically and those controlled abroad, rather than policy applied to all enterprises without regard to country of control. In practice it is sometimes difficult to maintain this distinction. For example, some policies which are apparently neutral with regard to ownership are intended to have an impact largely on foreign-owned enterprises, or are administered in ways which do so, and some industries or firms are largely or wholly foreign-owned. The word 'policy' is used in its widest sense to cover legislation, administrative processes and policy positions. In some countries the last two categories are more important than the first.

The evidence used in this study consists mainly of the experience of 15 developed countries. While these are among the higher-income countries, and while they follow a broadly market orientation for a significant part of production, they differ in many ways. Some are more home countries than host countries for MNEs, for example. There is significant variation in the size of the economies, in their degree of internationalization and in the role of government. Some details are given in Tables 1.1 to 1.3. All of this suggests the need for some caution in making comparisons between these countries. They may respond differently to the same problem or opportunity, for example, because of historic circumstances which blocked other policy choices. Such questions, which pervade all such comparative analyses, are perhaps reduced when similar types of policies are compared – for example, the design of procedures to review new investments and subsequent acquisitions. The problems in such an approach are also modified by the fact that each country's experience is examined separately in this study before an attempt is made to classify and analyse policies and related variables on a comparative basis. Nevertheless our varying familiarity with the economic experience and institutions of the countries involved necessarily leads to some unevenness in their treatment.

The focus in the country studies is on why policies were introduced, how they were designed to operate, and what the experience with them has been in practice. As a complement to these country studies we have attempted some overall analysis of two issues. First, how far can we explain the kinds of policies chosen, particularly the degree of restriction of foreign investment, by the characteristics of the countries and governments involved? Second, how effective are these policies if judged by their impact on investment? The key assumption in this case is that most governments included in this study are interested in preserving the flow of investment while denying access to certain sectors and regulating its effects in some respects.

In the communist countries, until recently, MNEs had to adopt other forms for the transfer of their knowledge. Government policies have been more restrictive in many developing countries which are mainly host countries to MNEs. We make no judgement on the appropriateness of policies in countries not included in this study. Most of the policy studies on MNEs are for such developing countries, but it is also of interest to consider the experience of the developed countries, since the great majority of the stocks and flows of MNE investments go to, or are located in, such countries, and since the range of policies they pursue has been quite wide.

This study is in three parts. Part I reviews some of the theoretical material. It begins in Chapter 2 with a closer look at explanations of what governments are trying to do when they make policy on MNEs or, indeed, on other matters. In Chapter 3 the constraints on policy are considered in terms of MNE strategies on investment. Chapter 4 considers the opportunities for and constraints on country policies more broadly. In Part II we review the country evidence, beginning in Chapter 5 with some methodological issues, then going on in succeeding chapters to examine the experience of various groups of countries. Part III summarizes what we have learned about the origins, nature and effectiveness of the policy instruments, both from the country

Table 1.1 Selected economic characteristics of countries surveyed, 1980

	Population (millions)[1]	*GDP bill$US*[2]	*GDP per capita US$*[2]	*Gov't outlays as % of GDP*[3]	*Exports as % of GDP*[3]	*Imports as % of GDP*[3]	*Primary commod as % of exports*[4]	*Stock of outward as % of Inward direct investment*[5]
Australia	14.7	149.0	10 137	32.1	17.1	17.8	68.0	17.6 A
Belgium	9.8	118.0	11 986	50.8	62.2	64.9	20.4[6]	62.4 B
Canada	24.1	263.2	10 934	40.5	28.5	26.6	45.2	41.9 A
Germany	61.6	813.7	13 216	48.3	26.5	27.1	11.1	103.6 A
France	53.9	664.6	12 335	46.4	22.2	24.0	23.8	111.2 B
Ireland	3.4	18.9	5 656	50.9	49.6	63.0	41.6	N/A
Italy	56.4	455.9	8 081	46.1	25.1	28.0	14.2	78.4 B
Japan	116.8	1 059.3	9 069	32.6	13.7	14.6	2.8	599.8 A
Netherlands	14.2	169.4	11 970	57.5	52.5	53.0	46.6	200.2 A
New Zealand	3.1	22.4	7 123	N/A	30.4	31.6	76.2	18.8 (1983)B
Norway	4.1	57.7	14 121	50.7	47.3	41.2	59.3	40.8 (1981)B
Sweden	8.3	124.2	14 938	61.6	29.8	31.7	18.6	396.5 B
Switzerland	6.4	101.7	15 920	29.3	36.7	40.3	5.1	455.3 D
United Kingdom	56.3	536.1	9 591	45.1	27.7	25.4	22.6	129.8 A
United States	227.8	2 688.5	11 804	33.7	10.2	10.7	29.8	259.3 A

Notes:
1. OECD, *Labour Force Statistics*, 1987.
2. OECD, *National Accounts: 1980 Prices and Exchange Rates*.
3. OECD, *Historical Statistics*.
4. OECD, *International Trade Statistics Yearbook(s)*.
5. (A) OECD (1987a).
   (B) Dunning and Cantwell (1987).
   (C) IMF, *Balance of Payments Statistics, Yearbooks*, Part I.
   (D) United Nations (1983). Average for 1975 and 1978.
6. Includes Luxembourg.

Table 1.2 Selected economic characteristics of countries surveyed, average 1975–80

	Population (millions)[1]	GDP bill$US[2]	GDP per capita US$[2]	Gov't outlays as % of GDP[3]	Exports as % of GDP[3]	Imports as % of GDP[3]	Primary commod as % of exports[4]	Stock of outward as % of inward direct investment[5]	
Australia	14.3	132.8	9 706	32.1	15.7	16.0	72.0	14.9	A
Belgium	9.8	109.5	11 175	47.3	56.9	57.9	18.2[6]	59.4	B
Canada	23.4	243.4	10 377	39.9	25.1	24.9	40.7	33.4	A
Germany	61.5	756.2	12 343	48.1	25.5	23.9	10.1	79.2	A,B
France	53.3	613.6	11 651	44.8	21.1	21.3	22.4	119.0	B
Ireland	3.3	17.0	5 250	46.4	47.9	58.4	45.7	N/A	
Italy	56.0	361.1	7 436	44.3	25.6	25.4	15.1	59.5	B
Japan	114.3	922.7	8 242	29.8	12.7	12.3	2.8	501.7	A
Netherlands	13.9	161.1	11 584	54.4	49.2	48.0	44.7	185.4	A
New Zealand	3.1	23.7	7 195	N/A	28.1	30.3	78.3	N/A	
Norway	4.0	51.8	12 773	51.5	42.5	45.7	40.9	55.0	B,C
Sweden	8.3	118.9	14 392	56.6	28.6	29.5	18.4	378.3	B
Switzerland	6.4	95.6	15 050	29.8	34.8	33.6	5.3	455.3	D
United Kingdom	56.2	521.6	9 297	44.4	28.2	28.0	17.3	141.1	A
United States	221.1	2 454.9	11 426	32.9	8.7	9.2	34.5	386.2	A

Notes:
See Table 1.1.

Table 1.3 Selected economic characteristics of countries surveyed, 1987

	Population (millions)[1]	*GDP bill$US*[2]	*GDPPC US$*[2]	*Gov't outlays as % of GDP*[3]	*Exports as % of GDP*[3]	*Imports as % of GDP*[3]	*Primary commod as % of GDP*[4]	*Stock of outward as % of inward direct investment*[7]	
Australia	16.3	183.3	11 282	35.9	16.4	17.7	75.2	37.4	
Belgium	9.8	127.0	12 867	52.5	69.7	66.5	19.6	66.9	(L&B)
Canada	25.7	325.1	12 674	45.5	26.5	25.3	36.3	50.3	
Germany	61.2	889.1	14 703	46.9	28.8	23.7	10.0	185.4	
France	55.6	745.9	13 409	51.3	20.8	20.6	23.9	187.5	
Ireland	3.5	22.3	6 286	53.4	59.0	52.4	30.0	N/A	
Italy	57.3	525.9	9 173	50.7	19.6	18.9	13.7	105.1	
Japan	122.1	1 370.6	11 226	33.4	10.5	7.3	1.8	853.9	
Netherlands	14.7	184.2	12 557	60.7	52.5	49.4	46.9	169.8	(1986)
New Zealand	3.3	25.9	7 820	—	28.1	28.2	71.3	18.8	(1983)
Norway	4.7	71.5	17 098	51.1	35.5	37.7	62.4	45.6	
Sweden	8.4	140.5	16 727	59.0	32.5	30.7	17.6	475.0	(1983)
Switzerland	6.6	114.4	17 276	30.1	35.5	34.7	5.0	535.9	(1984)
United Kingdom	56.9	628.7	11 044	43.2	25.9	27.0	30.6	153.1	
United States	243.9	3 301.3	13 535	36.9	7.9	11.1	24.4	115.6	

Notes:
See Table 1.1
7. From IMF, *Balance of Payments Statistics*, vol. 41 (1990) part 1, except for New Zealand, Norway, Sweden and Switzerland, which are from Dunning and Cantwell, 1987. The IMF data on stocks for Norway appear to be mispecified.
L&B = Luxembourg and Belgium.

studies and from some statistical measures, as evident particularly in experience up to about the mid-1980s. In Chapter 12 the new policies towards foreign direct investment are considered, policies which involve liberalization towards inward investment but also more selective regulation and an attempt to develop domestic MNEs. Some brief conclusions are contained in Chapter 13.

NOTE

1. Some writers prefer the term 'transnational corporations' in that it implies that the MNE keeps the identity of the home country. The term is particularly prevalent in the literature on MNEs in developing countries. By 'control' we mean effective voting control as defined in various countries's official data. It is well recognized that managerial control comes in ways other than by exercising voting powers. 'Parent firm' refers to the operations in the home country of the MNE, especially the headquarter's operations, while subsidiary (or unincorporated branch) refers to operations in the host country. 'Foreign direct investment' (FDI) refers to the financing of the international production involved. Correctly measured, both the flows and the stocks of FDI should include earnings retained by the subsidiary. We use the word 'techniques' for the skills involved in each of production, finance, marketing and organization, not just the first of these.

2. What Governments are Trying to Do

The governments of the industrial countries in this study all accept MNE investments and techniques and frequently attempt to attract them by using various policies. The sole general exception was Japan which, until the mid-1970s, favoured licensing of foreign techniques and Japanese-controlled joint ventures. These governments, in all cases, also attempt to influence the economic performance of MNEs, some going so far as to use general review mechanisms. All also attempt to reduce or prohibit foreign ownership in selected economic sectors.

A degree of ambivalence in policy – a love–hate relationship with the MNE – is thus the norm, though this ambivalence is far more acute in some countries. The first question which arises is just why these policies exist. What is it that governments are trying to achieve in accepting and even attracting MNEs while also regulating them and limiting entry in some sectors? This question dominates much of the analysis in this study. To attempt to answer it one must go well beyond what economic analysis usually considers, namely the maximizing (or, since constraints exist, optimizing) of individual, national or international economic welfare. As Caves (1982, xi) has remarked, 'I know no subject in economic policy in which the issues that excite public discussion bear so little relation to the welfare issues identified by normative economics.'

The literature on social science classifies the determinants of public policy in many ways. Lowi (1972), for example, argues that the most significant political fact about government is that it can apply coercion legitimately. He then proceeds to classify various types of policy according to the directness of that coercion, on the one hand, and the size of the unit to which it is applied, on the other. Dye (1972) uses a seven-fold classification of models derived from studies in political science. Policy is seen as the outcome of the nature of government institutions; as an equilibrium between group interests; as the reflection of the preferences of an elite; as an attempt to estimate and to maximize the net value of a community's preferences; as incremental variations on past policies; as a set of games between interdependent decision makers; and as a system where demands, on the one hand, and the acceptance of certain rules, on the other, lead to authoritative decisions. These categories clearly overlap and, as Dye notes, several could apply to any given situation.

Before indicating a classification for the present study we need to be explicit about those who are affected by MNE activities and by government responses to them. Standard economic theory has pointed, with some exceptions, to foreign trade and investment as *potentially* increasing the economic welfare of each nation as well as the amount of world production. The actual realization of such gains, and their precise distribution between countries, depends on assumptions about competition and other variables. The outcomes are not seen, generally, as zero-sum situations where some countries suffer absolute losses and others gain. Some of the literature takes exception to this view of the effects of trade and investment, as will become evident in Parts II and III. Some of the exceptions are on economic grounds – protection for new industries, improving the terms of trade, shifting excess profits between countries and avoiding so-called dependency effects. For present purposes what needs to be emphasized is that, in practice, all national governments will pay particular attention to national gains, with their support for international approaches conditional on ensuring or increasing such national gains. The situation becomes far more complex when one allows for non-economic objectives and for the ways in which different groups are affected by MNEs and by policies towards them. Various public and private groups in the home, host and third countries should be taken into account as well as the activities of MNE headquarters and their national subsidiaries.

With this in mind, we will utilize a four-fold classification of public decision making as a first approximation. The first two categories reflect the potential effects of MNEs on national economic and political welfare as seen in the analytical literature on such firms. These categories correspond to theories of public policy emphasizing attempts to increase a community's net economic wealth or independence. The other categories reflect the economic interests of private groups, on the one hand, and the electoral and ideological play of ideas in democratic states, on the other. While in the first two cases the objectives are to increase national income or independence, in the second two cases they are to redistribute income or power. The objectives may not correspond to the outcomes, however; the latter depend on constraints on policy, to be considered in the next two chapters.

These four objectives lend themselves in practice to many subdivisions, but two in each case seem particularly appropriate to the discussion of policy on MNEs. These subdivisions are noted in Table 2.1 and are discussed briefly below. They will be examined more fully at the relevant points of this study.

NATIONAL ECONOMIC WELFARE AND THE MNE

A major economic concern of host governments is whether the gains which are possible from multinational production are actually realized in practice. Such governments are particularly interested in whether these gains accrue to the firm, to home countries, or to third countries rather than to the host country. Another major economic concern is whether continued reliance on MNEs can lead to a structure of industry that is more favourable to home than to host countries. It is convenient to discuss these under the familiar headings of macroeconomic and microeconomic issues, although there is considerable overlap.

The most important macroeconomic objectives are efficient growth with an equity constraint. By the former we mean growth in income while avoiding inflationary, environmental and other distortions. Even when governments regard MNEs as engines of economic growth, they are concerned to capture as much of that growth as possible. They are particularly unlikely to leave the outcome of growth processes to large oligopolistic firms which are controlled abroad and which make some key decisions globally with a view to the effects on their international operations. In most countries the goal of efficient growth is subject to some kind of an equity constraint, at least to the extent that personal and regional income distribution should not worsen in the process and probably also that attempts should be made to reduce income inequality.

Table 2.1 Determinants of public policy on the MNE: possible objectives

National economic welfare: efficiency with an equity constraint (including rent capture)
Microeconomic effects
Macroeconomic effects
National political independence
Effects on policy-making capability
Extraterritorial extension of foreign law and policy
Distribution of income within the state
Group or sectoral interests
Regional effects
Distribution of power within the state
Electoral and bureaucratic processes
Ideas of state and firm: media processes

One particular aspect of the distribution of gains is seen in national efforts to capture more of the rents or quasi-rents which can arise especially (although not exclusively) in the exploitation of natural resources.[1] There are a number of economic reasons why governments are involved in natural resource investment decisions, including those made by MNEs (Mikesell, 1971b, ch. 2). The potential impact on a region or on other sectors can be substantial, depending on the linkages which can be developed with those sectors or regions. Governments are often expected to supply infrastructure, financing or other support. They may differ with firms on the acceptable rate of production and of environmental regulation. But much of the policy response to MNEs in natural resources has reflected an attempt to retain nationally a larger share of the rents involved. The policies of the natural resource-based countries in this study have strongly reflected these concerns and objectives.

Microeconomic objectives can be discussed in similar terms but some particular concerns have been expressed where there exists a large MNE presence. The theory of FDI, as noted further in the next chapter, is built around the idea of interdependence between oligopolistic firms. Many MNEs are large firms in industries with some barriers to entry. As a result, the possible anti-competitive effects have been a focus for some of the concerns about such firms. A partly related concern is just how far the advantages which an MNE may have are actually translated into increases in productivity in the host country's industrial structure. Much attention has focused on the effects on exports, imports and the technical capacities of subsidiary firms, all of which are important to the processes of economic adjustment and growth. The dependency literature, found in studies of Latin American experience in particular, has gained currency in some of the developed countries in this study. The argument is that a high degree of foreign ownership over a long period can lead to heavy reliance on imported techniques, either directly or through imports of goods which embody such techniques. The result may be that a country will not develop the capacity to produce many of these items. The concern is that this will dampen innovation and entrepreneurship generally. Even those host-country governments which do not accept such a dependency view of inward FDI place some emphasis on trying to capture more of the research of the MNE. In part this is a recognition of the tendency for such research to concentrate in larger or research-intensive countries when it is decentralized from the home countries of MNEs.

It is not only host countries which voice concerns about the economic activities of MNEs. Home-country governments and interest groups share some of these concerns. It has been argued, for example, that FDI abroad can have negative effects on the home country's income, employment and balance of payments in overall terms. Some have argued that the effects are distributional, in that MNE investment abroad creates a demand for high-skill jobs in the home country but reduces the demand for its lower-skilled workers. The nature and evidence on these arguments will be considered more fully in the country studies, especially that on the United States. Such claims have led home countries to turn increasingly to policies designed to retain more of the net gains from MNE activities.

The attempts by home and host countries to capture nationally more of the gains possible from MNE activities pose many problems. Nationally it is often difficult to sort out the evidence and to design effective policies. At the international level the policies may be welcomed where they are part of a bilateral or multilateral effort. Most policies are national, however, and sometimes reduce world income. They may lead to retaliation from other countries which believe their interests are affected negatively. Despite such problems, national governments are obviously going to address issues affecting national economic welfare. One interesting point is just how far such national economic welfare objectives, rather than others noted below, have influenced the development and the design of policies in this area.

POLITICAL INDEPENDENCE AND THE MNE

Governments and private interest groups are often critical of MNEs because of their concerns about national independence.[2] An obvious example is the defence sector, where countries typically restrict foreign MNE activities in some way. These concerns take many other forms, but two in particular are frequently noted. The first is the fear that the capacity to make or implement public policy is lessened by a large MNE presence or certain kinds of MNE activity. An example would be intervention by foreign governments or by foreign MNEs in political activity, going well beyond the lobbying in which all governments and many firms engage. Such would be the case in a formal protest against a policy regarding MNEs, presented to a host-country government by a home-country government, the implication being that some action will be taken by the latter if the response is not satisfactory. Among the countries in this study there is a more widespread concern that some types of MNEs are less responsive than are the more nationally-oriented firms to the government's regulatory, fiscal and monetary policies. The effect is to make some policy instruments inoperable, and also to require a higher investment in 'persuasion costs' by government for attaining any given objective (a phrase developed by Steuer *et al.*, 1973, ch. 8). Such issues are not restricted to host-country governments. Some home-country governments, such as the United States, have been affected at times by the negative political consequences of activities abroad by their MNEs.

The second major concern is the extension of law or policy abroad through the medium of MNEs. An example would be the attempt in the early 1980s by the US government to restrict the exports, through subsidiaries and licensees located abroad, of gas pipeline technology to the USSR. This type of issue can be regarded as a quarrel between sovereign governments with MNEs and independent licensees caught in the middle. Nevertheless host countries are likely to resent the diminution of their sovereignty over the subsidiaries at least as much as the home country laments its inability to prevent MNEs from circumventing its policies.

These issues clearly spill over into a broader set of concerns regarding the social impact of MNE activities. In cultures that are widely different, MNEs can lead to a rate of social change, and at times to a degree of homogenization of tastes and technology, which transform a society. The literature on some developing countries has explored these issues, with perhaps more emphasis on the negative than the positive aspects of such changes. With some exceptions these issues have not been emphasized in this study. For the countries covered here the social changes involved are frequently transmitted by trade, travel, communications and other means even in the absence of a significant MNE presence. Even where the MNE does not have an important overall presence in a country, it may still bring substantial social changes to some regions. Moreover it will be emphasized in what follows that governments do slow the rate of change for some types of industry, and attempt in particular to resist penetration by MNEs in sectors considered closely identified with national cultures or public policy.

There is a school of thought which would resist the view that net losses of independence are likely with a significant MNE presence. This view would argue that net national gains are possible in economic terms. To the extent that expanded economic wealth increases the scope for exercising political choices, the net effect of MNEs in terms of independence is believed to be positive. Much depends here on what one encompasses in the idea of national independence and how one weights the variables. For example, some would consider a repeated intrusion of foreign law and policy through the medium of MNEs so unacceptable that any tradeoff with economic gains would be rejected.

MNEs AND THE DISTRIBUTION OF INCOME WITHIN THE STATE

Normative analysis of the effects of MNEs concentrates on the implications for international and national welfare. In the latter case, policy is assumed to be directed to maintaining or increasing one or more of three objectives:

efficient resource allocation and economic growth, national independence, and equity in regional and personal income distribution.

It has been suggested above that national policy may be directed to redistributing income internationally; that is, to capturing for the nation more of the net social gains possible through MNE investments and operations. Such national policies may or may not reduce gains globally or in particular countries elsewhere.[3] The assumptions, however, are that the policies are intended to raise national income and succeed in doing so.

How valid are these assumptions? There is a significant literature in the social sciences, including that in economics, which argues that both the intention and the effect of public policy decision making are to redistribute income within a country. This literature also suggests that redistribution is not necessarily from higher to lower income groups. Policies on MNEs are subject to many of the same influences as policies in general. It is useful, therefore, to outline briefly some of the general literature on public decision making as a prelude to analysis of decision making about MNEs.

The earlier economic literature on regulation and fiscal policy was normative and often optimistic in terms of policy outcomes. Regulation was regarded largely as a response to market failure, reflecting such problems as national monopoly, common property resources and imperfect market information.[4] Public goods can be considered as a response to the most extreme form of market failure. Government fiscal policy was thought of in terms of the effects on overall social welfare and various theorems were developed on the maximization of social welfare.

Concepts such as these were challenged early by economists. Arrow (1951) argued that no rule could be formulated which would meet all of the conditions needed to derive a social welfare function.[5] Downs (1957) argued that the allocation of public expenditures so as to equalize votes at the margins, rather than to maximize social benefits, meant that the social rates of return to different public activities would vary widely. Buchanan and Tullock (1962) came to similar conclusions, noting especially that, short of a unanimity rule or identical preferences, both the coercion of some groups and the organization of pressure groups were inevitable. Olson (1965) analysed the organization of such pressure groups. He noted particularly the circumstances in which the costs of organization were exceeded by the expected benefits, so that the groups involved were more likely than others to organize and to press for policies in their favour.

A particularly strong position was taken by Stigler (1971) who argued that regulation was generally demanded by an industry and designed and operated for its benefit. Such regulation was supplied in the process of vote seeking and resource seeking by political parties, in situations where strong preferences and the ability to organize paid off. In examining the various types of policy support available to industry, he noted that cash will be preferred to control over entry to the industry or over its output only where the number of new entrants is likely to be small: where this is not the case, the available funds will have to be shared with such new entrants. Krueger (1974) put a similar point in a wider context by arguing that regulation creates rents and competition for these rents can lead to substantial waste of economic resources. In particular she argued that the welfare losses involved in import licenses are considerably larger than those imposed by tariffs, since the former require that resources be devoted to competing for the licences. Two such estimates of resource costs which she noted give significant portions of national income for the countries involved.

This listing is intended to be suggestive only.[6] We have emphasized contributions by economists to the behavioural analysis of public policy, but political scientists, organizational theorists and other social scientists have written along similar lines, the political scientists over a much longer period. For our purposes we can note that such studies emphasize two points. The first is the extent to which the self-interest of various groups dominates public decision making. Self-interest can be defined narrowly or broadly, depending on the circumstances. Two aspects stand out in the literature on collective decision making: economic self-interest and the seeking of power (including electoral success) or influence.[7] A third can be added which is particularly relevant to attitudes towards MNEs, though not only there: value systems. In particular a great deal of the argument over MNEs appears to reflect attitudes towards the appropriate role of the state and of the large oligopolistic firm. While these three determinants of public decision making can and do exist together, we can delineate economic self-interest as particularly useful for analysing private group interests while the pursuit of power is particularly useful in analysing electoral and bureaucratic aspects. The third determinant, value systems, runs through all of these groups and the interplay with other groups such as the media.

The second point emphasized in this literature is the extent to which apparently non-rational outcomes exist in public decision making. 'Rational' outcomes refer to consistent maximizing or, at least, optimizing of objectives, given the constraints involved. Such explanations involve clear specification of objectives, analysis of alternative ways to achieve these and of the consequences involved, and choosing the most preferred outcome. This approach involves a great deal of information, adequate time in which to assess the process and some agreement on the basic tradeoffs when objectives conflict. None of these may be available in some types of public decision making situations, notably, though not exclusively, in crisis situations. In such cases the outcomes may be dominated by the organizational pressures of bureaucracies and the interaction of key players in the process (Allison, 1971, 28–

35, 245–51). The decisions may be made in a context of ambiguous and changing alternatives, with a desire to avoid serious failure rather than to achieve maximizing of particular objectives (Anderson, 1983).

The influence of private group interests has certainly not been absent from the analysis of the MNE and of responses to it. Breton (1964) and Johnson (1965) developed models which analysed policies of economic nationalism in terms of the effects on group interests. Vernon (1971) devoted a chapter to the impact of the MNE on different groups within host countries, and some of the social science literature more generally can be interpreted in this way. Yet one must agree with Caves (1982, 290) that economists have been slow to apply behavioural models to analysis of policy on the MNE.

We propose to deal with such private group interests in terms of an attempt to affect income distribution, thought of in two ways. The first is income distribution between private interest groups classified as labour-capital- or resource-intensive, with further detail where necessary. One variant of this is the effect on sectors of industry, since it is the lobbying by and protection of particular industrial groups, involving different intensities of the factors of production, which is often the focus of policy. The second way to look at income distribution is on a regional basis. The differences in views on MNEs are likely to be particularly strong when regions of a country are at very different levels of development. In periods of slow economic growth, governments may attempt to attract investment to every region of a country. Nevertheless those who represent the lower-income regions, including central government departments concentrating on such regions, are likely to argue most strongly for MNE investments, if only because of the fewer options available to such regions. An extreme aspect of this can occur in federal states, where the division of powers between national and regional governments sometimes leads to direct policy conflicts on the treatment of MNEs.

An equity constraint usually accompanies the goal of economic growth, in that income distribution should not worsen in the process and some efforts may also be made to reduce the degree of income inequality. Such issues of equity or fairness should not be confused with income redistribution brought about by attempts to increase private rents whether through private actions or through influence on government policies. The object of the latter actions is not usually the reduction of income inequality, and much of the literature noted above suggests that the effects are usually the reverse of such a reduction.

THE MNE AND THE DISTRIBUTION OF POWER WITHIN THE STATE

Both the literature on public decision making and that on the MNE suggest that emphasis must also be given to electoral and bureaucratic processes and to differing views on the role of the firm and the state. The interaction between politicians and bureaucrats is clearly important, with the former striving to increase their chances of election or re-election and the latter developing policies which respond to this need while also reflecting the interests of the bureaucracy. It is obviously simplistic to think solely in terms of self-interest here, as if these groups had no interest in national or regional welfare independently of their own direct interests, or no views on the appropriate role of the state and the firm. Yet some such emphasis comparable to the self-interest of private groups would seem a useful assumption, judging by the literature noted above. Among other things it allows attention to be given to procedural and institutional questions; that is, to the way issues arise and how they are resolved. Such procedural issues often seem to dominate the uncertain and complex world of political and bureaucratic decision making, and to lead to outcomes which cannot be explained by approaches to policy which concentrate only on the substance of the issues.

Finally we suggest that competing ideas about the role of the state and of the large firm often determine policy. One could argue that this is already encompassed in the objectives of economic welfare, political independence and the self-interested seeking of income or power. The preferences which people have for public or private forms of activity should reflect their views on the way each form contributes to the realization of these specific objectives. Such a formulation does not capture adequately what is intended here, for it does not allow for the power of ideas to shape events, for the emotions which can be aroused by both nationalism and the MNE, for the influence of the media in shaping policy outcomes. Allowance for competing value systems permits consideration of the differences between the more and the less conservative political parties on the role of the government and of the large firm. Much of what is assumed to be a debate over the MNE may reflect such deeper differences. It is a useful hypothesis to suggest that such differences significantly affect policy in this area.

In summary, wealth and independence creation and wealth and power distribution are the broad determinants of policy which will be used in analysing decision making about MNEs. These categories, and the eight sub-categories shown in Table 2.1, clearly overlap, and are not mutually exclusive in examining any given policy. More refinement of categories is possible, and some will be evident as we consider the evidence in Part II below.

It is worth emphasizing that, at this point, we have simply stated, without analysing, how MNEs are believed to affect policy objectives. One view which is common is that net economic gains are possible nationally from MNEs, although not necessarily optimal without policy intervention. A more critical view is that the long-term effects of a large MNE presence may be negative even in economic terms. Another common view is that a net diminution of political independence is likely. This view in turn is challenged by those who associate economic wealth with independence and who believe economic wealth increases with a significant MNE presence. It is also worth noting that our outline of policy determinants has characterized the third and fourth group of determinants as simply redistributing income and power within the country. An argument can be made, however, that furtherance of the interests of domestic entrepreneurial groups, while probably involving short-term economic loss both overall and to other groups in it, might lead to long-term economic gains for a community. This is clearly an extension of arguments for infant industry protection against imports, in this case leading to infant entrepreneurial protection against competition from MNEs. This argument will be followed up in Part II.

We have set out above simply a set of hypotheses about the way policy decisions on MNEs are made, judging by the general literature on public decision making. Let us assume for the time being that governments are attempting to achieve the first two sets of objectives; that is, increasing national economic welfare and at least maintaining political independence. In that case there are important constraints on what can be achieved. One such constraint is the strategies of the MNEs. A second is the country's policy environment, particularly its capacity to attract or regulate such firms. Third, an emphasis in policy making on the other two objectives – the redistribution of income and power within the country – can limit what may be feasible in terms of increases in them. In the next two chapters we consider the related issues of MNE strategies and a country's policy environment, leaving the redistribution of income and power largely to Parts II and III.

NOTES

1. 'Rents' refer to returns beyond those considered necessary to retain the economic resources in the industry.
2. 'National independence' is used here to mean the capacity to make or implement public policy. 'Sovereignty' refers to the recognition of the right to make policy for a given population and territory.

3. For example, rent redistribution in itself should not reduce global gain but retaliation could lead to that result. Also, if one assumes that national policy corrects what would otherwise be resource misallocation through oligopolistic MNEs, there would be a global gain from national policy. We will refer again to the latter when discussing the actual effects of MNEs in the country studies.
4. It must be added that such efficiency-related issues dominated the US literature in particular, and especially before the 1970s. The literature in Canada, for example, also saw regulation as one form of income redistribution, one way to protect industries considered of particular cultural importance, and as an alternative to public ownership. For reviews of the development of the literature on regulation and on fiscal policy see, respectively, Cairns (1980) and Hartle (1976, ch. 1). A comprehensive statement on regulation is Trebilcock *et al.* (1982).
5. Such a function is a statement of society's objectives in which the level of well-being reflects the way in which resources are allocated. Arrow argues that it is valid only if derived from the preferences of the individuals in that society.
6. One significant extension is by Peltzman (1976) who sees regulators as striking a balance between the net benefits of the relevant interest groups, including regulators themselves.
7. In general, we use 'power' to refer to the ability of its holder to exact compliance from others. Electoral success involves still another dimension in that those involved assume the authority of the state. Value systems are included in this section in order to emphasize the distributional aspects, that is, the competition among values for acceptance. Other aspects of such value systems, including altruism, could be included under political and economic welfare as discussed above, or in categories not relevant to this study.

3. Constraints on National Policy: MNE Strategies

In Chapter 2 the determinants of government policy were summarized as the creation and distribution of wealth and power. What governments may wish to do or be pressed to do and what they can do in practice are quite different matters. For present purposes there are two broad sets of constraints on their policies, each of which also offers opportunities for realization of a government's domestic objectives. One is the characteristics of the country itself, which we consider in the next chapter. The other is the opportunities and constraints arising from the international involvement of the country, including those posed by the presence of MNEs.

The basic assumption about policy which is made here is that governments are mainly interested in attracting or holding MNE investments, except for certain sectors, and interested also in increasing net political and economic benefits nationally. Such a policy approach cannot even be attempted, much less successfully implemented, unless the investment and related decisions of MNEs are understood. Nor can the welfare effects of MNEs be analysed without such consideration.

This chapter examines what theory and evidence tell us about the way such MNE decisions are made. The effects on national and international welfare will begin to be evident in some respects as this analysis proceeds, but most of the evidence on such welfare issues is postponed to Part II. Here we concentrate on three issues. Why do MNEs exist at all, given the other ways in which firms can serve foreign markets? Given the existence of MNEs, how do they conceive of the competitive strategies which affect their investment decisions? Finally, what determines the particular country locations which they choose for new investment, or for expansion or reduction of existing investments?

Underlying such questions are views about the nature and objectives of firms in general and MNEs in particular. Economics offers various approaches to these issues. Traditional theory viewed firms as profit-maximizing entities. More recently managerial and behavioural theories have emphasized other objectives. The former have noted the consequences of the separation of ownership from control, leading to, for example, more emphasis on growth of sales or assets or on maintaining control as distinct from profit maximization. Behavioural theories tend to view the firm as a coalition of different interest groups – owners, managers, various groups of employees, trade unions and so on – aimed at achieving satisfactory aspiration levels for the groups involved rather than simply maximizing either (global) profits or any other single objective.

The question of objectives is closely related in practice to two other factors: the firm's strategy on how to export its knowledge (including a choice of organization structures) and the market structure within which the firm operates (see, for example, Caves, 1980). A firm has a set of assets or skills, both tangible and intangible. Its strategy reflects the managers' views on how best to exploit these skills so as to achieve its objectives. An organizational structure is chosen – for example, the relation between parent and subsidiary officers – which is most likely to serve that strategy. All of this is constrained and influenced by the market structure faced by the firm; that is, by such factors as the degree of competition from buyers and sellers, the nature of the product (especially with respect to product differentiation) and the nature of entry and exit barriers to the industry.

The final point to note is that many firms produce in more than one plant and often in plants which are relatively small. The choice of plant location and size is affected by many factors within a country, and an even larger number once the question arises of locating plant abroad.

In analysing the determinants of investment decisions by MNEs we shall follow the sequence just outlined: first, a look at the form in which a firm chooses to export its assets when going abroad (the issue of internalization); second, the industry setting it faces internationally in terms of competitive pressures (market structure); and, finally, elements of country situations which determine where it places plant (locational issues). In specifying firm, industry and country determinants we do not suggest they are fully independent of each other. For significant periods, for example, firms may retain their national characteristics, even to the extent of giving a margin of preference, unrelated to risk, for sourcing in the home country by units within the MNE.

Some of the outcomes of these investment decisions are shown in Tables 3.1 to 3.4. Table 3.1 highlights the fall in the share of the United States in the total outward stock of FDI, as well as the importance of such FDI to some smaller countries such as Switzerland and the Netherlands. Table 3.2 brings out the increased share of the United States in the world's inward stock of FDI. The more volatile flow figures in Table 3.3 show again the decrease of the US share on the outward side, with Japan and the United Kingdom increasing their shares substantially. The increase of the US share of flows on the inward side was accompanied by particularly large declines in the shares of Australia, Canada and West Germany up to 1988. When considering

Table 3.1 Outward stocks of foreign direct investment, by major home country and region, 1960–85 (billions of US dollars)

Countries/regions	1960 Value	1960 Percentage of total	1960 As percentage of GDP	1975 Value	1975 Percentage of total	1975 As percentage of GDP	1980 Value	1980 Percentage of total	1980 As percentage of GDP	1985 Value	1985 Percentage of total	1985 As percentage of GDP
Developed market economies	67.0	99.0	6.7	275.4	97.7	6.7	535.7	97.2	6.7	693.3	97.2	8.0
United States	31.9	47.1	6.2	124.2	44.0	8.1	220.3	40.0	8.2	250.7	35.1	6.4
United Kingdom	12.4	18.3	17.4	37.0	13.1	15.8	81.4	14.8	15.2	104.7	14.7	23.3
Japan	0.5	0.7	1.1	15.9	5.7	3.2	36.5	6.6	3.4	83.6	11.7	6.3
Germany, Federal Republic of	0.8	1.2	1.1	18.4	6.5	4.4	43.1	7.8	5.3	60.0	8.4	9.6
Switzerland	2.3	3.4	26.9	22.4	8.0	41.3	38.5	7.0	37.9	45.3	6.4	48.9
Netherlands	7.0	10.3	60.6	19.9	7.1	22.9	41.9	7.6	24.7	43.8	6.1	35.1
Canada	2.5	3.7	6.3	10.4	3.7	6.3	21.6	3.9	8.2	36.5	5.1	10.5
France	4.1	6.1	7.0	10.6	3.8	3.1	20.8	3.8	3.2	21.6	3.0	4.2
Italy	1.1	1.6	2.9	3.3	1.2	1.7	7.0	1.3	1.8	12.4	1.7	3.4
Sweden	0.4	0.6	2.9	4.7	1.7	6.4	7.2	1.3	5.8	9.0	1.3	9.0
Other[1]	4.0	5.9	3.1	8.5	3.0	1.7	17.4	3.2	1.9	25.6	3.6	3.3
Developing countries	0.7	1.0	—	6.6	2.3	—	15.3	2.8	—	19.2	2.7	—
Centrally planned economies of Europe	—	—	—	—	—	—	—	—	—	1.0[2]	0.1	—
Total	67.7	100.0	—	282.0	100.0	—	551.0	100.0	—	713.5	100.0	—

Notes:
1. Australia, Austria, Belgium, Denmark, Finland, Greece, Ireland, New Zealand, Norway, Portugal, South Africa, Spain.
2. 1983. Rough estimate.

Source: United Nations Centre on Transnational Corporations, based on J. Dunning and J. Cantwell, *IRM Directory of Statistics of International Investment and Production*, New York: New York University Press, 1987; and official national and international data, *The CTC Reporter*, No. 26, Autumn 1988, p. 7.

Table 3.2 Inward stocks of foreign direct investment, by major host region, 1975–85 (billions of US dollars)

	1975			1983			1985		
Countries/regions	*Value*	*Percentage of total*	*As percentage of GDP*	*Value*	*Percentage of total*	*As percentage of GDP*	*Value*	*Percentage of total*	*As percentage of GDP*
Developed market economies	185.3	75.1	4.5	401.0	75.6	5.1	478.2	75.0	5.5
Western Europe	100.6	40.8	5.8	159.6	30.1	5.6	184.3	28.9	6.6
United States	27.7	11.2	1.8	137.1	25.9	4.2	184.6	29.0	4.7
Other[1]	57.0	23.1	7.0	104.3	19.7	6.0	109.2	17.1	5.7
of which:									
Japan	1.5	0.6	0.3	5.0	0.9	0.4	6.1	1.0	0.5
Developing countries and areas	61.5	24.9	6.4	138.4	24.4	7.4	159.0	25.0	8.5
Africa[2]	16.5	6.7	15.7	19.6	3.7	9.4	22.3	3.5	10.8
Asia[3]	13.0	5.3	3.2	40.1	5.8	4.9	49.6	7.8	5.7
Latin America and the Caribbean[4]	29.7	12.0	8.9	73.2	13.8	11.9	80.5	12.6	13.6
Other[5]	2.3	0.9	2.1	5.4	1.0	2.4	6.6	1.0	3.4
Total[6]	246.8	100.0	4.9	539.4	100.0	5.5	637.2	100.0	6.1

Notes:
1. Australia, Canada, Japan, New Zealand, South Africa.
2. Botswana, Cameroon, Central African Republic, Congo, Côte d'Ivoire, Egypt, Gabon, Ghana, Kenya, Liberia, Libyan Arab Jamahiriya, Malawi, Mauritius, Morocco, Nigeria, Senegal, Seychelles, Sierra Leone, Togo, United Republic of Tanzania, Zaire, Zambia, Zimbabwe.
3. Bangladesh, China, Hong Kong, India, Indonesia, Malaysia, Pakistan, Philippines, Republic of Korea, Singapore, Sri Lanka, Taiwan Province, Thailand.
4. Argentina, Barbados, Brazil, Chile, Colombia, Dominican Republic, Ecuador, Guyana, Jamaica, Mexico, Panama, Paraguay, Peru, Trinidad and Tobago, Uruguay, Venezuela.
5. Fiji, Papua New Guinea, Saudi Arabia, Turkey, Yugoslavia.
6. Excluding the centrally planned economies of Europe, for which no precise data are available.

Source: See Table 1.1.

Table 3.3 *Inward and outward direct investment flows for OECD countries, 1961–88*[1]

Country	*Cumulative flows of inward direct investment (US $ million)*						*Cumulative flows of outward direct investment (US $ million)*					
	1961–70	*%*[2]	*1971–80*	*%*[2]	*1981–88*	*%*[2]	*1961–70*	*%*[2]	*1971–80*	*%*[2]	*1981–88*	*%*[2]
Australia	5 402	12.8	11 295	6.0	20 846	4.8	493	0.7	2 510	0.8	19 029	3.2
annual average	540		1 130		2 606		49		251		2 379	
Austria	360	0.9	1 455	0.8	2 061	0.5	55	0.1	578	0.2	1 591	0.3
annual average	36		146		258		6		58		199	
BLEU (Belg & Lux)	1 358[3]	3.2	9 215	4.9	13 290	3.1	323[3]	0.5	3 213	1.1	8 669	1.5
annual average	226		922		1 661		54		321		1 084	
Canada	5 489	13.1	5 534	2.9	3 665	0.8	1 483	2.1	11 335	3.7	29 440	5.0
annual average	549		553		458		148		1 134		3 680	
Denmark	698	1.7	1 561	0.8	308	0.1	103	0.1	1 063	0.4	476	0.1
annual average	70		156		39		10		106		60	
Finland	81	0.2	376	0.2	754	0.2	146	0.2	605	0.2	5 034	0.9
annual average	8		37		94		15		61		629	
France	2 804	6.7	16 908	9.0	24 127	5.6	2 641	3.7	13 940	4.6	40 556	6.9
annual average	280		1 690		3 016		264		1 394		5 070	
FRG	6 270	15.0	13 957	7.4	8 716	2.0	4 091	5.8	23 130	7.7	47 745	8.1
annual average	627		1 396		1 090		409		2 313		5 968	
Greece					4 388	1.0						
					549							
Ireland			1 659	0.9	1 028	0.2						
annual average			166		129							
Italy	3 634	8.6	5 698	3.0	16 148	3.7	1 667	2.4	3 597	1.2	33 255	5.7
annual average	363		570		2 019		167		360		4 157	

Japan	624	1.5	1 424	0.8	2 582	0.6	1 438	2.0	18 052	6.0	93 672	15.9
annual average	62		142		323		144		1 805		11 709	
Netherlands	2 294	5.5	10 822	5.8	17 721	4.1	2 692	3.8	27 829	9.2	36 926	6.3
annual average	230		1 082		2 215		270		2 783		4 616	
Norway	372	0.9	3 074	1.6	2 449	0.6	60	0.1	1 079	0.4	5 800	1.0
annual average	37		307		306		6		108		725	
Portugal			535[4]	0.3	2 352	0.5			38[4]		116	0.0
annual average			89		294				6		15	
Spain	1 201	2.9	7 060	3.8	16 870	3.9	90	0.1	1 274	0.4	2 654	0.5
annual average	120		706		2 109		9		127		332	
Sweden	889	2.1	897	0.5	2 840	0.7	1 074	1.5	4 597	1.5	16 687	2.8
annual average	89		90		355		107		460		2 086	
Switzerland[5]					4 595	1.1					8 873	1.5
					574						1 109	
United Kingdom	4 310	10.2	40 503	21.6	55 167	12.7	7 398	10.5	55 112	18.2	120 829	20.6
annual average	431		4 050		6 896		740		5 511		15 104	
United States	6 282	14.9	56 276	30.0	234 734	54.0	46 822	66.3	134 354	44.4	116 569	19.8
annual average	628		5 628		29 342		468		13 435		14 571	
TOTAL	42 060		187 873		434 641		70 576		302 306		587 921	

Notes:
1. Including reinvested earnings according to the source. However, this is not the case for some countries such as Canada.
2. Shares in percentage.
3. BLEU 65–70.
4. Portugal 1975–80.
5. Switzerland 1983–86.

Source:
OECD, 1989a, 1990.

comparisons among countries one must note that definitions of FDI are not standardized. Not all of the flow data shown in Table 3.3 include returned earnings, for example, although this should not deter comparisons over time. In Table 3.4 the different degrees of stock ownership used to classify control are shown, though one should add that some countries use further tests as well. Finally, Table 3.5 shows the very different levels of penetration of FDI into the OECD countries, as measured in terms of employment shares accounted for by foreign-owned firms. These tables will be utilized throughout the study.

INTERNALIZATION

The theoretical and empirical work on this subject, so far as it relates to MNEs, was stimulated by the work of Hymer (1960) and Caves (1971). Its starting-point was the question posed by Coase (1937) on why firms exist, in view of the fact that there are alternative ways to organize economic activity. This led to a literature on the failure of markets, a literature developed most fully by Williamson (for example, 1975). The firm is seen as a way of minimizing the transaction costs involved in markets and in cooperative modes of organization, such as licences or franchises. It is also seen as a way to capture the rents on the creation and use of knowledge more fully than would be possible with the other organizational forms. The main behavioural assumptions underlying these choices are bounded rationality and opportunism. The first of these notes that economic agents can act rationally only up to some limit, faced as they are with complex problems and with the costs of securing and processing information. Opportunistic behaviour goes beyond self-interest to include such actions as the strategic manipulation of information or the misrepresentation of intentions (Williamson, 1975, ch. 2).

When applied to MNEs, this approach asks why firms go abroad through fully-owned or at least controlled subsidiaries, given the problems involved in such investments and the existence of alternatives. Through exports, licences, or joint ventures controlled by other firms, for example, a firm can sell its knowledge while avoiding many of the costs of learning to cope with a different environment and with management in a subsidiary located abroad.

The answer provided by 'internalization' theory is that the specific advantage a firm has, especially in its less tangible factors of production, is often better exploited through subsidiaries than through markets or cooperative modes of organization. These intangible assets involve investment in quite specific property rights, such as patents, but can extend to knowledge acquired in any aspect of its production, research, management, marketing or financial activities.[1] Once that knowledge is available it has some of the characteristics

Table 3.4 Cut-off points for foreign ownership of stock in classifying FDI flows in OECD countries

	% foreign ownership		*% foreign ownership*
Australia	25	Japan	25
Austria	5	Netherlands	N/S
Belgium	10	Norway	10
Canada	10	Portugal	11
Denmark	10	Spain	50
Finland	20	Sweden	10
France	20	Turkey	N/S
FRG	25	UK	20
Greece	N/S	USA	10
Ireland	N/S		
Italy	N/S		

N/S = not specified.

Source: OECD (1987b) and Dunning and Cantwell (1987). More recent publications by the UN and OECD show virtually the same figures.

of a public good; it can find more uses and users without diminishing its availability to others. If it is easily imitated by others, however, the incentive to invest in such knowledge is reduced. The possession of such knowledge implies a degree of monopoly power, most commonly in an oligopolistic industry where each firm's actions influence those of the others.

Many specific advantages are conferred when a parent company decides to use a subsidiary. Markets for transferring the intangible assets just noted are often imperfect, where they exist at all, especially for the newer or more complex technologies. For example, such technologies may involve training or transfer of personnel or other forms of activity which are costly even within firms and more so outside them, as noted further below.

Another type of explanation for the preference often shown for subsidiaries over markets or cooperative modes is the fear of opportunistic behaviour by others, such as early imitation, if the non-subsidiary forms of transfer are used. Teece (1981) has noted that, when a firm licences its knowledge, it is likely to require certain restrictions both to ensure the success of the transfer technically (for example, how the technology is used) or to increase its profit (for example, tied purchases from the licensor and limitations on where the product is marketed). A striking example of this is the market restrictions

Table 3.5 *Employment in foreign-owned firms as percentage of all employment, manufacturing industries, OECD countries*

	Year	*Percentage of employment*
Australia	1981–2	22
Austria	1976	22
Belgium	1978	38
Canada	1981	37
Denmark		n.a.
Finland	1983	4
France	1980	19
FRG	1977	17
Greece		n.a.
Ireland[1]	1983	37
Italy[2]	1977	18
Japan	1978	2
New Zealand	1977–8	20
Netherlands		n.a.
Norway[2]	1983	9
Portugal		n.a.
Spain	1971	11
Sweden	1983	9
Switzerland		n.a.
Turkey		n.a.
UK	1981	13
US	1984	7

Notes:
1. OECD (1987c, p. 45).
2. By contrast, Dunning and Cantwell (1987, pp. 89, 161) show Italy and Norway at 8 per cent and 20 per cent respectively in 1981.

Sources: UN (1983, p. 350 and 1988, p. 529) based in turn on data from OECD and International Labour Organization.

placed on technology imports into Japan, a country which in the period up to the 1980s was noted for its bargaining strength in this regard. Data published by Japan's Science Technology Agency (1981, 27) showed that in 55 per cent of such contracts in that year the sales were restricted to Japan, and in only 24 per cent were sales allowed to all countries.

The firm may prefer a subsidiary also because this maximizes opportunities for opportunistic behaviour on its part. The advantages of internalization can extend to the use of differential pricing in various markets so as to take advantage of variations in demand conditions. Internalization minimizes or avoids the costs of bilateral bargaining or of buyer uncertainty which occur when dealing with independent suppliers. Subject to government controls and some other constraints, internalization permits prices to be chosen for parent–subsidiary exchanges so as to minimize the effects of tariffs, tax differences between countries, exchange controls and price controls.

There are costs to internalization, however, such as communication and administration problems within large or complex enterprises, and the increased probability of government intervention when internalization across national frontiers creates a foreign-controlled firm. Where buyers and sellers in different countries affect one another significantly but these costs are not large, one would expect wealth-maximizing behaviour by firms to lead to forms of organization which involve control of equity.

It is important to note that from the viewpoint of national or international welfare (as distinct from that of the firm) one cannot predict *a priori* whether internalization leads to positive outcomes. The presumption that it might not do so is evident in the work of Hymer (1960) who emphasized the ways in which firms might create market imperfections – for example, by restricting international competition – in order to increase the returns on their intangible assets. Many other writers have pointed to other problems arising from internalization, such as the international redistribution of income when related firms use non-market pricing on transactions between them so as to minimize the effects of government policies. However the presumption that internalization may increase welfare is evident in the work of writers who regard MNEs as a response to imperfections in either the markets for the factors transferred or those created by government policies (for example, Buckley and Casson, 1976; Rugman, 1982; Teece, 1981). A key aspect of the dilemma inherent in these two views was outlined by Joseph Schumpeter long ago. He emphasized the need for incentives, by way of temporary monopoly, to assist the creation of knowledge, while recognizing also that, once it was created, rapid distribution of such knowledge by way of competition or otherwise is usually socially desirable.[2] That the debate is not resolved, and perhaps not resolvable in an overall sense, is evident in the language used to refer to MNEs: some writers refer persistently to their monopolistic advantages, while others prefer to speak of their intangible assets; some refer to their superior technology, while others prefer to speak of their propensity to differentiate products excessively or to develop technologies which are too sophisticated, and so on.

We turn now to consider elements of market structure and location which complement internalization in explaining investment decisions of MNEs.

MARKET STRUCTURE AND FIRM STRATEGY

The competitive environment in which a firm operates is of obvious importance to its strategy on products, markets and organization. Porter (1980, ch. 1) has noted six major competitive forces: rivalry among current competitors, threats of entry to the industry and of substitution by new products or processes, and the bargaining power of suppliers and buyers. The strength of these forces can be assessed by examining barriers to entry and exit in the industry concerned. Government policies are one of the factors which affect such barriers; for example, by closing a sector to MNEs on the one hand, or regulating the terms of exit on the other. Many such barriers have to do with the nature of the product or market and the ways in which firms organize economic activity, including relations with affiliates. In some circumstances the barriers to entry are such that a monopoly can exist for relatively long periods even at a global level. Patent and brand protection sometimes offer such opportunities. In other cases a duopoly situation exists, or one firm for each country if more than two are involved. If these interact with one another a good deal, for example because one is a major seller to the other, internalization theory suggests that some form of affiliation is likely. Where entry is relatively easy but products are differentiated one might expect many firms in a state of monopolistic competition. Where barriers are higher, various forms of oligopoly can exist, either tightly knit and reaching a monopoly outcome at one limit or loosely knit with frequently strong competitive pressures.

All of these cases are capable of generating models of foreign direct investment.[3] The first, monopoly, can do so on the assumption of transport or other barriers to foreign trade, requiring FDI as the form of transfer of skills. In the second and third types of industry structure this reason can be supplemented by the existence of intangible assets which are assumed to be a fixed cost which can be exploited abroad. All that oligopoly theory requires is a high degree of interdependence between firms in separate countries, such as to encourage merger, or to lead to competition with the other firm by FDI as well as trade, or even to use the threat of such competition as a way of keeping the tactics of the other party under control.

Within its competitive environment the firm must make a number of decisions which commit substantial resources for significant periods, and do so in the face of considerable uncertainty, high costs of information and significant potential gains or losses for the first firm which is prepared to make a long-term commitment. For the analysis of policies on foreign investment, several strategic decisions on products, markets and organization are critical.

Product Orientation

In terms of product orientation, one distinction frequently made is that between the extractive industries, manufacturing and various service sectors, which has the convenience of availability of statistics and also the fact that governments frequently distinguish between them in policy terms. For example, governments have clearly taken a more interventionist position in natural resources and in most service sectors than in manufactures. Kobrin (1980, 75–8) notes that expropriations in the period 1960–76 were significantly higher, relative to stocks of direct investment, in the extractive, utilities and banking and insurance fields than in manufacturing and trade. This conclusion is reinforced by his finding that only five countries which undertook large-scale public ownership of the economy account for half of the cases in manufacturing. Moreover, as will be noted further in Part II of this study, sectors which are partly or wholly closed to foreign direct investment tend to be in the natural resource and service sectors, rather than manufacturing.

A more fundamental distinction for some purposes has been that of horizontal, vertical and diversified foreign direct investments.[4] Horizontal integration can be thought of as a method of exploiting intangible assets (notably product differentiation) through internal markets, in this case in a multiplant firm where the plants are located at the same stage of production in different countries. Vertical integration internalizes markets for intermediate products at different stages of a production or distribution process, thereby reducing bilateral bargaining and other contracting costs. The diversified MNE minimizes risk by product diversification, as well as by the geographic diversification inherent in all types of MNEs. There is obviously some overlap with the previous classification, notably in the relation between extractive activities and vertical integration. The advantage of the present categories is that they highlight the role of trade in intermediate products in the MNE, particularly for vertically integrated MNEs. It is worth emphasizing, however, that trade in intermediate products is an important characteristic of all types of MNEs.

The distinction between horizontal and vertical integration becomes blurred in practice. From a public policy point of view what is often of interest is precisely the attempt to require more domestic purchasing of supplies and other inputs, more external marketing of outputs, and more domestic processing than the MNE would plan, given its view of the appropriate degree of international integration. A conflict arises between a government's attempts to 'internalize' production nationally and the firm's to internalize some activities within the MNE internationally.

Still a further distinction on the product side is the degree of technological intensity, often defined in practice as a relatively high research and development (R&D) expenditure per unit of value added. Many MNEs tend to be relatively technology-intensive.[5] One advantage this confers from the firm's perspective is to inhibit entry because of the need to match such expenditures, while also encouraging internalized forms of technology transfer. It has also led some governments to attempt to maintain a domestic presence in some of these sectors, partly for reasons of national prestige and partly to try to capture the potentially high returns, both private and social.

Market Orientation

In terms of markets, the key decisions are which ones to enter or leave and whether by constructing new facilities or by merger; where to undertake major expansion or contraction among existing affiliates; and how much economic integration to establish between affiliates, especially with regard to domestic and external sourcing and marketing and the related decisions on R&D. We have already noted that governments are interested in the degree of integration nationally. The lever they sometimes use is the permission given to MNEs to enter the country for the first time, to expand then or later by merger, and sometimes the agreement to any expansion by existing MNEs into unrelated lines of business. Where governments are not inclined to intervene with foreign-owned firms in these ways they may still be able to affect all investments, wherever owned, by disincentives or incentives applied to all firms.[6]

Much of the leverage governments can bring to bear in securing such objectives depends in turn on the market orientation of the firm. Where the MNE is seeking simply to enter the domestic market the bargaining power of governments can be significant, especially for larger markets. Where the MNE also plans to export from that or alternative sites, the bargaining power of governments tends to fall, other things being equal. The bargaining power of governments falls further if a free trade area, customs union or common market is involved, since, in principle, the firm can locate elsewhere in that market and still trade into the country (Guisinger *et al.*, 1985, ch. 6).

Organizational Issues

The third strategic decision of the firm is the organizational structure needed to allocate responsibilities and secure information so as to best realize its objectives. In part the task is to define the combination of product (or divisional) structures with functional structures (production, finance, marketing, personnel) which best suits the particular firm at a particular stage in its development. This task is complicated for multiplant firms such as the MNE by a third dimension, that of the degree of geographic decentralization. The evolution of these structures and the complications of management involved have been outlined in a number of studies; see, for example, Stopford and Wells (1972) and Brooke and Remmers (1970). In Chapter 4 we will consider how MNEs organize these authority and reporting structures so as to cope with government intervention.

LOCATIONAL APPROACHES

International trade theory has long emphasized the importance of a nation's endowments of labour, capital and natural resources, relative to other countries, as determinants of its relative cost structure and hence of what it exports and imports. Differences in the levels of technological development and in consumer preferences also affect the pattern of trade. These decisions on exports, imports and non-traded products in turn help decide investment patterns. In recent years, by emphasizing imperfect competition and increasing returns to production, trade theory has incorporated MNEs into its predictions on trade and on investment. The link to the approach outlined in the previous sections is that some inputs exist, such as the intangible assets noted earlier, which can serve product lines abroad without being located there: that is, they reflect economies of multiplant operation.

Analysis of multiplant operation in turn has yielded further insights into the location decisions of MNEs. As Scherer *et al.* (1975) have noted, firms often operate plants which appear to be too small to secure all economies of scale, and they also operate many small plants rather than one or a few large plants. Such multiplant operation can reflect historical anomalies, such as mergers where rationalization has not yet occurred, but it also reflects rational behaviour. Small plants tend to be associated with small national markets, with large transportation costs relative to product value, with long-run unit production costs which are relatively flat and with the manufacture of speciality products, among other factors. Scherer *et al.* go on to note that the advantages of multiplant operation depend critically on how well market processes are working; those advantages tend to be small when markets work well (382–7).

There is one particular issue regarding location of MNE investments which deserves more research, namely the impact of exchange rates. There are a number of ways in which exchange rate changes can affect MNE decisions, but our focus is whether first-time investment and allocation of investment among existing subsidiaries will be affected. In principle the devaluation by a host country, if it is expected to be of significant duration, should tend to attract FDI in the same way as would trade protection. Devaluation of a home currency should stimulate production for export rather than MNE production abroad (Batra and Hadar, 1979). It should be added that Itagaki (1981) shows this is so with a more complex model involving, among other things, the expectation of depreciation of the home currency under exchange rate uncertainty. Such an approach is broadly consistent with the evidence one finds before and after 1971. The overvaluation of the US dollar before that date coincided with major US direct investment abroad. The subsequent drop in the dollar, and upward valuation of such currencies as the mark and yen, coincided with substantial direct investment in the United States. Such a simplified approach is harder to relate to the coincidence of an overvalued US currency in the early 1980s and continued large flows of FDI to that country. Clearly the other determinants of FDI flows and reinvestments, such as market growth and global competitive strategy, need to be brought into play.[7] There are few studies which include exchange rate variation as a determinant of location, along with other variables. Goldsbrough (1981) finds the price responsiveness of intra-firm trade to be lower than for conventional trade. As reasons for this he suggests the use of transfer pricing practices, the greater prevalence of differentiated products with fewer close substitutes and the need to adjust subsidiary plant and products with an eye to the effects elsewhere in the MNE.

Those using the internalization approach to FDI were slow to wed it to locational approaches.[8] There were important exceptions, of which two are noted here. Vernon and his associates combined such locational issues with oligopolistic competition between existing firms, notably by use of the product cycle (1971, ch. 3; 1979). This approach suggests innovations are tested close to home, transmitted abroad first through exports then FDI, imitated abroad as the technology is standardized, and imported eventually by the originating country. A later version of this model allows for more rapid maturing and imitation in a world of established MNEs. Having allowed for strategic competition by global MNEs, however, Vernon also questioned whether information and coordination costs would permit many such firms or industries, as distinct from MNEs whose operations are more decentralized and nationally oriented. Dunning (1977; 1979) has adopted an eclectic theory to explain international involvement. Ownership-specific endowments reflect advantages distinctive to a firm, location-specific advantages those which adhere to a country, while internalization advantages reflect the perceived efficiency of MNE hierarchies in administering the firm's assets. In terms of location-specific variables he includes not only the characteristics of markets, of the factors of production, and of government policy, but also 'psychic distance' – cultural differences such as language, custom and other social institutions which restrain the flow of goods, capital and techniques. A recent study by Porter (1990) can be regarded as combining internalization (including ownership) and locational approaches. Porter's 'diamond' of national competitive advantage focuses on four main variables (the nature of home demand, of national and created factor endowments, of inter-firm rivalry, and of related and supporting industries) and two which influence these (chance and government). It has been argued by Dunning (1990) that this approach significantly increases our understanding of the country-specific explanations of MNE production, both outward and inward. He goes on to suggest, however, that MNE activities might well have been treated as an exogenous factor, as in the case of government, and shows how such an approach affects the competitiveness of countries. Rugman (1991) has argued that this is at variance with Porter's emphasis in several respects, notably his sometimes negative views on inward FDI.

We can summarize the types of determinants involved in locational approaches for FDI in terms of four broad issues: the demand, supply and policy influences in national markets and the competitive strategy of the firm. First, other things being equal, larger, more rapidly growing and more sophisticated national markets should be more attractive because they are more likely to sustain an efficient plant and because the MNE is less likely to be able to afford letting competitors dominate that market.[9] Second, the comparative advantage of different countries or regions in terms of their natural or created factor endowments, leading to low unit costs of production, will determine trade (and hence influence FDI location decisions) in a wide variety of market situations. This is true even when scale economies and imperfect competition are explicitly introduced into the decision process, although scale economies offer an additional incentive for trade (Helpman and Krugman, 1985, ch. 14). Impediments to trade can generate MNE investments, as with transport or tariff costs.[10] Third, government policies can have an impact on investment decisions by affecting the demand and cost considerations noted. Finally, the MNEs' problem is to determine in which markets to commit resources for production, either for domestic sale or export, and which markets to continue to serve through exports or cooperative modes such as licensing, given the market, cost, government and competitive pressures involved. Once resources are committed, on-going decisions must be made about expansion or contraction of investment and, in some cases, partial or full divestment.

EVIDENCE ON A TRANSACTION COST–LOCATIONAL APPROACH

The analysis to this point can be summarized in terms of two distinct, though related, issues. One is the *forms* in which technologies are transferred – broadly, through subsidiaries, trade and cooperative modes. The other is the *countries* in which MNEs locate their investments, particularly in subsidiaries. For brevity, all of these issues together will be referred to as a transaction cost–locational approach to the MNEs' investment decisions. The evidence in support of this approach, and some qualifications to it, will be considered in the rest of this chapter.

A transactional–locational approach would point to the following determinants of particular country choices by MNEs once a decision has been taken to go abroad by direct investment, or of subsequent changes with regard to such investment. First, factor endowments would dominate many choices. Natural resource exports, or location to utilize low-cost labour or high-quality research, are just three important examples for particular kinds of products. Second, impediments to trade, such as transport costs and protection, would encourage MNE investments. Third, market size, growth and sophistication should be important. It is true that where economies of scale exist the firm would favour exports. Should there be impediments to exports, however, a firm would prefer large or growing markets, if only to allow for subsidiaries of more efficient scale. Fourth, other things being equal, one might expect MNEs from any one country to invest first, or relatively heavily, where cultural differences are smaller. US investments in Canada or Swiss and West German investments in adjoining areas of France are cases in point. Another example, extending beyond geographic proximity, is investments by an imperial power in present and former colonies. Fifth, strategic behaviour should affect the choice of market, depending on the nature of competition in the home and host countries and internationally. This could encompass a wide variety of market situations, ranging from a bandwagon effect following on the first investment abroad, where industries are moderately concentrated (see Knickerbocker, 1973), to various types of deterrence to entry at the international level. Finally, government policies could either act as incentives to investment (tariffs, tax concessions) or disincentives (sectors closed to MNE investments, or general instability of policy).

It bears repeating that the mode of transfer of technology is not divorced from such locational issues. Substantial cultural distance, smaller market size, government policy or strategic considerations such as the presence of strong local firms might well favour various cooperative forms in preference to controlled subsidiary investments.

There are now a substantial number of tests which broadly support an approach such as that outlined above.[11] During the decade of the 1960s a considerable number of tests were made of the determinants of US direct investments in general or in particular countries. These were done by interviews or questionnaires and varied in scope and quality (see the list in Dunning, 1973, and OECD, 1983). By and large these tests pointed to the market factors (especially size and growth of market) as the major determinant, with the cost and availability of factors of production not far behind. Trade barriers were some distance behind these. The influence of other national policies was not consistently measured in most of the tests or was weak, but the two largest samples gave such variables as the degree of political stability some influence. Despite a number of problems in the design and interpretation of these tests, these studies lend credibility to some of the more obvious locational factors noted earlier. More recent tests do so as well: for example, interviews by Grosse (1980) for FDI in Latin America, where market size, strategic behaviour by competitors, tariffs and various government regulations all play a role – more so, in each case, than cost conditions. Econometric tests give support to some of these findings, but not all. For example, Horst (1972) concluded that the height of the Canadian tariff had a significant effect on the choice by US parent companies between US exports and subsidiary sales in Canada, but subsequent research suggested the relationship was more complex (for example, Orr, 1975; and Caves, 1982, 40–43). In tests by Goldsbrough (1979) increased demand in the host country led to increased FDI inflows, while increased costs relative to other countries reduced the inflow.

Perhaps the most extensive testing has been with data collected for the Harvard project, covering US direct investment and technology transfers from 1945 to 1978. This testing to date has tended to corroborate the transaction cost approach noted earlier, though with some important exceptions. What the tests tend to show is a process whereby uncertainty is reduced and information costs are minimized. Thus W.H. Davidson showed that countries such as Canada, Mexico and the United Kingdom, where information costs were low, were heavily represented as locations for US investments, especially in the earlier years of the above period; M. Williams made a similar point regarding US investments in Mexico and Canada for the period 1890–1914 (both cited in Caves, 1982, 63 and 72). Further tests by Davidson and McFetridge (1984; 1985) have considerably extended these results. The probability of internal transfer via controlled subsidiaries is greater with newer technologies, for those with fewer previous transfers, and where the technology lies within the transferrer's principal line of business. The probability of internal transfer is also greater if there are similar linguistic and other cultural characteristics. The probability of internal transfer fell after 1970, however, a point which will be considered further below.

Other studies can be cited which point to similar conclusions.[12] Teece (1977) showed that transfer costs were significant even for internal transfer within MNEs, and were higher for first transfers and for newer technologies. Mansfield and Romeo (1980) concluded that the mean age of technologies transferred to overseas subsidiaries in developed countries was less than to those in developing countries, which in turn was less than transfers through channels other than subsidiaries. US multinationals also apparently most often divest their entire equity position in a subsidiary when economic circumstances or government policy reduce their foreign involvement (Chopra *et al.*, 1978). Minimization of transactional cost disadvantages has been reported an important factor for studies of MNEs from a number of other developed countries (Caves, 1982, 64).

As for the influence of policy variables, Davidson and McFetridge (1985) report that the existence of screening and ownership controls reduces the probability of internal transfer. Where either set of controls exists, however, the country tends to be later in the order in which transfers are made. It is not clear at this stage of their research just how much emphasis to put on this finding, since it does not seem to matter to the transfer order whether there are some controls or pervasive controls (McFetridge, 1987).

The manner in which strategic behaviour affects the decision to locate abroad and the choice of country has also been tested empirically, although perhaps not as systematically as some other determinants (Caves, 1982, ch. 4). The Knickerbocker study referred to earlier is one example. The extent to which rivalistic behaviour can lead to FDI was explored in detail by Franko (1977). European MNEs, faced by import penetration due to declining tariffs, responded with both export penetration and FDI into one another's markets. Non-tariff barriers played a role in encouraging such FDI, but Franko also notes a number of strategic responses by oligopolistic firms. Graham (1978) found that European FDI in the United States was partly induced by US direct investment in Europe. Caves and Mehra (1986) have confirmed that the large inflow of FDI to the United States in the 1970s was partly a catch-up game. MNEs located outside the United States were responding to increased shares of world markets by US multinationals by claiming, in turn, larger shares of US manufacturing activities.

QUALIFICATIONS TO THE CONVENTIONAL APPROACH

While these and other studies tend to support the transaction cost–locational approach, there are several important qualifications. Our approach as outlined in this chapter can be thought of as an attempt to combine the standard theory of multinational investment with some aspects of business strategy. It is the first of these which is considered here.

We can call it the standard theory in that by the early 1980s its main elements had been most widely accepted by those working on MNEs, certainly with regard to the developed countries. Dunning's 'eclectic paradigm' embodied its main elements.[13] Various ownership-specific assets reflected advantages which were distinctive to particular firms. Internalization advantages reflected, from the firm's perspective, the perceived efficiency of the MNE form compared with exports and cooperative forms in exploiting many of these advantages abroad. The location-specific advantages of countries determined where the MNE investments would be made. In discussing the MNE above we collapsed ownership and internalization into the latter and will continue that below.

One set of criticisms is that the eclectic approach lacks the explanatory value of a more simplified theory; that it is, as Dunning (1988) suggests, a paradigm rather than a theory. Buckley (1988) argues that it would be difficult to test the general theory of internalization except by more careful restriction of assumptions. He notes also the need for a more dynamic approach to such questions as the move by MNEs from externalization to internalization, or the reverse, over time. Itaki (1991) raises similar questions, noting the overlap in the concepts of ownership, internalization and location. Casson (for example, 1991) has argued that the dynamics of the theory should emphasize entrepreneurial qualities in the broadest sense, reflecting cultural as well as technological factors which differentiate MNEs from different countries or sectors thereof.

A second question has been the extent to which the conventional theory can cover FDI in services, which became the fastest-growing component of direct investment in the 1980s. Changes in information technologies in particular have brought major changes in the international provision of services. For example, in some areas of finance what was formerly a non-tradeable service requiring direct investment can now be traded. It is probably too soon to be certain of the way in which MNEs in services will modify existing theory. A study by Boddewyn *et al.* (1986) suggests that special definitions and theories are not needed but that the nature of ownership–internalization–location advantages will differ and the links between MNEs and FDI will be broken in some cases.

A third criticism is that the theory did not give sufficient attention to the differing nature and performance of particular MNEs, including those from particular countries or industrial sectors thereof. These topics did attract attention earlier. For example, non-US multinationals, both from developed and developing countries, have had a significantly smaller proportion of wholly-owned subsidiaries than the US multinationals (UN, 1978, 228–30). There has been much debate over this, as evident in Kojima's distinction between US-based and Japan-based MNEs and the criticisms of his position (for example, Kojima, 1982). Differences in the nature of the advantages of MNEs from different countries were also referred to in discussing internalization at the beginning of this chapter.

Such differences among firm and country-specific MNEs have received more attention in recent years. In part this reflects the closer attention paid by those interested in MNEs to the origins of the ownership–internalization–locational advantages of such firms. This stems in turn from two sources. First, the study of technical change has been linked more closely to the study of international technology transfer. Examples of this can be found in the volume by Dosi *et al.* (1988, especially Part IV) and the paper by Cantwell (1991). Just two of the insights from these studies will be noted. In the first study there is emphasis throughout on the continuing improvements in technology, well after the early research and development aspects. The effect is to collapse and otherwise modify the linear nature of the product cycle model of FDI, changes which are not fully reflected in the observation that many product cycles have become shorter. Cantwell (p. 53) notes, among other things, that a theory based on competence in high-technology production implies that MNEs would locate increasing amounts of even their more advanced research in countries with similar types of competence. The second source for the increased interest in the origins of MNE advantages is, of course, the renewed interest in the determinants of the competitive advantage of countries, and how these interact with the competitiveness of MNEs. This approach was discussed earlier in referring to Porter (1990). Such developments have contributed to making MNE theory more dynamic.

A fourth point, related to the preceding ones, is the recent spread in cooperative forms of economic organization, sometimes referred to as the 'new forms' of technology transfer.[14] In contrast with an MNE where majority equity ownership is usually involved, in cooperative ventures the foreign-held equity is often a minority or even non-existent. Table 3.6 shows the characteristics of some major types, moving from internalized organizational forms to those which are closer to market forms. Table 3.7, which covers only technology-intensive agreements, both within and between countries, shows a rapid increase in numbers during the 1980s.

The analysis presented above on internalization suggested a number of reasons why MNEs would resist such cooperative forms in their core business, for newer or more complex products and in other respects. Yet the internalization approach always recognized that such cooperative forms offered advantages to MNEs. It was argued, for example, that joint ventures and licences allowed risks to be shared, access to other firms' technologies,

Table 3.6 A typology of international industrial cooperation modes

Form of cooperation	*Equity or non-equity*	*Time limited or unlimited*	*Space limited*	*Transfer of resources and rights*	*Mode of transfer*
1. Wholly-owned foreign subsidiaries	Equity	Unlimited	At discretion of MNE	Whole range	Internal
2. Joint ventures	Equity	Unlimited	Agreed	Whole range?	Internal
3. Foreign minority holdings	Equity	Unlimited	Limited	Whole range?	Internal
4. 'Fade out' agreements	Equity	Limited	Nature of agreement	Whole range? For limited period	Internal changing to market
5. Licensing	Non-equity	Limited by contract	May include limitation in contract	Limited range	Market
6. Franchising	Non-equity	Limited by contract	Yes	Limited + support	Market
7. Management contracts	Non-equity	Limited by contract	May be specified	Limited	Market
8. 'Turnkey ventures'	Non-equity	Limited	Not usually	Limited in time	Market
9. 'Contractual joint ventures'	Non-equity	Limited	May be agreed	Specified by contract	Mixed
10. International subcontracting	Non-equity	Limited	Yes	Small	Market

Source: Buckley (1983, 208).

entrance to markets too small for a subsidiary or too difficult to penetrate in other respects and returns from mature technologies (see, for example, Caves 1982, 85–90; Telesio, 1979, ch. 9).

One should note there are advantages to the cooperative forms more generally, going beyond joint ventures and licences.[15] They may allow selective transfer of technologies or parts thereof which are too complex, too difficult to value, or too difficult to monitor for opportunistic behaviour when the licensing form is used. Such cooperative agreements may be cheaper than mergers since they involve cooperation in a limited set of products or processes while competition otherwise continues. In addition they obviously carry fewer financial and operational risks than acquisition of an entire firm. They may also involve fewer political risks, given the preferences of governments for local participation in high-technology sectors. All of this has to be set against the difficulties in operating them, including, for example, learning cooperative rather than competitive approaches, resolving differences in views on the net benefits to each party and problems due to differential bargaining positions.

Some authors argue that strategic partnerships must be distinguished from those with other motives, especially cost reduction. In Table 3.7, for example, joint ventures in R&D and other joint research arrangements, along with minority FDI holdings, are identified by the authors as largely driven by long-term considerations regarding market positions, while only a small part of the other three forms are so identified. Technological complementarity, reduction of innovation time, and access to markets are identified in that study as the most frequent motives for strategic partnerships. It is also emphasized that such partnerships are less likely to exist where there is a high degree of asset specificity or a high degree of strategic importance in the product and process.

Just why cooperative forms have increased in importance in recent years raises other issues. Changes in technological and policy environments are probably critical elements. The increased rapidity of technical change puts a premium on more flexible or shorter-term arrangements than licences or acquisitions. Cooperative forms would also be favoured over FDI or trade where, especially in high-technology products, governments have increased non-tariff barriers or selectively limited FDI. Each of these reasons has been elaborated in the literature. For example, various studies have emphasized increased uncertainty and costs of R&D, increased complexity and cross-fertilization of technological change, increased pressures to enter a variety of markets as tastes are standardized and other developments which put a premium on the flexibility which international cooperative agreements can offer.

Table 3.7 Increase in the number of inter-firm agreements by form of cooperation (absolute numbers and percentages)

Modes of Cooperation	*Before 1972*	*1973–6*	*1977–80*	*1981–4*	*1985–8*	*Total*
Joint ventures and research corporations	83	64	112	254	345	858
	53.2%	41.8%	23.6%	20.8%	17.8%	21.6%
Joint R&D	14	22	65	225	653	1 009
	9.0%	14.4%	13.1%	20.9%	33.7%	25.5%
Technology exchange arrangements	6	4	33	152	165	360
	3.8%	2.6%	6.7%	12.4%	8.5%	9.1%
Direct investment (minority and cross-holdings)	27	29	168	170	237	631
	17.3%	19.0%	33.9%	13.9%	12.2%	15.9%
Customer–supplier relationships	5	19	47	133	265	469
	3.2%	12.4%	9.5%	10.9%	13.7%	11.8%
One-directional technology flows	21	15	71	259	271	637
	13.5%	9.8%	14.3%	21.2%	14.0%	16.1%
Total for period	156	153	496	1 223	1 936	3 964
% distribution	100%	100%	100%	100%	100%	100%
% distribution over all periods	3.9%	3.9%	12.5%	30.9%	48.8%	100%

Source: Hagedoorn (1990), p. 20. About half of these agreements are within Western Europe, the USA and Japan, rather than between these areas. See Hagedoorn and Schakenraad (1990, p. 8). The data cover research and technology-intensive agreements, rather than production or marketing agreements.

Some writers have suggested that the rapid increases in cooperative forms in recent years could mean both FDI in general and international mergers in particular are declining in importance.[16] Our view is that one must suspend judgement on this question. The new forms appear to be in addition to the subsidiary form. The MNE is itself the major supplier of many of the new forms. Its preference for internal partners is still strong, judging by studies of its choices between alternative organizational forms (Bertin, 1987), the major recovery in FDI after the global problems of the early 1980s and its diversification into services. The great majority of the cooperative agreements were established in the 1980s, many appear to be short-term in nature and a majority of them involve US firms.

Our own preference at present is to continue to regard the MNE as the central private institution in international economic activity, utilizing markets (or intra-firm trade) and alliances as a variety of political, economic and technological circumstances dictate. There is obviously scope for improvement in the theory of MNEs. At a minimum, that theory should be able to encompass cooperative agreements convincingly, as well as accommodate some of the other changes noted above. This process is already well under way.[17] It is also clear that the newer forms of international involvement, along with newer competitors in the shape of MNEs from many countries, increase the possibilities for governments interested in pursuing access to non-subsidiary forms of technology transfer. Whether they pursue such possibilities successfully in developmental terms depends on a host of other factors: there are examples of great success and of failure to be observed (Oman, 1984, chs 1 and 5). We turn now to look more directly at the opportunities and the constraints involved.

NOTES

1. Rugman (1987b) has noted that the firm-specific advantages of the major Canadian-controlled MNEs lie in marketing and managerial skills rather than research intensity. Giddy and Young (1982) note that much foreign direct investment is carried out by small MNEs with little advantage in R&D, relying rather on entrepreneurial skills, adaptation of production techniques to local conditions, and location-specific advantages. Kindleberger (1969, ch. 1) classifies the monopolistic advantages which produce FDI as departures from perfect competition in goods or factor markets, internal and external economies of scale, and government limitations on output or entry.
2. See, for example, Johnson's (1970) application of these ideas to the problems of policy regarding MNEs. Schumpeter did not write about such firms, but clearly would have sided with the second viewpoint noted above.
3. Examples of such models include Helpman (1984), Helpman and Krugman (1985) and Markusen (1984).
4. See Caves (1982, ch. 1) which I have drawn on for what follows. His 1971 article did much to encourage this approach to the study of MNEs.
5. See, however, note 1.

6. The incentives or disincentives may be applied in principle to all firms. In practice, since large or more sensitive investments receive more attention, it may be possible to take ownership into account in less direct ways.
7. In addition it can be argued that firms would not base a foreign acquisition simply on the fact that it was less expensive in their home currency, since the discounted future returns which would help determine the price to be paid would be converted to the home currency.
8. There is a significant business literature on the selection of countries for FDI. For analysis of the techniques for specifying the countries to be examined more fully, see Ehrman and Hamburg (1986).
9. A particular aspect of this is the MNEs situated in small countries, which tend to put a relatively large part of their investment abroad, as distinct from direct export (Caves, 1982, 44).
10. Markusen (1984) shows that MNEs can exist even in the absence of factor price differences and impediments to trade. The economies of multiplant operation, based on joint use of intangible assets, suffice to generate such firms.
11. For more detail on tests of this approach, see Caves (1982, chs 1, 2 and 9) and Rugman (1982) as well as citations in the text.
12. Some of the earliest tests were for US direct investment in Canada. These are summarized in Safarian (1985a) 7–11.
13. Probably the best source is Dunning (1988) which restates the eclectic paradigm and also discusses a number of criticisms of it. See also Dunning 1977, 1979 and 1990.
14. See Safarian (1991a) for an analysis of data trends and issues involved in international cooperative agreements.
15. These advantages are developed in Mowery (1988, 9–17) and, especially for strategic alliances, Hagedoorn and Schackenraad (1990).
16. See, for example, several studies in Mytelka (ed.) (1991), notably those by Michalet and Ciborra.
17. Eden (1990) estimates that about one-quarter of the journal articles on international business in 1983–8 dealt with such newer issues, specifically, services, cooperative arrangements and MNEs in Japan and other countries in Asia.

4. untry Strategies: Opportunities and Constraints

In the preceding chapter we looked at the choice between subsidiary, market and mixed modes of technology transfer as the firm decided how to exploit its advantages. Three other types of strategic decisions were emphasized: the product and market specializations and the organizational structure appropriate to these, especially to the degree of economic integration involved. Brief consideration was given, finally, to the market and cost factors influencing the choice of particular countries, factors which reflect a wide variety of socioeconomic influences. All of this is conditioned by two types of pressures: first, the firm must consider competitive pressures, whether from other MNEs or local firms; second, government policies can condition the choice of national locations, both in terms of the nature of existing incentives and disincentives to investment and the risk of changes in them.

In Chapter 2, in outlining the determinants of public policy, we noted briefly a number of reasons why countries have policies on FDI. It is one thing to have concerns about the effects of FDI, it is quite a different matter to put the policies in place and apply them so that they increase net benefits from FDI. What this requires is that a country continue to be an attractive location for those investments which are desired while securing also the particular ownership and performance objectives set by the government. All of this depends in turn on the bargaining power of the government in relation to the firm.

The countries which are considered most fully in this study are similar in that they have relatively high per capita incomes and a broadly market orientation. They differ in many important respects for present purposes; for example, as home or host countries for MNEs, in terms of government ownership of industry and of government intervention generally, and in the size and the degree of internationalization of their economies. Tables 1.1 to 1.3 give some indication of these differences.

These differences in policy environments affect the bargaining power which governments can bring to bear on MNEs. We comment first on the scope for bargaining, then on the determinants of bargaining power in terms of country-specific issues and industry- and firm-specific issues. It will become evident that bargaining power varies not only by country, but also by industry and by type of firm.

SCOPE FOR BARGAINING

There are several opportunities when governments deal with MNEs, as noted in Chapter 2. In some cases national economic welfare may be improved: for example, by capturing rents on natural resources. In others, policies may increase or preserve sovereignty. In many cases the effect of policy is a redistribution of wealth or power within the state, accompanied perhaps by a reduction of overall wealth if investment is reduced. This outcome may be acceptable to governments because an emphasis on sovereignty or independence may enhance its chances of electoral success or because it prefers a composition of output (more oriented to jobs or high technology, for example) different from that resulting from decision making by MNEs.

In some of these cases there may be a cost in that foreign firms may react by altering the size or the nature of their operations in the country in ways which reduce national income. If such losses are possible, this poses a constraint on the country, depending in turn on the kind of bargaining power it can bring to bear in its dealings with MNEs. Other costs may be inherent in the policy used, such as the effect on resource allocation of a tariff or fiscal incentive.

There are two central ideas on bargaining in the literature. First, it is argued that there is a range within which policies can bring gains without reducing the volume of investment or its nature. Second, recognizing that some policies may bring economic losses in overall terms, it is also argued that these policies may realize a non-economic gain or a redistribution objective. For example, much of the literature on natural resources points to the probability of large rents on some types of projects, as well as considerable variability in rents by project, fluctuation in them over time, and uncertainty in measurement. In addition there is substantial scope for bargaining, both over the contribution by governments to the financing of such projects and to their impact on local development (Mikesell, 1971(b), ch. 2; McKern, 1976, ch. 2). Vaitsos (1970) argued that the imperfections and uncertainty in the market for technology allowed a range for bargaining in manufactures also, and the possibility of buying parts of a technology package from MNEs without allowing foreign control. Johnson (1970) also pointed to the economics of investment in knowledge as creating opportunities to secure existing knowledge at a low or zero marginal cost, while doubting the ability of governments to implement policies to that effect. Dunning and Gilman (1977) analysed the options of a host country in terms of a model in which governments captured some of the profits of MNEs while forcing them to move to less profitable forms of domestic involvement, for example from subsidiaries to joint ventures or licences. Lall and Streeten (1977, 209–13) noted that the return to increased investment is a steplike function rather than continuous; the limits are set by the special advantages of MNEs on the one hand, and the cost to the government of alternative access to these advantages or of doing without them, on the other. The outcome is that there is a range of returns acceptable to both firm and government.

For our purposes we will note a simple model based on assumptions common to much of the literature and also to government views on the national effects of FDI, as outlined in Part II, but note also some important views to the contrary. We assume that increased stocks of FDI and national wealth are positively correlated, but that as the stock of FDI rises the rate of increase in wealth slows. Similarly FDI and national independence are assumed to be negatively correlated and the more the stock of FDI rises relative to the stock of domestic investment the larger are the effects on independence.

The question we want to address in this chapter is what determines the degree of bargaining power for the country in dealing with MNEs; that is, the capacity to achieve an increase in wealth while preserving any desired degree of independence. Before discussing this issue, note should be taken of views contrary to the above on the relation of the variables involved. Some would regard some aspects of independence as a constraint which must not be violated at any cost. The concept of a tradeoff with wealth would not apply. Such might be the view with regard to the defence sector, where FDI is prohibited in many countries. It is more difficult to think of an example at the overall national level, but the issue of extraterritorial extension of law through FDI is a possible example. In addition some writers have argued the contrary, that FDI increases wealth and increased wealth allows more policy choice, including policies associated with independence. Hence the relation between FDI and independence is believed to be positive by such writers and not negative, as assumed above. Other writers have argued that continuing inflows of FDI create a situation of dependency which, over time, reduces wealth. Hence the relation between FDI and wealth is assumed to be negative. In Part II we shall have more to say about some of these questions, both at an aggregate and a sectoral level.

COUNTRY-SPECIFIC POLICY ENVIRONMENTS

Concentrating for the moment on country characteristics, bargaining power can be analysed in terms of the nature of the actual or potential assets the country can offer the MNE, its capacity to organize effective policies and the degree to which the country's international involvement constrains certain types of actions. These are considered in turn, although they are not fully separable.

Countries have very different assets to offer MNEs in return for access to their capabilities. MNEs are likely to be attracted by large and growing markets which they do not wish to serve by exporting, either because of impediments to trade or internalization advantages. Depending on the product, they may find availability of high skills or low-cost labour attractive, or access to particular natural resources as the key to investment. A variety of infrastructure investments is taken for granted in some countries and regions but requires major investments in others. As noted earlier, psychic distance in social and linguistic terms has influenced the choice of location. A great deal can be said about these locational advantages but, in general, it is the uniqueness of the assets involved – that is, the difficulty of substitution across countries – which is important. This uniqueness, along with the ability to define the terms of access to these assets, gives the government its bargaining power.

A second major influence on the degree of bargaining power is the country's capacity to organize its policies effectively. For the government, as for the firm, uncertainty about policy alternatives is created by the costs of information and satisficing which are necessary because of the needs and demands of competing interests. States differ widely in the capacities of private interest groups to affect policy, in the need to reconcile the interests of central and regional governments, in the degree of consensus on the roles of private and state-owned firms and of government intervention, in the quality and influence of their government bureaucracies; and in the public acceptance and mode of operation of their political processes. All of this gives a stock of organizational capacities which determines how quickly policies can be put in place and how well they can be operated. One of the ways in which this matters is the reputation the country has for the clarity and continuity of its policies, as distinct from the degree of restrictiveness of policy. Other things being equal, MNEs are likely to downgrade investments in countries where the rate of return is subject to substantial uncertainty because of frequent policy changes or extensive negotiation delays.

As a particular aspect of this second point, it is well to note that the range of options available to a country is limited by its traditions regarding policy, which in turn reflects its constitutional and political history. The checks and balances on the use of political power are very different in a loose federation such as Canada or Switzerland from those in unitary states such as Japan or France, and different again in each of these given factors such as the degrees of public ownership and the scope for informal regulation as distinct from detailed laws. Even where the problems created by MNEs are viewed similarly the responses are likely to be conditioned by these traditional policy parameters.

A third influence is the international constraints on use of bargaining power. A high degree of international economic involvement, in terms of trade and investment in relation to national income, is most likely to limit the scope for more restrictive policies.[1] The general reason for this is the stake the country has in preserving a more open system, although this need not prevent it from using protectionist policies designed to secure sectoral objectives. The more specific reasons are the treaty obligations such a country may have entered into on trade and investment and, with or without these, the very real risk of retaliation if others object to its restrictive policies. A particular variant of this case occurs in trading areas such as a customs union or common market, where the countries will have surrendered some degree of freedom in their capacity to set independent policies on trade and perhaps foreign investment. Thus a country in such a trading arrangement is constrained in the use of tariffs and some other border measures to attract FDI from other members. Moreover firms can locate elsewhere in the trading area and export to that country. The iikely outcome is that governments may have to resort more often to competitive incentives to attract investment. These points will be developed more fully in the section on France, which is the first EC country considered and the one which was most interested in the 1960s and 1970s in preserving some capacity to review inward FDI.

Such a bald statement on international constraints, while broadly correct, conceals some important qualifications. In terms of FDI, one can suggest that countries with large outward stocks in absolute terms, and particularly if these are also large relative to inward stocks, are likely to emphasize the need to maintain access by such firms to foreign markets, non-discriminatory treatment once they are located abroad, the freedom to repatriate income, adequate compensation for expropriation and so on. Those in the home countries who benefit from such outward MNE activities can be expected to urge governments to protect their stakes. The qualification comes from those who see exports and licences as creating more jobs and tax revenues at home, and who see these as effective alternatives to outward FDI, at least for a time. Organized labour in the United States and Europe has made this argument, notably, though not exclusively, in the case of the production by MNEs in low-wage countries for import to the home country.[2]

Similarly a country with a large inward stock of FDI, absolutely and especially relative to outward FDI, might be concerned about some of the potential negative effects of such reliance. Nevertheless it would also have to consider the effects of strongly restrictive policies. These could not only disrupt its access to funds and technology but lead to divestment and possibly even to retaliation in circumstances where it relied largely on one or a few sources. At the same time the knowledge that existing foreign-owned firms may not have options in the short or even medium term, and that retaliation from abroad could damage them also, puts such firms virtually in the position of hostages. For example, not a lot was heard publicly from the major MNEs in the Canadian petroleum industry in the early 1980s despite the substantial discrimination against them in the National Energy Program of 1981. By contrast, United States border broadcasting stations have for a great many years made life difficult for Canadian governments by attacking publicly legislation which effectively prohibited advertising by Canadian companies in such stations for broadcast to Canada. The difference in the two situations may have had something to do with the stakes remaining in Canada for each set of firms, which were much higher in the former case.

Much of the outcome in such situations depends, therefore, on what advantages the country has to offer MNEs, how skilfully it handles policy and how large are its international stakes. Much also depends on the firm-specific and industry-specific aspects of bargaining power, to which we now turn.

FIRM-SPECIFIC AND INDUSTRY-SPECIFIC BARGAINING ISSUES

Firms must make decisions on products, markets and organization involving substantial commitments of resources for significant periods, under conditions of considerable uncertainty. All of this is within the context of actual or possible competitive and public policy pressures which are relevant to their circumstances. Once these decisions and commitments are made, the firm has less flexibility in dealing with governments, although over time it can change these in ways allowing it more flexibility.

What particular aspects of these decisions on products, markets and organization affect the firm's bargaining power? Most of the empirical tests involve the developing countries, but the principles involved are similar to those in analyses of experience in developed countries. Some of the more common hypotheses in the literature are the following, which overlap to some degree:[3]

1. The firm's bargaining power should decrease with time. Once a commitment of resources has been made to the country and market penetration has been achieved, a government can put more pressure on it to secure domestic benefits. This is particularly likely to be the case in large-scale, long-term commitments in natural resources, assuming that the firm has a substantial capital stake or relies on the resource in its downstream facilities. Vernon (1971, 46) spoke of 'the obsolescing bargain' in commenting on the propensity of governments to renegotiate contracts in such cases over time.
2. The firm's bargaining power should decrease with the number of effective competitors, whether local firms or other foreign-owned firms.
3. A high technology content and rapid change in technology should make the firm resist reductions in its equity, limits on where it can buy and sell (knowledge-intensive) products, and other controls, for the reasons already noted in Chapter 3. Governments are less likely to be able to bring pressure on such firms since they often enjoy a temporary monopoly of knowledge. Conversely, at later stages of the product cycle where imitation is easier, the firm's bargaining power lessens, assuming it has not itself introduced a change in product or a substitute which makes such imitation difficult once more.
4. Earlier studies associated horizontal direct investment in particular with product differentiation (Caves, 1971). Such differentiation, often requiring large advertising and marketing expenditures, leads to internalization, for reasons similar to those with production technology. This may also pose a barrier to entry by other firms, increase the desire by parent firms to retain ownership and the rents involved, and also increase the capacity to bargain with governments.
5. Marketing skills for export, in particular, are one of the intangible assets an MNE may possess. Exports to affiliates, or through the MNE's marketing facilities to other customers, tend to reduce the risks associated with foreign trade. The costs of information and of contracting are reduced when dealing with known and affiliated parties, for example. That, in turn, gives a degree of bargaining power when dealing with governments, at least when exports are a large share of production.
6. The financial resources which an MNE can offer a subsidiary, or its guarantee when local or third-country borrowing is involved, might be thought to give it an advantage for larger or longer-term projects in particular, hence to increase its bargaining leverage somewhat.

One of the more convincing tests of bargaining power is that of Lecraw (1984) involving the analysis of data from 153 subsidiaries in five developing countries. The bargaining power of the firm is taken to be related to the level of equity ownership achieved by the MNE in the subsidiary. Lecraw found that actual equity ownership by the parent rose with increases in each of the following: the technological leadership of the parent; the ratio of advertising to sales in the subsidiary; the ratio of exports to sales in the subsidiary; and, less convincingly, the capital requirements of the subsidiary. The actual equity ownership by the parent declined as the attractiveness of the host country and the number of potential MNE investors rose, and also over time.

These results are all in the direction expected in the literature as noted briefly above. Lecraw and others have recognized the problems inherent in such a test, notably in the fact that equity ownership is not necessarily the same thing as effective control and that the parent can secure returns on its assets in a wide variety of ways other than by equity participation. Further tests suggested that MNEs may find it advantageous to trade off equity participation, as demanded by governments, in return for more effective control over a number of variables in production, finance and marketing which are critical to the MNEs' success. The one situation in which this did not pay off in Lecraw's sample was a roughly equal split in ownership and management (36–41).

Lecraw's tests were for manufacturing industries. It is possible to cite a variety of tests which confirm some of these findings in the natural resource sector (for example, the discussion and sources in Vernon, 1983). One particularly detailed study is that for Australia by McKern (1976, ch. 10). It is sometimes argued that natural resource industries are more likely to accede to government demands for local ownership, both because they are often willing to spread the large risks involved and also because their intangible assets (marketing and technical know-how) are less likely to be diluted by such demands than is the case with patents, product differentiation and proprietary information generally. McKern takes this further by distinguishing different types of natural resources and different stages of activity. His measures of the effects of foreign investment in resources show that the ratio of foreign gains to domestic gains rises as one goes from relatively low technology and competitive industries such as coal to relatively high technology and more oligopolistic industries such as aluminium. Further testing showed the bargain ratio noted was positively correlated with technological intensity in processing downstream (that is, with entry barriers there) and negatively correlated with the size and richness of Australian resources relative to world resources.

Some of the results of the tests noted above have been questioned by Gomes-Casseres (1990). This study, based in part on data from the Harvard Project, includes firms in both developed and developing countries. Gomes-Casseres argues that earlier studies have not sufficiently separated what the firm prefers in its ownership structure (the internalization issue) from what it can get given the opposite ownership preferences of governments (the issue of bargaining power). Synthesizing and testing these two approaches he finds little or no support for some variables thought to affect the bargaining process, such as R&D intensity, marketing intensity, and intra-firm sales. Some other factors, such as the attractiveness of the domestic market and the existence of a raw material investment, did have an effect on bargaining outcomes as reflected in ownership of the subsidiary. He goes on to note that some factors believed to affect the ownership outcome of negotiations can lead, instead, to a decision not to enter the country. Such a decision was particularly likely to be the case for the largest firms in an industry and where vertical integration was important, including investment in resource-based sectors.[4]

Market and product characteristics are two ways in which firm- and industry-specific characteristics can affect the bargaining outcome. A third is the organizational characteristics of the firm. What is at stake here from the point of view of government policy is the ways in which some of these characteristics make a subsidiary less amenable to host government directives, thereby increasing the 'persuasion costs' involved in implementing policy (Steuer *et al.*, 1973, 172).

The organizational characteristics of the MNE, especially the degree of centralized control of decision making, can be thought of in part as determined by the underlying market and product characteristics and the firm's competitive setting. In part also the degree of centralization is a response to the problem of dealing with pressures from government. Gates and Egelhoff (1986) tested a sample of 50 large US, UK and European MNEs to assess how the relation between the parent and subsidiaries varied in response to company-wide and subsidiary-level conditions. The company-wide conditions were much stronger in their effects on the degree of centralization. Thus they found that the degree of centralization of decision making in the parent fell as the following rose: the extent of foreign acquisitions; the extent of outside ownership of foreign subsidiaries; foreign product diversity; and product modification differences between subsidiaries. Such findings, nevertheless, leave room for the view that parent firms have some area of manoeuvre in deciding how best to organize so as to cope with government pressures. The study just noted, for example, contradicted the view sometimes heard that centralization grows with the size of foreign operations, gave mixed results in trying to find a negative relation between the size of the MNE and the degree of centralization, and did not find much support for the influence of subsidiary-level product and market conditions on the degree of centralization.

Granting that there is some scope for a choice among different approaches, these can be summarized in the first instance as centralization of decision making, decentralization and mixed strategies (Doz, 1980). In the first set of MNEs the economic imperatives of a global or regional strategy dominate, with substantial central management as one outcome. Scale economies beyond the national level and a high degree of global specialization and exchange among affiliates are likely to characterize these companies. In the second set the potential benefits of integration are to some extent forgone in favour of a higher degree of national responsiveness, with less centralized decision making as one outcome. A third set attempted to combine these approaches, emphasizing one or the other as circumstances suggested. Doz relates the choice of strategy particularly to market orientation, the competition faced and the technology used. In terms of the first two strategies the pattern varies from industries with free trade where all competitors follow a global or regional strategy to industries whose markets are largely state-controlled and where the strategy of national responsiveness is the norm. A mixed strategy imposes large management costs but can make sense in sectors where markets are partly regulated and partly subject to international competition. He discerns a pattern whereby increased technological intensity and new products allow a firm more scope for a multinational strategy, but some high technologies prompt governments to intervene in an attempt to enforce more national responsiveness.

This initial classification allows for a variety of extensions. For example, Doz and Pralahad (1980, 152–4) note that simple adaptation to government pressures or withdrawal from the country are two extreme responses. In between are a variety of 'counteractive responses' in which the firm seeks some concessions from government in return for acceding to its demands, a strategy which, on balance, may allow the firm to have a competitive advantage over other MNEs. Haner (1980, 219), beginning with either a cooperative or an independent approach to government plans, spells out the sequence of decisions and outcomes in the face of increasing government intervention. Such 'decision trees' can be laid out in a variety of contexts, both before and after entry to the country, as indeed can the games which underlie them. What they have in common is an evaluation by the players of each other's bargaining position and hence the choices given to them at each move.

Neither the country nor the firm is fixed in its strategy over time. In the short run there may be little that a government can do to affect the size and quality of the national assets which attract MNEs. Even its reputation in terms of the treatment of MNEs may be difficult to alter over shorter periods, whatever the change in its policies. The MNE faces similar constraints over shorter periods, given its commitments to markets, products and organization. Over time both institutions can change their positions, marginally in some respects, more fundamentally in others.

One way to look at this set of issues is to classify the reactions of a firm already located in a country to increased net disincentives due to government policies. Let us assume that a particular country has decided to adopt a policy of reducing incentives and increasing disincentives in general, although not necessarily evenly in every sector or (given the discretionary approaches often used) for every firm with given characteristics. In the short to medium term the firm has at least four ways to react which can be labelled voice, cope, accommodate and avoid. In the medium to longer term it has at least two other possibilities – insulate and exit.[5] Some of these can be used in combination for a time.

The firm may decide to try to protest the regulations, preferably before they are imposed and with a view at least to modifying them. A wide range of information devices may be used to attempt to predict such policy changes, including various devices to assess political risk both before entry and subsequently. A wide range of contacts can be brought into play, depending in part on the stakes involved, going from firm or industry lobbying all the way to appeals for pressure from home governments or international institutions.

A second option is to keep a lower profile and simply cope with the regulations' effects on rate of return and other variables, waiting for a more auspicious policy. In such circumstances the stakes are likely to be low. Alternatively the firm's advantages are so safe from challenge by other firms or even governments that it feels relatively immune from most of the probable policies or able to await a change in policy.

Third, firms may also decide to accept and even cooperate with government policies, whether regularly or on an occasional basis. A smaller MNE may decide, for example, that this secures state support and other advantages in competition with the leading MNE which takes a less cooperative position. But even larger MNEs may find such a policy unavoidable and not altogether painful. After Venezuela nationalized the oil concessions the president of Exxon Services in Caracas was quoted as follows: 'The government has gained control of the oil industry without risk, and we have found an attractive income for technology that we would have to develop anyway... This is the way the world is going and it is, in itself, a profitable business' (*Business Week*, 9 August 1976, 47, as quoted in Lipson (1985, 225).

Fourth, there are a variety of ways the MNE may avoid the effects of a regulation. If it is forced to share equity with local firms, for example, it can vary its trade, licensing and financing transactions with the global firm (perhaps with the help of transfer pricing practices on such transactions) so as to continue to appropriate its former return. Even when officials and joint venture partners are intent on enforcing arm's length transactions, they may find that the information and implementation costs are prohibitive. Bierstecker (1980) has noted, with reference to Nigeria's requirements for local equity participation, the wide variety of steps which a firm can take if it is determined to minimize or offset their intended effect. They include steps such as assuring a wide dispersion of local equity and arranging closely regulated technical service agreements with the subsidiary, all the way to outright disobedience if the stake in the country is small.

Two medium- and longer-term strategies stand out. An MNE becomes vulnerable to intervention when its particular assets, from whatever source, can be imitated. If it can reinforce its advantage over time it may be able to insulate itself to some degree both from competitive pressures and from government pressures. In terms of the product cycle, as its products or processes (or any other advantages) mature and become susceptible to imitation, it can improve on them or find new intangible assets. With time it can even move its product line into sectors or stages of production which are less susceptible to intervention, a point of particular importance if it happens to be located in a sector likely to attract government intervention. Poynter (1985) has developed the issues involved in this particular strategy for dealing with intervention. The strategy of increasing the costs of intervention by governments can be applied on a wide front. For example, Moran (1973) has shown how one firm in the mining sector set out to make arrangements with customers, creditors and governments which would increase the costs of nationalization. It did not escape nationalization, but came out of the experience more favourably than a competitor which did not take such steps. Such insulation can be costly but may be less so than having few defences against competitive or government pressures.

Failing all of these strategies, where its returns are substantially affected and little possibility exists that the government will modify its position, the firm may remove part or all of its operation in favour of more hospitable host countries. This is clearly at one extreme of the set of policies, if only because it may be difficult to recapture market share on any subsequent re-entry. A more moderate variant is simply to dampen the growth of the subsidiary for a period, in the hope of a change in policy. If a firm is not already located in a country, increased net disincentives might persuade it simply to invest elsewhere. This may be too costly in some circumstances, for example where the country in question is a particularly attractive market. Gomes-Casseres (1990) has noted that a decision not to enter in the face of restrictive policy was more likely to be the case for larger firms and where vertical integration was significant.

NOTES

1. One could extend the argument to other forms of reliance, such as for military security.
2. The argument is a complex one which turns in part on how easily and effectively the three modes can be substituted for one another in different types of industry and over the product cycle. See, for example, Bergsten *et al.* (1978), chs 3–4.
3. The various studies which examine these hypotheses are summarized in Encarnation and Wells (1985, 51–2). See also Fagre and Wells (1982).
4. These results are subject to several qualifications, such as difficulties in measuring the restrictiveness of policy and the fact that the negotiating outcome is still geared to ownership.
5. Some of the terms used here have been applied to consumer responses to problems of quality. See the title to Hirschman (1970). For another classification and analysis of responses, see Gladwin and Walter (1983).

PART II

Country Policies: Origins, Nature, Effectiveness

5. The Approach to the Country Studies

Part II presents a series of studies on the policies in 15 of the more developed countries.[1] In each case we examine the origins of policies, their nature and effectiveness.

Before considering the detail of the country studies, it is useful to summarize briefly the expectations regarding policy from the perspective of Part I. The approach to the country studies will then be considered, including a comment on sources.

Chapter 5 outlines the approach to the country studies and the nature of the sources used. Chapter 6 considers the natural resource-based economies, namely Australia, Canada, New Zealand, Norway and Sweden. Each of these has some form of review of inward FDI as well as policies on the natural resource sector. Chapter 7 considers two other countries, France and Japan, which have also had review mechanisms. In Chapter 8 three host countries lacking general review are considered – Belgium, Ireland and Italy. In Chapter 9 we concentrate on a number of home countries which also do not use general review mechanisms, namely the Federal Republic of Germany (hereafter FRG), the Netherlands, Switzerland, the United Kingdom (UK) and the United States of America (USA).

These studies concentrate very largely on the individual country, with occasional references to the others. In Part III the focus will be on overall comparisons of the origins, nature and effectiveness of policy.

SUMMARY OF PART I

In Chapter 2 the concerns of governments with regard to MNEs were noted, but without comment on the evidence with regard to these concerns. Many of the economic and political studies of MNEs assume that the goals of governments should be the creation of national wealth and the preservation of independence. Not a few studies assume that these are also the goals of governments in actual practice, or that they are among the major goals. Since we are trying to explain how policies have developed, and not only what they should be, we have added the distribution of wealth and of power as policy determinants. Our expectations would then be as follows:

1. National governments are interested in national wealth creation and the preservation of independence. Their support for international policy approaches is conditional on those outcomes. Such governments may welcome such investments because they believe wealth and jobs can be created thereby. But they also intervene with MNEs, partly because they do not trust markets to ensure international and especially national wealth creation, identifying such markets with oligopolistic restrictions on subsidiary activities or intervention by other governments. The latter governments are likely to regard such attempts as simply redistributing wealth at their expense, perhaps as reducing international wealth, and possibly as reducing their independence.
2. If one allows for the redistribution of wealth within countries these tendencies to contention over MNEs are re-enforced, both because the impact of MNEs is uneven across income groups and because there are different regional impacts. Allowance for rent seeking, whether by the state or private interest groups, re-enforces these tendencies further. Because MNEs have an impact on the creation and distribution of wealth and independence, they are likely to be caught up in the struggle over the distribution of power which goes on in any state.
3. What governments may wish to do or be urged to do and what they can do are not the same thing. There are two broad constraints, each of which also offers some opportunities. One of these is the degree of international involvement, including particularly that with MNEs. The other is the characteristics of the country. Both determine the bargaining power which a country can bring to bear on MNEs so as to secure investment or technology transfer on terms it considers more favourable.

The first of these constraints was considered in Chapter 3 using a transactions cost–locational approach to examine the investment decisions of MNEs. Available evidence tends to support such an approach but there are significant qualifications due to the spread of mixed forms of economic organization and the development of new sources of MNEs. The internalization approach suggests a preference by MNEs for the subsidiary form of organization in many circumstances, rather than markets or mixed modes, so as to maximize returns on their intangible assets. The critical strategic decisions are on product and market specializations and the organizational structures appropriate to these, especially the degree of global integration involved. These decisions commit resources for a period under conditions of uncertainty. The precise national locations chosen for subsidiaries depend on factor endowments, impediments to trade, market size and growth, cultural distance and – what runs through all of the above – the competitive situation in the industry and the views on present and future government policies.

In Chapter 4 we looked at the opportunities and constraints which all of this suggests for country bargaining strategies. The model which is most commonly implied in the literature is one where FDI is positively correlated with national wealth but negatively correlated with national independence, suggesting that tradeoffs of wealth and independence may be necessary. By contrast, the dependency view suggests a negative correlation with wealth in the long run, especially in some types of developing countries. Also some argue that there is a positive correlation with independence if the latter is thought to depend significantly on wealth and if wealth is positively correlated with FDI.

For our purposes the main assumptions regarding policy are, first, that there is a range for bargaining within which policies can bring national economic gain without reducing the volume of investment and, second, some policies may reduce national wealth overall but realize more independence or a redistribution objective. The bargaining outcome depends on country- firm- and industry-specific characteristics which were considered in Chapter 4. What is believed to be important to a country in such a bargaining process is the nature of the assets it can offer to MNEs. The outcome should be positively associated with its economic attractiveness in market and supply terms, its cultural similarity to the investing country and its capacity to organize its policies effectively (including here their clarity and continuity). There may be international constraints on its use of bargaining power, including those associated with the existence of its own MNEs abroad and the strategies of inward-investing MNEs. On the latter, if one adds the firm and industry characteristics already outlined in Chapter 3, the additional expectation is that the country's bargaining power is negatively correlated with the technological leadership of the parent, its degree of product differentiation, the ratio of export to sales in the subsidiary, the degree of centralization of decision making in the parent and (less certainly) the capital requirements of the subsidiary.[2] Such bargaining power is positively related to the number of potential rivals locally or from abroad, and to time so far as any particular investment is involved. Some of these variables are related. Both the state and the firm can modify their strategies or even change them with time.

In Part II we will be looking for, among other things, evidence on the extent to which the origins, nature and effectiveness of the policies on MNEs reflect wealth and power redistribution as distinct from wealth and independence creation or preservation. We will ask how far country strategies reflect the opportunities and constraints they face, given the differing firm, industry and country characteristics involved. If our view of the determinants of bargaining power is correct and the actors are rational, one would expect different reactions to a given policy by the types of firms involved and, hence, policies which took this into account.

RATIONALE FOR COUNTRY STUDIES

The country studies yield two types of information which should be useful for the purposes of this study. They should yield information which can be used to test some of the propositions just noted and they should allow the development and operation of policy to be put into their historic and institutional context.

The existing published material on national restrictions on MNEs will be used extensively in what follows. It has made a considerable contribution to this study. However the published material is not adequate for our purposes since, as noted further below, either it covers only one or a few of the countries in this study in any depth or it gives a comprehensive listing of policies at the expense of in-depth analysis. For example, the review of establishment by an MNE in a host country can vary from formal procedures to quite informal practices and can involve, in either case, anything from quite mild to very stringent requirements. What is done is often by way of administrative processes which cannot be understood except by close study. Thus measuring the degree of restrictiveness of review policies by existing material is likely to give estimates only for a few countries where studies exist or to yield less reliable but fuller coverage.

What is more important, country analysis deserves emphasis in its own right. It was noted earlier that the countries in this study have some things in common: they have relatively high per capita incomes and also a broadly market orientation for a significant part of production. However they differ in many respects which are germane to this study. In Chapter 4, for example, it was noted that a country's bargaining power was determined in part by certain country-specific characteristics, such as the actual or potential assets it can offer MNEs on both the demand and supply sides, its capacity to organize its policies effectively, and its international involvement. It is not difficult to develop more specific differences which are germane to this study, such as the status of a country as a home and as a host to MNEs, the role of government and of various private interest groups in the economy, and the historic circumstances which led to intervention in MNE activities. Some of these can be quantified, others can only be assessed. Country studies are necessary, in brief, both to yield information for more accurate generalization across countries and also to permit closer attention to country responses to MNEs than one is likely to get from a purely statistical assessment.

While country studies are useful, there are some difficulties in such an approach. One obvious problem is that, with limited language skills and other resources, the researcher relies too much on secondary sources. Our attempt to resolve this through interviews is noted further below. A second problem is that one can lose sight of the elements common to country concerns and strategies in detailed studies of this kind. A comparative approach such as that in Part III helps to compensate for this, although, inevitably, it glosses over important institutional and historical differences.

TYPES OF POLICY INSTRUMENTS

It was noted in Chapter 1 that a variety of policy instruments are used to influence the ownership and performance of the MNE, or to achieve related public policy objectives. These instruments are worth reviewing in order to help set the framework for the country studies. Subject to further analysis in Part III, they are listed in descending order of restrictiveness towards foreign direct investment.

The strongest policy is to close a sector to foreign-controlled MNEs. This can be done wholly, with or without a grandfather clause for existing foreign-controlled MNEs. In the absence of such a clause, the policy overlaps with nationalization of such firms. Public ownership of all private firms, while often serving other objectives than the diminution of foreign ownership, can have the same effect of barring MNEs. A less stringent approach allows MNEs to enter such restricted sectors but with some limitation, for example as minority joint venture partners. All of the countries in this study have some sectors in which entry by foreign-owned firms is limited, although the extent and method of limitation vary considerably. Such sectors will be denoted as 'restricted' in this study. Other terms often used to describe them, such as 'key' or 'strategic' or 'closed', give an inaccurate impression of what many of the sectors involve.

A second and more limited policy is to regulate the establishment of a new foreign-controlled firm or a merger involving an MNE. This often extends to mergers by MNEs already established in the country, and can even include some types of expansion within existing subsidiaries. While ownership objectives are frequently included, the emphasis in such regulation is largely on various performance objectives for MNEs. Foreign exchange control, apart from requiring improvement in the balance of payments, is sometimes the instrument which triggers a more general review process.

A third policy approach is to give more favourable treatment to domestically controlled firms than to those local firms which are controlled abroad; that is, to accord the latter something less than 'national treatment', which refers to 'treatment under their laws, regulations and administrative practices, consistent with international law and no less favourable than that accorded in like situations to domestic enterprises' (OECD, 1976, 8). The scope for non-national treatment is wide, ranging all the way from explicit tax or expenditure advantages to locally owned firms to opaque regulatory differentiation based on country of ownership. Sometimes such policies are given a positive emphasis in terms of attempts to develop local capabilities rather than the negative one often associated with discrimination against firms based on country of control.

Fourth, a government may choose to put the emphasis on fiscal and other incentives designed to attract MNE investments. This policy can stand on its own, but is often combined in practice with requirements that the economic performance of the firm meet certain specified objectives in return for the incentives. Such incentives may be available formally to all firms, regardless of ownership, but be designed nevertheless with a view largely to their effects on MNE investments.

Fifth, governments may choose to regulate or to protect MNEs by emphasizing bilateral approaches, such as investment or tax treaties with other countries. A further step is the development of multilateral instruments such as the OECD Declaration and Decisions on International Investment and Multinational Enterprises.

Finally, a government may prefer not to distinguish among firms according to nationality of ownership. In that case its tax, expenditure and regulatory policies are intended to induce firms, wherever owned, to respond to public policy objectives, such as to maximize revenue collection, to increase local research, or to encourage competition. All countries in this sample have many such policies.

In practice, however, governments may have designed what appear to be general policy measures but with a view to probable responses by MNEs in particular. They may believe, for example, that responses by MNEs to legislation in the areas just noted will differ in some significant ways from those of locally owned firms. This is a matter of no small consequence where such MNEs are a large part of the relevant population. Nevertheless policies which are applicable to all firms can be distinguished in principle from policies which differentiate between firms by the nationality of ownership. Where the distinction runs into problems is in those situations where governments aim their policies at particular industries or firms, which may be dominated either by locally owned firms or by MNEs. One particular version of this is the attempt to develop 'national champions' or 'chosen instruments' by government procurement and other policies favouring specific locally owned firms, either alone or in joint ventures with foreign firms.

The focus of this study is on those policies which distinguish between enterprises which are controlled domestically and those controlled abroad, rather than the much wider range of policy applied to all enterprises regardless of where they are controlled.[3] Because of the focus noted, we will give somewhat more attention to the first types of policy on our list, especially restricted sectors and review mechanisms, than to some of those which are less obviously directed at MNEs or are less highly developed. The word 'policy' is used in what follows in its widest sense to cover legislation, administrative processes and policy positions. In some countries the last two categories are more important than the first.

ORGANIZATION OF STUDIES

The countries studied can be grouped in various ways. One method is by one or more of the hypotheses emerging from Chapters 2 to 4 regarding probable responses of countries to the presence of MNEs: for example, that those countries which are mainly host countries are likely to be more restrictive than those which are mainly home countries, and even more so if the former are substantial producers of natural resources or have large domestic economies. Another classification would group together those countries which had a close trading arrangement before the early 1980s, in this case the European Economic Community and the European Free Trade Association (EC and EFTA).[4] It has been emphasized by Guisinger *et al.* (1985) that such countries have more difficulty in following restrictive policies on foreign investment since the firms can locate elsewhere in the trading area and export throughout it; indeed such countries must compete heavily with incentives in order to attract investment, since they cannot use tariffs. Any such classification is going to involve tradeoffs between the different issues raised earlier which one may wish to highlight. The particular classification chosen is not critical at this stage, since the major cross-country comparisons are done in Part III.

Given the focus of this study it seems best to classify countries by the major policy instruments involved and by several country-specific and industry-specific characteristics which might lead to distinctive policies. These characteristics are their status as home and host countries, the size of the domestic market and the presence of a large natural resource base.

All of the countries in this sample have a number of restricted sectors, so it is not possible *a priori* to distinguish them by this method. It is possible to indicate whether establishment in the country is reviewed in some way. Such a review can vary greatly in the degree of formality, coverage and stringency. If such an instrument exists, however, one can hypothesize that the country is prepared to emphasize disincentives rather than incentives in its approach to inward FDI, at least in relative terms. We further distinguish those countries with a significant natural resource base as likely to restrict access to it by non-residents – a partial introduction of the restricted sector approach – and also the larger economies which can offer a large market in negotiations with MNEs. The group of countries with some form of review on establishment includes a number of smaller natural resource-based countries (Australia, Canada, New Zealand, Norway and Sweden) and two larger countries without such a major natural resource base (France and Japan).

Countries without such a review mechanism include three smaller host countries, Belgium, Ireland and Italy, and also five mainly home countries: the FRG, the Netherlands, Switzerland, the UK and the USA, three of which are among the largest economies in the study.

Table 5.1 gives some data on these countries grouped as above. There are obviously some losses of information with this classification compared with other possibilities, at least with the statistics utilized. This is particularly the case for the home and host characteristic. For example, Sweden differs in several respects from the other four smaller natural resource countries, notably in its relatively high ratio of FDI abroad. France, the FRG and UK have a balance of inward and outward stocks of FDI quite different from the excess of outward stocks shown for the other large economies, Japan and the USA. Similar problems arise if the groupings are recast to reflect more fully the home and host countries or other possible characteristics. It is well to note also that some of the data in Table 1.1 for the year 1980 and even for the early 1980s have changed significantly since then. The ratio of inward to outward stock of FDI is particularly volatile. For example, the USA had come closer to a balance of its inward and outward stock of FDI by the late 1980s and several other countries' ratios had changed significantly (Table 1.3).

SOURCES OF INFORMATION

The published information used in this study has come from a wide variety of sources, including private research reports, government documents of various kinds, reports by international organizations, and information on particular firms. This material has proved to be quite uneven for present purposes. For some countries there are many relevant sources, for others very few. In almost all countries, moreover, the published information on the actual policy processes does not address some issues of interest to this study or does not do so in sufficient detail. Language has also been a limitation, in that we have concentrated on the literature in English and in French. In a few cases, as indicated in the text, translations from other languages have been made of government documents and reports dealing directly with the policy process.

The most important device used to cover these gaps in the published information was a series of interviews conducted in 1981–2 in each of the 15

Table 5.1 Classification used for country studies, 1980 data

	Stock of outward FDI as % of inward[1]	Primary goods as % of exports	GDP in US $ billions	% Mftg employment in foreign-controlled firms[2]
A. Review of establishment				
1. *Smaller primary resource (host) countries*				
Australia	18	68	149	22
Canada	42	45	263	37
New Zealand	19	76	22	20
Norway	41	59	58	9
Sweden	397	19	124	9
2. *Larger home countries*				
France	111	24	6	19
Japan	600	3	1 059	2
B. Entry largely unregulated				
1. *Smaller countries*				
Mainly home				
Netherlands	200	47	169	N/A
Switzerland	455	5	102	N/A
Mainly host				
Belgium	62	20	118	38
Italy	78	14	456	18
Ireland	N/A	42	19	37
2. *Larger countries*				
FRG	104	11	814	17
UK	130	23	536	13
USA	259	30	2 689	7

Notes:
1. Figures vary significantly according to year selected. See Table 1.2 for average of late 1970s and Table 1.3 for 1987.
2. Data refer to various years in mid-1970s and different definitions of control as shown in Tables 3.4 and 3.5.

Sources: First three columns from Table 1.1, fourth from Table 3.5.

countries in this study, followed up by further interviews from 1983 to 1985 in Canada, France, Japan and the United States. Correspondence with interviewees in these and several other countries, along with published information on policy changes, helped to update the information. The focus of this study is policy up to about the mid-1980s, with more selective attention to policy developments since then. For some purposes we have drawn also on a set of briefer interviews conducted in Western Europe in 1976–7 in connection with an earlier study (Safarian, 1978). The time actually spent in each country conducting interviews varied from a month for countries such as Japan and France, plus follow-ups of a week or two, to a week in countries such as the Netherlands. In each case there was extensive preparation beforehand and sometimes extensive communication shortly afterwards.

The interviews conducted in the early 1980s were with three sets of people. By far the largest group was officials of government agencies and departments dealing with FDI. A second set involved officers of parent and affiliated firms in MNEs. In a number of the MNEs an effort was made to interview officers of the same firm in different locations, going from parent to regional offices and national subsidiaries. Interviews were also held in each country with academics who had worked on national policy studies, and also with officials of several international organizations. A few interviews were with officials of industry associations and trade unions, as well as lawyers and bankers who had acted on behalf of firms seeking establishment or merger. Interviews were conducted in English or French, except in Japan where translators were necessary in some cases.

A list of the government agencies or departments involved is given in Appendix I, along with the numbers and nature of companies visited. Seven of the 23 parent firms were in Japan, nine in the EC and five in the United States, and 17 of the 27 affiliates were in the EC. Most of the interviews lasted from two to three hours. In many cases, it may be noted, more than one person was interviewed in a department, agency or company, often separately. In some cases, particularly in countries which had review mechanisms, a return visit (or visits) was arranged with particular individuals.

Virtually everyone who was asked to do so agreed to interviews or re-interviews and was able to schedule them within the time constraints of the country visits. A few interviews with particular company officials could not be arranged because of timing problems, but suitable substitutes were found. Several of those who were contacted directly in government or among private researchers and consultants declined an interview, and in some cases it also proved impossible to arrange interviews with officials in international agencies. The success in arranging visits was partly due to the help from others, such as industry associations, parent company officers and embassy officials, and partly to the contacts made during earlier studies.

In the light of earlier experience and of the preparation for the interviews, it was decided that a highly structural questionnaire would not be appropriate for the kinds of agencies and kinds of issues involved. It also seemed clear that the range of experience and of policies was too wide to allow such an approach, particularly in those situations where rather opaque and ad hoc procedures were common. We opted, therefore, for a broad set of questions which were distributed in advance to every public official interviewed, plus additional questions as suggested by preparatory research for each country, the particular responsibilities of the officials involved and any unusual information which arose in the interviews. Considerable preparation with published materials was done before each country visit, especially on a number of cases which had been researched and published or reported in business journals. These cases were not usually representative of policy in general – the more controversial ones tend to be reported publicly – but they sometimes helped to spur wider discussions with those officials who were more comfortable when discussing specifics. One of the major bonuses from the interviews was the access afforded to unpublished material, some of which was unlikely to be released on a written request alone.

It may be added that team interviews with a number of people from interested departments and agencies did not work well at the beginning of some country interviews and were given up. They worked very well at the end, on the few occasions when this could be arranged. Interviews with several people together in the same agency or department also worked very well. The best interviews were on return visits, whether with government officials or others, but that reflected the investment involved in the earlier visits.

The interviews with company officials explored their experience with national policies and some associated issues. They were not intended to explore a variety of other issues of interest to the study of such firms, such as parent–subsidiary relationships. Some broad questions were sent in advance of the interview, and particular experiences available in public sources were studied in advance whenever possible and followed up in the interview. The company studies were not as successful as the interviews with governments in the sense that time and resource constraints did not allow for them to be as fully executed, but they formed a useful complement to and cross-check on the other interviews. Those with related affiliates in different countries were particularly revealing.

Appendix II contains the list of questions and a statement on the study which was sent to officials in government and business, along with the common portions of the individual letters requesting interviews. Where follow-ups were involved, an additional set of more specific questions was developed for the particular agency or firm: this was so, for example, in dealing with some of the more developed review agencies and with firms where several affiliates were interviewed. Exchange control is not listed separately but interviews were arranged with the central bank and other agencies involved where relevant. Taxation of international capital is a large topic not covered in this study, except for some particular cases of tax discrimination and subsidization involving MNEs.

There is clearly some overlap among the groups of interviewees involved, both in experience and attitudes. Yet the three broad groups mainly involved – civil servants, company officials and researchers – bring generally different assumptions, methods, information and objectives to the issues in this study. This helps the study in two ways. First, it looks at particular issues such as the origin of a policy or the operation of a review mechanism from different perspectives. Second, it helps the researcher with one of the more difficult problems of the approach used here – just what conclusions to draw from what is being said. These problems exist in structured mail or interview questionnaires also, but are likely to be larger in less structured interview studies.

Some previous experience with questionnaire and interview techniques suggests it is impossible to be definitive about this issue and difficult to be convincing (Safarian, 1966, ch. 2). For the present it can be noted that the interviews are only one part of the information base used here, though an important one on some issues which are less well defined by published material. We have relied also on much published material which is closely related to the same set of issues. Not all of the published material is beyond criticism, but it has served to check the interview material and vice versa. More important, the interviews have themselves been used as a form of cross-checking of information, between agencies or departments, and between different types of interviewees. This has been important at times when inconsistencies in information were revealed. Every effort was made to reconcile such matters during visits to a country or subsequently. Most were reconciled but problems of interpretation remain. One example is the policies followed by Japan over time, as Chapter 7 will indicate. Differences in *attitudes* between different departments or groups of interviewees are not the issue, it may be added, since that is useful information.

All of this meant that a great deal of the material available on some important issues came only or mainly from interviews. These interviews were confidential, with regard both to the identity of individual participants and to any material supplied which was not already public and could not be released. The undertaking of confidentiality was given in the expectation, based on past experience, that it would lead to the release of more information and especially that it would be discussed more fully than would otherwise be the case. It is difficult to assess this undertaking in retrospect. Many interviewees in companies appeared to put some emphasis on confidentiality for parts of the interview, particularly in European countries. Many public officials, by contrast, put less emphasis on it – although in some of the most detailed and revealing interviews involving sensitive current issues the issue of confidentiality was emphasized. In any case the confidentiality was offered and must be respected. This leaves at least two problems.

The first problem is that anonymous interviews cannot be regarded as conclusive from the reader's viewpoint. Others cannot replicate the precise interviews in order to ascertain exactly what was said and what to make of the interpretation the author has put on it. Published sources must also be assessed in terms of relevance and quality, but in this case others can also make their assessments. There is no clear solution to this, given confidentiality. To cite both dates and agencies consistently on detailed points would certainly identify individuals in many cases, as well as lead to excessive referencing. In order to meet this constraint while indicating sources as fully as possible, several procedures were used which are worth noting. First, wherever there was a public source covering the same material as an interview or part of it, the former is cited. This was often the case for those countries with relatively well-defined agencies and published reports, and also for some countries in some periods where private studies exist. Second, agencies and departments which were visited in each country are listed in Appendix I, and the agencies which were relied on most heavily are italicized. In addition, on a few occasions where it appeared desirable to do so, an agency has been cited in a way which appeared consistent with confidentiality. My own interpretations are usually explicit. Thus the reader should be able to utilize two rules: first, if the source is not a published reference or the author's explicit judgement, it is likely to be from an interview; second, the agencies mainly relied on for non-referenced information are indicated. These rules are more likely to hold up with regard to the material on policies and procedures in effect in the early 1980s. While some of the earlier and later material is also from interviews, it relies heavily also on a number of published sources which are cited.

This raises a second point. The material on policies and procedures in the early 1980s is clearly the most reliable material from the interviews. The material on origins is less so the further back one goes, as are the earlier cases or experiences, even when the interviewee was a direct participant. The views of officials on the effects of the policies, including those on how well they reached their objectives, are also clearly more subjective. One must add that officials in some of the countries were quite explicit about the problems encountered with the policies, and departmental views on such matters were far from uniform. Nevertheless the uneven quality of the interview material is worth noting. As indicated earlier, other sources were also used for some of these points.

Given the timing of the interviews, this study deals most fully with the policies and procedures in effect in the early 1980s. Those in effect earlier are developed in the introductory sections of each chapter, while changes during the 1980s are noted in the later sections. A cut-off date for most of the material is inevitable in any study of this kind. That which is involved here, not entirely fortuitously, is one of those periods when major policy changes were about to take place. For some years before the early 1980s attitudes towards MNEs had begun to change to a more receptive and less restrictive approach. The timing varied by country and began earlier in the developed countries. The major changes came, however, during or after the great recession of the early 1980s. Thus the early 1980s mark something of a turning-point in attitudes to and policies respecting MNEs. In Chapter 12 we shall consider more systematically some of the reasons for and nature of the new policies.

NOTES

1. A brief survey of policies towards MNEs in the developed countries appeared in Safarian (1983a).
2. The first two results have been questioned by Gomes-Casseres (1990).
3. The series of United Nations studies entitled *National Legislation and Regulations Relating to Transnational Corporations* falls into the latter category, covering not only foreign investment regulations but those on such general topics as patents and taxation applicable to all firms.
4. The EC countries included in the study are Belgium, France, FRG, Ireland, Italy, the Netherlands and the UK. The EFTA countries which are included are Norway, Sweden and Switzerland. The EFTA established free trade in industrial products among its members and, in 1977, a customs union with the EC.

6. Establishment Review: The Natural Resource-Based Economies

AUSTRALIA[1]

As a major importer of business capital, a country rich in raw materials, and one which has had both Labour and Liberal–Country Party governments at the federal level, Australia offers a test of several of the propositions noted earlier on the determinants of public policy. The evolution of policy was somewhat haphazard in the late 1960s and early 1970s. By the mid-1970s a reasonably well-defined policy had emerged with emphasis on Australian participation in ownership of natural resource projects. That policy has been implemented at the margin, for new projects, thus avoiding the costs which repatriation of existing natural resource projects involved for some other countries in this study. It has led, however, to important questions about the distribution of the resource rents.

Australia is a major importer of direct investment capital and has been until recently a relatively minor home country. In the late 1970s the stock of direct investment abroad as a percentage of that in Australia was only 15 per cent. That situation began to change as a result of large direct investments abroad in the 1980s.

Direct investment inflows and retained earnings on such investments were positive and generally rising in absolute terms over the 1960s and 1970s, except for some interruption in the flows in the early 1970s (Table 6.1). In the fiscal year 1980–81, about 20 per cent of the flow of foreign investment went in each case to mining, to manufacturing and to the finance, property and business services industries, while wholesale and retail trade took 25 per cent. Two countries, the United States and the United Kingdom, each accounted for between 30 per cent and 35 per cent of the inflows plus retained earnings in the last half of the 1970s, and Japan accounted for just under 15 per cent.

The foreign ownership and control of Australian industry are among the highest for the countries in this study. Some measures by major sectors are given in Table 6.2. Higher figures are evident if one looks at sub-sectors.[2] In the early 1970s, for example, foreign control of fuel minerals was at 75 per cent, of petroleum exploration at 74 per cent, and of manufactures of petro-

Table 6.1 Inward foreign investment in enterprises in Australia by type of investment, 1960–87 ($A million)

	Direct investment		*Portfolio and institutional loans*	*Total*
	Undistributed income	*Other direct investment*		
1960–1	113	262	96	473
1961–2	66	155	76	297
1962–3	109	275	83	467
1963–4	138	287	28	453
1964–5	124	416	44	584
1965–6	125	387	182	694
1966–7	115	249	153	516
1967–8	228	333	420	964
1968–9[a]	250	349	405	1 004
1969–70	221	514	305	1 040
1970–1	238	657	695	1 590
1971–2	224	646	584	1 454
1972–3	307	93	70	471
1973–4	430	185	-120	496
1974–5	246	411	346	1 003
1975–6	614	-38	282	858
1976–7	655	412	482	1 549
1977–8	662	386	282	1 330
1978–9	814	633	612	2 059
1979–80	1 017	521	1 543	3 081
1980–1	829	1 559	3 679	6 068
1981–2	358	1 984	7 206	9 548
1982–3	-586	1 481	8 357	9 252
1983–4	553	1 385	7 388	9 326
1984–5	610	2 001	10 662	13 273
1985–6	936	883	14 681	16 500
1986–7	650	3 362	17 601	21 613

Note:
[a]Some discontinuity in the treatment of mining and petroleum expenditures occurs prior to 1968–9 and from then on, while some insurance items are placed in the current account after that date. See the 1979–80 report of Australia, Bureau of Investment, 38. Prior to 1979–80 the definition of direct investment was 25 per cent or more control of voting stock; after that it was 10 per cent or more. This changes the levels of FDI flow by between 2 and 5 per cent (FIRB, 1985–6, 21).

Sources: Australian Bureau of Investment, *Foreign Investment 1981–2* (1983 preliminary) and earlier issues. For 1979–80 on see Australia, FIRB (1984–5, 21 and 1986–7, 36).

leum, chemical and coal at 75 per cent. In several other manufacturing industries foreign control of value added was between 33 and 55 per cent – 33 in the case of each of food and beverages, textiles and miscellaneous manufactures, 38 for base-metal products, 42 for other machinery and equipment, and 55 for transport equipment. The data on foreign ownership and control were discontinued for several years in the late 1970s and early 1980s. More detail will be given below on the primary sector.

The long-term change in the role of foreign business investment in Australia is most simply summarized by a measure of the foreign-owned proportion of the total capital stock. This shows a figure of 18.2 per cent in 1970–74, declining to 12.3 in 1975–9, then rising to 16.6 in 1980–84. The figure rose each year from 11.4 to 20.8 in the last five-year period just noted. Such aggregative measures are subject to a number of statistical problems (Australia, FIRB Report 1984–5, 39).

Table 6.2 Selected data on foreign ownership of Australian industry, 1972–3 to 1983–4

	1972–3 (%)	*1983–4[a] (%)*
Mining	50	45
Minerals processing	40	46
Manufacturing	32	32
Life insurance	37	40
General insurance	45	35
Registered financial corporations	—	36
Agricultural land	—	6
Transport	—	5
Banking	—	21

Note:
[a]The fiscal years are 1984–5 in mining, 1981–2 in mineral processing, 1982–3 in manufacturing, and 1986 in banking. Data are based on value added in manufacturing, mining, processing and transport, premiums received in life insurance, number of hectares in agriculture and financial corporate assets and bank assets.

Sources: FIRB Report (1987–8, 22–3), as derived from various publications of the Australian Bureau of Statistics.

The Development of Policies on Key Sectors and Screening

Table 6.3 summarizes the history since 1939 of federal policy towards inward FDI. Exchange control was in effect from 1939 until 1984. It is not a

Table 6.3 Development of federal government policies on inward direct investment in Australia

1939–84	*Exchange control* in effect, varying degrees of severity.
1942	*Broadcasting* and TV licenses limited to citizens or Australian–controlled firms.
1945	Foreign interests not to be licensed to carry on *banking* or purchase a bank, except for those already in existence. Ten per cent limit on shareholding by any one person or company, whether owned locally or abroad. Representative offices allowed for liaison purposes.
1947	*Airline* service within Australia restricted to British subjects resident in Australia.
1965–9	Overseas firms to consult with Federal Reserve Bank on plans to *borrow* in Australia (1965). For new ventures, access to loans linked to provision made for equity participation by Australians (1968). Companies allowed to raise in Australia a proportion of their total new Australian-held equity in the company, with the latter weighted on a four-to-three basis (1969). These measures ended in 1972.
1967	Establishment of Australian Resources Development Bank.
1968	Foreign ownership of individual *life insurance* companies limited to 40 per cent overall, and 20 per cent for any given foreign shareholder.
1969	Government reserves the right to prevent foreign *takeovers* considered to be contrary to the national interest.
1970	Establishment of Australian Industry Development Corporation. Foreign ownership of two mining firms with *uranium* interests limited to 20 per cent overall and 5 per cent for individual shareholders.
1972	Companies (Foreign Takeovers) Act empowers Treasurer to prohibit takeover by s*hare acquisitions* if judged not to be in national interest. Interdepartmental Committee on Foreign Takeovers examines proposals where 15 per cent or more of voting stock held by a foreign person or corporation or 40 per cent or more if two or more such persons or corporations. Guidelines on criteria of national interest issued by government.

1973	Foreign purchases of *real estate* prohibited except for certain industrial or residential purchases.
1974	Foreign Investment Committee established to review, on a non-statutory basis, foreign *acquisition of assets* of Australian firms or new businesses established by foreign interests. Guidelines set for more Australian ownership and control in *mining*.
1975	*Foreign Takeovers Act* covers both share and asset acquisitions, some other forms of takeover, and increases of 15 per cent in foreign ownership even if already controlled. Interdepartmental Committee to review all of this on basis of revised set of criteria of national interest. New *mineral projects* to have no less than 50 per cent Australian ownership, and similar Australian participation to be encouraged in exploration. New *uranium* projects to be 100 per cent locally owned. Screening extended to non-bank financial institutions, insurance companies and real estate.
1976	*Foreign Investment Review Board* replaces Interdepartmental Committee; 50 per cent Australian equity requirement extended to *agriculture, forestry, fishing and pastoral industry*; Australian ownership in uranium lowered to 75 per cent.
1978	'*Naturalizing*' companies with 25 per cent domestic equity, a majority Australian board, and a commitment to proceed to 51 per cent Australian ownership were allowed to proceed with new projects under the 50 per cent investment guidelines for natural resources. *Uranium projects* with at least 50 per cent local equity allowed, subject to some qualifications.
1983	Modest general tightening up of existing procedures and criteria for takeovers, new firms and naturalizing companies.
1983–4	Local equity limits raised for uranium projects. Exchange control requirements removed.
1985	Foreign-controlled trading banks and merchant banks allowed. Fifty per cent (later 100 per cent) foreign ownership of stockbroking companies allowed.
1986–7	Review criteria modified and asset threshold levels for review raised, except for restricted sectors. Fifty per cent local ownership rule ended for new oil and gas projects. Easing of some restrictions on real estate investment; reverse for developed residential real estate.

Sources: Sexton and Adamovich (1981, ch. 2) and various policy statements and FIRB Reports noted in the text of the present study.

primary objective of exchange controls to perform an economic review of individual instances of direct investment, but they can be used to supplement such a review – for example, in bringing important takeovers to the attention of the government, and in assuring compliance with non-statutory policy. Until the late 1960s, Australia maintained an open door towards FDI although a few sectors were partially or wholly closed and financing institutions were established to enable Australians to participate more fully in natural resource and industrial development. The Liberal–Country Party governments in power since 1949 tended to view FDI as contributing to the process of economic growth and viewed the latter as a necessary adjunct to policies encouraging immigration.

While a welcoming attitude remained, what had evolved at the end of the 1960s and in the first half of the 1970s was a policy of closing additional sectors to FDI, of ensuring Australian participation in the ownership of natural resources in particular and of attempting moderately to increase net economic benefit in other respects through a review process. These policies were initiated somewhat hesitantly by Liberal–Country Party governments until 1972. They were developed with much more enthusiasm and some initial confusion by a Labour Party government that fell in 1975. The present form of the policies dates from legislation passed in 1976, when a Liberal–Country government was in power; however the antecedents of this legislation may be traced to the previous government, as Table 6.3 makes clear. The Labour government elected in 1983 continued the established policies in the main for a few years. It then began a process of significant liberalization.

Certainly there had been concerns about the economic impact of direct investment before the mid-1960s, as witnessed by an early study for the federal (Commonwealth) government of the limitations on exports of such firms (Arndt and Sherk, 1959) and the concern over the substantial payments abroad by General Motors–Holden (Penrose, 1956). However the government of Australia at the time, led by Sir Robert Menzies, with Harold Holt as Treasurer, was not prepared to intervene directly and extensively, whether for macro- or microeconomic reasons, as witness its rejection of the proposals in 1965–66 by the Vernon Committee that all foreign takeovers be screened and that the future inflow of direct investment be kept at the average of several past years.

What increasingly interested the government was the desire to ensure more Australian participation in the resource boom of the late 1960s, a desire which led to much of the policy and eventual legislation which developed, often in an ad hoc manner. An early turning-point was the guidelines issued in 1965 (which lacked legislative backing) requesting companies owned overseas to consult the Federal Reserve Bank before borrowing in Australia. This was a response to the guidelines issued, first by the US government, then by the UK government, urging their companies, among other things, to finance overseas investment by borrowing overseas (Goldberg and Kindleberger, 1970). The degree to which there was local equity in the company played a part in determining the amount of Australian borrowing allowed, but there is some ambiguity about how consistently this was applied. In 1969, however, quite specific guidelines were issued in this regard by Prime Minister J.G. Gorton and the Treasurer, W. McMahon, as noted in Table 6.3.[3]

Another approach was to strengthen Australia's financial capacity to undertake more of her investments. The Australian Resources Development Bank was established in 1967 to borrow capital in Australia or abroad so as to enable Australians to establish commercially viable large-scale enterprises in the natural resources sector in particular. It was intended that the Bank operate in situations where (minority) foreign equity owners are involved but to give a preference to Australian ownership. It operated by refinancing loans made by the trading banks. The concern was that, without such an institution, Australians might finance even fewer of the larger-scale resource projects, or do so at a higher interest cost or smaller equity involvement. There was some initial subsidy by the Reserve Bank by way of a contribution to its equity and support for interim loan financing. The longer-term costs would be reflected in any crowding out of private Australian financing or of the public expenditures which might have been financed at the lower interest rate involved. In addition the Australian Industry Development Corporation was established in 1970 to provide both loan and equity finance for processing, manufacturing and distributing industries. While it was not restricted to majority Australian-controlled firms it had as a major objective the maximum achievable participation by Australian residents. Once again the emphasis was on borrowing abroad to ensure more Australian equity at home – although the minister who introduced it took a decidedly more critical approach to MNEs than did those who spoke for the Development Bank.[4]

It was noted above that the government led by Sir Robert Menzies had rejected proposals that all foreign takeovers be screened. The possibility of overseas takeovers of a large insurance company in 1968 and of a mining firm with uranium interests in 1970 prompted legislation to limit foreign ownership in these sectors. More generally, Prime Minister Gorton, who had become increasingly critical of foreign direct investment, announced on 16 September 1969 that the government was reserving the right to prevent foreign takeovers where these were considered to be contrary to the national interest. This was couched in good part in terms of improvement in takeover procedures generally in order to protect shareholder interests. There was specific reference also to the need to block foreign takeovers at times in major firms, although the criteria of national interest were not spelled out.

Over the next few years and especially during the election of 1972 the opposition Labour Party drew a good deal of public attention to issues involving MNEs and to policy questions. Gorton's successor, Prime Minister McMahon, announced in September 1972 a foreign takeovers act with a review body to enforce it, and also stated in some detail what the applicable criteria of national interest involved. The Companies (Foreign Takeovers) Act which went into operation in November 1972 dealt only with share acquisitions. It was left to the Labour government which won office the next month to implement this legislation. In the period December 1972 to August 1974, some 450 takeover proposals were notified under the Act. About three-quarters were deemed not subject to the Act or not objectionable. Of the remainder which received more detailed review, 11 were considered to be against the national interest, 39 were found to be unobjectionable or outside the Act, 20 were withdrawn before conclusions were reached, and about 40 were still being investigated at the end of the period (Sexton, 1974, 251–2).

Prime Minister Whitlam's government went much further than this, however. It extended review on a non-statutory basis to the foreign acquisition of assets in June 1974. Then in August 1975 it passed the Foreign Takeovers Act and organized the review process not only to cover the various forms of foreign takeover but new investment as well, on the basis of a more extensive set of criteria. Moreover review was extended to cover real estate, non-bank financial institutions and insurance companies. Finally new mineral projects were to have no less than 50 per cent Australian participation, except for uranium, where 100 per cent local participation was necessary.

The Labour government lost power in December 1975, shortly after some of these changes had been implemented or announced. The succeeding Liberal–Country Party government continued the measures just noted, and extended the 50 per cent local equity requirements to several other primary resource sectors. Yet, even after allowing for the confusion inherent in the introduction of such complex measures in a federal state, there is no mistaking the difference in attitude of the Whitlam government towards foreign direct investment from that of the governments which followed and preceded it. It is true that Prime Minister Gorton, in contrast with preceding governments, and despite his rejection of the Vernon Committee proposals, had eventually adopted a more critical stance towards foreign takeovers in particular, and that Prime Minister McMahon moved on foreign takeovers late during his tenure. Yet it was clearly the Labour opposition which had dramatized the issues in the resources field in particular, both before and after it took power. And the Whitlam government, if sometimes clumsily, brought a range of instruments into play which have continued since, though falling well short of what it hoped to achieve and not always operating as Labour intended. For example, a government-owned authority designed to help finance exploration activity ran into constitutional difficulties, with two states going so far as to refuse to extend any cooperation to private firms associated with the federal government plan. One senior minister resigned and one was dismissed in 1975 in connection with attempts to borrow massively abroad on government account so as to finance Australian control of resource investments.[5]

The new government moved quickly to attempt both to complete the policy position as it saw fit and to remove some of the uncertainty surrounding policy which characterized the previous period. Early in 1976 the Foreign Investment Review Board replaced the previous committee, the 50 per cent rule on Australian equity participation in new mineral projects was extended to several other primary sectors, and the requirement for Australian control in uranium was dropped to 75 per cent. Over the next eight years, until the election of a Labour government in 1983, the fundamentals of policy changed very little. Australia's policies were characterized by a high degree of stability along with an emphasis on Australian participation in ownership in the resource field in particular. The government's position also reflected the almost universal ambivalence towards MNEs, as witnessed by the following statement by the Treasurer in 1981:

> We have come a long way from the days when mindless appeals to prejudices against multinational companies were the stuff of foreign investment debates. Nevertheless there does exist in Australia a very strong and thoroughly natural desire to see this country, its citizens and its companies, command a proper share of Australia's resources of all kinds.[6]

The Foreign Investment Review Board (FIRB) in the Early 1980s

Before considering the operations of the FIRB, it is worth noting that substantial financial deregulation occurred in the early 1980s under both Liberal–Country and Labour governments, but especially the latter. In December 1983 the exchange rate was freed. Most remaining restrictions on portfolio investment abroad were removed, as were those remaining on borrowing in Australia by overseas firms. As far as direct investment was concerned, the main effect of such controls in the immediately preceding years had been that new investors could not borrow in Australia to purchase shares or assets. It is also worth noting that the amount of information issued by FIRB is unmatched by any other such agency in this study, although in the late 1970s Canada was a close second.

The screening process in Australia is based on the Foreign Takeovers Act of 1975, which, as noted above, had antecedents dating back to 1972. However, the establishment of new foreign-controlled businesses is covered only by policy statements and guidelines, not by statute. While compliance with these guidelines has been technically voluntary, the government has had a number of weapons that it could use against those who tried to circumvent its clearly stated policy. For example, it could withhold foreign exchange approval and export permits unless its requirements were met. What follows describes the system in effect until 1983; the changes introduced thereafter, including the ending of exchange control in 1983–4 and a sharp reduction in FIRB's activities in 1986, are noted briefly in the next section.

The Treasury Department bears the main responsibility for policy and operation in the area of foreign investment.[7] Its pre-eminence in this field may explain the relative consistency of policy despite changes in government and despite some experimentation, particularly in the early 1970s. The Treasury's Foreign Investment Division makes its recommendation on each application to the FIRB, an administrative agency not mentioned in the Foreign Takeovers Act. The FIRB, in turn, acts as the primary source of advice to the minister. In the early 1980s the FIRB had two part-time members (including the chairman), recruited from the business community, and a full-time executive member, who headed the Foreign Investment Division; in 1984 a trade union member was added to the board. Perhaps half of the cases that came before the FIRB in the early 1980s involved routine situations in real estate and other sectors where allowance was indicated; such cases were, in effect, decided by the executive member, while the remaining cases were referred to the board in its weekly meetings. All departments and agencies that have a policy interest see each proposal before the FIRB recommends it to the Treasurer. The Act does not require consultation with the state governments, but in practice the states are consulted on relevant and non-routine cases. It is rare for cases to go to cabinet, although the Treasurer does consult the Prime Minister and other ministers directly on major or sensitive cases. Once the Treasurer receives notice of a takeover proposal, he has 30 days in which to issue a final order or an interim 90-day order, plus ten days in each case for publication in the *Gazette*, or a maximum of 140 days in total.[8] Approval of some major natural resource projects has taken much longer than this.

The screening process covers takeovers from abroad and within Australia, new direct investment, expansion into new lines of business, and proposals by single or associated foreign interests to increase an equity holding by 15 per cent or more even where control has not changed.[9] 'Offshore takeovers', where a parent company abroad is acquired by another firm abroad, are reviewable with respect to the Australian subsidiary, but in this case the national interest criterion noted below does not normally apply. It should be noted that real estate transactions are subject to review. The concerns here were to limit foreign investment in rural land (such investment is allowed only if the case for it is strong) to prevent rapid increases in the price of housing through speculation or to allow Australians to capture such increases, and to ensure Australian participation in major property development. For most new businesses, no review was undertaken unless the investment amounted to Australian $5 million or more; however notice had to be given of all proposals for new businesses in certain restricted sectors. Notice also had to be given of all takeovers, although in most cases no action was taken if the amount involved in the takeover was under Australian $2 million. In addition notice was necessary for all real estate transactions amounting to Australian $350 000 or more. Until 1978 the limits were Australian $1 million in the first two cases and $250 000 in the third. These limits were raised to $5 million on takeovers and $10 million on new investments in 1985, and further revised subsequently, as noted in the next section.

In order to prohibit an investment, the Treasurer must decide that it is 'contrary to the national interest'. What constitutes 'the national interest' is not spelled out in the legislation, but policy statements have been issued that converted this formula into a test of the potential net economic benefit for Australia if a given proposal were approved.[10] A summary of the criteria used is given in Table 6.4. The evaluation process had two stages. The first involved a necessary condition of net economic benefit in relation to the competition and other effects noted in part (a) of the table. If the proposal was not contrary to the national interest in these terms, then additional criteria were applied as noted in part (b).

It may appear to be extremely difficult to evaluate a proposal in these terms, given the complexity of the issues and the time frame involved. The actual decision-making process was greatly simplified in two ways, apart from the fact that many cases were regarded as routine and handled accordingly. First, an attempt was made to look at the key variable or variables in given cases, such as the taxation issue in some export cases or the effects on competition in an industry. No attempt was made, at least explicitly, to assign weights or priorities in some standardized way from case to case for all of the variables noted. More importantly the examination process was simplified by the fact that the key tradeoff between ownership and other benefits had been defined. Like many other countries, Australia is highly receptive to new investments, although some sectors are closed and there are some Australian participation requirements. Since new investments, unlike takeovers, do not mean the loss of domestic control of existing firms, the attitude to new investments is that there is a prima facie case for benefits. In takeover situations, by contrast, the view is that there should be other benefits to compensate for the loss of Australian ownership and control. Should the FIRB judge these other benefits to be low, it will recommend the retention of some measure of Australian ownership. If the benefits are high, or if

Table 6.4 Criteria for examination of proposals, Australia, 1982

(a) Whether, against the background of existing circumstances in the relevant industry, the proposal would produce, either directly or indirectly, net economic benefits to Australia in relation to the following matters:
- competition, price levels and efficiency;
- introduction of technology or managerial or workforce skills new to Australia;
- improvement in the industrial or commercial structure of the economy, or in the quality and variety of goods and services available in Australia; and
- development of or access to new export markets.

If a proposal is judged to be not contrary to the national interest on the basis of the above criteria, the following additional criteria are taken into account:

(b) whether the business or project concerned could be expected to be conducted in a manner consistent with Australia's best interests in matters such as:
- local processing of materials and the utilization of Australian components and services;
- involvement of Australians on policy–making boards of businesses;
- research and development;
- royalty, licensing and patent arrangements; and
- industrial relations and employment opportunities;

(c) whether the proposal would be in conformity with other government economic and industrial policies and with the broad objectives of national policies concerned with such matters as Australia's defence and security, Aboriginal interests, decentralization and the environment, as well as with Australia's obligations under international treaties;
(d) the extent to which Australian equity participation has been sought and of the level of Australian management and control following implementation of the proposal;
(e) taxation considerations (including the manner in which the proposal is to be financed);
(f) the interests of Australian shareholders, employees, creditors, and policy holders affected by the proposal.

Foreign investment proposals do not have to satisfy all of the examination criteria listed above in order to warrant approval. The list is drawn upon to the extent appropriate to the circumstances of each proposal and the importance of each criterion; and the extent to which proposals are required to meet the criteria varies from case to case.

Where proposals concern areas of the economy in which foreign ownership and control are already extensive or would become extensive as a result of their implementation, the government expects the proposals to provide for significant economic benefits and/or significant Australian equity participation before approval is granted. Special requirements and guidelines apply to proposed foreign investment in the natural resources sector and in real estate, finance and insurance, the media and civil aviation.

Note:
In 1983 the criteria were extended to include explicitly the opportunities for Australian contractors and consultants to engage in construction, the introduction and diffusion of technology and other skills, and limitations on export franchises. In 1986–7 the less demanding and less specific criterion of national interest was substituted for net economic benefit as measured above, except for the still restricted sectors. See Table 6.5 for policy in effect in 1988.

Source: Australia, Department of Treasury (1982, 6–7).

the foreign firm faces problems in revealing proprietary technologies or information, the FIRB will agree to full foreign equity ownership.

The FIRB is prepared to accept the view that in high-technology industries and in the case of MNEs whose international operations are highly integrated it is necessary to grant full foreign ownership in order to protect proprietary rights and the related organizational structure.[11] This is of interest, given the internalization theory of MNE strategies noted in Chapter 3 above. The exceptions for both new and takeover investments are important, and in both cases these exceptions relate to the emphasis on Australian ownership in some sectors. First, certain sectors are closed in part or whole to foreign investors. Second, there is a requirement of 50 per cent Australian participation in new resource projects; in certain circumstances, Australian participation is also required in finance, insurance, real estate and rural properties. Third, where foreign ownership of an industry is already high, the firm is expected either to show large other benefits or to agree to Australian participation.

A clear policy had evolved in the natural resource sector by the mid-1970s, although concern about Australian participation and some ad hoc policy had emerged long before then. In the areas of minerals, agriculture, fishing and forestry, Australian policy required that all but the smallest new projects involving foreign ownership (a) be determined not to be against the national interest and (b) generally have at least 50 per cent Australian equity and Australian voting strength on the board. The latter requirements were waived if the lack of Australian capital could seriously delay development, but efforts had to be made to ensure the future achievement of the 50 per cent objectives. Australian participation is not required for exploration activities, although it is actively encouraged; at the development stage the requirements just noted for Australian participation come into effect. Uranium projects required 75 per cent domestic equity and control, although 50 per cent might be permitted in some cases.

One point to note is that approval is for new natural resource projects. To this extent the activities of existing foreign-owned firms in their usual lines of business are subject to review. The FIRB has noted that 32 of the 55 new natural resource projects that came before it from 1976 to 1982 provided for at least the minimum guideline level of Australian equity, and 20 more were required to provide for it as a condition of approval. Four of the 20 later met the guideline or had clear plans to sell equity, while eight were required to meet the guideline before they started production 'or as soon thereafter as possible' (Australia, FIRB Report, 1982, 67). It is evident that the FIRB, while pressing for adherence to the guideline, also recognized that efforts made to satisfy it 'will depend on the commercial feasibility of a change in equity structure' (ibid.).

In 1978 an additional approach was introduced as a result of negotiations between Conzinc Riotinto of Australia Limited and the Australian government. Briefly, 'naturalized' and 'naturalizing' companies can go ahead with new projects, other than projects in defined restricted sectors, on their own or in partnership with similar firms or with Australian companies, providing the 'resultant mix' reaches the 50 per cent equity level where applicable. The Foreign Takeovers Act still applies, however. A naturalized foreign investor has at least 51 per cent Australian ownership and a board with a majority of Australians. Naturalizing investors have at least 25 per cent Australian equity and a board with an Australian majority; moreover they have made a public commitment, which is subject to regular review, to proceed to 51 per cent Australian ownership. This type of phased ownership is voluntary. Until 1981, fewer than ten firms had opted for it, including several large ones (Australia, Department of Treasury, 1982, 9–11). The lack of a fixed date for achieving the 51 per cent figure is one feature of this arrangement that has attracted criticism (Anderson, 1984, 97–8).

Just how Australian participation was to be achieved, beyond the natural resource sector and the others noted above, is not entirely clear. In Canada, the Foreign Investment Review Agency (FIRA) did not formally publish private takeover offers, although the business grapevine often spread the information quickly.[12] In 1980 the Liberal government of Canada announced its intention to require that all takeover bids, public or private, be publicized and that competing bids from Canadian owners be subsidized – plans that were withdrawn in response to the furore over the National Energy Program (NEP). In France, the relevant departments search for competing domestic offers more or less routinely when significant foreign takeover bids emerge. The Australian policy prior to 1986–7, as described in some detail in the FIRB's reports for 1982 (41–5) and 1983 (14–15) was far less systematic than either of these approaches, but it did have some structure.[13] It was customary to ask those involved in a foreign takeover bid to announce their proposals publicly, something that is not normally done in a private takeover offer. The announcement was solicited early enough in the discussions with the FIRB to allow interested Australian parties to make a bid and interested third parties to express their concerns. A public announcement was not expected in the case of takeovers involving less than Australian $2 million or in those considered routine. The same procedure was followed in the case of a proposed purchase of rural property, where some care was taken to ensure that Australians were given an adequate opportunity to purchase before the foreign acquisition was approved.

It is not difficult to envisage the problems that such an approach raised: in effect, the government and the FIRB determined the division of property rights among the vendor and one or more domestic or foreign bidders. In the circumstances some ambivalence in policy was inevitable.[14] The FIRB appears to have attempted to resolve the problems involved in such situations by concentrating its attention on only the more significant cases and by being prepared to give much weight to arguments about normal commercial considerations. Particular attention was paid to sectors in which foreign ownership was already large, and to those in which Australian equity guidelines or other restrictions applied. The FIRB also attempted to avoid appearing to negotiate for one party or the other, although this must sometimes have led to situations reminiscent of the British television series entitled 'Yes, Minister'. For example, an officer of the FIRB began a long statement on this point as follows: 'The short answer is that FIRB does not act as any kind of arbiter at all between competing bids. That is not to say that FIRB takes no account of views put before it by those who wish to do so' (Harvey, 1981, 188).

In concluding this section, a few comments are in order about Australian policy on outward direct investment.[15] Australia has not been a substantial exporter of capital until recently. During the 1976–83 period, the policies with the largest effect on capital export were those related to exchange control. Approval for capital export was given if the investment involved Australian managerial participation and export of skills, promoted Australian exports, or protected an existing investment abroad. These criteria were designed to test whether a direct investment rather than a portfolio investment was involved; portfolio investments were limited by exchange control. Trade considerations also played a part in determining policy towards capital export, as is shown by the second of the above criteria and by the government's unfavourable view of direct investments set up outside Australia for the purpose of promoting exports to Australia. Investments by financial enterprises abroad were scrutinized closely to ensure that the controls on foreign borrowing in Australia were not evaded. Current income could be retained abroad provided it was demonstrated that this income was needed for development purposes. There was no attempt, however, to evaluate the broader economic effects on Australia of outward direct investment, including the question of whether the firm might be able to export instead. The few rejections of applications in the years noted were related to questions about whether a direct investment was actually involved. Restrictions on portfolio and direct investments abroad by residents of Australia, which had been eased earlier, were removed in 1983–4.

Meanwhile the picture of Australia as very largely a host country for FDI was beginning to change significantly. A growing rate of merger activity in Australia in the 1980s spilled over into major foreign acquisitions, with entrepreneurs in the resource companies and media groups leading the way.[16] Many of these outward direct investments had encountered serious financial problems by the end of the decade. The difficulties in broadcasting and newspapers, prompting sales of assets to non-residents, severely challenged Australian policies aimed at retaining domestic control in these sectors. Outward FDI continued to be substantial. One estimate suggests Australia ranked eighth in outward mergers and acquisitions in the first nine months of 1990 (*World Deal Review*, 1991, 47–8).

Recent Developments in Australian Policy

The election of a Labour Party government in March 1983 might have been expected to change the situation significantly. Before Labour formed the government, its position on the regulation of MNEs had certainly been stronger than the policies in effect in 1976–83, despite the fact that most of the important aspects of that policy, which had evolved in the mid-1970s, incorporated changes introduced by the previous Labour government and enjoyed the support of the major parties. In the election campaign of 1983 the Labour Party called for the following measures (*The Economist*, 26 February 1983, 74):

1. a requirement of at least 50 per cent Australian participation not only in new mineral projects, as before, but also in new investments in other industries;
2. stronger efforts to ensure 50 per cent local ownership in new mineral projects, including government participation in some cases; a reversal of the Fraser government's decision to license up to ten foreign-owned banks;
3. the restoration of higher domestic ownership ratios in uranium; and
4. stronger controls on foreign investment in rural and urban land.

The Labour governments of Prime Minister Bob Hawke not only stopped well short of implementing these proposals but, especially in 1986–7, liberalized the existing policy substantially. It is useful to cover, first, the changes in 1983–5, which were modest except for finance.

A review of foreign investment policy left the main elements of the existing policies unchanged, while underlining both the 'significant contribution' that foreign capital can make and the need to ensure Australian participation in development. In particular, the government 'decided that it would not be appropriate or desirable to establish specific Australian equity guidelines for all sectors of the economy, nor to require majority Australian equity for new projects or businesses' (in sectors other than those in which this policy was already in effect). In other respects some tightening up of the existing provisions is evident. The criteria for examining foreign investment proposals were extended to include opportunities for Australian contractors and consultants to engage in construction, the introduction and diffusion of new technology and other skills, and limitations on export franchises. These additions were at least implicit in the existing criteria (Table 6.4 (a) and (b)). A timetable for naturalization was to be worked out in consultation with the companies involved, and the government announced that two additional members, including a trade unionist, were to be appointed to the FIRB. It was also emphasized that the FIRB was to 'continue to provide to the Government an independent and business-oriented source of advice'.[17] The government also announced it would raise the domestic ownership requirements for mining and production of uranium.

It was in finance, however, that major changes were brought in. The Campbell Committee had recommended in 1981 that many aspects of the financial system, domestic and external, be deregulated. Exchange controls were largely ended in 1983–4. The Fraser government announced in January 1983 that it would issue up to ten new foreign commercial bank licences, subject to certain conditions. Despite the opposition of some segments of the Labour Party, the new government issued trading-bank licences for 16 such banks, subject to varying conditions on services and ownership. Nine of the banks had no local equity (*The Economist*, 2 March 1985, 76). Also the Australian Associated Stock Exchanges began to amend their rules in 1984 so as to allow member firms to incorporate, and also to allow 'outside interests', foreign or Australian, to acquire ownership. At first the government applied the Foreign Takeovers Act, but in December 1984 it applied the maximum 50 per cent foreign ownership rule to acquisitions in this industry, where individual and total foreign ownership had been limited to 15 and 40 per cent respectively.[18] In September 1984, in an effort to speed restructuring of the industry, the government waived for 12 months a requirement that new merchant banks have 50 per cent Australian ownership and involve at least joint control.

Late in 1985 a new phase began which led over the next two years to a substantial liberalization of policy. In part this was a continuation of the deregulation begun earlier, particularly in the financial sector. However the major impetus was the sharply deteriorating position of Australia's external economic position – a considerable increase in the trade deficit and in foreign debt as a percentage of gross national product and a sharp fall in the value of the Australian dollar. The collapse of primary product prices in the early 1980s would fall particularly hard on a country with agricultural exports and mineral products each at about 40 per cent of total exports and a manufacturing sector still notoriously inefficient. A surge in business borrowing for investment and takeovers at home and abroad played an important role in the late 1980s. This is not the place to attempt to assess how far both short-term and long-term policies contributed to the problems Australia faced in the 1980s. For present purposes what needs to be emphasized is the changes in policy on inward FDI, apart from those involved in 1983–4 in the abolition of exchange control requirements for direct and other investors. Table 6.5 summarizes policy as of June 1988. The major changes were as follows.[19]

1. The opportunities test was discontinued. As noted earlier, this involved a demonstration that potential Australian investors had been given opportunities to express interest in or bid for the assets being acquired. The test was not applied systematically, as already noted. Indeed it was the government's view that 'it had made little difference to the level of Australian ownership and control of resources and industries over the years' (FIRB Report, 1985–6, 11).
2. The criterion of 'not contrary to the national interest' became the policy norm, replacing 'net economic benefit' in most sectors of the economy. However specific guidelines for review continued to apply in the still restricted sectors: banking, civil aviation, media, minerals and developed urban real estate.
3. The review process continued, with the changes just noted, but the asset thresholds for review under the provisions of the Foreign Takeovers Act were raised to Australian \$3 million and \$5 million for rural properties and acquisitions respectively. New investment proposals were reviewed if they were over \$10 million in most sectors of the economy, including manufacturing, services, resource processing and non-bank financial institutions. Subsequent revisions meant takeovers of Australian \$4 million were reviewed (\$2.4 million in the rural sector), the threshold for new businesses became \$8 million and that for commercial real estate became \$4 million (*World Deal Review,* 1991, 47).
4. In terms of sectoral restrictions, the government also announced:
   (a) In restricted sectors such as civil aviation and media, review would occur regardless of the size of the investment.
   (b) The 50 per cent and national interest criteria continue in mining with an economic benefits test for acquisitions. The 50 per cent rule was abolished for new oil and gas projects, although the national interest criterion remained for those over \$10 million. The government took the view that the introduction of resource rent taxes and royalties ensured that Australians participated in the returns in the oil and gas industry, hence the ownership requirements were unnecessary.[20] Finally the terms involved for naturalized and naturalizing companies were eased.
   (c) Contrary to the trend in most other sectors, the requirements for purchase of developed residential real estate were tightened in

some respects. In particular, the removal in September 1987 of the $600 000 cumulative exemption threshold for developed urban real estate purchases by non-residents led to a substantial increase in the number of such investments subject to examination. In 1987–8 there were 1219 such proposals, compared to 88 in the previous year (FIRB, 1987–8, 14). The 50 per cent rule on foreign acquisition of undeveloped real estate was removed, subject to not more than half the residential units in any one development being sold to foreign interests. The restriction on foreign acquisition of developed non-residential real estate was eased, subject to a (flexible) 50 per cent Australian ownership rule.

It will be evident from the above that the FIRB process and sectoral restrictions, while continuing, have been significantly eased – first in finance, then more generally in 1986 and 1987. Among other things, these changes affect any reading of the statistical series on FIRB's performance for 1987–8 and later. For example, the routine tax conditions imposed earlier on accepted proposals were discontinued. Residential real estate proposals grew rapidly, while other proposals declined as thresholds were increased. The sharp increase in the number of rejections in 1987–8 must be qualified by the fact that all but one involved the acquisition of real estate (Table 6.6).

Finally it should be noted that significant changes have occurred in policy areas related to those emphasized here. In order to encourage the inflow of capital, the federal government abolished in 1987 both the withholding tax on dividends paid abroad and the branch profits tax (payable in addition to income tax) on foreign firms operating in Australia in that form. Moreover the offsets policy which had been directed to defence industries was broadened in the mid-1980s to encompass many other industries and to encourage the development of internationally competitive firms with a focus on technological development. In essence, larger government contracts which involve imports require offsets of 30 per cent of the import content. Such offsets are assessed in terms of long-term competitiveness, technical sophistication and augmentation of the overseas suppliers activities in Australia. This programme is in addition to a variety of grants and tax concessions introduced or extended in the 1990s as Australia, like other countries, attempted to increase research-intensive and internationally competitive industries (see InterData, 1988, 22–6).

An Evaluation of Policy

The roots of Australian policy for the 1970s and 1980s lie in the Companies (Foreign Takeovers) Act of 1972. Some of the policies under consideration

Table 6.5 Summary of Australia's foreign investment policy, as at June 1988

General

The government's foreign investment policy is framed and administered with a view to encouraging foreign investment in Australia and ensuring that such investment is consistent with the needs of the community. The Government recognizes the substantial contribution foreign investment makes to the development of Australia's industries and resources. Capital from other countries supplements domestic savings and provides scope for higher rates of economic activity and employment. Foreign capital also provides access to new technology, management skills and overseas markets.

Examination

The following types of proposals by foreign interests to invest in Australia are subject to examination:

- acquisitions of substantial interests in existing Australian businesses, as provided in the Foreign Takeovers Act 1975 (FTA). The government has announced that the FTA will be amended to exempt proposals in respect of businesses with total assets of less than $5 million (less than $3 million for rural properties) from the provisions of the Act;
- proposals for the establishment of new businesses involving total investment of $10 million or more;
- proposals for investment in civil aviation and the media irrespective of size;
- direct investments by foreign governments or their agencies; and
- proposals to acquire real estate. The government has announced that the FTA will be amended to bring all acquisitions of urban real estate within its provisions.

Sectoral guidelines

The policy applicable to investment proposals subject to examination is outlined below:

Manufacturing, Services, Resource Processing, Non-Bank Financial Institutions, Insurance, Sharebroking, Tourism (Hotels and Resorts), Rural Properties, Primary Industry (other than non-oil and gas mining)
The Government approves proposals to acquire existing businesses or to establish new businesses over $10 million, unless the proposal is contrary to the national interest.

Real estate
Acquisitions of real estate for development are approved unless they are contrary to the national interest. Foreign interests are normally given approval to buy vacant residential land (providing a dwelling is built within 12 months) and to buy home units, townhouses etc 'off the plan' or under construction, providing no more than half of the units in any one development are sold to foreign interests.

Acquisitions of developed non-residential commercial real estate are permitted, subject to the acquisition being made with 50 per cent Australian equity participation. Where Australian equity is not available, 100 per cent acquisitions by foreign interests are approved unless they are contrary to the national interest.

Acquisitions of developed residential real estate are not permitted except in the case of Australian citizens abroad, intending migrants who have received approval from the immigration authorities to take up permanent residence in Australia, and foreign companies buying for their senior executives resident in Australia.

Mining
A proposal for a new (non-oil and gas) mining project involving expenditure of $10 million or more is allowed to proceed if it is not contrary to the national interest and it provides for a minimum 50 per cent Australian equity and joint control. The Australian equity and control guideline is applied flexibly. Proposals for acquisitions of existing mining businesses (other than oil and gas) need to demonstrate net economic benefits.

Banking
The Government does not envisage issuing further banking authorities to foreign interests not already holding a banking authority in Australia. Foreign investment in the banking sector needs to be consistent with the Banks (Shareholdings) Act and banking policy, including prudential requirements.

Civil aviation
All proposals to establish a business or take over a business relating to civil aviation are subject to case-by-case assessment.

Radio and television
Foreign investment in radio and television is governed by the Broadcasting and Television Act 1942. The Act provides that a 'foreign person', as defined in that Act, may not hold or control, directly or indirectly, more than 15 per cent of the issued capital or voting rights in a licensee company, and that two or more 'foreign persons' may not hold or control in aggregate more than 20 per cent of the issued capital or voting rights in a licensee company.

Newspapers
Foreign investment in mass circulation newspapers is restricted. All proposals by foreign interests to establish a newspaper in Australia are subject to case-by-case examination.

Uranium
Foreign interests may explore for uranium and are not required to seek Australian participation in their exploration activities. With respect to development of uranium projects, the government's policy provides for the continuing operation of the existing Ranger and Nabarlek projects in the Northern Territory and the development of the Olympic Dam copper/uranium/gold deposit in South Australia, but for no other uranium mines to be developed.

Naturalization

A company may be granted naturalized status if (i) it is at least 51 per cent Australian owned; (ii) its Articles of Association provide for a majority of board members to be Australian citizens; and (iii) general understandings have been reached about the company's autonomy and to ensure that its operations and policies are determined by the Australian board. A naturalizing company must be at least 25 per cent Australian owned and have given a public commitment to increase Australian equity to 51 per cent on a generally agreed timetable. It must also meet conditions (ii) and (iii) for naturalized companies.

The only criterion for approval of examinable proposals by naturalized and naturalizing companies (other than in the uranium, civil aviation, media and banking sectors) is that proposals be judged not contrary to the national interest, except that in establishing new mining projects over $10 million in partnership with other foreign interests the naturalized/naturalizing companies should hold at least 50 per cent of the equity in the joint venture. For purposes of calculating Australian ownership levels, a naturalizing company is given prior credit for achieving 51 per cent Australian ownership.

Source: Australia (FIRB, 1987–8, 31–3).

Table 6.6 Conditional approvals and rejections of foreign investment proposals, Australia, 1976–7 to 1987–8

Type of proposal	*1976–7*[a]	*1977–8*	*1978–9*	*1979–80*	*1980–81*	*1981–2*	*1982–3*	*Total to 1982–3*	*1983–4*	*1984–5*	*1985–6*	*1986–7*	*1987–8*
Approved without conditions	692	764	591	757	710	847	800	5 161	781	770	580	529	1 641
Conditionally approved	450	312	287	329	462	362	310	2 512	427	482	710	818	1 450
Total approved	1 142	1 076	878	1 086	1 172	1 209	1 110	7 673	1 208	1 252	1 290	1 347	3 091
Rejected	7	9	6	20	40	47	60	189	54	34	20	5	100
Total decided	1 149	1 085	884	1 106	1 212	1 256	1 170	7 862	1 262	1 286	1 310	1 352	3 191
Not requiring approval under Act or policy	252	228	168	360	447	140	108	1 703	36	26	17	6	—
Withdrawn	58	29	24	51	74	77	85	398	67	66	51	54	139
As % of total decided													
Conditionally approved	39.2	28.8	32.5	29.7	38.1	28.9	26.5	32.0	33.8	37.5	54.2	60.5	45.4
Rejected	0.6	0.8	0.7	1.8	3.3	3.7	5.1	2.4	4.2	2.6	1.5	0.3	3.1
Withdrawn	5.0	2.7	2.7	5.1	6.1	6.1	7.3	5.1	5.3	5.1	3.9	4.0	4.4

Notes:
In 1981–2 and 1982–3 there were 272 and 218 proposals, respectively, for urban real estate and rural land together. All but one of the rejected proposals in 1987–8 involved acquisition of real estate.
[a] 1 April 1976 to 30 June 1977.

Source: Australia, *FIRB Reports* (1982, 82; 1985–6, 42; 1987–8, 5, 37).

in 1972–5 anticipated a much more restrictive policy towards FDI. What has been in effect since the early 1970s – most clearly since 1975 – is a policy which accepts the need for such investment combined with, first, a number of partly or wholly restricted sectors and, second, an attempt to ensure Australian participation in new resource projects and a few other sectors. At no time, despite much rhetoric, has there been a substantial change in the framework of this policy, such as significant reliance on imports of technology by means other than FDI. When significant change did occur after 1985 it was to make policy less restrictive, in line with developments in other countries. Moreover the yet more open approach left in place the main policy instruments – FIRB, restricted sectors and Australian participation in selected sectors.

For at least the period 1975–85 and, on some interpretations 1972 to the present, Australian policy has been relatively stable, relatively clear in its priorities and (given that it had a review mechanism) relatively open to FDI. This is a judgement which depends on one's views on policies in the other countries yet to be considered. In particular some vagueness in the area of takeovers was noted above. Deferring comparative analysis to Part III, one can note here considerable evidence (apart from policy statements) for the description of policy just given and also point to some reasons why a relatively stable and clear policy developed.

One piece of evidence on the welcoming attitude to FDI is the fact that in the years 1976–85 only about one-third of the approved applications had conditions attached to them (Table 6.6). Moreover, in the great majority of cases, these conditions referred to equity participation by Australians (notably in minerals), resale of an acquisition (mainly in real estate) or taxation agreements; or they drew attention to the participation requirements that would apply should exploration lead to development (Table 6.7). The taxation conditions usually referred to the ways in which restructuring or financing of the firm occurred; these conditions were discontinued in 1986–7 when the government developed other ways to deal with the tax effects. Consultation and reporting conditions generally involved following up those with respect to equity participation and taxation. These conditions should not be confused, therefore, with the undertakings on employment, foreign trade, research and other aspects of economic performance imposed by some other screening agencies.[21] Indeed FIRB (1984–5, 5) put it very strongly:

> The Board has avoided recommending the imposition of conditions that would require the parties to alter aspects of their proposed investments relating to the operations and conduct of their businesses; such 'performance requirements' would not be in the commercial interests of the parties to proposals and would represent an unwarranted incursion of foreign investment policy into business affairs.

Table 6.7 *Conditions applied to approved foreign investment proposals, Australia, 1977–8 to 1986–7*

	1977–8 to 1982–3					*1983–4 to 1986–7*		
	Real estate (1978 & 1979)	*Mineral exploration (1977–82)*	*Acquisition (includes real estate 1980–83)*	*New business*	*Total*	*Acquisitions*	*New Business*	*Total*
No. of conditionally approved proposals	155	451	1 319	145	2 070	2 195	242	2 437
Conditions								
Resale	144	5	507	4	660	269	1	270
Australian equity	2	449	306	71	828	121	29	150
Taxation	—	1	329	32	362	2 007	284	2 291
Periodic reporting	70	5	399	52	526	224	18	242
Consultation	15	7	161	32	215	65	9	74
Development and zoning	24	6	69	43	142	84	16	100
Environment	10	9	42	22	83	23	2	25
Other	2	6	97	34	139	136	32	168

Notes:
Data for 1976–7 are not included since the classification system was more limited then. Taxation was not a separate category in 1977–8 and 1978–9. Real estate covers 1977–8 and 1978–9, since data were not shown separately for later years. Many proposals have more than one condition attached.

Source: Compiled from Australia (various years) FIRB Reports.

As for the monitoring process, it should be noted that conditional approvals are not part of the Foreign Takeovers Act and that the practice of screening new businesses is based on a policy statement rather than on legislation. Thus there is no statutory basis for conditional approvals, although the government did have a number of policy guidelines and ways to enforce them, as noted earlier. In order to enforce its conditions, the FIRB relies on publicity, on formal reporting in connection with matters such as major equity participation by Australians, and on encouragement to firms to report major subsequent developments to the FIRB. It is important to underline, therefore, that for the most part there is no intention either to exact detailed undertakings on various aspects of economic performance or to monitor their subsequent achievement.[22] The economic benefits claimed by the firms on entry, and considered and published by the FIRB, are not generally reported or enforced later.

Further evidence that Australian policy was reasonably stable and favoured direct investment is the fact that the rejection rate rose to a peak of only 5.1 per cent in 1982–3 and declined thereafter. In the period before the process of liberalization began, rejections averaged only 2.4 per cent and withdrawals of applications averaged 5.1 per cent. Withdrawals were made for a wide variety of reasons, but some portion certainly reflected a recognition that the proposal would be rejected unless it was modified to meet government policies. It is important to note that private parties often engage in extensive discussion with FIRB officers before they submit a formal proposal, in order to ascertain what is likely to be acceptable; moreover, in the course of examining formal proposals, the FIRB often suggests modifications or conditions that lead to acceptance of proposals that would otherwise be rejected. While these considerations must be taken into account in any assessment of rejection rates, it is interesting to note the small size of formal rejections under a system, like Canada's, but unlike those in some other countries such as France and Japan, in which the authorities are not attempting to avoid outright rejection altogether.

Having said that, one must add that the rejection rates of agencies of this kind are notoriously unreliable indicators of the degree of stringency of the system, even for a country such as Australia where data are made public. Specifically about 75 per cent of approved acquisitions in 1983–4 did *not* lead to changes in control from Australian to foreign interests. These involved, for example, changes in control between foreign interests, restructuring or financing of companies with possible tax consequences but without a change in control, or partial acquisitions of 15 per cent or more which must be reported. Rejection rates were not given separately for the category of proposed acquisitions where changes in control were involved, although it is clear that FIRB paid particular attention to these proposals. The annual reports of FIRB after the early 1980s began to give more detail on proposals which were rejected. Such rejection became rare, except in real estate as a result of policy changes in 1987–8. In 1987–8, for example, all but one of the 100 rejections involved acquisition of real estate (Australia, FIRB, 1983–4, 9–10; 1987–8, 5.)

A number of other factors support the view that policy after 1975 was both reasonably stable and quite favourable towards direct investment. The FIRB and its support group had only 35 professional employees and 15 others in the later years of this period. This may seem large in relation to the small staffs to be noted later for Norway and Sweden, but a quite large caseload and more structure and reporting are involved for Australia. Also, at various times when the structure or the responsibilities of the FIRB might have changed significantly, the government clearly chose to avoid such changes. The decision not to have a register of foreign investment proposals is a case in point. This measure had been promised in the 1976 guidelines, but on the advice of the FIRB it was never instituted. The government also avoided a plausible opportunity to change its approach when it decided not to issue a more detailed set of economic guidelines; the FIRB argued that the adherence to the OECD guidelines for MNEs eliminated any need for such a step (Harvey, 1981, 179–84). The OECD guidelines, let it be noted, are voluntary and reflect in their highly qualified wording the different viewpoints of home and host countries, MNEs and trade unions. A review completed by the government in 1982 left the main features of the FIRB unchanged (Australia, FIRB Report, 1982, Attachment C). Policy changes afterwards were in the direction of simplifying and easing restrictions, with some exceptions.

If Australian policy towards inward direct investment was both generally favourable and reasonably stable after 1975, it does not follow that this policy was consistent or free of conflict. Harvey (1981) and Sexton and Adamovich (1981) have underlined the lack of a legal basis for new investment regulation, the weak enforcement process and uncertainty about some aspects of policy. Long delays in approving major resource projects occurred at times; environmental control considerations provided one reason for these delays, but they were also caused by efforts to ensure 50 per cent Australian ownership.[23] In 1981 the Treasurer pressed Shell Australia to sell 25 per cent of the equity of the existing firm, a move quite distinct from the policy of 50 per cent participation in new projects; however, upon running into objections, the Treasurer did not push ahead with his proposal. The major problem, however, was reconciliation of the emphasis on ownership with other policy objectives, as noted at the end of this section. There are four explanations for the development of this reasonably stable and reasonably clear policy: a political consensus between the major parties, the particular role of the

Treasury, the concerns about the maintenance of the inflow of capital and the development of a major decision criterion for FIRB.

There is of course a great deal of political rhetoric involved in an issue as large and sensitive as MNE activities. In addition there were differences on these issues between ministers of the same government which should not be underestimated in terms of policy development. In terms of what was done, as distinct from what was said, the Whitlam Labour government stands out from the rest as most determined to change the policy setting for such investment. It is difficult to know whether this period was the somewhat awkward genesis of policies which were to become accepted by other parties or, had the then Labour government continued in power, the commencement of a very different set of policies from anything seen before or since. In any case the succeeding government continued the major policies developed in this period, while reducing the uncertainty and underlining the welcome for FDI, while the Labour government that followed did not significantly change the policies until 1986–7.

Quite apart from the debate over the substance of the issues and the position taken by the political parties and government ministers involved, one should note the influence that senior officials have had on the resolution of the issues associated with MNEs. The views of department officials on these issues vary considerably. For example, departments of regional development tend to be very favourably disposed to such firms, given their mandate and the fewer options for less developed regions. Departments involved in technical development tend to be less favourably disposed mainly because of a preference for developing research locally rather than importing it. Finally Treasury officials often play a consensus role, and, in any case, are interested in the possible tax revenue and other macro gains from FDI.

It has been suggested that the Australian Treasury played a key role in insulating policy changes against political fluctuations.[24] More specifically, Treasury officials in 1972 and later recognized the need to accommodate the political concerns about MNEs but attempted to minimize intervention. It appears that Treasury officials prepared a policy in 1972 in response to the political demand and helped keep a fairly consistent policy despite political changes – and also despite some reservations they had about the then current critique of the effects of FDI, if one can judge by the Treasury study of this issue noted below. Responsibility for assessment in the Treasury probably also meant more emphasis on macro and general equilibrium concerns than if the assessment had been done in the Department of Industry. The predecessor committees of the FIRB, while interdepartmental in composition, were all serviced by the Treasury. The executive member of the FIRB heads the Foreign Investment Division in the Treasury.

A third possible reason for the relatively stable and open policy is the view that Australia needs to encourage a capital inflow for developmental purposes. It is easy enough to argue this *ex post*, given the data noted earlier on the extent to which the country has depended on such flows, especially when resource investments were heavy, and particularly if one leans towards a market-oriented development emphasis, as did the Country–Liberal Party coalition governments. In various periods the exchange control apparatus has been used to limit access to the Australian market or to ensure capital inflow in the case of FDI. Some institutions have been developed, as noted above, to borrow at home and abroad so as to reduce reliance on equity investments. There is concern about the effects of the inflow on monetary management and especially on the cost structure of the heavily protected and generally inefficient manufacturing sector. Yet the view that Australia benefits from the capital inflow has been echoed by ministers of all parties in recent years.[25]

This view may be based in part on the experience of the early and mid-1970s, when the inflow of capital fell sharply (Table 6.1). In the late 1960s and early 1970s Australia was enjoying a resource boom, the influx of foreign investment was substantially higher than it had been and relatively full employment existed. All that had changed by the mid-1970s, and, specifically, the capital inflow was substantially lower for several years after 1972. There were several reasons for this: the resource boom had run into problems, there was substantial currency speculation in 1975–6 and policy on portfolio account was somewhat erratic in this period. Nevertheless the proposals and actions of the Whitlam government had thoroughly alarmed foreign investors. Both the Prime Minister and Minister of Minerals and Energy had stated more than once their opposition to further foreign involvement in mining and tried to enforce requirements which made that clear.[26] Towards the end of its period in office the Whitlam government had modified its position on these issues, and the Fraser government which succeeded it made a determined effort both to stabilize policy and to seek foreign capital. The experience of these years lingered, whatever the role of policy in creating the decline, and despite the temptation at times by governments to exploit the issues for electoral reasons. The deterioration of Australia's external economic situation in the mid-1980s had a similar effect.

The fourth reason for the relatively stable and clear policy was the development of a decision criterion for FIRB, specifically the emphasis on Australian participation in natural resource development and real estate. Before examining some of the consequences of this criterion, one should note that there was an alternative emphasis which might have been given to policy, namely, to concentrate on securing more economic benefit in areas such as employment effects, technical change, competition and foreign trade. It was noted above that until the mid-1980s economic benefits were a necessary part of the process of approval and assumed larger importance as the foreign ownership of the industry increased (Table 6.4). However this should not be interpreted as an automatic bargaining process to increase net benefits beyond those which most proposals would point to.[27] It was noted that only the key variables were examined, and then only in non-routine cases; that most conditional approvals did not relate to economic performance; and that, in any case, the tradeoff of equity participation and economic performance was quite explicit in the assessment process.

In some other countries with review on establishment one finds a major emphasis on attempting to increase net economic benefit, or at least ensuring that net economic benefit does occur by imposing and monitoring conditions on subsequent economic performance. This is often accompanied by a view that the performance of foreign-owned firms would otherwise be inconsistent with the national interest, in comparison with national firms which escape such review. The problems alleged to be associated with such firms are many. In essence they amount to a view that the subsidiaries are dependent on the parent or other affiliates abroad for a range of functions which might otherwise be performed locally, with negative effects on innovation and industrial efficiency (little local research and development, a high propensity to import and a limited right to export) and that decision making in an MNE may at times be inconsistent with national interest (greater mobility out as well as in, and the ability to transfer price so as to minimize taxes or escape government regulation). For example, the basis of the Foreign Investment Review Agency in Canada is a concept known as 'truncation', which reflects such views, and it is a concept one finds frequently in discussions with government officials in France and other countries with screening.

Whatever one's conclusion on this point, the idea that MNEs retard domestic innovation and efficiency received little support either in the published literature on Australia or from most Australian government officials who were interviewed, despite a great deal of public concern about this issue in the 1960s and later.[28] Brash (1966) conducted the most thorough empirical and theoretical study of alleged problems at the micro level, while not neglecting macro effects. His conclusion was that Australia does benefit from FDI but may not be maximizing the benefits. He suggests that net benefits can be increased by reducing tariffs, attacking restrictive practices and tax avoidance, modifying imperfections in Australian capital markets and reducing state subsidies to FDI (pages vi and 275; see also Brash, 1975). The Australian Committee of Economic Enquiry (the Vernon Committee), which issued its report in 1965, took a critical stance on a number of important issues regarding foreign investment – a stance that was rejected by the government of the day. Mainly because of concerns about the balance of payments, the committee did not wish to see an increase in the level of 'new' capital inflow (total investment less undistributed profit). It also called for a review of takeovers and for Australian equity (especially joint ventures) in natural resources and was concerned about a further substantial increase of foreign ownership. On the question of MNEs' effect on innovation and efficiency, however, it took a more cautious line, noting that the evidence on restrictive export franchises was inconclusive and that FDI had made 'a very great technological contribution' (Australia, 1965, 1, 291).

A major analytical study by the Australian Treasury is also instructive in this regard (Australia, Department of the Treasury, 1972). Chapter 4 of this study dealt with microeconomic effects. Its findings in this regard are in contrast to those for the Gray Report in Canada, which appeared at the same time, and which the Australian study cites (Canada, 1972). The Treasury study does not find the export or research performance of subsidiaries inferior to that of domestic firms; it regards the high import propensity of subsidiaries as an aspect of technology importation; it suggests that foreign investments have expanded management opportunities; and more generally, it attributes the problems of Australian manufacturing to extensive protection against imports and to other domestic policy positions. The study's conclusion on the microeconomic effects of FDI, while qualified on some points, seems to suggest they are favourable on balance, or at least not negative, and that where particular negative results exist or net benefits are not maximized the usual cause is inappropriate domestic policies (ibid., 76–7 and 125–6). This view is reflected in other private empirical studies of the period, such as Sheridan (1975) and Carr (1978). There are qualifications, of course; thus Carr points to the problems of assessing the net benefit of FDI in a dynamic sense and to some possible stifling of innovative capacity. A detailed empirical study by Parry and Watson (1979) is inconclusive on the latter point.[29] Several government or government-sponsored reports on manufacturing in the 1970s have little to say on the subject of direct investment.[30]

None of the above should be taken to mean that concern has not been expressed about particular microeconomic effects of FDI, including some by the authors noted. The Australian Labour Party has been critical of some of these effects also, as is indicated by the addition of the issue of limited export franchises to the FIRB's evaluation criteria in 1983. Some of the Australian literature is reminiscent of the dependency theories of direct investment that appear frequently in the Latin American literature on MNEs,[31] an approach that yields both negative economic and negative political effects over time. My point is simply that such views have not played a major role in the FIRB process, in contrast with the issue of Australian participation.

What does enter into the FIRB process as the major decision criterion and bargaining instrument is the attempt to get 50 per cent ownership in new natural resources projects and to preserve a degree of local ownership in takeovers in sectors where foreign ownership is already high. If a form of nationalism related to manufacturing is relatively weak, nationalist issues with regard to the resources sector are strongly felt more generally. In government statements, public and private sharing of the rents generated by resource booms are repeatedly emphasized as the basic reasons for the policy. While a desire to exercise domestic *control* over economic and social developments in Australia is also emphasized, and 50 per cent of voting strength on the board had to be held by Australian interests, this consideration can only be regarded as secondary: there is nothing in FIRB's criteria or procedures to ensure that the Australian 50 per cent is held by an effective partner.

Gaps in the data make it difficult to know just how foreign ownership, and especially control, changed after the 50 per cent rule went into effect. In the decade before 1972–3, foreign ownership of Australian mining had doubled (McKern, 1976, 37). The government discontinued the collection of data on foreign ownership during the period 1978–82. Table 6.8 indicates that, after the adoption of the 50 per cent rule in the mid-1970s, direct foreign ownership of minerals fell by five percentage points (1974–5 to 1981–2). The decline is likely to have continued in subsequent years.[32] It is more difficult to trace the degree of control, since detail on various types of control is lacking for the years before 1981–2, when 30 per cent of the industry was in firms whose equity was 100 per cent controlled abroad.

The Australian concentration on domestic participation in new projects is not costless, of course. The capital used has an opportunity cost, and must be imported in non-equity forms when Australians cannot supply it. The late 1970s and the 1980s were periods of high real interest rates, and the recommendation often made earlier to rely less on foreign equity and more on debt financing from abroad does not look as attractive as it once did. Moreover there are important income distribution issues associated with both the Australian and the Canadian approaches to ownership issues.[33]

The Australian policy does not require joint venture partners or even majority domestic ownership. As Caves (1982, 91–3) has noted, this is not an ideal way to collect rent. A knowledgeable joint venture partner has some possibility of sharing rents, particularly if supplying technology or markets for the project. Where competitive stock markets are involved, the MNE can capitalize rents when it sells shares in its subsidiary, and the local shareholders will get only a normal return. In Australia, the parties involved have been generally left to themselves to come to a commercial decision on the precise timing and terms of local participation.

Table 6.8 Foreign ownership and control of Australian mining

	1972–3 (%)	*1974–5 (%)*	*1981–2 (%)*	*1984–5 (%)*
Ownership				
Foreign ownership				
direct foreign ownership	37.5	40.9	35.7	44.7
other identified foreign ownership	12.0	10.9	15.6	
Australian ownership	50.5	48.2	48.8	55.3
Total[a]	100.0	100.0	100.0	100.0
Control				
Foreign-control			29.8	15.2
Joint foreign and Australian control	57.7	60.1	22.4	24.8
Naturalized or naturalizing			5.8	11.5
Australian control	42.3	39.9	42.1	48.5
Total[a]	100.0	100.0	100.0	100.0

Note:
[a]Totals may not add, owing to rounding.

Source: Australian Bureau of Statistics (1981–2) *Foreign Ownership and Control of the Mining Industry and Selected Mineral Processing Industries, Australia, 1981–2*, reproduced from Australia, *FIRB Reports* (1983, 34 and 1986–7, 48). Data based on value added.

The fact that the policy exists and that the market was not always competitive means that some rents may have been shared with local investors. Australian equity markets and joint venture partners were not well developed in the 1960s and early 1970s, with the result that a few financial institutions such as insurance companies took up large parts of the Australian equity involved.[34] A study of major resource projects for the 1960s suggests that Australians investing through the market paid more for their equity in foreign-owned projects than the foreign owners paid. By contrast, cases in which Australian firms were directly involved show Australian participation at par (McKern, 1976, 46). These estimates apply to the period before the 50 per cent Australian participation rule was adopted.

The view often heard from Australian officials is that Australia had no capital gains tax (such a tax was not introduced until 1985) and that, while the states collect royalties, some states subsidize projects too heavily because of competition for the investments. Thus the policy of 50 per cent Australian participation in new projects serves as a net for capturing some of the rents that might otherwise escape. Yet a government that wishes to capture economic rents has at hand a more effective and equitable instrument than the 50 per cent rule – to tax the rents through either general tax policy or policy aimed specifically at resource rents. Taxation is not only more likely to collect the rents; it also ensures that the public at large receives the larger share of the benefits of resource development, rather than the institutional investors, domestic mining firms or the equity market more generally.

There has also been some concern in Australia about the effects that a boom in resources has on other sectors, by increasing wage and other costs, raising the exchange rate and thus increasing import competition, and absorbing huge capital and tax outlays. The question of an appropriate policy response to a resource boom is complex, but one aspect is closely related to the present focus. The 50 per cent rule adds to the pressures that the resource boom has on other sectors. Combined with subsidies to resource investment, the 50 per cent rule tends to steer large amounts of domestic equity financing to the resource sector. Presumably this raises capital costs to other sectors or increases the import of capital in non-equity forms. Australian investors, as a consequence, are more heavily involved in resource investments and (assuming the savings rate is stable) foreign debt instruments than they would be in the absence of the 50 per cent rule. Whether such a degree of involvement is desirable or not depends on assumptions one makes about the alternative investments and outcomes, but it appears to be a fairly direct result of present policies. This issue was raised as early as 1972 by a Treasury Economic Paper:

> Although the question of local equity participation in foreign-owned subsidiaries, like that of foreign takeovers, raises important non-economic considerations, it needs to be recognized, nevertheless, that such participation cannot, in general, add to Australia's total capital resources and extend Australian ownership of domestic assets *unless it occurs via an increase in the rate of domestic saving or is financed by overseas borrowing*. It can, in fact, reduce these resources – though not Australian ownership – if Australian equity participation (financed by a given level of domestic savings) in new enterprises displaces overseas capital that would otherwise have come in for these enterprises or if overseas capital released by Australian equity investment in existing foreign subsidiaries moves out of the country. (Australia, Department of the Treasury, 1972, 96, emphasis in original)

The paper went on to note that by using well-timed share issues the MNE could increase the size and profits of its subsidiary while maintaining control and investing less than it would otherwise invest. Such outcomes are not uncommon in mining, in particular, and do not necessarily yield a higher return than alternative uses of Australian savings (ibid., 97).

Partly because of the high degree of foreign ownership, there has been an extensive debate in Australia on the taxation of resource rents. The crucial question is how to determine and tax economic rents; that is, without distorting production decisions. Just how this might be done has been examined in some detail by Garnaut and Ross (1978, 1983). The Labour government in the early 1980s proposed a resource rent tax for new oil and mineral developments, a tax that was implemented despite strong opposition from the states with such resources.[35]

Natural resource development is the direct responsibility of the state governments, which supply infrastructure and collect royalty income. It is the state governments that bargain with the firms on these matters, while the responsibility for regulating ownership and exports rests with the central government (although the FIRB has a policy of consulting state governments about significant cases). In fact several states have passed ownership legislation of their own. Thus New South Wales attempts to secure at least 51 per cent Australian equity on new projects, rather than 50 per cent, Victoria has legislation (rarely used) allowing it to examine foreign takeovers that affect the 'general public interest', and Queensland has moved at times to protect local firms against both inter-state and overseas bids. These policies did not lead to serious federal–state conflicts (Sexton and Adamovich, 1981, 190–95), but the state governments, when dealing with foreign investors, are not averse to pressuring the national government to ensure that the investments occur, to that extent reducing any bargaining power that the national government may have.[36]

What has led to difficulties, especially between the Commonwealth government and the governments of Queensland and West Australia, is a range of other issues. The federal government has control over exports. Through the federal–state loan council it can exercise control over state borrowings abroad.[37] Only the federal government levies income tax; hence the way in which it makes financial grants to the state governments can significantly affect financing for major resource projects. Conflict arises because of differences in the views of governments over the pace of the resource boom, who gains from it, and how it should be managed. Thus the federal government has tried at times to moderate the pace of development in one or two states because of the impact on non-resource sectors and on macro management of the economy, for example, on interest rates. The central government has also indicated concern that the benefits to Australia from major resource projects have at times been reduced by low charges for electricity, royalty rates, freight rates and infrastructure costs generally, low charges that are sometimes brought on by competition for investments between the states. The states in turn believe that the central government's policies favour the more populous and developed sectors.

It will be recalled that a number of approvals by the FIRB have been conditional on appropriate arrangements being made on tax questions. Such arrangements are often important in the case of natural resource projects where, despite the political difficulty involved in delaying projects, the federal power over exports has been used to ensure acceptable prices and also to deal with environmental concerns. The federal government is anxious to avoid low export prices, which would reduce Australian tax revenue. In the area of raw material exports, unlike some types of manufactures, there is often a market price for comparable products that can be used for price comparisons, and projects are frequently large enough to warrant close comparisons. However, since a number of firms may be participating with different profit, tax and other variables to take into account, the government may find it has to deal with several export prices.

CANADA[38]

For most of the period under review Canada has had the highest degree of foreign ownership of industry of all of the countries in this study.[39] Since the 1950s there has been widespread resort to federal and provincial policies in response partly to concerns about the effects of such a high degree of foreign ownership (Table 6.9). Two major policy instruments are of particular interest for present purposes: the Foreign Investment Review Agency (FIRA) and the National Energy Program (NEP). In addition there have been important differences in views on the effects of FDI and on the appropriate policies, as witnessed partly by the major changes in the instruments just noted during the period under study.

The data on foreign control of the capital employed in Canadian industry are of considerable interest, both because they are available in some detail for a reasonably long period and for the changes they show. In the late 1970s close to 80 per cent of the stock of FDI in Canada was in US-controlled firms. Foreign control has been concentrated particularly heavily in manufacturing, mining and petroleum industries. In these sectors, shown in Table 6.10, foreign control rose very considerably from 1926 to 1948, and again from 1948 to the late 1960s. These increases appear to have reached their peak in 1970 for manufacturing, and in 1971 for each of mining and petroleum. Thereafter they fell almost without interruption, and quite significantly, until

Table 6.9 A selective outline of the development of federal government policy in Canada

1957	Amendments to Canadian and British Insurance Companies Act to ensure majority of board members are Canadian and to allow firms to buy their shares and convert to mutual companies. In 1964–5 limited foreign ownership of Canadian-controlled federally incorporated firms to 25 per cent with no single foreign shareholder to have over 10 per cent.
1958	Eisenhower–Diefenbaker Joint Statement on Export Policies.
1958	Broadcasting licences restricted to Canadian-controlled firms: extended to cable television in 1964.
1960	Leases for mineral exploration in Yukon, North West Territories and offshore limited to Canadian citizens or resident corporations provided 50 per cent of shares owned by citizens or companies are listed on a Canadian stock exchange.
1964–7	Foreign ownership in Canadian-controlled chartered banks, trust, loan and investment companies limited to 25 per cent of equity and no single foreign shareholder to own over 10 per cent. Citizenship and residency requirements for majority of Directors. (Subsequently the domestic assets of foreign bank subsidiaries were limited to a percentage of total domestic assets of all banks.) Ontario, Alberta and Manitoba prohibit the incorporation of foreign-controlled trust and loan companies.
1965	Amendments to Income Tax Act and Customs Act effectively prevent new foreign-controlled newspapers and periodicals and foreign takeover of existing newspapers and periodicals under Canadian control. Exemptions allowed for *Time* and *Readers' Digest*, but the former eventually withdrew its Canadian edition and the latter underwent major restructuring.
1966	Issuance of Voluntary Guidelines for Good Corporate Citizenship and reporting on these by larger subsidiaries.
1968	Canada exempted from US balance of payments measures on FDI, while agreeing to monitor any evasion of restrictions through Canada.

1968	Report of the Task Force on the Structure of Canadian Industry recommending a variety of policies.
1970	Foreign ownership of uranium limited.
1971	Establishment of Canada Development Corporation.
1972	Report of the working group on Foreign Direct Investment in Canada recommending FIRA, among other measures.
1974–5	Canada Business Corporations Act requires majority of directors of federally incorporated companies be resident Canadians by 1980.
1975	Amendments to Combines Investigation Act to nullify effect in Canada of foreign court orders under certain circumstances.
1973–4	Foreign Investment Review Act: first phase on acquisition of control of Canadian businesses effective 9 April 1974, second phase on establishment of new businesses effective 15 October 1975.
1975	Establishment of Petro-Canada.
1980–81	National Energy Program announced 1980 and put into effect 1981.
1985	Investment Canada Act (effective in June) replaces FIRA.
1985–6	Major provisions of NEP regarding MNEs terminated.
1989	Canada–US Free Trade Agreement raises review limits of Investment Canada and removes banking restrictions (see text).

1987. At the end of 1970 companies whose equity was controlled abroad accounted for 61 per cent of the capital employed in manufacturing, 76 per cent of that in petroleum and natural gas, and 70 per cent of that in mining and smelting. By the end of 1987 these figures had fallen to 49, 34 and 27 per cent respectively. The most inclusive measure of foreign control of all (non-financial) industry had fallen from 36 per cent to 23 per cent over the same period. It is worth noting that the considerable fall in foreign control of capital employed in petroleum was well under way before government-sponsored purchase of foreign firms was instituted in 1978, as noted further below. In 1988–90 foreign control began to rise again.

Two other aspects of Canada's changing circumstances in the 1970s are worth noting. First, Canada's role as the primary target for direct investment changed considerably. In 1961–70 Canada attracted 13.1 per cent of the flows of FDI from developed market economies, which in turn accounted for the great bulk of such flows: this proportion had fallen to 2.9 per cent in 1971–80. It fell to only 0.8 per cent of such flows in 1981–8, in part because of the effects of the NEP in the first half of this period (Table 3.3).

Second, while Canadian concerns and policies have concentrated on the issues raised for host countries, Canada has become a significant home country in a short period of time.[40] The net outward flow of FDI exceeded the net inward flow after the mid-1970s, and well before the substantial outflows associated with the NEP (Tables 6.11 and 6.12, especially column 7). Of course the absolute stock of FDI in Canada continued to rise because of substantial retained earnings as well as increased inward flows in some sectors. Nevertheless the flow and retained earnings figures taken together as reflected in the stock of FDI show a remarkable change. From 1975 to 1980 Canada's direct investment stock abroad rose from $10.5 billion to $27.0 billion, then rose further to $72.2 billion in 1988. For the same years the stock of foreign direct investment in Canada rose from $37.4 billion to $61.7 billion and $110.1 billion respectively. Hence the ratio of Canada's outward stock abroad to the inward stock, a ratio which had been between 20 and 30 per cent for decades, rose rapidly to 44 per cent in 1980 and 66 per cent in 1988 (Table 6.13). Looked at in still another way, Canada's share of FDI outflows for the developed market economies noted in Table 3.3 rose from 2.1 per cent in the 1960s and 3.7 per cent in the 1970s to 5.0 per cent in 1981–8.

In brief, throughout the 1970s there was a significant reduction in the degree of foreign control of industry in Canada, while at the same time Canada developed into a significant home country. It is interesting to note that the FIRA, which was Canada's major experiment in trying to change the economic performance of foreign-controlled firms, did not begin operations until 1974, and the major attempt to reduce ownership did not take effect until the 1978–80 period. Such lags in policy responses are not surprising. While Canada has good data on FDI flows and stocks compared with almost all other countries in this study, there are long lags in the preparation of data on stocks and the country of control. The foreign control figures remained relatively high, while falling, and the petroleum sector attracted growing attention everywhere with the price increases and supply problems of the 1970s. Moreover policy consensus on a topic as complex as this takes time

Table 6.10 *Control of capital employed*[a] *in non-financial industries, Canada, 1926–90 (percentages)*

	Manufacturing			*Petroleum and natural gas*[b]			*Mining and smelting*			*All non-financial industries*[c]		
	US	*Other*	*Canada*	*US*	*Other*	*Canada*	*US*	*Other*	*Canada*	*US*	*Other*	*Canada*
1926	30	5	65	—	—	—	32	6	62	15	2	83
1948	39	4	57	—	—	—	37	3	60	22	3	75
1960	44	15	41	64	9	27	53	8	39	26	7	67
1969	47	13	40	60	14	26	59	11	30	28	8	64
1970	47	14	39	61	15	24	59	11	30	28	8	64
1971	44	14	42	61	16	23	59	12	29	27	9	64
1972	44	15	41	58	17	25	47	11	42	26	9	65
1973	43	15	42	59	16	25	45	13	42	26	8	66
1974	43	14	43	59	16	25	45	13	42	26	7	67
1975	42	13	45	59	15	26	46	14	40	26	7	67
1976	42	13	45	54	14	32	41	14	45	24	7	69
1977	42	12	46	51	13	36	40	13	47	24	6	70
1978	41	12	47	41	13	46	38	13	49	22	6	72
1979	39	12	49	40	13	47	37	14	49	21	7	72
1980	40	11	49	38	12	50	29	12	59	21	6	73
1981	36	11	53	30	8	62	27	12	61	19	6	75
1982	37	12	51	28	8	64	22	12	66	18	6	76
1983	36	12	52	28	8	64	21	15	64	18	6	76
1984	36	12	52	28	8	64	20	13	67	18	6	76
1985	37	12	51	27	8	65	17	15	68	18	6	76
1986	34	15	51	27	7	66	12	15	73	16	7	77
1987[d]	34	15	51	27	7	66	12	15	73	16	7	77
1988[d]	34	15	51	34	8	58	11	17	72	17	7	76
1989[d]	35	16	49	33	8	59	9	18	73	18	7	75
1990[d]	35	17	48	33	10	57	9	18	73	17	8	75

Notes:
[a]Based on book value of long-term debt and equity (including retained earnings) employed in enterprises in Canada.
[b]Petroleum and natural gas not available separately before 1954.
[c]Includes the three sectors shown, railways, utilities, merchandising and (from 1948 on) corporations in the construction industry.
[d]Pro forma projections.

Sources: Statistics Canada, *Canada's International Investment Position, 1971–1973*, 134; *1979 and 1980*, 32; *1986*, 84–5; *1988–90*, 88–9.

Table 6.11 *Flows and retained earnings of direct investment to and from Canada, 1960–90 (Can. $ millions)*

	Inward			Outward			Difference	
	Flow[a] (1)	*Change in retained earnings* (2)	*Total* (3)	*Flow* (4)	*Change in retained earnings* (5)	*Total* (6)	*Flow (1–4)* (7)	*Total (3–6)* (8)
1960	670	280	950	50	N/A	—	620	N/A
1961	560	240	800	80	N/A	—	480	N/A
1962	505	325	830	105	N/A	—	400	N/A
1963	280	435	715	135	N/A	—	145	N/A
1964	270	480	750	95	N/A	—	175	N/A
1965	535	735	1 270	125	N/A	—	410	N/A
1966	790	640	1 430	5	N/A	—	785	N/A
1967	691	845	1 536	125	N/A	—	566	N/A
1968	590	810	1 400	225	167	392	365	1 008
1969	720	1 045	1 765	370	105	475	350	1 290
1970	905	830	1 735	315	342	657	590	1 078
1971	925	1 335	2 260	230	333	563	695	1 697
1972	620	1 545	2 165	400	-65	335	220	1 830
1973	830	2 165	2 995	770	571	1 341	60	1 654
1974	845	2 730	3 575	810	493	1 303	35	2 272

1975	725	2 556	3 281	915	487	1 402	-190	1 879
1976	-300	2 756	2 456	590	199	789	-890	1 667
1977	475	2 983	3 458	740	985	1 735	-265	1 723
1978	135	3 732	3 867	2 325	811	3 136	-2 190	731
1979	750	4 795	5 555	2 550	1 570	4 120	-1 800	1 420
1980	800	5 454	6 264	3 150	808	3 958	-2 350	2 306
1981	-4 400	4 480	80	6 900	-350	6 550	-11 300	-6 470
1982	-1 025	928	-97	875	-2 940	-2 065	-1 900	1 968
1983	300	3 838	4 138	3 400	-1 134	2 266	-3 100	1 872
1984	1 700	4 273	5 973	2 949	2 473	5 422	-1 249	551
1985	-2 800	6 641	3 841	3 900	201	4 101	-6 700	-260
1986	1 375	3 800	5 175	5 650	-1 044	4 606	-4 275	569
1987	4 600	4 706	9 306	9 375	N/A	N/A	-4 775	N/A
1988	4 406	3 814	8 220	6 800	N/A	N/A	-2 394	N/A
1989	4 200	4 956	9 156	5 290	N/A	N/A	-1 090	N/A
1990	6 600	2 388	8 988	1 450	N/A	N/A	5 150	N/A

Note:
[a]Column 1 is gross inflows minus gross outflows, including in the latter acquisitions of direct investment interests in Canada from non-residents; a similar interpretation applies to outward flows in column 4. See also Table 6.12.

Sources: Statistics Canada, *Canada's International Investment Position*, Cat. no. 67–202, various issues. See also source for Table 6.12, p. 65.

Table 6.12 FDI gross flows to and from Canada (Can. $ millions)

	FDI in Canada			*Canadian FDI abroad*		
	Gross inflows	*Gross outflows*	*Net inflow*[a]	*Gross outflows*	*Gross inflows*	*Net outflow*[a]
1979	2 909	2 159	750	3 714	1 164	-2 550
1980	4 227	3 427	800	4 916	1 766	-3 150
1981	4 801	9 201	-4 400	8 176	1 276	-6 900
1982	4 120	5 145	-1 025	4 458	3 583	-875
1983	4 012	3 712	300	5 840	2 440	-3 400
1984	3 743	2 043	1 700	5 343	2 392	-2 950
1985	3 910	6 710	-2 800	6 754	2 854	-3 900
1986	8 050	6 675	1 375	9 558	3 908	-5 650
1987	10 595	5 995	4 600	12 973	3 598	-9 375
1988	9 141	4 735	4 406	12 385	5 585	-6 800
1989	14 238	10 038	4 200	12 899	7 609	-5 290
1990	8 947	2 347	6 600	7 245	5 795	-1 450

Note:
[a]See also Table 6.11, columns 1 and 4.

Source: Statistics Canada, *Canada's Balance of International Payments*, 1926 to 1990, 176, 185 (Ottawa, 1991, catalogue 67–508).

to develop: indeed, while policy did develop on a large scale in Canada, a political consensus did not. In the 1980s the NEP was partly dismantled, so far as the foreign ownership aspects were concerned, and the FIRA gave way to the more welcoming Investment Canada.

How did these policy responses develop? There had been concerns about foreign control of Canadian industry in earlier periods of Canadian history. There has been a significant presence of US firms in Canada since the early part of the nineteenth century, a presence which has led to conflict from time to time. Yet it is fair to say that Canadians generally, including governments, were not seriously interested in the topic until the second half of the 1950s, despite the high levels of foreign control of industry noted in Table 6.10. Academic interest was even less evident. The ideas in Hymer's famous doctoral thesis (1960) led a largely underground existence for some years thereafter, and the first major empirical analysis of the Canadian experience after that by Marshall *et al.* (1936) was not until Safarian (1966).[41]

One person, Walter Gordon, successfully sounded the alarm on foreign control of Canadian industry and exercised a remarkable influence on both

Table 6.13 Inward and outward stock of FDI, Canada

	Inward Stock	*Outward Stock*	*Out as % of In*
		($ billions)	
1926	1.8	0.4	22.2
1930	2.4	0.4	16.7
1939	2.3	0.7	30.4
1945	2.7	0.7	25.9
1950	4.0	1.0	25.0
1955	7.7	1.7	22.0
1960	12.9	2.5	19.4
1965	17.4	3.5	20.1
1970	26.4	6.2	23.5
1975	37.4	10.5	28.1
1977	43.7	13.5	30.9
1978	48.3	16.4	34.0
1979	54.3	20.5	37.8
1980	61.7	27.0	44.0
1981	66.6	33.8	50.8
1982	68.9	35.6	51.7
1983	77.4	39.9	51.6
1984	83.4	47.4	56.8
1985	87.2	54.1	62.0
1986	92.4	58.5	63.3
1987	101.5	65.9	64.9
1988	110.1	72.2	65.6
1989	118.5	79.9	67.4
1990	126.6	84.8	67.0

Sources: Statistics Canada, *Canada's International Investment Position, 1986*, 28–9; *1988–90*, 43.

public opinion and policy development for the next 30 years. As Chairman of the Royal Commission on Canada's Economic Prospects in the mid-1950s he was mildly critical of the performance of foreign-controlled firms. The Commission urged subsidiary firms to employ Canadians in senior positions, to do more purchasing in Canada and to publish financial statements. It also suggested that fiscal incentives be given to such firms to sell a minority of their shares in Canada (Canada, *Preliminary Report*, 1956, 90–93).

As Minister of Finance for the Government of Canada, Gordon introduced tax incentives in 1963 to encourage such minority share issues. He also attempted at that time to introduce a tax on foreign acquisitions of Canadian-owned firms but was dissuaded by widespread criticism, not least from the Canadian financial community. He was the central figure in the decision to attempt to block or at least modify the takeover of the Mercantile Bank of Canada, then owned by Dutch interests, by First National Citibank of New York, an episode which led to ownership restrictions on banks.[42] He was instrumental in commissioning a study for the Government of Canada which became known as the Watkins Report (Canada, *Foreign Ownership*, 1968) and highly influential in persuading federal and provincial politicians, among others, to support more restrictive policies on FDI. With time he himself favoured increasingly strong policies, such as the repatriation of major foreign-owned firms.

Both economic and political issues were emphasized as the concerns on FDI mounted. One recurring theme was whether the microeconomic performance of firms was in Canada's best interests given that decisions about the Canadian facilities were made with a view to the global interests of the parent. It was usually acknowledged that such decision making could lead to short-run gains through the import of capital and technology and because of market connections. In the longer run, it was argued, it led to 'truncation', that is, to firms which lacked entrepreneurial development and independent innovative capacity. Such firms, it was argued, were unlikely to be research- or export-intensive (except for raw materials) and likely to be highly import-intensive, especially in goods and services embodying the knowledge of the parent. They were likely also to develop an excessive number of product lines and high production costs. The long-run effects, in brief, were said to be anti-developmental. This was the argument made by Levitt (1970), picked up by another report for the Government (Canada, *Foreign Direct Investment*, 1972) and incorporated into FIRA, emphasized in various publications of the Science Council of Canada (for example, Britton and Gilmour, 1978) and underlined again in the debate leading up to the National Energy Program (for example, Government of Canada, *Energy*, 1980, 47). It is well to add that the NEP's major concern regarding FDI was the capture of rents which would otherwise accrue to foreign firms.

A second theme, often dominating Canadian policy reactions, is the concern about sovereignty and independence. This concern reflects in part the historic Canadian worries about how to manage her relationship with her huge and (for most practical purposes) only neighbour, a relationship involving a high degree of Canadian dependence on foreign trade, defence and communications spillover, as well as investment and other ties. The issues associated with direct investment have reflected a series of particular concerns.

Three of these have strongly influenced Canadian attitudes and, through this, the policy-making process.

First, earliest and most aggravating were the issues involving extraterritorial application of US law and policy to Canada and other countries. No one would argue that other countries, including Canada, do not engage in extraterritoriality. It remains true that the issues which have been most widely reported, and which have been particularly prominent in Canada, given the large US investment presence there, are a series of US efforts to extend law and policies to subsidiaries located abroad. Trade with North Korea, China, Cuba and North Vietnam all raised problems between Canada and the USA, given the latter's determination to prevent trade with such countries at various points of time, including that by subsidiaries located abroad, and the equal determination by Canada and other countries to allow (non-military) trade by firms located within their jurisdictions. This was a quarrel between sovereigns, with the management of parent and subsidiary firms caught in between. It was a quarrel which permitted only short-term and eventually unreliable political solutions. From the late 1950s onward, a series of such trading incidents exacerbated relations between the two countries. The problem was extended from the early 1960s to a series of US anti-trust decisions which had an impact on Canada. Here Canada eventually took action, as did several other countries, by enacting legislation in 1975 to nullify the effect on Canada of decisions by foreign tribunals under specified circumstances.

Second, while different in character, the attempts by the United States and the United Kingdom to solve their balance of payments problems by direct controls led to similar concerns in Australia, Canada and elsewhere in the 1960s. The Canadian government took exception to such measures, particularly those in the major US market, as sharply limiting whatever control a small open economy had on retained earnings and other financial flows. As with the interest equalization tax imposed in 1963 on foreign capital borrowing in the USA, Canada was able to secure an exemption from the 'guidelines' restricting FDI abroad by larger US firms.

Third, however, one should note that no such exemption was available when the US government decided to impose a temporary tax on imports at the beginning of the 1970s, as part of a larger programme to deal with her balance of payments problem. While not directly related to restrictions on FDI, the 'Nixon shock' was something of a turning-point in relations between the two countries. It encouraged the Canadian government to think of a strategy to strengthen the Canadian economy and other aspects of its national life and in the process to reduce its vulnerability to external forces, if only by a relative decline in its dependence on the United States (Sharp, 1972). One could make a good case that over the next decade Canada's high economic dependence on the United States actually increased. Nevertheless this type of thinking influenced such actions as the establishment of the FIRA and perhaps other policies.

The initial response to the set of economic and political concerns noted above was threefold. First, Canada attempted to negotiate the broader political issues with the United States. Second, an attempt was made to strengthen Canadian capacities to undertake more investment. Third, a whole range of industries was partly or wholly closed to foreign firms. We shall note briefly the developments under these headings before turning to the major instruments of the FIRA and the NEP.[43] It is worth emphasizing that Liberal governments have been in power at the federal level in Canada for the entire period since the Second World War, except for 1957–63, 1979–80, and since 1984; the Liberal governments of 1963–68 and 1972–4 were minority governments.

In the past Canada has attempted to work out with the United States agreed procedures on some issues involving extraterritoriality. One agreement was for prior notification when anti-trust rulings would affect the other country's residents. Another was an arrangement whereby a subsidiary's officers could apply to the US government, through the parent, for approval of a particular export order where the United States did not allow its own residents to export to the country involved. Not much is known about the way these procedures have worked in practice, but the eruption of the issues from time to time suggests that they have remained unsolved. Amendments to Canada's Combines Investigation Act in 1975 empowered the relevant Commission to nullify the effect in Canada of decisions by foreign courts or tribunals which adversely affect Canadian interests. In December 1984 the federal government passed legislation which would allow it to prohibit a Canadian subsidiary of a foreign-owned firm from complying with extraterritorial measures more generally. The legislation also empowered the government to seize records in Canada for safekeeping if deemed necessary. This legislation was aimed in part at prohibiting in Canada a fact-finding process which is an important part of US anti-trust law. Several other countries have similar laws. Britain, for example, has passed legislation to prohibit disclosure of information in foreign anti-trust cases and to allow recovery of treble damage awards in British courts.

There are a considerable number of federal and provincial measures in effect which are explicitly directed to the performance of foreign-owned firms or to influencing their ownership or control. The attempt to increase the capacity of Canadians to undertake more of the investment which takes place in Canada has been a motive for many types of policy. Sometimes it is voiced indirectly or as an accompaniment to other objectives: for example, investment in education and skills, improvements in capital markets and general support for technical improvements. On occasion these measures to increase Canadian capacities are linked fairly directly to the desire to limit non-resident ownership or to increase that by residents. The arguments for dividend tax credits, and the limitations on investment abroad by pension funds, each reflected such objectives. An even more direct link was the decision to allow the deduction, as an expense for purposes of taxation, of the interest paid on funds borrowed to finance the purchase of shares in other firms – a procedure permitted in the United States well before it was allowed in Canada. The easing of rules on equity investments by various types of financial institutions in recent decades was partly for similar reasons. The establishment of institutions such as the Canada Development Corporation was predicated in part on the view that there were deficiencies in Canadian capital markets, namely, a scarcity of large-scale venture capital vehicles under Canadian control.[44] This type of measure overlaps with those explicitly directed to increasing domestic ownership and control.

A wide range of measures specifically aimed at ownership and control are in effect. By far the most important device is partly or wholly to close a sector to foreign ownership, sometimes with a grandfather clause for existing firms. There is now a significant number of such restricted sectors. In the case of the federal government there are limitations on the foreign ownership of companies in broadcasting, newspapers, book publishing, insurance, trust and loan companies, air transport and chartered banks. In the last of these an attempt was made also to limit foreign ownership of any one bank to 25 per cent, but this gave way to legislation limiting the size and growth of the foreign-owned bank sector and also subjecting it to central bank regulations. Limitations on foreign ownership are written into legislation in a number of other industries: for example, mining leases in the Northwest Territories are restricted to Canadians and to firms with 50 per cent share ownership by Canadians, and fishing licences or leases are not given to foreign-owned firms.

The provinces have also instituted ownership policies. Examples are book and magazine distribution in Ontario and Quebec, transportation companies in Ontario, financial sectors under provincial jurisdiction in most provinces, and access to public land in some cases. Several provinces restrict 'foreign' ownership of land, or levy higher taxes on transfers of land to or between foreign owners, including both individuals and foreign-owned subsidiaries: in some cases the restriction on ownership is extraprovincial and not simply non-Canadian. Foreign investment is limited in many government-controlled corporations.

Domestic ownership can be influenced by tax measures also. The 1963 budget gave a modest boost in this direction by lowering the withholding tax on investment income paid abroad for companies with a degree of Canadian ownership, namely, 25 per cent or more. Limitation of advertising expense deductions from taxable income for periodicals deemed not to be Canadian, along with other measures, were used in a protracted effort to support Canadian-owned periodicals.

It should be emphasized that much of the legislation noted above, including that on energy, is aimed at achieving effective control of the organization by residents, and not simply ownership of shares.

Improved information and voluntary guidelines of behaviour were developed prior to enactment of the FIRA, particularly through the Corporations and Labour Unions Returns Act. This latter Act is applicable to all non-financial firms above a certain size but gives some detail on those owned abroad. One can note also the federal and some provincial requirements that, with some qualifications, a majority of the directors of a business corporation must be resident Canadians.

Some examples of different treatment of an MNE after it is established in the host country include higher tax on transfers of real estate to non-residents and to foreign-controlled firms in Ontario and Quebec, and the federal treatment of licences for fisheries. Other examples are measures to exclude foreign-owned firms from enjoying a lower rate of federal tax for small business, various agricultural subsidies, grants for mineral exploration in northern federal territories, government advertising contracts by the Ontario and federal governments and (until 1989) underwriting of Canadian government debt (OECD 1985a, 68–75; 1987b, 35–7).

The most important attempts to influence performance and to affect ownership were contained in the FIRA and the NEP. We now turn to a closer look at the origins, operations and effects of these policy instruments.

The Foreign Investment Review Agency (FIRA)

The Foreign Investment Review Act became law in December 1973. The first phase, relating to acquisition of control of Canadian businesses, took effect in April 1974, while the sections of the Act dealing with new businesses took effect in October 1975.

While both performance and ownership approaches existed in the way the agency operated, the former supplied the dominant overall motive. Concerns about the economic performance of subsidiaries were of long standing. In 1966 the Government of Canada issued voluntary guidelines of good corporate citizenship and asked for voluntary reporting on these by the larger subsidiaries.[45] This was in part a response to the balance of payments guidelines issued by the US government, limiting FDI abroad and otherwise trying to affect the performance of MNEs. A report prepared for the Government of Canada (*Foreign Ownership*, 1968, 403) recommended the creation of an agency to coordinate policies on MNEs, but more particularly to make these guiding principles operational and otherwise 'countervail the economic power of foreign-controlled oligopolists'. It remained, however, for a further report prepared for the Government of Canada (*Foreign Direct Investment*, 1972) to develop an integrated approach to the possible negative effects on industrial structure due to excessive reliance on MNEs and the related case for a review mechanism. This report rejected other general approaches based on ownership, including proposals for a broad extension of key sectors or mandatory Canadian shareholdings (chs. 25–7).

The timing of the decision to introduce FIRA may have had something to do with the Canadian government's disillusion with US balance of payments policies in the late 1960s and particularly the import restrictions in 1971. Both the timing and the form were probably influenced also by the existence of a minority Liberal government subject to pressure from the New Democratic Party in particular, as well as to its own significant nationalist wing. The New Democratic Party took a stronger stand on MNE issues than did the Conservative Party and the Liberal Party in the 1970s and 1980s. It has been argued that FIRA was stronger than originally planned by the Liberal government, in part as the price for support from the New Democratic Party. The legislation introduced before the election of 1972 covered takeovers only, a move criticized by the New Democrats. The minority Liberal government after the election introduced a more comprehensive bill (see Fayerweather, 1973, 163–5, and C. McMillan, as quoted in Harvey, 1981, 35.) As noted below, similar electoral pressures helped shape the NEP.

It must be underlined, however, that the way for FIRA was prepared by developments noted above over a decade and a half which led many to question the economic performance of subsidiaries. The 'truncation' hypothesis was firmly embedded in the 1972 Report, often called The Gray Report, and in the legislation underlying FIRA. The senior officers of the FIRA, both in 1978 and 1983 – that is, before and after the major changes in its operations described below – believed firmly that FIRA's task was to correct for truncation. In brief FIRA could correct for everything from ignorance of Canadian possibilities in MNE headquarters to the pressures within a global oligopoly to favour locations elsewhere.[46] Many Canadian politicians are on record as favouring a similar view.

Review was necessary under FIRA for all acquisitions and for every establishment of a new business in Canada by foreign-controlled entities, except in the cases of (a) an acquired business in a field related to that of an established Canadian business of the acquiror with gross assets not exceeding $250 000 and gross revenues not exceeding $3 million (these limits were raised in 1982, as noted below); and (b) a new business in a field related to that of an established Canadian business. The FIRA did not review the major activity of foreign-owned firms – that is, their expansion in existing lines of business – except when mergers occurred involving sums beyond the limits noted or when ownership of the foreign parent company changed. The application passed automatically after 60 days unless it was denied by the Cabinet. A request for further representations could prolong the review period without limit. In the late 1970s the average number of days required to process cases under the standard procedure, which applied to businesses not in the small business category, varied from 80 in 1977 to 120 in 1979 (Schultz *et al.*, 1980, 65). However several interviewees noted cases where more than a year was involved and at least one pointed to a much longer delay.

To obtain approval the investor had to satisfy the government that the investment would be of significant benefit to Canada. The FIRA was required to monitor the detailed undertakings provided by the investors in their applications. Some undertakings were renegotiated as a result of the monitoring process, but no prosecutions were actually launched for failure to comply with them. Significant benefit was determined on the basis of five factors specified in the act:

1. The effect of the investment on the level and nature of economic activity in Canada, including employment, resource processing, domestic sourcing and exports.
2. The degree and significance of Canadian participation in the business enterprise and in the industry sector to which the enterprise belonged.
3. The effect on productivity, industrial efficiency, technological development, innovation and product variety in Canada.
4. The effect on competition in Canada.
5. The compatibility of the investment with national industrial and economic policies, taking into consideration the industrial and economic policy objectives of the province(s) likely to be significantly affected by the investment.

It is important to note that decisions on individual cases were made by Cabinet after the recommendation of the relevant minister: that minister, in turn, was advised by a specific agency with legal status; there was an Act spelling out procedures and penalties; and there was a staff of 130, of whom about half were professional and technical staff. The FIRA process was a very specific and formal one in comparison with all of the other review processes in this study. One aspect was the necessary consultation in every case with the province or provinces involved, which could not exercise a veto but could exert pressure on FIRA or on the federal Cabinet.[47] One reason why FIRA had to be spelled out so fully was the requirements of a decentralized federal system such as Canada's. Indeed the minister's recommendation to Cabinet included any representations submitted by the province affected. On the whole the agency developed a close and good working relationship with the provinces, perhaps in part because it gave close attention to regional development effects. It is true that at times the provincial governments were critical of FIRA, including one occasion in the early 1980s when the premiers of eight of the ten provinces publicly announced their opposition. It is difficult to reconcile this opposition with what is known of the process.[48]

The burden for the firms and for FIRA in such a detailed review process was reduced by the development of a short-form procedure in 1977 to speed up smaller investment proposals. Small business cases, which were 55 per cent of the total in the late 1970s, were reviewed by a special committee of Cabinet, and another 20 per cent could go there if a province or federal department did not object (Schultz *et al.*, 1980, 73–6). In 1982 the ceilings for these proposals were raised to $5 million and 200 employees for acquisitions and new business proposals, and three times that where the control changed from one foreign parent to another.

Unlike the other agencies or procedures discussed in this chapter, the FIRA was given the task of ensuring improved economic performance on a wide range of issues, well beyond the natural resource sector. This difference accounts for its larger staff, its stronger monitoring and enforcement features and, ultimately, the different perception of it by investors and foreign governments.

Those putting proposals to FIRA were expected to note the benefits for Canada in terms of the criteria noted above. These 'undertakings' became legally binding once the minister conveyed them to the firm in writing. The FIRA monitored the firm's adherence to its undertakings and was prepared to enforce them. Many of the undertakings given by firms and confirmed in the letters from the minister were very general statements of intentions, or they were hedged by conditions that made them amount to little more than a pledge by the firm to do its best.[49] Obviously it would have been difficult to hold firms to undertakings of this kind. However, judging by the more important cases that have been made public, many other undertakings were unqualified and specific (Appendix III). Moreover the FIRA surveyed these more rigorous undertakings each year until they were met, utilized random audits to confirm the reports, and spent considerable time in deciding what to do in case of non-compliance (Harvey, 1981, 144–5, 174–7). The minister could begin legal proceedings if the investor failed to file notice as required by the Act, failed to carry out the conditions set out in the investment notice or the undertakings connected with it, or failed to comply with an order of disallowance. A number of companies challenged the applicability of the Act in particular cases. The government, for its part, initiated legal proceedings against a few firms which failed to file notice and also in order to enforce a disallowed investment (FIRB Reports, 1980–81 to 1984–5).

It was emphasized above that from at least 1976 on the FIRB enjoyed a fairly clear mandate for its emphasis on Australian participation and on defining the key tradeoff between ownership and performance. The FIRA had no such clear mandate. Its many objectives were not assigned relative priorities and, in particular, the question of what constituted an acceptable tradeoff between performance and ownership was never clearly answered.[50] For much of the FIRA's existence the outcome of this lack of a clear mandate was considerable uncertainty among potential investors about what was necessary to achieve entry, significant delays at times and a review process that was widely regarded as being too legalistic and bureaucratic. It is perhaps of interest that during interviews abroad in 1981–2 – admittedly a difficult period for FIRA, partly because of the NEP – not only company personnel but government officials in countries with a variety of policies towards FDI were almost uniformly critical of FIRA.

The difficulty with an approach such as FIRA's is evident from its own description of its operations a few years after these began (Government of Canada, FIRA 1977, Appendix B). The criteria of benefit noted above are varied and phrased very generally. The weights assigned to these criteria are said to be variable. Nothing is said about the resolution of tradeoffs between conflicting criteria. Undertakings are described as both absolute and contingent, both precise and general, but not standard for any of the benefits assessed. Until the reforms in its procedures instituted in the early 1980s, the clear impression left was that the officers might well try to negotiate more undertakings than the firms offered, and that it was not clear which new undertakings would satisfy the agency since the weights to the criteria (hence the tradeoffs) were not evident. These matters were ones which the agency attempted to clarify for its own purposes. But the task of the FIRA was greatly complicated by the failure of the Cabinet to clarify the mandate and priorities of the agency, despite repeated requests that it do so. This failure in turn meant that it was difficult for the agency to let firms know what was expected of them. It also raises a question whether the agency was in a position to assess net benefit so as to ensure positive welfare outcomes.[51]

It is interesting to note that FIRA's disallowance rate was significantly higher than that of any other review agency in this study. The rate averaged 2.7 per cent for Australia during 1976–84 and 7.0 per cent for Canada during 1975–84; it was less than 1 per cent for most of the other agencies, though in some of these efforts were made to avoid an outright refusal. Such comparisons are difficult for other reasons also – for example, varying coverage of total investment, and opportunities to influence outcomes in preliminary discussions. In Canada's case one can note that 40 per cent of withdrawals in the earlier years were made in expectation of disallowance (Canada, FIRA, 1978–9, Supplement to the Annual Report). Withdrawal rates, like rejection rates, were much higher for Canada, averaging 9.6 per cent up to 1984, compared with 5.1 per cent for Australia. (Data for Canada are available for a longer period than data for Australia.) It appears also that the Canadian rejection rate was more variable than the Australian rate, showing significant decreases in 1978 and 1983 and a significant increase in 1981.[52] The Australian rate rose steadily after the first few years; although it fluctuated greatly in percentage terms, it was under 4 per cent except in 1982–4.

Not all of the public criticism of FIRA urged an easing of its policies. Some pointed to the fact that the original intention had been to monitor licensing agreements, as well as new businesses and acquisitions, but this was never put into effect (*Globe and Mail*, 28 November 1973, B2). Others argued that the agency did not give sufficient weight among its criteria to Canadian ownership and failed to review the major activity of established foreign-owned firms, namely expansion within existing lines of business. In 1980 the government indicated its intention to institute systematic publicizing of proposed takeovers by foreign-owned firms and subsidizing of competing bids by Canadian-owned firms, as well as periodic performance reviews for the larger existing foreign-owned firms.

The former proposal has no exact equivalent among the countries in this study, although any review process offers some situations where, because of denial of approval or for other reasons, opportunities arise for counter-offers. It may be noted that the French authorities do frequently attempt to find a French partner when a foreign firm proposes a merger, but this is done through a search by the ministries rather than publicizing the proposed takeover. It was noted earlier that the Australian agency did in some circumstances require companies to announce bids, which would have a similar effect, but this was not done systematically. A plan to register foreign-owned firms and takeovers was not put in place, partly on the advice of FIRB.

The kinds of problems FIRB was having even with its limited involvement in this respect would have been magnified in the Canadian version. One should not overemphasize the difference from existing practice. News of a proposed foreign takeover of a firm spreads rapidly in the media and in other ways; apparently there were enquiries from Canadian-owned firms to FIRA in most such cases (FIRA interview, April 1981). Nevertheless FIRA would have been put in the position of having to deal directly and continuously with the tradeoff of the Canadian seller's potential loss through a lower price, on the one hand, and the gains in Canadian ownership and any other effects, on the other. One of the more influential officials in Ottawa stated in an interview in 1981 that the best thing FIRA had done was to create some room for Canadian-owned firms to buy other firms 'at a discount', thereby developing more integrated and more innovative firms. Any losses to Canadian sellers were presumably offset by such gains. He held strongly to the view that the big difference between Canadian-owned and foreign-owned firms was that the former were far more likely to be led by people who were innovative, including in that phrase the accommodation of government interests, while the latter were 'bureaucrats, who just managed a business'.

As for the second proposal, that there be periodic performance reviews restricted to the larger foreign-owned firms, much depends on what was intended by this procedure. Assuming it was to be something more than collecting data or encouragement to meet general obligations applicable to all firms, then at least two points can be made. Such monitoring has the potential for some far-reaching direct regulation of industry, given the extent of foreign ownership and the interdependence with the Canadian-owned sector. Some very close coordination with the provinces would have been necessary, given their constitutional powers. No country in this study has attempted such reviews limited to the foreign-owned sector alone, so that parallels, if applicable, cannot be drawn.

In the event, the government announced it would not proceed with these changes for the time being, partly because of the criticisms at home and especially abroad of the NEP and of FIRA, but also because of doubts about the desirability of the policies as internal evaluations proceeded. On the contrary these pressures, and the recession of the early 1980s, led to a sharp change in FIRA operations in 1982–3 under a re-elected Liberal government, a change intended to clarify the bases for its decisions and to simplify and speed up its procedures. For example, a new procedure for small business proposals speeded these up, and an attempt was made to indicate quickly to each applicant what was necessary to obtain a favourable recommendation. In the fiscal year ending 31 March 1983 the disallowance rate was cut in half, and it was halved again in the next fiscal year (Table 6.14).

In the meantime criticisms from abroad had led to a reference to the General Agreement on Tariffs and Trade (GATT) about the undertakings on exports and imports made by firms to the FIRA. The United States in particular argued that these 'trade-related investment measures' were similar to tariffs, quotas or subsidies and that they distorted trade. Canada took the position that the undertakings were needed to counter a bias by MNEs against Canadian production and, in any case, were not formal requirements. Late in 1983 the Council of the GATT ruled that the undertakings contradicted treaty obligations for imports but not for exports. Canada accepted this finding and indicated it would modify the FIRA's procedures in line with it. In October 1984 the US Congress enacted a bill that, among other things, authorizes the president to negotiate the reduction or elimination of any export performance requirement that is established by another country as a condition for US investment and that is determined to affect US economic interests adversely. The bill also grants authority to impose duties or other

Table 6.14 Rate of allowance of foreign investment proposals, Canada, 1975–84[a]

	1975	*1976*	*1977*	*1978*	*1979*	*1980*	*1981*	*1982*	*1983*	*1984*	*1975–84*
Reviewable new cases and carryover	150	228	493	727	838	963	897	1 050	1 218	1 112	6 203
Applications											
Resolved	92	159	398	602	659	797	586	719	1 079	961	6 052
Allowed	63	114	319	541	576	687	448	513	924	585	5 043
Disallowed	12	22	33	25	44	58	63	81	60	27	425
Withdrawn	17	23	46	36	39	52	75	125	95	76	584
Carried over	58	69	95	125	179	166	311	331	139	151	—
Per cent of those resolved											
Disallowed	13.0	13.8	8.3	4.2	6.7	7.3	10.8	11.3	5.6	2.8	7.0
Withdrawn	18.5	14.5	11.6	6.7	5.9	6.5	12.8	17.4	12.9	15.7	9.6
Per cent disallowed for											
New business	b	0.0	6.8	4.2	5.6	7.1	9.2	11.1	8.4	4.5	7.1
Acquisitions	13.0	14.4	9.9	4.2	7.7	7.5	12.3	11.5	2.5	1.1	6.9

Notes:
[a]Fiscal years ending 31 March for the year shown.
[b]New businesses were reviewed beginning on 15 October 1975.

Source: Canada (various years) Foreign Investment Review Act, *Annual Reports*.

restrictions on goods or services from the foreign country and to deny importation of products that are subject to export performance requirements. This bill, it should be added, is aimed at many countries, not just Canada: some developing countries in particular are far more demanding and explicit in this regard. Judging by US Senate hearings on the subject, however, the FIRA played a significant role in highlighting the issue (US Senate, 1982). Developments in this area later in the 1980s will be noted in Chapter 9.

The changes which were made in FIRA in the early 1980s were not enough for the Conservative government elected in September 1984. In the following September FIRA was replaced by Investment Canada, whose objectives and design are substantially different. The mandate of Investment Canada is to encourage and facilitate investment by both Canadians and non-Canadians. The minister and the agency provide a number of investment services to that end. The review process is no longer required in the great majority of cases. Specifically notification rather than review is all that is usually required when non-residents establish new Canadian businesses or make direct acquisitions of Canadian businesses with assets under $5 million. Nor will review normally be required for most 'indirect acquisitions' of businesses with assets under $50 million, that is, when control of the parent changes outside Canada; however the $5 million threshold applies in this case also if the Canadian business represents more than 50 per cent of the assets involved in the total international transaction.

Review of new businesses and acquisitions can occur regardless of size in a set of activities related to Canada's cultural heritage or national identity. These activities, which were specified when the Act came into effect (the list can be amended), include the production, distribution, sale or exhibition of books, magazines, periodicals and newspapers; film and video products; audio and video music recordings; and music in print or machine-readable form. The Minister of Energy subsequently announced that upstream oil and gas production assets in excess of $5 million would be available for acquisition by non-residents only if the firms were 'in clear financial difficulties' (*Globe and Mail*, 11 August 1987, 182).

What also remains subject to review are all direct acquisitions of control of Canadian businesses with assets of $5 million or more, and indirect acquisitions as just noted. Recommendations to the minister no longer have to go to the Cabinet. A specific time limit is set for review, namely 75 days, unless both parties agree to extend it. The criterion of significant benefit has been changed to one of net benefit. However the detailed criteria noted above for the FIRA are virtually unchanged except for the addition of the effect on Canada's ability to compete in world markets, and firms will still be expected to make undertakings in some cases. Moreover, taking takeovers and new business proposals together, it appears that the review process has covered about 80 per cent of assets while applying to only about 20 per cent of the numbers involved.

In general the language of the Investment Canada Act implies a more welcoming attitude to FDI and a set of procedures less complex than those implied by the previous Act – although, as noted, many of the changes were anticipated by the procedures used after 1982 and especially after the election of 1984. Like all such review mechanisms, of course, the new Act can be applied more or less restrictively in practice. To date it has been an agency far more interested in attracting investment than in the potentially restrictive aspects, with the exception of the sectors noted. While it rejected no formal application in the period up to 1990, it did require undertakings of firms on the basis of the criteria already noted.

In the four years after 30 June 1985 Investment Canada reviewed 696 acquisitions and negotiated 276 undertakings in 11 per cent of these.[53] Since some of the undertakings involved more than one factor of assessment, the latter are referred to 359 times in Table 6.15. Economic activity was the most important factor of assessment (162 times) and conformity with government policy next at 95 times. Competition issues are presumably left largely to the competition authorities. In terms of rationales for the undertakings, compliance with a specific government policy is the largest category – the oil and gas acquisitions policy and the book publishing policy would be important examples. Greater assurance that the investor will implement agreed conditions ranked second. In 42 cases the undertakings were considered by Investment Canada to be essential to determining net benefit and were apparently not in the business plan of the investor. However it is hard to know exactly how to categorize these since some of the undertakings in other categories could fit this description. Voluntary undertakings were not required for approval. A few public interest undertakings go beyond specific policies.[54]

Many proposals are now treated fairly routinely, but two groups involve a great deal of effort. One is the small number of proposals in the cultural sector which, particularly in book publishing and distribution, are often difficult to resolve. The other group is a few substantial acquisitions in petroleum and some other sectors, and several foreign acquisitions of high-technology companies. One such case which attracted much attention in 1989–90 was the sale of Connaught Biosciences to a foreign firm. Investment Canada approved both of the foreign bids for Connaught, subject to a long list of undertakings in each case. Such a long list reflects many concerns, apart from the opportunity afforded by two proposals from abroad; for example, concerns about maintaining R&D, given acquisition by a competitor, and the fact that one of the bidders was owned by a foreign government. Institut Mérieux SA, which subsequently acquired control of Connaught,

Table 6.15 *Undertakings to Investment Canada, June 1985–June 1989*

	Category of Rationale					
	Certainty	*Specific policy*	*Substantive negotiation*	*Voluntary*	*Public interest*	*Total*
Factors of assessment						
Econ. activity	71	50	17	20	4	162
Cdn. participation	24	23	9	4	0	60
Productivity	16	0	5	1	1	23
Competition	0	0	5	0	0	5
Govt. policy	2	90	0	0	3	95
Int. competitiveness	3	4	6	1	0	14
Total	116	167	42	26	8	359

Source: Supplied by Investment Canada.

agreed to some undertakings over a ten-year period and some indefinitely, as reproduced in Appendix III. These undertakings were designed to maintain or increase research in Canada, maintain a high degree of Canadian identity and influence in Connaught, encourage employment and access to exports, and ensure vaccine and other supplies to Canada. It remains to be seen how fully such a long list of undertakings, both general and specific, can be implemented and monitored.

The National Energy Program (NEP)

Unlike several other countries in this study, Canada began only recently to treat its natural resource sector as a key sector. Foreign ownership in uranium was limited in 1970. In the early 1970s a Canada Development Corporation was established under federal ownership to invest in, among other industries, the natural resource sector. In the late 1970s Petro-Canada was established to further ownership and other government objectives in the oil and gas sector, and was given preferences in the acquisition of oil and gas rights in federal lands. In June 1974 the Prime Minister stated as an objective of his party and his government that 'at least 50 per cent and preferably 60 per cent Canadian equity ownership' should be attained in new major projects in the field of natural resources (Canada, FIRA, 1979, 9). However, except for federal lands, it is the provinces which have jurisdiction over and management of natural resources. The provinces have developed areas of public participation and of public ownership, as well as a wide range of regulation, but generally have welcomed resource investments from abroad.

Had the 1974 objective been implemented formally, a matter that would have required some difficult negotiations with the provinces, the outcomes would have been similar to subsequent Australian policy. It appears that the minister responsible for the FIRA was expected to work towards this goal where feasible, both before 1980 but especially after, without the benefit of either legislative support or public clarification.[55] The Canadian federal position, while it had some antecedents in both the provincial and the federal spheres, was not fully developed until 1980–81. It applied to the petroleum and natural gas sector, not to natural resources as a whole. It encouraged public and private repatriation of entire firms or parts thereof. It aimed for control, both private and public, and not just ownership. It differed in these respects from the Australian policy.

The NEP was intended to address a number of issues arising from the turbulence in energy markets in the 1970s. The federal government had undertaken a number of major initiatives in reacting to the energy problem, notably in the decision to keep Canadian oil and gas prices well below world levels and in the establishment of Petro-Canada and the Petroleum Monitoring Agency. All of this culminated in the NEP in 1980. This programme involved a considerable number of objectives, including increases in prices and in taxation revenues (especially the federal share), greater federal control of the industry and a shift in its focus to federal lands, and a substantial increase in Canadian ownership and control of oil and gas revenues.

The stated major reason for the planned increase in Canadian ownership of the industry was the desire to capture more of the economic rent in Canada. The government's position was that the major planned price increases would give substantial rent to an industry which was largely foreign-owned. It was also argued that the existing system of depletion allowances, which was available to all firms but utilized mainly by integrated MNEs with downstream profits, meant that the latter were the major beneficiaries. A further objective was greater domestic control of petroleum firms, as distinct from ownership; specifically the government wished to have more influence on the direction and speed of development of the industry, and to have assurance of more domestic purchasing and research than it believed would otherwise occur (Canada, Department of Energy, Mines and Resources, 1980).

The specific objective set was to reduce the 70 per cent foreign ownership of oil and gas revenues to 50 per cent by 1990.[56] This was to be achieved partly by expanding the public sector, specifically by introducing a special energy tax to be used by Petro-Canada or other government-owned firms to buy some of the MNEs. In addition the system of depletion allowances for exploration and development was largely replaced by incentive grants. In areas of federal jurisdiction these grants were to increase for companies having more than 50 per cent Canadian ownership, to the point where a company with 75 per cent Canadian ownership could get 80 per cent of exploration and development expenses paid by the government. There must be 50 per cent Canadian ownership at the production stage in the case of such federal lands.[57] Finally provision was made to reserve a 25 per cent Crown interest in all petroleum rights for all firms on federal lands (including those held by private Canadian interests) with some payments for work done to date. This was an extension of a policy which had been in effect with respect to Petro-Canada.

The NEP approach involved substantial fiscal incentives for both government and private firms to purchase foreign-owned assets. The overall costs of such purchases depend on a number of variables, specifically:

- the price paid for the asset;
- the discounted expected value of the income from the asset;
- the interest cost of capital used for the purchase;
- the cost of resources used directly to administer the policy; and

- the extent of retaliation by or disruption in relations with other countries.

As it turned out, the variables moved in the wrong direction, given the purposes of the NEP, with economically depressing effects which lingered for years. In a number of cases the prices paid for firms appear to have been well over the premiums above stock market prices customary for such mergers, a result attributable in part to the euphoria about rising rents. The expected value of income from the assets fell as recession arrived and oil prices declined. Interest rates shot up in 1981 in both real and nominal terms and stayed high in real terms. It turned out to be quite complex and costly to administer the detailed ownership requirements and some other aspects of the programme. Canadian policy invoked a very hostile response in the US press and in Congress, and relations between Canada and the United States deteriorated significantly for a time. The US government ultimately decided against direct and explicit retaliation, although, as noted above, it cited some aspects of the FIRA as violations of the GATT.

The costs of the repatriations under the NEP in the early 1980s were significant. In the absence of a federal government surplus or the prospect of soaring resource revenues, and given the weakening international situation at the time, the outflows involved in repatriation put much downward pressure on the exchange rate and upward pressure on interest rates in a period of rising unemployment.[58] From a longer-term perspective, the effects of these repatriations on the foreign share of net rents may have been negligible if one assumes a real after-tax opportunity cost of 7 per cent. The prices paid for the takeovers were apparently too high to allow such a return in the years afterwards (Helliwell *et al.*, 1984, 28). The exploration incentives did favour rent recapture, however.

One of the anticipated major benefits of the programme was to increase Canadian ownership and control of the industry's revenues, including public sector ownership. In 1981 alone the Canadian ownership of petroleum revenues rose almost seven percentage points. Payments for identified repatriations amounted to $7.5 billion in that year. About 60 per cent of this increase in Canadian ownership was in the public sector. Canadian ownership and control continued to rise, more slowly, for several years. Petro-Canada became a major integrated firm. Control of one of the largest integrated foreign-owned subsidiaries was purchased by a Canadian-controlled firm in 1985, after the revisions to the NEP noted below had been announced. This purchase resulted in part from a change in the controlling interest abroad, which automatically led to review in Canada, and also from the new parent firm's desire to reduce the debt associated with its merger abroad.

The Liberal government did not change the fundamental aspects of this part of the NEP, but it did increase payments for the 25 per cent Crown interest, underline that this was a special programme designed to cope with problems in a major sector rather than a prelude to similar programmes elsewhere, and made a number of ad hoc exceptions to the rules to allow particular projects to proceed. It also set aside plans to strengthen the FIRA. The objective of increased leverage on domestic purchasing for major energy projects had to be modified as well, in part because the possibility of realizing this objective melted away with the declining price of oil and in part because the pursuit of such leverage was contrary to the government purchasing code in the GATT. Like other countries, however, Canada does require that domestic sources of supply be considered on a competitive basis by firms that undertake major resource projects.

The Conservative government elected late in 1984 went further. Early in 1985 it reached an accord with the three western petroleum-producing provinces that, over the next few years, effectively phased out much of the National Energy Program enacted in 1980–81. Among other things the new accord deregulated oil prices and significantly reduced taxation of the industry. Three major NEP policies of direct relevance to this study were repealed. The special energy tax for buying MNE assets was ended. The provision for a 25 per cent Crown interest in petroleum rights on federal lands, applicable to all private investors, was withdrawn. The incentive grants for exploration and development, which were geared to the degree of Canadian ownership of the company, were ended on 31 March 1986, subject to transition arrangements. However the Conservative government remained willing to assist efforts to increase Canadian ownership of the petroleum industry, as evident in the permission given to Petro-Canada in mid-1985 to help Canadian investors purchase a major foreign-owned petroleum firm. Such episodic involvement is some distance from the concerted policies for Canadianization pursued by the preceding government.

The Canada–US Free Trade Agreement

In 1989 a free trade agreement took effect between Canada and the United States which included, among many other things, a number of decisions on the treatment of direct investment and MNEs. The provisions of the agreement in these respects were as follows.[59]

1. National treatment will be provided to each country's investors with respect to establishing new business, acquiring existing business and conducting, operating and selling established business. Each country agreed, more specifically, that (a) it will not require that minimum levels

of equity be held by nationals; (b) it will not require forced divestiture; (c) there will be fair standards for expropriation and compensation; and (d) it will not impose export, local content, local sourcing or import substitution requirements on the other's investors.

2. However, all *existing* laws, regulations and published policies and practices that do not conform with these obligations can be retained.
3. Canada agreed to raise progressively the exemption level for review of US acquisitions of Canadian-owned firms from $5 million in gross assets to $150 million in 1992 constant dollars. Canada also agreed to phase out review of indirect acquisitions, that is, where the parent's ownership changes. As noted earlier, Investment Canada requires only notification for new investments.
4. Acquisitions in certain sectors, such as the cultural industries and upstream oil and gas, will continue to be reviewed at the general thresholds rather than those just noted.
5. Canada agreed to give US firms national treatment with respect to ownership of Canadian financial institutions. This will end the 25 per cent limit on foreign ownership of Canadian bank assets, though not the 10 per cent limit for any one domestic or foreign owner, and also end the limit on total domestic assets of US bank subsidiaries. The United States agreed to give Canadian financial institutions the same treatment as US institutions when the Glass-Steagall Act limitations on bank ownership of securities firms are ended.
6. There is broad agreement to attempt to cover a number of service sectors later, using the principles of the agreement on investment and some other parts of the overall agreement – national treatment, right of establishment, right of commercial presence, transparency and dispute settlement.

In some respects rather little has been changed by the agreement. Existing laws, regulations and published policies and practices are continued if the countries so desire. This includes restricted sectors and non-national treatment in both countries, plus review of larger acquisitions by Investment Canada on all the criteria previously in use, except for those noted in the first point listed above.[60] However the future actions of both governments are significantly constrained. Canada, for example, could not re-institute review of new investments, nor could the United States institute a review process so far as Canada is concerned.[61] It is clear also that Canada gave up more in this section of the agreement, presumably in return for concessions elsewhere.

Conclusions

In Part I of this study the motives for government policy were noted under four headings, and the bargaining power of governments relative to MNEs was related to various variables. Canadian experience offers a particularly good test of these ideas, given the high degree of foreign control of industry and the recency and strength of the policies involved. In addition there is a rich literature on FDI in Canada, although that on the effects of policy is not as strong as one would wish.[62]

Each of the four hypotheses about the motives for policy which were considered in Chapter 2 would receive some support from the Canadian experience. In terms of wealth maximization, several estimates of macroeconomic effects of FDI conclude that they are positive and that the tax benefits in particular are substantial. Moreover studies of the effects of foreign ownership on productivity show a positive association, although this is not a uniform conclusion. It is the microeconomic effects which have attracted the most attention, however, with the fear of truncation forming a basis for policy, as noted earlier. One cannot deny that this concern is widespread in Canada, and particularly among many politicians and civil servants responsible for deciding and implementing policy. Yet one must also note that a substantial body of empirical research has not confirmed this position in the Canadian context.

There are a number of ways to test the underlying concept of truncation which was described earlier. In Canada, various writers focused on exports, imports and research and development spending in Canada as proxies for the variables involved, despite the ambiguities in welfare terms of changes in these. The ideas were first tested by Safarian (1966) who, while emphasizing a number of important differences in other respects, concluded that average performance on exports and on research and development was not statistically different between domestic and foreign-owned firms, but that imports were higher for the latter. There have been many tests since, some with more sophisticated data and models, which tend to confirm the results on exports and on imports, but which give mixed results on research and development. The debate was much advanced by a series of studies by the Economic Council of Canada (1983) which shifted the emphasis from research and development to the much broader issue of the generation and diffusion of innovations. The Council's work gave a more optimistic view of technical capacity and activity in Canada than did earlier studies. This resulted in part from recognition of the differences in industry structure in Canada and abroad, the importance of access to knowledge (including that from abroad) and its rapid dissemination, and the different roles played by domestic and foreign-owned firms in the process of producing and distributing knowledge.

That being said, it is important to add that some of the results noted can be interpreted as evidence of comparatively poor performance by both sets of firms. Moreover evidence about the same US firms in Europe would not support a claim of poor economic performance compared with domestic firms: the contrary has often been the case (Safarian, 1979, 325). Finally there is other evidence that Canada may not have optimized the potential gain from technology diffusion which arises from a large MNE presence, probably in part for reasons noted in the next paragraph.

One of the more serious problems with the truncation approach is that there is an alternative explanation for the observed problems of economic performance, an explanation which has had substantial and usually positive tests over time. What is often called the Eastman–Stykolt (1967) hypothesis indicates that oligopolistic decision making in a small protected market with weak competition policies is likely to encourage entry at an inefficient scale, the multiplication of product lines and high unit costs. Such firms are likely to have problems in competing internationally and to have less incentive to introduce innovations. Inappropriate industrial policies rather than FDI are seen in this case as the primary reason for poor economic performance by all firms, domestic and foreign-owned. There is a long list of tests one can cite leading to these conclusions, apart from that by Eastman and Stykolt: most recently and comprehensively, those by Harris and Cox (1983) and Baldwin and Gorecki (1983, 108–16). The last of these is particularly emphatic in rejecting foreign ownership as a reason for the excessive product diversity and short production runs in Canadian industry.

As for the NEP, some have argued that what went wrong was simply an incorrect forecast of energy prices. Even if the government had correctly foreseen the decline in prices of oil and the recession, however, there was still a problem. If the price paid for a nationalized or repatriated asset fully reflects the expected profit stream of that asset, discounted into present dollars, one must ask where the gain lies. Funds so invested have other uses which also show a stream of profits or benefits. A government can always try to pay less than the discounted capitalized value of the future income stream – there is scope for differences of view on how to measure this – and hope that the reactions of the firms and home governments are not too negative. Some would argue that that is what the government did since, given the tax changes already noted, the assets then became relatively more valuable to domestic owners. It is doubtful that Canada's situation permitted a large leeway in this respect, judging from the premiums over market prices actually paid in public and private buy-outs.

Unless one argues that even these premiums were well below the expected values of the assets, what the argument for nationalization and repatriation becomes is an argument that there were benefits in terms of more Canadian ownership, benefits beyond the costs imposed and which exceeded those to be realized by investing similar sums and similar policy costs in other activities. If the issue was greater taxation of rising profits, this could have been done in any case, and was done in the NEP. If performance of firms was the issue, one would have to demonstrate that Canadian ownership was a better route than more effective application of the substantial regulatory requirements and administrative processes already in place. What was done by way of ensuring that domestic suppliers could bid on projects was feasible, and to some extent already in practice, before the NEP. And it is not self-evident that Canadian ownership would guarantee the degree of self-sufficiency in this or other respects that a particular Canadian government thought desirable. Government officials complain from time to time that even government-owned corporations, including Petro-Canada, act too much like privately owned corporations, a quite unsurprising outcome when government also insists that such firms show profits, look to the market for funding, and so on.

It was emphasized above that concerns about the effect on independence of a substantial MNE presence, especially given other links to the United States, played an early and major role in the development of Canadian policies, notably in closing off some sectors to FDI. It is difficult to test an issue of this kind in any systematic way. Leyton-Brown (1974) examined in detail 21 cases of conflict between Canada and the USA during 1945–71. He concluded that the Canadian government was satisfied with the outcome of a majority of the more important cases, despite the discrepancy in power involved. No comparable study exists for recent years, when the relations between the two countries have been less predictable. In any case, such studies do not deny the public pressure on politicians from issues involving independence, to which Canadians remain highly sensitive.

Nor is it difficult to find support in Canada's experience for the view that policy has the effect of redistributing income within the country. Some Canadian sellers of firms would lose in price terms by having the FIRA process interposed between them and MNE purchases, while, as noted earlier, potential Canadian buyers gained in this process. The NEP was designed to create incentives for foreign firms to sell assets to Canadians or to engage in joint ventures with them, a process which gave the *potential* for securing substantial gains for the Canadians involved. One interesting point is whether these transfers reduced overall real income, a point taken up later. Another is the interest and capacity of the groups involved to influence the legislation. Obviously the sellers or potential sellers of firms were unable to prevent the establishment of the FIRA. The Canadian-owned sector would be split on an issue of this kind with some being attracted by the added protection from entry by foreign firms and the opportunity to buy assets more cheaply. There was no concerted effort by that sector to stop the enactment of FIRA, of the kind, for example, which blocked the passage of stronger competition laws on five occasions throughout the 1970s and early 1980s. Such a concerted effort might not have succeeded in any case, given the strength of the demand for policy on FDI in the early 1970s. In the case of the NEP, where the energy problems and opportunities of the 1970s had created a fertile field for intervention, the MNE opposition was accompanied by vehement opposition by some of the provinces and by smaller Canadian-owned energy firms.

Finally we note that the distribution of political power was central in both cases. The enactment of FIRA, particularly in its strengthened form, owed something to the position and efforts of the New Democratic Party as well as the nationalist wing of the Liberal Party. The enactment of the NEP and the plans to strengthen FIRA owed a great deal to the need for the Liberal Party to win in Ontario if it was to form a government in 1980.[63] Indeed one of the more interesting aspects of the election in that year was the conversion of the leader of the Liberal Party, who was not noted for his nationalist views, to something like an economic nationalist position. Both FIRA and the NEP were substantially modified by the Liberal government in the early 1980s as recession struck and retaliation became a strong possibility, but they were undone by the election of a Conservative government.

The points which remain to be considered are what effects the policies had in practice and, what is related, how effective they were in reaching their objectives. The question of effects is important because it sheds light on the issue as to whether the policies succeeded in transferring rents and other benefits to Canadians from foreigners or simply reduced resources in real terms. As to effects, no really satisfactory study exists of the effects of an instrument such as the FIRA. Globerman (1984b) has outlined the requirements of such a study, emphasizing particularly the need to measure the general equilibrium effects. As noted earlier, acceptance rates alone do not begin to tell the story of FIRA's effects, nor does a simple statement of the undertakings given by firms. Globerman notes that, on the one hand, FIRA tended to reduce net returns to the firm or increase the uncertainty associated with them in a situation where returns are not significantly higher than in the United States and where Canada's share of world and US direct investment was falling. On the other hand, where the supply of FDI is increasing, the extra undertakings extracted from investors are a form of rent which is shifted to Canada. Globerman suggests that the pursuit of such rents by Canadian-owned firms can have positive growth effects (ibid., 24–6). His overall conclusion is that FIRA probably imposed net costs on the Canadian economy, but the sources of these costs are complex and the size difficult to document (see also Globerman, 1979). Other studies have come to similar conclusions while being limited in the effects measured (for example, MacDowell, 1984). The changes in FIRA in the early 1980s and the shift to Investment Canada addressed some of the problems raised by these studies.

No doubt similar problems would arise from any attempt at an overall assessment of the effects of the NEP. But in this case the evidence presented above suggests that, *in the circumstances of the early 1980s*, the NEP reduced real national wealth. It is difficult to know what other assessment to make of a programme which induced substantial Canadian purchases, at high real interest rates, of an asset whose value declined drastically, and which led to upward pressure on interest rates for a time in a period of recession. To offset such negative effects one would have to give major weight to the increase in Canadian ownership per se, or demonstrate that it brought economic advantages not otherwise obtainable.

As to effectiveness of policies, the bargaining power of governments in such situations depends on many factors. Four of these are highlighted here. One consideration is timing: if such policies can be introduced while resource rents are rising, the bargaining power of host countries is much enhanced. A second factor is the extent to which the policies are consistent with the strategies of MNEs, and hence less likely to run into resistance or evasion. A third consideration is the design of the instruments – specifically, how likely they are to achieve the objectives involved without negative side-effects. Finally, there is the issue of retaliation, or threats of it, by foreign governments that believe their interests are damaged or that come under significant pressure from the affected firms. It is of interest to look at these briefly in comparisons with Australian policy, a country which has characteristics similar to Canada's: a federal state; a small, open economy; a large degree of foreign ownership in manufacturing and resources; and a good deal of policy development in the 1970s and early 1980s.

In terms of timing, it can be noted that the debate in Canada over policy on FDI extended all through the 1960s and early 1970s, producing a significant number of policy changes by sectors and otherwise, as noted. FIRA was not fully operational until the end of 1975, however, and some important parts of its operation were left unclarified. The details of NEP were not announced until early in 1981, and resistance and discussions with some provinces then required many months. The timing in both cases caused difficulties, in the first because Canada's share of world FDI was falling rapidly as MNEs redirected investments to the EC but especially to southeast Asia and the United States, in the second because of the collapse of energy prices. In Australia, a policy on review with a fairly clear mandate and extending to natural resources was in place by at least 1976. The sequence of policy development was similar but Canada's took longer, in part because of greater regional differences (Stevenson, 1976).

As to the strategies of the MNEs, the internalization theory examined in Chapter 3 suggested that firms would be more likely to give undertakings for their relatively mature products and processes and also for the types of activities they are prepared to locate outside their regional or global headquarters. One would also expect that, insofar as FDI means a reduction of parent ownership (as distinct from loss of control), it will be undertaken more readily by firms in many natural resource industries than by firms in many manufacturing sectors and some service sectors. The intangible assets that a firm in the natural resource industries may try to protect are likely to be in marketing and technical know-how, for example, which are left relatively intact by some diminution in ownership. The intangible assets of a manufacturing firm are likely to be in patents, product differentiation and proprietary information, for which the rents are harder to realize when ownership is diluted, even when the firm is able to impose and enforce many restrictions on the subsidiary or independent user. Important qualifications occur in each case, of course, particularly as one disaggregates these sectors. As noted in Chapter 3, there is more scope now than there was earlier for transfers of technology outside and between MNEs.

The FIRA challenged the concept of internalization by attempting either to decentralize or to capture for Canada a range of activities that many MNEs prefer either to centralize (such as many kinds of R&D) or to have some central say in allocating (such as some types of exports).[64] Undertakings or performance guarantees of the type required by the FIRA were disincentives to investment from the firm's viewpoint, since they tended to reduce its overall rate of return. They were also, in effect, the price that the firm had to pay in order to gain entry to Canada, to merge or to expand in unrelated lines of activity. As noted earlier, available data and studies do not permit a full assessment of how far FIRA reduced net profit and investment, on the one hand, or increased net benefits from FDI, on the other.

The approach adopted in the National Energy Program also posed a challenge to the internalization thesis, since it substituted domestic government and private ownership and control for part or all of the assets of the MNE. There are qualifications one should make here: some of the incentives in the NEP tended to encourage joint ventures with independent Canadian firms rather than supersede MNEs, and some tended to encourage the creation of Canadian-controlled MNEs. Nevertheless the contrast with the Australian case is unmistakable. There is no integrated major public firm comparable to Petro-Canada engaged in the natural resource sector in Australia. The effect of Australian policy is to leave control of the subsidiary with the MNE, while diluting equity in particular projects. It is generally up to the MNE to decide on the form of domestic participation. It decides on the price it will charge local participants, and hence how far it will go in trying to capture any rents.

The effectiveness of the approaches used by the FIRA or the NEP is clearly not simply a question of the likely response of firms, but also of the timing issues already noted and of the way in which policies are designed and implemented. While it is difficult to disentangle the various elements noted, some aspects of the design of the policies and the reactions to them are worth noting.

FIRA was a more structured and, potentially, more far-reaching review process than any in this study, with the exception of Japan in the earlier post-war period. First, it was based on a specific law which, along with various guidelines, spelled out the scope, procedures and criteria of significant benefit more explicitly than anything existing in other countries, with the possible exception of Australia. Second, FIRA was very comprehensive, applying to all new businesses by foreign persons (with special procedures for most small-business proposals) and all but the smallest acquisitions. Expansion of existing foreign-owned firms was not reviewed, however, unless it was in a non-related area of business. Unlike most other countries considered here, the change of a foreign parent, with no change in the degree of foreign ownership, led to a review of the subsidiary or branch. Third, while decisions were made by Cabinet after recommendation by the relevant minister, a specific agency existed, with legal status and a large staff. The relevant province or provinces also had to be consulted in each case, but did not exercise a veto. Fourth, considerable detail was published on the type of decisions reached and related matters, although not on specific companies unless the minister so decided. It can be noted, for example, that the allowances and disallowances were published by company each year, as were the principal factors of assessment indicating significant benefits expected for Canada for each of the allowed cases. Among the review agencies in this study, only that for Australia published more information. Finally, the rejection rate was well over that of the other countries in this study.

It is a difficult thing under the best of circumstances to operate a policy as ambitious as this. It becomes much more complex when the process is as politicized as it was, with every decision at least potentially subject to pressure at the provincial and federal cabinet levels, as well as earlier. The uncertainty of outcomes was unnecessarily complicated by the failure, at least in public, to assign relative priorities to its several objectives and to define what constituted an acceptable tradeoff between performance and ownership.[65] Schultz *et al.* (1980) suggest that the failure to set clearer policy guidelines reflected the fact that Cabinet was bogged down by the sheer number of cases. One can also ask whether any of the major economics ministries or the provinces would be prepared to accept the consequences of a clearer setting of priorities and tradeoffs. Such clarification would imply the decentralization of many decisions to the one ministry and even, in practice, to the FIRA, or at least a more difficult task in challenging recommendations by the agency and ministry directly involved. The creation of an agency with that much power was unlikely to be welcomed by other agencies and departments. Two of the deputy ministers of the major economics ministries did not believe the agency was needed in any case, and the ministry responsible for drafting the Act is said to have believed it should be 'self-complying and self-assuring', somewhat like the income tax act. Whatever else one may make of such views, the result was likely to be a complex and uncertain process.[66] FIRA was required, in effect, to implement an industrial strategy, but without sufficient clarification of the priorities and tradeoffs which such a strategy requires.

We note also that the design of the NEP took major risks in at least three respects: in terms of the likely reaction of the provinces, especially Alberta; in terms of the changes in the economic variables, notably oil prices and interest rates; and in terms of the probable reaction of both MNEs and home governments. Certainly the problems of the late 1970s in attempting to cope with the price, supply, tax and regional problems of energy development had formed a prelude for the NEP. The election of a Liberal government on a nationalist platform, and rising rents, gave a particular focus to these attempts in 1980. Although the NEP was preceded by a government policy paper and presented in a government budget document, it was to a considerable extent the creation of the Department of Energy, Mines and Resources. Normally one would expect the Finance Minister and his officials to play the leading role on such a major financial measure. Moreover, because the NEP's precise form was introduced in a budget document, the input from other departments was limited and that from the private sector came largely after the programme was announced. Relations with Alberta had to be ironed out over many months afterwards, and concessions made to the private sector as problems and pressures in that area became evident. One defence of such an approach, made by one of the responsible ministers, was that little would have occurred if the government had opted for a more consultative route, since opposition would have mounted. The same minister noted that events would have been very different if the forecasts of oil prices had been correct. Perhaps the only response to the latter point is to invoke Murphy's law. The Canadian programme gave the possibility of far greater and faster capture of rents, and of Canadian control, than did the Australian approach, but it also ran far greater risks with little downside protection built into it.

We can deal with retaliation briefly in view of the comments above. Both the Canadian and Australian approaches to foreign ownership can be said to involve elements of non-national treatment; that is, treatment given to foreign-owned firms which differs from that accorded nationally-owned companies. However Canadian policies that can be considered discriminatory or retroactive in their treatment of foreign-owned firms have drawn more attention from the firms' home countries than their Australian equivalents. Criticism of the FIRA abroad, while not as strong as it became in 1980–81, was frequently voiced in the late 1970s. Canada's proximity to the United States and the fact that so much of the FDI in Canada was from that country guaranteed a stronger reaction there to Canadian than to Australian policy initiatives. Yet British, West German and (with less justification) French and Japanese criticisms of Canada's policies were no less pointed even before 1980–81, and certainly thereafter. All of these countries, with the Netherlands and Belgium, registered complaints against Canada with the OECD (*Globe and Mail*, 20 January 1982, B2).

Quite apart from the effect of Canada's proximity to the United States, the design of the NEP made it much more likely than the Australian approach to invite retaliation. The petroleum incentive payments were geared to the degree of Canadian ownership of the firm and hence were explicitly discriminatory towards established foreign-owned firms. Both Australian and Canadian tax law had been used in ways that distinguished established firms by nationality of ownership, but nothing on the scale of the NEP had been attempted before. The provision for a 25 per cent Crown interest in all petroleum rights for all firms on federal lands, while it applied to Canadian-owned as well as to foreign-owned firms and involved some payment for work done to date, was strongly criticized as a retroactive measure. It is true that some other countries, such as Norway, took far larger shares and allocated them administratively, but the shares were not changed during the course of the lease. Despite particular problems on specific projects, neither the FIRB nor the requirements for Australian participation attracted anything like the criticism Canada received abroad.

NEW ZEALAND

New Zealand is one of the smallest countries in this study in terms of national income. It relies heavily on agricultural and other natural resources production and export. By 1980 it had attracted foreign ownership of about one-quarter of its manufacturing production, as well as significant foreign ownership of its commercial and financial sectors. It had also developed a distinctive set of policies on inward direct investment, policies inspired originally by the attempted takeover of a newspaper in 1964 by a Canadian newspaper magnate who was resident in the United Kingdom, and also in response to the regulation of direct investment abroad by the United Kingdom and United States in the 1960s (Table 6.16). Antedating these was a desire to

Table 6.16 Development of New Zealand's policies on inward direct investment

1938–85	Exchange control and quantitative import controls in effect with varying degrees of severity.
1964	Overseas Takeover Regulations. Ministerial approval needed for foreign acquisition of 25 per cent or more of voting shares of a local company, including such acquisition by foreign-controlled subsidiaries already in New Zealand.
1965	News Media Ownership Act limiting foreign ownership of radio, television, newspapers.
1965	Capital Issues (Overseas) Regulations. Ministerial approval needed for commencement of business in New Zealand by overseas firms, and borrowing in New Zealand by all companies.
1968	Supreme Court approval needed for some types of foreign purchase of non-farmland. Measures in effect (1952) to prevent undue concentration of farmlands from any source.
1973	Overseas Investment Commission established to consider all overseas investment proposals (see criteria in Table 6.19).
1974	Overseas Investment Regulations amend and consolidate 1964–5 regulations.
1979	Statement by Minister of Finance, 27 July, with new guidelines for Overseas Investment Commission (see Table 6.19).
1984	Exchange controls ended. Restrictions on the levels of foreign ownership removed for financial institutions and some other sectors, partly as part of extensive privatization.
1987	New banks registered, including some controlled overseas.
1985–7	Trigger point for review raised to $NZ 500 000, then $NZ 2 million. Review process streamlined in 1987. Subsequently the figure became $NZ 5.8 million.

Note:
See text for further details.

avoid concentration of ownership of rural land, which extended eventually to controls on non-rural land also.

Some measures of the role of inward direct investment in New Zealand are shown in Table 6.17. Of course comparisons of direct investment flows with national investment and product data must be treated with caution, but the three series shown all suggest a broadly increasing role for FDI over the period noted. Three countries accounted for the bulk of the inflows. The share of the United Kingdom in such inflows declined from about 70 to 41 per cent from the 1950s to the 1970s. For the same periods the Australian share rose from 15 per cent to 30 per cent and that of the United States and Canada together from 10 per cent to 24 per cent (New Zealand Reserve Bank, 1981, 21).

Table 6.17 Inward direct investment[a] in New Zealand and income earned, comparisons with national accounts, 1951–80

		IDI as a % of[c]		
Year ending 31 March	*$NZ mill.[b]*	*Total domestic investment*	*Gross domestic product*	*Income on direct investment as % GDP[d]*
1951–55	83.0	5.0	1.05	1.10
1956–60	105.1	4.4	0.97	1.07
1961–65	207.3	6.2	1.36	1.47
1966–70	234.9	4.8	1.09	1.47
1971–75	666.3	7.8	1.76	1.41
1976–80	1159.4	—	—	—

Notes:
[a]Net of repatriations.
[b]Includes retained earnings.
[c]National accounts,old basis.
[d]Net of income and withholding tax.

Source: Reserve Bank (1981, 27).

Data on the stocks of inward and outward FDI are not available from public sources, and those on foreign ownership and control of industry are sparse. Table 6.18 shows taxation data for the shares of overseas companies in various aggregates. Such firms accounted for 24 per cent of net output (measured as wages plus gross profits) in all industries covered by tax returns, and 20 per cent for manufacturing alone, in the fiscal year 1977–8.

Table 6.18 Share of overseas companies in overall company activity, New Zealand, 1977–8

Overseas companies as % of all companies	*No. of returns*	*Salaries and wages (%)*	*Income tax assessed*	*Total shareholders' funds*
Agriculture, forestry hunting & fishing	0.4	4.0	2.7	1.3
Mining & quarrying	11.8	13.9	22.7	76.8
Manufacturing				
Food, beverages & tobacco	5.4	20.2	21.8	19.5
Textiles, wearing apparel & made-up textiles	2.8	13.2	12.9	15.2
Wood, paper & chemical products and miscellaneous manufacturing	5.1	20.7	46.5	30.9
Metals & metal products	4.8	31.7	50.2	30.9
Total manufacturing	4.8	22.8	40.8	28.3
Construction, electricity, gas, water & sanitary services	0.3	3.5	10.2	2.9
Commerce – wholesale & retail	1.6	12.0	32.3	19.9
Commerce – other	2.0	60.7	40.7	16.3
Transport, storage & communication	1.5	8.3	16.3	16.6
Community, social & personal services	0.7	3.6	26.1	16.8
Total all industries	1.8	17.8	35.3	22.1

Source: Reserve Bank (1981, 18). Data derived from company income tax statistics; available for later years on a different industrial classification.

Very approximate estimates using balance sheet data have been constructed for 21 industry categories for 1980: they show that foreign-controlled firms accounted for over half of the assets of companies in clothing, drugs and chemicals, metals and machinery, electrical machinery and appliances, miscellaneous manufacturing, other finance, and non-life insurance; they accounted for one-third or more of assets in other food, construction and transport (Reserve Bank, 1981, 11, 34–5). It is possible, of course, to get higher and lower foreign ownership ratios, depending on the question posed. A survey in 1973 of the 63 largest companies in New Zealand, for example, showed that almost 60 per cent were at least 40 per cent foreign-controlled (quoted in Sexton, 1979, 120). A very rough estimate of all measured economic activity, corporate and non-corporate, private and public, suggested about 10 per cent for the role of overseas-owned firms (Deane, 1975, 64).

The year 1964 appears to have been the turning-point in terms of restrictions on inward direct investment. It is true that exchange control was instituted in 1938 and that the Wartime Emergency Regulations of 1940 required the minister's consent for the registration of any company, for any increase or issue of capital, and also for the commencement of business by any overseas company in New Zealand.[67] These provisions were not revoked until 1964–5. Nevertheless the Aliens Act of 1948 provided that real property could be acquired and disposed of by aliens in the same manner in all respects as by New Zealanders and other British subjects. An exception was the Shipping and Seamen Act of 1952 prohibiting alien (non-British) ownership of ships of New Zealand registry.

All of this changed in 1964. What appears to have triggered the closing of another sector and also the more general concerns about foreign control of industry was the attempt by a British group headed by Lord Thomson to acquire one of the national daily newspapers. In addition, UK and US guidelines restricting the outflow of FDI and/or requiring repatriation of earnings played a role in the development of regulation in New Zealand in the mid-1960s.[68] The News Media Ownership Act of 1965 provided that companies incorporated outside New Zealand could not establish or operate a radio or television station or publish a newspaper. In addition, no more than 15 per cent of the voting power in any corporation operating a radio or television station or a newspaper could be controlled by persons not resident in or closely connected with New Zealand. The opposition to the bill involved a diverse array of interests – the Stock Exchange Association of New Zealand, a committee of 50 Auckland lawyers and the New Zealand Journalists Association – and also attracted the criticism of the Labour opposition party as a limitation of the freedom of the press and as preserving an insular and monopolistic industry. The government in turn argued that an industry which was 'part of the fabric of our social and cultural life' could not be considered simply in economic terms (Paterson, 1975b, 195).

The Reserve Bank of New Zealand Act for 1964 provided for a wide variety of controls on foreign exchange and other transactions affecting overseas resources. This included approval of FDI abroad by residents and prohibition of portfolio investment (OECD, 1979, 48). What is of interest in this Act for present purposes is the Overseas Takeover Regulations of 1964 and the Capital Issues (Overseas) Regulations of September 1965. The former required registration of notice at the Reserve Bank, and the Minister of Finance's consent, when an overseas resident or its local subsidiary acquired 25 per cent or more of the voting shares of a New Zealand company. The latter, replacing the 1940 Regulations, required ministerial consent for the commencement of business in New Zealand by an overseas company or the borrowing overseas by all companies operating in New Zealand. These regulations were administered by an ad hoc committee drawn from the central bank, the Treasury and the Department of Trade and Industry. In effect New Zealand had acquired a review mechanism a decade before Australia and Canada.

New Zealand had passed an Act in 1952 limiting undue concentration of ownership of rural land in an attempt to ensure availability of land for those starting first farms. In response to some concerns about foreign acquisition of land by aliens, especially in wilderness and semi-rural areas, the 1952 Act was amended in 1968 so that the consent of the Administrative Division of the Supreme Court was required for some types of real property purchases by foreign interests (Paterson, 1975b, 182–4).

The 1960s legislation just noted had been passed by National Party governments. The Labour Party government elected at the end of 1972 proceeded to consolidate this legislation and to reject larger numbers of takeover proposals, but left much of the letter and the spirit of the earlier legislation unchanged. The Overseas Investment Act of 1973 established the Overseas Investment Commission, enlarging the committee of officials by two private members. The Overseas Investment Regulations passed under this Act consolidated and amended the 1964–5 Regulations noted above. The operations under this Act continued under the National Party governments of 1975–84 and will be considered more fully below. The Labour government also enacted legislation to allow the state to take a 51 per cent interest in the development of petroleum reserves.

It is important to note that the controls on borrowing in New Zealand under the 1965 Regulations distinguished between resident firms by the degree of foreign ownership. If the firm had more than 50 per cent New Zealand ownership it could borrow locally without restriction, although approval was needed. If foreign ownership was 50 per cent or more, however, the borrowing was related to annual turnover and/or the extent of foreign ownership in relation to the proportion of funds raised outside New Zealand. These criteria were applied flexibly in particular cases, and significantly liberalized in 1979. Nevertheless they can be interpreted as giving a modest incentive to some firms to maintain local equity holdings. Payment of earnings to non-residents and repatriation of capital required approval, but appear to have been given readily where evidence of source of earnings and original capital inflow was available (New Zealand Reserve Bank, 1981, 6–7).

What evolved in the 1960s was a system of monitoring foreign ownership and control with four objectives: to permit review of investment proposals so as to promote benefits and decline undesirable investments; to control the level of FDI in natural resources; to provide similar control in other sensitive sectors such as media; and to allay public concerns about FDI which would arise in the absence of such policies (New Zealand Reserve Bank, 1987a, 1). Many of the review policies which were developed in the 1960s were still in existence in the late 1980s. The following sections consider them in more detail.

The Overseas Investment Commission (OIC) up to the early 1980s

The Minister of Finance is responsible for policy in this area according to The OIC Act of 1973. This authority is delegated to a commission of five, two of whom are businessmen from the private sector, one of whom acts as chairman, while the other three are officials representing the Reserve Bank of New Zealand, the Treasury and the Department of Trade and Industry. The secretariat is provided by the Reserve Bank, which also administered exchange control. Thus the members are part-time, except for the secretary. The OIC, in addition to determining whether specific proposals are in the national interest, is also empowered to advise the government on all other aspects of overseas investment in New Zealand. This includes advising the government on how to get the fullest possible benefit for New Zealand from FDI and keeping track of the level and extent of foreign ownership and control.

As of 1973, takeovers of 25 per cent or more of any class of shares or of assets by an 'overseas person' required approval where the consideration exceeded $NZ 100 000, although, as of 1979, purchases of less than $NZ 500 000 would normally be approved automatically. Decisions on takeovers were to be made within six weeks of an application. In practice, consent could be given in a week or two, particularly for smaller applications which were clearly within the criteria. The commencement of new businesses by an overseas person also required approval, as did expansion into an area of activity not related to that involved in the original consent. An 'overseas person' could be an individual or firm not resident in New Zealand, or a resident firm when 25 per cent or more of any class of shares is owned abroad. Both the earlier administration and that under the Labour Party automatically granted consent to transfers of New Zealand interests between overseas companies (Paterson, 1975b, 203).

Approval of a proposal was conditional on assessment of benefits to New Zealand as outlined in a set of criteria. The 1973 criteria were revised in 1979, as noted in Table 6.19.[69] While most of the earlier criteria were repeated, the overall simplification was intended to sound a more welcoming note to FDI. That was also the intent of a clarification of the 25 per cent level of foreign ownership as simply triggering review rather than, as some firms apparently believed, indicating the maximum level permitted. Indeed, the OIC then went so far as to declare that 'the level of equity participation is only a relatively minor factor in the assessment of any proposal' (OIC, 1980, 6, 10; see, however, the section below on the natural resource sector). The last of the 1979 criteria is of interest in that it makes explicit one problem in operating such review mechanisms, that is, the desire of domestic owners to dispose of their shares favourably.

While the OIC is an advisory body, in practice it makes almost all of the decisions on applications. It has been estimated that only about 5 per cent of these were considered by the minister, comprising usually the larger or politically sensitive cases (OIC interview, 1981). The very small size limits suggest most applications would not require much attention in any case, so that the minister may have been involved in most of the important ones. Other departments would be consulted as a matter of course if their interests were involved.

The OIC itself did not undertake systematic cost–benefit analyses of the effects of the proposals, or attempt to negotiate undertakings on the various economic benefits noted in the guidelines. This could hardly be undertaken systematically by part-time members and a small staff of six. The conditions attached to approvals, as noted below, are on other issues. Even the criterion of local equity involvement, whatever emphasis it received before, was sharply downgraded in the 1979 statement. Indeed opposition party critics were quite emphatic in interviews that the National Party government of the late 1970s and early 1980s had moved some way from the original reasons for the OIC, which, in their view, envisaged a more active negotiating stance on economic commitments. Since formal commitments on economic performance were not required in most cases, a subsequent monitoring process was not necessary.

Several qualifications are necessary to this interpretation of the role of the OIC. It encouraged preliminary discussions with applicants, and these could

Table 6.19 Criteria for examination of proposals, New Zealand, 1973 and 1979

January 1973 Statement

The Government's major objectives in supervising overseas investment were stated as:

(a) to ensure that New Zealand's natural and human resources are developed to the benefit of New Zealand, in a manner which accords with the best interests of New Zealand and consistently with the preservation of a social and physical environment which promotes the well-being of all New Zealanders;

(b) Within this over-riding objective, to maximize the benefit to New Zealand available from the international transfer of capital and technology, and thus to ensure that overseas investment contributes to the maintenance of a satisfactory rate of economic growth in New Zealand, while making certain that ownership and control of New Zealand resources is not unwisely or unnecessarily transferred to overseas residents.

The detailed criteria applied to each case were as follows:

(1) The extent to which New Zealand resources of raw materials and human skills would be combined and developed to the most advanced stage which is economically feasible or desirable and having regard to the impact on employment opportunities.

(2) The compatibility of the proposal with Government policies on the protection of the environment and regional development.

(3) The degree to which the proposal would extend New Zealand's access to technological developments and scientific research conducted overseas and the extent to which research and development would be stimulated in New Zealand.

(4) The extent to which the proposal would promote New Zealand's industrial growth and efficiency by increasing the degree of export orientation and helping to provide access to new or extended export markets.

(5) The impact of the proposal on productivity, with particular reference to the effects on costs and prices in New Zealand.

(6) The impact of the proposal on the structure and competitiveness of the industry or industries of which it would form part, and on linkages with other New Zealand industries.

(7) The contribution to product innovation, marketing expertise and consumer choice in New Zealand.

(8) Where the interests concerned with the proposal are operating on a multinational basis, the role of the New Zealand proposal in their total operations, with particular regard to the firm's export and pricing policies, its other international strategies and New Zealand participation.

(9) The taxation yield to New Zealand in relation to the benefits which the overseas company derives from its New Zealand activities, with particu-

lar reference to the taxation aspects of its pricing policies and the ratio of equity to loan capital.

(10) The balance of payments implications of its proposal, including the cost of servicing the investment, the amount of capital inflow and the extent to which this supplements or adds to the overseas capital available through other channels, either to the Government or to the private sector in New Zealand.

(11) The degree and significance of participation by New Zealand shareholders in relation to the nature of the individual overseas enterprise and the competing needs of New Zealand-owned enterprises for local equity capital.

(12) Overseas interests wishing to acquire control of an existing New Zealand firm are required to demonstrate that their proposal will bring substantial new benefits to the New Zealand economy which would not be provided by continued local ownership. Due consideration is given in individual cases to the relative opportunities for the disposal of the assets to other New Zealanders.

July 1979 Statement

The aim of this revision was to make it quite clear that the Government welcomed foreign investment that can contribute to the development of New Zealand, and especially to underline that the 25 per cent level of foreign equity simply triggered commission involvement rather than required local equity participation. The criteria to be applied to each case were as follows:

1. added competition to local industry, lower prices and greater efficiency;
2. the introduction of new technology, managerial or technical skills;
3. the development of new export markets or increased market access;
4. the extent to which the proposal is likely to make a net positive contribution to the balance of payments;
5. the creation of new job opportunities;
6. the promotion of New Zealand's economic growth.

In weighing up the benefits of a proposal the following factors will also be taken into account:

1. the degree of equity participation by local shareholders in relation to proposals which involve the ownership and control of New Zealand's natural resources;
2. potential impact of the proposal on the environment and on regional development;
3. the implications of the proposal for the Government's other economic and industrial policies and any other national policies which might be affected by the proposal;
4. the relative opportunities of shareholders in small private companies to dispose of their shares to the best advantage.

Sources: Carey (1975, Appendix) for 1973 Statement of Minister of Finance; Sexton (1979, Appendix B) for 1979 Statement of Minister of Finance; and Reserve Bank (1987a).

lead either to modifications in proposals or a decision not to submit a formal proposal. More importantly, the larger or more sensitive cases, which were few in number, would be analysed at some length by the Treasury and involve political decision making as well, as noted further below. In addition the Department of Trade and Industry apparently used its control over import licences prior to the establishment of the OIC, and its responsibility for various investment incentives subsequently, to persuade a number of foreign corporations to include or increase the local equity in a proposal.[70]

In assessing the rejection rate for formal proposals it is important to recall that the OIC emphasized that it 'welcomes enquiries on any aspect of overseas investment policy and assists investors in the preparation of applications.... The successful operation of this service in the past has meant that the vast majority of proposals submitted to the Commission have been approved' (OIC, 1980, 8). Put differently, we do not know how many proposals did not materialize because either published information on New Zealand policies or preliminary discussions indicated probable rejection. Actual rejections of proposals in the early 1980s also consisted 'largely', according to the OIC, of attempts to increase imports rather than to establish FDI: trading companies attempting to buy out their New Zealand distributor, for example, or an attempt to set up a subsidiary largely as an import mechanism. It is apparent that, while the OIC was not engaged in extracting economic performance requirements, it was prepared to limit organizational forms which were essentially import-oriented – a pattern evident in other review mechanisms.

The rates for rejection of formal applications given in Table 6.20, while qualified as noted, suggest a significant increase in rejections under the Labour government from November 1972 to November 1975. Moreover the number of takeover applications fell sharply after 1973. All of this would be consistent with the Labour government's declared policy of examining foreign investment proposals more critically. Such comparisons with rejections by the preceding government are complicated by the fact there is another explanation for the increased rate, namely the removal of tax incentives to purchase firms with accumulated losses, purchases the Reserve Bank had automatically approved. Such purchases were about a quarter of all applications before March 1972 (Paterson, 1975b, 204). It may be significant that the rate of refusal was close to zero under the succeeding National Party government in the late 1970s.

For reasons of confidentiality information is not published on individual approvals or refusals, much less the conditions attached to them. It appears that all approvals have conditions attached to them in the sense of limiting takeover targets to the existing fields and limiting new firms to those specified in the application (Sexton, 1979, 13; information from OIC). Beyond that, the conditions largely refer to such things as the length of time for

Table 6.20 *Approval rates for overseas new business proposals and takeovers, New Zealand, 1965–85*

	Commencing Business				*Acquisitions*			
	Applications[a]	*Withdrawn, declined*[b]	*Approved*	*Withdrawn, declined (%)*	*Applications*[a]	*Withdrawn, declined*[c]	*Approved*	*Withdrawn, declined (%)*
1965					68	1	67	1.5
1966					58	2	56	3.4
1967					66	3	63	4.5
1968					85	8	77	9.4
1969					129	9	120	7.0
1970	162	9	153	5.6	180	9	171	5.0
1971	123	4	119	3.3	160	9	151	5.6
1972	146	8	138	5.5	166	21	145	12.7
1973	179	11	168	6.1	206	45	161	21.8
1974	171	8	163	4.7	104	7	97	6.7
1975	202	31	171	15.3	137	11	126	8.0
1976	171	15	156	8.8	132	27	105	20.5
1977	185	10	175	5.4	146	12	134	8.2
1978	183	3	180	1.6	131	3	128	2.3
1979	202	—	202	—	164	3	161	1.8
1980	198	5	193	2.5	179	—	179	—
Total to 1980	1 922	104	1 818	5.4	2 111	170	1 941	8.1
1981	308	7	301	2.3	234	4	230	1.7
1982	324	9	315	2.8	210	7	203	3.3
1983	346	67	279	19.4	193	33	160	17.1
1984	603	26	577	4.3	336	22	314	6.5
1985	451	2	449	0.4	287	1	286	0.3
Total to 1985	3 954	215	3 739	5.4	3 371	237	3 134	7.0

Notes:
[a]Excludes applications for name protection which do not involve commencement of business and are readily approved according to OIC (1980, 13). Applications to increase capital shares were almost always approved up to 1975, according to Paterson, (1975a, 81). If they are excluded, the rejection rate for 1970–80 rises to 6.9 per cent from 5.4 per cent but the year-by-year pattern is very similar.
[b]One or no withdrawals, except for five in 1970 and three in 1974 and 1985.
[c]Only zero to three cases were withdrawn each year, except 1973, when they rose to eight.

Source: Reserve Bank (1981, 15–16) and Reserve Bank (1987b).

completion of the investment, or funds to be brought in and profit remittances as required by exchange control. As noted above, they do not cover commitments on economic performance or on local equity. However the few cases of larger or politically sensitive projects which are decided elsewhere, and on which some information has become available, have involved conditions going beyond those noted above.

Key Sectors and Major Projects up to the Early 1980s

It was noted that laws which close sectors to overseas ownership have been relatively few in New Zealand compared to some other countries in this study. The government would not allow further entry of commercial banks: three of the five were already foreign-controlled. While more permissive in the case of other financial institutions, the OIC tended to insist on 50 per cent local equity for new or takeover investments in merchant banks and insurance (Sexton, 1979, 156). Significant foreign investment in most rural and non-rural land was effectively blocked. Long-term forestry leases could be ended if the lessees became foreign-controlled (OECD, 1978, 118). An effort has been made to favour joint ventures in the 200 mile exclusive economic zone introduced around New Zealand in 1978. Foreign ownership of individual newspapers was limited to 15 per cent. In common with most other countries, New Zealand reserves the coastal trade to national flag carriers and non-national airlines are not allowed to carry passengers from one national point to another.

All of this is in addition to sectors which have been closed to both foreign and domestic private investment because of public, mixed or privately-operated monopolies. The first category includes post and telegraph, railways, electricity generation and television stations, the second includes air transport and radio stations. New Zealand governments have also attempted to increase the capacity of New Zealanders to invest in industry in a context where capital markets were controlled for long periods. This has sometimes occurred through direct state ownership in some firms normally left to the private sector, but more generally through the Development Finance Corporation established in 1964 and various export vehicles such as the Export–Import Corporation established in 1974. These agencies are available to foreign investors in New Zealand but size limitations and other factors may make them more readily helpful to companies controlled in New Zealand.

Of more interest for present purposes are the major projects, mostly in natural resources, which receive special analysis and treatment, or which come into the public eye because of their more controversial nature. In such areas as energy, mining and forestry there has been a general concern about the impact of large corporations and major projects on a small country, particularly if the country lacks policies which allow it to deal with the resulting problems effectively. Other concerns are very specific, such as government claims of tax avoidance from excessive import-pricing policies for petroleum in the early 1970s – claims which the international oil companies settled out of court, but which went to the Privy Council in the case made against the only New Zealand-owned oil distributor (Carey, 1975, 14). It should be noted that New Zealand had no capital gains tax. The lack of this was sometimes an incentive to governments to favour local equity participation.

In petroleum and natural gas the government required 50 or 51 per cent ownership through the public New Zealand Petroleum Corporation (Petrocorp) or one of its subsidiaries. More flexibility was allowed at the exploration stage, however. Government in the early 1980s contributed 40 per cent of exploration costs and 51 per cent of development costs and in return took 51 per cent of gross revenues. The 51 per cent rule on public participation was not retroactively applied to outstanding leases and it was planned to apply it to future participation in the industry by New Zealand private interests. On other major natural resource projects there was not specific legislation, as there was in petroleum and gas, and governments did not follow a firm rule. Nevertheless the clear policy of both the Labour and National governments of the 1970s and early 1980s was to try to secure 51 per cent New Zealand participation, private or public. Thus the government had a 50 per cent interest in the Maori natural gas field, 75 per cent interest in a project to produce methanol, a joint venture in aluminium, one in liquid fuels, and so on.

In terms of procedures, the Treasury undertakes a detailed cost–benefit analysis and also attempts to secure information on the firm's activities elsewhere – information not always readily available. Attempts are made to increase to the extent feasible the domestic input into such major projects as well as to maximize processing and downstream use of the resource. These measures, it should be noted, would be applied to all major projects, though most would have a significant foreign presence. Departmental coordination is attempted through a committee of officials, which recommends to the Cabinet Economic Committee chaired by the Deputy Prime Minister but including the Prime Minister. In order to speed up what is often a long and complex matter, the National Development Act was passed to allow the thirty or so necessary approvals to be done together under a 'fast-track' mechanism.

The entire process had become highly politicized by the early 1980s, as in many other countries. The Prime Minister played a direct and significant role; the firms involved lobbied the politicians and the departmental officials vigorously; private groups sued the government in the courts on both environmental and economic grounds. By the early 1980s these controversies were not so much on issues involving foreign investment, given the laws and policies then in effect. The questions centred more on the developmental approach of the then government, particularly the fear that the very capital-intensive projects involved would have a major opportunity cost in terms of more job- or skill-intensive activities, and the concerns about damage to the environment in some of the projects. Moreover there was a concern that insistence on New Zealand equity participation in major projects would lead to increased capital imports in the form of debt. Finally the Labour Party in particular, while continuing to favour joint ventures in some cases, developed quite early some important reservations about the equity participation route – noting, for example, that it often did not give control commensurate to the equity involved, sometimes diverted funds from alternatives with higher returns and led to capital export (Rowling, 1975, 23). These types of concerns were widely echoed among opposition parties and the public in the early 1980s.

It might be noted that, where local participation is required, and where the foreign firm believes the local participants are not supplying inputs of various kinds commensurate with their ownership, there is an incentive for foreign firms to practise transfer pricing. Apart from general tax supervision, the New Zealand position on this, where the government was directly involved, was to write detailed arrangements on responsibilities and payments and to audit these. In joint ventures with private New Zealand participants, the latter were relied on to protect themselves against such practices.

Related Policies

In common with other countries, New Zealand has had for some time an extensive set of fiscal incentives for investment with particular objectives in view. These objectives are diversification from agriculture to manufacturing, export promotion, strengthening innovative capacities and regional development. One important method employed was suspensory loans for exports and for regional development; that is, loans which are converted to grants as predetermined targets are achieved or maintained. Taxable income could also be reduced as such objectives were achieved. Some of these measures have had to be modified or terminated as a result of the 1980 GATT agreement and the 'Closer Economic Relationship' with Australia, and also because of the liberalization noted below. In principle, the incentives have been available to firms regardless of ownership (OECD, 1983, 170–75).

Tax policy is used only modestly to distinguish individuals or firms by country of ownership. Higher rates of tax are paid by absentee individuals and company shareholders who own land in New Zealand. Special bases of assessment of taxable income exist for films, insurance and shipping where non-residents are involved.

In concluding this section it is important to note that New Zealand had import controls and financial controls throughout the period under review here. These controls in themselves helped determine the policy position on inward FDI. A system of import licensing creates excess profits or rents caused by the shortages involved. Such rents can be secured by the government if the licences are auctioned off; otherwise they accrue to private owners of the licence. Governments are likely to try to keep private foreign firms out of such sectors, so as to keep the rents internally, or they are tempted to demand economic performance of certain kinds in return for access to the rents. When the licences pass on to others the rents are likely to be capitalized in the price paid for the underlying assets, and not be available to the new owners. Similar problems arise from the extensive financial regulation in New Zealand, designed among other things to keep interest rates low. Since this would tempt foreigners to borrow in New Zealand or New Zealanders to invest overseas, exchange controls must be put in place to prevent this. Among other things, import controls and exchange controls can lead to an overvalued exchange rate – one which would fall rapidly for a time if such controls are removed. Those who would be negatively affected by the removal of the controls resist such a move. Despite this, New Zealand had begun to move away from controls through the 1970s. One major change was made in 1976, when interest rate controls began to be removed. The successive moves in this direction in later years were to culminate in the removal of controls on borrowing and lending abroad.

We note these points to underline the fact that controls on FDI are to some extent second-best policies, designed to correct for distortions produced by other policies which governments may have problems in ending. When New Zealand did dismantle its other controls, however, those on FDI were maintained, though in a weakened state.

Recent Policy Developments[71]

Some of the tight economic controls which characterized New Zealand governments, both Labour and National, were being eased before 1984. However the Labour government elected in that year and re-elected in 1987 launched a sharp and far-reaching break from earlier economic policies. The break was not only from the policies of the previous government, such as income controls and major public investment projects financed by substantial increases in foreign debt; it extended also to extreme government regulation of the economy extending back to the 1930s.

Shortly after its election in 1984 the government devalued, then floated the exchange rate and ended the long-standing controls on outward and inward foreign exchange transactions. It began the process of ending wage and price control, including those on interest rates. Various types of subsidies to industry, agriculture, exports and state corporations were ended or sharply reduced. Quotas on imports were phased out, except in a number of industries where sectoral adjustments were planned, and the process of reducing very high tariff rates was begun. The government also overhauled the taxation system, placing much more reliance on a value added tax and much less on income tax, and slowly began reform of the labour market. State ownership of industry was reduced and the remaining state-owned corporations were required to follow a more market-oriented set of rules. It may be noted that the government appeared prepared to sell the stock in state firms to foreign buyers, but in at least one case, Petrocorp, the government's plan to sell the stock to a UK firm met such strong opposition that a New Zealand firm won out. Sensitivity to sales of public firms, especially to foreign interests, continued in the 1980s. It appears to have played a role in the decision by the US firms which bought Telecom New Zealand to reduce their ownership to 49.9 per cent through offerings on the New Zealand and international markets (*Globe and Mail*, 16 July 1990).

Such changes reflected in part a response to foreign exchange problems in 1984 but, more fundamentally, to longer-term problems of poor economic performance by international standards.[72] For present purposes the changes in policies on FDI are of most interest. The long-standing control of foreign exchange transactions applied to both inward and outward FDI as well as other investors. In October 1984 the government lifted rules which restricted private domestic borrowers' ability to raise funds overseas. In November overseas-owned companies operating in New Zealand were given unrestricted access to the domestic capital market. In December exchange controls were effectively removed.

The number of restricted sectors, which was not extensive in relative terms, was significantly reduced by the Labour government elected in 1984. At the same time that it ended exchange controls it removed the maximum levels of foreign ownership in advertising agencies, land-based fishing plants and financial institutions. Foreign airlines were permitted to purchase up to 50 per cent of domestic airlines and the government indicated that it would consider 100 per cent foreign ownership of a domestic airline where reciprocity existed in the home country of the foreign firm. The objective in this case was to introduce competition to an industry where, in effect, a monopoly was involved. Air New Zealand was privatized and sold to a consortium which included several foreign airlines. Restrictions on the degree of foreign ownership continue in broadcasting, domestic airlines, as just noted, and exploitation of certain natural resources such as deep-sea fishing. The purchase of rural land (including farms, scenic reserve land and offshore islands) is closely monitored to ensure significant economic benefit to New Zealand. Purchases of commercial property by overseas interests for rental purposes would not be allowed. Foreign investment in large-scale natural resource projects requires case-by-case authorization (OECD, 1987b, 51).

An overhaul of banking policies has recognized that the activities of banks and non-bank financial institutions have overlapped. New registered banks are being authorized so long as they meet certain criteria based on issued capital and financial experience and standing.[73] The only additional criterion for applicants from overseas is reciprocal rights of access in their home market. Eight registered banks were licensed in 1987, including some owned overseas. Australian banks have recently purchased two New Zealand banks.

By contrast, relatively minor changes were made in the regulations of the Overseas Investment Commission. The trigger point for review of acquisitions by overseas persons, which had been set at $NZ 100 000 in 1973, was raised to $NZ 500 000 in 1985 and $NZ 2 million in 1987. If the overseas persons had not already received consent to carry on business in New Zealand, however, the $NZ 500 000 level remained in effect. The most important change was to increase considerably the proposals for foreign investment which are processed by the secretariat, although, as before, the commission or minister retained the power actually to decline applications. The Treasury member of the OIC was replaced by a private sector member. More recently the threshold level for review of a takeover has been raised to $NZ 5.8 million.

It will be noted from Table 6.20 that there was a significant increase in the number of applications both to commence business and for acquisitions in the 1980s, but especially in 1984 and 1985. The sharp but temporary increase in the rejection rates shown in that table for 1983–4 resulted from the embargo the then government placed on some applications from Australia. This was an attempt to persuade the Australian authorities to allow greater access for New Zealand FDI in Australia.[74] Foreign takeover proposals to the OIC rose sharply after the stock market crash of 1987. In 1985–9 there were 3478 such proposals, only two of which were rejected (*World Deal Review*, 1991, 501).

It should be added that a new Commerce Act in 1986 included stronger provisions for anti-competitive behaviour than existed before and also a merger law which required prior notification to a Commerce Commission. While directed at all firms and at the issue of market dominance, such a change can also involve a form of regulation of larger MNEs or those in highly concentrated sectors.

At the end of the 1970s New Zealand had one of the most regulated and protected economies in the OECD. Much of that regulation and protection was removed in the 1980s, but macroeconomic growth also slowed. Many reasons have been advanced for this apparent lack of response at the macro level, both external (strong agricultural protection abroad) to internal (either too much or too little deregulation). Whatever the reasons, the National Party government elected in October 1990 apparently decided further change was needed, for its first measures were designed to cut public spending, especially in social welfare, and to end both compulsory unionism and the centralized pay award system (*The Economist*, 23 March 1991, 79–80).

Conclusions

In Part I of this study we outlined four explanations for public policy decisions, as well as the kinds of strategies different types of countries could follow in dealing with MNEs. This section notes briefly the experience of New Zealand within this framework, while deferring generalizations to the point where our sample of countries has been covered.

The extensive system of exchange controls still in existence in 1964–5 provided the setting within which approvals on inward FDI were instituted. This was partly a defensive move against controls on outward FDI elsewhere. Concern over a particular takeover attempt in a sensitive sector also played a role in developing controls on inward FDI.

The regulations passed at that time were consolidated and extended in 1973 with the establishment of the OIC. What were the circumstances which led to such a move? The existence of import controls and the maintenance of low rates of interest would tend to prolong the exchange controls and at least some of the controls on FDI. The election of a Labour Party government, with the concerns such parties then had about large private corporations, might be expected to favour such a prolongation – although one should add that this particular Labour government showed more pragmatism than its counterpart in Australia at this time. Note should be taken also of an extensive public debate on the effects of MNEs, very similar to that which was occurring elsewhere throughout the late 1960s and early 1970s. That debate was as inconclusive in New Zealand as it was elsewhere, and for similar reasons. The economic effects of MNEs became intertwined with the political effects and these in turn became in part synonymous with the social effects of large corporations and of government policies towards them.

Perhaps the point can be made by reference to the few larger studies on the subject, then and later. By far the most comprehensive economic analysis was published in 1970 (Deane) and it still remains the only major economic analysis of the subject. The conclusions of that study, put briefly, were that foreign investment had made a substantial contribution to New Zealand economic growth; that the economic problems attributed to it were either minor in nature or involved issues pertinent to the entire economy, not just to foreign-owned firms; and that adequate overall and industrial policies, rather than treatment directed to FDI, were the keys to increasing benefits from both foreign and domestic firms (Deane, 1970, ch. 13).

Perhaps the study did have an effect on public policy. Certainly the OIC avoided the detailed extraction of performance commitments typical of some other review mechanisms in countries where negative industrial performance was believed to be closely associated with MNEs. Nevertheless more popularly written and more autarchic views were widely disseminated, notably those of Sutch (1972), a long-time senior civil servant in what became the Trade and Industry Department. His argument pointed to the risk of loss of control of the New Zealand economy because of dependence on outside direct investment, whatever the country sources of such investment, and a plea for domestic control in all sectors as necessary to the development of a distinctive society. Such polarization of views is useful for those who make policy, since it gives them even more freedom to pursue their own preferences. One can note, for example, the statement of the Finance Minister (later Prime Minister) W.E. Rowling:

> The two most comprehensive sources of information are both private studies from which, I am bound to admit, the learned doctors responsible manage to reach diametrically opposite conclusions. Despite this precedent, I am hopeful that the existence of comprehensive, continually updated information will lead to discussion on this topic being based rather more on fact and rather less on emotion. (Rowling, 1975, 21)

One would hardly have concluded from this statement that the two studies he noted differed substantially in this respect.

One might ask what the regulation of FDI was accomplishing by the early 1980s, apart from the control over larger natural resource projects. There was no bargaining with most firms over performance requirements, and little systematic monitoring except to prevent entry into fields other than those approved. Few applications were declined. The stance of the OIC was pragmatic and, indeed, welcoming to FDI. Related policies, such as the award of incentives, remaining controls on foreign exchange and import licensing, were being handled by other agencies and were ended or reduced after 1984. The debate on FDI had become less vigorous by the early 1980s, if not before, with attention focusing more narrowly on the problems of large projects, especially in natural resources. With the election in 1984 of a government which was dedicated to sweeping away many other regulations and relying on framework policies, one would expect that foreign investment regulation would be questioned.

In fact a review of its role was undertaken by the OIC in 1986, in part to determine whether to move to a notification system with full review reserved for only the most significant proposals. In the event it was decided, with the concurrence of government, to maintain a general review system, significantly streamlined in operation, as noted above. It appears that the public costs of the two systems were not very different, while the modified general review system offered more flexibility over time, especially in handling contentious cases. It may be added that New Zealand, unlike other countries noted in this study, could afford to take such a view in part because her general review policies were not notably restrictive and hence did not have to undergo major liberalization in response to the changed circumstances of the 1980s. New Zealand's policies, in fact, showed considerable continuity over the 1970s and 1980s, in contrast to the experience of other countries with review mechanisms.

NORWAY

Norway has seen very large fluctuations in foreign ownership of its capital stock over the past century. In the first two decades of this century it developed a strong set of policies directed in part at foreign ownership and in part at the impact of large corporations generally. The increased activity in petroleum and gas in the past two decades has led it to adopt a distinctive set of policies in that industry involving both domestic ownership and economic performance objectives (Table 6.21).

Foreign direct investments were prominent in Norway in the last three decades of the nineteenth century. By the turn of the century UK investors dominated the paper industry and Swedish investors dominated mining – the two largest export industries. By 1909 fully 39 per cent of the industrial capital stock (mining and manufacturing) was owned by foreign investors, rising as high as 80 to 85 per cent in mining and in chemicals, and between 30 and 45 per cent in several other manufacturing sectors. The figure of 39 per cent fell sharply, to 15 per cent, in 1919. Despite the policies on foreign control it rose to 26 per cent in 1939, but again fell back to 15 per cent in 1962.

Foreign ownership of the corporate sector as a whole rose from about 7 per cent in 1919 to 11 per cent and 16 per cent in 1928 and 1936, falling to 10 per cent in 1950, then rising to 17 per cent in 1972. It might be noted that these are significant underestimates for some purposes.[75]

Table 6.21 Summary of policy development in Norway

1906	Temporary prohibition of foreign acquisitions of waterfalls, mines, forests.
1909	Prohibition of foreign acquisition of forests.
1917	Concession Act of 1917 regulates acquisition of waterfalls, mines, other real estate by foreign interests, and of waterfalls and mines by fully Norwegian-owned firms.
	Laws regulating foreign acquisition of marshland (1913), limestone deposits (1914), mountain and meadowland (1915), agricultural land (1920), quartz deposits (1949).
1950	Inflows and outflows of capital regulated by law.
1961–3	Policy statements by government on foreign direct investment and on the review process.
1963	Law regulating exploration and exploitation of coastal natural resources.
1970	Updating of Act of 1917.
1972	Establishment of state-owned Statoil.
1985	Foreign bank subsidiaries permitted on a reciprocity basis.

Sources: Norway, Industry Department 1974–5; *Business International*, Norway, May 1986.

More recently foreign ownership of Norwegian industry has been relatively high in a few sectors only, notably metals, chemicals and electrical products; in the early 1970s these were the only ones in the 30–40 per cent range for foreign ownership, with others at 10 per cent or less. Over the period from 1929 to the 1970s no home country ever accounted for more than 30 per cent of the total foreign capital in Norway. In the early 1970s the USA accounted for 26 per cent of total FDI stock and the next two largest shares, those of Sweden and the UK, were 12 and 10 per cent respectively (Einarsen, 1970, 162–3; Kresl, 1976, 23–4). The percentage of sales accounted for by foreign-based firms in Norway in 1981 was 31, 13, 13 and 15 respectively for primary goods, manufactures, construction, and trade and distribution (Dunning and Cantwell, 1987, 161).

What led to the early development of policy on this subject? As noted above, by the turn of the century foreign investors dominated two major industries. Some 'concession' laws were in effect as early as 1883. What seems to have triggered an extensive discussion and legislation, however, was the rapid acquisition of waterfalls by domestic and foreign interests; that is, of the hydro-electric power which was becoming the basis of much new industry. In addition Norway was in a strongly nationalist phase politically. It had achieved political independence of Denmark in 1814 but its union with Sweden did not end until 1905. Moreover Norway was determined to maintain its neutrality, which some felt was compromised by the attempts of some subsidiaries to continue normal business relations with parent firms and customers during the First World War (Stonehill, 1965, 153).[76] It also became clear during the debates on this issue that labour groups and others were concerned about the effects of absentee ownership on wage rates, social conditions and other aspects of domestic economic policies, and particularly about the effects of major industrial projects on remote agricultural regions.

As these concerns mounted, however, they began to reflect the view that private domestic, as well as foreign, interests could cause similar difficulties. The emphasis shifted to some extent to the need for more general regulatory instruments to control the social and economic impact of large firms in natural resources, as well as a method to review inward FDI. A law was passed in 1906, temporarily preventing foreign acquisitions of waterfalls, mines and forests. In 1909 the foreign ownership of forests was permanently forbidden. A more general law of 1917, directed to some extent at both (large-scale) domestic and foreign interests, formed the basis of the concession system.

These laws do not, however, appear to have been the main factor in the substantial drop in foreign ownership of industry during and after the First World War. While the actual causes are somewhat obscure, they seem to centre on the development of a large current account surplus during the war, part of which was used to repatriate firms owned abroad (Stonehill, 1965, 452).

The concession laws obviously allowed for a great deal of flexibility, since, as noted earlier, foreign ownership rose significantly in the inter-war period. Another opportunity for repatriation arose with the ending of the Second World War. Norway was occupied by German forces during that war. As reparations afterwards, all German holdings in Norway were acquired. The most important acquisition was Norsk Hydro, about half of which was acquired by the state, with the remainder in private foreign and domestic ownership. Norway also gained control of the major iron ore mining companies (Stonehill, 1965, 59–70). Such reparations led to a substantial decline in foreign ownership, as noted earlier.

Since the 1950s there has been a renewed interest in investment in Norway, and particularly large investments have occurred in petroleum and natural gas with the price increases of the 1970s (Table 6.22). A number of policy statements have set the background against which such investments have occurred.

Table 6.22 Inward and outward flows of FDI in Norway, 1970–87 (kroner million)

	Inward	*Outward*
1970	457	229
1971	664	226
1972	794	N/A
1973	1 203	289
1974	1 919	820
1975	1 130	889
1976	2 035	1 027
1977	4 077	665
1978	2 547	341
1979	2 028	223
1980	296	1 254
1981	3 912	1 049
1982	2 850	1 967
1983	2 426	2 597
1984	-1 648	4 476
1985	-114	8 895
1986	6 628	9 430
1987	1 316	6 125

Sources: Dunning and Cantwell (1987, 157) for 1970–82; thereafter, IMF, *Balance of Payments Yearbook*, 1988, part 1, converted from SDRs to kroner. Excludes retained earnings.

Concession Law of 1917 and Regulation of Establishment

The Act of 1917 requires foreigners and foreign-controlled Norwegian companies to secure a special permit or concession in order to acquire waterfalls, mines and other real properties, whether buildings or land, and without regard to the purpose for which the property was to be used.[77] Concessions are required also for leases of property for industrial uses. Such foreign interests must have a concession also to acquire more than 10 per cent of the share capital of a company owning or leasing real property which is subject to concession. A foreign-controlled Norwegian company is one where more than 20 per cent of the voting rights or share capital is owned by foreigners or foreign-controlled companies or where at least one member of the board is an alien. It should be added that, if the company wishes to purchase electric power beyond a small amount, it must be incorporated in Norway and the majority of its executive board, including the chairman, must be citizens of Norway.[78] In such cases, if the concessionaire has any aliens on its executive board or any basic capital held outside Norway, the concession may include a provision for the state to purchase within 40 years the factory using the power and the associated land and facilities. A similar provision applies to mining.

The Concession Act of 1917 as amended contains a number of 'basic rules' to be met by the firms involved. It is particularly to be noted that Norwegian-owned corporations are also subject to the Act in connection with the development of waterfalls and mines. The basic rules involved in these cases are:

1. regulation of the capital structure of the firm, including the proportion of equity to the total;
2. Norwegian labour, insurance companies and materials 'should preferably be used';
3. any approved exports (imports) be at prices no lower (higher) than normal world market prices;
4. processing in Norway to the extent stipulated by the government;
5. approval by the ministry of any agreement regarding payment for financial, technical and commercial assistance.

There are also provisions that the firm supply social capital such as education and health services in remote areas, that production fees be paid and that part of the supply be made available to local and central governments.

Concessions on 'other real property' are not required for Norwegians in the 1917 Act. Foreigners who wish access to these, which effectively means those who wish to conduct other types of business, must have an executive board whose majority, including the chairman, are Norwegians. They are subject to each of the five basic rules noted above, except for the second, and any other rules provided in their concession 'as may in each separate case be considered necessary on account of the public interest or in order to safeguard any private interests that are harmed' (Act of 1917, official translation, 27).

The concession can provide that the property not be used for other purposes than those stipulated.

What is clear from the above is that the concession laws not only maintained a degree of domestic control over natural resources, depending on how firmly the laws were applied, but also provided the basis for the review of incoming FDI or merger by established foreign-owned firms, whatever the nature of the activity. Further clarifications of policy occurred in the 1960s as an expansion of FDI was under way in Norway (see Kresl, 1976, 8–12; Stonehill, 1965, 56–7). In 1961 the government declared that it was prepared to encourage direct investment in Norway in areas where Norway did not have the capability to develop independent production. It was especially interested in securing access to newer knowledge, export markets, and to raw materials and intermediate goods. In 1962 a further statement was made by government on the water power and water power-intensive industries. It favoured loan financing for the development of electric power. In the case of industries utilizing such power, it favoured joint ventures where feasible with the Norwegian interest, 'effectively organized', accounting for at least 50 per cent ownership. The statement also underlined some of the national interest provisions of the 1917 Act. In 1963 the Department of Industry outlined the specific criteria which are taken into account in evaluating an application for a concession. These are as follows:

1. The effects on income, production and employment.
2. Location of the project with regard especially to areas of low income development.
3. The extent of foreign financing, and especially the need to import capital in large, capital-intensive projects.
4. The development of new types of production.
5. The possibility of receiving new knowledge.
6. The possibility of cooperating with international concerns to secure better or more stable prices and guaranteed access to raw materials or exports.
7. The extent to which the domestic sector is already developed.
8. The extent of competition on the home market with established Norwegian firms and the danger of monopoly practices.

Review Procedures[79]

Norway has had exchange controls for the post-Second World War period, as well as a policy of encouraging low domestic interest rates. These controls were liberally administered by the early 1980s, thanks in part to oil revenues, and interest rates were being allowed to move upwards. Foreign companies in Norway still needed permission to borrow abroad, including parent-company loans or guarantees.

The responsibility for examining inward direct investment is divided among several agencies, with coordination achieved through consultation rather than a formal mechanism. The Department of Agriculture is responsible for several parts of the concession laws, as is the Department of Industry, while the central bank manages the exchange control aspects and approval for trading companies and some areas of finance, and the industries on the continental shelf (particularly petroleum and gas) are the responsibility of the Department of Energy. In what follows we will concentrate on the Departments of Industry and of Energy.

It is the Department of Industry which has the main responsibility for the concession laws. What these laws amount to in terms of the topics in this study is an authorization for new direct investment from abroad, acquisitions (including those by established foreign-owned firms) and expansion into new lines of activity. Authorization is also needed for expansion of existing lines if this involves the purchase of real estate containing buildings, but in this case approval is virtually automatic. Authorization is needed to transfer shares to another foreigner but again this seems to be given quite readily. So far as industrial activities are concerned, it is evident that the concession laws place authorization requirements on foreign-owned firms which would not be applied to domestically owned firms. The latter would not require authorization for acquisitions, for example, except in connection with competition effects or other laws applied to all firms.

To obtain a concession an investor in most cases will use the services of a lawyer specializing in this service, since little precise information is available on the particular conditions the ministry will require. Informal consultations will occur with the ministry to determine how to present the case, and possibly with local government officials and other ministries also. A formal and detailed letter to the ministry follows. Major projects may be submitted to an ad hoc committee drawn from several ministries and may go to Cabinet. In some cases, as required by law or the importance of the case, parliament itself is involved. But most cases are evaluated in the ministry, with consultation as needed. A formal concession agreement will then be issued in the form of a letter from the ministry, containing some of the agreed conditions. A response to an application must be made in 90 days, a period which can be extended for specified reasons.

The criteria by which authorization is given are not published, apart from the information in the Concession Acts and policy statements noted above. The letters from the minister contain a number of standard items, as shown in Appendix III, but specific conditions may also be attached. Some of the phrases in the standard conditions, such as 'sound business practice' and 'realistic pricing', have their equivalents in tax and company laws applicable to all companies. Under the concession laws, as already noted, preferences are to be given to Norwegian labour and materials, foreign trade must be at normal world market prices and payments to the parent for technical and other assistance are subject to approval. These conditions have been given particular attention in the petroleum sector, as noted further below.

There is no detailed information on the specific conditions attached to particular firms apart from the standard items. It does seem clear that what occurs is an attempt to indicate which aspects of the proposal need to be revised if it is to prove acceptable rather than a process of bargaining in a systematic attempt to maximize gains. This is certainly the case for most proposals – a staff of three in the Industry Department, with other duties as well, is hardly optimal for a bargaining process. Even on major projects a series of ad hoc committees is not likely to accumulate the information needed to bargain strategically. It is important to add that officials in other departments bear the responsibility for particular items or industries (National Revenue for transfer pricing, Energy for petroleum); hence expertise is brought to bear on particular points. To some extent this large task is made more manageable because of emphasis on particular government objectives at particular points of time: on regional development and technological improvement in the 1970s, for example, when unemployment rates were very low. Rejection rates for formal applications are not available but such rejections are infrequent – not surprisingly, given the significant informal consultation process which would discourage unacceptable applications.

Acquisitions by foreign firms receive closer scrutiny than new investments, particularly the larger cases. This concern arises partly because of the fear that MNEs may reorganize an acquired plant or division so as to increase imports. An attempt may be made, therefore, to locate a Norwegian partner for the selling firm, or to end up with a joint venture arrangement with the foreign firm. The maximum holding by the foreign firm will be written into the concession and a change requires consent.

The conditions in these concessions are not systematically monitored in order to ascertain if they are being implemented. Rather reliance is placed on the contacts firms have with government agencies – for example, a further application to exchange control authorities. Fines can be levied if the conditions are not met, but only six or so such cases had occurred up to the early 1980s.[80]

Key Sectors and Petroleum

In Table 11.3 we note the industries which are public monopolies or privately-operated monopolies, thus closed to private ownership, whether Norwegian or foreign. As for sectors closed specifically to foreign ownership, some are those closed elsewhere, others those of particular interest to Norway. Foreign investment in Norwegian-owned banks was generally limited to 10 per cent, but 25 per cent could be authorized. As of 1985, subsidiaries of foreign banks have been allowed on a reciprocity basis. With occasional exemptions, foreign-controlled firms could not own ships of Norwegian registry, engage in fishing, operate travel agencies, engage in air transport within Norway or establish or operate free warehouses or free ports. In most of these cases, along with the requirement that a majority of shares remain in Norwegian hands, there are requirements for Norwegian directors as well (OECD, 1985a, 1987b). Moreover the review process has discouraged entry into certain industries where capacity was already developed, an example being the pulp and paper industry (Stonehill, 1965, 65). As already noted, the Concession Act of 1917 limits foreign ownership of waterfalls and mines: in such cases government is likely to negotiate extensive Norwegian ownership and management if it agrees to a concession at all.

The most important set of regulations concern petroleum and gas, an industry which accounted for one-third of the value of exports and one-sixth of state revenue by the early 1980s. It is well to note again that Norway had a long experience with concessions on electric power and some other resources, an experience which helped it to avoid very long-term and unconditional types of concessions. It appears, for example, that one of the major participating MNEs in the early 1960s wanted a concession for the entire North Sea, but had to accept instead a concession system based on detailed proposals by companies for each block. It is true that the lack of expertise in petroleum development in Norway meant substantial reliance on MNEs in the early years. The first licence, which was awarded in 1965, gave a multinational firm 100 per cent ownership of production and Norwegian firms took relatively small shares of production in the late 1960s. Progressively larger shares were given to Norwegian firms, however, as new licences were issued thereafter, and Norwegian firms also became operators of large shares of the blocks.[81] The establishment of Statoil in 1972, wholly owned by the state, is particularly noteworthy. Since 1973 it has been allocated by law a minimum 50 per cent of production and can be allocated up to 85 per cent on a sliding scale, depending on the richness of the field. In 1985 Statoil began the process of taking over from a foreign MNE as operator of Statfjord, the major field in Norway. It should be noted that, in addition to production participation, the state also takes substantial taxes and royalties and an effort is made to ensure domestic sourcing of supplies for the industry.

The allocation of blocks is quite different from the auction system used in some other jurisdictions, allowing the government not only to secure economic rent but also to exercise some control over various activities and to allow local firms to gain experience (Noreng, 1980, 116–27). Government makes choices from among detailed company proposals for the development of a particular portion of a field which is available for concession. The system is highly subjective in the sense that it is not known just how the government makes choices, particularly among MNEs. It also has the effect of putting the government in a strong position in dealing with MNEs, given the richness of the Norwegian fields and the political stability of the country. As noted, Statoil got 50 per cent in each case, going up to 85 per cent on some of the more prosperous blocks. Two of the larger Norwegian firms might get 15 to 20 per cent in a typical case, the MNEs would get 15 to 20 per cent, and about 5 per cent could be reserved for smaller Norwegian firms. In some cases, however, 100 per cent was allocated to Norwegian firms. The two larger Norwegian firms are Norsk Hydro and Saga Petroleum, the former being 51 per cent state-owned and 35 per cent foreign-owned, the latter a private consortium of many Norwegian firms. In the early 1980s concessions for oil to foreign firms reverted fully to the state after 40 years; 25 per cent of the area reverted to the government after an initial period and a further 25 per cent after another three years.

The proposals to exploit a particular block do not include local content provisions. Rather, as a firm works on a concession, it provides information on all larger contract proposals or purchase orders so that the government can be assured that potential local bidders are given a fair chance to bid. The performance in this respect is reviewed after the event. It will be recalled that the Concession Law of 1917 included a preference for Norwegian labour and materials. This has been applied more firmly in recent years, especially with regard to North Sea oil. The first field to be developed had only 20 per cent local content, while one developed in the late 1970s had about 80 per cent. The latter figure falls to about 50 per cent if allowance is made for imports by the Norwegian firms (interview with Statoil, August 1982).

One should add that foreign companies were encouraged to submit proposals for industrial cooperation with Norwegian firms when applying for rights to develop a block. Many of these attempts to develop industry by taking advantage of MNE sales and production contacts did not work out profitably. On the other hand, a number of joint research proposals, especially those related to energy, were more promising.

Taxation is a separate issue from that of participation in production. Some backtracking was necessary in 1974, when the government proposed an excess profit tax at a level considered unacceptable to the companies, but by mid-1975 both production participation and special taxes were important policy instruments (Noreng, 1980, 52–3). Such taxes were paid on a price set by a government committee every six months so as to reflect the international price. To some extent this system offset any tendency to transfer pricing, that is to having MNEs take the oil at a lower price into their downstream operations abroad.

From the point of view of the MNEs this system involved some problems. Statoil in particular was given two major advantages. First, after the early years it did not pay any exploration costs on its share of the concession, costs which were therefore the responsibility of the other firms. Second, when particularly encouraging results appeared from exploration the government was likely to favour Statoil, and sometimes the other two larger Norwegian firms, in allocating the promising adjacent blocks, rather than the firm or firms which had succeeded in making the discovery. From another perspective these advantages to Norwegian firms could be seen as simply the terms on which the owner, in this case the state, extracts rents on its property. This argument is convincing in the case of Statoil which is wholly owned by the state, less so for the case of privately-owned Saga, unless one is prepared to make a case for the income redistribution involved, and not at all for the 35 per cent portion of Norsk Hydro which is foreign-owned.

One should add that, while the MNE officers who were interviewed complained that the terms of exploration involved too much discretion and were very stiff, they did not consider them to have been applied retroactively: changes were introduced on new concessions. In this regard they drew a distinction with efforts by Canada to increase rents in the industry in the early 1980s. It is also worth noting that the election of a Conservative (minority) government in 1981 did not lead to substantial changes in the role of Statoil with regard to allocation of blocks or in most other ways, except as the collector of petroleum revenues for the state (*The Economist*, 5 November 1983, 5–6).

This brief comment does not take account of the major issue so far as most Norwegians are concerned; that is, the socioeconomic impact of the development of oil and gas. A white paper presented to parliament in 1974 emphasized the need for a controlled and moderate pace of production, a slow introduction of the use of revenues into domestic consumption and significant government participation at different stages of the industry. The first two objectives reflected fears about the environmental effects of large-scale development, a desire to maintain full employment and also regional balance, the problems of spending large revenues wisely, and the effects on other industry from a rising cost structure. These concerns did not disappear but the 'hasten slowly' policy ran into difficulties in the late 1970s, as development led to various economic imbalances, and again in the recession of the early 1980s, when more rapid expansion of oil and gas was encouraged. Norway was not successful in achieving the objectives it set for balanced development, any more than other major beneficiaries of a resource boom based on oil and gas.

In concluding this section we note that approval of outward direct investment was the responsibility of the central bank as an aspect of its exchange control function, with consultation with various government departments as needed. The representatives of workers on the board of the company making the investment would also be consulted. The objectives of the control process appeared to be those associated with exchange control, such as assurance that the investment is not simply a vehicle to export portfolio capital or accumulate profits abroad, rather than consistent reviews of investments in terms of their overall economic desirability. Outward investment increased significantly after 1974, when controls on such investment were eased, and especially in the 1980s (Table 6.22). In 1981 the output of manufacturing affiliates abroad as a percentage of domestic manufacturing output was 15 per cent. Norwegian MNEs accounted for 52 per cent of manufactured exports from Norway in that year (Dunning and Cantwell, 1987, 102).

Conclusions

Norway does not possess an extensive set of studies on the economic effects of FDI, despite the long history of policy. Stonehill (1965) remains the most detailed general historical study. Part II of that study examines for 1952–62 the performance record of firms with three types of ownership: 50 per cent and 20 per cent foreign ownership and Norwegian-owned enterprises. On most of the tests – the growth pattern, stability of production and employment, returns to factors – the empirical results did not support negative views of the effects of MNEs, while in some cases, such as balance of payments effects and regional development, the results were indeterminate. Stonehill went on to note, however, that the main concerns about FDI in Norway had been the effects on political independence, in ways already noted above with regard to the First World War (for example 89–90, 153–6). Nevertheless Norwegian policy was fairly open toward inward FDI in the period after the Second World War, partly because of the general desire for industrialization, partly because some of the early fears of the economic effects of FDI had not materialized, but also because the existence of the concession laws assuaged the concerns about FDI (Einarsen, 1970, 174–6).

It must be added that the concession laws had some defects as a method of reviewing inward FDI in the 1970s and 1980s. It is somewhat surprising that a different mechanism was not under active consideration, as was the case in Sweden. Very little information is made public – there are no data on applications, rejections or reasons involved in the latter. The staff in the Industry Department is too small for assessment purposes, and the ad hoc interdepartmental committees do not appear to allow for a sufficient learning process. The conditions in the concessions are not monitored and, for the most part, tend to be fairly standardized phrases that exist in company law, tax law and competition law applied to all firms. Since the process was administered quite liberally in the early 1980s, according to interviewees in government and in several firms with concessions, the question arises whether it would have made much difference in terms of economic welfare if the concession system had ended, outside petroleum, natural resources and takeovers in a few sensitive areas. Alternatively the system was not well defined for those who favoured a systematic review of new or merger activity by foreign firms.

The political dimension of the relationship of a small state to MNEs did receive attention in an unusual research programme financed by government on the distribution of power in Norway. This study was begun in 1972 and presented to the government a decade later (Heum, 1979, 1982). The central argument of these studies is that many MNEs are internationally integrated units, at least in some important respects, so that the Norwegian subsidiaries are subject to the strategic considerations of the entire concern; that the subsidiaries in most cases account for a relatively small share of the entire MNE operation, and in some significant ways are only weakly integrated into the Norwegian economy; and that it is difficult in the typical case for Norway *acting alone* to influence the actions of subsidiaries, including those of Norwegian MNEs, where this conflicts with the overall objectives of the firms. The findings for the Nordic Council (Knudsen and Landmark, 1980, chs 12–13 especially) and by the Council's project leader on MNEs (Knudsen, 1980) reinforce these conclusions so far as Norway is concerned. The latter addresses the exposure of the Nordic countries to the political influence of MNEs in part by examining the geographic dispersal of the MNEs. The greater the dispersal, it is reasoned, the greater is the MNE bargaining power with respect to host countries – at least when given a degree of centralized decision making in MNEs. In the sample of MNEs used, Norway was the Nordic country with by far the largest proportion of foreign-owned subsidiaries with parent firms whose activities were widely dispersed geographically. The main report called, therefore, for more information on such firms, more international coordination of policy and more worker and state involvement in MNE decisions.

The Knudsen measures, it should be emphasized, are for manufacturing industries. A somewhat different perspective is needed with regard to petroleum and gas, as will be evident from the comments above. Because of the electric power boom early in the century, Norway had substantial experience with closing some natural resource sectors to MNEs and regulating most other FDI. Moreover a clear set of policy objectives was enunciated in the late 1960s and early 1970s as the petroleum boom got under way: control over the rate of production and of the use of revenues, state participation in the various phases of the industry and capturing for Norway some of the developmental effects, particularly by way of acting as suppliers to the industry. Finally Norway consumed a relatively small part of what turned out to be a very productive set of oil fields in high demand through the 1970s in particular. In brief it was in a strong position to attract petroleum investment and to deal with MNEs from a strategic viewpoint. Put differently, it was in a strong position to resolve in its favour the various tensions in state–MNE relations in natural resources which were noted in Chapter 2.

In terms of the first of these tensions, securing the economic rent from the resource, some success can be claimed. The production participation arrangements noted above were strong instruments to this end, and substantial tax and royalty payments were involved in addition. The MNEs disliked the high degree of discretion in the production participation system but were unable to do much about it, among other reasons because of the political sensitivity of such issues. It is one thing to argue about the effects of a particular set of taxes, where these have an impact on all firms, including Statoil, quite another to line up against the government, the state petroleum company and the private Norwegian sector on what you believe to be allocations which discriminate against MNEs, in a system where the criteria for decision taking are not clear in any case.

A second objective, the developmental effects in terms of encouragement of local sourcing, are also a significant part of the process of awarding concessions. However attempts to encourage industrial collaboration with local firms appear to have met with limited success. The other two tensions inherent in MNE–state relations in natural resources are somewhat more complex. First, the attempt for a variety of socioeconomic reasons to control the pace of development was not notably successful, an experience repeated in other countries with a resource boom. The upward pressure on wage rates and other costs and, despite this, the appreciation of the exchange rate at times in response to rising oil exports, created serious problems for manufacturing and some primary resource producers. Indeed manufacturing output was stable in the last half of the 1970s, despite the efforts to link the oil boom with increased demands for some types of local manufacturing. There was renewed effort to attract investment in oil so as to maintain jobs, regional development and other objectives in the 1980s as global recession in the early part of the decade and lower oil prices reduced inward FDI.

One might think that the other objective, state participation, was achieved on a large scale, given the major role of Statoil. This became a problem in itself in the sense that the Conservative government of the early 1980s, despite its expressed desires to reduce the scope of Statoil, found itself unable to do so in a significant way.[82] The political popularity of state participation, combined with the need to deal with MNEs on a broad front, appears to have curbed the government's professed wishes. By the late 1980s the Labour government was considering sale of some of its shares in North Sea oil, partly on the grounds that such direct participation was too large a risk for society.

These decisions clearly involved some factors beyond the control of a national government. But it is well to add that the objectives set by the government in a complex area such as oil are implemented by a variety of agencies with different views of these objectives and purposes of their own. One commentator, in reviewing Norway's experience in this regard, concluded: 'There may not be any such thing as a consistent oil policy, or a consistent policy for dealing with the impact of oil' (Smith, 1981, 766). Some Canadians, among others, might be inclined to agree.

SWEDEN

Sweden has had concession laws since 1916. A major effort was made in the 1970s to update those laws, based in part on a substantial research programme on MNEs. That effort produced only modest changes in the actual policies regarding MNEs. Where Norway faced the challenge of developing policy for North Sea oil, the challenge facing Sweden was whether a review process was desirable and feasible for the substantial outward investment by Swedish MNEs.

Sweden is more a home than a host country so far as MNEs are concerned. On the inward side, Table 6.23 shows that enterprises with 50 per cent of voting capital held by a firm or group abroad had from 5 per cent to 10 per cent of total enterprise activity in 1979, depending on the measure used. If one looks at enterprises where 20 per cent or more of the voting capital was held by non-residents, the proportions rise to 8 to 13 per cent. It will be noted that almost all of these measures show an increase for the decade as a whole. Nevertheless Table 3.5 shows Sweden has had a relatively low degree of foreign ownership, measured by employment in foreign-owned manufacturing industries. The low overall ownership by foreign interests may be due in part to the small size of the market and the presence of strong Swedish MNEs in a number of sectors. Sweden has also kept tariffs low, thus limiting the scope for the tariff-induced type of subsidiary. Also an overvalued exchange rate until the late 1970s inhibited inward investment while encouraging outward investment (Swedenborg, 1985, 221–2).

In 1979 enterprises which were 50 per cent or more owned abroad accounted for 6 per cent of manufacturing employment, 20 per cent of em-

Table 6.23 Foreign-owned enterprises as a percentage of total enterprise activity, Sweden 1971 and 1979

Activity	*Enterprises 20% or more owned abroad*		*Enterprises 50% or more owned abroad*	
	1971	*1979*	*1971*	*1979*
Employment	7.1	8.2	4.3	5.0
Value added	8.1	9.7	5.3	6.3
Investment	7.1	7.8	4.4	5.2
Company taxes	13.2	13.3	10.2	9.5
Net profit	9.6	10.1	6.8	7.5
Assets	8.2	9.1	4.9	6.1

Source: National Central Bureau of Statistics, *Foreign-Owned Enterprises*, 1978 and 1979 (25 September 1981) and 1972 and 1973 (9 June 1975), Stockholm.

ployment in wholesale trade and only 1 or 2 per cent of employment in agriculture and mining, finance and insurance, and transport and communication. In manufactures, about half of the employment in foreign-owned firms was in the engineering industries (metal products, machinery, electrical), while chemicals and foodstuffs account for another one-third (Swedenborg, 1985, 225). The United States was the largest single investor with about one-third of the assets in the mid-1970s, with the United Kingdom the other major investor with about one-quarter. The other Nordic countries, along with France and West Germany, also had significant investments in the late 1970s.

The impact on Sweden of her own MNEs, by contrast, is potentially much larger (Swedenborg, 1985, 215–27, 247). Sweden is a highly industrialized and highly internationalized economy. Exports were about 30 per cent of gross domestic product (GDP) in 1980. Manufacturing plants located abroad account for about one-third of Swedish industry's total sales. This investment is largely concentrated in the metals, machinery and electrical products industries. Two-thirds of it is in the EC and the United States. One can recapitulate for manufacturing alone by noting that, in 1978, there were in total 875 000 workers in Sweden; Swedish MNEs had 416 000 workers, of which 228 000 were in their foreign affiliates, and foreign MNEs in Swedish manufacturing had 51 000 workers. Net outward FDI has substantially exceeded net inward since 1969 (Table 6.24). In the early 1980s, more than half of the employees of Sweden's ten biggest firms were working abroad (*The Economist*, 6 November 1984, 16). This large outward investment has been explained by the fact that Sweden has a relatively large stock of human capital vital to the development of MNEs and also a home market which is too small to exploit economies of scale (Swedenborg, 1985, 221–2).

The 1916 Concession Act states that alien individuals and companies need the permission of the government to acquire real property or to engage in

Table 6.24 Net outward and inward direct investment in Sweden, 1961–87 (million Skr at current prices)

	Outward	*Inward*
1961	154	64
1962	310	280
1963	338	463
1964	483	203
1965	528	450
1966	612	719
1967	569	524
1968	229	542
1969	1 225	799
1970	1 103	557
1971	900	423
1972	1 256	325
1973	1 267	320
1974	1 913	357
1975	1 812	323
1976	2 578	17
1977	3 016	313
1978	1 888	312
1979	2 596	476
1980	2 648	1 054
1981	4 227	915
1982	5 979	1 131
1983	8 081	418
1984	8 640	1 289
1985	11 025	2 298
1986	21 837	5 800
1987	19 898	1 861

Source: Swedenborg (1985, 247) until 1980, then IMF, *Balance of Payments Statistics Yearbook*, 1988, converted from SDRs. Includes incomplete estimates for reinvested earnings up to 1974, and small amounts for such earnings on the outward side thereafter.

mining activity.[83] The Act was apparently a response to, and intended to regulate, foreign acquisitions of Swedish natural wealth such as mines, forests and water power, either directly or by acquiring Swedish companies which had such assets. Such foreign acquisitions were significant in the late nineteenth century and the period preceding the First World War. Sweden was particularly concerned at the time about the effects on her neutrality of acquisitions of firms in these sectors by actual or potential belligerents. It should be noted that the Act was *not* generally intended to prevent foreign acquisition of real estate.

The Act also applied to certain Swedish entities, including Swedish joint stock companies. However a Swedish company is exempted from the Act for most purposes if its articles of association state that aliens may only acquire less than 20 per cent of its voting shares and less than 40 per cent of its share capital. About 80 per cent of the Swedish companies listed on the Stock Exchange have such clauses prohibiting alien ownership. If a company wished to remove this clause so that larger parts of its shares could be acquired by aliens, it needed the permission of the government or, in some cases, of the National Industrial Board.

Thus, while the 1916 Act protected natural resources from foreign acquisition, it did not clearly allow the government to prevent foreign acquisition of firms which did not have such resources. This omitted some of Sweden's present-day major firms. An Act in 1968 required government permission for aliens to form or become a partner in a trading company. An amendment to the 1916 Act in 1973 indicated that the government would allow removal or modification of the aliens clause from a company's articles of association, whether 'real estate' was involved or not, but only if it was satisfied that acquisition by foreigners did not conflict with an essential public interest.

The 1973 amendment was regarded by the government as provisional since it left unresolved a number of questions on coverage of the 1916 Act. The 1916 Act generally did not apply to joint stock companies which lacked an aliens clause. It did not cover establishment of new companies.[84] It did not cover the performance of existing foreign-owned firms, a matter which had become a concern as FDI in Sweden increased in the 1960s. And it did not specify what was meant by essential public interests. Two important results from this uncertain position were, first, the launching of a considerable range of studies to determine appropriate policies and, second, a quite liberal approach in the meantime to approval of requests to remove the aliens clause.

Three of these studies are of particular interest for present purposes. In 1973 a Commission was appointed with three objectives: to consider a general system for controlling the establishment and the activities of foreign-owned firms in Sweden; to determine whether the system of dealing in shares could be used to improve information on foreign-owned firms in Sweden; and to propose special legislation on controlling foreign acquisitions of land and natural resources. The Commission members disagreed fundamentally on the major issues before it, the control of inward direct investment and the activities of the existing firms (Sweden, 1978, ch. 2). One group, reflecting the views of many trade union leaders and elements of the Social Democratic party, favoured what was known as the control alternative. It argued that the Swedish policies favouring community and employee participation in company activities often cannot be effective with regard to subsidiaries of MNEs, because information is lacking on overall MNE activities and because the bargaining power of the relatively small Swedish firm within the MNE is usually small. This group argued for a strong system of concessions with conditions to be monitored after approval of establishment, a high degree of information and of trade union consultation, and strong penalties where conditions of approval were not met. A second group, reflecting the views of the conservative parties and a number of business groups, favoured what was called the equality-of-treatment alternative. It regarded critiques of MNEs largely as unproven, the problems associated with them largely those affecting firms in general, and that other countries would likely retaliate if Sweden became more restrictive. In terms of new policy initiatives it favoured strengthening policies applicable to all companies, such as general control of mergers and voluntary codes of good behaviour. A third position, the so-called negotiation alternative, was favoured by elements of the liberal and centrist parties. This group believed the problems encountered with MNEs were likely to be episodic, hence it disagreed with the first group on the need to regulate MNEs after establishment. Apart from control of establishment, it recommended that negotiations be undertaken by the National Industrial Board at the request of employees and, if necessary, subsequently by a government department, if the public interest was disregarded.

The Commission did recommend that the control of foreign acquisitions of land and natural resources continue under a new law much like the 1916 Act. However the split along political lines blunted the effects of the Commission's report. In 1983 a new law required government approval of all foreign takeovers, and not just those of firms with an alien's clause in their charters. This law, which is considered further below, was closer to the positions of those on the Commission who argued for equality-of-treatment and negotiation than those who favoured more control of MNEs. It should be noted that a long period of Social Democratic government ended in 1976 just before the Commission reported, but this party did form the government again after the early 1980s.

A report completed in 1975 for the government took a somewhat different approach (Sweden, 1975, 297–324). This study had been commissioned in part because a study of concentration of industry in the 1970s had not said much about FDI. What the 1975 report did was to concentrate on analysing the relevant theory and existing data on the history, nature and economic effects of MNEs, as a basis for understanding appropriate policy responses. Its conclusions can be summarized briefly in three quotations:

> The overall picture which emerges from our study is the lack of a scientific basis for a great deal of the praise and criticism of international corporations. ... Both of these factors presumably help to explain our inclination to criticize or praise international corporations for phenomena which emanate from large private firms and foreign dependence in general, but not from international corporations in particular. ... Contrary to popular viewpoint, perhaps the future belongs to the modern nation state, whereas international corporations may well be nearing the end of an era. (322–4)

These and other conclusions led to a variety of reactions to the report, from praise for putting the issues in perspective to criticisms of the lack of relevant empirical research. The trade unions in particular were critical of the conclusions and the Swedish Confederation of Trade Unions demanded a new investigation.[85]

A third major study was commissioned by government in 1977 to consider the long-term effects on industrial policy of both inward and outward investment (Sweden, 1983).[86] This committee undertook a number of detailed studies at the level of firms and industries, as well as considering overall effects. One set of studies concentrated on comparisons, generally for the period 1965–77, of the economic performance of Swedish MNEs, foreign-owned subsidiaries and branches in Sweden, and Swedish national firms.[87] These comparisons were standardized for size of firm and industry, but not for other variables. Intensity of R&D was lowest in the national firms, about twice as high in the foreign-owned, and twice as high again for Swedish MNEs. Both the return on equity and value added were higher for the foreign-owned firms over the period noted than for either of the other two. Exports as a percentage of value added were 62 per cent for Swedish MNEs, 38 per cent for foreign-owned firms and 25 per cent for national firms. The foreign-owned firms were more import-intensive, with imports as a percentage of sales at 30 per cent, compared with 19 and 11 for the Swedish MNEs and national firms. This comparison does not take into account imports for resale which are likely to be especially large in the first group (Hörnell and Vahlne, 1986, 32). This is a problem which calls into question similar comparisons in most other countries.[88] The data on employment were considered for identical enterprises and excluded the changes due to acquisition and divestment of companies over the period. They show absolute domestic employment rising by 2 per cent for the foreign-owned firms and by 1 per cent for the national firms, while falling by from 3 to 4 per cent for Swedish MNEs. Meanwhile actual employment abroad in Swedish MNEs, not adjusted as above, rose considerably over the period.[89]

One should be careful about assessing the overall welfare effects of such comparisons: a high import propensity, for example, is not negative in welfare terms if it reduces costs, supplies competition, increases export competitiveness, and so on. Nevertheless these and other studies led the Committee to conclude:

> There is no general answer to the question of whether foreign investments in Sweden are beneficial or otherwise for industrial policy in the longer run: this depends in large measure on the extent to which the Swedish subsidiaries are given resources and the freedom to develop their competitiveness. ... There is no evidence that the entities which used to be in Swedish hands have developed less well after their acquisition by foreign owners. (Sweden, 1983, VI, 21)

In particular, they do not support the concern that foreign takeovers lead to the technological weakening of the Swedish firms involved.

As for the Swedish MNEs, the Committee noted that production abroad had accounted for a growing share of their sales abroad, rising from 42 to 52 per cent between 1970 and 1978. However the studies of particular enterprises and industries pointed to no consistent short-run effect, whether positive or negative, of investment abroad on exports. Despite the major expansion abroad the Swedish MNEs continued to do the greater part of their R&D in Sweden: specifically 86 per cent in 1978 for all MNEs and also for the 20 largest MNEs. The committee acknowledged a beneficial R&D effect from the international sales of Swedish MNEs. However the ten enterprises with more than half of their production abroad averaged about 30 per cent of R&D abroad, and the proportion was higher still for machinery manufacturing. The committee took the view that FDI abroad was largely unavoidable and desirable, given the problems with exports in a world of trade barriers and with mixed modes of technology transfer in some circumstances. The effects on Sweden depended on the subsidiary's position in the MNE. 'The positive effects of investments abroad diminish for Sweden when production abroad starts to predominate, and they disappear entirely if central functions of the enterprise are relocated outside Sweden' (Sweden, 1983, VI, 25–6). The committee was concerned that this shift was beginning to happen in some large Swedish MNEs.

The Committee took the position that substantial government restriction of Swedish FDI abroad would probably harm the national interest. It called instead for more effective international cooperation to reduce import barriers which increase FDI abroad, improvements in Swedish industrial policies, and better statistical and analytical systems regarding the effects of FDI. However, given its unease about the actual and potential shift of MNE central functions abroad, including R&D, it proposed that the scrutiny of FDI abroad through the exchange control system continue, with the development of some assessment criteria for the effects on Sweden. It also proposed that the government and at least the 20 largest MNEs engage in a 'system of deliberations' whereby information on their investment strategies, including that on FDI, could be related in a flexible way to industrial policy (Sweden, 1983, 27; Vahlne, 1983, 215–17).

One of the studies for the committee took a less micro approach in the sense of applying econometric tests to a large postal survey and other data. This approach yielded results which can be interpreted as even more positive in terms of the effects of Swedish MNEs, and as supporting a non-interventionist policy towards MNE involvement. The findings by the author in this and other studies have tended to confirm that foreign production and the resulting trade flows are determined by a country's comparative advantage, on the one hand, and by barriers to trade and factor productivity, on the other.[90] For our purposes, the main finding is that investment abroad has increased the output of goods in Sweden which are complementary to foreign production, but decreased such output where the goods were competitive with or independent of foreign production. Overall the effect on Swedish exports was mildly positive. Swedenborg is critical in any case of attempts to relate foreign production and the export of jobs, arguing that the level of employment in a country depends not on MNEs but on economic policy (1985, 234–7, 243).

One outcome of the research and discussions was a new law which took effect on 1 January 1983, requiring government approval when foreign interests acquired more than 10 per cent of a Swedish firm's shares, and a further review or reviews if the percentages rose above 20, 40 or 50. Approval could be withheld if an essential national interest was threatened. In effect the new law meant all takeovers could be reviewed, not just those firms with an aliens clause. New FDI, as before, was exempt, except in terms of exchange control regulations. The Social Democrats in particular wanted a stronger law – especially a more formal process involving the attachment and monitoring of conditions for approval, and some application to existing foreign-controlled firms – but failed to get the agreement of the parties which formed the government.

Finally we note that Sweden has had exchange controls since 1939, administered by the central bank. Controls on direct investment abroad in particular were tightened in 1969, partly because of concerns about the long-term effects on the balance of payments. Approval of such investment was contingent on consequent improvement in the balance of payments, and part or all of the financing needs had to be supplied abroad. Approval was also needed for capital transactions on inward FDI; for example, that a certain portion (normally half) of the investment be financed from abroad and that loans between the subsidiary and foreign affiliates be approved. Current commercial transactions in or out of the country were generally unrestricted. The exchange control restrictions on outward FDI were partially lifted in 1981 and further eased in 1986. The most important aspect of these policies from our perspective is the attempts to apply criteria other than for exchange control to outward FDI, a process which will be taken up in the next section.

Approval for Inward and Outward Direct Investment[91]

(a) Inward FDI

As is evident from the above, Swedish policy on inward direct investment has remained quite open, despite some doubts on this in some of the studies and political parties. Except for exchange control issues, new investments and expansion in existing lines have not been reviewed. A minority of takeovers by foreign interests, in firms without an aliens clause, also escaped formal review. In 1983, however, all takeovers by foreign interests became subject to review, as did increases in foreign ownership of a company above specified limits.

Reviews are conducted by the Department of Industry with input from other departments as necessary. There is no formal structure involved, such as an interdepartmental committee meeting regularly and having its own secretariat. In fact in the early 1980s two people who had other responsibilities undertook the task, acting under the senior officers of the department. It is true that there were not a large number of takeovers by foreign interests (80 in 1979, according to the source in Table 6.23) and that local governments could approve the smaller and less important mergers. Nevertheless the small size of staff clearly reflects a limited approach to review and follow-up.

There are no published criteria on the approval process, apart from those in the 1916 Act and the broad terms already noted in the 1973 amendment and 1983 law. The procedure, confirmed by the law of 1983, is one where the firms, after preliminary discussions with government and other affected groups, declare the commitments they are prepared to make when they merge with the Swedish company. The main interest in the review is the structural changes at the commencement of takeover, when reorganizations are frequent. The emphasis is on protecting Swedish interests at this point, for example, where the merger might involve closing a plant, changing product lines, significant layoffs or a major change in local sources of supply. Since the unions and professional workers' federations must be consulted in any case – particularly as regards employment, investment plans and employee participation – the government encourages negotiations with them.[92] At times the buyer may also be asked to work out an agreement with other firms which are strongly affected. If the seller, the union or others affected have reached an agreement with the buyer, and the government concurs, it adds the agreement to its own decisions. These have involved cases where it was suggested that a joint venture be retained, or less than 50 per cent foreign ownership be the outcome; however 100 per cent takeovers are common. Efforts are also made on occasion to find a domestic merger partner in place of the foreign merger, where, for example, the Swedish government or business is anxious to preserve a technological capacity. These efforts have major limits, given the problem of matching the technical and other capacities of the firms involved.

These agreements are deposited with the ministry and are at least morally binding. However it would be a mistake to confuse them with the formal and detailed process which was in effect, say, in Canada under the Foreign Investment Review Act. The commitments are relatively few and are considered binding for three to five years. Everyone concerned recognizes that a company's circumstances can change and require further structural changes. Moreover rejections of applications are rare, no doubt in good part because of the preliminary discussions with government on possible commitments and the discouragement given to unacceptable applications at this stage. Very little attempt is made to follow up systematically on the commitments. The size of staff alone would make this impossible and, as noted, strong business and political opposition would be brought to bear against such an approach. No doubt any short-term and major departure from the commitments would be brought to government attention through the private parties involved in any case.

It should be added that the law which took effect in 1983 confirms that these commitments may not be tied to an approval. However it also states that, where they are voluntarily undertaken by the foreign firm, they help government to decide on approvals of acquisitions. This delicate phrasing, often used in other countries, allows government to claim that it is not exacting performance requirements as the price of takeover, while affirming the previous government practice of encouraging 'voluntary' commitments by the firms.

All of this may appear to be an ad hoc and unstructured approach well short of a systematic review process, but one should put it in context. There is not a substantial degree of foreign ownership in Sweden, except for a few industries, as noted; hence there is not a widespread and on-going concern about inward FDI. No doubt this reflects both economic circumstances –

Sweden's market is relatively small – and past policy, such as the 1916 law protecting the resource sector, the aliens clauses in company charters and the set of policies and entrepreneurial activities which created a large Swedish MNE presence in several major sectors.

(b) Outward FDI

Much larger issues exist with regard to Sweden's substantial direct investments abroad. There has been a major debate for almost two decades on the long-term employment and other effects of such investments, and on appropriate policies. We will note some of the research findings after outlining policies which have been in effect. The issues involved are both complex and sensitive. One notes, for example, the widespread concern over the closure of one factory employing 35 workers in 1980 – this in a country where major industries were in serious trouble at the time. But the Swedish parent company, Alfa-Laval, was one of the score or so large international engineering firms which Sweden has developed, with substantial production abroad as well as in Sweden; the factory it closed had been highly automated just two years earlier; and the production of the marine oil separators involved was now to be transferred to Spain, Italy and a new factory in Japan. The ensuing debate reflected all the concerns about Swedish competitiveness, the effects of domestic and external policy, as well as the decisions of MNEs (*The Economist*, 4 April 1981, 78–9).

Policy on outward direct investment has been an offshoot of the exchange control regulations, as noted above. The restrictions on outward FDI were based on an exception, lasting until 1987, to the OECD Code on Liberalization of Capital Movements, an exception Sweden invoked because of balance of payments problems. The regulations were eased significantly in the 1980s. For example, until 1981 FDI abroad was approved only if it was considered favourable to the Swedish balance of payments. This requirement eased thereafter, though approval was still needed for the investment.

The interesting question for purposes of this study is whether, given the large Swedish investments abroad and the concerns about their effects on jobs and investment *in Sweden*, the government developed the elements of a review process on the outward side. The answer appears to be that Sweden flirted with such an approach but abandoned it in 1981. It was a law which took effect in July, 1974 which empowered the government to review outward FDI.[93] Something much broader was envisaged than the existing power of exchange control authorities to review investment for balance of payments reasons. Among other objectives, it was an attempt to address the concerns of blue-collar workers, worried about the effects on Swedish employment of FDI in low-wage European countries, and also of white-collar workers who might suffer from exports of technology. The Exchange Control Board of the central bank approved individual applications for FDI abroad, receiving advice from a committee which had representation from the Ministries of Labour and Industry as well as representatives of business and labour. It is well to recall that organized labour would be consulted in any case, given Swedish laws on labour participation on boards and on consultation, not to mention the direct recourse to government should such participation procedures break down. Thus the process has been one where management has to persuade the other parties that the investment is desirable or inevitable or both.

In economic terms, as noted further below, what all this involved was two issues: first, a question whether FDI abroad is unavoidable, given the possibility that other firms may take or enter that market – and whether such a competitive response needs to be made shortly or can be put off for some years; and, second, whether the FDI, once made, will substitute for the exports previously made from Sweden, or will actually encourage further exports. One can imagine the firms arguing that the investment is unavoidable, urgent and likely to protect or enhance established export positions, while the others concerned attempt to assess this information within the context of this specific firm and the usual time constraints on such decisions.

The strengthened exchange control provisions in 1969 involved a criterion that outward FDI, to secure approval, should promote exports from Sweden or be favourable to the balance of payments in some other way. In addition, from 1975 to 1986 the investment was to be financed by loans abroad with an average life of at least five years. Some exceptions were allowed to these two rules: for example, investments in developing countries which were the main recipients of Swedish foreign aid. The Act of 1974 went further and allowed the Exchange Control Board to consider also aspects of employment and industrial policy when deciding on such investments. However the central bank could refuse an application on these latter grounds only if the investment 'would inflict extraordinary harm on the country's interests'. No application appears to have been rejected on these grounds, although some may have been withdrawn.[94] Presumably this is partly because, the criteria being known, applications would be made where approval was likely. Also revisions of plans are possible at some stage in the process. In one case, for example, the union representative in a firm was able to put forward a detailed alternative to a plan for direct investment abroad, an alternative which won Board approval. Information and timing problems would usually militate against such major reversals.

There are significant differences in views on the control of FDI abroad, with trade unions and Social Democrats generally favouring stronger policies. Research for a commission on the foreign exchange regulations concluded otherwise, pointing both to the high information costs of making welfare judgements on firms going abroad and to the probability that the effects of FDI abroad on Swedish exports were positive. Moreover the existing regulations had had little effect on the level and composition of foreign manufacturing investment.[95] In 1981 the foreign exchange law was changed to reflect such views, so that only the financing aspects were taken into account thereafter.

Related Policies

In terms of key sectors, it was noted above that Sweden moved early to limit foreign ownership in natural resources, which, at the time, was the major sector of industry. Foreign control was prohibited also for banks, brokerage firms and firms supplying credit information. The rules on banking were changed in the mid-1980s to allow foreign-controlled subsidiaries, partly in response to pressure from Norway, which had begun to allow entry by foreign banks. Other sectors which are closed to some degree or completely are some aspects of maritime transport and airlines, insurance, the manufacture of munitions, and trading partnerships.

Sweden has the usual list of public utilities which are closed to private ownership, whether domestic or foreign (Table 11.3). In addition the state or its agencies have invested in a number of sectors, notably in order to rationalize some larger and older industries such as shipbuilding which were depressed, but also to encourage growth sectors and small businesses. In relative terms Swedish policies in this respect are not a substantial obstacle to foreign direct investment, judging by Table 11.3 and the fact that less than 10 per cent of the work force is in utilities and state-owned firms. What may perhaps be a larger obstacle is the judgement among some civil servants that the political parties, even the conservatives, would probably resist a foreign takeover of a major Swedish firm. In fact several larger firms which requested removal of the aliens clause from their charters were refused, although in one of these cases the government later agreed to a modified proposal which kept effective voting control in Sweden. Also a major firm with a high profile is likely to attract particular attention, as in other countries. Norway's acquisition of a 40 per cent interest in Volvo in 1978 involved extensive negotiations in an attempt to assure both countries of benefits: specifically, increased industrial activity, including research, in Norway and more energy security in Sweden (*The Economist*, 16 December 1978, 101). These attitudes and policies may not survive Sweden's decision to apply for membership in the EC, as noted in the conclusions below.

Sweden is one of three European countries in this study, along with Norway and Switzerland, which has nationality requirements for directors and chief executive officers of limited companies and cooperative societies, whether these are controlled in Sweden or abroad. Normally Board members, the chairman and the managing director must all be resident Swedish subjects. In practice exceptions are readily granted in the case of managing directors and up to one-third of the Board.

It was noted above that Sweden has had for some time various legal provisions for labour participation in corporate decision making. During 1984–90 Swedish firms were required to pay taxes on a portion of net profits and on total payrolls into five regional funds (*The Economist*, 6 November 1984). These 'wage earner funds', which are associated with the state national pension insurance fund, each have nine board members nominated by government, five of whom are trade unionists. Each fund can buy up to 8 per cent of a company's shares, while the pension insurance fund can buy up to 10 per cent. These funds were not directed against FDI as such – various motives appear to have been involved, such as further labour participation in industry, reduction of concentration and a brake on union pay claims. They would tend at the least to increase trade union influence where foreign entry by takeover was involved.

Finally Sweden had developed a substantial set of investment incentives by the early 1980s, geared to regional development, structural adjustment of declining industries, help for growth sectors, small business development and all of the consequent labour adjustment. These and other incentives carry a number of performance conditions. However these programmes and conditions are available to firms without regard to nationality of ownership and hence are not of direct interest here.

Conclusions

From some perspectives Sweden's policies on foreign direct investment can be judged successful. If the object was to maintain domestic ownership of the major 'key sector' – in this case natural resources – this was achieved early in the century. Foreign ownership of manufacturing is also among the lowest for the countries in this study. An industrial environment was created where a number of Swedish MNEs successfully penetrated foreign markets. As inward and especially outward FDI speeded up in the 1960s, however, one important objective of public policy was to develop the reasoning and instrumentalities for a more comprehensive and more sophisticated set of policies regarding such investments. One outcome was some uncertainty in the 1970s and early 1980s of the probable directions of future policy, a situation not conducive to strategic planning by either firms or governments. Quite substantial differences were exposed or accentuated on the way to treat MNEs, differences which continue. In the event, the policies which were adopted involved relatively minor changes to what was already being done. The instruments exist to review particular cases of inward takeovers and outward FDI where this is considered necessary, but there is not systematic review of either of these in practice. More than a decade of intensive research and, at times, vigorous public debate failed, apparently, to yield agreement on appropriate policies towards MNEs.

There are several reasons for this. One, noted earlier in discussing the various commission reports, was, broadly, the different views of the trade unions and Social Democrats, on the one hand, and the other political parties and business federations, on the other. A second reason is the change in circumstances: there was probably more scope for policy experimentation on FDI in the full-employment world of the early 1970s when these reviews commenced than in the slower-growth world of the early 1980s when decisions on such policy had to be made. And the long period of Social Democratic government ended in the mid-1970s, to be replaced for a time by more conservative or more cautious consensus-type governments.

It would be a mistake to place undue emphasis, given all this, on the importance of research findings to these outcomes. Yet the fact remains that government launched a number of major studies, involving business and labour cooperation and innovative research. One should be careful in drawing conclusions from a literature which is much more substantial than suggested here and available, in some important cases, only in Swedish. Yet the impression one is left with, despite much original empirical work, is a confirmation of much of the agnosticism of the findings in the 1975 study. The study completed in 1983, while urging that scrutiny through exchange control continue, did not believe that the investment problem in Sweden could be solved by controlling outward FDI, nor did it recommend stronger controls on inward FDI. The essential differences in viewpoint which emerged in the analytical work have centred on two issues. First, should one add up particular microeconomic decisions to achieve a macroeconomic effect, especially with regard to employment? Despite disclaimers about the welfare conclusions implied, that is frequently what is done in practice. Second, and related, there is a basic difference between those who emphasize that employment and growth require essentially macroeconomic policies, and those who, doubting their effectiveness or having reservations about the resulting composition of output, prefer some stronger approaches through industrial policies. That difference can be found in other countries in this study, including some where the debate has been far less sophisticated.

A decade of study and debate led to some extension of existing law but no fundamental changes (Table 6.25). In part this was due to the end of a long period of continuous Social Democratic government. Even after their return to power, however, the trend, if anything, was to liberalize existing controls – for example, to admit foreign banks – as part of the response to the

Table 6.25 Policy development in Sweden

1916	Concession Act requires government permission for alien acquisitions of real property and mines (i.e. natural resources). Applies also to Swedish joint stock companies unless articles of association restrict alien holdings of voting rights and share capital to less than 20 per cent and less than 40 per cent, respectively.
1939	Exchange controls; tightened in 1969 on outward side, including FDI.
1973	Amendment of 1916 Act allows removal or modification of aliens clause in a company charter where government decides this does not conflict with an essential national interest.
1974	Law allows review of outward FDI on broader economic grounds than balance of payments effects, a policy largely abandoned in early 1980s.
1983	Government's approval needed of *all acquisitions* by foreign interests of more than 10 per cent of a company's shares, and also when percentages rise above 20, 40 or 50 per cent. New investment continued to be free of such approval.
1981, 1986	Exchange controls eased (see text).

changed economic circumstances of the early 1980s. Moreover the many studies questioned whether some major concerns about MNE activities were valid, whether other concerns reflected unavoidable international demand and cost changes facing all firms and countries, and whether the remaining problems could be tackled by detailed regulatory approaches involving case-by-case review.

What impact did existing policy have on the strategies of MNEs, particularly on investment flows and microeconomic performance? If one judges by the nature of the policies and of the flows, a preliminary assessment would be that there was little impact, apart from the sectoral limitations on the inward side. Sweden did not have the set of circumstances which would have allowed a strong bargaining stance on the inward side had the government wished to follow that approach: she was not prepared to allow widespread access to natural resources which, in any case, were no longer the basis for much of her industry; her low tariff policy removed this as a method of attracting FDI to some sectors; there was not much point in developing other major fiscal incentives geared to FDI, as in Ireland and Belgium, given the strength of her own MNEs; and the small size of the market, with much larger markets and skilled labour forces nearby, would not be attractive to foreign MNEs. While FDI in absolute terms increased sharply over the 1960s and 1970s, in real terms the increases were modest. As for influencing microeconomic performance, the FDI establishment process was geared to aspects of industrial structure that could be controlled in a three to five year context. There was certainly little effort expended towards using this process to control longer-term industrial change, whether on establishment or for on-going companies, despite the wishes of some groups for exactly such a procedure. One must look elsewhere in Swedish policy for this type of influence.

On the outward side the influence of policy was equally weak. Exchange controls, particularly the requirement for financing abroad, would tend to slow the process of outward FDI. Until 1981 such outflows had to meet a further test in the sense of a positive contribution to exports or some other aspect of the balance of payments. Despite such controls the outflows increased far faster than the rate of inflation, and the globalization of Swedish firms was considerably increased. Refusals of applications for outward investment were rare. Attempts were made to constrain the effects of such FDI on Sweden; for example, it appears that the Exchange Control Board exerted pressure through the approval process to retain R&D in Sweden. For most Swedish firms, however, the advantages in so doing would favour such a choice in any case (Swedenborg, 1985, 238). There is no evidence that the Board exercised such a review process on a systematic and broad front, and the basis for it in exchange control regulations was largely eroded in the early 1980s.

Finally Sweden's decision in 1990 to apply for membership of the EC is likely to bring important changes in policy on FDI, both directly and indirectly. If membership results the direct consequence will be the end of review, on the basis of the rules on inward FDI, adopted in 1983, of acquisitions by EC firms. The indirect effects are likely to be even more important. Sweden, like several other countries noted later, allows dual voting shares, cross-shareholdings and other devices which permit both a high degree of concentration of corporate control and also substantial protection against hostile takeovers. One corporate group accounts for 35 per cent of the entire capitalization of the Swedish stock market. Swedish firms were highly active in acquiring European investments in the late 1980s, while EC firms found it difficult to react by penetrating Sweden. With entry to the EC, Sweden would have to live with the more standardized Community rules for mergers and acquisitions which came under consideration in the early 1990s. The coalition government which took office late in 1991 announced that it would end in 1992 the need for government approval of foreign purchases in Swedish firms (see *The Economist*, 23 June 1990, 73–5; 2 March 1991, 62; 16 November 1991, 62.)

NOTES

1. Parts of this section appeared originally in A.E. Safarian (1985c) 'FIRA and FIRB: Canadian and Australian Policies on Foreign Direct Investment', Toronto: Ontario Economic Council, Discussion Paper Series.
2. See Safarian (1985c) for further details, including sources. 'Foreign control' refers to situations where 25 per cent of the equity is held by a foreign investor and an Australian investor does not have more than this. These data are at the two-digit level. At the next level of classification in manufacturing at least 75 per cent control existed in basic chemicals, non-ferrous basic metal products, and motor vehicles and parts.
3. See Sexton and Adamovich (1981, 11–12) and the speeches by Gorton and McMahon in the Parliamentary Debates, 16 and 25 September 1969.
4. See the statement on the Australian Industry Development Corporation Bill 1970 by the Minister for Trade and Industry, J. McEwen, Parliamentary Debates, 5 May 1970.
5. The attitudes of the various Prime Ministers and some of the problems encountered by the Whitlam government in particular are well described in *The Economist*, 22 April 1969, 73; 30 September 1972, 96; 26 July 1975, 89. For more detail on policy development in the early 1970s see Neilson (1973), Bell (1975), Arndt (1977) and Anderson (1984, ch. 4).
6. Some of the more important policy statements are the speech by the Treasurer, P.P. Lynch, on Foreign Investment in Australia, Parliamentary Debates, 1 April 1976 and the statements by the Treasurer, J. Howard (Press Releases no. 42 and no. 87, 1978 and 1981). The last offers a particularly detailed assessment of the then situation.
7. For published statements of the procedures involved, see Australia, FIRB Report (1982, ch. 5); Australia, Treasury (1982); Anderson (1983, ch. 5); Sexton and Adamovich (1981, chs 6 to 10); and Harvey (1981, chs 2 to 4). More recent statements are Australia, Treasury (1987) and FIRB Report 1987–8.
8. In the last four years of the 1970s it took on average about 20 days to settle takeovers without conditions, 23 days when approval was conditional, and about 40 days when takeovers were rejected. For new businesses, where maximum times are not set, the averages were about 33, 42 and 70 days respectively. In 1981–2 and 1982–3, about three-quarters of all cases were resolved within 30 days. Many such cases were relatively routine real estate transactions. It is important to note that preliminary consultation before formal notice, which is common, would tend to reduce these times (Sexton and Adamovich, 1981, 99, 117 and 124; and Australia, FIRB Report 1982, 1–4 and 1983, 3).
9. What must be reported, and may be reviewed, is a 15 per cent or larger ownership of voting stock by a single foreign interest or associated interests, or 40 per cent for two or more non-associated interests.
10. In 1986–7 the review criteria were eased to a national interest test, except for the restricted sectors, as noted further below.
11. In any case the firm might get high marks for the introduction of high technology and some of the efficiency gains of a specialized operation (interview with officers of the FIRB, 18 June 1981).
12. The FIRA's treatment of third-party intervention by potential buyers and others is outlined in Schultz (1980, 67–71).
13. As noted further below, the policy was abolished in 1986–7.

14. 'It is clearly not the intention of the foreign investment policy to override reasonable commercial concerns to ensure the efficient and harmonious functioning of a business or a joint venture operation. Equally clearly it is not acceptable from a foreign investment policy viewpoint for a potential Australian participant in a business or joint venture to be vetoed without good cause'. (FIRB Report, 1982, 46). Everything depends on the interpretation given to the adjectives in these sentences in particular cases.
15. Based on Reserve Bank of Australia (1980, 14) and interviews with Reserve Bank and Treasury officials.
16. One ironic example is the experience of Rupert Murdoch, who owns major media interests in Australia, the United States and the United Kingdom, among other places. It has been reported that he changed his citizenship in order to comply with US ownership laws so as to acquire a number of US television stations. Subsequently he won control of Australia's largest newspaper company, which also has broadcasting interests. Some restructuring of his Australian acquisitions then became necessary to meet the limitations Australia has on foreign ownership of media (*Globe and Mail*, 17 January 1987 and 12 February 1987. See also *The Economist*, 4 January 1986, 57–64).
17. The outcome of the review was reported in a statement by the Treasurer, Paul Keating, 20 December 1983. The quotations are from pages 1, 2, and 10 of that statement.
18. Subsequently 100 per cent acquisitions were allowed.
19. A full statement is available in FIRB reports as follows: 1985–6, 37–9; 1986–7, 52–5; 1987–8, 28, 33. See also Department of the Treasury, 1987.
20. Treasury Press release, 20 January 1988.
21. The one exception is the relatively small number of undertakings, outside real estate, which required resale of assets if the other basic conditions attached to a proposal could not be met (Australia, FIRB, 1983, 7).
22. Sexton and Adamovich (1981, 116) state that no regular monitoring of conditions exists, but major cases are investigated for possible breaches, as are cases where problems come to notice. They go on to note that many conditions are longer-term and would not be in breach at the time of writing.
23. The handling of the Oaky Creek coking coal project and the Blair Athol steam coal project, both in Queensland, are cases in point. See *The Economist*, 11 April 1980, 74.
24. See Harvey (1981, 37–40) on the positions of senior officials in Australia and Canada. The phrasing on policy insulation is from Sexton and Adamovich (1981, 198). Several officials outside the Treasury whom I interviewed took a similar view of the Australian situation.
25. The statement of 20 December 1983 by the Treasurer for the Labour Party government begins by saying policy will continue to be based on the 'twin pillars', the first of which is 'a recognition of the significant contribution that foreign capital can make to the development of Australia's industries and resources'. See also the opening paragraph of the 1988 summary, Table 6.5.
26. For example, the assertion that future mining would be 100 per cent Australian-owned, as reflected in Labour Party policy at the time; the mysterious attempt to borrow large amounts abroad for unknown purposes, but presumed by some to be for purchase of firms; and the attempt to set up a government authority to participate in exploration. See *The Economist*, 26 July 1975, 90; 21 September 1976, 62–3; 27 March 1976, Survey.
27. FIRB publishes a long list of benefits claimed by new and takeover investments. Approval does not require benefits in all categories. It is hard to imagine many *bona fide* investment proposals where a number of these benefits could not be claimed. It should be added that they were examined in two stages, as noted in Table 6.4. See FIRB, Report, 1982, 87–8.
28. The contrast between the FIRB and the FIRA on this point can be underlined by noting the comment made by an official of the former agency during an interview in 1981. He stated that specific conditions (on exports and local research in manufacturing sectors) were not required, since the firms would undertake these if they made commercial sense and, if they did not, the government should not impose such conditions. Canadian officials, in the appeal to GATT on the FIRA and elsewhere, have emphasized the need

for corrections to the distortions in markets resulting from the decisions of large oligopolistic firms.

29. Parry and Watson conclude, among other things, that a large proportion of the sample subsidiaries conducted R&D within the Australian enterprise, that some of these resources went to modifying overseas technology, that restrictions on exports were significant but much less so than in the case of technology agreements with non-affiliates, and that subsidiaries' exports of technology were significant. Comparable data for locally owned firms were not collected, however.
30. See Australia (1977; 1979).
31. See, for example, Crough and Wheelwright (1981) and a number of other publications of the Transnational Corporations Research Project, University of Sydney, Canberra. The research for this project is described in a note by Wheelwright in the *CTC Reporter*, Autumn 1986, 56–7.
32. One observer estimated that Australian ownership of mining industry assets would rise to 53 per cent by June 1985, from 47 per cent in 1979–80. The Australian ownership of major newer projects is estimated at 56 per cent. Cited by Anderson (1984, 100–1) from a study by Bruce McKern.
33. The effects of the Australian policy on the distribution of the gains are considered more fully in McKern (1976, ch. 10) and Anderson (1984, 108–18). Parry (1983, 25–30) has also criticized this and other aspects of the policy on local equity.
34. McKern (1976, 13, 22, and 186) notes that in the early 1960s Australia had only three firms that could undertake major mining projects, and that none of the Australian-owned participants in minerals in the mid-1970s was an MNE, given a definition of an MNE as a firm that operates in seven or more countries and whose foreign-source income is 25 per cent of its total income.
35. A resource rent tax is essentially a profits tax that is collected when a given rate of return is realized, and that can be raised progressively as higher rates of return are realized. See Garnaut and Ross (1978, 1983) and also Australia (1984) and *The Economist*, 4 February 1984, 72–3.
36. An example of the type of jockeying that goes on is provided by a report in *The Financial Australian* (22 June 1981, 131) that Japanese steel mills decided to reconsider plans for a new iron ore mine after the West Australian Minister for Mines and Energy met their officials to clarify the foreign investment guidelines. 'Canberra statements have left an impression here that any new project will have to have 50 per cent Australian equity,' he is quoted as saying. 'If this was an obstacle to their decision making, I have been able to correct it.'
37. If the state governments and firms are prepared to go ahead with the projects, the effect of this control may be simply to shift emphasis to private borrowing abroad.
38. Parts of this section, especially those on the FIRA and NEP, draw on A.E. Safarian (1985b) 'Government Control of Foreign Business Investment', in J. Whalley (ed.), *Domestic Policies in the International Economic Environment*, Toronto, University of Toronto Press and A.E. Safarian (1985c) 'FIRA and FIRB: Canadian and Australian Policies on Foreign Direct Investment', Toronto, Ontario Economic Council.
39. The qualification is necessary because countries such as Australia and Ireland, which also have very high foreign ownership of some major sectors and overall, do not publish as complete and recent data as does Canada.
40. The reasons for this development are examined in Rugman (1987b).
41. A good early review of the data and the issues is Aitken (1961).
42. A detailed study of this appears in Fayerweather (1974).
43. The outline of policies which follows is from Safarian (1985b, 27–32). For a detailed statement of the legislation at the federal and provincial levels, see Foreign Investment Review Agency (1977), parts I and II. The laws relating to the NEP and to Investment Canada are the major changes since then.
44. Canada Development Corporation, later Polysar Energy and Chemical Corporation, became a major player in a number of fields. It had difficulty at times reconciling the views of its major owner, the Government of Canada, with its private sector objectives.

In 1985–6 the government's ownership was cut from 48 per cent to 10 per cent. Nova Corporation acquired the company in 1988 (*Globe and Mail*, 30 August 1988, B1).

45. The guidelines are reproduced in Canada, *Foreign Direct Investment* (1972, 324–5).
46. These views were put to me at some length in interviews in June 1978 and June 1983. It is perhaps of interest to note again that the comparable officers of the Australian and New Zealand agencies had little enthusiasm for such views during my interviews with them.
47. Several provinces in 1981 sent senior representatives to Western Europe with the message that the important thing for businessmen was to work closely with the provinces, which would then intercede with FIRA.
48. The Commissioner of FIRA noted in a letter to the *Globe and Mail*, 21 March 1981, that the decision of the federal government differed from provincial government views in fewer than 3 per cent of the 3000 cases dealt with to date. See also Schultz (1979, 59–61). At the time the eight provinces announced their opposition in 1982 the provincial rate of recommendation for disallowance apparently exceeded that by FIRA.
49. There was no requirement that the Minister publish the letters, but in some cases the undertakings were published in detail. For a further analysis of 'performance requirements', see Safarian (1983b). It is of interest to note that, while the FIRB published a tabular summary of the 'benefits' stated by the firms and used in the assessment, the FIRA published them by individual companies for all allowed cases by ten categories.
50. See Safarian (1978), Schultz *et a*l. (1980) and Harvey (1981, especially 163–71). Harvey notes several unsuccessful attempts by the FIRA to clarify its mandate. His list of factors emphasized in negotiations demonstrates this lack of clarity, since it raises more questions than it answers. Is it literally true, for example, that the FIRA began with the position that investors are 'not wanted if they would merely duplicate an existing business' (167)?
51. One officer of the agency described its procedures in 1978 as follows. The assessments looked at measurable activities such as employment undertakings, qualitative matters such as possible productivity changes, and Canadian participation. If there was a positive effect on all three, approval was recommended. If there was a problem in one of these an improved offer was requested in that general area. The agency's officers used data on industry performance as a method of checking the undertakings. There was a strong emphasis on regional development; in low-income regions any positive effect in one of the three categories was likely to mean approval was recommended. Moreover, if a new firm in a high-income region threatened the existence of a firm in a low-income region, the agency was likely to recommend refusal, while in the reverse case it was likely to recommend approval. Greater weight was given to new export creation than to import substitution and more weight to export creation than either new domestic consumption or production. Finally rejections were largely in distribution-type activities which would increase imports rather than create directly new employment and investment.

    Two points can be made about such a process. First, to the extent that these procedures were consistently followed internally, this was not always evident externally, even with the benefit of legal advice. Several officers of companies indicated that they went through up to a year of discussions in which undertakings were progressively increased, and only at the end of the process was it clear what FIRA's officers considered acceptable. The second point is that there are rather strong assumptions here which affect one's views of the welfare effects, for example the preference for exports over both import substitution and production for domestic consumption.
52. These are fiscal years. See Globerman (1984a) for a more detailed analysis of the variability of the Canadian rate.
53. The information in this paragraph and the data in Table 6.15 were supplied by Investment Canada.
54. Investment Canada has also ranked the undertakings by their average importance in determining net benefit using a scale of 1 for least important to 10 for most important. In terms of factors of assessment, government policy received the highest weight (8.7) and international competitiveness was next (7.6) while the other factors received weights

ranging from 5.8 to 6.6. In terms of the rationale for the undertakings, the largest weight was specific policy (8.8), substantive negotiation was next (7.5), certainty and public interest received weights of 5.1 and 6.9 respectively, while voluntary undertakings were given a weight of 1.1.

55. See Anderson (1984, 4–5, 42, and 46–7) on the rather uncertain status of the 1974 announcement. The Anderson study's primary focus is on the effects of applying such an approach to Canada.
56. The figures given earlier for foreign ownership and control of this industry are much lower because they are based on capital invested rather than revenues, and involve a comprehensive definition of the industry, including sectors (reserves, transmission and distribution) where Canadian ownership and control are higher.
57. It should be noted that foreign-controlled firms could become eligible for significant grants by taking Canadian partners at earlier stages.
58. See Table 6.11 for FDI flows in this period. A clearer view is available from Table 6.12, which shows gross inflows separate from gross outflows. These short-term effects, and other aspects of the NEP, are discussed more fully in Safarian (1985c).
59. For an assessment of the investment aspects of the agreement, including the effects on investment flows, see Safarian (1988).
60. About two-thirds of total Canadian-controlled assets remained reviewable under the new threshold for direct acquisitions.
61. The Exon-Florio provision of the 1988 Trade Act, which is discussed in the section on the United States, does apply to Canada. There are also national security exemptions under the Free Trade Agreement.
62. Studies on the theory and effects of FDI with particular reference to Canada are covered in some detail in Safarian (1979, 1985a, b, c). The paragraphs which follow are drawn from the third and fourth of these.
63. See, for example, notes for remarks by the Right Honourable P.E. Trudeau in Toronto, 12 February 1980, and in Windsor, 14 February 1980, presaging both the strengthening of FIRA and enactment of something like the NEP.
64. See Pearce (1989), Caves (1982, 198–200) and Cantwell (1991) for analyses of the degree to which R&D is centralized and the conditions that determine its decentralization to subsidiaries; Rugman (1981b) for a criticism of R&D policies in Canada in this context; Safarian (1966, ch. 4) for a discussion of the comparable issues in connection with export allocation and performance; and Safarian (1983b) for an analysis of trade-related performance requirements.
65. Harvey (1981, especially 163–71) notes several unsuccessful attempts by the FIRA to clarify its mandate, so the failure may have been reflected in private as well. See also Schultz *et al.* (1980) and Safarian (1978).
66. See Harvey (1981) for the positions of senior officers. One of the views noted was expressed in an interview with the present author: Ottawa, 1981.
67. In the period just before and after 1920 the criticisms of foreign control of colonial trade led to investigations and controls on shipping and the export of meat (Carey, 1975, 8).
68. Sexton (1979, 121); Paterson (1975a, 77); Rowling (1975, 24); and interviews with Overseas Investment Commission, June 1981.
69. The 1973 criteria in turn were an expanded and updated version of those earlier published by the National Government, according to Paterson (1975a, 30).
70. The former point is examined at some length, and critically, in Deane (1970, ch. 4). See also Sexton (1979, 134–5).
71. This section has benefited from correspondence with, and publications and other documents made available by, the OIC and other government agencies during 1987. As always, the interpretations placed on this material are entirely my own.
72. The policy changes are noted in detail in the OECD annual economic surveys of New Zealand, and also in Reserve Bank, 'New Zealand Economy Information', May 1987 (mimeo). See also *The Economist*, 1 June 1985, 17–20; 21 November 1987, 21–4; and 5 March 1988, 68.

73. No new commercial banks were registered earlier although merchant banks, investment banks and others were allowed.
74. The effects on the data are spelled out in New Zealand Reserve Bank (1987b, 4).
75. Estimates are from Stonehill (1965, Part I) and (for 1972) from Norway Industry Department (1974–5). Stonehill (69–71) revises some of these for the omission of unincorporated branches and other foreign investments. The 1962 figure for manufacturing and mining would rise to 23 per cent from 15 per cent according to his revised measure. However the figure falls back to 17 per cent if only the clearly foreign-controlled group is considered by omitting those firms with less than 50 per cent foreign ownership. Estimates for the group of 'foreign-controlled' firms with less than 50 per cent foreign-ownership are not very meaningful since the data are dominated by Norsk Hydro, which is about 50 per cent state-owned while having a large foreign ownership. Stonehill warns that the underlying data reflect serious valuation questions, and only broad trends can be taken from the historical series.
76. Kindleberger (1984, 36) quotes Edvard Bull to the effect that Norway limited foreign ownership of natural resources in 1905 (1906?) because of fears that British investments would furnish an excuse for the British government to intervene in order to protect its citizens, along the lines of the Jameson Raid in the Boer War. Einarsen (1970, 171) refers only to several references in the Storting to a comparable situation in South Africa.
77. Act of 14 December 1917 (no. 16), Relating to the Acquisition of Waterfalls, Mines and Other Real Property etc. (as Amended). Official translation from Norwegian, October 1970, Royal Ministry of Norwegian Affairs, Oslo.
78. In addition the Companies Act of 1976 requires that the manager in a joint stock company, at least half of the board, the corporate assembly and the committee of representatives must have resided in Norway for the previous two years. The corporate assembly is partly elected by shareholders and partly by employees. It elects the board of directors and also approves major investment and structural changes in the company's operations.
79. This and the succeeding section draw particularly heavily on interviews in the early 1980s, as noted in Appendix I. This includes interviews with MNEs investing in Norway as well as Norwegian-owned firms and government officials.
80. In a press release dated 26 April 1976 the Department of Industry claimed that only 75 breaches of conditions, most quite minor, had occurred in a study it had made of 1100 concession agreements.
81. The evolution of the Norwegian concession policy with respect to petroleum and the details of the taxation system are analysed at length in Noreng (1980): see the summaries on pp. 126 and 171. See also Grayson (1981, ch. 8).
82. For the growth in Statoil's influence and some conflicts with government see Grayson (1981, ch. 8).
83. Act of 30 May 1916 concerning restrictions on the rights to acquire real property, mines or shares in certain companies. The historical section which follows is based largely on Eckerberg (1978) and interviews with government officials.
84. There is other legislation covering this, such as the Freedom of Trade Act of 1864, but it is confined to the financial standing of applicants rather than economic or social effects (*The Economist*, 14 August 1965, 627).
85. See Vahlne (1983, 212). In response to growing unrest among unions about inward and outward FDI in the early 1970s, the Swedish Confederation of Trade Unions (Lansorganisationen i Sverige) published a report on the union movement and MNEs for its 1976 congress and followed this up in 1979 with a detailed handbook for union activities in MNEs. The views of Swedish unions on this issue in the early 1970s are explored in Hedlund and Otterbeck (1977, ch. 5).
86. These three studies by no means exhaust the list of studies in Sweden. To mention just two others, in 1976 the National Industrial Board was asked to consider the effects of the MNE on the development of Swedish industrial technology, and a committee ap-

pointed in 1977 to revise foreign-exchange controls was asked to consider also Swedish policy on FDI abroad.

87. The committee's studies are in six volumes. The work is in Swedish, but volume 6, pp. 19–28, has a summary in English. I am indebted to the committee's research director, Jan-Erik Vahlne, for an outline of the studies. See also Vahlne (1983) and Part II of Hörnell and Vahlne (1986).
88. See MacCharles, 1987, ch. 4, for analysis of this point with regard to Canada.
89. Data are approximate because of small exclusions. The comparisons of the various types of firms are from volume 3 of the committee's reports, p. 88 for exports, 92 for imports and 104 for adjusted employment.
90. See volume IV of the Committee's reports, which was principally the work of B. Swedenborg. This study was a follow-up to her earlier major study (Swedenborg, 1979). See also Swedenborg (1985) for a shorter statement of some of her findings. While confirming much of the theory of FDI outlined in Chapter 3 above, Swedenborg has also used comparisons between Swedish, UK and US multinationals to challenge some earlier findings. Specifically her work does not support the idea that MNEs from different lands tend to concentrate in the same industries; rather they produce abroad what their comparative advantage at home suggests; and smaller Swedish firms go abroad as frequently as larger ones, if you look at this in terms of the proportionate size of each to begin with.
91. This section is largely based on the interviews noted in Appendix I and subsequent follow-up by correspondence.
92. Sweden's laws provide labour participation in corporate decision making. For example, unions in joint stock companies with 25 or more employees have the right to appoint at least two representatives to the Board, as well as two deputy directors without vote and a representative to any Board committee. Also a joint economic committee of management and employees keeps employees informed of company operations. If this does not work to the employees' satisfaction, they may also appoint a consultant from their ranks. As noted earlier when discussing the Commission appointed in 1973, this does not necessarily mean that unions believe they can get enough information to understand and influence the direct investment decision, inward or outward. During 1984–90 a new factor was introduced with the provision to give unions funds to buy company shares, as noted further below.
93. For the early history of this law see Bergsten *et al.* (1978) 38–40. They note that the law refers to the objectives of economic policy, rather than specifically to unemployment, because of concern over conflict with Sweden's commitments to the OECD. My interviews suggest that, in practice, the committee was attempting to consider quite specific issues.
94. The rest of this paragraph is based on interviews with a trade union official, as well as government officials, in August 1982. Vahlne (1983, 211) notes that only 13 of 1340 applications to the Board were refused in 1977, but these would include those refused on other grounds. Swedenborg (1985, 222) also notes that approval was almost always granted for investment by manufacturing firms. Some direct investment abroad did not require approval: for example, if it was financed abroad and not guaranteed by the Swedish parent.
95. This conclusion reflects that reached by Swedenborg (1985, 222) based on a study of the foreign exchange control act and its effects on manufacturing investment inside and outside Sweden.

7. Other Countries with Review: France and Japan

FRANCE

Of the ten West European countries being considered here, France has had the most highly-developed policies towards inward FDI. By comparison with most of the countries in this study, France has also had a reasonably well-developed approach to industrial planning. That has involved a set of long-term goals on industrial policy which overlap with policy on FDI; for example, a concern for technical development, control of sources of raw materials, export development and more balanced regional economic growth. Carlson (1980, ch. 2) has described the key elements of this approach as *étatisme, dirigisme* and *élitisme*. The publicly-owned sector of industry is large. Much of the private industrial sector is dominated by large groups, whether French or multinational. Government control of industry is extensive, including control of finance through public ownership of banks and direct grants, an extensive system of industrial support and considerable specification and negotiation of industry or firm objectives. Since 1945 a system of overall planning has also influenced the pattern of sectoral development. Finally the links between the senior civil service and industrial leadership are close, not only in terms of working relationships but in the fact that both are drawn largely from a narrow list of educational institutions.[1] One of the issues of major interest here is how successfully this approach to industrial planning has integrated the international aspects, particularly policy on FDI.

Policy Developments Prior to 1965

French data on FDI leave something to be desired, especially on the outward side. Comprehensive official data on stocks are not available, and coverage of flows has had a way of changing which is abrupt even for this field. Nevertheless some major aspects are reasonably clear. Until recently the French performance on outward FDI has been weak by comparison with other major industrial countries.[2] In 1985 France had 3.0 per cent of the world stock of outward FDI, compared with 3.8 per cent in 1975 and 6.1 per cent in 1960 (Table 3.1). It is true that many larger French firms were operating on a highly multinational basis by the early 1980s, but this process had still not gone as far as in most other major industrial countries at that time. In the late 1980s, however, there was a surge in outward FDI.

By contrast, since 1960 direct investment inflows have played a somewhat larger role in France than in many other industrial countries, particularly the larger economies. Employment in foreign-owned firms has been higher than in the other larger European countries (Table 3.5). More tellingly for the French authorities, a measure of the foreign ownership of manufacturing in the six most heavily industrialized and technology-intensive economies (United States, Japan, FRG, United Kingdom, Sweden and France) showed France at the head of the list (France, Conseil Economique et Social, 1981, 91–2).

It is true that the degree of foreign ownership of manufacturing and of industry did not change much in the 1970s. The concerns of the French authorities date from the 1960s, however, when foreign ownership of industry was rising rapidly and MNEs from the United States dominated inflows. The percentage of French industry under foreign control doubled for the decade after 1962 (Bertin, 1975, 38). Over 30 per cent of FDI inflows in the 1960s were from the USA, a figure which fell sharply to 20 per cent in the 1970s. Meanwhile, EC investments increased their share of inflows from 37 per cent to about 50 per cent in these two periods (Michalet and Chevallier, 1985, 101). However the US share of sales, employees and investment in the inward *stock* of FDI was closer to 40 per cent in the early 1970s (Delapierre and Michalet, 1976, 89). What also attracted attention was the concentration of foreign firms in a number of technology-intensive sectors where the French government was attempting to maintain a domestic presence, as outlined in Tables 7.1 and 7.2 and examined further below.

French policy towards inward FDI was liberal before the early 1960s.[3] From 1939 on the French government had the legal authority to control inward FDI because of governmental authorization of foreign exchange transactions. The Ministry of Finance led the review of applications for FDI and looked with particular favour on those which appeared to assist the balance of payments or encouraged the less well developed sectors of the economy. There is no record of any US investment being permanently blocked in the period 1957–62 (Johnstone, 1965, 23–4).

Policy changed quite perceptibly to a more restrictive stance from late in 1962 until early in 1964 under a centre-right government led by Premier Georges Pompidou. While policy became less restrictive thereafter, in 1966 France adopted a foreign investment control policy, as distinct from having an exchange control policy which could be used, somewhat awkwardly, to review FDI. For the period through the 1970s the policy on FDI might be described as 'selective encouragement' (US Department of Commerce, 1978).

Table 7.1 Manufacturing sectors where foreign affiliates exceed 30 per cent of sales, France, 1980

	Per cent
Computers and data processing equipment	74.1
Agricultural machinery	57.8
Miscellaneous chemicals	53.3
Crude oil and natural gas	51.5
Pharmaceutical products	43.6
Miscellaneous (and other) products	42.1
Oils and animal fats	37.2
Precision and scientific instruments	36.2
Mechanical handling equipment	35.2
Basic chemicals	31.5
Domestic and industrial electronic equipment	30.8
Footwear	30.3

Source: Michalet and Chevallier (1985, 104).

Table 7.2 Percentage share in French industry of firms with foreign participation, 1972 and 1980

	1972	*1980*
Manufacturing (excluding energy)		
Number of firms	6.1	9.0
Employment	18.6	19.3
Total sales	23.5	24.1
Gross value added	N/A	22.6
Investment	24.7	29.3
Total Industry (including energy)		
Employment	18.0	18.5
Total sales	25.8	26.6
Investment	24.1	19.1

Source: Michalet and Chevallier (1985, 103).

The change in policy in the early 1960s to a more restrictive stance, and thereafter to a somewhat cautious encouragement, can be related to a number of factors. First, in broad terms, the balance of payments had improved after the late 1950s and the economy was stronger: France could afford to be more selective on inward FDI. Second, such inflows had increased, though more so to some other European countries than to France. This raised concern in some quarters in France about the lack of a European policy on FDI with the advent of the European Common Market. In principle, at least, the Treaty of Rome forbade controls on capital movements except for specified reasons. This raised the possibility of firms from outside the Common Market locating elsewhere in it and exporting to France, or even investing in France, without restraint. We shall have more to say on this below. Third, while the gross inflows of the 1960s were only 3 per cent or less of gross capital formation they were concentrated in commerce and in some relatively high capital and skilled labour-intensive sectors, where they formed high percentages of control. Moreover the United States accounted for between 30 and 40 per cent of inflows in the mid-1960s and significantly more than this if the inflows for the larger firms only are considered (Bertin, 1975, 14). The US share of inflows fell sharply during the late 1960s and the 1970s, as EC investments rose and as US balance of payments controls and devaluation took effect. The concern with the US share reflected a fear of US technological superiority and control of a number of science-based industries in France and in Europe. In turn, it was believed, this would leave Europe vulnerable to US government pressure on military issues and to MNE pressure in resisting the industrial plans of some West European governments (Gilpin, 1968, ch. 3). The statement by President Charles de Gaulle in 1964 is particularly telling in this respect:

> It is clear that it is necessary to produce always more and always better, to save and to invest constantly and, even more, to push relentlessly our technical and scientific research, in order to avoid sinking into a bitter mediocrity and being colonized by the activities, inventions and capacities of other countries. (Quoted in Gilpin, 1968, p. 39)

One can be critical of such views with the benefit of hindsight. *The American Challenge*, to use the title of Servan-Schreiber's well-known book, did not look as formidable in the 1980s as it did in the 1960s, not even for French industry which, after a slow start, joined other industry in penetrating sectors of the US market. These general fears were supported, however, by a number of concrete incidents which gave a certain credence to them, even when the 'facts' were sometimes less one-sided than the popular press and the government made them out to be.

Several US companies were involved in well-publicized incidents in 1962–4 which helped to provoke the change in French attitudes. In two cases this involved substantial layoffs of workers with little or no prior consultation with the French authorities of the kind customary in France. In another case a US automobile firm acquired control of the third largest French automobile producer by buying their foreign-held shares through a Swiss bank; since the owners were not French, approval was not necessary under existing French law.

Particularly galling for the government, however, was acquiescence in 1964 to the takeover of part ownership of France's largest computer firm by a US company. An attempt by Machines Bull to sell 20 per cent of its stock to General Electric Company was blocked by President de Gaulle. The French government emphasized that IBM France was already dominant in the French market, accounting for about half of French output in an industry considered essential for defence. It proved impossible, however, to find a partner or partners for Machines Bull, even with substantial financial help from the government. General Electric then acquired from 49 to 51 per cent of the stock in three subsidiaries created to carry on Bull's activities but none of the stock in a fourth subsidiary to carry on defence work of a classified nature (Johnstone, 1965, 25–6; Dickie, 1970, 68–71).

Early in 1966 the issue of foreign control of the computer industry flared up again with the refusal of the US government to allow the sale of two large computers to the French Atomic Energy Commission. While the USA eventually allowed the sale to go ahead, provided the computers were not used in France's nuclear weapons programme, the entire incident was deeply resented by President de Gaulle and other French leaders. It led directly to the decision to create a French computer industry as support for its independent strategic capability, in what became known as *le plan calcul* (Gilpin, 1968, 53–4; McArthur and Scott, 1969, 360–69).

Still other tensions over MNEs clouded French–American relations in this period. In 1965, for example, the US Treasury ordered a US firm to suspend a contract by its French subsidiary to deliver vans to a French firm for shipment to China. The French minority directors of the subsidiary successfully sued in the French courts to execute the contract (Goldberg and Kindleberger, 1970). France also reacted to the US balance of payments guidelines of 1965, as did other countries. The government now required contributions to a new FDI inflow immediately, and in cash, with French funds limited to less than half of the total finance. Moreover the review of individual investments passing through the exchange control apparatus was tightened. For a time the Minister of Finance personally reviewed every application for investment by a US firm. During 1965 a large proportion of applications were delayed by the authorities, effectively leading to their rejection (Dickie, 1970, 66; US Senate, 1975, 197).

In 1966 a new law was introduced consolidating the policy on control of direct foreign investment flows. In the process the scope of investments subject to prior declaration was greatly increased to include the transfer of ownership of firms located in France from one foreign owner to another, the merger of two foreign firms if one owned a French subsidiary, and expansion of existing subsidiaries using new capital from abroad. At the same time it was decided that the Ministry of Industry must approve acquisitions of foreign industrial property rights, know-how or technical assistance, and related expenses must be reported annually. The foreign investment law was challenged by the Commission of the EC and submitted to the Court of Justice of the European Communities. France exempted the EC from the foreign investment law but insisted on applying exchange control measures to investment from the EC in ways which some members believed led to the same result. Finally we note that the various ministers of the French government clarified its policy stance in this period, notably by emphasizing the preference for new investment over takeovers, and by spelling out which types or sectors of takeovers were unlikely to be approved.

It is important to note that French policy became less restrictive after the events of 1964–6. But it is also clear that these events led to a series of laws, decrees and policy statements putting in place a foreign investment policy – a process of encouraging such investment in some sectors and circumstances but discouraging it in others. To a considerable degree this openness was unavoidable, given the competition for such investment within the EC and the pressures making for internationalization of industry. At the same time the government had in place an apparatus for influencing those pressures so as to serve its industrial policies. We turn now to consider how it has used that apparatus in practice.

Review of Inward Direct Investment

In what follows we describe the system which was in operation in the early 1980s, with recent changes noted at the end of the section. The basis for the system was authorizations under exchange control regulations, plus the law of 1966 and subsequent measures implementing and extending it. Generally a prior declaration of any direct investment, regardless of its size, had to be filed with the Ministry of Economy and Finance, Treasury Department.[4] Such direct investment includes establishing a new business, taking control of an existing one, whether from abroad or by a subsidiary in France, or increasing control of an existing business. An expansion of a company under control would require prior declaration if it was into new lines of business including new product lines, or in existing lines also if external financing was necessary.[5] Acquisition of 20 per cent or more of the voting stock or capital of a firm listed on the stock exchange requires prior declaration, as does a one-third acquisition if the firm is not listed.[6] Transfers of ownership between non-residents require such declaration when a direct investment is involved, but a review would be undertaken only if it appeared to conflict with French policy. The financial transactions related to the foregoing have been subject to prior authorization through the prior declaration. Approval extended to loans and loan guarantees by parent firms.

The prior declaration requested information on the investor and the French firm, a description of the activities planned in France with a statement of the sources of the funds, reasons for the investment, and the effects on the French economy. For a new company, cash flow projections were also needed for four years.[7] The declaration was presented to the Ministry for Economy and Finance, Treasury Directorate. It went automatically to an interdepartmental Committee on Foreign Investment if the capital stock involved 5 million francs or more, while highly sensitive proposals could go to the office of the Premier or even the President. Smaller applications might involve only informal consultation between Departments if of interest to an industry plan or for some other reason.

The law specifies that the government has two months to make a decision once a declaration is received. It could allow the investment to proceed, could begin discussions with a view to modification of the proposal, or ask for a postponement. The last of these might be to allow negotiations to continue, but could also lead to an indefinite postponement as a way of banning an investment. No reason need be given for such postponements. In the process of discussion the proposal can be significantly changed in scope or content to meet the objectives set by government for the industry. Much steering may be accomplished through discussion of planned public support for the project.

Apart from the financing and foreign exchange requirements, the criteria of benefit to France are set out only in very general terms, mostly enunciated in the late 1960s and 1970s by ministerial policy statements. An early summary of policy by two members of the planning commission emphasized the attempt to link FDI policy with general and industrial objectives. Four criteria were noted as guiding the Committee on Foreign Investment: first, the nationality of the investor, with a particularly favourable reception for EC investments except where these were by firms controlled outside the community; second, the effects on economic growth, including employment, regional balance and the development of research capacity; third, the effects on the structure of industry, involving such issues as the degree of foreign ownership and the strength of local firms, and especially the effect on government attempts to create French-controlled industrial groups capable of becoming multinational; finally, the effects on the balance of trade or (if financing requirements are taken into account) the balance of payments, especially on the development of export capacity (Bonnaud and Bosser, 1973, 520–21). It should be added that in certain periods there was also a tendency to look negatively on investments controlled in the United States, especially during the 1960s, as already discussed above (Bertin, 1977, 89, 95). Also export development was emphasized rather than import substitution, in part because the latter could lead to problems with EC and GATT obligations. Investments which appeared mainly to be a vehicle to import products would not be looked on favourably because of concern that they could reduce employment.[8]

Interviews conducted in the years 1981–3, as noted in Appendix I, indicated that there was no formal list of criteria or standard criteria against which investments were evaluated. None was made known in advance to firms, and none apparently existed internally either – although the persons involved would discuss the effects noted above. Official statements referred very broadly to conditions on investment designed to maintain or create jobs, or to encourage regional development or exports (OECD, 1982, 22). Nor were there tradeoffs specified between the objectives where they conflicted. Without clearly specified criteria and tradeoffs, no consistent cost–benefit analysis could be made internally, nor could clear signals be given to the firms as to what was necessary for approval.

It is well to add several points in interpreting this. While no formal list of criteria on the acceptability of FDI existed, there was certainly discussion of the trade effect, the employment effect and so on. This arose because both overall plans and often industrial plans exist; what was at issue was the consistency of the foreign investment decisions with such plans. The second and related point is the variation in emphasis on certain criteria over time. In the 1960s and early 1970s there was a deliberate emphasis on technological development, in the early 1980s on the creation of investment and jobs even if they were not highly skilled, at various points of time on improvement of the balance of payments. Insofar as these reflected the preferences of the planners, they amounted to a rough specification of tradeoffs or priorities with regard to other criteria which were used, hence an approach, however broad, to welfare effects. We return to this in our conclusions.

Conditions attached to an approval were conveyed in writing but were not publicly known in general. They were usually of relatively short duration and quite specific: for example, to finance from abroad in certain ways, to undertake a certain amount of real investment by a certain date, or to maintain employment for at least a certain time. They could also be more detailed in some cases, such as agreeing to maintain a product line or a research facility, or not to increase imports. The emphasis was on setting conditions which were short-run and specific, hence capable of being realized and checked. Interviewees took the view that anything more lengthy was difficult to enforce as circumstances changed so much with time. The monitoring system was not well developed in any case, often involving simply a request for a progress report on a building plan or a balance sheet. There are no penalties under law for firms which fail to meet these commitments and cannot explain this failure to the satisfaction of the authorities. It is well to note, however, that most undertakings involve some government support, financial or regulatory, and there is a great deal of on-going contact between firm and government in France. Firms which must come back to government or a government agency for the second instalment of a grant or credit for expansion are likely to meet commitments or at least to try to have satisfactory explanations for not doing so. Some of the interviewees made a distinction between those requirements that the firm make an investment or hire a certain number of persons, often assisted by a grant, and those 'conditions' which are simply an indication of the firm's plans and which cannot have the force of law. The distinction may be more apparent than real, however, if one considers that particular French ministries may take exception to the investment and either require changes or counsel non-acceptance if their interests are not satisfied.

One must be careful of words such as 'non-acceptance' and especially 'rejection' in the French context. In the first nine months of 1965 fully 47 of 138 applications were 'rejected', mostly by indefinite delay which led investors to abandon their plans.[9] A later estimate suggested that less than 5 per cent of applications were rejected, even in periods of greater restrictiveness, and most of these were on purely technical grounds (Bertin, 1977, 82). One interviewee in the private sector with long experience of such applications could recall only one outright refusal. Interviewees in three government departments or agencies represented on the Committee on Foreign Investment thought the figure was zero or practically zero in the early 1980s once a formal application was filed. There are several reasons for this, apart from the fact that policy favoured inward direct investment in the early 1980s, subject to some qualifications noted below. Firms are unlikely to go ahead with formal proposals if previous discussions indicate that an application will not be welcomed. And the government can discourage an applicant from continuing with discussions by many means. One is to set conditions on performance and finance which the firm is quite unprepared to accept. In effect the firm is put in the position of deciding not to enter, rather than facing a formal and public refusal. While the outcome is the same, the psychology for the applicant – and the political context for its home government if it is involved – are different in the two cases.[10]

As in several other countries noted earlier, the interests of the different ministries can significantly influence the outcomes of particular cases and the sources of the process overall. Before commenting on the ministries, it may be noted that the attitudes of both French parliamentarians and civil servants towards MNEs were much more critical than was the case in the United Kingdom. The overall effects on France were believed to be negative in a high proportion of both groups in a survey conducted in 1975, with members of the Socialist Party particularly concerned about negative effects (Graham, 1982, 241–6).

The Ministry of Economy and Finance chairs the Foreign Investment Committee and is most likely to emphasize macro issues such as the financing of the project (especially the necessary import of capital) and the effects on the overall balance of payments and economic growth. DATAR is charged with supplying information to foreign investors and controls much of the financial incentives which are available. It is likely to favour investments where job creation occurs, especially when firms locate in relatively less developed areas.[11] The Ministry of Industry is most likely to reflect a micro approach, for example, to insist that benefits be verified, that the competition with established firms be considered, and especially that specific technological development be given weight. One established firm which made a (partial) acquisition in the early 1980s noted in the interview that Finance seemed satisfied when the regulations regarding import of capital were met, DATAR by the fact that the firm was outside Paris, while Industry was the most demanding, with questions about the impact on employment, exports and technological development. There are other interests on the Committee, but the potential for conflict seems largest among these, as will be noted further below.[12]

There were 10 professional people in the Treasury in the early 1980s dealing with applications, three in Industry, one or two in DATAR, and one or two elsewhere. These are people who are knowledgeable about the FDI authorization process; obviously there are others involved in other aspects, such as DATAR's staff at home and abroad on the information side, and Industry and Finance specialists knowledgeable about particular sectors. The number of applications of all kinds listed above averaged about 25 a week. Many of these were quite small or routine. The existence of industrial and general plans suggests some guidelines, even if broad, on how to evaluate applications. Nevertheless this number of professionals is small by comparison with several of the countries noted earlier, especially since many of the officials had other important responsibilities with regard to external economic issues.

Treatment of FDI from the EC countries was a major problem until 1980. Subject to some exceptions noted below, the Treaty of Rome can be read to establish free movement of capital among its members. Shortly after the French veto of UK membership in the EC, French officials proposed consideration of a Common Market policy towards investments from outside that Market. Meetings of the finance ministers of the EC in March 1963 and later could not agree on such an approach, preferring national policies and the EC competition policy (Dickie, 1970, 72–3; Johnstone, 1965, 18, 21–2). France then took the position that her developing policies applied to all foreign investors including those in the EC, and most particularly to EC investors where control lay outside the Community. French concerns were partly due to a desire to ensure consistency of foreign investment policy with industrial policy, but also to ensure that entry by US and other non-EC investors into the less restrictive parts of the Community would not then circumvent her developing foreign investment policy. The EC Commission took the view that this conflicted with the Treaty of Rome and took the issue to the European Court of Justice in 1969.[13] In February 1971 a compromise was reached whereby the French government exempted EC members from filing prior declarations for authorizations under her direct investment controls but simultaneously subjected such proposals to her exchange control system. In effect EC investments would be scrutinized under balance of payments controls.[14] This was a 'colourable device' which continued to be an issue between France and her partners. To be sure, France often gave preference to EC investment if only as a way of strengthening various joint undertakings and diminishing reliance on US capital. Nevertheless, during the 1970s, the French authorities did not hesitate to bar investors with parent companies in the EC from acquiring French firms if such acquisitions did not fit in with their plans. For example, such acquisitions were barred in the biscuit and the paint industries because foreign ownership was already high in those sectors (Bertin, 1977, 94–5).

In 1980 France agreed to relax the rules on acquisitions from EC partners. These would require only prior notification while the general review process for other countries continued to involve prior authorization, with some exceptions noted below. However the Minister of Economics may notify the firms that they fall within certain categories subject to the general review process, even for investments from EC countries – namely, investments affecting public order, health, security and defence materials, or operations which could obstruct the application of French regulations or laws, or sectors which participate ('even only occasionally') in the administration of public authority. There is clearly some scope for elasticity of interpretation in such phrases. Investments by firms located in EC countries, but with 20 per cent or more of the capital owned by residents outside the EC, continued to be subject to the general review procedures (OECD, 1982, 21).[15] All external investments were also subject, of course, to exchange control requirements until the late 1980s.

One of the more important aspects of French policy has been the attempt to preserve a French presence in some sectors, and to do so in ways which encourage an internationally competitive industry. This could be a declining industry which was being restructured or a new or growing sector the government wished to encourage. The origins of this policy go back at least to the mid-1960s and a variety of ministerial statements over the years confirm it. The policy utilized many instruments, such as government procurement favouring French-owned firms in some sectors. The position is expressed partly in a strong preference for new investments compared with acquisitions, a position which most interviewees in government and business emphasized. This preference was expressed in various policies; for example, in some periods a new investment required less external financing than a takeover, and a takeover would be considered more closely. Most interviewees also agreed that a 'French solution' was always considered, and not just in the case of sensitive sectors. It was acknowledged that, from 1980, investors with control lying in the EC could be barred from takeover only in certain circumstances, but, as noted, these were elastically defined. It was also acknowledged that in the great majority of cases it was not possible to find a French firm as a suitable partner, even where special government financing was made available.

It was emphasized repeatedly in interviews that there are no clear or consistent rules on how to react to takeovers, even in sensitive areas. Despite some unconditional statements on the nature of the French solution in the literature and even from some of those involved in policy, the reasons for the lack of clear rules are easily comprehended. Suppose the welcome for new investment was unqualified. A highly competitive new investor could play havoc with established firms. Suppose that acquisitions were simply unwelcome. Important changes in techniques known to outside investors but not yet to the relevant French firms would have to be imported by licences and other non-controlling devices which could prove unsatisfactory. Firms which were about to fail or be sharply reduced in size would find fewer alternatives. One can easily construct other situations in which the French authorities and even the rest of the industry might consider acquisitions or perhaps joint ventures as superior.

For these types of reasons the policy could only be one where the particular industry situation was considered. A detailed review of an application could be triggered for a variety of reasons. One commonly stressed in the literature is that foreign ownership was already high. However this presupposes that there is a view on what needs to be done in order to preserve a French presence in the industry, and that the relevant investment of public resources is warranted. Hence one aspect of an industrial plan might be to preserve French firms; that is, to seek a French solution if a firm is in difficulty, to reorganize the structure of the industry with public support if necessary, and so on. We shall note below a number of restricted sectors where this is, or was, the case. But much of what passes for a French solution is far more ad hoc than this. A search for a French bidder by contacting the banks (largely government-owned) and large industrial groups (some in the public sector) triggers several outcomes. It necessarily spreads information on the existence of an offer to acquire the firm, although confidentiality issues presumably limit what can be made known (see Carlson, 1980, 42–3). It gives potential competitors of the acquiring firm, including some in the public sector, an opportunity to make their concerns and desires known. Some of these concerns might be resisted by the authorities who are using the FDI as a way to bring desired changes to the industry.[16] Other conditions may appeal to them and find their way into conditions on the application, if approved. The possibilities here have already been considered in earlier country studies where it was pointed out that all sorts of rent-seeking behaviour might be followed by local firms to limit competition, to try to secure part or all of the target firm at a favourable price, to increase public financial or regulatory support, and so on. The possibilities are stronger than in, say, Canada or Australia, given the closer contacts between government and business and the virtual absence of any desire in France to request equity issues on the market, which allows the MNE to capture any rents.[17] We emphasize again that in the great majority of cases the authorities have concluded that a viable merger is not feasible and a takeover is allowed. Details are not made public but such government–private sector arrangements designed to forestall an acquisition by FDI do reach the press.[18]

The system described above had been formally loosened up by the mid-1980s. Prior *authorization* was still required for non-EC investors, except that only prior *notification* was required for creation of new enterprises or for participation under 10 million francs in an existing French firm. In these latter two cases, however, the Minister of Economics and Finance had the option in special cases of postponement of the investment within one month, rather than two as in the case of acquisition. Also, if the investment falls into any of the sensitive categories listed earlier in discussing EC investments, then prior authorization is needed for both EC and non-EC investment, and the Minister has one month to declare that such prior authorization is needed. For both EC and non-EC investments neither prior notification nor authorization was needed for investments or acquisitions where at least 75 per cent of the equity was already foreign-controlled (OECD, 1987b, 19–20). Apart from formal changes in the system, it had been liberalized in practice as well. One heard much less of pressures for local participation by joint ventures, or of whether existing foreign ownership of a sector was already too large, and so on. As one government interviewee remarked in 1983, 'There are too many problems these days to be dogmatic on such matters' – a remark which perhaps understated the degree of pragmatism earlier. The system of exchange controls was further eased at the end of the 1980s, retaining only notification for FDI in existing foreign-owned firms except for the sensitive categories already noted above.[19]

Early in 1990 the regulations were further relaxed. The time allowed for the Ministry of Finance to decide on a review was reduced to two weeks for EC investments and four weeks for larger non-EC investments. EC firms with turnover over one billion francs and which were at least three years old no longer required even notification for acquisitions. Neither notification nor declaration is needed for greenfields investments, expansion of a firm's activities, or increases in shareholdings beyond two-thirds, although a report must be submitted within 20 days. A variety of smaller investments, and financial arrangements between affiliates, were exempted from reporting (Bailey *et al.*, 1991a, 31).

None of this means, however, that the French government has lost its interest in the sensitive sectors, including a significant number of state-owned firms or sectors. Such state ownership, along with less formal links to privately-owned firms, ensures many opportunities to influence the structure of industry, including nationality of ownership, for governments which are so inclined. Moreover, as in a number of other countries in this study, the law allows firms in France an extensive set of protective devices to ward off undesired takeover offers (see, for example, *The Economist*, 1 June 1991, 75–6). Such devices can be used, of course, against both domestic and foreign firms, hence they are not explicitly directed against the latter. Where countries differ significantly in law and acceptable practice on such matters, however, pressures for reciprocity of treatment are likely to arise if only because some firms or sectors threatened by entry from abroad cannot retaliate in kind. This subject will be taken up again in Chapters 11 and 12.

Restricted Sectors and Nationalization

As in most of the other countries in this study a number of public and privately operated (or mixed) monopolies exist which effectively close off FDI as well as other private investment (OECD, 1982; 1987b). In addition there is a rather long list of industries where the establishment by foreigners or foreign-controlled firms is limited. These are shown in Table 11.3 and include, among others, defence industries, aspects of transport and agriculture, a number of cultural activities and various financial sectors. The incidence of these limitations is reduced by exemptions for EC nationals in some cases and reciprocity provisions in others.

It is necessary to add that France has attempted to maintain a position in some major high-technology sectors, especially where close relations with the government are involved. This has been an important aspect of French policy since at least the early 1960s, reflecting her desire to ensure major power status in the era of the scientific state, to use Robert Gilpin's term (Gillespie, 1972, 425–7, 430–31). One of the best known examples is the attempt to maintain a French presence in the computer industry, particularly as distinct from IBM France Ltd. That firm had the advantages of having arrived in France as early as 1914, of having secured a major share of the market, including the important government market, and of being a large employer and exporter. The attempt to maintain a French presence in large computers has had a chequered history involving on occasion tradeoffs of a significant degree of independence for access to the technology of other US-owned firms. We noted above the inability of the government to prevent a partial merger of General Electric and Machines Bull in 1964. In 1970 the US firm, Honeywell, bought out the General Electric interest.

In 1975 French interests, in the form of a firm established by government a decade earlier, were merged with Honeywell–Bull. The establishment of CII–Honeywell–Bull in effect ended attempts for a time to develop a European firm or a purely French firm in the large computer area. Along the way a considerable amount of government support has been involved through direct subsidy and government procurement favouring this firm. The result was a significant drop in IBM France's share of public sector sales, although important parts of the public sector continued to buy from that firm or to import. However the Bull group was still in considerable financial difficulty at the beginning of the 1990s. In 1991 the Japanese firm, NEC, took a 4.7 per cent ownership interest in the Bull group. Early in 1992 IBM took a 5.7 per cent interest in a deal which also involved important technical and commercial links (*Financial Times*, 29 January 1992, 1; Bailey *et al.*, 1991a, 38).

Similar efforts have been made to establish or maintain a distinct French presence in such sectors as aerospace, nuclear industries and telephone systems, sometimes by easing out US-owned firms as French capacities increased (*The Economist*, 10 September 1977, 20–21; 29 May 1976; 17 November 1979). The French government made no secret of the fact that it retained the right to grant official subsidies, guarantees, loans or preferential purchasing to enterprises in certain sectors, and to regulate conditions in such sectors, even if this involved distinctions by national origin of the firm (OECD, 1978, 61–2). The authorization system has been used at times to preserve a French presence in areas where it was feared that foreign-controlled firms were becoming dominant, such as electronics, pharmaceuticals, food processing and paper (US Department of Commerce, 1978). Industries considered part of the national heritage, as noted earlier, would also be protected. Thus the proposed sale of the prestigious Château-Margaux vineyards to a US company was blocked, much to the distress of the financially pressed owners, who were being offered only half the amount involved by prospective French buyers – and who pointed out at once the need for government financial support (*Toronto Star*, 25 August 1976). In more recent years industries such as biotechnology and automated machine tools have been sectors where France has attempted to maintain a domestic presence (*Business International*, ILT, May 1986, 3).

Finally we note that, since 1928, France has had a system of import quotas for crude oil designed to promote refining in France but also having the effect of limiting the number of firms while lessening dependence on foreign-owned majors. France, lacking the natural resource, has used control of the domestic market to also pursue over time several objectives in addition to those just noted, such as assurance of supply by diversification of sources, improvement of the balance of payments and development of two state-controlled MNEs. Like other states in the 1970s, France intervened more heavily still in petroleum markets. In essence French policy attempted to preserve about 50 per cent of the market for the French-owned firms over very long periods. This policy had to be modified somewhat in the early 1980s to take account of EC objections over many years to the discrimination against firms owned in the Community. French objectives have involved a variety of measures which discriminated against foreign-owned firms in the attempt to develop a domestic and state-owned presence, measures which sometimes damaged the interests of independent French distributors also.[20]

In addition to the above, there has long been a substantial publicly-owned sector which was considerably extended in the early 1980s. In the 1930s most aircraft companies and firms manufacturing military materials were nationalized. After the Second World War the state took part or entire ownership of a number of other firms, including the largest automobile manufacturer, the three largest commercial banks, the major insurance companies, the largest coal mines and most of the electric power and natural gas utilities. The nationalizations of 1982–3 substantially increased the publicly-owned sector of industry, from 18 per cent to 32 per cent of total turnover. For the largest industrial companies, with 2000 or more employees, the nationalized firms account for 47 per cent of sales. This includes considerable increases in a number of sectors where MNEs, whether French or foreign, have played a significant role internationally; for example, increases of 20 percentage points or more in base chemicals, pharmaceuticals, computer and office equipment, power generating equipment, electronics, consumer durables and aircraft. Almost all of the private banking sector was brought under public ownership, a notable exception being the foreign-owned banks.[21]

The motives for the 1982 nationalizations were complex. They were one aspect of a major set of policies designed to improve industrial competitiveness through economic restructuring. A number of the French groups which were nationalized were in financial difficulty in the late 1970s, even before the recession of the early 1980s. Some were in declining sectors (steel); others offered growth opportunities which France was anxious to seize. With respect to the latter, one may note that in 1979 French authorities identified offshore petroleum, office automation, biotechnology, electronics and energy-saving technology as areas in which to encourage national firms. A new interministerial committee was given funding to encourage such development (Mytelka, 1986, 159). Nationalization was expected to accomplish a number of objectives in this regard. It would allow restructuring of much of this and other industry, and the resultant financing, more directly in terms of control than would the considerable but often indirect controls already in place. And it would do so without necessarily reverting to internationalization, which the socialist government believed was otherwise inevitable and undesirable. In defending the nationalizations in 1981, for example, President Mitterrand not only claimed a better investment record of the public than the private sector in recent years but also claimed nationalization would forestall internationalization. The implication clearly was that investment abroad by the newly nationalized groups would not be encouraged (*The Economist*, 27 February 1982, 16; *Daily Telegraph*, London, 28 September 1981, editorial). The Minister of Industry, Jean-Pierre Chevènement, believed major firms were on the verge of failure and would have had to sell off assets to foreign interests (*Business Week*, 10 January 1983, 55).

It should be emphasized that the major interests which were affected by the nationalizations were French rather than foreign. Nevertheless there were foreign shareholders of nationalized companies, and both joint ventures with and subsidiaries of foreign-owned firms were involved in the nationalizations. Discussions with the three major foreign interests affected – Hoechst, Honeywell and ITT – were all resolved but only after some difficult negotiations with the first of these in particular, which left the leading French producer of pharmaceuticals under Hoechst management and control while the state acquired 34 per cent. Honeywell's holding was reduced from 47 per cent to 20 per cent but important links were maintained with CII–Honeywell–Bull. The government also took 100 per cent control of subsidiaries of ITT but left a dozen others as they were, once again increasing its ownership but maintaining ITT participation in the French economy (Savary, 1984, 159; Doyle, 1983, 61).

Nationalizations on the scale involved in France are likely to raise substantial dissent politically, from the local and foreign interests being nationalized, and sometimes from foreign governments. The procedures used in the French nationalizations, in terms of consistency with French law and international law, led to relatively few problems in these respects, in part because the French government quickly accepted the changes proposed by the French Constitutional Council (Doyle, 1983, 67, 71–2). The associated expansionary fiscal policies soon had to be reversed, however, in the face of international recession.

The result of the nationalizations was to leave an even larger set of industries where publicly-owned firms and foreign-owned firms competed, both in France and abroad. One result of this is to raise even more widely questions about subsidized and often opaque competition by the state: for example, government procurement favouring state firms, financing of state firms at less than market rates and other subsidies which are difficult to determine from consolidated accounts.[22] The US government in particular raised questions about the entry of French nationalized firms to the US market, or competition by them in other markets, based partly on the issue of such alleged subsidies but also on the question as to whether reciprocal access to the French market by US firms was possible, given the nationalizations.

In any case various ministers of the socialist government were not long in making it known that they welcomed inward FDI which met the broad criteria already in effect, and that incentives would be given to such investment even more generously than in the past (Savary, 1984, 169 and *International Herald Tribune*, 9 November 1981, p. 1; 9 February 1982, p. 2). They had several reasons for adopting such a position. One was that, having nationalized a number of firms and groups where they wished to exert more control, they could afford to be somewhat less restrictive elsewhere. In any case the government was concerned that the nationalizations proceed as smoothly as possible, in terms of both internal and external effects; witness, for example, the decision to allow effective control of Roussel-Uclaf by Hoechst. Second, with the reappearance of balance of payments pressures and the international recession, the government was anxious to encourage inward FDI.

It is difficult to know how much of the steep declines in inward and outward FDI after 1980–81, however measured, to attribute to the nationalizations and to the reservations the government had about outward FDI (Table 7.3). Recession would affect these totals, as would the significant delays of particular investments in 1981–2 while the direction of industrial policies was being determined. What seems clear is that the government soon showed a considerable willingness to allow inward and outward FDI, contrary to the positions and concerns of some of its most influential mem-

Table 7.3 Flows of direct investment, France, 1967–86

	In Francs		*In SDRs*		*In US dollars*	
	Outward	*Inward*	*Outward*	*Inward*	*Outward*	*Inward*
			(millions of units)			
1967	—	—	354	341	—	—
1968	1 680	981	343	196	—	—
1969	1 031	1 599	193	295	—	—
1970	2 079	3 461	373	622	373	626
1971	2 196	2 910	396	524	399	528
1972	2 995	3 467	546	632	594	687
1973	4 163	5 011	784	945	935	1 125
1974	3 754	8 882	650	1 541	781	1 847
1975	6 122	6 247	1 300	1 281	1 428	1 457
1976	8 184	5 022	1 428	920	1 712	1 051
1977	5 885	8 670	856	1 619	1 198	1 765
1978	8 095	11 031	1 510	1 960	1 794	2 445
1979	8 395	11 579	1 535	2 003	1 973	2 722
1980	13 100	13 903	2 382	2 528	3 138	3 327
1981	24 909	13 355	3 887	2 084	4 615	2 426
1982	18 691	10 492	2 576	1 446	3 063	1 563
1983	12 951	13 215	1 590	1 622	1 699	1 733
1984	18 650	21 051	2 082	2 350	2 134	2 409
1985	20 007	23 227	2 193	2 546	2 201	2 526
1986	36 979	22 288	4 551	2 743	5 339	3 218
1987	54 577	30 553	7 022	3 931	—	—

Source: OECD (1987a, pp. 58–60, 108–9), updated after 1980 from IMF, *Balance of Payments Statistics*.

bers while in opposition. It is also clear that there was a significant revival of such flows by 1984.[23]

In 1986 the French legislature, now controlled by a conservative government, passed legislation to turn 65 state-owned firms over to the private sector over a five-year period. These included not only the six large industrial groups nationalized in 1982 but banking, insurance and several other state-owned enterprises. The process began in November 1986 with the sale of one of the industrial groups, Saint-Gobain. The government had intended to impose a 15 per cent limit on foreign investment in such firms during an undefined transition period, a position criticized by the EC Commission as discriminating against Community members. The amended bill raised the limit to 20 per cent in line with the point at which foreign purchases of publicly listed firms are reviewed. It also limited the right of the government to intervene, in order to maintain this share, to five years and to strategic companies, as well as limiting individual French holdings in such firms to 10 per cent. The return of a socialist government in the late 1980s resulted in a cessation of privatization and opened a debate on core groups. It appears that up to 30 per cent of the shares of privatized firms had been placed with groups of friendly shareholders, each having up to five percentage points. These groups had agreed to maintain their holdings for up to five years and to grant each other the first right of refusal on selling. One view of this provision was that it was intended to protect newly privatized firms from hostile takeovers for a few years. Members of the new government argued that it put in control of the firms various interests which were hostile to them, and they proceeded therefore to seek ways to unseat some of the core groups (*The Economist*, 15 March 1986; *Globe and Mail*, 1 August 1986; 20 February 1989).

In addition significant deregulation of internal and external financial markets was undertaken, beginning in 1984–5 under the socialist government, but accelerating under its conservative successor. One aspect of this was the abandonment by the end of the 1980s of most of the remaining foreign-exchange restrictions affecting companies, including many of those on inward and outward direct investment. The review process, which is distinct from the exchange control process, continued (*The Economist*, 29 November 1986, 75–6). Another aspect of the financial deregulation was to allow foreign firms into some sectors previously closed to them, subject in some cases to reciprocity considerations for non-EC countries (Table 7.4).

Related Policies

We discuss briefly here three policy areas related to those on inward FDI, namely, outward FDI, technology transfer, and fiscal incentives.[24]

(a) Outward FDI

For most of the post- Second World War period French MNEs have tended to be less prominent than those of other major industrial countries. Studies of the multinationalization process completed in the early 1970s emphasized the limited extent of multinational production even for major firms, the emphasis by firms and governments on developing exports rather than subsidiaries abroad, and the problems such strategies raise when other countries' firms are moving more aggressively into FDI (Michalet and Delapierre,

Policy development in France

	Exchange control law, 9 September, supplies legal foundation for government control of new FDI in France.
1966	Law of 28 December, Article 3: government can require reporting, authorization and control of monetary operations and capital movements in and out of France, including FDI. The decree of 27 January 1967 implementing this law specifically refers to acquisitions, increases in control and expansion, as well as new firms. The decree of 24 November 1968 requires that FDI must be effected through intermediaries approved by Ministry of Finance. Most commercial banks are approved.
1971	22 February, EC investors not required to file prior declaration on FDI but must get approval under foreign exchange procedures.
1974	January. Authorization needed for purchases over 20 per cent of stock of firms in stock market.
1980	4 August, FDI from EC free to enter in principle, with stated exceptions requiring authorization.
1982	As part of the nationalization of major French industrial groups, three large foreign-owned firms nationalized (in two cases, partially). Subsequent privatizations placed temporary limits on foreign ownership.
Mid-1980s	General easing of review for non-EC investors: for example, prior notification only in the case of new investments and participation under 10 million francs, except special circumstances.
1985–7	Foreign exchange controls on inward and outward FDI substantially liberalized; largely ended for companies by 1989.
1988–90	Further liberalization, including exemption of greenfields FDI from notification or declaration, exemption of acquisitions by large EC firms even from notification, shorter time for approvals.

1973, ch. 9; Bertin, 1975, ch. 3). Perhaps as a consequence of all this, until recently the quality of French data on outward FDI did not compare well with that of many other countries in this study.

In the early 1970s in particular the government began to encourage FDI abroad more systematically as part of its industrial planning process (Bonnaud and Bosser, 1973, 523–8). There was a broader recognition in this period of the advantages of such firms and, in particular, that exports and external FDI were not simply alternatives but, to some extent, complements. More particularly the substantial increases in inward FDI during the 1960s led the government to emphasize the development of French firms which were less vulnerable to takeover by foreign interests and more likely to be multinational in their own right. This policy was not without risk, in that French MNEs might prove to be less susceptible to government control than would more nationally oriented firms. Nevertheless all governments since then have encouraged this multinationalization of French firms, with the brief exception of a period during the 1980s nationalizations. One aspect of the change was to broaden to larger firms, in 1972, the financial support which had been available to smaller firms investing abroad since 1965. The export orientation of such firms remained a key to the level of support given, however (Rainelli, 1984, 495–7). More importantly, as noted earlier, substantial financial aid was available to firms undergoing reorganization as an aspect of the government's attempt to preserve a French presence in selected sectors of industry.

By the early 1980s, at least the leading French firms were engaged in foreign production on a large scale. The multinationalization of French firms still remained relatively less extensive than those of other, larger industrial powers. The Economic and Social Council, on reviewing the reasons for and effects of FDI, went on to recommend that such outflows be doubled again by 1985, and that particular attention be given to increasing the French MNE presence in the United States (France, Conseil Economique et Social, 1981, 93–4). With the nationalizations in 1981, stronger foreign exchange controls for a time, and some propensity for the new government to emphasize the domestic market, there was a view that investment abroad would slow down. In fact, after the early 1980s, FDI abroad rose substantially. In 1988 and 1989 acquisitions abroad by French firms soared to 76 billion francs and 108 billion francs respectively, reflecting such factors as the end of exchange controls, a strong profit and debt position, and the merger activity associated with increased European integration (*The Financial Times*, 9 May 1990, 20). By 1990 French companies led all others, including US and Japanese firms, in both the number and value of cross-border mergers and acquisitions in Europe (*World Deal Review*, 1991, 11).

Approval for outward FDI depended on the same dual process of exchange control approval and foreign investment approval described earlier for inward FDI. However consideration by the Committee on Foreign Investment appears to have been much more broadly based than for inward FDI. Balance of payments effects and domestic employment effects were factors taken into account, the latter in part by examining investment plans by the firm at home and abroad. In the case of nationalized firms the relevant trade unions would be consulted by management with regard to an investment abroad. It appears from interviews and from government documents noted earlier that the limitation on outward investment was not substantial, apart from the need at times to satisfy exchange control requirements. As noted above, exchange controls as they affected direct investment were largely removed in the late 1980s. Moreover governments generally favoured outward FDI after the early 1970s, and increasingly appeared to accept the firms' views that they had to invest abroad if they were to sell abroad. What was more important than these on-going approval processes was the support by particular governments of major FDI projects, which dominate both overall and sectoral data. Many of these decisions involved state-owned firms, particularly after the nationalizations of 1982. Thus the largest oil and chemicals group in France, Elf Aquitaine, was owned two-thirds by the state. In 1980 its bid of $4 billion for a US firm, Kerr-Addison, was vetoed by the French government, which wanted Elf to devote more of its resources to France. In 1981, however, the government approved its $2.5 billion bid for the US firm Texasgulf, which was part of Elf's move out of its Canadian operations (*The Economist*, 26 May 1983, 66–7).

(b) Technology transfer

Licensing and technical assistance agreements and renewals of agreements must be reported to the Institut National de la Propriété Industrielle, which is part of the Ministry of Industry. In part this is for information. However the Institut does express reservations in less than 10 per cent of the cases, reservations largely with respect to royalty rates which are considered excessive. The Ministry of Economy and Finance, while not bound by Institut reservations, can forbid any excess amount of royalty from being deducted for tax purposes (*Business International*, France, December 1982, 15). It is not clear whether and how far the reporting system is used for other policy purposes.

(c) Fiscal incentives

French objectives with regard to investment incentives have been described as regional development; industrial restructuring; adherence to quantitative targets with respect to research, pollution control, savings in energy and improvement of working conditions; and the development of strategic sectors, mainly the computer and scientific instrument industries and ship and aircraft building (OECD, 1983, 115). The study goes on to note that some of the wide range of assistance is tied to performance, such as creation or preservation of jobs. Inward FDI had to be financed in foreign currency until recently, generally wholly so in the case of an acquisition and partly so for a new investment: 'Apart from this obligation, the same undertakings as to results are required whether the firms are French and resident or non-resident, and regardless of the sector in which they are set up' (ibid., p. 121).

This summary underlines the point made earlier that industrial policy has played a larger role in France than in most other countries in this study and that an attempt is made to integrate policy on inward FDI with industrial policy affecting all firms. It does not go far enough, however, in indicating that governments do distinguish between firms by ownership when incentives are given and performance requirements are set. Moreover governments find these distinctions consistent with policy positions which state that national treatment is involved; that is, that enterprises controlled by non-residents are treated no less favourably than domestic enterprises in like situations.

Two short steps are involved in evaluating this process. One is to acknowledge the discretionary nature of many fiscal incentives. The following statement is explicit on this.

> The French Government considers that the application of national treatment can in no way constrain it to grant official subsidies, guarantees or loans to enterprises other than those of its own choosing, in the absence of a general regime applicable to a whole category of enterprises. It moreover reserves the right to limit the conditions under which companies are allowed to operate in sectors which may receive aid from the State or from public authorities. (OECD, 1978, 61)

The second step is to recognize that an industrial policy designed in part to preserve French-owned firms in certain sectors is likely to involve discrimination against some or all of the foreign-owned firms already in that sector. The point need not be laboured, since it has been made more than once above, for example with regard to the petroleum and computer sectors. Every government in this study engages in practices similar to those noted here, in the sense of closing a sector in part to foreign-owned firms and offering financial incentives or other aid to local firms not available to their foreign-owned competitors. Sometimes this occurs because of the existence of public ownership. What distinguishes the French situation from the others is a higher degree of intervention and state ownership at the sectoral level, hence more opportunity to assert ownership goals, among others, and perhaps also a greater willingness to state its position to international agencies.

Programmes can be defined so as to exclude foreign-owned firms, in part or whole, without actually breaching the principle of national treatment. Support programmes geared to smaller firms have this effect, even if foreign-owned firms are not explicitly excluded, since the latter tend to be larger. In France two programmes are worth noting (Mytelka, 1986, 160). An interministerial committee for the adaptation of industrial structures (French acronym CIASI) was established in 1974 to provide support to firms in financial difficulty. It does not assist firms which are part of an industrial or financial group, that is, subsidiaries of MNEs or larger French firms. An interministerial committee for the development of investment and maintenance of employment (CIDISE) created in 1979 takes the same position, since it supports only independent firms, on the argument that the diversified French or foreign firm already has access to financial resources.

Conclusions on FDI and Industrial Policy

French concerns about FDI focused on a number of issues, both political and economic, at both the macroeconomic and industry levels. Rather than review these again, it is useful to look at the evidence and viewpoints on one of the major issues – the foreign trade associated with MNEs. One must begin by noting that there does not appear to be a study for France (or, indeed, for most other countries included here) comparable in theoretical and empirical terms with those noted for Sweden. Nevertheless, a number of measures can be noted.

The concern about the effectiveness of government export and import policies within the context of MNEs is of long standing and has received some support in the literature. Perhaps the most extensive study was by the Ministry of Industry for the year 1978, reflecting a survey of firms accounting for half of all exports. Exports as a percentage of output were higher for independent French firms than for foreign-owned subsidiaries in France – 23 per cent against 18 per cent in manufacturing. This difference appears to have closed by 1979 (*Journal Officiel*, 1981, 105–6; Michalet and Chevallier, 1985, 117–9). However it was also concluded that the import propensity of the subsidiaries was considerably higher at 27 per cent against 15 per cent. In discussing the Swedish data we have alluded to the statistical and welfare problems associated with interpreting them. Nevertheless they have played a significant role in views on MNEs. Indeed Savary (1984, 29–32, 118–9) goes further. In his sample, foreign-controlled firms export less than those controlled in France, and he expects the positive trade effect of French MNEs to diminish over time.

In these and other published sources, both private and public, as well as in interviews, there was frequent reference to the lack of 'equilibrium' or of 'symmetry' in exports and imports, which in turn raises two major concerns: the balance of payments effects, on the one hand, and the possible loss of capacity to plan industrial investment and employment if the trade balances by sectors cannot be controlled. The view that equilibrium in the balance of payments should be determined by monetary and fiscal policies does not seem attractive to those officials anywhere who are involved in planning at the industry level, and even less so to those who, as in France, have substantial planning instruments at their control. The view that aiming at sectoral trade balances could involve efficiency losses would also be unconvincing for officials engaged in preserving or enhancing a French presence in designated sectors as a matter of public policy.[25] Their objective is to ensure that the presence of foreign MNEs and the growing international production of French MNEs do not together impede the development of a high and integrated value added structure in specific sectors. Thus Messerlin (1987) notes the use of a wide range of protective devices to induce Japanese firms to produce in France and to export, as a way of offsetting growing imports in electronics. He notes also the possibility of welfare losses as a result of inducing inward FDI under conditions of protection.

What is at issue here, in other words, is the objectives and the quality of French industrial planning and, in particular, the integration of decisions on FDI with industrial policy. As noted often above, French officials generally took the position that the approval of inward FDI and subsequent merger and expansion was one aspect of policy for the industry involved: this link was referred to, for example, in discussing the criteria for authorization and the lack of any distinct follow-up with regard to the conditions applied to FDI approvals. How effectively was this integration of FDI policy and industrial policy carried out? We are not attempting to assess the effectiveness of French industrial policies in general, of course, for that is another and much larger issue.

Clarity and consistency are two of the characteristics one would expect from a well-defined and well-operated review process. The French review process left much to be desired in both respects. There is no lack of statements by the authorities on the objectives of such a process, but the actual operation can only be called opaque. The highly internalized nature of the process is indicated by, for example, the very limited information on the specific criteria for approval, the treatment of unacceptable proposals, and the lack of published data on the review process. Among the countries examined so far only Norway has less published information on such matters, and in that country the review process (petroleum excluded) is far less ambitious in nature. In terms of integration with the planning process, one can note also the relative lack of general data on FDI. As is evident from the sources listed above, detailed analytical studies with a substantial data base did not appear until about the mid-1970s and a comprehensive official report of similar quality only in 1980. These dates are a decade or so after the appearance of similar publications in most of the other countries noted above.

It may be that public information was kept low in order to increase the bargaining power of the authorities and a conscious decision made to accept any loss involved in a lack of clarity. However the actual review process as described above, including the nature of the conditions for approval, does not conform well with the idea that the authorities systematically bargained to increase net benefits.

As to continuity, the evidence points to cycles of more and less restriction of FDI, which suggests either frequent changes in industrial policy or in the way this was applied to FDI. The publications noted above point to variability, with a single exception.[26] We noted earlier the swings in policy from less to more restriction and back to less in the 1960s. This is not a good test, in the sense that policy in this area was still relatively new. Partly because of that experience and the work in this area in connection with the Sixth Plan, one would expect a more consistent and well thought out policy after the early 1970s. There are certainly elements of such a policy: for example, successive attempts to modernize sectors of French industry with the assistance of FDI and to reduce reliance on the USA in this respect by turning more to EC partners and later to Japan (Bertin, 1977, 89–90). In terms of policy consistency one can point in either direction, depending on the example used: there was not much consistency in the computer sector, and more in the petroleum sector. In overall terms, however, a major study in the mid-1970s concluded that there was a need to recognize the degree to which French industry had become internationalized and to redefine its role accordingly (Bertin, 1975, 97). In the late 1970s, as we have noted, there was a substantial expansion of both inward and outward FDI, raising concerns once again about the impact on the structure of French industry. The election of a socialist government in 1981 led to nationalization of a number of major industrial groups. It also led to an attempt to redefine industrial policy, hence policy on FDI, to allow more domestic control of the adjustments being brought by multinationalization. We do not know where that might have led in terms of policy on inward and outward FDI, since it gave way quickly to the more immediate problems of coping with macroeconomic management in an international recession. Writing a decade after Bertin, although their analyses differ somewhat, Michalet and Chevallier (1985, 123–4) come to a very similar conclusion: 'The real problem for the 1980s is to devise industrial and economic policies which might be adapted to the new technological and other developments including the multinationalization phenomenon.' In a similar vein, Rainelli (1984) concludes that domestic and foreign MNEs are changing French industry in ways that differ from the aims of industrial policy.

It must be added that almost all of the interviews in the period 1981–3, whether with businessmen, academics or government officials, came to the view that policy on FDI had had and continued to have a large element of pragmatism in it. This case-by-case approach was well suited to the discretionary and opaque nature of the review process. It was not well suited to the implementation of industrial planning, which presumes some consistency by sectors and in terms of the macro effects of micro decisions. One frequent view in the interviews and in some of the published sources was that the system was not really restrictive at all but quite open in practice, in part because of the lack of well-defined policies over time (Michalet and Chevallier, 1985, 123).[27]

There are several reasons for this apparent lack of a well-defined policy or of consistency in it, in a country where relatively more definition and consistency might have been expected. One reason was the attempt to adjust industrial planning to external shocks: the reconstruction needs of the immediate post-war period, adjustment to the EC, the monetary and oil price shocks of the early 1970s, and the great recession of the early 1980s. If industrial planning is simply a response to such exogenous forces, it is difficult to see why the phrase has any meaning: the attraction of the idea is precisely the possibility of influencing the outcome at the national and regional level, in part through policy on MNEs. There were differences in approach between governments over time, of course, on an issue as complex as this and in a political setting as diverse as that of France. Yet civil services have the potential to supply continuity of policy even in an area as contentious as this, as we saw with regard to Australia. Several of the interviewees, both inside and outside government, suggested that departmental differences had at times been a serious impediment to developing consistent policy, particularly in situations where the political arm failed to give leadership on the issue.[28] The very structure of the review procedures would ensure that departmental views played a dominant role: that is, an interdepartmental committee without a secretariat meeting fortnightly, telephone contact in the interim, and a relatively small group of specialists on this topic located in the various departments. Such a process is also likely to make it more difficult than others noted above to focus both the research and operational aspects of a review procedure.

In closing this comment on industrial policy it should be noted that, after the nationalizations and other interventions of the early 1980s, France moved to substantial deregulation of the economy under both socialist and conservative governments. These changes have swept away many instruments associated with central planning at a sectoral level, such as credit controls. They have also reduced the scope for macro intervention, given a policy of maintaining the franc's parity in the European Monetary System. How far all of this will lead to fundamental changes in the attitudes and roles of government and business remains to be seen.

One must also ask whether the obligations involved in EC membership limited policy development. This is often expressed in the literature as a concern that firms would locate elsewhere and export to the French market if the French authorities proved over-demanding in dealing with FDI. There is some truth to this and some limitations, consequently, on an independent strategy. As we saw, the French government was unable to get agreement on a community policy in the mid-1960s, and actual or potential displacement of several investments to other countries in the EC raised concerns at an important moment in policy determination (Mytelka, 1986, 157). Nevertheless it turned out that France had considerable leeway on policy making in this area. Non-tariff barriers, both fiscal and regulatory, have continued to play a significant role in the EC while internal tariffs have ended. France maintained a substantial power to review EC investments right up to 1980. EC investments with ultimate control elsewhere could still be reviewed and, as noted, ways could be found to review even investments by firms controlled in the EC if that was deemed important in particular cases.[29] What probably became of greater importance in the 1980s as a limiting factor on French policy was the *competition* for FDI within the broad limits of the EC controls on fiscal incentives. Such competition between countries in the same region can be an effective constraint on policy in particular cases, as we shall note for other EC countries.

JAPAN

The policies of Japan regarding inward direct investment are the most difficult to characterize adequately in a study of the industrial countries. This is partly because of Japan's distinctive socioeconomic institutions and experience. As in other aspects of her economic development, one often finds that Japan is the exception to the rule. Her ratio of outward to inward stock of direct investment, for example, was larger than that of any country in this study (Table 1.1). For much of the period after the Second World War, and, indeed, before then, Japan followed a highly restrictive approach towards inward FDI, concentrating on the import of technology by other means: at the same time, Japan continued to be a significant investor in the developing countries of south-east Asia in particular. Another reason, however, why it is hard to characterize Japan is that her policies, her investments and her economic status have changed so much. From the late 1960s, and especially after 1980, Japan liberalized her policies on the inward side, and in the 1980s she became an increasingly important direct investor in the developed countries. Over the same period Japan's economy was transformed, with per capita gross domestic product in US dollars rising from about 25 per cent of the US level in 1965 to about 80 per cent in 1987.

These trends are shown in Tables 7.5 and 7.6. There are two quite different sets of data on direct investment, one reporting approvals of investment and the other using balance of payments definitions.[30] They tell a similar story, however. Inward direct investment has been quite small throughout the post-Second World War period. It picked up considerably after the legal changes in 1980, although this was more apparent in approvals than in balance of payments data. Depending on the series used, outward direct investment was from two to four times larger than inward before the 1970s; that margin grew rapidly in the 1970s and especially in the 1980s as outward direct investment soared. Japan's share of inward direct investment flows for OECD countries remained low, at 1.5 per cent and less for the period from the 1960s up to 1988 (Table 3.3). Over the same period her share of outward direct investment flows rose rapidly from 2 per cent in the 1960s to 16 per cent in 1981–88.

This material can be put in perspective by noting that the sales of Japanese firms whose equity was at least 25 per cent owned by foreign interests have been quite small, generally about 5 per cent or less of each sector of manufacturing, including sectors such as chemicals and electrical machinery where FDI is extensive in most other countries in this study. The two exceptions are petroleum and rubber products, where the ratios fell from about 60 per cent and 20 per cent in the mid-1960s to about 40 per cent and 10 per cent at the beginning of the 1980s. In 1980 only 4.7 per cent of overall manufacturing sales were in such foreign-owned enterprises, compared with 2.5 per cent in the mid-1960s. For all industries the percentage was 2.1 per cent in 1980 (Ozawa, 1985, 162–3).

There was more multinationalization on the outward side than the inward by the late 1970s, but Japan's outward FDI as a percentage of domestic activity was still less than that of many other countries in this study. In 1979 the sales of Japan's foreign affiliates as a percentage of the firms' sales in Japan were only 5.9 per cent for manufacturing as a whole, although the figure was 21.7 for food and drink and 41.9 for paper and allied industries. In the services sector the figure was much higher at 32.4, and the primary sector was also highly multinationalized (Dunning and Cantwell, 1987, 293). Judging by data in Table 7.6, the multinationalization of the Japanese economy progressed more rapidly on the outward side than the inward during the 1980s. Yet by 1987 production by Japanese manufacturing firms abroad as a percentage of production in Japan was still only 3.9 per cent, while production by foreign-controlled firms accounted in 1986 for only 1.3 per cent of manufacturing production in Japan (data supplied by Ministry of International Trade and Industry, or MITI). Most of Japanese FDI abroad has been in

Table 7.5 *Direct investment flows (Ministry of Finance), Japan 1950–87*[a] *($US millions)*

Fiscal Year[b]	*Inward*	*Outward*
1950–55[c]	29	} 447
1956–60[c]	62	
1961–65[c]	181	494
1966–70[c]	324	2 628
1951–69[c]	596	2 672
1970	94	904
1971	210	858
1972	169	2 338
1973	-42	3 494
1974	202	2 395
1975	167	3 280
1976	196	3 462
1977	224	2 806
1978	236	4 598
1979	524	4 995
1980	300	4 693
1981	432	8 906
1982	749	7 703
1983	813	8 145
1984	493	10 155
1985	930	12 217
1986	940	22 321
1987	2 214	33 364

Notes:
[a]Inflows are based on balance of payments definitions to 1974, then on acquisitions of stocks for participation in management of companies. Outflows are from balance of payments data until 1969, then on approved and reported cases. No minimum percentage ownership is acknowledged on the inward side, but 25 per cent of equity or more was used on the outward side before 1980 and 10 per cent or more since then. Dunning and Cantwell (1987, 297) indicate 25 per cent has been used on the inward side also.
[b]1 April to 31 March.
[c]Cumulated total for period.

Source: Ministry of Finance, as reported in OECD (1987a, 58 and 60) carried backward and forward with MOF data and Sakamoto (1989, 65).

Table 7.6 *Net direct investment flows and stocks (balance of payments), Japan, 1961–87[a] ($US millions)*

Year or year end	Flows (net)		Stocks[b]	
	Inward	Outward	Inward	Outward
1961	44	93		
1962	45	77		
1963	89	122		
1964	84	57		
1965	47	77		
1966	30	107		
1967	45	123		
1968	76	220		
1969	72	206		
1970	94	355		
1971	210	360		
1972	169	723	1 645	2 574
1973	-42	1 904	1 602	4 546
1974	202	1 878	1 867	6 559
1975	226	1 763	2 084	8 322
1976	113	1 991	2 208	10 313
1977	21	1 645	2 229	11 958
1978	8	2 584	2 841	14 329
1979	239	2 898	3 422	17 227
1980	278	2 385	3 270	19 612
1981	189	4 894	3 915	24 506
1982	439	4 540	3 998	28 969
1983	416	3 612	4 364	32 178
1984	-10	5 695	4 460	37 921
1985	630	6 452	4 745	43 974
1986	235	14 480	6 507	58 071
1987	1 190	19 519	—	—

Notes:
[a]Based on balance of payments definitions. Excluding reinvested earnings.
[b]Largely derived from cumulation of flows.

Source: Bank of Japan, as reported in OECD (1987a, 130); from 1984 on updated from IMF, *Balance of Payments 1988*, and Sakamoto (1989, 65).

services, notably finance and insurance, along with large investments in real property.

Finally it is important to add that technology transfer through licensing, as distinct from inward FDI, has played a significant role in Japan's development. This influence has decreased as Japanese firms have expanded their own research efforts in recent years.

Background

Even a brief account of Japanese policies on direct investment would be incomplete without mention of several related characteristics of Japanese society. The attempt to explain the rapid economic growth of Japan has become a growth sector in its own right. We note only a few aspects which are particularly relevant to what follows.

First, many writers have noted the remarkable extent to which Japanese society seems capable of acquiring knowledge and of reaching a consensus on major aspects of policy at any given time, while also accepting vigorous competition within those parameters (for example, Vogel, 1979, chs 3–4). This applies also in varying degrees at the level of industry as well, whether through industry associations or agreements among the larger firms. This capacity for informed consensus has been ascribed to many factors, which are both cause and effect: for example, a greater degree of cultural homogeneity than elsewhere without, however, this dulling a keen competitive instinct; a close business–government relationship,[31] which involves substantial political stability as well; and company unions and a relatively docile work force, in part predicated on understandings about employment stability in the larger firms. A second characteristic is the power of the bureaucracy and in particular the role of 'administrative guidance' in influencing industrial development.

It is easy to overstate these characteristics. By conventional measures of the role of public spending the influence of government is less than that of most other countries in this study (Table 1.1). The role of government was often to initiate and to help set objectives rather than to detail the means, which would be left to larger firms or to industry associations. Moreover the influence of a commitment to overall growth and employment, and the emphasis on overtaking the main industrial countries, in themselves played critical roles in policy determination. Nevertheless sectoral policies as such, with an emphasis on developing technical capacity and export shares and with various forms of regulatory support from the state, were important in achieving such overall objectives. No less important was the capacity to adjust out of declining sectors in ways which avoided large-scale continuing unemployment and social dissent.

The full significance of these and other characteristics of Japanese society and the relationship to economic growth and welfare are matters of some complexity. Some writers, for example, would emphasize the negative aspects, such as the poor quality of housing. For present purposes a few links to foreign investment policy can be noted. First, Japan's unusually high saving rate has been frequently noted. What has been less remarked is the very early development of institutions such as the Bank of Japan in 1882 and the Industrial Development Bank in the first decade of the twentieth century. One reason for such institutions was a desire to ensure coordinated foreign borrowing so as to limit the contacts which local governments and private firms had with overseas capital markets (Okita and Miki, 1967, 141–9). Second, while technological imports played a substantial role in Japanese development they were channelled through licensing and joint ventures rather than FDI. Coupled with these imports were substantial investment by both firms and governments in mechanisms to search for technology and the training and education needed to utilize it successfully.

Third, in terms of administrative guidance as it affected inward FDI, the influence of the Ministry of International Trade and Industry (MITI) is worth particular attention. MITI played a significant role in the successful attempt to catch up with the leading industrial countries, both in persuading older industries to adjust downwards and newer ones to develop.[32] In the process some formidable barriers to inward FDI and to imports were enforced, both by MITI and by other agencies of government. The 1979 report of the Fair Trade Commission (FTC), for example, notes in detail the guidance given to anti-recession cartels in many industries, cartels which often jointly control imports as well as other aspects of economic activity. As late as 1988 the FTC exempted 276 cartels, only two of which were recession cartels (*The Economist*, 16 September 1989, 80).

It is important to add that some of these aspects of Japanese society have undergone significant change in the 1970s and especially in the 1980s. For example, trade and FDI were substantially liberalized and the role of MITI has correspondingly altered. However the characteristics noted above played a significant role during much of the period studied here, as the detailed review of policies will make clear.

History of Policy[33]

Japan's highly restrictive policies towards inward FDI after the Second World War reflected a long-standing determination to modernize in ways which maintain a large degree of economic and political independence. It was a policy implemented by highly discretionary measures, unlike the more legalistic approaches evident in some of the countries discussed earlier. A process of liberalization began in the late 1960s, however, which by the early 1980s had removed most of the explicit legal and regulatory barriers to inward FDI.

While FDI was prominent in several industries before the Second World War, a long and fairly consistent policy of avoiding foreign-controlled firms kept such FDI to a minimum (see especially Henderson, 1973, 10–17). Reliance on external forces was by way of borrowing on government credit and the import of technology in ways other than through FDI.

In the early years after the Meiji restoration of 1868, when industrial development was actively pursued, the few established foreign manufacturing firms were purchased. Most of the foreign businesses in Japan thereafter were concentrated in trading, shipping and banking, but Japanese control in these areas was also established in the early decades of the century. A number of foreign-controlled manufacturing firms were established in the period between the two world wars, including US-controlled assembly firms which accounted for three-quarters of Japanese automobile production in the mid-1930s. Under pressure from locally owned firms, and also for military and balance of payments reasons, the government passed the Automobile Manufacturing Law of 1936. This eliminated the foreign-controlled firms. The government then gave substantial support to the remaining local firms (Bloomfield, 1978, 227–8; Maxcy 1981; *The Economist*, 29 October 1983, 88). By 1941 foreign capital accounted for only 0.3 per cent of the paid-up capital of all Japanese companies (Lockwood, 1968, 260).

The difficult period of reconstruction immediately after the Second World War passed relatively quickly, thanks in part to the economic policies of the occupying power, policies which strike one as somewhat ironic from the perspective of the late 1980s.[34] The key to Japanese policy on FDI for much of the period after 1950 was the Foreign Exchange and Foreign Trade Control Law of 1949 and the Foreign Investment Law of 1950. Until 1967 this policy favoured licensing or, at most, joint ventures controlled in Japan. An important exception in the period 1956 to 1963 was the 'yen-based companies' which allowed 100 per cent foreign ownership subject to conditions noted below. A series of liberalizations of restrictions on FDI began in the mid-1960s and continued through the 1970s. In 1980 the laws of 1949 and 1950 were changed to reflect the more open set of policies in effect. Substantial liberalization of regulations on outward FDI, and on portfolio investments, also took effect in the 1970s and early 1980s. We examine these policy developments more fully below.

The Foreign Exchange and Foreign Trade Control Law required that all payments in yen or foreign currency between residents and non-residents be approved, including deposits and credits. The Foreign Investment Law required approval of foreign acquisitions of shares and other proprietary interests in domestic firms, beneficial certificates, assets arising from loans, debentures and licences under technological assistance contracts. A Foreign Investment Council under the Ministry of Finance, along with the Ministry related to the industry of the applicant (usually MITI), had formal authority to validate applications. Articles 1 and 2 of the law stated its general purposes as follows:

> Article 1. The purpose of this law is to create a sound basis for foreign investment in Japan, by limiting the induction of foreign investment to that which will contribute to the self-support and sound development of the Japanese economy and to the improvement of the international balance of payments, and by providing for adequate protection for such investments.
>
> Article 2. Foreign investment in Japan shall be permitted to be as free as possible, and the system of validation pursuant to the provisions of this law shall be relaxed and eliminated gradually as the necessity for such measures decreases.

As Henderson (1973, 217–18) notes in quoting these articles, one interpretation is that this law temporarily protected the Japanese balance of payments in a period, up to the mid-1960s, when exchange shortages were general. Approved investments were guaranteed repatriation of principal and profits, regardless of the state of the balance of payments. Quite another interpretation Henderson notes is that many officials had little faith in such 'free market' approaches and saw the law as a method for importing technology selectively and on government terms, and also protecting and guiding domestic industry. Capital liberalization, in this view, would be allowed only in step with the strengthening of domestic firms to the point where they could compete effectively with FDI. Both interpretations receive support from Article 8 of the Foreign Investment Law which notes the standards which the relevant minister must follow in approving contracts. Priority is given to those contracts which quickly improve the international balance of payments, but the standards also emphasize contributions to 'essential industries or public enterprises', contracts which are 'fair', which do not 'adversely' affect the rehabilitation of the Japanese economy, and so on – standards which, as Henderson (p. 228) notes, vary with the 'length of the chancellor's foot'.

More specifically, MITI required that foreign investment projects (a) make a clear contribution to technological development of Japanese industry, (b) make a contribution to exports or a saving on imports, (c) involve no significant competition with Japanese industry, and (d) involve a percentage of equity less than 50 per cent (*The Economist*, 14 August 1965, 626–7). One foreign businessman described the experience of foreign investors prior to 1967 by stating that 'to receive approval ... the product or process of production should be new to the country, may not be "unfairly" competitive with existing locally-owned counterparts, and should fit into the overall plans for the expansion of Japanese industry. The product ... should be exportable or import replacing. ... The most important criterion is that the product should not compete with deeply entrenched local manufacturers'[35] The process of obtaining validation was described as 'cumbersome and time-consuming, characterized by ambiguity, uncertainty, red tape, and protracted delay'.[36] Many potential investors simply gave up trying, which meant that no formal denial was on record.

With one significant exception, the result of such a policy was that few foreign-controlled firms entered Japan in the 1950s and 1960s. The important policy exception was the yen-based companies which were allowed from 1956 to 1963. These were wholly-owned subsidiaries which, unlike the largely Japanese-controlled joint ventures formed under the 1950 law, did not enjoy an unconditional guarantee of repatriation of earnings and principal. According to a government study noted by Komiya (1972, 151), there were 289 companies established under this provision, including some of the largest foreign-controlled firms, compared with about 150 authorized under the Foreign Investment Law. The provision for such yen-based firms was ended in 1963 as Japan was about to accept IMF obligations requiring guaranteed repatriation of earnings. These obligations would mean that the only difference between the yen-based firms and other foreign-owned firms would be in liquidation procedures. MITI was apparently alarmed enough at this prospect to press for the abolition of the provision for yen-based firms (Komiya, 1972, 151–2; Henderson, 1975, 18–19).

Apart from such investments, policy favoured technology licensing. Joint ventures were limited to 49 per cent foreign control in the earlier years, where allowed at all, but 50 per cent was more common later in this period. In addition to the yen-based companies, only 209 joint ventures were approved during 1950-64,[37] of which 4 per cent were actually wholly-owned subsidiaries, 9 per cent were 51 per cent foreign-owned, 17 per cent were 50 per cent foreign-owned and 70 per cent had less than 50 per cent foreign ownership. By contrast, over the same period Japan approved about 3000 foreign technical-assistance contracts, a figure which rose to almost 12 000 by the end of 1972 (Japan Ministry of Finance, 1974, 28).

Japan joined the OECD in 1964, while maintaining many reservations in the OECD's Code of Liberalization of Capital Movements. Signs of changes in foreign investment policy were evident as early as 1963, when the criteria for screening inward FDI changed from admitting only those which made contributions to the Japanese economy to prohibiting those deemed to have negative effects. More specifically, such investment must not '(1) unduly oppress small-size enterprises; (2) seriously disturb industrial order; (3)

seriously impede the domestic development of industrial techniques' (Yoshino, 1975, 246).

Liberalization began more broadly early in 1967 when the Foreign Investment Council was reorganized so that it consisted entirely of business and academic people rather than government officials. The Council was asked to consider the type of liberalization policy which Japan should follow. (Validation of applications, it should be added, was delegated to the Foreign Investment Management Committee, composed mainly of administrative vice-ministers from the ministries which had formal authority (Henderson, 1973, 224).) On the basis of widespread discussion and consensus seeking in government and through the private sector, a series of phased liberalizations were put into effect. What began as a rather modest two phases of liberalization gradually stretched out to five phases and, despite much qualification along the way, a decade of substantial liberalization.

In the first stage, which went into effect in July 1967, new firms with up to 50 per cent foreign ownership were allowed in a limited number of industries without individual screening, provided a number of measures, noted below, were taken to ensure effective Japanese control.[38] Purchases of shares in existing firms were allowed only if foreign ownership did not exceed 20 per cent (or 15 per cent in certain sectors, such as banking) and no single foreign shareholder had over 7 per cent.

A second round of liberalization in the late 1960s was equally modest. Indeed, in the period June 1967 to August 1970, only nine investments were made in the liberalized industries (Yoshino, 1975, 285). The third stage which went into effect in August 1970 was more extensive in the number of products included. The fourth stage, in mid-1971, took the step of indicating the industries which required individual screening, rather than the earlier approach of indicating those which were being liberalized. Up to that point Japan had been the only OECD country using the latter approach; it now joined Spain and Portugal in using the former approach (Yoshino, 1975, 286). In May 1973 a further round took a much larger step. Except for a few industries, 100 per cent foreign ownership of newly established firms was allowed. Industrial screening continued in a few industries: agriculture, forestry, fishing; petroleum refining and sale; leather goods; mining; and retail chains. The last of these was removed from the list in 1975. In 17 further industries the allowance of 100 per cent foreign ownership through new firms was to be phased in over three years. Some of these, such as the computer industry, were of considerable interest to foreign firms. The stringent restrictions on takeovers were also removed, with the important proviso that the consent of the firm being acquired was needed. This proviso was formally ended when the 1980 amendments were put into effect.

Virtually all those who have examined the liberalization note that it was aimed, especially in the early rounds, at areas where Japanese firms were well entrenched. For example, with regard to the first round, it appears that 100 per cent foreign ownership was allowed only in industries where Japanese firms were believed to be as efficient as foreign, joint ventures where this was believed to be almost so, and screening where Japanese firms were considered less efficient technologically (Allen, 1968, as cited by Pearl, 1972, 1, 65). More generally, in the first three rounds, one finds industries being liberalized where the definition of industry was such as to limit newcomers to inefficient technology, where production was concentrated in a few Japanese firms, where government purchases were large and unlikely to be directed to foreign-owned firms, or domestic specialities which were of little interest to foreigners (Pearl, 1972, 1, 68–75). Again Komiya (1972, 153) described the first two rounds of liberalization as amounting to little, while expecting substantial changes from the third.

There were substantial conditions for 'automatic' validation of 50–50 joint ventures, particularly relevant for the early rounds of liberalization where 100 per cent foreign control was limited. Among other things they required that such a joint venture: (a) must not be exceptionally harmful to Japan's interests (which would include the effects on local competition); (b) must not lead to merger or to receiving, by transfer or lease, any business from a pre-existing firm; (c) must involve a Japanese partner in the same business as the new company and possessing one-third or more of the total shares; (d) must involve directors elected by the Japanese firms at least in proportion to the Japanese shareholding; and (e) must not require the consent of a specific officer or of all stockholders in order to conduct business (Henderson, 1973, 245–6; Pearl, 1972, 1, 75–9). These provisions clearly strengthened the hand of the Japanese partners in overall management, as well as averting merger with existing firms.

It was noted above that, except for certain sectors, the stringent restrictions on acquisitions were removed from 1973 to 1976, but the consent of the firm being acquired was necessary. If consent was not forthcoming, acquiring stock with a view to participation in management was given close scrutiny. This scrutiny began where individual foreign investors acquired 10 per cent or more of the stock in an existing firm, or all foreign investors acquired 25 per cent or more. For a restricted group of industries the latter figure was 15 per cent or more. This restricted group involved 19 industries, including various utilities; transportation by rail, marine, air and commercial road transport; broadcasting; and banking and various other credit institutions.[39]

It needs to be emphasized, then, that a number of sectors remained closed or largely so to foreign control, as in other countries. Moreover conditions could be set by the authorities in 'automatically' approving joint ventures or fully owned foreign firms, given the broad wording noted above. Takeovers of Japanese firms remained difficult in view of the general need for consent of the Japanese firm and the continuing reservations of many public officials regarding such takeovers. Nevertheless, by 1978, well over half of the new foreign firms which were being established in Japan were fully owned by foreign capital, in contrast with less than one-third in 1973 (*The Economist*, 2 February 1980, 71).

Reasons for Policies

The reasons for the policies adopted have varied over time. The highly restrictive policies followed up to the mid-1960s have been justified in terms of protection during the period of reconstruction and the development of technically-oriented industries but, as noted earlier, they can be seen also as an extension of a long-standing aversion to foreign control. What needs explaining is the change to a more liberal policy after the mid-1960s, at first very slowly, but with gathering momentum through the 1970s, in the face of these long-standing reservations about inward FDI.

Something of the nature of these reservations can be shown by noting the informal guidelines issued by the Ministry of Finance in September 1967, at the beginning of the liberalization process, to indicate what was expected of foreign firms. They made the following points:[40]

1. Seek coexistence and prosperity with Japanese enterprises through joint ventures on an equal partnership basis.
2. Avoid concentration of investment in specific industries.
3. Avoid suppressing small enterprises when entering into industries characterized by small firms.
4. Cooperate voluntarily with the Japanese effort to maintain proper industrial order.
5. Avoid entering into unduly restrictive arrangements with parent companies abroad, and do not resort to unreasonable restrictions concerning transactions or to unfair competition.
6. Take positive steps towards developing Japanese technology, and do not hamper the efforts of Japanese industries to develop their own technology.
7. Contribute to the improvement of the nation's balance of payments through exports and other means.
8. Appoint Japanese to the board of directors and top management positions and make shares of company stock available to the public.
9. Avoid closures of plants, mass dismissal, and unnecessary confusion in

employment and wage practices by paying due regard to the prevailing Japanese practices.
10. Conform to the government's economic policy.

Such a list reflects in part the Japanese government's desire to continue to maintain close control over the processes of economic change through various forms of 'administrative guidance'. In particular many officials doubted whether foreign-controlled firms would be as responsive as domestic firms to such influences. This was a point of view encountered several times even in interviews in the early 1980s, although none of those who made it opposed the liberalization process. While foreigners often see this as a desire to protect industry from foreign competition, Japanese officials and important elements of the public emphasized the social need for orderly change (see, for example, US Senate, 1975, 212–13).

It is quite clear that pressure from the United States government in particular, and those of a number of other OECD countries in general, played an important role in the liberalization, both in the beginning and especially in the important fifth round.[41] These governments argued that Japan's improving economic status, thanks in part to access to other countries' markets, obliged it to reciprocate by opening its own markets further to trade and investment. In practice, of course, this led to what proved to be difficult and prolonged negotiations with other countries on opening up trade and investment, particularly in automobiles, computers and some other manufactures, yet the main directions of change were set. Some senior politicians and business leaders in larger firms supported the changes, as did the Federation of Economic Organizations (Keidanren) which represents the larger firms and a substantial number of national business associations. A number of senior civil servants also supported change, notably those in the Ministry of Foreign Affairs. Officials in the Ministry of Finance and in MITI were divided, with strong resistance in middle management levels in the latter. Departments such as Agriculture generally opposed the changes, as did many medium and smaller businesses. As Henderson notes (1973, 243) the need to get consensus on a contentious issue slows policy changes, so that the lag between the announcements of 1967 and the more significant third phase of liberalization is not surprising.

The changes, in brief, were not simply a response to external economic and political pressures. They reflected also, particularly as one gets further into the 1970s, the view of some important domestic interests that Japan would benefit economically from a more open economy and that it was now in a position to compete effectively in that economy. On the first point it was noted that it was increasingly difficult to attract advanced technology by licensing alone, that too restrictive policies could redirect investment to other countries nearby, and that some sectors of Japanese industry needed access to foreign technology to modernize. The counter-arguments were, as in the 1950s, that the Japanese industries involved should be rationalized first so that they could withstand the pressure from foreign competition. Strength in the balance of payments for much of the period after the late 1960s encouraged liberalization of outward FDI in particular, but also reduced fears that the payments associated with inward FDI might strain the balance of payments. It might be added that in the 1970s and especially the 1980s a more general decontrol on capital markets and international capital flows accompanied, somewhat slowly, the reduction of controls on FDI.

The Laws of 1979–80: An Overview

In the second half of the 1970s there were further pressures to liberalize, stemming in part from the growth in net exports. The latter was a remarkable phenomenon considering the dependence on oil imports. Early in 1978 the Prime Minister announced that the government was considering changing the foreign exchange control legislation to emphasize the freedom in principle of external transactions, except where approval or licences were explicitly required – an objective emphasized also later that year in economic negotiations with the United States and with the European Community. It had become clear that the general system of licensing, established in 1949–50, of prohibiting external transactions in principle while allowing administrative agencies to relax them at their discretion had become a complex anachronism, inconsistent with liberalization and leading to a great deal of confusion and criticism from foreigners.[42] The next two years were spent in revising the legislation, with the assistance of an Advisory Committee, and in steering it through the Diet. Legislation was finally passed in December 1979 and put into effect in 1980, in the form of a combined Foreign Exchange and Foreign Trade Law, incorporating revisions in practice which had occurred over the years, as well as some new steps (Japan, Ministry of Finance, 1980a, 1980b, 1981).

This included liberalization of foreign exchange controls, although the prior notification requirement remained for capital transactions. With regard to inward direct investment the formal entry restrictions disappeared and, with the sectoral exceptions noted in Table 7.7, majority or 100 per cent foreign control by way of new firms and acquisitions became possible. The mechanisms were maintained, however, not abolished, moving in the terminology of government documents from 'prohibition in principle' to 'freedom in principle', with certain exceptions. For purposes of direct investment, a foreign investor was defined as having 50 per cent foreign ownership of voting shares, directly or indirectly, or 50 per cent or more of the Board

Table 7.7 Japan's policies on foreign direct investment, 1949–80

	Establishing new firm (number of industries)			*Shares in existing firms (percentages)*		
		Foreign Ownership		*Total foreign investment*		
	Not Liberalized	*50%*	*100%*	*Maximum per investor*	*Not restricted*	*Restricted*
Yen-based companies 1956–63			All			
Foreign Exchange and Foreign Trade Control Law 1949						
September 1952	All[1]				8	5
June 1960	All[1]			5	15	10
Liberalization programme						
1. July 1967	Rest	33	17	7	20	15
2. March 1969	Rest	160	44	7	20	15
3. September 1970	Rest	447	77	7	< 25	15
(Auto & related April 71)	Rest	453	77	7	< 25	15
4. August 1971	7[2]	All but 17[3]	228	< 10	< 25	15
5. May 1973	5	17	22	100 with consent and notice, with exceptions[4]		
Follow-up to May 1976	5	Notification		100 with consent and notice, with exceptions[4]		
Foreign Exchange and Foreign Trade Control Law 1980	4	Notification		100 with notice		

Notes:
1. Foreign ownership rarely in excess of 49 per cent, except for yen-based companies, until 1960s.
2. These seven include some very broad categories: oil refining and sales, electronic computer and peripheral equipment, data processing, leather and products, retail chains of more than 11 stores, agriculture–fishery–forestry, and real estate. The 5 shown in later years exclude electronics and data processing but include mining. Retail chains were dropped in 1980. Note that this is *in addition* to several sectors closed to foreign firms, as noted under restricted sectors below.
3. 562 other industries came under the 50 per cent rule.
4. Consent of the company being acquired, and notice to the government if stock of an unlisted firm is planned or over 10 per cent of a listed firm. Prior notice was also needed for purchases of stock of 11 listed firms where foreign ownership was 25 per cent or more.

Sources: Pearl (1972, Part I); Henderson (1973, chs 6–7); American Chamber of Commerce (1979, part II, especially 17–18).

consisting of non-residents. A notification system for FDI was kept in order to monitor specified exceptions to liberalization and also for statistical purposes. Prior notice must be given to the Bank of Japan in the first instance, and to the Ministry of Finance and the ministry for the industry involved, when direct investment occurs by way of new investment or the acquisition of shares beyond certain limits, substantial change in the business purpose of the company where the consent of an investor holding a third or more of the shares is required, and a variety of other situations which may involve control. Transfers of technology were also included in this process, as well as acquisitions of immovable property. Notice is also required to establish an unincorporated branch. In the old law there was no provision for formal approval of such branches, although regulation of external transfers of funds effectively limited such investment.

Most acquisitions were expected to involve no special issues and to be dealt with in two weeks in the case of FDI, and less time in the case of technology transfer. Review of particular cases was to take place within 30 days, but extensions up to another four months could occur where the criteria for review were applicable.

The former Foreign Investment Council was replaced by a Committee on Foreign Exchange and Other Transactions as an advisory group to the Department of Finance. It is made up of 15 people 'of learning and experience' appointed by the minister from outside government and serving on a part-time basis. The Committee deals with broad policy issues while a group composed largely of senior government officials deals with specific applications. However the Committee's opinion is required before recommendation is made to alter or suspend a proposed direct investment. An appeal to the courts is possible only after an objection to a ministerial decision or a request for re-investigation has been given a public hearing.

Acquisition of stock of unlisted companies is subject to prior notice, as are acquisitions of stock of a listed company by foreign-owned firms or investors which raises their holdings of a company above 10 per cent.[43] In addition, under Supplementary Provisions of the Foreign Exchange and Foreign Trade Control Law, prior notice had to be given of further foreign purchases of the stock of a group of 11 listed companies, where foreign ownership of stock was already 25 per cent or more, in order to determine how the national interest might be affected. Most of these companies were in oil refining or electrical goods. Given this list, and since the requirement for consent of an acquired firm was being dropped, it was no longer necessary to have the trigger points on foreign stock ownership to scrutinize hostile stock acquisitions with a view to management participation. We shall have more to say on this below.

It should be noted that a significant liberalization of portfolio capital flows accompanied that on FDI in the late 1970s, both for residents and non-residents.[44] Moreover, in 1991 the Japanese government decided that the second criteria noted below under Article 27 would apply only to national security or related interests as described in the OECD Code of Liberalization of Capital Movements. In addition, apart from such interests and the reservations under that Code, the requirements for prior notification would be replaced by *ex-post facto* reporting procedures.

Inward Direct Investment Under the 1980 Law

The old law had prohibited foreign transactions in very broad terms, leaving authorized exceptions to a wide range of administrative decrees. The new law set out in detail what was covered; transactions were to be unrestricted except as otherwise specified in law. While a number of relatively minor exceptions existed, the essence of the system was to preserve notification of inward direct investment so that judgements could be made following specified criteria. These judgements were of two sorts: those involving restricted sectors or companies, to be dealt with more fully in the next section; and other cases which might fit the criteria specified.

The *criteria* which are used to determine whether a transaction should be accepted, modified or rejected were outlined in several articles of the 1980 law (all references are to Japan, Ministry of Finance, 1980a). Under Article 9 there is a general provision that the relevant minister can suspend any transaction in an emergency ('when a drastic change emerges in the international economic situation'). Under Article 27 the minister could institute an enquiry during the four-month waiting period if it was believed of the foreign investment that:

1. 'It might imperil the national security, disturb the maintenance of public order, or hamper the safety of the general public',
2. 'It might adversely and seriously affect activities of our business enterprises engaging in a line of business similar or related to the one to which the direct domestic investment, etc., is to be made, or the smooth performance of our national economy.'

A third paragraph of Article 27 goes on to say that reciprocity of treatment of Japanese direct investment by the home country is a factor in the treatment of direct investment. This would apply to situations where the home country had not concluded treaties or international agreements with Japan. A fourth paragraph refers to situations where approval of related capital transactions is involved, which could invoke Article 21, 2; that is, emergency consideration of any negative effects on maintaining equilibrium in the balance of payments, the exchange rate or capital market.

It might be noted that the first of the four criteria noted above is consistent with the OECD Code on Liberalization of Capital Movements to which Japan is a signatory. It could cover sectors such as nuclear power, weapons or special vaccines. The third does not appear consistent with the Code. The wording in the second appears unusual, but, as noted in the next section, is generally considered by the Japanese authorities to apply only to the few non-liberalized industries. Only the first two criteria would apply to technology importation and to the 11 designated firms noted earlier.

The changed position on foreign acquisitions is worth noting. The aversion of the Japanese authorities to foreign takeovers of existing firms is evident throughout the previous discussion of policy. New investment is preferred in other countries also, but the lengths to which Japan has gone to avoid such takeovers is noteworthy. In part this reflects opposition to takeovers more generally, short of situations where it is an alternative to bankruptcy. Takeovers can upset the balance of interests involved in a company – for example, traditional practices on security of employment for workers and management alike, or interruption of traditional financial or supplier arrangements. Foreign takeovers had the added problem, in Japanese eyes, of firms less likely to accept administrative guidance from government or cartel-like arrangements in trade associations.[45]

The cautious approach to acquisitions was often justified also by the argument that Japanese firms had a relatively high debt to equity ratio hence stock purchases designed to give management control could be easily effected. This view would have to be reconciled with the fact that a significant portion of the small equity was closely held by banks and other firms associated in some way with the company, who would not surrender such control easily. Moreover recent research has raised some questions about the idea that Japanese firms are more highly leveraged than US firms. Kester (1988, 263–4) concluded that when leverage is measured on a market value basis there is not a significant difference from the United States, other things being equal. Leverage on a book value basis is much higher for Japan, but this is concentrated in mature heavy industries. Whatever the view one takes of this, nothing like the merger mania evident in other countries has occurred in Japan. In 1986, for example, mergers and acquisitions totalled only $3 billion, and many were intra-group rationalizations. In the United States in that year mergers and acquisitions totalled $300 billion (*The Economist*, 21 March 1987, 94).

The fundamental concern raised in recent years in other countries is that a combination of factors – continued private and public aversion to foreign control, weak anti-trust policy and the concentration of share ownership –

makes it very difficult for foreign firms to penetrate the Japanese market through acquisitions. The last of these has attracted particular attention, not least as Japanese FDI has expanded abroad, and despite the fact that much of that expansion has been through new investment or non-hostile takeovers. It has been estimated that the six largest *keiretsu* account for 61 per cent of the capitalization on the Japanese stock market.[46] Such groups of affiliated firms, sometimes centred on banks, involve a variety of collaborative arrangements in terms of cross-shareholdings, financing, purchasing and other arrangements.[47] There are many consequences of such organizational forms, whether in Japan or elsewhere; one is to make hostile takeovers of members of the group all but impossible, whether from domestic or foreign sources.

There are signs of change in the attitude towards hostile takeovers, but they are quite modest and do not extend to takeovers from abroad. Hostile takeovers are not absent in Japan but they are concentrated in the smaller firms and conducted less openly than in countries such as the United States or the United Kingdom. The mergers one sees in the data tend generally to involve the approval of the group of companies associated with the Japanese merger partner, including its bank, trading company and other significant owners. This began to change in the late 1980s, but only slowly.[48] Change was triggered in part by the attempt by a few foreign firms to launch unwanted takeovers, or to acquire enough stock to press for a voice in the affairs of Japanese firms which were not small. The latter was the case with a 26 per cent acquisition by T. Boone Pickens in a Japanese automobile parts maker, one which led to considerable controversy and publicity. A further important development was the successful court challenge by a Japanese investor of the practice of issuing low-priced shares to friendly investors so as to dilute holdings below the one-third needed to challenge management decisions.

It can be argued that all of this is not a barrier to foreign direct investors as such, since the constraints on hostile takeovers of larger firms apply to Japanese investors also. It is clear also that the price of many of these firms would be very high and the set of inter-company relationships difficult to unravel. Nevertheless the characteristics noted above differentiate entry by merger into Japan from some – by no means all – other industrial countries. Moreover entry by merger is the preferred form of entry by many MNEs, far more so in the case of entry to the main host country, the United States, as will be noted below. And Japanese banks have been important players in helping leverage buy-outs abroad in markets more susceptible to hostile takeovers. In any case both US and EC officials have begun to press the Japanese government to change some of the circumstances surrounding investment entry by merger into Japan, including some of the business practices of the *keiretsu* which are believed to be exclusionary. In the case of the United States the pressure has been exerted especially through the talks held under the Structural Impediments Initiative arising from the US Trade Act of 1988 (Bailey *et al.*, 1991c, 44–5).

As noted earlier, by the mid-1970s in all but a few industries it was possible for foreigners to acquire majority or 100 per cent control of a Japanese firm, provided the consent of the board was forthcoming. If this condition was not met, the authorities would review acquisitions by single foreign investors of 10 per cent or more of the stock of an existing firm, or where 25 per cent or more was acquired by all foreign investors. The same was true for 19 designated utility, transport and finance industries, if foreigners acquired 15 per cent or more of the stock. The 15 and 25 per cent limits were ended in 1980, as was the requirement for consent of the acquired firm. The exceptions were four broad sectors already noted, various acts placing some restraints on foreign firms in many of the 19 industries, and 11 designated larger firms. It is unusual to specify such 'key firms' in law. The firms so specified and the degree of foreign ownership beyond which foreign purchases would be scrutinized (in these cases, also the actual percentage of foreign ownership) were as follows: Sanyo Pharmaceutical (25), Katakura Industries (25), Arabian Oil (25), Fuji Electric (26), Hitachi (30), Tokyo Precision Instrument (32), General Oil (49), Showa Oil (50), Mitsubishi Oil (50), Toa Nenryo Kogyo K.K. (50) and Koa Oil (50) (Bank of Japan, 1981, 7-8). The prior notice and time for review in such cases followed the rules for direct investment, and the scrutiny used the first two of the four criteria noted earlier.

It appears there was considerable discussion and different views on how far to go in liberalizing takeovers beyond that of the mid-1970s, and this set of designated firms was a compromise arrangement involving especially a number of oil firms and also electrical product firms with some defence production. Once 25 per cent of a firm's stock was held abroad, the Minister of Finance and the minister for the industry involved were empowered to stipulate a threshold ratio of foreign ownership, beyond which acquisition of the firm's stock by non-residents required a review and could be stopped under the two criteria noted earlier. In the event other firms were not named, partly because of some questions raised by other countries in the OECD and perhaps partly because a lawsuit was initiated by a foreign firm with respect to the effect on it of the designation of one such firm,[49] Katakura Industries, a textile producer (Japan, Ministry of Finance, 1980a, 47–50; Smith, 1983, 10; Japan, MITI, 1983, 23–36). The designated companies list was ended in 1984 (*Business International*, Japan, May 1986, 6).

In terms of the way in which the review process is conducted, it is simply not possible to get from official sources any meaningful data, on approval rates or on conditions attached to approved applications, similar to those for some other countries in this study for which authorization in some form or other is needed. Indeed some Japanese officials insisted in interviews conducted in 1983 that such concepts were no longer relevant after the 1980 law, since, except for the sectors and firms noted, the issue is notification rather than approval. According to government officials, no application in the non-restricted sectors under the new law has been declined. The officials were quite specific, however, in noting that the ministry relevant to the industry would often be approached before an application was made, especially if it was believed there would be a problem, and that applications were unlikely if the problem could not be resolved. Birembaum and Zackula (1988) confirm that, while no application under the 1980 law has been suspended indefinitely or required formal amendment, this may reflect the important role of the informal prenotification process which is essential in non-routine cases (noted in Bailey *et al.*, 1991c), 31–2).

The difficulty in assessing the Japanese review system is evident when one notes that applications were not declined in the period *before* the 1980 liberalization law either. In the three fiscal years 1975 to 1977, for example, there were 1898 applications for inward direct investment, of which 28 were withdrawn on the initiative of the investor, and only one application was refused. Moreover no conditional applications are reported for these years, since 'customary and explanatory conditions attached to authorization are not considered as conditions' (OECD, 1979, 66).[50] It might be argued that no change in approval rates would be evident after the mid-1970s, since Japan had already completed most of the liberalization process by then. It seems apparent, however, that the officials involved preferred to signal that an application was unlikely to succeed, or to avoid outright rejection of applications. For example, they preferred to attach conditions over periods of time not unusual in negotiations in Japan, but which must have appeared to some outsiders as the equivalent of rejection. One must allow here for quite significant differences in business and government cultures. Some Japanese businessmen indicated in interviews, for example, that they were surprised when applications to acquire assets in Canada were actually declined, at least partly because they expected further negotiations. The following excerpt from a talk by a senior official of MITI states rather well what various officials and writers had to say about the pre-1980 system in this regard:[51]

> More specifically, I was asked to respond to the following question: Can you mention a case, as an example, in which entry by a foreign firm into Japan was rejected in the bad old days but would not have been subjected to the same treatment under the present policy?
>
> There are actually two answers to this question: a formal one and less formal one. Despite the language used, however, both of them are honest answers.

The first answer is: 'No, there hasn't been such a case.' No application has been rejected formally, except one, which happened two years ago. This case involved a joint venture between a state-owned transportation company from a communist country and a Japanese firm. The application was rejected for various reasons. Since the investor was from a communist country, the case has no relevance to the scope of today's discussion which is concerned with investment by OECD or IMF member nations. Now, here is my second answer. Most of you in this room know that no application for foreign investment has ever been turned down formally. What happens is that a foreign investor is 'advised' to withdraw the application, or more often, to make amendments in the application regarding the equity share, the rate of royalty, etc. If the foreign investor disagrees, the application then simply becomes 'pending'.

But I suspect that only a few of you may know how difficult it was for me to find a case appropriate to this question. Not because there were many to select from but, rather, most foreign investors found their ways into Japan, one way or another. Some did have to make 'suggested' amendments on their applications. I am not saying that they were happy to do so. The rigorous screening process might have scared potential investors away even before knocking on the door; we have no way of knowing. But the fact remains – most of the foreign investors who really knocked on the door did enter Japan.

The most famous case of a failure to enter Japan is the case involving Yale, the world-famous cylinder door-lock manufacturer. Their application was filed on October 22nd, 1964 and was formally withdrawn on May 25th, 1972, some eight years later. I would like to make several comments regarding this case.

First, the question WHY. It was because the cylinder door-lock industry in Japan was, and still is, one in which small and medium sized companies were dominant. And they did carry significant political clout despite the relatively small number of people engaged in the industry. You know the politics of democracy. They were frightened by the proposed entry by Yale and made their opposition known.

Second, MITI tried its best to pave the way for smooth entry and to take the political steam off. MITI told the industry that Yale would only produce the highest grade products, and that they would not compete head on with Japanese manufacturers who have been producing goods of lesser quality. It was a time-consuming process of persuasion.

Third, long before withdrawing their application formally in 1972, Yale got fed up. I couldn't figure out when that was; most probably no later than 1967. I am not blaming Yale for being short-tempered. They had legitimate reasons to get fed up. But if Yale had persisted for another year or so, they might be operating in Japan today.

Fourth, imports of cylinder door-locks currently account for approximately 4 per cent of the Japanese market. Most of them are of the top class grade and 50 per cent of the imports are supplied by Yale – the rest by other major foreign manufacturers such as Corbin and Schrage: You often find them in places like five-star hotels such as the Imperial, or the Okura, and in high-class residential

> areas. When you go home tonight, you may want to check the door-lock of your flat. If you find it's not made by Yale or other foreign manufacturers, you should write for an increase in your accommodation allowance and look for another house.
>
> Finally, if Yale would like to reconsider entering Japan, here is our message for them: 'The door is open, and there's no lock on it.'

Restricted Sectors

Three types of restricted sectors can be distinguished in Japan. One is a set of 11 key firms, as already noted above. The limitation on foreign ownership in these firms was removed in 1984 as part of a further liberalization of international capital markets. A second set involves the four sectors which were not liberalized in 1980. A third set involves a group of industries in which foreign ownership was limited or prohibited by various laws of long standing.

The four non-liberalized sectors were part of a longer list which was shortened throughout the 1970s. It was not impossible to increase foreign ownership in parts of these four sectors, but close review would be involved. These exceptions fall under the second criterion noted earlier in the 1980 law, that is, investments which might adversely and seriously affect local firms or the performance of the national economy. The Cabinet decision implementing the policy on inward direct investment stated that this and the other criteria were to be applied in a way consistent with the OECD Code on Liberalization of Capital Movements.[52] The Ministry of Finance (1980b, 36) specifically notes that the second criterion would apply only to the few excepted industries, a point emphasized in a number of interviews as well. One must add, however, that, as allowed by the OECD Code, the criterion could be extended to investments which have 'an exceptionally detrimental effect' on the interests of the country (OECD, 1982, 27).

The four broad sectoral exceptions were primary industry related to agriculture, forestry and fisheries, including land other than for residential or direct investment purposes; mining; petroleum; and leather and leather products manufacturing. Under the Treaty of Friendship, Commerce and Navigation signed with the United States in 1953, both countries had reserved the right to limit foreign ownership in land or other natural resources, as well as public utilities, shipbuilding, air and water transport, and banking involving depositing or fiduciary functions (Kim and Peters, 1975, 554). The Japanese government's propensity to protect weaker industries from foreign investment until they have been strengthened by various forms of government support (or, in some cases, significantly reduced) was noted earlier. High adjustment costs in some types of small-scale agriculture is a reason given in many countries for the protection extended to it. Nor is it unusual for agriculture to have an inordinately large effect on the political process, although in Japan the influence of this sector on the politics of the ruling party has been particularly strong. Mining was already protected from foreign investment by a law passed in 1950. Under the current provisions, up to 50 per cent ownership in new mining enterprises has been possible. In these cases and in the petroleum sector the national security provisions of international treaties have also been noted by a country highly sensitive to its dependence on imports of natural resources. Foreign-controlled firms in the petroleum industry had accounted for about 60 per cent of total sales in the early 1960s. This ratio had fallen to 34–8 per cent in the years 1975–80, although the share of profits was substantially larger (Ozawa, 1985, 162–3). The decline in the share of sales reflected government responses to the oil crises of the early 1970s, including government support for domestic private firms and a government petroleum company, direct dealing with Organization of Petroleum-Exporting Countries (OPEC) suppliers and a policy of not permitting over 50 per cent foreign ownership in joint ventures in oil refining (Federal Reserve Bank, 1979–80, 31). In principle, however, the authorizations for oil refineries and oil distribution apply to both residents and non-residents (OECD, 1987b, 47).

The leather industries could also be included under those where adjustment costs are high and some slowing of the process of trade or investment competition is considered desirable. An additional factor, however, was the desire to preserve employment opportunity for a group of Japanese who have suffered from social discrimination.[53]

A third set of restricted sectors are those protected by long-standing laws reflecting exceptions recognized in bilateral treaties and international agreements. In Japan's case this involves limiting to a minority or prohibiting foreign ownership of firms in maritime and air transport between Japanese points, radio and television broadcasting, cable television facilities, telecommunications, atomic energy, armaments and narcotics. The establishment of branches and subsidiaries in banking and the securities business requires authorization and may be subject to reciprocity requirements. Public monopolies in several areas, such as tobacco manufactures and all aspects of the salt industry, prohibit private enterprise, domestic and foreign. These sectors are similar to those evident in other countries, and most come under the national security, public order or similar exceptions allowed in various treaties.

In the area of finance Japan, like other countries, has gone through a process of liberalization in the 1980s in response to her growing financial presence internationally, the pressures of globalization in this sector as financial markets are increasingly integrated, and reciprocity requirements and similar pressures from countries such as the United States, the United Kingdom and West Germany. The liberalization has involved, among other things, reducing the long-established division between banking and securities firms.

In December 1968 there were 16 foreign banks with full services in Japan, eight from the pre-war period. Establishment of banks from industrial countries was discouraged in the period up to 1968. Many such banks entered Japan in the 1970s but their operations were restricted in a number of ways. By 1981 there were 65 foreign banks in Japan, all authorized as foreign exchange banks, but with only 3 per cent of Japan's loan market and 1 per cent of deposits (Smith, 1983, 25; McFarlane, 1977, 33). The Bank Act of 1981 which began the process of liberalization for domestic financial markets also extended that process for foreign banking.[54] It was not until 1985 that such banks and foreign firms in the securities business were given a number of important concessions, as noted in Table 7.8. These concessions were motivated in part by threats to enforce or introduce reciprocity provisions in major markets abroad. These and other steps in the late 1980s left a number of barriers to foreign participation in the Japanese financial markets. However it is well to add that 'reciprocity', as always, is in the eye of the beholder. In allowing foreign banking subsidiaries to act as brokers, for example, Japan went farther than it allowed its own banks to go and farther than the United States had gone pending reform of the Glass-Steagall Act.[55]

Licensing and the Fair Trade Commission

Unlike the other countries in this study, Japan has regarded technological assistance contracts (involving patents, trademarks and know-how licences) as a form of foreign direct investment.[56] Such contracts were included under the Foreign Investment Law, although, if payment or performance was under one year, they were handled under the Foreign Exchange Control Law. Technological assistance contracts are not costless, but they allow access to foreign technology while limiting foreign ownership and management control. Moreover, by reviewing such contracts and by controlling import permits in earlier decades, considerable pressure could be placed on foreign direct investments which are highly dependent on both. In many cases a denial of (or strong conditions attached to) technological assistance contracts or import permits could make such an investment impractical.

While there were many variations, policy in this area can broadly be set in three phases. Until the liberalization of FDI policy which began in the late 1960s, emphasis was put on technology imports as distinct from FDI, but with review of the former. Often, based on administrative guidance, conditions were imposed. The terms under consideration by the foreign and Japanese

Table 7.8 Liberalization of securities markets in Japan

1960	Foreign investment in Japanese securities permitted up to 25 per cent.
1970–73	Japanese allowed to buy foreign securities.
1971	Foreign securities firms can open branches in Tokyo.
1972	Foreign mutual funds cleared for sale in Japan.
1973–7	Japanese banned from investment in foreign securities; ban lifted April 1977.
1979	Non-residents freed to buy yen bonds. Foreign private firms allowed to issue yen bonds in Japan (Samurai).
1980	Foreign Exchange and Foreign Trade law lifts exchange controls. The 25 per cent ceiling on foreign ownership of Japanese stocks lifted.
1981	Foreign firms permitted to have seats on the Tokyo Stock Exchange; none available.
1982	Foreign brokers' branches granted equal status to Japanese brokers that are not members of the stock exchange.
1984	Banks permitted to deal directly in foreign exchange.
1985 April	Six foreign banks admitted to government-bond underwriting syndicate.
1985 June	Nine foreign banks permitted to enter trust banking.
1985 end	Foreign banks permitted to open 50 per cent-owned securities branch; six foreign firms win seats on the Tokyo Stock Exchange.

Source: *The Economist*, 7 December 1985, 91. See also note 55 of this chapter.

firms could be altered or rejected outright if, for example, the charges for it were too high or the financial stability of local competitors was threatened (Hay, 1971, 181). For the period March 1962 to March 1966 the rejection rate was 5 per cent, while another 5 per cent were still under consideration as late as October 1967 (Komiya, 1972, 157). One observer of this process described it as follows:

> Because of their early importance to Japan. ... technological assistance applications have been carefully handled by the 'case-by-case' method of screening, which as noted earlier has been characterized as a 'two-against-one' contract process, whereby (after the parties sign) a second round of redrafting and renegotiation is imposed to accommodate MITI views, often in practice indirectly conveyed through the Japanese licensee. Most liaison lawyers in the field have examples of contracts previously signed by the parties but returned after preliminary talks with MITI, replete with interlineations of (1) reduced duration; (2) reduced royalty rates; (3) deletions of license-back and territorial clauses; and (4) reductions of items covered. This practice is dying out but is still likely to reappear whenever critical technology is involved. (Henderson, 1973, 230–31)

How extensive this use of foreign technology had become is suggested by the estimate that 28 per cent of the investment in machinery and equipment made by technology-importing firms in the manufacturing sector was directly related to the import of technology (Ozawa, 1985, 159). There are differing ways to consider the costs involved. One author notes that Japanese firms signed over 17 600 licensing contracts with foreign firms during 1950–72, 'for which they paid a staggering sum of $3.3 billion' (Yoshino, 1975, 273–4). From another perspective, a study prepared for the US government, in commenting on technology sales, describes the situation as 'a disaster' from the US viewpoint. It notes that the 25 000 contracts it considered involved much of the technology the USA and other countries had to offer and was secured for only $5 billion ('little more than 10 per cent of the annual R&D of the United States'). In adds that this technology developed strong competitors who subsequently entered the US market (US Treasury, 1978, 26).[57]

This first phase was bound to change, for several reasons. Japan's liberalization of trade and investment, for reasons already noted, would also affect technology contracts. Moreover Japanese firms, which were becoming increasingly effective competitors in many lines based on technology contracts, found themselves limited by the accompanying territorial restrictions on exports (see below). Also the foreign firms increasingly insisted on at least an equity stake, and often on majority and management control. This was particularly so in the case of the newer or more advanced technologies, where their bargaining power was greater, and which the increasingly technologically advanced Japanese firms required. In the event, in the mid-1960s the government and industry began a programme to raise indigenous R&D from the relatively low proportion of GNP then involved. R&D expenditures as a percentage of national income were only 0.8 per cent in 1953 and 1.4 per cent in 1960. By 1970 they were 2.0 per cent, and by 1980, 2.4 per cent. The last figure compares with 2.6 per cent and 2.7 per cent for the United States and West Germany (Ozawa, 1985, 172).

A second phase involved liberalization of technological inflows, along with FDI, beginning in 1968 (Henderson, 1973, 231–2). Contracts with compensation of up to $50 000 were approved almost automatically by the Bank of Japan. The relevant ministers were informed of larger contracts and could, within one month, ask the Bank of Japan to withhold validation if they believed 'grave harm' might occur to Japanese industry. Case-by-case screening was continued (a) for cross-licensing between foreign and domestic firms; (b) between parent firms and their subsidiaries in Japan; and (c) for technology related to seven industries involving defence computers and petrochemicals. The third category appears to have been merged with the general screening process in the period up to the mid-1970s.

A third phase began with the general change in the laws on foreign investment and exchange in 1980–81 (Japan, Ministry of Finance 1980a, 29–32; 1981, 11–16). While prior notification, rather than government approval, was the emphasis of the new procedures, the power to review and decline contracts was retained. The distinction between short-term and longer-term contracts was ended. The procedures were similar in many ways to those for inward FDI, involving prior notice to the Minister of Finance and the minister for the industry or industries involved; information about parties involved, the nature, timing, reasons for and conditions attached to the contract; an initial period of 30 days for decision, but which could be extended up to a further four months if the Minister believed an inquiry was needed; consultation with the Committee on Foreign Exchange and Other Transactions in cases of deferral; and the possibility of alteration or rejection of the contract. The criteria on which an inquiry could be required are the first two of the three noted earlier with regard to inward FDI, namely those related to national security, public order or safety, on the one hand, and adverse effects on business enterprises or the national economy, on the other. Generally the approval would be within a few days, but in 12 sectors with contract values over 100 million yen a more careful look at the relevant technology is involved. Many of these sectors involve categories where the criteria just noted clearly apply, while others depend on a fairly broad interpretation or can be interpreted to apply to a wide range of industries.[58]

One measure of Japan's changing technological situation is the ratio of international receipts to payments for royalties and fees. This ratio has risen

Table 7.9 International royalty receipts and payments, Japan, 1970–84

	Receipts	Payments	Receipts as % of payments
	($US millions)		
1970	59	433	13.6
1971	60	488	12.3
1972	74	572	12.9
1973	88	715	12.3
1974	113	718	15.7
1975	161	712	22.6
1976	173	846	20.4
1977	233	1 027	22.7
1978	274	1 241	22.1
1979	342	1 260	27.1
1980	378	1 439	26.3
1981	477	1 688	28.6
1982	563	1 754	32.1
1983	555	1 937	28.7
1984	657	2 176	30.2

Source: 1970–80 from Ozawa (1985, 157) using data from the Science and Technology Agency of Japan; 1981–4 from Dunning and Cantwell (1987, 294), using data from IMF and MITI. The two sets of data are close in magnitude but not identical.

from about 13 per cent in the early 1970s to 26 per cent by the end of the decade and about 30 per cent in the early 1980s (Table 7.9). In new contracts Japan became a net exporter of technology in the early 1980s (Ozawa, 1985, 157). A broader measure relating various types of international technological receipts to payments suggests the ratio rose from 24 per cent in 1972 to 65 per cent in 1982 (Madeuf, 1987, 40).

In addition to the constraints on international licensing just noted, one should note that the Anti-monopoly Act of 1947 prohibited practices which substantially lessened competition or unreasonably restrained trade. This applied to domestic trade as well as internationally.[59] Of particular interest for present purposes is the prohibition of international agreements which could substantially reduce competition or unreasonably restrain trade. Like the domestic practices, such international agreements had to be filed for consideration by the Fair Trade Commission. Prior to the liberalization of direct investment in the late 1960s there were few such violations of the Anti-monopoly Act in the agreements filed with the Commission since screening under the Foreign Investment law modified or removed these. With liberalization, the Commission's role became more important. In 1968 it prepared and published a set of guidelines to firms with respect to such international agreements. These guidelines apply to international licensing agreements on patent rights, utility model rights and know-how. They list in some detail the types of restrictions which may be invalid and also those limitations considered acceptable in enforcing patent rights and other recognized rights (Japan, Fair Trade Commission, 1968).

It should be noted that the Commission's formal procedures are distinct from those considered above on notification and possible review which are undertaken by the government ministries. The Commission can issue a warning ('guidance') calling for changes in the prospective agreement within 60 days of its receipt. Virtually all such warnings are resolved by discussions.[60] The company or the Commission can resort to the courts, but this is rare. It should be noted that the Commission urges consultation prior to notification in difficult cases, involving discussion with the Japanese firm, foreign investor, government officials and even other affected parties such as industry groups or rival manufacturers. The Commission can also review earlier agreements upon receiving complaints from companies (Fair Trade Commission, 1968; *Business International*, May 1986, ILT Japan, 6, 11–12).

The Fair Trade Commission gives some interesting data on the 'guidance' given firms involved with international contracts.[61] In 1979 the number of international contracts registered with it on the inward side amounted to 4618, with 1499 in the case of technology inflows, 912 for import agents, 629 for loans, 71 for joint management, 209 for trademarks and 1298 for other contracts. The number of guidance items issued for all such contracts was 359, or 7.8 per cent of the total of 4618. In the case of technology contracts, the number was 224, or 14.9 per cent of the total of 1499. The nature of the restrictions which were challenged is shown in Table 7.10, which shows larger totals than those given above because more than one business practice was cited in some contracts. Almost one-third of the practices which were challenged were in technology improvement and another large group was in the handling of competitive goods. An example of the former would be where the rights to any improvement by the recipient reverted to the originator. An example of the latter would be a joint venture contract to manufacture construction machinery which unduly restricted the use of competitive goods by local businessmen (Japan, Fair Trade Commission, 1979, 172).

As noted earlier, the guidelines issued by the Commission not only noted the restrictions which would be involved but also those which were allowed by patent and other rights. Territorial restrictions are one of the allowed rights. Thus the guidelines prohibit restrictions on price, quantity and territory

Table 7.10 Guidance in international contracts, Japan, Fair Trade Commission, 1979 (number of contracts)

Nature of restriction	*All contracts*	*Inward technology contracts only*
Technology improvement	156	149
Handling competitive goods	107	44
Source of purchases	6	6
Markets	50	39
Resale price	47	20
Overestimated price	4	3
Quality	16	15
Parallel imports[a]	15	0
Advertising	20	10
Method of sale	8	0
Business activity	2	1
Other	51	33
Total	482	320

Notes:
Only inward contracts are shown. See text for further details. The figures exceed the actual number of contracts since several business practices were registered for some contracts.
[a]Imports other than by sole import distributorship of same goods from same origin.

Source: Fair Trade Commission, *Annual Report*, 1979, 173–6. Unofficial translation for the author.

of the licensee's export sales but allow exceptions if the licensor has registered patent rights in the territory involved, the licensor is selling the particular goods there, or the licensor has given a third party an exclusive right to sell the goods in that territory. Table 7.11 shows the territorial restrictions on the 2076 technology import contracts registered in fiscal year 1981. In 55 per cent of the contracts the licensors' sales of the products involved were limited to Japan, while, at the other extreme, there were no territorial limitations in 24 per cent of the cases. Similar data have been noted for other countries.[62]

All of this must be put in the context of a society where, at least until recently, a more tolerant view has been taken of cartel-like arrangements approved by government than has been the case, for example, in the United States, and in particular a considerable role for industry associations under the guidance of MITI in particular.

Table 7.11 *Territorial restrictions on technology import contracts, Japan, fiscal 1981*

Export sales allowed to	*Percentage of contracts*[a]
No countries	54.5
Korea and Taiwan	2.6
South East Asia	9.4
Europe	0.9
Other countries	8.1
All countries	24.4

Note:
[a]The total number of agreements with duration of one year or more was 2076.

Source: Science Technology Agency, *Annual Report on Introduction of Foreign Technology*, 1981 (unofficial translation).

National Treatment: Industrial Policy as Protection

At the beginning of this section on Japan's policies it was noted that industrial policy has played a special role in Japan. It is true that government intervention is not large if measured by conventional measures, such as government spending as a percentage of national income. It can also be argued that much of the success of Japan in economic terms can be traced to macroeconomic policies geared to economic growth, such as the tax and credit policies favouring saving and investment. Yet the propensity of the Japanese bureaucracy to support a sector at critical moments in its growth path (both 'sunrise' and 'sunset') is well documented, even if it is also true that guidance has sometimes been misdirected. The support given industry in negotiations with Texas Instruments in the mid-1960s is an example of the former. Despite a strong bargaining position, the firm had to settle for 50 per cent ownership rather than the 100 per cent it insisted on, as well as other conditions (Baker and Kondo, 1970, 13; Bailey *et al.*, 1991c, 22). An example of misdirected (and unaccepted) guidance was that intended to keep Honda out of automobiles and consolidate the industry further (Schultze, 1983, 7).

For present purposes what is at issue is industrial policies which discriminate against foreign-owned firms after establishment. This is an aspect of the larger issue of national treatment. It is an issue which is difficult to deal with in Japan since her market and society have so many features which are distinct from those of most (or all) other countries in this study. Foreign firms which encounter these 'internal obstacles' often argue that they are being discriminated against, when, in fact, Japanese firms face or have faced the same problems. What the Japanese firms have also had, however, is a considerable amount of government support in overcoming these obstacles, and what some of the foreign firms have faced are handicaps imposed by government which reduced their competitive power and market share.

Some broad observations can be made by noting the conclusions of two scholars on the nature of Japanese industrial policy, before proceeding to examine some specific examples involving foreign firms. Yamamura (1986) does not deny the factors which made rapid growth possible in Japan apart from direct government intervention, such as the catch-up process reflecting borrowing of technology from more developed countries, and a generally buoyant world economy until the early 1970s. But he goes on to develop a model in which protection of the domestic market and encouragement of oligopolistic firms played a large role in public policy. In addition what gave competitive viability to this process of protection was coordination or guidance on investment by government ministries and strong export promotion policies. In terms of competition with foreign multinationals three policies are particularly noteworthy; the Ministry of Finance made low-interest loans available through the banks to the larger innovating firms; MITI could allocate foreign exchange selectively for imports of raw materials and competing products; and MITI also approved imports of technology (Yamamura, 1986, 172–3). Such guidance was not as influential after the mid-1970s as liberalization spread on the import side and Japanese firms themselves became more multinational. It did not disappear, however, but rather shifted its form, for example to research consortia supported by government.

The point which is relevant here is that the trade and investment protection involved in such policies, along with the particular characteristics of industrial organization in Japan, together proved a formidable barrier to entry by foreign firms. Industrial organization differs significantly from that in most other countries in this study in the degree of networking involved, helped along by a high degree of freedom from anti-trust laws. Okimoto (1987) is one source detailing the organizational links between banks and industrial firms, between such firms and their subcontractors and distributors, the cooperation in industrial associations and various legal cartels, and so on. He notes the difficulties for importers in penetrating these networks, especially in intermediate goods, but also for consumer goods, given the high degree of both horizontal and vertical integration, the on-going collusion in overall market shares and the protective policies of government departments and agencies.[63] Difficulties in importing goods limit direct investment since they are complementary to a degree. The legal obstacles to mergers up to 1980 and the customary opposition to hostile takeovers (both domestic and foreign) limited the most popular form of direct investment. After liberalization, FDI did not expand much as a percentage of Japanese industry because of a variety of other problems in penetrating Japanese industry (Okimoto, 1987, 104–15). Both Yamamura and Okimoto recognize the formidable competitive advantages which some important industrial sectors in Japan have developed. Their point is that direct intervention and the character of industrial organization have played important roles in limiting some types of imports and much direct investment. While liberalization, multinationalization and slower growth have all occurred since the early 1970s, these influences limiting imports and direct investment have not disappeared.

Having said that, the great importance of macroeconomic forces, especially national savings patterns between countries, should be noted. There are various estimates, for example, of the effect on US exports of import barriers in Japan. They range from a low of one or two billion dollars to a high of $10 billion out of a US trade deficit of $40 billion with Japan in 1984 (cited in Okimoto, 1987, 88).

Once one turns to specific examples of alleged non-national treatment, the issues are further clouded by the need to distinguish those obstacles to business faced by all firms from those confronting foreign-owned firms. Distribution, for example, is often cited as an obstacle to FDI in Japan. It is a multilayered and small-scale system on the whole. Three-quarters of retail sales are through small speciality and small family-run stores. This partly reflects a pattern of daily shopping for basic needs, but also shows the influence of a law which virtually allows small retailers a veto in the construction of larger new stores and the expansion of existing ones. Wholesalers, especially trading firms, serve in more ways than linking manufacturers and retailers, supplying, for example, financing and a variety of other services. The ratio of wholesale to retail sales in 1986 was 4:1, compared with 1.8:1 in the United States and West Germany. The costs to consumers as well as to potential new entrants are obviously high in such a system, with criticism directed particularly at tolerance of cartels, resale price maintenance and captive distribution networks (*The Economist*, 31 January 1987, 62–3; 13 August 1988, 55–6; 28 January 1989, 15).

There are obviously problems in such a distribution system for new entry by both foreign and domestically-owned manufacturers. The latter can attempt to establish their own distribution systems, including vertically integrated systems, and thus get around the complexities and costs of the wholesale and retail systems. Foreign manufacturers or foreign-owned firms can attempt the same, or if they are unwilling to undertake the costs of such an investment, can try to serve a non-competitive manufacturer as a distributor. The existence of high costs of distribution or of entry to distribution does not in itself establish discrimination against FDI. It is when government guidance is given to the domestic firms and both government and industry are blocking foreign entry that the question of national treatment arises. The history of the development of the television set industry in Japan is an example of such a policy, involving research support to domestic firms, protection against imports and collusion in distribution mechanisms which raised the costs of foreign entry (Yamamura, 1986, 178–85).

Japan's retail laws are beginning to change in ways which could increase both imports and inward FDI, as well as lower domestic prices. In part the changes reflect pressure from the United States under the Structural Impediments Initiative of its 1988 Trade Act, but the changes also coincide with the interests of some Japanese manufacturers. The Fair Trade Commission, for example, has decided to abolish resale price maintenance in 1992 (*The Economist*, 21 December 1991, 79–80).

Discrimination against imports has been documented in a considerable number of case studies of restrictive interpretations of customs regulations and of product approval procedures, government procurement policies, administrative guidance limiting imports and other measures (for example, Weil and Glick, 1979). Documentation on non-national treatment, that is, discrimination against established foreign-controlled firms, is much harder to cite. An examination of the studies on national treatment and on controls on direct investment published by the OECD from 1978 to 1987 proved unrewarding in the case of Japan: the review (later notification) system for FDI is noted, as are the sectoral limitations, but nothing is shown under exceptions to national treatment with regard to access to financing, governmental procurement or official aids and subsidies.[64] In the late 1970s most government procurement was not by public tender and government agencies were responsible for many services, a system which began to change in the 1980s under a variety of domestic and international pressures. Both foreign-owned firms and some domestically owned firms lost out in some of these sectors where particular suppliers were favoured. This was particularly likely to be the case where the government was trying to build up the Japanese-controlled firms, or some of them. The computer, pharmaceutical and telecommunications industries are some of those where established foreign-controlled firms – and sometimes locally controlled firms – found themselves disadvantaged (American Chamber of Commerce in Japan, 1979, 142–4). One of the better known cases is that of IBM Japan. It succeeded in taking a significant share of the Japanese computer market, estimated at 40 per cent in the early 1980s (Okimoto, 1987, 110). Several interviewees in the government tended to view that as an example of the ability of strong foreign firms to thrive in the Japanese market. It is also true that IBM's share used to be substantially higher than that figure, and that the government made a concerted and successful effort to develop Japanese firms by, among other things, declining to make government purchases from IBM. In 1979, only

2.8 per cent of all computers in central government agencies were of foreign origin (American Chamber of Commerce in Japan, 1979, 143). The government also funded a number of major research projects in this area, which did not extend to foreign-controlled firms. In these respects, one might add, Japanese efforts differed from British and French experience mainly in being more successful in excluding foreign-controlled firms and in establishing early on some strong Japanese firms. More recently the government has encouraged and helped fund research consortia in newer technologies, consortia which rarely include foreign-owned firms. Such consortia also discriminate in some cases against excluded Japanese firms as well.[65]

Some evidence of non-national treatment is also evident in a questionnaire survey for the year 1981–2. In 29 per cent of the responses the firms indicated that government subsidies were available to their line of business or to customers and clients. Among these, 39 per cent indicated that the government assistance was given on a discriminatory basis. Government procurement practices were said to favour Japanese firms in 27 per cent of the cases.[66] Other examples of discriminatory treatment with respect to access to credit and to government procurement are cited in a number of sources.[67]

The informal understandings between business, finance and government which affect such decisions for companies are not absent in some of the other countries in this study. There may be more scope for them in a relatively well-integrated society such as Japan, however, and correspondingly less scope for outsiders.

Outward Direct Investment

Japan has drawn substantial benefit from inward technology flows. In terms of direct investment, however, it is the outward side which has played the major role. While the pace of multinationalization by Japanese firms had been increasing, Japanese FDI was still some distance behind those of other major industrial powers in the mid-1980s. At the end of 1986 Japan's stock of FDI was estimated as $58 billion, which was less than that for the UK, West Germany and Holland and under one-quarter the figure of $260 billion for the United States. A rough estimate suggested that about 4 per cent of the production of Japanese firms was made outside Japan at that time, compared with 20 per cent for West German firms and 17 per cent for United States firms.[68] Another contrast arises in the sectoral distribution of FDI. On the inflow side it has been overwhelmingly manufacturers which have dominated. On the outflow side, however, investments in primary resources, in trade and in the finance–insurance–real estate category have been important, along with manufacturing. In the last case, some labour-intensive industries such as textiles have been particularly prominent in the degree to which they have become multinational in their production.

Outward investment has reflected a variety of forces over time.[69] Some early pressures arose from the drive for exports with a consequent heavy investment in trade-related commercial facilities abroad. Natural resource investments on a large scale reflected the attempt to secure low-cost access to such supplies in a resource-poor country. In the 1970s a surge of overseas investment occurred as Japanese firms located some labour-intensive sectors in Asian developing countries especially. This surge was strongly aided by the search for relatively low labour and land costs, growing pollution problems and a variety of restraints on imports from Japan in the developing countries. Such import restraints have played an important role also in the increase in Japanese direct investment in manufactures in the more developed countries from the mid-1970s onward.[70] In the 1980s many of Japan's financial institutions also made direct investments abroad, partly tracking their industrial and commercial clients as they moved abroad but also to better manage raising capital and selling bonds and equities to Japanese and foreign customers. The appreciation of the yen also speeded outward FDI in some areas, as did liberalization of foreign exchange controls.

The motive for control of outward FDI was, in the first instance, the balance of payments pressures after the Second World War. The 1949 Foreign Exchange Control Law contained a series of restrictions on foreign exchange transactions, including outward FDI. Various regulations by the Cabinet and ministries spelt out the details. Case-by-case screening was in effect for every such new investment and also for additions to the capital of existing subsidiaries abroad. The decisions were made by the Finance Ministry after consultation with other affected ministries, notably MITI. No criteria for approval were made public, but the following have been cited as those informally in effect: FDI must lead to export promotion or development of natural resource imports; it must not damage the competitive position of other Japanese firms in Japan; it must not limit the effectiveness of monetary policy.[71]

A second phase began in the mid-1960s. It was triggered by an improvement after 1967 in the balance of trade and balance of payments and an attempt to keep the yen from appreciating too rapidly, but it reflected also some of the underlying forces noted earlier, such as the shifting of mature labour-intensive industries to developing countries and the obligation to liberalize involved in Japan's membership in the International Monetary Fund (IMF) and OECD. The liberalization began in 1964 with a decision to allow automatic approval by the Bank of Japan for investments under $40 000. This limit was gradually raised to $200 000 in 1969 and to $1 million in 1970, then removed entirely in 1971. The definition of FDI was also widened in

1971 and again in 1972 through lowering the equity ownership required in the foreign subsidiary. However the 1972 changes required that, where the equity ownership was less than 25 per cent, 'automatic approval' was given only if one of several conditions was fulfilled, presumably to verify that the restrictions on portfolio outflows were not circumvented.[72] 'Automatic approval' did not mean that outward FDI was not screened. Some sectors, such as fishing and the pearl nursery industry, banking and securities brokerage operations, were monitored, because of domestic law or policy or international obligations. In addition care was taken to avoid investments which could have 'grave adverse effects on the Japanese economy' (Japan, MITI, 1974, 13–14). Moreover, as noted further below, MITI did not hesitate to urge the larger firms to follow certain procedures, in the developing countries in particular, some of which were very sensitive to Japanese exports and FDI.

Japan not only began to liberalize outward FDI measures in this period but also reduced in various ways the costs of such investments for the firms involved, including favourable tax treatment in some industries for loss reserves set aside in connection with FDI. This was in addition to a generous general system of overseas investment insurance. Government assistance to developing countries was given in ways which assisted Japanese direct investment abroad, including participation in the implementation of investment projects. A range of government or government-related institutions helped with the financing costs of overseas business, including interest-free loans for overseas joint ventures in the case of smaller firms. Substantial public subsidies were provided for technical trainees in such firms and for research and information costs in connection with overseas FDI.[73]

The liberalization process slowed after 1974 with the increase in oil prices and the consequent recurrence of balance of payments pressures. Restrictions were reimposed on overseas investment in real estate, and attempts made to persuade business to postpone some other projects. These restrictions were removed in 1977 and a broad liberalization of many types of investment abroad, direct and otherwise, got under way. In 1978 a system of prior notification on outward FDI replaced the approval process. In 1980 the long-standing legislation on foreign exchange and on FDI was revised to bring it more into line with current practice.

The 1980 law provided for continuation of a procedure of prior notification to the Bank of Japan for outward FDI exceeding 3 million yen, raised to 10 million yen in 1984, as well as for some other forms of outward capital movement. Direct overseas investment was defined as either more than 10 per cent Japanese ownership or as a long-term economic relation with the investor as specified by various criteria. The Minister of Finance was also notified and, along with other relevant ministries where necessary, had 20 days in which to decide whether alterations or suspension of execution of the proposal were called for. The criteria for any such recommendations are:

1. 'It might adversely affect the international money market or derogate from the international reputation of our country';
2. 'It might adversely affect our money or capital market';
3. 'It might adversely affect the business activities of a certain sector of our industries or the smooth performance of our national economy'; or
4. 'It might disturb the faithful performance of treaties or other international agreements concluded by our country, or imperil the international peace and security, or disturb the maintenance of public order.'[74]

The purpose of such prior notification of outward capital flows was primarily to monitor investments in a few industries. Prior notification served also a reporting role with a view to the introduction of emergency controls, sectoral or overall, for the reasons just noted. So far as FDI was concerned, in certain 'exceptional industries' investment of any amount at all required (and might not receive) authorization. These industries included investment by or in the banking or securities industries and in the other finance sectors; investments in the fishing, cultured pearl, leather, textiles, weapons and drug industries; investments in the Republic of South Africa or Namibia; and investment projects of $20 million or more per case. These restrictions reflected a variety of motives. Some, such as banking and securities, were in sectors which were still undergoing liberalization or which could serve as vehicles for avoiding continuing regulations. Some were clearly covered by national law or policy, or by international treaty – South Africa and fisheries, for example. Other exceptions, such as weapons and drugs, were allowed in international conventions such as the OECD code on liberalization of capital. Still others were more clearly intended to maintain protection for industries undergoing competitive adjustments.[75]

Up to mid-1983 no suspensions of formal applications had been made. Interviewees in government ministries in that year confirmed that firms would approach the departments concerned, prior to notification, if they expected a problem, and were unlikely to apply if the problem could not be resolved. If a prior notification revealed a problem, attempts would be made to work this out with the firm rather than recommend that the proposal be suspended.

The growing overseas direct investment by Japan has been accompanied by a number of effects, at home and abroad, which warrant brief comment here. As elsewhere, there has been concern about the effects on domestic industry. Much of this concern has centred on the employment effects on the textile industry, particularly in the many smaller firms. Another major concern has been the hostility to some types of Japanese investment in host countries. In part this reflects the strong bargaining power which Japan as a major purchaser brought to some of the natural resource projects, where the sellers are likely to complain about the Japanese attempts to keep prices low while the buyers bemoan their substantial dependency on foreign suppliers. With regard to manufactures, conflict was inevitable, given the relocation of mature industry to countries which, in many cases, were suspicious of foreign direct investment from any source, but particularly from a former occupying power. That suspicion was enhanced in the early years by the close working relations Japanese direct investors developed with local Chinese interests. These were often an outgrowth of earlier contacts, such as the latter's role as import agents, but the outcome was often that the Japanese also felt the resentment which Chinese interests met in countries such as Indonesia, Malaysia and Thailand (Ozawa, 1979, 222).

One result of these difficulties was a set of guidelines to firms investing abroad, emphasizing corporate behaviour considered acceptable to the Japanese government. These guidelines were drawn up by Japanese business organizations with the direct involvement of MITI. They emphasized, for example, the inclusion of local investors in Japanese firms abroad and the employment of local personnel at all levels. At one point in 1973 MITI was considering enforcing numerical guidelines on such matters on the larger Japanese direct investors in the developing countries, but this idea appears to have given way to individual attempts at moral suasion.[76]

There are significant differences in the pressure for and patterns of investment abroad in a country such as Japan, compared with other direct investors. Resource dependency is more extreme than most, for example. In manufactures, Japan in the 1960s and 1970s was exporting to or through her subsidiaries a more mature technology, frequently imported in earlier years, than was the case for countries such as the United States. This has led to an interesting debate on the effects of Japanese FDI abroad. Kojima (1978) argued that Japanese direct investors tended to be smaller than those from other countries, to be concentrated more in developing countries, and to produce more standardized and low-technology products. Two important consequences were that local partners found it relatively easy to enter joint ventures with Japanese firms and to develop an export orientation. Both these points were set forth in comparison with the model of direct investment developed from US experience, emphasizing larger oligopolistic firms with firm-specific advantages they would prefer to exploit in wholly-owned subsidiaries, a model emphasized in Chapter 3 above. Kojima agreed that, in part at least, the difference reflected different stages of development: Japanese firms with more developed technologies, and those going to industrial countries, might resemble the conventional model. Nevertheless he believed that Japanese firms were more likely to invest abroad in areas of growing comparative disadvantage, and to this extent reflect trade creation, either through import of natural resources or the developing countries' exports of standardized manufactures. US firms, by contrast, were more likely to invest abroad in areas reflecting US comparative advantage, such as more advanced technology-based products for local markets, hence to be trade destroying. This theory, as noted, may be less relevant as Japanese direct investment increasingly reflects a variety of firm-specific advantages (which may involve many variables other than research intensity) and concentrates more on the industrial countries. It has been criticized in other respects also.[77]

Interviews with a small number of firms add one or two points of interest. These are all among the largest manufacturing firms and are also major exporters or direct investors. The size of the sample is so small, however, that not much should be made of the inferences drawn. The two from textiles are from industries which made substantial investments abroad in the 1960s, the three from electrical products did so in the 1970s, and the automobile producer is in an industry which has been making large foreign investments in the 1980s. With one or two qualifications, these firms' preferred ways of going abroad, in declining order, were exports, wholly-owned subsidiaries, joint ventures and licences. The qualifications were with regard to joint ventures. In the case of many developing countries they preferred these to wholly-owned subsidiaries (quite apart from legal requirements) because political risks were high and they wished to have local management and partners who could deal effectively with host-country governments. In a number of industrial countries they also preferred joint ventures because of the technical and other access it gave to partner assets. To this point, the company executives sounded very similar to those interviewed in the United States. However there are two points of difference. Those Japanese executives who had wide experience of joint ventures did not regard them as unstable. Continuity of the joint venture is assured by provisions to rewrite agreements as technology or other factors change, by various contract clauses which constrain the partner from opportunistic behaviour, and by clear understandings that the Japanese firm controls technology, quality, supplier arrangements and so on. Such techniques are used in other countries also, but the attitude to the effectiveness of joint ventures is often less optimistic. The other difference from US multinationals is the greater reluctance to move from exports to direct investment, even when protection or the threat of protection is significant. Protection in the form of 'voluntary export restraints' often raised the per unit profit or led the firms to produce higher value added items. Beyond these incentives to stay with exports, however, labour relations and supplier arrangements in Japan provided large incentives to continue to export rather than invest abroad. Japanese firms in the automobile industry and some others have been trying to transfer these arrangements abroad (see, for example, Clark, 1979; Fuss and Waverman, 1987).

Conclusions

The increased economic strength of Japan and the liberalization of policy on direct investment are reflected in substantial increases in direct investment flows, both inward and outward, in the 1980s. Moves to privatize industry have also created new opportunities for foreign-owned firms, though not without strong differences of opinion within government on the merits of allowing such firms to participate and various qualifications in practice – the privatization of the tobacco marketing monopoly and the deregulation of Japan's telecommunications market in the last half of the 1980s are cases in point (*Business International*, Japan, 1986, 5). In addition attitudes on incentives to investment are changing. It was noted earlier that Japan had made strenuous efforts to develop sectors of newer Japanese-owned industry which would be competitive with foreign firms. While policy on incentives has remained formally non-discriminatory, as it was before, both MITI and many prefectures in the 1980s were offering many forms of support, including incentives, to foreign firms as well as domestic firms which located research or advanced-technology production outside Tokyo and Osaka. Access to a wider range of industries has allowed firms with a foreign equity to secure subsidized loans from the Japan Development Bank, something that would have been more difficult in earlier years (*Business International*, Japan, 1986, 17–18).

It was noted earlier, however, that the foreign-owned sector of manufacturing and of industry remained low, the lowest of any of the countries in this study. Both on trade and on direct investment there also remains a view in many countries that Japan's protective practices have changed less than her laws. This is not always a balanced appraisal of Japanese policies, as was noted earlier in drawing the distinction between policies which are designed to discriminate against foreign firms and those which are impediments to business in a foreign culture. In part, however, the appraisal reflects the slowness of change in Japan, a slowness due at least as much to views on what was appropriate to Japan as to the desire to prevent foreign penetration of industry. Circumstances always differ, of course, but one can note the controlled process of economic adjustment after the Second World War, even well after the occupation period, in contrast with the more rapid dismantling of such controls in several European countries such as West Germany. A more relevant comparison might be the abolition of the monitoring of inward FDI by the United Kingdom in 1978 at the time it removed its existing exchange controls, compared with the retention of a system of prior notification in Japan. Prior notification, implying prior approval, was retained until 1991 when, with exceptions, it was replaced by notification *ex post facto*. Japanese authorities have repeatedly stated that this system is for information purposes, in order to review investments in some defined sectors, and for emergency situations. Despite this stated intent to operate the system liberally, some foreign governments and some foreign investors remain concerned about the potential for restrictiveness, given the discretionary nature of such a reporting system and the broad nature of the criteria, and given also a society where recourse to the courts, while possible, is frowned upon.

More than any other country in this study the Japanese authorities have succeeded in developing a consistent view of policy on foreign direct investment, both inward and outward, and of the links with domestic economic policy, while also showing the ability gradually to change policy as new pressures or opportunities required. What is perhaps equally remarkable is that this system in practice has been based on a large degree of discretion in decision making, with the legal basis set in very broad terms. Public objectives were achieved to a great extent, while Japanese firms had some consistency in practice – all in the face of considerable opposition from foreign firms and governments.

Certain points stand out in considering the four broad bases for policy discussed in Chapter 2. As the review of historical experience suggested, there is no mistaking the long-standing and widely held view of the need to maintain domestic control of industry as an aspect of preserving the independence and distinctiveness of Japan. In the period after the Second World War this found expression also in a drive to achieve economic growth, seen in many Japanese quarters as a way of recovering from the humiliation of defeat and occupation (for example, Yamamura, 1986, 109). In terms of the distribution of political power, Japan has also been unique in this study. One party has governed throughout the post-Second World War period, albeit one in which the factions compete vigorously for power. That political continuity contrasts, nevertheless, with a country such as France, which has also attempted to regulate inward investment and to relate this to domestic policies, in part through discretionary methods.

In terms of explanations of public policy which emphasize group interests, at first sight some winners and losers seem apparent. The major winners might be expected to be the management interests in larger firms and in government, and the political interests, which together controlled development. The possibilities for successful negotiations and consensus between such groups were much enhanced by the fact that they overlapped; senior bureaucrats, for example, often moved to industry or into the political arena. The struggles over the distribution of the proceeds of rapid economic growth which have occurred in other industrial societies have been more muted than elsewhere as a consequence of the consensus on growth and the control of decision making by these groups. This does not mean that other interests have been neglected. The large corporations have exercised their paternalism in ways often beneficial to their employees, including a substantial degree of employment security and other benefits. The ruling party's strong base in agriculture and small business has ensured considerable attention to the adjustment and other needs of such groups. More particularly, however, rapid economic growth has increased opportunities for many who might otherwise have had much to protest about in an industrial society which requires discipline and adherence to tradition in an unusual degree. Nevertheless a case can be made that significant losses were borne by consumers and many smaller firms; that housing, pollution and social infrastructure were often neglected; and that significant adjustment costs were imposed on labour and capital abroad by the emphasis on market penetration (Yamamura, 1986; Baldwin and Krugman, 1988).

One of the points of interest for present purposes is how all of this affects the first possible determinant of policy which was noted in Table 2.1, the increase in a nation's wealth. The focus on growth has already been emphasized. It has also been emphasized that there are many features of Japanese society which impinge on growth which are unusual, at least in degree, in comparison with the other countries in this study. Nevertheless it is worth asking how far the relatively high growth and development process witnessed in Japan for most of the period since the Second World War can be traced to industrial policies, particularly those on foreign investment. What is involved here is a Schumpeterian focus on innovations, in this case the introduction of foreign technology without foreign control, geared to an entrepreneurial class owing something to both the protection and the guidance of the state. In principle such a model of rapid development can be made to work very effectively; indeed some simulation studies suggest that in growth terms the innovators lose out to those capable of successful early imitation (Nelson and Winter, 1982, 130). In addition, at the next stage, market penetration abroad occurs on a large scale, benefiting in part from these borrowed and improved technologies.

There are two questions one should pose here. The first is the counter-hypothesis: how far did Japan's rapid growth reflect macroeconomic policies in the context of rapid world economic growth up to the mid-1970s? Some writers have suggested that Japan's economic growth would have been substantial even without the industrial policies noted earlier, and have also put more emphasis on business decision making than on administrative guidance. Rapid growth is then related to factors such as the high rate of saving, as well as the lower cost of relying on borrowed technology as distinct from creating new knowledge and the cooperative nature of labour–management relations (for example, Schultze, 1983, Krugman, 1984).

What is at issue here is not whether industrial policy can make a difference to economic growth – most writers agree that it can in principle, though perhaps not as much or as consistently as some proponents have suggested. The more relevant point for present purposes is what determines the capacity to carry out effective industrial policies, which achieve rapid growth while constraining the costs of such policies over time. More specifically, in terms of the topic of this study, what were the circumstances which allowed Japan to secure and adopt technology through licensing and Japanese-controlled joint ventures for such a long period and so successfully? The theory of the multinational enterprise outlined in Chapter 3 suggests that such firms would accept the transfer of relatively mature and easily imitated technology in these ways – this is what Japan borrowed in earlier years. Such firms would prefer fully-owned subsidiaries or joint ventures they controlled when technology was difficult to transfer or when rents could be preserved longer by these organizational forms. These circumstances would certainly apply where Japanese producers were beginning to be formidable competitors, a capacity they had already demonstrated in some of the older industries in the 1960s, if not before. The circumstances would also apply where Japanese producers increasingly wished to have access to more advanced technology.

It is interesting to consider the industries where FDI and licensing contracts were concentrated. Table 7.12 shows that 54.5 per cent of the licensing contracts in manufacturing were concentrated in the chemicals, machinery and electrical machinery industries during 1950–80. This percentage had fallen over the years, but was still 51.2 per cent in 1975–80.[78] The proportion of FDI in manufactures fell from 98.9 per cent to 77.0 per cent from 1955–9 to 1975–80. Machinery, chemicals and petroleum were the only sectors in manufacturing to exceed 10 per cent of the total, together accounting for 60.1 per cent over the period 1950–80, and commerce and foreign trade the only non-manufacturing sector to exceed 10 per cent. Licensing is in numbers of contracts, FDI in dollar values. Nevertheless, the concentration of both licensing contracts and FDI in certain sectors where FDI is traditionally concentrated suggests that Japan had a considerable capacity *over the entire period* to use licensing contracts to secure foreign technology.[79]

This capacity to absorb foreign technology so successfully depends on sociocultural and historical factors, some of which were touched on above.[80] Before looking further at some of these reasons, it bears emphasis that many foreign investors would hesitate to build new plants in Japan in the 1970s, given the problems of recruiting personnel, developing relations with suppliers and governments, establishing distribution, and so on. Entry by merger or acquisition would offer many attractions under such circumstances, but was

Table 7.12 Industry distribution of licensing contracts and inward direct investment, Japan, 1950–80

Licensing contracts (numbers in manufacturing)	*1955–59*	*1975–80*	*1950–80*
		(percentages)	
Chemicals	20.2	10.3	13.0
Non-electrical machinery	20.9	22.4	24.0
Electrical machinery	19.0	18.5	17.5
Other manufactures	4.7	13.6	12.4
Foreign direct investment (values, in all industry)		*(percentages)*	
Machinery	23.4	26.6	18.2
Chemicals	33.1	18.0	27.2
Petroleum	16.0	11.9	14.7
Manufacturing	98.9	77.0	73.8
Commerce and foreign trade	0.1	15.5	13.2

Source: Adapted from Ozawa (1985, 180–83), based on data from MITI and Japan's Science and Technology Agency

often not feasible, for reasons noted above. Thus joint ventures would offer many attractions, even if the risks of instability or development of competitors were significant. A survey undertaken in the late 1970s showed that 58 per cent of US firms in Japan preferred the joint venture form, although only 20 per cent of these preferred minority ownership while 34 and 46 per cent preferred equal and majority ownership respectively. Another 40 per cent preferred wholly-owned subsidiaries or branches (American Chamber of Commerce in Japan, 1979, 181).[81]

Having said that, we can note that Japan was strongly placed to spur development through licensing contracts and joint ventures. Unlike many other countries which have attempted this, Japan in the 1950s could offer strong Japanese partners and technical skills, both in the joint venture partner and the industry involved, capable of absorbing, adapting and spreading the imported technologies. In brief Japan at the time was not in the position of many developing countries which have been less successful with such policies. In addition Japan could offer a large domestic market for exploitation of such technologies, including the import substitution which often went with them. The measured return on investment for foreign investors in that market was unusually high, an additional bargaining lever for the Japanese authorities and joint venture partners.[82] But it needs also to be emphasized that Japanese government officials and joint venture partners used their potential bargaining power very skilfully. The consensus seeking on the basic industrial parameters within which competition would proceed was as marked here as in other areas of industrial policy. Japan in the 1980s became a more open society, both on trade and investment, both inward and outward. The scope for administrative guidance in such a society could weaken, even in Japan. Yet the head start given its own industries could be expected to have effects well beyond the control period. One need only consider, for example, that foreign multinationals were long constrained in one of the most effective forms of response to trade or investment entry to their home markets: namely, to engage in both trade and merger entry to the other party's market.

NOTES

1. On several occasions an interviewee's name card bore the school of graduation, a practice not encountered anywhere else among the countries in this study.
2. This conclusion was reached by Savary (1984); Muchielli (1985); and Michalet and Chevallier (1985, 92–100). See also last columns of Tables 1.1 and 1.2.
3. For the history of French policy, see especially Johnstone (1965, chs 2–3); Dickie (1970); Kindleberger (1969, ch. 3); Gillespie (1972, 403–18); Boddewyn (1974); Bertin (1977); and Carlson (1980, chs 4–5).
4. Once authorization was secured, up to 5 million francs per year could be brought in without further authorization provided it was financed by foreign currency and did not increase the degree of foreign ownership. This figure rose to 10 million francs in the 1980s.
5. The definition of new lines of business is spelt out very fully and publicly in Canada, and so broadly that most firms would find this a small barrier. In France much more attention is paid to new product lines by the Industry Ministry.
6. Under French law 66.66 per cent is necessary to have 'an absolute majority' so that action can be taken independently of the minority partner, so long as it or they are treated fairly.
7. The prior declaration is reproduced in Dickie (1970, 117–20). It had not changed much by the late 1970s.
8. Dickie (1970, 72–92) gives a similar list based in part on the experience of particular firms and sectors with the approval process. See also Rainelli (1984, 493); and *Business International*, ILT, France (December 1982, 8–9).
9. US Senate (1975, 197–8), based on Manuali (1967, 47) and Dickie (1970, 42).
10. This was a point made in several interviews with government officials in both France and Japan, and also by officials in a number of French and Japanese MNEs who had faced outright rejections by Canada's FIRA. There clearly is another viewpoint on this, however. Marc E. Leland, Assistant Secretary for International Affairs, US Department of the Treasury, stated before a sub-committee of the US Senate, 'But I think the answer is investing in France has never been the easiest thing in the world, ... you have to get the permission of the French Government to invest in France and often requests languish. This has been true for years ... in this case it is a method to say 'No' ... it just sits and you never know what is going on with it.' (US Senate, 1982, 249).
11. Délégation à l'Aménagement du Territoire et à l'Action Régionale, freely translated as

the Commission on Land-Use Planning and Regional Development. One may note a comment made by an official of one of the regions which echoes views heard in several other countries: 'A la limite, la localisation du centre de décision à Paris ou à l'étranger n'est pas, dans un contexte régional, différemment ressentie'. (DATAR, 1974, 65). This is not far removed from the view of a Canadian federal cabinet minister from one of the maritime provinces who remarked to me that 'The only thing wrong with foreign direct investment is that we don't get enough of it.'

12. This description of departmental attitudes is from Boddewyn (1972, 431–2) but it fits my experience in the interviews. In the mid-1980s the other ministries on the Committee were Interior, Defence, Foreign Trade and Foreign Office (*Business International*, ILT, May 1986, 5).
13. Other international agreements, such as bilateral treaties of establishment and the OECD code on liberalization of capital movements, would also appear to restrain national policies in this regard, but these do not appear to have disturbed France to quite the same extent.
14. See Boddewyn (1974, 46–8), for a discussion of the issues involved and the relevant sections of the Treaty of Rome.
15. In 1988 the French government temporarily blocked, then approved with conditions, the proposed acquisition of a French newspaper by a UK publisher on the grounds that the latter might be acquired by a non-EC publisher (Globe and Mail, 23 February 1988, 23 April 1988).
16. In the case of a new investment one might note that by Mitel in 1981 which was strongly resisted by the industry but approved for regional development reasons and because it was expected to bring jobs, technical development and exports.
17. It should be noted that the proposal would go to the Competition Commission. It is well known, however, that in France and several other EC countries there is more tolerance of market sharing and similar devices provided they are known and acceptable to the authorities and, in France, consistent with plans for that industry. The French authorities appear to be fairly pragmatic on this, sometimes encouraging competition, thus allowing FDI, and sometimes deciding such competition is not desirable or necessary.
18. See, for example, the case of Richier in the *Financial Times*, London, 16 November 1979, and of Locatel in *Wall Street Journal*, 25 February 1980, as well as the next section on restricted sectors.
19. *Journal officiel de la République Française*, 16 January 1990, 650–51.
20. For a fuller development of these policies from the First World War until 1980, see Grayson (1981, ch. 2). See also McArthur and Scott (1969, 353–6).
21. Data above from *Business International*, ILT France, December 1982, 5–7, May 1986, 4.
22. These are in one sense reversals of claims often heard from national firms with regard to their MNE competitors; that is, that parent or subsidiary firms are preferred suppliers or give financing at preferred rates.
23. Mytelka (1986, 157–62) concludes that there is no (simple) correlation between regulatory changes and flows of FDI in the period 1960–80 in the case of both France and Australia.
24. French law, decrees and other instruments on FDI are very detailed. For a fuller description see France, *Journal Officiel*, 'Relations Financières avec l'Etranger, Investissements Directs et Emprunts à l'Etranger' (Paris: Imprimerie des Journaux Officiels) 15 August 1980 and later editions.
25. It should be noted that we are referring to publications and interviews in or preceding the early 1980s, before strategic trade policy gained wider academic respectability. This will be taken up again in Chapter 12.
26. Carlson (1980, 49–50) finds continuity of policy to be one of the major strengths of the French approach, although he also finds problems in the constant supervision associated with it.
27. It may be thought that such views conflict with ours, which is that the French system on the whole was one of the more restrictive with regard to inward investment of the

countries in this study. Our basis for comparison is what other countries have actually attempted in terms of FDI policies of all kinds, not what might be the case with a more fully defined industrial policy in France.

28. As one knowledgeable outsider put it in an interview: 'The result is that industrial plans do not work well because you cannot reconcile departmental differences, and you get political compromises which cannot be sustained economically.' For treatment of some recent cases as well as an historical review, see Bailey *et al.*, 1991b.
29. We shall be making the point later that this is not a peculiarity of French policy. *All* countries in this study, whatever their general position on FDI, can and do find ways to block or review individual investments in exceptional circumstances. Even many of the exceptions agreed by treaty, as noted earlier, are broadly phrased and leave considerable scope for interpretation. For treatment of some recent cases, as well as an historical review, see Bailey *et al.*, 1991b.
30. Data on FDI flows and stocks, always troublesome, are particularly so in the case of Japan. The approvals data far exceed the balance of payments figures. For a comment on this discrepancy and recent efforts to improve the data, see Sakamoto (1989).
31. This phrase should be interpreted to include businessmen, bureaucrats and politicians, since there is significant overlap in career patterns among all three groups in Japan.
32. A thorough statement of the role of MITI can be found in Johnson (1977).
33. There is a brief historical survey in Yoshino (1975) and a more detailed one in Henderson (1975 ch. 1, 6 and 7). Other useful historical sources are Okita and Miki (1967), Kobayashi (1970), Hay (1971), Pearl (1972), Sekiguchi and Matsuba (1975) and Japan, Ministry of Finance (1974). I have also relied on interviews, which largely confirm these and other sources. As it happens, I also conducted a month of interviews in 1967 with Japanese officials and businessmen, during their intensive discussions on the proposed liberalization policy.
34. From 1946 to 1950 financial aid from the United States covered 70 per cent of Japan's imports. Inflation was halted and the yen–dollar exchange rate stabilized by the so-called Dodge Line put into effect by the occupying authorities to encourage economic self-reliance (Okita and Miki, 1967, 157–8).
35. L. Blundeberg of the Bank of America, speaking in May 1964, reproduced in US Government Hearings (1975, 219). Others reached similar conclusions on the role of MITI: for example, Baker and Kondo (1970, 8–9).
36. US Senate (1975, 220).
37. The difference between this estimate and that noted in the previous paragraph is due in part to the different time periods involved,with the latter involving two extra years.
38. The classification of 'industry' which is at the core of the liberalization includes many broad categories. See the notes to Table 7.7. The total number of industries appears to have grown over time.
39. Japan, Ministry of Finance, 1974, 9–10.
40. From Yoshino (1975, 279). The phrase 'maintain proper industrial order' in point four can best be understood as the avoidance of 'excessive' competition.
41. What follows on the history of policy summarizes views expressed in interviews in 1981–3 with officers of MITI, Finance, External Relations and the Bank of Japan, as well as a number of academics and businessmen familiar with the liberalization process. Some of these items were checked again with officers of MITI and Finance in 1989. Pearl (1972, 265–6) concludes that such pressure played the key role in liberalization and suggests that Japanese business and government were unenthusiastic about reform, at least up to the early 1970s. Henderson (1973, 237) and Komiya (1972, 158) also appear to place more emphasis on international standards and pressures than on perceived domestic benefits, at least at the time.
42. See, for example, Japan, Ministry of Finance, 1980b, 2–3.
43. Portfolio acquisitions of listed companies, that is, under 10 per cent, also require notice, but are judged by a more limited set of criteria than those over 10 per cent, which are regarded as direct investment. In the case of such portfolio acquisitions notice need not be given if the acquisition is through a registered securities firm. It should be noted that

a number of foreign investors could each acquire less than 10 per cent and thus win a large part of a firm without any notice, except for the 11 designated companies and the closed sectors.

44. However, foreign borrowing of yen funds remained regulated for a time.
45. Several interviewees associated with US firms in Japan indicated that such associations could raise questions with anti-trust in the United States.
46. Articles by Edith Terry, *Globe and Mail*, 22, 24, 25 September 1990. Hay (1971, 80) notes a study which showed that average holdings of the largest shareholders in listed companies was only 8 to 9 per cent of the listed stock. This does not preclude several owners having effective control if the rest is widespread. See also Pearl (1972, 1, 86) on the concept of 'working stockholders'. A study by the Fair Trade Commission of 193 firms in six bank-led groups which account for one-quarter of all sales in Japan showed the average interlocking shareholding of each *keiretsu* was 22.7 per cent in 1987 and 25.5 per cent in 1981 (*The Economist*, 19 September 1989, 63).
47. The revisions of the anti-monopoly law in 1977 and 1984 meant, among other things, that banks could own only 5 per cent of the shares of a single firm. They can have a larger influence than this through ownership of other firms within their group (*The Economist*, 7 January 1989, 70).
48. For further details on these developments see *The Economist*, 19 July 1989, 68 and 29 July 1989, 64.
49. Other firms were clearly interested in being so designated. Yamato Transport Company, which operates an express cargo delivery system, was denied such 'protective designation' in 1981 after foreign ownership rose from 1.4 per cent to 21.6 per cent of its stock, on the grounds that a takeover would not disrupt public order since the industry is not oligopolistic (*Japan Economic Journal*, 9 July 1981).
50. It appears that until about 1967 information was published on the conditions attached to inward direct investment.
51. From a talk by the Director, International Business Affairs Division, MITI, to the American Chamber of Commerce, Tokyo (Japan, MITI, 1980, 26–8).
52. On Implementation of a Policy on Inward Direct Investment, Cabinet decision, December 1980, unofficial translation.
53. The Burakumin (village dwellers) have traditionally been involved in the meat and leather industries, which other Japanese considered as degrading occupations. There continue to be persistent reports of discrimination against the descendants of such people. Not all are poor, however, since control of meat imports has created substantial rents. See *The Economist*, 18 June 1977, 94; *Globe and Mail*, 10 April 1982, 14; and Sekiguchi and Matsuba (1975, 56).
54. Foreign securities firms had been allowed to establish branches since 1971, but only four had done so by 1982. Another 50 had representative offices in Japan (Malcolm Smith, 1983, 26).
55. The process of financial liberalization is further described in *The Economist*, 20 December 1986, 15–16; 23 April 1988, 78–9.
56. Some others, such as France, required foreign licences to be registered, but did not engage in the review processes noted below.
57. The measures shown here differ from some used earlier because (a) contracts under one year may be included; (b) renewals may be involved; and (c) the items included in technology transfer can vary.
58. Technologies relating to aircraft, weapons, explosives, atomic energy, space development, electronic computers, electronic parts of computers for the next generation, machinery and tools related to laser processing and light communication, innovatory materials (especially involving superconductivity), salt electrolysis by non-mercurial method, off-shore petroleum production, and leather and leather products (Bank of Japan, 1981, 10).
59. There are other important provisions of the law which are not as directly relevant here, such as the considerable modification of anti-monopoly provisions to allow for various types of cartels – depression cartels, rationalization cartels, foreign trade cartels, and

those to prevent small and medium-sized businesses from being overwhelmed by large firms. The anti-monopoly law was revised and tightened up in 1977 and 1984. Among other things, the government was given power to limit one firm's ownership in other. Banks were restricted to 5 per cent ownership of the shares in a single firm, while insurance companies were limited to 10 per cent ownership.

60. In Table 7.10 there are 482 warnings or guidance items. (The interviewee used the term 'warning', while the translator specified guidance.) I was informed that at least one-third of these were resolved before formal notification and up to one-third during investigation by the Commission subsequent to such notification.
61. The term 'contract' can sometimes be read as business practice.
62. The economic implications of such restrictions are discussed for Canada in Safarian (1964; 1966, 117–19, 139–44) and for Australia in Brash (1966, 223–40). For another view of this subject, see Williams (1986).
63. Once again we should note that corporate groupings in financial terms which affect real transactions are not uncommon in other countries: they can be one way to reduce uncertainty in the Williamson (1975) sense. It is their scope and continuity which are believed to distinguish Japan, rather than their mere existence.
64. See OECD (1978 and 1985a especially; also 1982 and 1987b). It should be noted that reporting was not very thorough for some other countries also, especially in the 1978 study.
65. See Yamamura (1986, 194–6) for more on these points. He shows a list of MITI projects in semiconductors and computers, for 1966–80, including the firms involved, as compiled from US International Trade Commission sources. Cross-licensing may allow foreign firms to gain access to the technology in some cases. Gotlieb and Zeman (1980) provide details on the way in which the government developed a domestic computer and communications industry, using support for local firms and restraints on foreign-owned firms, including particularly IBM (for example pp. 165–6).
66. American Chamber of Commerce in Japan (1982). The survey covered 495 members in Japan, with 147 usable replies. The respondents replying that they did not know the answer to the subsidies and procurement questions were 37 per cent and 15 per cent respectively.
67. For example, by the Business and Industry Advisory Committee, OECD (1982) *Statement on National Treatment.*
68. Both sets of estimates are by the Japan External Trade Organization, as reported in *The Economist*, 7 February 1987, 59 and 20 February 1988, 75. The second ratio is based on a quite different measure from that by Ozawa noted at the beginning of this section on Japan.
69. See Ozawa (1979, ch. 1; 1985, 165–9) and Komiya (1988) for an account of the factors influencing expansion abroad. Komiya also notes some differences to FDI from other countries, which may reflect the recency of much Japanese FDI.
70. For example, Messerlin (1987) gives a detailed account of the attempts by French authorities to induce investment and technical transfer in electronics. The European Community has attempted to set a variety of local content requirements in deciding when such direct investments in particular European countries qualify for duty-free entry into others. The Japanese government has appealed such rulings to the GATT (*Globe and Mail,* 8 September 1988, B24).
71. Ozawa (1979, 13) citing Frank and Hirono (eds) (1974, 59). For further details on the liberalization process described below see Japan, MITI (1981), and Sakamoto (1989).
72. The conditions included the dispatch of Japanese executives to the affiliate, provision of manufacturing technology, a supply of raw materials, purchase of manufactures, financial support, conclusion of a sole agency agreement, or establishment of permanent economic relations with the recipient (Japan, MITI, 1981, 13).
73. Details on Japanese government support are available in Ozawa (1979, 33–8); Japan, MITI (1981, 9–11); Robinson (1976, 302–3); and Ishimine (1978).
74. Japan, Ministry of Finance (1980a, 16–17). See also Japan, MITI (1981, 14–15).
75. Leather was discussed earlier. In textiles, interviewees in two major ministries in 1983

stated that approval would not be given to overseas FDI or joint ventures which involved the import of textiles to Japan.

76. The guidelines are reproduced as Appendix H to Robinson (1976) and their application discussed on pp. 308–14. See also Yanagihara (1976, 18).
77. Kojima and Ozawa (1985) review some of these criticisms and offer a clarification of their position.
78. Ozawa (1979, 159, 174–5) suggests that the authorities aimed initially to develop the producer goods industries through technology import contracts. His data show that that concentration continued throughout the next three decades.
79. One should recall that foreign-owned firms' shares of sales in Japan in the late 1970s were generally 5 per cent or less in each manufacturing sector except for petroleum (about 40 per cent) and rubber (about 10 per cent).
80. See Ozawa (1981) for a more extended analysis.
81. A survey by MITI in 1974 concluded that in 85 per cent of joint ventures the Japanese partners dominated the actual decision-making processes. (Reported in *The Economist*, 14 May 1974, 101.)
82. The average return on investment can be measured in various ways and is open to various objections, given valuation and other problems. One measure based on US direct investment abroad in 1966–77 shows the average return highest in Japan at 19.0 per cent, second in Germany at 18.0 per cent, and nine other major hosts with average returns of 13 per cent or less (American Chamber of Commerce in Japan, 1979, 65).

8. Host Countries Lacking Review

BELGIUM

The foreign investment policies of Belgium have been dominated by several factors. One has been the need for a smaller economic power which is highly dependent on foreign trade to adjust to participation in the EC. Another has been an emphasis on rapid industrial growth with an eye particularly to more balanced growth between the Walloon south and Flemish north. The slowdown in the economy more generally in the mid-1970s, and the recession of the early 1980s were accompanied by some divestment. In such circumstances policy has emphasized both restructuring older industries and attracting newer ones. A very open position on foreign direct investment, with generous tax concessions, has been an important aspect of policy throughout the past several decades of economic change.

Experience with Direct Investment

Belgium has had experience both as a home and a host country for MNEs, but has been predominantly a host country since the 1950s. Belgian MNEs were prominent both in the industrial and less developed countries before the Second World War, notably, in the latter group, in what is now Zaire. In the 1970s there was an acceleration of outward flows, particularly to EC countries (Van Den Bulcke, 1985, 249–51, 263). In 1975 employment in Belgian affiliates abroad was equal to 16.5 per cent of domestic manufacturing employment (Dunning and Cantwell, 1987, 18).

The inward stock has been almost twice the size of the outward in the early 1980s, while inflows have been substantially in excess of outflows for many years (Table 8.1). In 1975 the foreign-controlled firms in manufacturing accounted for 33 per cent of employment in manufacturing, and 44 per cent of both sales and exports.[1] In a range of manufacturing industries inward FDI accounted for the major shares of employment – 78 per cent in oil refining, 56 per cent in chemicals, 66 per cent in man-made fibres, 58 per cent in mechanical engineering, 87 per cent in electrical engineering, 55 per cent of motor vehicles and parts, and 60 per cent in rubber and plastics. Moreover foreign banks located in the wholesale sector accounted for 8 per

Table 8.1 *Overall development of direct investment, Belgium–Luxembourg (FB billion)*

	Stocks		*Flows*	
	Inward	*Outward*	*Inward*	*Outward*
1965			7.1	2.0
1966			7.0	0.4
1967			11.5	2.6
1968			12.5	2.6
1969			13.8	0.7
1970			15.9	7.8
1971			21.8	8.8
1972			17.7	6.5
1973			27.5	6.7
1974			41.8	14.5
1975			33.9	5.5
1976			30.6	11.3
1977			40.0	12.7
1978	276.5	155.5	40.8	11.4
1979	306.0	214.3	29.5	32.8
1980	348.5	217.5	42.5	1.8
1981	398.7	219.5	50.2	1.1
1982	462.2	216.0	63.5	-3.5
1983	505.5	234.3	65.0	18.3
1984			21.0	16.0
1985			57.0	14.0
1986			28.0	73.0

Source: Banque Nationale de Belgique for flows, Dunning and Cantwell (1987, 10) for stocks. Flows exclude retained earnings.

cent of employment and one-third of all bank assets, foreign-owned advertising firms accounted for 40 per cent of employment and two-thirds of sales in that sector; and foreign insurance firms accounted for about 40 per cent of the total premiums (Van Den Bulcke, 1985, 253–6).

Among the European countries covered in this study only Ireland bears comparison with such high figures. Belgium is in the position of being one of the smaller countries in the EC but, at least since the Second World War, without the strong nationally based MNEs of countries such as Sweden and Switzerland. She has been in an excellent position to take advantage of the EC. About 100 million people, including the populations of some of the most heavily industrialized parts of Europe, are within a radius of 200 miles of Belgium (*The Economist*, 12 February 1986, 3). Belgium was also faced with a long-standing economic and political problem in the discrepancy in development in her major linguistic regions, specifically a lag in industrialization in the Flemish north. All of this led from about 1960 onwards to a highly open economy with substantial fiscal incentives designed to attract FDI.

The result was a phenomenal overall expansion until about the mid-1970s, but a substantial slowdown thereafter, well before the great recession of the early 1980s.[2] Belgian output and employment grew rapidly in the period to 1973 as her traditional heavy industry took advantage of the EC. Inward FDI played an important role in the Belgian expansion, as witnessed by the fact that the ratio of the flow of inward FDI to gross capital formation was from 5 to 8.5 per cent from 1967 on. This ratio did not exceed 3 per cent for Western European countries (Van Den Bulcke, 1985, 251). US firms played a major role in investment by MNEs, accounting in 1975 for 40 per cent of the latter's industrial employment. Inward FDI was heavily concentrated in newer industries and in the less developed northern part of the country, thus tending to even out regional discrepancies in average income as well as to reduce the overall weight in the economy of the traditional steel and metal-working industries of the southern region. Several studies of the motives for inward FDI highlight similar factors as important – the central geographic location with its access to the EC market, most aspects of labour markets, infrastructure advantages such as excellent transport systems, the fiscal system and incentives, and credit facilities (Van Den Bulcke, 1985, 262).

This period of overall expansion ended in 1973. In the next five years the labour force in industry fell by about one-fifth. Inward FDI, which had risen six-fold in a decade, fell off in the late 1970s. By 1981, Belgium had developed one of the largest public sector deficits in the OECD and a substantial deficit on current account. The issue which needs to be addressed here is the contribution of inward FDI to the problems after 1973, and the performance of such firms more generally, but first we examine policy on inward FDI.

Policy on Inward FDI[3]

In common with most other countries, Belgium has a number of public and privately-operated monopolies in areas such as transportation and communication. Only a few sectors are reserved for resident investors. About the closest one comes to this is a limitation on the acquisition of Belgian-flag vessels when the firm does not have its principal office in Belgium, and a reciprocity requirement for non-EC insurance firms. Restrictions have been in effect in one or two other sectors, such as exchange dealers, at some points in the past. The proposed foreign takeover of a few 'key' firms has been turned away, as noted below.

There have been few controls on inward FDI (OECD, 1982, 20; 1987b, 18). Transfer of direct investment through the open exchange market was automatically approved once an application was made to a designated bank. If the direct investor so preferred, authorization of the exchange control authority could be requested. This authorization, which was rarely refused, allowed capital transfer through the official exchange market when the rate was more favourable than on the free exchange market. The two-tier exchange market was ended early in 1990.

The Ministries of Finance and of Economic Affairs must be notified in advance of any sale to non-residents or to non-resident controlled firms of one-third or more of the ownership of all but the smaller Belgian firms. This is for disclosure reasons rather than in order to seek prior permission. It appears that the first draft of the 1970 economic expansion law provided for the latter, but this was revised when the US government pointed out that it would be inconsistent with the standard treaty between the two countries governing commerce, establishment rights and other matters. Not all countries with such treaties have been as careful to honour them, perhaps because few were as enthusiastic as Belgium about the investments (Boddewyn, 1974, 22 and 26). For example, the Belgian government's response to mandatory restrictions on the export of US capital in 1968 was to offer US investors up to 100 per cent finance. This was done through non-voting equity and guaranteed loans, subject to short-term participation requirements, as noted further below.

In addition the Finance Ministry must approve *public* takeover or exchange bids by non-residents (except for those in an EC country) or by firms in Belgium controlled by non-EC enterprises.[4] This takeover procedure for publicly listed firms has not been used generally to discriminate against such firms, but there have been exceptions. Boddewyn (1974, 73) notes one such case of a 'prestige company' in economic difficulty where the government acquired the firm rather than allow a US firm to do so. Four other cases were noted in interviews with government officials, two involving substantial Belgian firms.

It should be noted that, under its EC obligations, the government could not directly turn down a public takeover bid from investors based in the Community. The Belgian private sector is bound by no such obligation. This can be important in a relatively small business community such as that of the indigenous Belgian firms. The maximum challenge to Belgium's open system and to its business community came with the announcement early in 1988 by Carlo De Benedetti, Chairman of Olivetti, that his French holding company had acquired 18.6 per cent of the stock of Société Générale de Belgique and planned to acquire a further 15 per cent.[5] Société Générale has been closely identified with the industrial revolution in Belgium and with the colonization of the Belgian Congo, now Zaire. A huge conglomerate, it controlled firms accounting, by some estimates, for one-third of Belgian economic activity. It had also had low growth and profits and a management style which appeared unable to turn these around.

Apparently De Benedetti was asked by the Minister of Finance if he was prepared to keep his stake below 25 per cent, the level needed to block major corporate decisions, and replied affirmatively. A major bidding war soon developed, however, with many of the tactics customary in such circumstances. Shares were issued to dilute the acquirer's equity and this was promptly and repeatedly challenged in the courts. White knights were sought in Belgium. One of them, a Flemish conglomerate, insisted that the Société Générale give a greater role both to shareholders and to Flemish-speaking Belgians – and eventually ended up as an ally of De Benedetti. In the event, a group led by France's Banque Indosuez, and involving a major Belgian insurance company, secured control. The De Benedetti interests retained minority positions in shares and on the Board, and major changes in management structure and personnel were undertaken. While the attempt by De Benedetti to secure a controlling interest was turned away, the outcome was that strategic decisions about Société Générale could not be made without the agreement of non-Belgian (especially French) interests. Since Indosuez acquired control a new management team has strengthened the influence of Société Générale's headquarters and attempted to bring more focus to the conglomerate's widespread activities. In 1991 De Benedetti sold his remaining stake to Indosuez, raising the latter's ownership to 60 per cent.

Belgium has assisted industry very substantially with tax concessions and expenditure programmes, so much so that, at times, it has run into considerable criticism and scrutiny from the EC Commission (Boddewyn, 1974, 25). Some milestones include the Economic Expansion Acts of 1959 and 1970, the former at a national level and the latter also emphasizing regional development. The provisions of the latter Act had to be modified in response to objections from a number of EC countries. To meet the problems of the mid-1970s some emphasis was placed in the support programmes on restructuring older industries, but development of more high-technology goods was also encouraged. In the early 1980s two new programmes were added. Small new firms set up in designated areas of high unemployment and involving research or high-technology products were given ten-year tax holidays and other tax concessions. Tax incentives were also given to coordination centres performing services exclusively for other companies in the group (Van Den Bulcke, 1985, 276–7; *Business International*, Belgium, 1987, 14–16). It should be added that, where interest subsidies are large, a condition of state aid has been the issue of convertible bonds to the government, and state agencies may participate in joint ventures. In the latter case the state equity must be taken up by the private firm on a predetermined schedule. Moreover financial support is given on a variety of conditions determined by the Act involved. Depending on Belgium's objectives at any given time, these extend to evaluation of the firm's plans for employment creation, introduction of the products and technology and a variety of other economic, social and financial criteria (OECD, 1979, 64; 1983, 88).

These supports have generally been equally available to resident and non-resident firms. There are a few exceptions. For example, foreign senior management, supervisors and researchers working in Belgium receive a personal income tax deduction of 30 per cent of gross income for from five to eight years. A number of business interviewees, both in Belgium and elsewhere, suggested this was one reason for the decision to locate European headquarters of non-EC firms in Brussels. The coordination centres would clearly be more attractive to MNEs. More generally it has been argued that the more mobile foreign firms were more likely than domestic firms to be influenced by regional policy incentives. A study by Van Den Bulcke suggests that after 1959 the lower-income regions received a considerably larger share of foreign production units (cited in Dunning, 1981, 251).

The Problem of Divestment

The Belgian economy ran into difficulties from the mid-1970s onwards, difficulties added to by the global recession of the early 1980s. The economic slowdown was accompanied by a high degree of political instability, including, for example, five coalition governments in 1979–81 and accentuation of regional and linguistic differences. Government responded in a variety of ways, some of which have already been touched on. In the late 1970s and early 1980s policies were adopted to encourage new high-technology industries. Strong macro policies were adopted in 1981 and later to reduce the growing debt and current account deficit. Some devolution of political and economic power was put in place, including that for industrial policy, except for five problem industries (*The Economist*, 22 February 1980, Survey).

The substantial increases in inward FDI flows in the 1960s and early 1970s were not repeated after 1973. While the stock continued to grow with retained earnings, the flow stabilized at about 30–40 billion Belgian francs in 1973–80 inclusive. In the first half of the 1980s it rose to 50–60 billion francs, except for sharp declines in 1984 and 1986.[6] Clearly the stimulus from rapid expansion was over for the time being. Indeed disinvestment by a considerable number of foreign firms became a major concern from the mid-1970s.

The slowdown in inflows of FDI and the disinvestment by some firms raised questions about the reliance on FDI for growth. These questions centred on two issues: the relative economic performance of subsidiaries in general and the employment changes which went with restructuring of industry in particular.[7] Studies have been made of these issues using samples which distinguish between the uninational Belgian firms, Belgian MNEs and foreign-owned subsidiaries in Belgium, and standardizing for product mix. In terms of productivity, profitability, high-skill employment, competitive position and export intensity the studies point to the strongest performance for foreign-owned subsidiaries (notably those owned by US multinationals), followed by Belgian MNEs and uninational firms. The results for exports occur despite intra-firm restrictions on exports. The foreign-owned subsidiaries were also significantly more import-intensive and moderately less oriented to performing research in Belgium. Accepting that economic welfare is increased by the signs implied here (for example, that welfare is reduced by more imports) it would be difficult to fault the overall performance of the subsidiaries by such studies.

The same conclusion applies to job losses, an issue which was dramatized by the Badger case in the mid-1970s.[8] Overall data show that during 1968–75 net new employment (excluding takeovers) rose by 79 000 in foreign subsidiaries while that in Belgian firms fell by 91 500. In 1975–8 the figures were an increase of 2400 and a decline of 120 000 jobs respectively (Van Den Bulcke and Halsberghe, 1976, 65–6). MNEs did move more quickly in the slowdown. The *number* of closures as a percentage of total number of plants was higher for MNEs than for locally owned firms in the mid-1970s, but this difference declined over the next few years. The smaller job losses experienced with MNE closures reflected greater capital intensity in their plants, a phenomenon which narrowed in relation to Belgian plants as layoffs raised the latter's capital intensity.

The Belgian approach to investment has not been without its critics. Hannequart (1974) has argued that it was too heavily oriented in practice to attracting foreign firms, even to the point where the governmental authority to deal with such firms was more centralized than in the case of domestic firms. While a great deal of development occurred, it was the foreign firms that took most advantage of the available aids. In terms of assistance for new investment or plant expansion in the late 1970s, for example, foreign or foreign-controlled firms took 43 to 53 per cent of the incentives in all but one year (OECD, 1983, 88).[9] Hannequart's point is that policy was not sufficiently oriented to the technical and marketing needs of national industry in establishing or maintaining strong EC positions. As noted earlier, a number of new industrial policies were developed in the late 1970s and early 1980s. These policies included support for restructuring and modernizing traditional (Belgian-owned) industry. They also included diversification to more high-technology sectors with emphasis on applied research and innovation. In the process, new methods of organizing support were developed, such as temporary state participation in equity where state and private joint ventures were involved, and some aid was devolved to regional granting institutions. However it would be difficult to regard this new approach as changing the liberal orientation of Belgian policy towards foreign direct investment or discriminating against such firms. Some of the new policies, such as the coordination centres, would be particularly attractive for MNE service activity.

IRELAND

Policy in Ireland has been designed to serve the needs of a country with a small domestic market, a relatively low per capita income and a long-term problem of unemployment. Until 1958 government policy attempted to keep control of industry in Ireland. Almost all restrictions on foreign ownership of industry were removed over the next decade. Since the 1950s policy has offered generous incentives for new manufacturing industries, and also welcomed particularly those multinational firms with an orientation to exports. A great deal of multinational investment was attracted to Ireland through the 1970s, with some clearly beneficial effects but without resolving some important development issues. Grants for new investment have been made somewhat more selectively in the 1980s, and stronger efforts made to encourage Irish entrepreneurs.

History of Policy: Trade, Investment, Incentives

Policies on trade protection and on protection against foreign ownership of industry began to be reversed in the late 1950s (Table 8.2).[10] When negotiations with the EC failed in 1963, two unilateral tariff cuts of 10 per cent each were undertaken. These were followed by a free trade agreement in manufactures with the United Kingdom, to be implemented from 1965 to 1975. Entry to the EC was secured in 1973, with free trade in almost all manufactures to be completed by 1978. In 1966 Ireland had relatively high protection;

Table 8.2 Trade and investment policy development in Ireland

1932	Control of Manufacturers Acts, intended to keep foreign ownership and board membership in minority positions.
1949–50	Industrial Development Authority established.
1952	Cash grants for investment in designated undeveloped areas, extended to new industrial projects in 1956, and enlarged and consolidated in IDA through the 1960s.
1956	Tax relief at 50 per cent for profits from export increases: raised to 100 per cent in 1958, and profits from export business at Shannon exempted from tax.
1958	Easing of restrictions in Control of Manufacturers Acts: Industrial Development (Encouragement of External Investment) Act.
1964	Repeal of Control of Manufacturers Acts, to take effect fully by 1968.
1965	Anglo-Irish Free Trade Area Agreement in manufactures, to be established over ten years.
1967	Free depreciation introduced, extended in 1971.
1973	Membership of EC, free trade in manufactures to be established over five years.
1978	Decision to replace export profits tax relief with 10 per cent corporation profit tax for manufactures, 1981–2000.
1981	International services programme introduced. National Enterprise Agency (superseded by National Development Corporation in 1986).
1984	White Paper on Industrial Policy supports more selective grant policies emphasizing integrated and skill-intensive projects, as well as more emphasis on indigenous Irish industry.
1986–7	Implementation of various policies to develop internationally competitive indigenous industry, promotion of cooperation of foreign and locally-owned firms through National Linkages Programme, reduction of capital intensity bias of investment incentives.

Source: Largely O'Malley (1980, 88–91) which contains a much more detailed outline of the development of the grant system in particular.

average nominal tariffs in manufactures were 25 per cent, average effective tariffs 79 per cent. A decade later the level of protection had declined by four-fifths (O'Malley, 1980, 7, quoting studies by McAleese). Ireland entered the European Monetary System in 1979.

The policy of trade protection adopted in 1932 was accompanied by legislation restricting foreign ownership and board membership of Irish manufacturing firms to minority positions. At the same time the government established an Industrial Credit Company to help finance new industries. The Control of Manufacturers Acts were eased in 1958, then repealed in 1964, with their phasing out completed in 1968. An Industrial Development Authority (IDA) was established in 1950, designed in part to attract foreign firms. The Industrial Development (Encouragement of External Investment) Act of 1958 also allowed the IDA to go further in encouraging inward direct investment.

Liberalization of trade and ownership laws was accompanied by the development of a generous grant and tax scheme. Non-repayable cash grants were made to firms establishing in designated undeveloped areas in the west (1952), new firms anywhere in the country (1958) and major expansion of existing plants (1959). The distinction between designated and non-designated areas was ended in 1963 for larger grants.

In addition, beginning in 1956, profits on increases in export sales were given 50 per cent tax remission, raised in 1958 to 100 per cent. In 1960 the duration of this relief from corporation income tax was raised from 10 years to 15 years, and could extend for a further five years on a falling scale. In 1978 this was replaced by a 10 per cent corporation profit tax on all manufacturing in the years 1981–2000, although export profits tax relief could continue until 1990 for those qualifying before 1981.

In 1969 the legal maxima on grants were reduced, but a new set of incentives, such as interest subsidies and loan guarantees, was added. A considerable number of other programmes have been instituted, including grants for training workers and managers and for housing workers. Some idea of the range of programmes undertaken by the IDA can be grasped by considering the programme titles, which overlap to some degree (Table 8.3).

It should be noted that Ireland has continued with exchange controls, which means that prior authorization is needed for FDI. Exchange control approval for foreign investment is readily given if the investment is considered to be genuine inward direct investment. Except for certain sectors noted in the next section, investment by established foreign-controlled firms does not require approval. Except for investors from the EC, foreign direct investors would be expected to introduce funds from abroad in order to finance fixed assets. Approval for income remittances is routinely given at the time the investment is approved, and is generally without limit, although the size

Table 8.3 IDA programmes, 1977–80

Grouping	*Titles*
Job creation	New industry Service industry
Enterprise and innovation	Small industry Project identification[a] Joint ventures Product and process development
Job maintenance	Re-equipment and restructuring Rescue

Note:
[a]To identify opportunities for supply from domestic sources, including inputs for industrial construction.

Source: O'Malley (1980, 10).

of royalties and fees on licensing contracts can be questioned. The administrative requirements involved in exchange controls were further eased in 1990.

The liberalization of trade and investment policies which began in the 1950s was undertaken partly with a view to applying for membership in the EC. It was also a response to a series of concerns which received increasing attention in the 1950s, including an influential study released in 1958 by the Department of Finance. While import substitution in a small economy had given an industrial base, it was one-sided and inefficient: in particular, production of capital goods and consumer durable goods could not be efficiently established, and manufactured exports were small. Infrastructure investments in public services, transport and other areas were relatively well developed, but large-scale unemployment and emigration persisted. Trade and investment liberalization, and increased subsidization of industry, were the new strategies (O'Hagan and McStay, 1981, 18–21).

Manufacturing employment had risen from about 9 per cent of total employment in the late 1930s to only 12 per cent in the early 1950s;[11] by 1970 it was 19 per cent, a figure at which it stabilized throughout the 1970s. In absolute terms for these same years employment in manufacturing rose from 100 000 in 1938 to almost 145 000 in the early 1950s and stabilized at about 200 000 in the 1970s (O'Hagan and McStay, 1981, 39, 56). Over the period 1958–73 the traditional industries performed poorly, notably in the case of textiles, clothing, footwear and food. By contrast, newer sectors, relying particularly heavily on foreign ownership, did very well in terms of output and employment – sectors such as chemicals, minerals, metal and engineering, and other manufactures. McAleese (1978) notes that the ratio of exports to gross output was almost static in this period for traditional industries, at 19 per cent, but was 72 per cent for new industry.

Ireland's membership in the EC from 1973 might be expected to increase the opportunities for export-led direct investment as well as import competition in some of the traditional sectors especially. The period was also marked by considerable economic turbulence, including recession in 1974–5 and 1979. Manufacturing output continued to expand rapidly but employment growth stagnated. The traditional sectors generally showed slow increases or even declines in output, and declines in employment.

The official data on stocks and flows of direct investment are rather limited, and non-existent on the outward side. Direct investment inflows (Table 8.4) increased after the first two years of the sixties, then were fairly stable until the early 1970s. It is only after entry into the EC that inward

Table 8.4 Direct investment flows to Ireland, 1960–87

	£Ir	*$US*		*£Ir*	*$US*
	(millions)			*(millions)*	
1960	1	2	1974	22	51
1961	3	7	1975	72	158
1962	16	44	1976	96	173
1963	15	41	1977	78	136
1964	21	58	1978	196	375
1965	16	45	1979	165	337
1966	4	12	1980	139	286
1967	13	35	1981	126	203
1968	15	36	1982	170	242
1969	-13	-30	1983	134	170
1970	13	32	1984	110	121
1971	10	25	1985	154	164
1972	13	31	1986	-32	-43
1973	22	52	1987	60	89
Averages (£ Ir = millions)					
1960–64	11		1975–79	121	
1965–69	7		1980–84	136	
1970–74	16		1985–87	61	

Sources: International Monetary Fund, *Yearbooks* for US dollars, Dunning and Cantwell (1987) for Irish pounds (converted from US$ 1960–69, 1985–7).

direct investment rises sharply. This upward trend was reversed in the early 1980s. Inward flows remained weak in the late 1980s. Ireland's share of the capital expenditures of US-owned subsidiaries in the EC had fallen from a peak of 2.6 per cent in 1981 to 1.4 per cent by 1985 (OECD, *Ireland*, 1985b, 57).

Considering the three major inward direct investors which account for the great majority of inward FDI – the United States, the United Kingdom, and West Germany – some further information can be ascertained (Dunning and Cantwell, 1987, 72–81). In 1981 these countries accounted for 63, 32 and 5 per cent respectively of their combined inward stock. Fully 75 per cent of this stock was in manufacturing, 25 per cent in tertiary industries, 3 per cent in the primary sector.[12] The inward stock of FDI for these three countries, in book value, was 22 per cent of Gross National Product (GNP) at factor cost in 1981. Employment in such foreign affiliates was 38 per cent of all employment in manufacturing in 1978.[13] This figure was as high as 80 per cent in chemicals; 49 per cent in the combined sectors of metals, mechanical engineering and electrical equipment; 38 per cent in textiles; and 32 per cent in other manufactures. Fully 70 per cent of manufacturing exports in 1979 were from such affiliates.

Sectoral Limitations

Ireland has a relatively small set of sectors where foreign direct investment is treated differently from domestic. Certain sectors or investments are closed to direct investment: both flour milling and (effectively) agricultural land in the case of non-EC investors, and air transport. In some other cases various regulatory measures are applied more restrictively to non-residents. Non-EC insurers must make special deposits, are subject to a different rule for localization of assets, and may face reciprocity requirements. Licences allowing foreign banks to establish themselves may involve local share ownership or board membership requirements, a demonstration of net benefit and reciprocity requirements, some of which do not apply to EC members. There are reciprocity or, alternatively, local incorporation requirements for shipping vessels registered in Ireland (OECD, 1987b, 45–6).

There are no limitations on foreign ownership of shares in manufacturing firms, although it should be added that state-owned firms exist in sectors such as steel, nitrogen fertilizers, sugar and some areas of chemicals. Most of the state holdings date from the 1950s. The IDA has a section which encourages joint ventures with local firms, but there is no requirement to engage in a joint venture. The state owns most of the mining rights and has made some leases which involve a state-owned share. In petroleum in the early 1980s exploration contracts provided for a government share in any profits, ranging from 25 per cent in marginal fields up to 50 per cent, with zero being possible in extreme cases (*Business International*, Ireland, 1987, 2, 5).

Taxes and Other Incentives: The Industrial Development Authority

Ireland is at one extreme of the countries in this study. For reasons noted earlier, it embarked on a programme of attracting FDI which has led to a very generous scheme of incentives. The critical components of this policy have been the tax system and a group of government agencies, of which the IDA has been the most important.

As noted above, in the late 1950s a system of 'export sales relief' was introduced which gave 100 per cent tax remission on profits earned on export sales over a base period. Relief was given for 15 years and, on a diminishing scale, a further five years. This relief, which extended to 1980, was not applied to new projects after 1981. Instead all manufacturing profits, whether for export or the domestic market, were to be taxed at a maximum rate of 10 per cent from 1 January 1981 to 31 December 2000, as distinct from the normal rate of 35 per cent on the first Irish £25 000 and 45 per cent thereafter.[14] Because machinery and industrial buildings could be depreciated at 100 per cent in the first year under 'free depreciation' rules, the effective tax rate could be as low as zero in the initial years of a project.

The tax changes noted here were made for various reasons. In joining the EC Ireland had secured agreement that it could continue grant incentives and, indeed, it was the only entire country designated to offer the maximum level of state aids available under Community rules. There was doubt, however, whether the tax incentives were sustainable after Ireland entered the EC in 1973. Indeed the European Commission had limited the extension of export sales relief from 1979 to 1981 and also ruled that such relief was not available to new firms after 1981. Moreover export sales relief was to end in 1990 and had already run out for many firms. Firms which were no longer entitled to export sales relief could utilize the new scheme, and those which were still entitled could switch if this was to their advantage (Forbes, 1979, 352–3). In addition the change removed the discrimination against manufacturing production for the domestic market inherent in the earlier scheme. The discrimination against non-manufacturing production continued although the low rate of tax was extended to data processing and software development in 1984.

In addition to low tax rates, however, one should note a series of expenditure programmes involving capital grants, training costs, grants for hiring unemployed workers, interest subsidies, loan guarantees, R&D grants, technology-acquisition grants, ready-to-occupy factories, rent reduction in industrial parks and industrial housing. Great care was taken in the promotion of these programmes. For example, there were extensive advertising and information services, programmes were designed to fit different needs, many programmes were centralized in one state agency and advisory services were also provided after establishment.

These types of services can be found among many of the other countries in this study, but the degree to which they existed in Ireland, not to mention the enthusiasm and expertise with which they have been promoted, is exceptional.[15] At least three studies, including one by the Economic Commission for Europe, concluded in the early 1970s that the group of incentives for export industries was the most attractive in Europe or the OECD countries. De Meirleir (1976) concluded that Ireland's incentives were the most attractive of those of EC countries for small labour-intensive plants, second or third for large labour-intensive plants and small capital-intensive plants (Northern Ireland or Italy ranking ahead) and average for large capital-intensive plants (studies cited in O'Malley, 1980, 13).

The concentration of much of the aid programme in the IDA is worth particular attention. An autonomous state agency reporting to the Department of Industry and Energy, the IDA was originally intended to be a promotional agency, but was merged with the existing grant-giving agency in 1969. The range of functions it developed is evident from Table 8.3 above. The largest budget expenditure has been for non-repayable capital grants of up to 60 per cent of fixed capital costs in the western designated areas and 45 per cent elsewhere. The subsidization of rent, leasing and interest costs has been the next largest cost in terms of budgetary expenditures. IDA works closely with another state agency, the Industrial Training Authority, which has a number of innovative programmes providing grants of up to 100 per cent of training costs for personnel at all levels.

In procedural terms any grant application up to Irish £2.5 million can be dealt with by IDA on its own authority. Requests for larger grants go to other government departments and can go up to the Cabinet. The latter can reject a proposal but, most often, if it comments, it does so by way of questions on the proposal. The IDA then carries out all of the negotiation with the firm on the size of the grant and other matters. Liaison with the Department of Industry is maintained through the Assistant Secretary of the Department of Industry and Energy, who is on the IDA Board and also on its executive committee. Approval within two weeks is likely if the project is small and IDA criteria are satisfied, but grants over Irish £2.5 million may require up to three months for approval. The IDA does not hesitate to discourage or reject applications which do not appear to be viable commercially, which may prove unacceptable for environmental reasons, or do not tie in well in terms of its criteria. However it is likely to try to persuade a firm to adjust a project rather than simply to turn it down.

Both the payment of grant and the level of payment are discretionary. The question then concerns how the IDA determines the best return on the public funds it allocates. A detailed statement of the way such decisions have been made is available from an official of the IDA (McKeon, 1980) as summarized below. In essence the primary objective is job creation. IDA staff negotiated with the investor in order to minimize 'grant cost per job' while securing the investment desired.

1. All projects are evaluated for *commercial viability*; that is, ability to generate profits necessary for reinvestment and for shareholders without further recourse to state aid. This in turn involves examining the production, marketing, finance and management capabilities of the firm. The basic guideline is the grant cost per job, but grant levels can increase also with the level of value added, skill content of jobs, speed of build-up, long-term growth potential, expansion of desirable sectors, whether R&D or marketing functions are in Ireland, use of local natural resources, and spin-offs for existing firms.
2. The next step in the evaluation is to compare the *fiscal threshold* with the proposed level of aid. The government will receive cash flows from the project in terms of extra tax income and social welfare contributions, as well as some reduction in payments for unemployment. This measures only direct labour employed on the project, and is based on studies of how labour is recruited into firms receiving grants. These benefits are calculated over 15 years and discounted at 10 per cent per annum. This fiscal threshold is then compared with the proposed financial aid measured by the present value of the various grants, and also of any equity and infrastructure investment by the government. The project is accepted if it is commercially viable and the grant cost per job is less than the fiscal threshold. In practice this includes over 95 per cent of the projects which are presented.
3. There is a *complete economic evaluation* for larger projects and for those where the required grant level is close to the fiscal threshold. This involves estimating net domestic value added for each project and comparing it with the costs incurred by the state on its behalf, appropriately discounted. An important part of the exercise is to ascertain what alternative uses (if any) of the labour, capital and foreign exchange are forgone in going ahead with this project. Some evaluations will not go beyond the first of these since it is considered to be the largest source of value added.

Such cost–benefit analyses are usually used to select from among different projects. The IDA normally has the task of generating *more* projects, and also of ensuring that the tests are understandable and capable of being completed in the negotiating periods involved. Estimates by the IDA suggest that the average grant per job has been kept well below the fiscal threshold, as well as (necessarily) the legal limits. In 1979 the grant approved per job was Irish £5500, the legal limits were Irish £8700 and Irish £6500 for designated and non-designated areas, and the fiscal threshold was Irish £14 600. The average pay-back period to the state was estimated at three years if based on labour directly employed, but less than two and a half if indirect and other effects are taken into account (McKeon, 1980, 18 and 20).

Several questions have been raised about the incentive policies noted here. A number of writers have argued that the granting system combined with forgone tax revenue involves a significant reduction in the cost of capital. This would tend to reduce the rate of employment creation in some sectors where input ratios for factors of production are not fixed – and more so, given any increases in labour costs.[16] This is quite apart from the need to finance the grants and forgone tax revenue through higher taxes on other businesses and individuals, with effects there in terms of lost employment or reduced work incentives. Some writers, such as Ruane (1979, 1980) have supported a criterion of social profitability, which incorporates a measure of growth components and of income distribution as well as net domestic value added. One concern is that, without such a broad measure, competition with other countries for multinational investment could dominate the outcome in some projects which could not pass the other tests.

The sectoral emphasis of the IDA, and the tax incentives as well, have come in for criticism. Both were concentrated in manufacturing, although the IDA gave some grants in the 1970s to non-manufacturing or service firms providing employment in Ireland. In the 1980s there has been a more concentrated attempt to attract and expand firms in international services trade, such as data processing and software development, consulting services and financial services. Not only were grants made available more broadly to such sectors, but they were based on employment and the 10 per cent corporate tax was extended to them under certain circumstances (*Business International*, Ireland, 1987, 15–16). Moreover, in its promotion activities and other ways, a strong effort was made in the late 1970s and later to develop some sectors such as electronics, which were considered particularly suitable for Ireland. Increasingly the IDA reports and other government sources emphasized high-skill jobs, attraction of R&D and marketing facilities to Ireland, increased linkage to the domestic economy and other variables suggesting a more selective approach. Some of the other aspects of a more selective approach are noted in the next section.

Incentives and FDI

Most of the governments of the countries covered in this study would argue that their incentives were available to all companies which qualified, regardless of nationality, except for certain restricted sectors. No doubt the Irish authorities would take the same position: they are hardly likely to promote subsidies available only to firms controlled abroad. Yet there is a good case for regarding the grants and even the low tax on manufactures as devices geared in large part to attracting foreign-owned firms. Much of the public and private literature on Ireland argues that this is what they were primarily intended to do. Moreover, despite strong efforts to stimulate domestic entrepreneurship, it was foreign-owned firms which responded most often to the incentives. Most governments in this study are concerned, with some sectoral exceptions, to attract and steer FDI rather than to keep it out. Especially in the 1980s considerable incentives were offered to these ends. The fiscal incentives offered by the IDA can be considered at one extreme of those in this study, with the emphasis on attracting investment rather than a strong steering function. A great deal of information on probable performance had to be submitted as a basis for judging whether the discretionary grants should be given and how large they would be. A limited form of cost–benefit analysis has been used, as noted. There is follow-up, particularly in terms of suggesting areas where import substitution can be increased. On the larger grants or projects in particular there is follow-up to ensure that the commitments to hire labour or buy Irish goods are being met. A more planned and integrated approach is taken in promotion and grants to a priority area such as microelectronics. All of this is some way, however, from case-by-case negotiations to extract performance undertakings, application of standardized ratios on such commitments, and subsequent monitoring. Case studies indicate a lack of performance requirements, as normally understood, except for providing the agreed number of jobs (for example, Guisinger *et al.*, 1985, 191, 223, 227).[17]

It is also important to note that studies of the reasons for location of so much FDI in Ireland put more emphasis on factors other than grants and low taxes, although such incentives show up as quite significant (O'Malley, 1980, 36–41).[18] Low labour costs adjusted for quality are considered critical in such studies. For the period up to the late 1970s Ireland's wage rates were low relative to those of other industrialized countries. This position has been increasingly eroded by some developing countries producing similar products, as well as relatively rapid wage increases in Ireland. However Ireland's access to the EC in particular was rated as a major factor for locating there in most studies. Also rated highly was the long and intensive promotion in such culturally close sources of investment as the United States. On the minus side, a number of costs were relatively high by EC standards, including some relating to state-owned industries (*The Economist*, 16 January 1988, 23–4).

However one rates these factors, FDI inflows grew significantly after the early 1960s, and again after the early 1970s. The relatively rapid expansion of the newer industries in the 1960s and 1970s was noted earlier. In 1975–80 the growth of Irish manufacturing production exceeded that of all OECD countries except Portugal, and continued to be positive for the next few years despite a growing international recession. Electronic products and chemicals grew to over 50 per cent of non-food manufactured exports: indeed Ireland developed the largest share of electronics in such exports for all OECD countries. The weak spot was employment in manufactures, which fell off after the early 1980s (OECD, *Ireland*, 1985b, 45–7).

Much of the long-term growth noted above can be traced to FDI in Ireland, and particularly to US-owned firms which displaced the United Kingdom as the major source of FDI. A study by McAleese (1977), among others, has highlighted these effects in some detail. By 1974, for example, more than a quarter of manufacturing employment was in new industries, and about 60 per cent of the employment in new industries was in multinational firms. The drive for export promotion through FDI had certainly succeeded: by 1979 multinational firms were exporting about three-quarters of their production, compared with about 30 per cent for Irish firms (OECD, *Ireland*, 1985b, 55).[19] All of this was accompanied, of course, by rapid increases in foreign ownership of Irish industry, as noted earlier.

Profiles of new grant-aided industry, both foreign-owned and domestic, are useful in spelling out these and other characteristics.[20] The export propensity of new foreign-owned firms has exceeded that of new Irish-owned firms. It appears that this was also true for import orientation even after allowing for the food sector, where local content is high (O'Malley, 1980, 46; O'Loughlin and O'Farrell, 1980, 173). These export and import ratios have fallen over time, suggesting more domestic linkage.[21] For example, McAleese suggests the decline in the export ratio is 3 per cent over a decade, O'Loughlin and O'Farrell suggest it could be twice that figure. While overseas firms are concentrated in industries with high capital and technical intensity, this difference disappears once one allows for industry sector.[22] Many of the overseas firms appear to have relatively small MNE parents and to be producing in fairly standardized ways compared with new Irish firms. In most cases such functions as research and marketing are located elsewhere in the EC, in Brussels, for example. There is little difference in the propensity of foreign and Irish projects to be located in designated lower-income areas (O'Farrell, 1980). There does not appear to be a difference by nationality of ownership in plant closures due to recession, but a rising trend in closures raised concerns even in the 1970s about the long-term instability of some of the new industry (O'Malley, 1980, 42–3, O'Hagan and McStay, 1981, 48–9).

This summary is a somewhat oversimplified picture of what the studies show, but it helps to highlight certain issues. In particular, questions have been raised about the size of the incentives offered and about the slow development of domestic linkage, both of which affect the net national gains from FDI. There is also the issue of older Irish industry, which was unable to utilize the incentives to the same degree and went into absolute decline quite early.

The question of the size of subsidy is inherent in all such programmes where the objective is to give the minimum overall concessions needed to attract the investment. In negotiations with the firms the IDA has the benefit of its own long experience and some knowledge of what the other countries offer, but its information is necessarily less than that of the firm and particularly of a multinational firm. This issue is of considerable importance since most studies suggest that the profits which are taxed locally, rather than retained by the firm, are one of the major potential benefits from inward FDI.[23]

One cannot judge whether the grants and tax relief are too high simply by reference to the estimates noted above that they are about the most generous in the EC, or that they amounted to a rather high figure of about 6 per cent of GNP in 1983 (OECD, *Ireland*, 1985b, 48). Such measures not only neglect the benefit side, they do not address the question as to whether they were necessary in order to attract and retain the investment. The IDA could argue, for example, that the relative lack of some infrastructure investments, the small domestic market, transfer costs and other disadvantages required some compensation by way of grants and tax relief in order to attract investment.[24] The fact that profits to FDI are very high by international standards is inconclusive, for similar reasons. In the period 1974–9 US manufacturing firms had an average return on book value of investment of 29 per cent, compared with 6 per cent for such firms in the other EC countries and 14 per cent in all countries. The difference was maintained in the early 1980s.[25] Such persistent and large differences could suggest considerable transfer pricing practices; that is, locating profits in the low tax jurisdiction by the pricing and composition of exports and imports. Unfortunately there does not appear to be a convincing study on this practice, although Stewart (1985) argues that the available evidence is consistent with such transfer pricing.

Given what the IDA was attempting to do – to attract and retain FDI with the minimum grant per job – it is significant that US manufacturing investment rose far more rapidly in the case of Ireland than for the other EC countries in 1974–9, namely by an annual rate of 32 per cent against 12 per cent. This was a period when grant cost per job in 1979 was fairly stable at

$6114 for 1974 (9 months) and $5559 for 1979 (McKeon, 1980, 20). However, as noted earlier, Ireland's share of US manufacturing firms' capital expenditures fell significantly in the first half of the 1980s, a period when economic recession led to an easing of restrictions and increased subsidy competition for FDI globally. We do not, unfortunately, have a test which allows sufficiently for other determinants of investment in order to know how much of the success as well as the failure to ascribe to the Irish incentives.

Ultimately, with present information and measures, it seems unlikely that one could decide whether the package of incentives was too high or too low. In any case, phrasing the question in this way emphasizes the objective of attracting FDI, usually in manufacturing, in competition with the incentive schemes of other countries. As noted earlier, critics have also suggested that the design of the grants programme needed consideration – that it was too oriented to capital subsidy, especially when combined with the low rate of corporation tax, and geared too much to value added rather than growth and distribution issues. A consultancy study, known as the Telesis Report, prepared for the National Economic and Social Council in 1982, concluded that incentives were higher than necessary in most cases and that average grants should be reduced by one-third. This proposal was rejected by the government, which feared Ireland would lose out to other countries in the 1980s when subsidy competition was increasing (Ireland, *White Paper*, 1984, 62–3).

Linkage is a closely related aspect of this topic. For want of better measures, decreased percentages of imports in purchases and of exports in sales are taken as evidence of increased backward and forward linkage, respectively. The domestic welfare implications of such measures are not easy to assess. Whether increased linkage is desirable depends, for example, on how it is achieved. And some would argue that *increased* export propensities were desirable in terms of promoting output growth, assuming again that there is no better alternative available.

Accepting that increased linkage is desired, it was noted above that new Irish firms had both lower import and export propensities, thus creating more linkage than new foreign-owned firms. It was also noted that more linkage was developed over time, but not fast enough to satisfy the authorities. Just why linkage was low is difficult to explain – everything from the insufficiency of skills and of entrepreneurial capacities to transfer pricing by MNEs has been noted.[26] But the effort to increase domestic purchases and to increase processing or assembly in Ireland has been long-standing. The IDA Project Identification Unit established in 1975 had this type of objective, as did its efforts in industries such as timber and electronics. Linkage was certainly one factor considered by IDA, as will be evident from the criteria for grants outlined above. In a detailed study of linkages, O'Farrell and O'Loughlin (1980, 59–60) suggested a three-fold strategy for the IDA. They recommended that, in negotiating the incentive package with overseas firms, IDA should put more emphasis on increased purchasing autonomy for the subsidiaries and on the input requirements of the projects. In addition, to develop forward linkage, there should be more concentration on a number of natural resource sectors where Ireland has some advantages, as well as on the electronics sector.

A More Selective Approach

One more important issue needs to be noted. Whatever successes may be claimed for new industry, much of older industry continued to suffer a long decline, especially in employment.[27] These older industries, it may be noted, coexisted with new industries in many sectors of production. Much of the old industry was established in good part in response to earlier high levels of protection. Much exhibited the small-scale, short production runs and broad product lines characteristic of production in a small and highly protected market where imperfect competition exists.[28] What was particularly disturbing was the limited adjustment of considerable segments of such old industry to the development of freer trade in the 1960s and 1970s. Numerous private and public studies have been made of the phenomenon, pointing to a variety of possible reasons: for example, unsuitability of some of the protected firms or sectors even to changing Irish resource characteristics; excessive reliance on imported technology along with inadequate investment in science and technology in Ireland; and inadequate investment in such infrastructure items as road transport and telecommunications. It has also been suggested that the existing fiscal incentives system was more likely to be utilized by new firms, especially those controlled abroad, although efforts were made by adaptation grants and other means to assist the older firms.

The persistence of the problems of old industry and such issues as low linkage and lack of skill development in the new had led to modifications in IDA policies well before the 1980s, generally towards more directing of its financial and other support to the needs of different kinds of applicants. A still more selective approach has developed in the 1980s, in part because of the criticisms of the performance of overseas firms contained in the 1982 Telesis Report and other sources, and in line with the recommendations of a White Paper (Ireland, 1984). While recognizing that subsidy competition was increasing, the White Paper also stated that IDA would concentrate more in future on those overseas projects which were less reliant on the parent firm, which had strong demands for skilled labour, both in their own operations and through linkage with other domestic firms, and involved import substitution in sectors which Irish firms were unlikely to enter (Ireland, *White Paper*, 1984, 64). A National Linkages Programme instituted in

1986 has attempted to develop highly-skilled inputs as well as otherwise encouraging linkage.

As noted above, a concerted effort was also launched in the early 1980s to attract more international service projects, with employment grants from IDA and in other ways. The financial services sector in particular has expanded rapidly. In response in part to the criticisms of the Telesis Report the size of the grant given by IDA takes account of domestic spending, in the sense that the latter must be at least four times the size of the former (*The Economist*, 16 January 1988, 18).

A National Enterprise Agency was established in 1981 to exploit business opportunities which private enterprise alone would not undertake, but this was superseded by the National Development Corporation, which began operations in 1986. IDA had been investing in the equity of some firms and a considerable state-owned sector existed. The new Corporation had the more ambitious tasks of investing in the private sector with a view particularly to advancing technology, promoting strong Irish firms, strengthening the indigenous resource sector and improving services to smaller firms. It could also stimulate projects in the existing public sector. While it could engage in joint ventures with both Irish and overseas firms, the emphasis on development of the former is clear. Its investment decisions were to be guided by the need to achieve, after an initial period, a real rate of return equal to the cost of the invested funds (Ireland, *White Paper*, 1984, ch. 12).

Ireland had run into serious economic imbalances in the 1970s, with rising unemployment and inflation and increasing ratios to GNP of both public debt and the external current account deficit. These problems worsened in the 1980s, with unemployment rising to almost the highest rate for the OECD. A number of policies were adopted in 1987 in particular in an attempt to reverse these problems, notably to stabilize the debt to GNP ratio, and to reduce inflation, interest rates and direct taxation (IMF, *Survey*, 22 January 1990). In surveying the reasons for the high unemployment, the OECD examined the contribution of a number of factors: weak international demand, inflexible labour markets and excessive taxation and reliance on social security. It went on to note, as in past surveys, that MNEs were less likely to favour employment in Ireland and more likely to make large income payments abroad, given an industrial policy favouring capital-intensive firms. Issues such as low domestic linkage and unusually large pay-outs abroad would be a problem under any circumstances, but showed up even more sharply in the context of the mid-1980s. The OECD's own presentation of data, however, as well as its reasoning, suggest that much of the blame for the employment problem lay elsewhere (OECD, Ireland, 1987c, 34, 46).

Manufacturing employment (000s), by nationality

	1970	1980	1986
Irish firms	157	166	127
Foreign-owned	62	87	79

This conclusion is reinforced if one considers average annual employment loss rates in indigenous and foreign enterprises between 1973 and 1980 measured by IDA grant categories. In the case of new industry grants the overall loss rates for industry were 4.1 per cent and 4.2 per cent for indigenous and foreign enterprises respectively, closure loss rates 1.7 and 1.9 per cent. For re-equipment grants the overall rates were 5.1 and 4.0 per cent respectively, while closure loss rates were 2.0 and 1.8 per cent respectively (OECD, 1985b, 65, citing a study by M. O'Suilleabhain for the ILO).

Conclusions

As is the case elsewhere in this study, the focus on direct investment policy necessarily understates macro variables which can be critical to development. It must also be emphasized that the IDA, even in the 1980s, should not be treated simply as one end of a spectrum of screening agencies for FDI. While most countries give incentives, IDA has been far too incentive-oriented, and its basic decision criteria too systematic and well known, to be confused with other agencies in this study.

The policies followed in Ireland have been dominated by the concerns with high long-term unemployment and emigration plus the perceived need for access to a larger market. High protection on both trade and investment until the 1950s was accompanied by industrial expansion, but also by an inefficient structure of industry. One decision made at that time was to move to both trade and investment liberalization. Another, however, was to move in stages to an aggressive policy of promotion of manufactured exports, most of which turned out to be from foreign-owned firms, through generous grants, tax relief and other policies. The transition from protection to liberalization of trade was not as sharp as appears at first sight. Bond and Guisinger (1985) have noted that investment incentives can be regarded as an alternative form of protection, of particular importance to a country which cannot change its (EC) tariffs or use direct export subsidies.[29] Nevertheless a switch from import protection to export development was achieved on a considerable scale, along with a substantial expansion of grant-aided new industry, over two-thirds foreign-controlled.

This pattern of development left some serious problems in its wake. One was the state of the older industries, many of which made an incomplete adjustment to freer trade despite public support of various kinds. Another was the high import propensity of new industry, particularly the overseas component, and particularly in the skills-oriented products and services Ireland was emphasizing.

Despite some evident sectoral successes the problems which had led to the policy changes have not been resolved. It is not clear why this is so – whether because of defects in policy design, or overemphasis on 'export-platform' standardized technologies in FDI which have low linkages and can be reproduced in developing countries, or slower international growth for a time along with increased subsidy competition from other countries.[30] The reasonably consistent policies of the 1960s and 1970s began to change in the 1980s, but not abruptly, to more selective encouragement of FDI and to more direct and selective encouragement of Irish-owned industry. The outcomes of this new evolutionary approach remain to be seen.

ITALY

Italian governments have retained a relatively liberal policy towards inward FDI over the post-Second World War period, despite major economic swings from the early 1970s onwards. Variations in policy have been small – as one source noted, from seeking and encouraging it in the 1950s and early 1960s to merely welcoming it later (OECD, 1979, 17). In good part this policy has reflected a desire for development in the southern half of Italy. The continuing severity of Italy's regional problem is evident from the fact that it had four of the richest 25 regions in Europe and seven of the poorest 25 (*The Economist*, 19 February 1988, 23). More recently the desire to play a larger role in newer sectors of industry, in part through joint ventures with state-owned firms, has also favoured liberal policies. The policy followed has been one of notification and exchange control, rather than screening as such. Essentially this has been the case for outward FDI as well.

These liberal policies have not been without criticism, nor has Italy been free of problems involving foreign-controlled MNEs. Both the government and trade unions have attempted to safeguard jobs by seizing companies which were about to close down.[31] In the 1970s two petroleum firms left Italy and a third threatened to do so, in part because of the way in which price controls were administered. From time to time, transfer pricing policies which violate Italian law have been ascribed to MNEs. Firms owned in Italy, it may be noted, have not been immune to similar criticisms or charges. Nevertheless the fact that costs as well as benefits are associated with FDI and the presence of MNEs has led some to suggest a more selective and regulatory approach (for example, Acocella, 1979), though there has not been widespread political support for such overall regulation. Italian Communist party experts, for example, indicated in the mid-1970s, when criticism of MNEs was frequent, that there would not be discrimination against them within their planning framework (*The Times*, 6 March 1976).

Despite the liberal approach, the role of both inward and outward FDI has been relatively low in comparison with other larger European countries such as France, the United Kingdom and West Germany, and, indeed, most of the developed countries. This is not the case for foreign trade: exports and imports are broadly of similar importance in the economies of these large countries and Italy (Table 1.1). An outline of the data on FDI will underline this point.

Both flows and stocks of FDI remained low in the 1970s, especially in contrast with what was happening in a number of other European countries (Table 8.5). The inward stock remained substantially in excess of the outward throughout that decade. Both inward and particularly outward flows speeded up in the early 1980s. On the outward side, Italian investors consist of a few major groups and a considerable number of smaller firms, with medium-sized firms not common except for a few sectors such as food and beverages. The smaller firms in particular prefer to take a minority or 50 per cent stake in their ventures abroad, with the result that such forms of investment abroad are unusually high in Italy's outward FDI (Viesti, 1988, 36–45). As a percentage of gross domestic product the outward stock of FDI fell from 2.9 per cent in 1960 to 1.8 in 1980. This percentage rose sharply to 3.4 in 1985, but remained well below that of the other major developed countries (Table 3.1). Employment in affiliates abroad as a percentage of domestic employment in 1981 was only 1.6 per cent for all industry and 2.1 for manufactures (Dunning and Cantwell, 1987, 90). Sectorally, of course, there are important exceptions to this low representation abroad relative to that at home, office equipment and rubber and plastics being cases in point. The state-owned firms, it may be added, played a major role in outward FDI only in petroleum, with significant representation in a few other sectors such as steel. In the former case they were encouraged by government, as in France, in order to reduce Italy's reliance on Anglo-American firms (Franko, 1976, 62; Onida and Viesti, 1988, 152).

Outward FDI was constrained by the exchange control authorities in some periods in a variety of ways, not least in the bureaucratic procedures involved. Most outward flows, including FDI, required in 1980 a deposit of 50 per cent in a non-interest-bearing account. This was reduced to 25 per cent in the mid-1980s in the case of OECD countries, as Italy began a process of significant liberalization of controls on outward capital flows.

On the inward side, both the flow and stock figures showed weakness after the early 1970s. This was a period when the Italian economy was especially

Table 8.5 Overall development of direct investment in Italy (billions lire)

Year or end of year	*Direct investment capital flows*[a]		*Stock of direct investment*	
	Inward (net)	*Outward (net)*	*Inward*	*Outward*
1970	378	70		
1971	324	249	3 253	1 377
1972	364	125	3 585	1 948
1973	366	149	4 127	1 939
1974	393	130	5 449	2 285
1975	412	227	6 230	2 255
1976	78	132	4 990	2 941
1977	1 002	486	6 014	3 607
1978	433	143	6 667	3 956
1979	301	452	7 302	4 704
1980	503	646	8 274	6 486
1981	1 303	1 596	9 273	8 857
1982	860	1 387	10 106	11 118
1983	1 807	3 230	12 148	14 098
1984	2 251	3 471	18 031	20 498
1985	1 916	3 502		
1986	-122	3 998		
1987	5 284	3 027		

Note:
[a]Excludes reinvested profits.

Source: OECD (1987a, 120) updated after 1983 from IMF, *Balance of Payments Statistics*, 1988, converted to lire.

vulnerable, given its substantial dependence on imported energy, and when sociopolitical problems were particularly severe. While FDI does not play as important a role in Italy as in other major European countries, that role is still significant, particularly in manufacturing. In the early 1980s foreign affiliates (including minority and 50 per cent joint ventures) accounted for 20 per cent of industry output. They accounted for 6.5 per cent of industry employment and 8.3 per cent of manufacturing employment.[32] Their role in the primary and services sector has been much smaller, except for the distributive trades and finance. However, for industrial concerns with at least 500 employees, the share of employment is much higher; one estimate places it at nearly 23 per cent in the mid-1980s (Dunning and Cantwell, 1987, 89; Mariotti, 1988, 136).

The relatively low propensity for both outward and inward FDI has been explained in several ways. Italian industry includes a large number of smaller firms, many in traditional consumer goods such as clothing where exports are an effective means of foreign penetration. Many of these smaller firms also venture abroad in other ways but prefer methods involving less than full or majority ownership. The large state-owned sector is required to give preference to investment in the less developed south of Italy while the private sector is given significant incentives to invest there: in a sense, investment in the south has been an alternative to outward FDI. Monetary problems also played a role at times, in the sense of burdensome regulations on exchange control. On the inward side the presence of a large state-owned sector and control of many firms by a few families and individuals have limited FDI in many sectors. Problems with public infrastructure and with complex administrative procedures, along with serious sociopolitical difficulties in the 1970s, also played a role (Viesti, 1988, 46–8, Mariotti, 1988, 146–8). In recent years the major efforts by some of Italy's larger private investors to expand abroad have been frustrated on occasion by close holdings of the shares of the target firms, among other factors. The cases of Société Générale de Belgique and Continental of Germany are noted in the sections on those countries. Nevertheless Italy's share of OECD outward flows was 5.7 per cent in 1981–8, compared with 2.4 in the 1960s. This contrasts with a decline to 3.7 per cent from 8.6 per cent on the inward side over the same periods (Table 3.3).

Policy on Inward Direct Investment[33]

Major industrial investments in Italy, whether under foreign or domestic control, require approval by an interministerial committee on industrial policy. This can take up to six months but acts more quickly if the investment is not in the industrialized north and centre of Italy. In the late 1970s, so far as one could ascertain, the process did not involve much sorting out of projects to determine which were more desirable or to increase net benefits.

In terms of inward FDI, except for certain sectors the exchange control provisions have been the key. These are administered by the Ministry of Foreign Trade's Italian Exchange Office, but involve also the Treasury's approval of a firm's status as a 'productive' enterprise. These inward provisions have not involved an authorization process as such for direct investment but rather a notification process through banks or other financial institutions, plus a decision by the investor on the procedure to use. Two procedures are possible under the relevant law of 1956. One is for 'productive' new investment or the expansion of an existing operation.[34] If so designated, the income paid abroad and any eventual divestment can be made virtually without limit at the official rate of exchange. However such firms must accept certain limits on their borrowing rights in Italy, and any subsequent purchase of shares involving control of other firms would need Treasury approval.

The other procedure applies to acquisitions of existing firms or other forms of FDI. Firms which cannot be designated as productive or do not request it can enter in any case, and their income and capital transfers abroad are guaranteed at the official rate. However such guaranteed income transfers are limited to 8 per cent annually of the capital, while the export of capital can occur only after a period of two years and only in the amount of currency originally imported.

In practice, the distinction between these two procedures does not appear to have been large, even when balance of payments problems have been severe. In part this is due to the many exceptions allowed: for example, an acquisition from abroad could be treated as productive if the operation acquired was to be modernized or expanded with imported capital. More importantly, foreign investors can open a capital account in lira and borrow and invest freely. They can then transfer profits and liquidate capital through these accounts, thus escaping the limits noted above for non-productive investments. This is an administrative procedure, unlike the legal guarantees involved in the law of 1956, and hence could be reversed if the balance of payments situation or other factors so required. However for the past two decades this has not occurred.

Italy's exchange controls were tightened in the 1970s as capital flight intensified. In the 1980s the trend has been to liberalization with occasional interruptions. A new law and approach came into effect in 1988 with the adoption of the position that all transactions are to be permitted except for those regulated or prohibited, which reverses the previous policy position. Some power is to be retained to deal with emergency exchange or balance of payments situations. While the liberalization was to be gradual in some respects, restrictions on outward investments in particular were substantially eased. Further liberalization occurred in 1990.

Turning to key sectors, the first point to note is the substantial presence of state-owned firms. Apart from monopolies in sectors such as telecommunications, rail transport and the supply of electricity and gas, the state owns or controls three large holding companies with many interests, as well as a number of other entities with more specific objectives. The three largest industrial groups, IRI, ENI and EFIM, accounted for about 10 per cent of GDP in the mid-1980s (*The Economist*, 27 February 1988, 30). State-owned firms are common in other countries in this study, but their incidence has been larger in Italy. Moreover privatization of such firms in the 1980s proceeded at a much more modest pace than in several other EC countries.

A number of complaints which are sometimes difficult to verify have been made by other firms regarding the privileges enjoyed by such state firms: favouritism in allocating government contracts, subsidies not available to private firms, and so on. There are offsets, of course, in terms of government intervention in the decisions of such firms for public purposes: for example, state firms are under strong pressure to place 40 per cent of their new investment in the south of Italy and 30 per cent of overall budget purchases (*Business International*, Italy, 1986, 5, 14–15; OECD, 1983, 147–54). Many private firms, foreign and domestic, enter into joint ventures with the state firms. Nevertheless a tendency to reduced inward FDI as well as private investment more generally might be expected in sectors where state-owned or -controlled firms are very active.

Italy has a significant set of industries where entry from abroad or by established foreign-controlled firms is either prohibited or limited in some way. Foreign majority participation is not allowed in shipping, maritime transport, fishing and ownership of aircraft. There are reciprocity requirements for non-EC investors in banking and insurance, and shares of banks 'of national interest' can only be held by Italian citizens and EC residents. Branches of foreign banks are restricted in the volume of their lending. They are also restricted to lending in the region of their location, except for foreign enterprises or their subsidiaries (OECD, 1985a, 96). Italian-owned banks, it may be added, have also been greatly restricted in the term of loans, in the opening of branches and in participation in merchant banking activities, among other things. Many such restrictions are likely to disappear in the unified EC market after 1992, since otherwise the banks in the less restricted EC countries would be at an advantage.

In the energy sector, Italy has used the threat of trade barriers combined with subsidies in order to ensure the development of refinery capacity. Various laws ensure that the state holding company, ENI, has a preferred position in exploration and development of hydrocarbons and that any production is available for domestic consumption.[35] It is of interest to note that Italy does not have laws dealing with mergers. Nor does its Civil Code have much by way of limitations on restrictive practices, although some restrictions among EC firms would need to be registered with the Community. In many other countries, as noted earlier, merger laws can act as a brake on MNEs even if not specifically distinguishing them from other firms.

As in other countries, the authorities would prefer to examine the takeover of a major Italian firm by foreign interests, but there is no law or stated policy on the subject and private companies are not obliged to inform the government that such negotiations are about to be concluded. There are at least two instruments which the government could use to forestall an unwelcome takeover by foreign interests, whether from abroad or by a foreign-owned subsidiary. One is through influencing acquisitions by the appropriate state-owned firm, particularly in the case of public takeovers. The other has been through the provision of exchange control and related capital market requirements, some aspect of which was likely to have an impact on any acquisition, at least until recently. Thus careful consideration was given in 1976 to the proposed acquisition of a 14.5 per cent stake in Fiat by the Libyan government in return for a $400 million injection of capital. The acquisition, which went ahead, needed the approval of the government in at least two respects: the approval of a new share issue and also of a long-term foreign loan involving interest payments abroad. The stock was repurchased in 1986 for $3.2 billion, at a time when Libya's relationships with both Italy and the United States had deteriorated sharply and when Fiat was interested in increasing its sales of armaments, in particular to the United States (*The Economist*, 27 September 1986, 69). One should also note that, as in some other European countries, hostile takeovers through stock market raids are avoided by the country's financial elite, which prefers that takeovers be negotiated privately. Such hostile takeovers do occur occasionally, but they are limited by the combination of widespread state-company holdings and concentration among several private groups. One consequence in recent years is to encourage the latter to expand in Western Europe rather than to challenge one another's holdings (*The Economist* , 4 February 1988, 55–6).

While the treatment of inward FDI has been quite liberal from an exchange control perspective, there has been until recently an element of non-national treatment in subsequent access to the domestic capital market. Enterprises classified as productive, hence guaranteed income and capital repatriation at the official rate, were limited in their local borrowing. However they had the option of entering without such classification or of using special capital accounts, as already noted.

The desire for investment in the lower-income regions, especially in the south, has been central to the strategy of openness towards FDI. Part of that strategy involves substantial fiscal incentives, combined at times with actual or threatened trade barriers to persuade firms to enter. Along with general support for industrial development and restructuring, generous support has been directed to the south. In the mid-1980s, for example, companies locating there were allowed full exemption from corporate income tax for 10 years and full exemption from local tax on reinvested profits; in the late 1970s these exemptions were 50 per cent and 70 per cent respectively. Cash grants, long-term loans at low interest, reductions in social security payments and support for physical infrastructure and training were among the other forms of assistance. Public agencies and state-owned firms are encouraged to make purchases in the south, as already noted.

In principle these aids are available to foreign-owned firms without discrimination. In practice one observer has argued that they have been difficult for foreign investors to secure, in part because of delays and other bureaucratic problems. They have not attracted the substantial foreign investment evident in Scotland and Ireland (Mariotti, 1988, 147).

NOTES

1. The 1968 and 1978 figures for employment have been estimated at 18 and 38 per cent respectively (OECD, 1985c, 62).
2. The paragraph which follows is based on Van Den Bulcke (1983, 251–4).
3. The actual procedures used to process applications are described in Boddewyn (1974, 22–8).
4. This provision extends to firms incorporated in the EC but which do not have their registered office, central administration or principal establishment in the Community. Note that the provision would not apply in the absence of a public bid. In July 1989 a law was passed requiring *all* investors, wherever located, to disclose a holding of more than 5 per cent of any Belgian firm which has shareholder funds exceeding 250 million Belgian francs.
5. The account which follows is based on *Globe and Mail*, 20 January 1988, 6 September 1988, 6 February 1989; and *The Economist*, 20 January 1990, 84–5, 16 February 1991, 69.
6. Much of the increase reflects exchange rate devaluation after 1981.
7. The studies noted below are Van Den Bulcke and Halsberghe (1976) and Van Den Bulcke (1983, 1985).
8. Badger Belgium, a small engineering subsidiary of a US firm, was closed with insufficient assets in the Belgian subsidiary to pay for the high redundancy payments required by Belgian law. Pressure from the unions and Belgian government, and an appeal to the OECD Declaration on Multinationals, led to an enhanced settlement with the parent firm.
9. It is important to add that domestic and foreign firms appear to have been largely complementary, with the former concentrating in more standardized and semi-finished goods and the latter in more differentiated final goods (Sleuwaegen, 1988, 163–4).
10. This historical section draws heavily on O'Malley (1980, especially Section III, 6–19) and O'Hagan and McStay (1981, 18–39).
11. The next two paragraphs draw on O'Hagan and McStay (1981).
12. These estimates are for the three major investors. They would miss, for example, major primary sector and related investments by countries such as Canada.
13. By way of comparison, the ratio of inward FDI stock to GNP as measured above was 12 per cent and 20 per cent for Belgium and Canada, while employment in foreign-owned manufacturing affiliates was 38 and 37 per cent respectively (Table 3.5).
14. Changed later to 40 per cent and 50 per cent. Profits from certain trading operations carried out at the customs-free area of Shannon Airport were exempt from the tax up to 1990. This incentive was not offered after 1 January 1981.
15. There are a number of references to the professionalism of the IDA by the firms studied in Guisinger *et al.* (1985, 223). This effort extended beyond the IDA. In 1982, on requesting from a bank clerk an unusually attractive bank calendar, the author of the present study quickly found himself in the bank manager's office being plied with information on the benefit of locating in Ireland, presumably on the chance that even an itinerant scholar might be useful in attracting industry to Ireland.

16. See O'Malley (1980, 29–33) for a discussion of these studies; also Ruane and John (1984). A study by Flynn and Honohan cited in OECD, *Economic Survey for Ireland*, 1983–4, 40, suggests that, after allowing for inflation, the cost of capital in the early 1980s was about half that in the early 1970s.
17. In the late 1970s and later the amount of domestic spending was given more emphasis in making grants, as noted further below.
18. For example, a survey in 1967, while emphasizing that it was difficult to assess any one factor accurately, noted that firms employing 32 per cent of the labour involved gave availability of labour as the primary factor in the investment decision; 24 per cent listed market access; grants and export tax relief were next at 13 and 15 per cent, and availability of local raw materials (largely food-processing) at 13 per cent (O'Malley, 1980, 41).
19. The export orientation of foreign new industry appears also to have been higher than that of domestic new industry (McAleese, 1977, 84).
20. These generalizations are based partly on studies by McAleese (1977) and O'Loughlin and O'Farrell (1980), as well as those cited below.
21. Strictly speaking, forward linkage refers to sales of intermediate goods. Lacking such data, most writers infer that reduction in the ratio of export sales to output means increased forward linkage. The detailed study by O'Farrell and O'Loughlin (1980) does show intermediate sales.
22. O'Loughlin and O'Farrell (1980).
23. Spinoffs or linkages to the domestic economy are another major potential benefit, as noted further below. See MacDougall (1960) on the theory and Jenkins (1979) for a measure of possible tax benefits in the case of Canada.
24. It may seem odd that one would refer to the small Irish market given access to the EC, but the assumption here is that, from the firm's viewpoint, the access is not perfect. The EC drive for improved access by 1992 points in the same direction. According to IDA sources, larger European states have not hesitated to emphasize assured access to the domestic market in bargaining with larger MNEs which are considering alternative EC sites.
25. These are US Department of Commerce data. One should note that royalty and fee payments to US parents, as a percentage of the stock of US investment, were about the same as for the EC as a whole (OECD, *Ireland*, 1985b, 56).
26. Transfer pricing possibilities would tend, other things being equal, to shift profits to the relatively low-tax Irish jurisdiction, but also to keep in other higher-tax jurisdictions such things as marketing, research facilities and higher-priced component purchases.
27. This paragraph is based largely on O'Malley (1980, sections IV.4 and 5). In the mid-1970s about a third of grant-aided new industry jobs were in Irish firms, while a substantial minority of old industry was foreign owned (O'Malley, 1980, 53).
28. Stykolt and Eastman (1960) and Eastman and Stykolt (1967) developed and tested a model of growth under such circumstances, one which has received considerable confirmation in subsequent studies of Canadian experience.
29. They went on to show, for 11 Irish manufacturing industries, that effective rates of protection to labour fell in all cases from 1966 to 1977 as tariffs came down, but the protection accorded to labour fell more slowly than that to value added. In some industries, factor-based incentives accounted for as much as 40 per cent of total investment incentives.
30. We neglect here macro-type explanations dealing with overall fiscal, monetary and income policies as noted in the previous section.
31. For example, in 1968 the government seized a US-controlled firm making cathode ray and vacuum tubes, whose liquidation had been announced. The unions seized a British-controlled motor factory in 1975 for the same reasons (*Globe and Mail*, 27 November 1975 and 12 February 1987).
32. Onida and Viesti (1988, 156) suggest the former figure may have risen to about 12 per cent by the mid-1980s. By contrast, the OECD estimate given in Table 3.5 suggests 18 per cent of manufacturing employment was in foreign-owned affiliates in 1977.

33. Major sources for this section, apart from interviews, are *Business International*, Italy (1986), ABECOR (1976) and an unofficial translation of the following documents on investment of foreign capital in Italy: Law Number 43 of 7 February 1956; Presidential Decree Number 758 of 6 July 1956; and various circulars issued in 1956 under Law Number 43. See also OECD (1982, 1985a, 1987b).
34. The concept of 'productive' investment appears to be intended to minimize temporary or speculative investments. Such investments must 'have as their object the production of goods or services such as undertakings which for the purpose of carrying out their activity require land reclamation and improvement, the construction of factories, shipyards, generators and energy transmission lines, the excavation of shafts and galleries, the use of ships and aircraft, the construction of buildings, including buildings to be used as hotels, and roads' (OECD, 1979, 17 quoting the relevant law).
35. See Franko (1976, 154) and *Business International*, Italy (1986, 4, 6). In this respect OECD (1987b, 47), citing reciprocity requirements only, appears to be an understatement.

9. Home Countries Lacking Review

FEDERAL REPUBLIC OF GERMANY (PRE-UNIFICATION)

The Federal Republic of Germany has been among the most liberal countries in this study so far as foreign ownership of industry is concerned. Few sectors are closed to foreign direct investment. In a significant number of sectors public ownership is large or exclusive, providing limitations on entry to all private firms. There is no authorization or screening of firms on entry, or of foreign takeovers, apart from merger policy directed to all firms. The central bank has had to require notification or restriction of capital movements at times in the 1970s for international monetary reasons, once again directed to all relevant firms.

This liberal position can be traced in part to the favourable view of business in general on the part of FRG governments and the desire to rebuild industry rapidly after the Second World War. A view of 'social markets' was encouraged; that is, of private enterprise with some sense of community values and interests. Worker participation in supervisory boards is one aspect of this. While some MNE managements have been concerned about the way such participation would affect international investment decisions, the MNEs were also beneficiaries of the favourable attitude to business implied by social markets.

In 1945 a moratorium was imposed on FDI in West Germany, in part because the reparations issue had not yet been resolved and in part because of problems of assessing asset values, given the prevailing monetary disturbances (Kindleberger, 1969, 38–41). The moratorium was lifted in 1949. Inward FDI, especially from the United States, soon became a significant component of economic growth. By 1960 the stock of inward FDI was more than double that of outward, and the inward stock exceeded the outward until 1980.[1] FDI inflows, with and without retained earnings, were substantially in excess of outflows until the late 1960s. This situation began to reverse itself in the early 1970s. From the mid-1970s onwards the outward flows substantially exceeded the inward flows. Almost 80 per cent of the outflow in 1983 was to Western Europe and the United States.

The West German economy had become highly internationalized by the early 1980s. Employment in foreign-controlled firms in manufacturing was 17 per cent (Table 3.5). However, the share of foreign firms in manufacturing output was significantly higher at 26 per cent. Employment in foreign manufacturing affiliates abroad was equal to 18 per cent of domestic manufacturing employment – as high as 58 per cent in chemicals and allied products and 29 per cent in motor vehicles (Dunning and Cantwell, 1987, 56–7). As noted in Table 9.1 and above, outward FDI grew more rapidly than inward after the early 1970s. Measured in US dollars, West Germany's share of the world's outward stock of FDI in 1985 exceeded that of all countries except the United States, United Kingdom and Japan (Table 3.1).

The position the government has taken towards outward FDI can best be described as neutral, in the sense of avoiding policies which would restrict or increase it. Two exceptions can be noted. First, the federal government has had standby authority for controls on direct and other international investment when balance of payments or capital market problems occurred. Such controls were in effect in the early 1970s, but had been largely removed by the mid-1970s and fully so shortly afterwards. Second, there have been considerable efforts to encourage FDI in developing countries. These efforts include, among other measures, a large number of bilateral investment protection agreements providing legal safeguards for investors; guarantees against political risks for approved investments; and special tax incentives for investment in less developed countries – notably for employment-intensive investments.[2] Despite such efforts, FRG investments have been very largely in the United States and Europe.

It should be added that, like other governments, the West German government has been concerned about transfer pricing practices. In 1973 Germany passed a law controlling transfer pricing of exports and also providing for the income of German affiliates in tax-haven countries to be taxed as if it had been paid to the parent firm (Franko, 1976, 227).

Policy on Inward Direct Investment

In terms of the policy instruments considered to date for other countries, the FRG is remarkably free of investment controls. Exchange controls were dismantled in the mid-1970s and, in any case, were directed in 1973 at a balance of payments surplus. There is no review process for new investment or acquisitions. A foreign investor acquiring over 25 per cent of an existing firm's assets must report this to the state branches of the Bundesbank. This is a statistical requirement, rather than an approval process.[3] The federal government, under the law on foreign economic relations, can restrict foreign direct investment when necessary to fulfil its international commitments,

Table 9.1 Direct investment stocks and flows, Federal Republic of Germany, 1960–87

Year or End of year	Direct Investment Capital Flows				Stock of Direct Investment	
	Inward (net)	Of which retained earnings (DM million)	Outward (net)	Of which retained earnings	Inward	Outward (DM billion)
1960	900	190	587	100	7.00	3.20
1961	1 332	280	821	130		
1962	1 444	370	1 141	200		
1963	2 010	480	866	220		
1964	2 532	410	1 193	270		
1965	3 660	370	1 241	190	19.56	7.85
1966	4 061	620	1 428	200		
1967	3 361	550	1 342	300		
1968	2 163	600	1 979	390		
1969	2 067	710	2 788	670		
1970	2 176	640	3 194	690	35.11	17.33
1971	3 905	730	3 656	900		
1972	6 157	1 350	4 988	930		
1973	5 324	1 090	4 417	860		
1974	5 495	400	4 595	1 160		
1975	1 690	400	4 940	1 110	60.51	37.64
1976	3 378	31	6 179	1 300	63.53	43.10
1977	2 249	560	5 122	309	62.31	46.54
1978	3 270	600	7 242	1 400	66.91	52.70
1979	3 194	1 850	8 235	1 070	70.27	61.76
1980	757	-1 112	7 310	567	71.76	74.35
1981	693	-3 065	8 741	-1 119	74.74	88.43
1982	1 956	-1 152	6 001	-1 581	76.36	95.40
1983	4 040	109	8 134	519	80.59	106.05
1984	1 575	-438	12 369	3 057		
1985	1 674	-449	14 437	3 079		
1986	2 165	-1 121	20 839	3 235		
1987	3 510	3 510	16 548	3 021		

Source: OECD (1987a, 114) for flows 1960–79, and IMF, *Balance of Payments Statistics*, 1988, for flows 1980–87. Stocks from 1960–83 are from Dunning and Cantwell (1987, 49). See also note 1 on accompanying text.

preserve domestic economic stability, or for national security reasons. Exceptional situations such as these are recognized by various international accords, such as the OECD Declaration on International Investment and Multinational Enterprise. The restrictions must be limited to specific purposes and can be reviewed by the legislature.

The same pattern of openness appears if one looks at key sectors. There is a list of public monopolies which includes sectors common to various countries, such as telephone and telegraph, various forms of transport, airports, gambling and broadcasting. There are nationality or reciprocity restrictions in airline licences, German-flag vessels and coastal trade, and foreign credit institutions. Foreign banks located in West Germany were not allowed to lead-manage D-mark Eurobond issues until the financial deregulation of the mid-1980s. Such banks were also then allowed to join federal government and public sector bond syndicates. Some discrimination has occurred also against foreign-controlled firms in government purchases of telecommunications equipment and in government financial support for tourism (OECD, 1985a, 86–7; 1987b, 43–4).

There are three other factors to be taken into account in assessing the FRG policy on FDI – government ownership, bank ownership and anti-trust policy. First, government ownership is high in some firms and sectors so that, while foreign firms can enter, they may hesitate to do so in competition with federal or state governments. Partial or full government ownership extends across a wide range of firms in banking and other service sectors, mining and manufacturing, as well as various utilities and transportation. Privatization plans for various firms were introduced by the federal government in 1983, but have proceeded more slowly than in the United Kingdom. Second, the banks have been significant holders of equity in industrial enterprise – estimates suggest that 12 to 15 per cent of all corporate equities were held by banks in the late 1980s. Many larger German firms are in a position where one of the three major banks owns a significant portion of their equity and is represented on the supervisory board. In addition, by law, the banks can exercise proxy votes for those unable or unwilling to attend shareholders meetings. Deutsche Bank, for example, owns 28 per cent of Daimler-Benz AG, the largest conglomerate in the FRG, and is reputed to appoint close to 400 directors of West German companies. It has played a prominent role in the support and reorganization of a number of major firms in the 1980s. Taking account of both direct ownership and proxies, the banks are believed to control about half of all German shares.[4]

This system has been criticized by the German Monopolies Commission as limiting competition, and by the Academic Advisory Council as involving conflicts of interest. Others have defended it, arguing that it lends longer-term stability to a firm's position both because hostile takeovers are more difficult and because banks as creditors are more likely to come to the support of a firm in difficulty. For present purposes the key point is the way in which government and bank ownership of equity helps to limit hostile takeovers, including those from abroad. Indeed mergers and acquisitions in West Germany are generally negotiated, in contrast with the frequently hostile takeover of listed firms which occurs in some other countries.

It is clear that both the banks and governments occasionally intervene to protect West German firms from foreign takeovers.[5] As noted earlier, West Germany is highly reliant on foreign-owned petroleum firms. In the late 1960s the government objected to foreign takeovers of petroleum companies on two occasions, in one case successfully finding a German buyer (Gillespie, 1972, 415–16; Franko, 1976, 154–5). More extensive concerns arose in the mid-1970s. During and after the petroleum crisis of 1973 there was considerable discussion on the need for a policy position or law with regard to the takeover of key firms by foreign interests. The word 'key' is not well defined here or elsewhere, but appears to refer to those which are economically important, technologically advanced, or simply much in the public eye. There was a particular concern, much exaggerated as it turned out, that Middle-Eastern governments, with their newly-acquired oil wealth, would come to dominate some sectors of German industry. Iran's acquisition of a 25 per cent interest in Krupp aroused great interest, but it was the acquisition of a 14 per cent interest in Daimler-Benz by the Government of Kuwait which touched off a storm. German firms organized a holding company to acquire Daimler shares.[6]

The government's response was to establish an informal notification system in which the banks and major firms report to the government any *impending* sales of companies or large blocks of stock to foreigners, particularly OPEC governments or their agencies. In addition, gentlemen's agreements were established with Iran, Kuwait and Saudi Arabia, to the effect that these countries would inform the West German government if they intended to take a large position in a West German firm. Finally it appears that in a few cases the government encouraged German investors to buy the equity being offered for sale (*Financial Times*, 4 June 1975; Federal Reserve Bank, 1979–80). It is not clear whether this informal system of prior notification continued after the concerns of the 1970s had passed.

The fear of takeover in the mid-1970s led a number of firms to limit shareholder voting rights even further than they were. It was possible in a joint stock firm, for example, to require the approval of the board of directors for the sale of registered shares, a practice often used in the insurance and power industries. A device allowed in company law and increasingly utilized in the 1970s was the limitation of any one shareholder's voting rights to not more than 5 per cent of the total equity. This was particularly useful against unwelcome takeover attempts when the shareholdings were widely held. Among the larger firms which adopted such a clause were Deutsche Bank, Mannesmann, Veba, Bayer and BASF. Still another device in limited liability companies is the provision by which other shareholders, who have the right of first refusal, must consent to share transfers (Haggeney, 1976, 63).

All of this means that it is extremely difficult for a hostile takeover of a larger firm to occur, either from abroad or domestically, if the banks and some larger firms decide to oppose it. A recent example was the unsuccessful attempt by Pirelli of Italy to secure control of Continental, a major producer of tyres, through a hostile bid. The long and complex manoeuvres failed for a variety of reasons, including some errors by the bidder, and Deutsche Bank ultimately remained neutral. But the set of protective devices noted, and the support of other German firms, played a role in the outcome (*World Deal Review*, 1991, 232–8; *The Economist*, 7 December 1991, 81).

Apart from government and bank ownership and other cross-holdings, we should note, third, that West Germany has what may be the most stringent anti-trust policy in Europe. While not discriminating against multinational firms the laws and decisions quite explicitly take into account the effects of MNEs on competition. Both the other firm and the Cartel Office must be informed if a firm acquires 25 per cent participation. In the case of mergers, a 1980 law stated that the Cartel Office must be notified if at least one merging enterprise has *worldwide* sales exceeding D-marks 2 billion and if the merger has an effect on West Germany. The latter is presumed to be the case if one of the partners has a 'presence' in Germany, including, for example, even a sales promotion activity. Thus the merger provisions apply explicitly to transborder transactions, and they have been used to deny or limit such mergers when they create or strengthen a dominant position in Germany. The types of situations involving market dominance are spelled out in statistical terms. The Economics Ministry can overrule Cartel Office decisions, and appeals to the courts are possible. Some MNEs have had to give up or to restructure proposed mergers as a consequence of Cartel Office decisions.

These and other provisions have allowed the Cartel Office to claim extra-territorial powers over German firms abroad and, indeed, to reach non-German firms if there is a 'presence' in West Germany and an adverse competitive effect on Germany through trade, investment or in some other way. One of the more interesting provisions, which was established by a court case involving a foreign-owned petroleum company, is the right of the cartel authority to demand information through the German subsidiary from a foreign firm when an abuse occurs in Germany. This judgement runs up against laws in a number of countries prohibiting such information transfers. In 1982 the Cartel Office also prohibited on competition grounds a merger in

Germany resulting from the merger abroad of two parent firms. This is a power which exists in some other countries, such as Canada, by reason of investment review, but in such cases the decision criteria go far beyond competition effects. This particular decision of the Cartel Office has been appealed.[7] The Cartel Office has also considered the ways in which outward FDI can have an impact on Germany. Thus it limited the shareholding which a German firm could take in an Italian competitor because of concern about the effect of a larger shareholding on the price of imports to Germany (Franko, 1976, 157).

West Germany also has a substantial programme of fiscal incentives at the federal, state and local level which, like those of most other countries, is not explicitly geared to MNEs. Such incentives are in part discretionary, however, and hence allow room for dealing with such firms. Such incentives have been given some credit, for example, for the considerable number of foreign-owned refineries which chose to locate in the FRG, and have been used to help persuade automobile firms to remain within a state and within the country (Franko, 1976, 154; *The Economist*, 6 December 1986, 14).

West German incentives are well documented since a federal law passed in 1967 requires systematic reporting to parliament. Federal, state and local incentives have been geared in part to regional development, especially to border areas with East Germany and to West Berlin. EC objections to the size of the West German population covered by such subsidies, 35 per cent of the total, led in the mid-1980s to some reduction in coverage (OECD, 1983).

It has been suggested, finally, that worker participation in supervisory boards has influenced foreign investment decisions. In 1974, for example, when Volkswagen asked its supervisory board to consider a proposal to establish a plant in the United States, there was considerable opposition from union and local government officials on the board (Franko, 1976, 23–31). Their objections delayed but did not prevent the decision. Some foreign-controlled firms in West Germany have expressed concerns about the effects of codetermination, while others have welcomed it. Whether the system of codetermination has significantly affected FDI decisions here or elsewhere is unclear. What does seem clear is that the West German economy has remained free of most of the restrictions on FDI examined elsewhere in this study. This does not mean it is lacking in a capability to resist unwanted foreign takeovers.

NETHERLANDS

The Netherlands ranks next to Belgium and Ireland in the countries in this study in terms of the high ratio of exports and imports to GDP. It has a far larger stake in outward FDI (Table 1.1). This openness has created difficulties for the Netherlands in the past two decades of great volatility in the international economy. That volatility was compounded by a set of problems frequently experienced in natural resource development, in this case natural gas, which has been characterized as 'the Dutch disease'. Essentially this involves problems in international competitiveness because of the impact of the boom in gas exports. Such problems include, among other things, a high exchange rate and rising labour costs because of the development and export of natural gas. The problems can extend, as they did in the Netherlands, to the undertaking of large, continuing public expenditures on the basis of a volatile stream of natural resource revenues.

There has been remarkable consistency of policy on FDI in the face of large economic and social changes in the 1970s and 1980s. The Netherlands remains among the most liberal of the countries in this study. This position also existed, it may be added, when more interventionist ideas were more influential before the 1980s. As with some other countries in this study, however, Dutch law allows a formidable list of defences against hostile takeovers, whether internal or from abroad.

Outward Direct Investment

The Netherlands has a long history of outward direct investment in large part associated with its imperial past. In recent times the Anglo-Dutch firms Royal Dutch Shell and Unilever, along with Philips and two chemical firms, have dominated the data on outward FDI, but there are many smaller firms including a considerable number in services (Dunning and Cantwell, 1987, 107). The outward stock was consistently about twice the size of the inward in the 1980s. In *absolute* terms the Netherlands stock of outward FDI ranked after that of the United States and United Kingdom in 1960, and it was still the sixth largest in 1985 (Table 3.1). Employment in affiliates abroad as a percentage of domestic manufacturing employment was 30 per cent in 1980, a figure which, according to Dunning and Cantwell, put it just ahead of countries like Sweden and the United States.

Discussions with both government and company officials emphasized that the substantial stake in outward FDI and in foreign trade were major reasons for the liberal position on the inward side (see De Jong, 1973, 294 for a similar view). Moreover it has been noted that the existence of a small group of MNEs of great size has meant that they do not compete often with other

Dutch MNEs. One consequence is that Dutch governments, when considering the effect of tax or other policies on firms abroad, need not be as concerned about the effects on other Dutch firms as would be the case, for example, in the United States (Vernon, 1977, 183). Moreover, through their holdings in Royal Dutch Shell, the Netherlands could claim whatever security came from having 'full-fledged membership in the Anglo-Saxon oil club', (Franko, 1976, 61). As noted earlier, France's sense of exclusion from this group had led to strong policies on MNEs in petroleum as early as the 1920s.

Policy on Inward Direct Investment

On the inward side the rapid increase in inflows in the 1960s is particularly noteworthy (Table 9.2). The position of the Netherlands in the EC, its strength in entrepot trade, and a strong labour supply position were important aspects of its attractiveness to inward FDI. Indeed problems of pollution and congestion led the government to play down efforts to attract FDI in the late 1960s. A decline in the relative attractiveness of the Netherlands as a locale for investment had occurred by the early 1970s. Throughout the 1970s the inflow of FDI as a percentage of GDP stopped growing for most European countries, but fell sharply for the Netherlands. Increases in labour and social security costs and strong environmental controls appear to have played a role in this relative decline. By the late 1970s the Netherlands government was again actively seeking inward FDI (Kemper and De Smidt, 1980; *The Economist*, 9 December 1978, 86–7). By 1980 employment in foreign-based firms accounted for 19 per cent of manufacturing employment and about twice that in sectors such as chemicals and metals (Dunning and Cantwell, 1987, 103).

On inward FDI the Netherlands has followed a notification process. One part of this is notification to the Ministry of Economic Affairs to secure building and residency permits, and environmental and other approvals required of all firms. The other part is exchange control approval for international capital transfers. This was quite liberal by the early 1970s, involving largely formal notifications and procedures, except for some sectors such as banks and some types of operations such as short-term loans to affiliates.

Dutch restrictions on FDI in certain sectors tend to follow a conventional pattern. There are ownership restrictions for ships flying the Netherlands flag and for airlines based in the Netherlands. The government can prohibit foreign-owned firms from producing defence supplies. Approval is required for mergers of credit institutions and for acquisitions in excess of 5 per cent of share capital; while this applies to both domestic and foreign owners, reciprocity provisions may apply to non-EC investors. Licences for insurance

Table 9.2 Foreign direct investment, Netherlands (million DFl)

Year or end of year	Direct investment capital flows: Inward (net)	Direct investment capital flows: Outward (net)	Stock of direct investment: Inward	Stock of direct investment: Outward	Direct investment earnings[a]: Debit	Direct investment earnings[a]: Credit
1960	162	526			160	766
1961	222	576			193	1 002
1962	441	595			258	902
1963	381	423			202	1 111
1964	594	422			171	1 255
1965	556	538			212	1 372
1966	571	929			259	1 156
1967	921	1 079			290	1 555
1968	1 174	1 240			543	1 685
1969	1 496	-1 942			507	1 834
1970	1 942	1 995			808	1 862
1971	2 065	1 747			1 227	2 268
1972	1 939	2 356			867	2 208
1973	2 363	2 526	21 206	44 047	1 308	2 664
1974	2 602	4 607	23 994	47 386	2 129	3 308
1975	2 470	4 172	26 957	51 328	3 168	2 739
1976	936	2 967	29 159	50 225	2 627	3 163
1977	877	3 715	30 960	55 917	2 625	3 042
1978	1 444	3 781	32 546	59 417	2 952	3 142
1979	2 581	4 709	37 741	70 293	3 530	4 481
1980	3 894	6 495	42 468	85 030	4 569	5 273
1981	3 512	2 180	46 879	95 793	4 240	5 371
1982	1 563	5 168	48 473	99 694	4 335	4 539
1983	1 948	4 401	51 865	119 886	5 040	5 260
1984			53 265	128 086		

Note:
[a]Excluding interest.

Source: De Nederlandsche Bank. From OECD (1987a, 136) except stocks for 1983 and 1984 which are from Dunning and Cantwell (1987, 48). The latter source gives much larger flow data than those shown here, especially on the outward side after 1977. This difference cannot be reconciled by the available data on retained earnings.

appear to require some rules for foreign-based insurers which differ from those of domestically based firms (OECD 1982, 1987b).

Some governments before the 1980s indicated a preference for joint ventures controlled by Dutch nationals, but nothing appears to have been done to enforce such a policy. Indeed legislation exists empowering the government to prohibit investment in any industry where the national interest requires this but, as in the United Kingdom, this law has never been invoked (*Business International*, 1986, 4; Netherlands, Ministry of Economic Affairs, 1).

While there is no screening of inward FDI as such, both foreign-owned firms and those owned locally must observe guidelines established for mergers and acquisitions. The guidelines are voluntary, but various types of pressures are exerted on transgressors. Along with notification procedures the guidelines contain rules designed to protect the interests of shareholders. In addition the trade union is given the opportunity to comment on the merger as it affects employees. It should be noted that Dutch firms with over 100 employees are required to have an elected works council. This advises the company on a number of matters, such as mergers and closures, and must agree on a number of others, such as pensions and working hours. The works council would be consulted on significant outward FDI as well.

There is obviously scope in the various approvals noted above for a government to stop or to modify foreign acquisitions. It does not appear to have used these powers for such purposes. It should be noted that the Dutch commercial code gives firms significant protection against hostile takeovers. Corporations can stipulate that appointments to the Board must be decided by the Board itself. More importantly, because of provisions requiring the assent of at least two-thirds of individual shareholders, majority ownership of voting shares does not guarantee control. These and other provisions have allowed many larger firms to guard against hostile takeovers. Many of these defences were built by firms in response to a wave of takeovers in the 1960s. Others are more recent. In 1989, for example, Philips increased its list of takeover defences by instituting a method to issue preference shares so as to offset the voting power of ordinary shares (*The Economist*, 19 May 1990, 16).

As in other countries with a booming natural resource, special policies have been in effect with respect to natural gas in particular. Concession permits are necessary to explore for oil and gas on the mainland or the Dutch sector of the North Sea. Such concessions involved agreement to use local suppliers to a degree. Apart from taxing a substantial share of profits from gas, gentlemen's agreements were made in 1980 with the two major firms with respect to reinvestment of what were considered excess profits in the Netherlands over the next decade. These investment commitments were made in return for an undertaking from government not to increase its share of gas profits. As with oil, the assumptions about gas prices and markets underlying these agreements changed radically thereafter.

One should note, finally, that the Netherlands instituted a generous system of tax bonuses known as WIR in 1978 in place of a number of existing fiscal incentives to investment. These are available both for construction of new buildings or buying existing ones, as well as for tools and equipment, transport equipment and other facilities. About 70 per cent of private investment benefits from this scheme (OECD, 1983, 177). The basic tax credit is 12.5 per cent but can be adjusted upward for a variety of reasons, such as energy conservation, employment generation and small business investments. These tax bonuses are automatic in the sense that they are based on well-defined legal criteria. In addition there are significant regional development incentives which are given on a more discretionary basis. While the OECD states that the various investment incentives were not designed to attract FDI, and they are available to all eligible firms, the timing of WIR in particular coincides with the renewed interest in attracting FDI as noted earlier. There seems to be agreement that they have affected the investment decisions of a number of direct investors (OECD, 1983, 179; *Business International*, Netherlands 1980, 14). This may be even more the case if one allows for a number of favourable corporation tax provisions of Dutch law relative to those of neighbouring countries.

SWITZERLAND

An examination of Tables 1.1 and 1.3 reveals that Switzerland is at one extreme among the countries in this study. It has one of the smallest populations, but the highest per capita income. It is among the most dependent on foreign trade. It vies with Japan in terms of lack of natural resources, the low ratio of government outlays to total income, and the ratio of outward to inward stock of capital.

The policies of Switzerland on FDI have been heavily influenced by this lack of most natural resources and by her small domestic market. The country has relied heavily on foreign trade and on outward direct investment in a largely successful attempt to secure specialized development on a world scale. While there are counter-pressures from smaller national firms and other sources, the larger business and financial institutions have usually succeeded in persuading the federal government to adopt itself, and press others to pursue, liberal approaches to trade and investment. These efforts have been aided by the fact that Switzerland is a highly decentralized federal state with a substantial amount of direct democracy. One result is to limit the extent to which the federal government, and sometimes government in general, can intervene directly in the economy, and to increase the emphasis on consensus seeking among the different interest groups in the economy.

At the same time Switzerland has not hesitated to protect its distinctive society in the face of the vulnerability to which a small open economy is subjected.[8] Adaptation has come in part through a flexible economic response internationally – through building up newer sectors as older or less competitive ones declined. As is well known, however, a very large part of the costs of international adjustment have fallen on foreign labour, which rose to about a third of the labour force in the boom of the 1960s but took the brunt of the unemployment increases in periods when growth slowed. Swiss governments and the private sector have also taken action to protect some types of industry from foreign control on the inward side, partly as an aspect of Swiss neutrality but partly also simply to minimize such control.

Experience with Outward Direct Investment

Before developing the policy position on inward FDI, a brief look at the data is useful. It must be said that, on a topic for which data are often poor, Switzerland, one of the major home countries, is unusually badly served by data on FDI.[9] The major OECD statistical studies (1981, 1987a) show virtually nothing for Switzerland. The IMF series begins in 1983. One must rely on a few private studies for the period covered here. However the overall statistical picture on FDI is clear.

Switzerland shares with Japan the distinction of having the largest ratio of outward to inward stock for the countries in this study, averaging 4.6 in the late 1970s and 5.4 in 1984. If outward stock is expressed as a percentage of GNP, Switzerland had the highest ratio for the ten major home countries for 1975, 1980 and 1985. This ratio was 49 per cent in 1985, compared with the average for the developed countries of 8 per cent. In 1985 Switzerland accounted for about 6.4 per cent of global outward stocks of FDI (Table 3.1).

It is not clear just what proportion of domestic industry is owned by non-resident interests. The reliance on outward investment, however, is striking. For the 87 largest Swiss MNEs in 1980, employment in foreign affiliates was 18 per cent of domestic employment for all industry and fully 79 per cent for manufacturing alone (Dunning and Cantwell, 1987, 212). This activity is heavily concentrated in the 15 largest Swiss industrial firms, which accounted for at least 80 per cent of foreign personnel and production in 1980 for all Swiss MNEs. The characteristics of these firms have been studied in some detail. Some aspects are shown in Table 9.3.

The Swiss economy, already highly internationalized before 1970, became even more so during the 1970s. Employment in the 15 largest MNEs was stable at home but rose rapidly abroad, while overall employment in Switzerland for all firms fell sharply. This trend to greater internationalization by the larger firms slowed down in the 1980s (Borner *et al.*, 1985, 84–8). Nevertheless questions were raised about the effects on Switzerland of such rapid further internationalization, as well as its causes.

Table 9.3 The geographical distribution of the activities of the 15 largest Swiss industrial MNEs, 1980

	Switzerland	*Industrialized countries*	*Developing countries*	*Total abroad*
Employment	24.9	59.5	15.6	75.1
Investment stock	32.4	58.5	9.1	67.6
Production	25.6	59.6	14.8	74.4
R&D	62.0	35.0	3.0	38.0

Source: Borner *et al.* (1985, 93).

Studies of the motives for such outward investment emphasize factors which are familiar from the analysis in Chapter 3 above. In the host countries these include demand factors in the larger or rapidly growing host countries combined with fiscal and other incentives favouring investment rather than import. In Switzerland the factors involved in outward FDI appear in part to be beyond the control of a national government: for example, a very tight labour market at home relative to those in the host countries, and various costs associated with a federal form of government (Bürgenmeier, 1991, 106–7 and Appendixes). Economic analysis of the consequences of such large outward FDI has concluded broadly that it was both unavoidable and desirable. For example, Niehans (1977) examines the determinants of FDI for five major Swiss MNEs, then asks what would happen to them if MNEs were suppressed but the market imperfections and policy interventions which foster them continued. He concludes that, in such circumstances, Swiss incomes would be significantly reduced. Borner *et al.*, (1985, 93–5) arrive at broadly similar conclusions, namely, that increased multinationalization was unavoidable if the firms' competitive positions were to be maintained, both in the 1970s and later.

For our purposes the main point is that no attempt was made to review outward FDI to ensure employment and other benefits to Switzerland, despite massive internationalization of company operations, in the 1970s especially. Controls on international investment in the late 1970s were intended to stabilize the exchange rate rather than to influence the firms' economic performance. The basic position of its governments has been that the freedom to invest abroad, while it might cause short-term disturbances in employment and other respects, was very much in the Swiss long-term interest as an efficient world-scale producer. That view, repeatedly emphasized in interviews with government officials and managers in the larger business and financial firms, has not prevented some restraints on inward investment.

Policy on Inward Direct Investment

Switzerland has been among the most open of the countries in this study so far as inward investment is concerned. Exchange control, imposed in 1978, was largely removed over the next two years. Authorization is not required for inward direct investment or that by firms already established. Restricted sectors exist but they are reasonably well defined. Policy on inward FDI is by no means absent, however, and sometimes appears in indirect ways.

Throughout the 1970s Switzerland had to take a variety of steps to stem the inflow of foreign exchange, with its strong upward pressure on the franc. These measures were particularly extensive in 1972 and in 1978. In each case most of them were removed within a few years, but some were retained. For example, while the foreign exchange market was largely free after 1980, gentlemen's agreements were made between the National Bank and commercial banks in which the latter undertook to avoid transactions which encourage speculation against the Swiss franc. While this and other measures are not intended to discriminate between firms by country of ownership, they do supply the authorities with a good deal of advance information on major international transactions.

There is a significant list of sectors largely or solely reserved for citizens or residents, or involving reciprocity provisions (OECD, 1985a, 1987b; Briner, 1976). The restrictions on water power date from 1916, many of the others from the Second World War, and reflect in part the Swiss policy of neutrality. There are citizenship, ownership or headquarters limitations in, for example, nuclear power installations, facilities transmitting oil and gas across national frontiers and (in ten cantons) oil and gas production. Similar restrictions apply to air, maritime and rail transport, and a few other sectors such as motion picture distribution. Reciprocity was introduced into Swiss banking law in 1971, partly because of an influx of foreign banks and also to protect the strong position of Swiss banks abroad. Foreign-controlled banks cannot operate unless legal and de facto reciprocity is granted in the home country. In 1975 the three largest Swiss banks issued registered shares for the first time; the significance of this is noted below.

Investment in real estate by foreigners has been significantly limited since the late 1960s, reflecting Swiss concern at the substantial foreign acquisition of residential real estate. Approval would usually be granted by the relevant cantonal authority for land purchases to establish a commercial or industrial subsidiary. Limitations on the acquisitions by foreigners of secondary residences have been tightened over time and were subjected to an overall limit in 1985. In a number of other sectors, statutory monopolies exist at the federal or cantonal level, effectively blocking foreign and other private Swiss interests. In addition to closed sectors, Switzerland restricts membership on the board of directors of all joint stock companies. They must have a majority of members permanently resident in Switzerland and also having Swiss nationality.

This generally liberal approach to foreign ownership must be qualified in three ways. First, although no law exists to this effect, many Swiss officials are of the view that the Swiss government would not allow foreign interests to purchase a major firm without at least reviewing the effects on the community. Governments can always find a way to do so, even without specific laws allowing review. In the case of Switzerland, for example, acquisition of real estate could be a pretext for examining a takeover of an industrial firm.

Second, there is a long history of attempts to limit the importation of foreign workers, an issue involving many economic and social questions. Since 1973 the federal government has limited the number of authorizations granted to foreigners who intend to carry on a remunerative activity in Switzerland. Work permits are issued both by the cantons and by the federal authorities. While the issuance of work permits applies to all firms, wherever owned, including the large Swiss MNEs, they have a particularly heavy impact on those foreign-owned firms which plan for a time to import significant numbers of workers from abroad. Interviewees of quite different backgrounds – both Swiss and foreign, industrial, financial and legal – emphasized that such controls significantly limited the amount of inward FDI, and cited specific examples of firms which located elsewhere in Europe because of the failure to secure work permits for technical and other personnel. Some of them believed the cantons in particular have used this power at times to block inward FDI, although this can be appealed to the federal government, which has a quota at its disposal. Residency and work permits for foreign staff are required in other countries, of course, but they are often more easily secured, for technical personnel in particular.

Third, and most important, Swiss firms have erected a formidable set of barriers to prevent hostile takeovers, both from outside the country and within. There is no provision in Swiss law preventing such takeovers, whatever the source, except for the sectors noted above. There are provisions which allow firms which wish to do so to make a hostile takeover impossible from abroad and very difficult from within Switzerland. These provisions go well beyond the limitations on share purchases over significant periods of time as an aspect of the attempt to control huge inflows of capital. Briefly Swiss law on limited companies allows both bearer and registered shares. The latter can be designated by the firm as tenable only by Swiss nationals and firms. Such a designation was made by many firms in the 1940s and 1970s.[10] They also converted bearer shares to registered, or increased the latter, and issued various types of non-voting shares so as to concentrate voting power in the registered shares. In addition firms enjoy considerable latitude in the registration provisions. Firms can set a limit on shares held by any one shareholder. They can also give themselves the power to refuse to register new shareholders, without explanation. The Swiss banks, it may be added, assist firms in monitoring the registration process. Under such a system even Swiss nationals and Swiss-controlled firms who succeed in acquiring a significant proportion of the registered shares of a firm may be unable to exercise control because of refusal by the firm to register the shares. In 1987 the Swiss firms, Hero and Sulzer, in each case were able to ward off domestic takeover attempts by this method (*The Economist*, 18 January 1989, 69).

Both the legal basis for the measures noted above and their actual implementation by the firms have had something to do with concerns about the effects of foreign control of the larger firms for a country with a policy of neutrality. These are continuing concerns, but were particularly important in the 1940s with regard to German firms and, in the 1970s, firms associated with governments in the OPEC countries. The federal government made it clear in the mid-1970s that, if such 'voluntary' methods to protect the Swiss character of limited companies should fail to do so, it was prepared to consider further measures (Briner, 1976, 73–7). There has been considerable resistance by many larger firms to efforts to reform company law in the 1970s and 1980s so as to modify some of these provisions in Swiss law. Switzerland has come under some pressure from other governments in this regard, including particularly those where Swiss firms have made major acquisitions which are sometimes contested. Perhaps more important, domestic interests are also pressing for changes, in part because the undervaluation of firm assets which results affects stock values and the ability to secure capital. Perhaps the most startling change recently has been the decision by Nestlé, whose shares amount to over 10 per cent of the capitalization of the Swiss stock market, to give foreigners the same shareholding rights as Swiss investors. The company also indicated that it would limit the holdings of any one shareholder (*The Economist*, 26 November 1988, 74–5).

Share registration, much less a wide variety of takeover defences, are hardly unknown elsewhere. In the United States especially, but increasingly in some other countries, the 1980s in particular have witnessed the issue of shares with different voting rights, share acquisition ratios which trigger various protective devices against hostile takeovers, and many other devices limited only by the ingenuity of the lawyers and financiers involved, the financial stake of their clients and the often vague limits imposed by law. Nevertheless two things distinguish the Swiss experience. Such protective devices began much earlier as a widespread phenomenon, at least among the larger firms. And Swiss protection of shareholder's rights appears to have lagged significantly behind that in other countries (Table 11.5).

One should also add that Switzerland, like most other industrial countries, is interested in attracting certain types of FDI. In the mid-1960s a Commission which favoured cutting government subsidies had some trouble locating industrial subsidies for this purpose (Katzenstein, 1980, 517). That was certainly not the situation with respect to competition among the cantons to attract firms with the lure of low tax rates. And by the late 1970s it was also not the situation with respect to subsidies to industry. A wide range of subsidies had become available at the cantonal level in particular, where much of the responsibility for industry establishment lay. The federal government also offered subsidies for more limited purposes, such as for diversification or innovation in low-income regimes and those dependent on a single industry. These programmes do not distinguish between firms by nationality of ownership, with a few exceptions dependent on reciprocity in the firm's home country. It should be added that the range of tax and other concessions available at the federal, cantonal and municipal level would allow for significant discretion between firms, wherever owned (OECD, 1983, 213–18; *Business International*, Switzerland, 1987, 14).

UNITED KINGDOM

Policy Position

Policy towards inward FDI in the United Kingdom could be described until 1979 as one of 'qualified welcome' (Steuer *et al.*, 1973, 180). There is virtually no law on direct investment as such, and the general policy is one of securing adherence to key industrial policies, such as regional development, by all firms. The existence of exchange control provided an early warning system on direct investment, which allowed various agencies to intervene occasionally with such investment or to support competing firms controlled in the United Kingdom. The strength of exchange controls was much reduced in the 1970s. With the election of a Conservative government and the ending of exchange controls in 1979 the emphasis shifted to the welcoming aspect but not unconditionally – one study refers to the 1980s as a period of 'bounded prejudice', of liberalism with an occasional resort to intervention (Young *et al.*, 1988, 197). The policies potentially directed to FDI consist of a number of restricted sector limitations, notably in petroleum, and a provision of the Industry Act in 1975 empowering the minister to prohibit proposed foreign takeovers in manufacturing. This provision has never been used. Ad hoc support continues to be given in order to maintain a domestic presence in some sectors or firms, and legislation on monopolies and other policies is very occasionally used with a similar effect. Deregulation and privatization have opened some publicly owned firms to private investors, while often limiting the stake of foreign investors.

As with other countries, what follows concentrates largely on policies directed to foreign-owned firms. There are other impediments to acquisitions of firms, whether by domestic or foreign investors, reflecting takeover defences allowed by law, close holdings, rights of minority shareholders and other factors. The United Kingdom appears to be relatively open in terms of these other impediments (for example, Table 11.5). In the late 1980s it was by far the largest target for cross-border acquisitions by value in Europe (*World Deal Review*, 1991, 14).

On the outward side the United Kingdom authorities have often moved to protect the interests of a major home country. The UK government has been very active in supporting UK firms on specific issues, such as opposition to unitary tax measures in the United States, various extraterritorial policies such as those noted in Chapter 2 in connection with Soviet gas exports to Western Europe, and the Vredeling proposals of the EC regarding consultation with employees (Stopford and Turner, 1985, 203–18).

One can certainly point to considerable differences in the rhetoric and to some differences in the policies of the two major political parties with regard to industrial policy in general and FDI in particular. Significant differences in philosophy and approach can be cited in the approach to industrial restructuring and the treatment of the petroleum industry, for example, though the international circumstances and other factors also conditioned such approaches. Nevertheless a generally liberal policy towards inward FDI has broadly characterized both Conservative and Labour governments. Similarities in policy can be related to the concern that retaliation against the large UK interest abroad might follow any restrictive UK policies; to a perception among most politicians and civil servants that foreign investment is beneficial, with few serious problems; and to immediate balance of payments pressures for most of the post-war period (Hodges, 1974, 7; Gillespie, 1972, 400–3; and interviews in 1982 with government officials). Some elements of the Labour Party have taken a more critical view of direct investment.

Outward Direct Investment

The United Kingdom was for long the major direct investor abroad. In 1914 and 1928, for example, the UK stock of FDI abroad has been estimated at 46 per cent and 40 per cent, respectively, of the total world stock. By 1960 that figure had fallen to 16 per cent (Dunning, 1983, 87). Much of that change had to do, first, with the decline in UK assets abroad during the Second World War, then with the surge in US direct investment abroad.

In the period after the Second World War the United Kingdom also became a major host country, notably for US firms. It has been estimated that the United Kingdom's stock of outward FDI exceeded the inward stock by about 30 times in 1914 and 15 times in 1938 (Dunning, 1985b, 16). By 1962 it was only about two and a half times as large and stayed below that ratio for most of the next two decades (Table 9.4).

Table 9.4 Direct investment stocks, United Kingdom, 1962–87 (£ billions)

	Excluding oil, banking and insurance		*Including oil, banking and insurance*	
	Inward	*Outward*	*Inward*	*Outward*
1962	1.4	3.4	2.1	4.9
1965	2.0	4.2	—	—
1966	—	—	3.1	6.3
1968	2.7	5.6	—	—
1970	3.3	6.4	4.8	8.9
1971	7.8	6.7	5.4	9.3
1972	4.1	7.9	5.8	10.8
1973	5.4	8.7	7.5	11.6
1974	6.6	10.1	9.5	13.1
1975	7.0	11.5	11.1	15.0
1976	7.6	14.6	12.9	19.6
1977	8.7	14.8	14.7	20.1
1978	11.0	19.2	17.1	25.5
1979	13.3	19.7	21.3	30.7
1980	15.9	20.6	26.4	33.2
1981	17.0	28.6	30.0	44.9
1982	17.5	34.1	32.3	52.0
1983	19.5	37.9	37.2	57.8
1984	—	—	40.1	79.1
1985	—	—	43.5	74.4
1986	—	—	48.2	88.0
1987	—	—	53.4	91.4

Note:
Data are book values of net assets.

Source: OECD (1987b, 165, 161) except Dunning and Cantwell (1987, 111) for 1962 and 1966 and IMF, *Balance of Payments Statistics* 1988, 739 for 1980–87 (including oil etc).

Nevertheless outward FDI has remained a major factor in the UK economy, as is evident in a variety of statistics (Dunning and Cantwell, 1987, 119). Employment in foreign affiliates of UK multinationals was equal to 23 per cent of employment in domestic manufacturing in 1981. As noted in Table 9.5, the assets of UK multinationals abroad were equal to 15 to 34 per cent of domestic assets in a considerable range of industries. These percentages would go much higher with finer breakdowns of industry.

In recent decades the questions raised about the effects of outward direct investment on the home country have been very similar to those raised in other home countries. In political terms, for example, the extensive UK

Table 9.5 Industrial distribution of foreign firms in United Kingdom and UK firms abroad, 1978 (percentages)

	Foreign firms' shares of UK assets	*UK firms' assets abroad as percentage of domestic assets*
Primary		
Agriculture	N/A	34.4
Mining & quarrying	N/A	29.5
Oil	37.9	30.3
Manufacturing		
Food & drink	8.0	23.4
Chemicals & allied	15.2	34.4
Metals	16.4	23.7
Mechanical engineering	21.9	8.7
Electrical equipment	17.0	10.2
Motor vehicles	24.1	6.1
Other transportation equipment	N/A	32.7
Textiles & clothing	2.4	16.1
Paper & allied	10.6	21.9
Other manufacture	9.0	15.4
Services		
Construction	2.3	10.5
Transport, communications	4.2	18.8
Trade & distribution	10.3	22.8
Banking & finance	N/A	13.0
Other services	6.9	12.4

Source: Dunning and Cantwell (1987, 117–19).

investments abroad were inevitably involved in many of the nationalizations by newly independent states after the Second World War. In the 1960s, for example, about half of all reported nationalizations involved UK affiliates (Hood and Young, 1979, 257–8). On the whole these appear to have been handled in a more accommodating way by the UK authorities than has been the case in the United States; there is no UK counterpart to the US Hickenlooper Amendment (Stopford and Turner, 1985, 201). In economic terms, the closing of tax havens and other tax issues involving UK multinationals have exercised many UK governments (see, for example, *The Economist*, 26 March 1983, 16). The continued substantial outward investment has often raised the question whether it reflected a relative increase in the competitiveness of UK multinationals or a decline in the locational attractions of the United Kingdom.[11]

One of the dominant economic issues has been that which is examined with regard to Sweden and the United States, namely, the effect of outward FDI on employment and on the balance of payments of the United Kingdom. These issues are related, as noted in connection with the studies for the other countries. In considering these issues, it is important to keep in mind that the United Kingdom maintained exchange controls throughout the post-Second World War period until 1979. Outward direct investment required permission from the Bank of England. The object of such controls was to ensure that the financing of direct investment abroad was done in ways which minimized the cost to the foreign exchange reserves. In general terms what this meant was the following:

1. Where an outward direct investment met a 'super criterion' it could be financed with official exchange up to the greater of £250 000 or 50 per cent of the cost of the investment. This meant it could secure foreign exchange at the official rate rather than pay the premium involved in the market for investment currency. Such outward investments were expected directly to promote UK exports and bring other benefits to the balance of payments which equalled within 18 months the value of the investment. More generous terms were provided for EC investments and sterling area investments could be made freely.
2. Where an outward investment did not meet this criterion it could still be made by the purchase of investment currency, borrowing foreign currency (subject to certain rules), export of capital equipment and other ways as approved by the Bank of England.
3. The Bank of England reviewed the performance of UK-controlled subsidiaries and normally required that two-thirds of the net earnings be repatriated each year.[12]

It is our understanding from the interviews that outward direct investment was not monitored except for exchange control reasons, notably to ensure the repatriation to the UK of a certain portion of profits. However those planning large direct investments abroad were informally asked by government officials whether they had considered options more favourable to United Kingdom employment and other objectives.

There was considerable debate over the effects of such controls on the balance of payments. In 1968 two comprehensive studies were published on the effects of outward FDI on the home country's balance of payments: Hufbauer and Adler for US firms and Reddaway *et al.* for UK firms. These studies differed in a number of ways. For example, the US study relied on published data and analysis of a broad range of effects, while the UK study concentrated on information from 65 major UK firms, including differential effects of UK and other ownership. In addition the UK study assumed that competitive firms would undertake investments forgone by UK firms, while the US study made some alternative assumptions. If one compares the assumption common to both studies, it appears that UK overseas investment took longer than did US investments to generate an equivalent pay-back effect on the balance of payments. In general the studies seemed to suggest that outward FDI in manufacturing was helpful to the home country's balance of payments after a relatively short period, particularly for the United States, and that continued controls were damaging to the home country's balance of payments.

Whatever one's position on these and other studies, the fact is that the UK continued exchange controls for a decade after their completion. By then the oil from the North Sea had reduced the balance of payments pressures felt for so long, but it was the election of a Conservative government in 1979 which finally ended the controls. There was some doubt in any case about their effectiveness, given the ability of larger firms in particular to borrow abroad, not least because of the growth of Eurocurrency and Eurobond markets (Hood and Young, 1979, 310). Nevertheless there was a brief post-control increase in outflows, as noted in Table 9.6, especially if one deducts retained earnings.

Inward Direct Investment

The importance of FDI in the United Kingdom can be shown in various ways. Foreign-controlled firms accounted in 1981 for 38 per cent of UK assets in the petroleum industry and from 15 to 24 per cent of assets in the chemicals, metals, mechanical engineering, electrical and automobile industries (Dunning and Cantwell, 1987, 117).[13]. Such firms accounted for 13 per cent of overall employment in manufacturing (Table 3.5). This percentage

Table 9.6 Direct investment flows, United Kingdom, 1960–84 (£ million)

Year	*Direct investment capital flows*[a]			
	Inward (net)	*Of which retained earnings*	*Outward (net)*	*Of which retained earnings*
1960	135	67	250	85
1961	236	37	226	14
1962	130	58	209	95
1963	160	90	236	118
1964	162	80	263	147
1965	197	118	308	167
1966	196	93	276	183
1967	170	97	281	190
1968	274	176	410	277
1969	322	133	549	321
1970	363	180	546	322
1971	450	184	676	329
1972	408	304	737	465
1973	734	344	1 621	840
1974	854	251	1 576	851
1975	615	247	1 171	879
1976	799	541	2 145	1 454
1977	1 326	838	1 885	1 292
1978	1 261	720	2 710	1 260
1979	1 740	1 226	3 035	1 622
1980	2 541	689	3 317	1 634
1981	998	638	5 134	2 032
1982	1 074	770	2 529	1 662
1983	2 196	1 097	3 535	2 181
1984	2 689	1 743	2 999	2 360

Note:
[a]Excludes oil companies.

Source: OECD (1987b, 161) until 1980, Dunning and Cantwell (1987, 112) for remainder.

had approximately doubled from 1963 to 1981. The United States has been the dominant investor on the inward side.

UK policy on inward FDI (Table 9.7) has evolved in part in response to changes in government with differing views of the effectiveness of state intervention in industry. Such intervention, however, is itself the result of issues believed to be associated with growing foreign control of certain

Table 9.7 Some aspects of UK policy on inward FDI

1947	Exchange Control Act allows loose scope for review beyond exchange control aspects: provisions reduced in scope in 1970s, ended 1979.
1966	Industrial Reorganization Corporation created, partly with a view to reducing reliance on FDI; along with new Ministry of Technology, leads to direct intervention in several sectors (e.g. motor cars, computers).
1967	Companies Act provides for more disclosure by MNEs.
1975	British National Oil Corporation created; government control of oil and gas industry strengthened.
1975	Industry Act empowers minister to prohibit foreign takeovers in manufacturing.
1979	Exchange controls end.
1980s	Privatizations of state-owned firms include golden share provisions restricting holdings of any one shareholder, domestic and foreign. Various ad hoc FDI interventions by sectors, partly involving trade and incentive issues.
1986	Significant financial deregulation also eases access by foreign-owned firms.
1987	Banking Bill gives Bank of England power to block purchase of over 15 per cent shares of a UK bank from any source.

Note:
See text for more details.

industries. As background to the sections on particular policies, these two issues are considered in turn.

In terms of the issues involved, a very comprehensive study of economic and political issues by Steuer *et al.* (1973) broke new ground in some areas, such as industrial relations, and still warrants rereading, despite the growth in the literature since its publication.[14] Its conclusions (pp. 12–15) were hedged by the lack of information and the possibility that others would see the economic and non-economic issues differently. Nevertheless they state that 'On economic grounds and grounds of national autonomy we express few arguments against inward direct investment' (p. 15). The strongest recommendations were: (a) collecting more information on MNE activities; (b) some sympathy on non-economic grounds for an overall general limit, but not for selecting applicants; and (c) action to improve the balance of payments so that UK firms could participate more fully in international investment.

The pioneering study of the effects of inward investment in the period after the Second World War was that by Dunning (1958) on the impact of US investment on UK manufacturing. He continued with many other studies on MNEs, some of which are collected in Dunning (1981). For present purposes we concentrate on his 1985b study of the characteristics of three sets of firms, namely, the production of foreign-owned firms in the United Kingdom, of UK multinationals outside the United Kingdom, and of uninational UK firms.[15] Analysis of data for 1971 and 1979, while subject to a number of statistical qualifications, suggest two broad conclusions. In the first place, the ownership-specific advantages of MNEs have helped the United Kingdom to adjust to sectors in which it is most competitive, and also to improve the efficiency of existing sectors. Second, MNEs have adjusted to the changing locational advantages of the United Kingdom more than have uninational firms. In terms of adaptation to market needs, for example, both foreign firms in the United Kingdom and UK firms abroad are much more likely to invest in growth sectors (especially when growth includes exports from the United Kingdom) than is the case for uninational UK firms.

Comparisons limited to the UK-owned firms manufacturing in the United Kingdom and foreign-owned affiliates in the United Kingdom tend to favour the latter. Thus such foreign affiliates produced in sectors with above-average productivity or profit and were better represented in growth sectors (especially if defined to include exports). They were also more highly represented in sectors where the average concentration ratio was higher.

The policy conclusions one draws from this type of analysis depend on what else one takes into account. Dunning notes that these favourable effects on the economic structure have been accompanied by interdependence between national markets, and increased vulnerability to international changes in the UK economy. This and other issues where private and public national interests can diverge, notably in the exercise of monopoly power by multinationals and the effects of the policies of other governments, led him to recommend that MNE activities be monitored and some effort made to ensure consistency with national objectives (Dunning, 1985b, 47–50 and ch. 13).

A comprehensive recent review of the economic impact of inward FDI on the United Kingdom (Young *et al.*, 1988) tended to confirm the conclusion of the earlier studies that the net impact was probably beneficial, but did so with more qualifications. The cyclical variability and relative decline in competitiveness of the major source, US multinationals, was one concern. Another is the lack of strong linkage to domestically owned firms in most sectors, an issue which the authors note has at least as much to do with UK competitiveness as with multinationals. The independent decision-making capacity of the subsidiary, particularly with regard to innovations, is also an issue, given the centralized control which goes with some types of global rationalization (Young *et al.*, 1988, chs 3 and 5).

Some groups in the United Kingdom, notably some elements of the Labour Party and the trade union movement, have advocated stronger positions than those taken by any of the post-Second World War governments to date. Their concerns are many, but two which appear often are the perception of diminished government power over the national economy and the effects of MNE investment decisions on jobs. The Trades Union Congress, for example, has stated that inward FDI should be encouraged provided it is on the right terms, but that outward investment should be limited to cases where it does not compete with UK industry. It has repeatedly recommended either more social ownership to counter such firms or more accountability, including a Foreign Investment Review Agency to deal with individual cases.[16]

Studies of the perceptions of UK elite groups suggest that the great majority believe that the overall effects of MNEs on the United Kingdom are beneficial. This was true both of British members of parliament and of civil servants, although more so of the latter. The results are in contrast with the views of their French counterparts, which were decidedly more negative in both cases. The surveys were made in 1973, after some academic studies and individual cases had highlighted problems with MNEs in both countries (Graham, 1982, 239–49). Surveys in 1969–71 had also confirmed that most UK civil servants and politicians believed inward FDI was beneficial to the UK economy and led to few serious problems. Among the principal gains which were seen were support for the balance of payments and access to technological and managerial skills. Back-bench Labour parliamentarians were more critical, however, than their front-bench colleagues (Hodges, 1974, ch. 4).

In terms of policy on inward FDI, it was noted earlier that exchange control was in effect until 1979. Such control provided that inward investment be financed by a capital inflow rather than borrowing in London, and also that Treasury permission be secured before a foreign firm took control of the stock of a domestic company. The Conservative government of the 1950s and early 1960s took a very liberal view of the substantial increase in inward FDI during this period.[17] As long as it made a contribution to the balance of payments – an issue of some importance given the UK's problems in that respect – little seems to have been done of a restrictive nature beyond attaching conditions to some major takeovers. For example, the purchase of Trinidad Oil Company by the Texas Company in 1956 was strongly protested by the Labour party, partly on the grounds that this gave the US firm control of Trinidad Oil's significant Canadian holdings. The government approved the deal subject to certain conditions intended to assure full use of the operations in Trinidad. The purchase by US Ford of the minority interest in UK Ford in 1960 was also approved, subject to conditions noted below. Gillespie (1972, 400) concluded that formal disapproval of proposals for investments were small in number or perhaps non-existent, although he adds that unwanted proposals could be withdrawn or discouraged.

The Labour government of 1964–70 took a different perspective on the issue of state intervention in industry in general and with regard to some types of MNE activities in particular. As had happened a few years earlier in France, concern grew about a technological gap with the United States and the penetration of US firms in large or rapidly growing sectors. Legislative support was given to mergers and to industrial reorganization with a view to increasing the competitiveness of UK firms, but also in the hope that this would make it less likely that they would be absorbed by foreign firms. Thus the Mergers and Monopolies Act of 1965 and the Industrial Reorganization Act of 1966 could both be regarded in part as designed to minimize foreign takeovers, although not explicitly designed to discriminate against foreign firms, and certainly highly involved with local firms. The Industrial Reorganization Corporation did play a role both directly and indirectly in attempting to reduce reliance on foreign investors. For example, it supported Stokes in the formation of British Leyland, and it stopped the Swedish multinational, SKF, from acquiring the leading UK firm in ball-bearings.[18] A new Ministry of Technology also took a close interest in the impact of FDI, urging the Treasury to take into account performance other than the balance of payments effects where foreign takeovers occurred in industries considered important. Trade union concerns about MNEs led the government to urge the OECD in 1970 to consider the problems raised by such firms. The Companies Act of 1967 provided for more disclosure of information by MNEs (Graham, 1982, 262–3).

It would be a mistake to differentiate sharply the Labour government's policies from those which followed. Steuer *et al.* (1973, 179–80) note that

> In no case of any importance, where the applicant has been prepared to meet the conditions of finance, has permission for any genuine manufacturing or service investment been refused, and in general refusals of permission have been extremely rare.

They ascribed this outcome partly to the fact that exchange control criteria were well known and those who could not meet them would not apply, and partly to the fact that in a few important cases the firms had given performance undertakings beyond those necessary for exchange control reasons.[19]

Again, in a study concentrating on the UK government's policies in 1964–70, Hodges (1974, 285) concludes that the Labour government did not distinguish between the foreign-controlled and domestic firms in its policies in most important respects. He suggests that this attitude was the result of several factors: a desire to protect the much larger outward stock of FDI from retaliation; the fact that US firms, which dominated the inward side, were considered (perhaps incorrectly) more acceptable than those from other countries; and the persistence of balance of payments problems. He also suggests that the division of responsibility on FDI among government departments led to a view that the problems associated with such firms were limited in relation to the benefits. The exceptions to this were in automobiles and computers where the Ministry of Technology had jurisdiction and some steps were taken to regulate the industries (ibid., 286–93).

The Conservative government of 1970–74, despite public concerns about MNEs in automobile and other sectors, took little further action against such firms. The Industrial Reorganization Corporation was replaced by a weaker body. With the return of a Labour government in 1974, responsibility for government industrial policy was centred in the new Industry Department. An Industry Act of 1975 contained two provisions worth noting here. One was a provision allowing the government to block the foreign takeover of a firm in manufacturing, a provision not used to date. The other was a provision for government–industry planning of industry sectors, involving both foreign-owned and indigenous firms. The government showed considerable preoccupation with industrial structuring, through organizations such as the National Enterprise Board and the National Economic Development Council. With the escalation of oil prices in 1973–4 a Crown Corporation was established in 1975 so as to share more fully in oil rents and to control development of the industry. Yet the policy of this Labour government towards MNE investments in general was not notably more restrictive than that of the preceding government. Faced by possible disinvestment in

Chrysler's UK factories, for example, it approved a large aid package. The government opposed EC efforts to regulate MNEs, while supporting a largely voluntary OECD declaration and guidelines on MNEs (Graham, 1982, 267–69). The newly elected Conservative government in 1979 ended exchange controls, proceeded to deregulate some sectors and particularly to reduce state ownership in a number of major firms, including petroleum.

Restricted Sectors and Key Firms

A few sectors or firms are protected by law from foreign ownership, in whole or in part, or involve reciprocity provisions in the home country if a takeover is involved. Air transport licences are granted only to nationals or firms controlled by nationals unless the government determines otherwise. Acquisition of UK-flag vessels is similarly restricted. Broadcasting is restricted to nationals of the United Kingdom or the EC or firms incorporated in and having their head office in those countries. Some sectors of banking, finance and insurance had reciprocity requirements in the home country in the early 1980s. Support for films and consultancy contracts on overseas aid were restricted to nationals (OECD, 1982, 1983, 1987b).

In privatizing various public firms in the 1980s the Conservative government included a 'golden share', allowing it to limit the size of a shareholding in a privatized firm or to insist on British directors. The golden share could be used to stop any single investor, domestic or foreign, from taking more than a specified amount of shares, usually 15 per cent. This provision normally lasted five years. Firms such as British Aerospace, Jaguar and Rolls-Royce were privatized with provision for such a share. In 1988 the EC asked the UK government to justify the 15 per cent limit. Member governments of the EC are allowed to discriminate against nationals of other members, so far as capital transactions are concerned, only in particular circumstances such as national security issues.

In understanding the UK approach to restricted sectors, it is important to add that special support has been given to some major companies in order to maintain a UK presence in certain industries in competition with foreign-controlled firms. This support goes beyond those industries which tend to be public monopolies generally. The automobile and computer industries deserve specific comment. In addition two sectors, finance and energy, have involved special forms of support or protection. These four industries are considered below.

The three larger US-owned automobile firms had all gained a strong presence in the UK by the late 1960s. In the case of Ford's takeover of the minority UK shares (1960) and Chrysler's takeover of the controlling interest in Rootes (1967), a number of assurances were sought before permission was given by the government.[20] Moreover, in the belief that the British-owned firms might not survive the competition, the government gave considerable encouragement, including financial support, for their merger during 1964–8 into British Leyland Motor Corporation. As noted earlier, the Chrysler operations in the United Kingdom, experiencing considerable losses, were given substantial further support in 1975 in the face of possible disinvestment. A government which was attempting to gain public support for industrial restructuring found itself supporting what was widely regarded as a losing cause, thanks to pressure from groups such as trade unions and Scottish nationalists anxious to avoid immediate plant closures and trading partners anxious to avoid any imposition of import controls (*The Economist*, 13 December 1975, 87–8 and 20 December 1975, 75–83). Despite this and other support, the government agreed in 1978 to allow Peugeot to buy Chrysler UK. The growing financial problems of the US parent, as well as industrial relations problems in the UK industry, were important aspects of this sale.

Meanwhile British Leyland, by now state-owned, was also in difficulty. Significant state aid was made available in the late 1970s, which had totalled £3.8 billion in grants and guarantees by 1986. Various proposals for partial or full sale to non-residents were under consideration in the early 1980s, including a proposal to sell to Ford and General Motors which was abandoned by the government early in 1986, at least in part because of a public outcry at thus disposing of yet another UK-controlled motor firm.[21] In the meantime attention had shifted to attempts to attract Japanese firms into local production, a topic which will be touched on below when considering the review process.

While policy on automobiles often involved agreeing to foreign affiliation in order to avoid bankruptcy or to slow employment declines, policy on computers raised a different issue – the desire to maintain a domestic presence in a dynamic high-technology sector closely related to many other such sectors and to military development. The problem faced by the Labour government elected in 1964 and by the British-owned firms was the very strong position of International Business Machines (IBM) in the UK market and, indeed, in the world market. As the Managing Director of International Computers put it a few years later, 'There is no problem in the computer business which could not be solved by the demise of IBM' (Hodges, 1974, 227). In 1964 the four British-owned firms had 41 per cent of the UK market, IBM had 40 per cent and other US firms had 10 per cent. At the world level IBM had had 60 per cent since the 1950s (Hodges, 1974, 228).

The first policy attempted was a price preference for computers purchased by government from UK-owned computer firms. By 1968 the government had decided to merge the major UK-owned firms into International Computers Limited (ICL) and to place government orders for large computer systems with it without tenders from other firms. In 1965–9 the share of ICL in the public sector market rose from 39 per cent to 73 per cent, while its share in the private sector market rose from 29 to 40 per cent. IBM's public sector share fell from 23 per cent to 9 per cent (Hodges, 1974, 233–6). Government support for ICL was given in other ways, such as 10 per cent ownership of its shares, support for its R&D, and support for mergers involving the firm. This support was not unlimited, however, for UK governments clearly intended to maintain access to foreign technology, and were not prepared to favour ICL without some regard for price and quality of product. At the same time the support was considered justifiable not only in terms of the importance of the industry but also to help offset the substantial support US firms received from their home government's military and space programmes.

Support for ICL continued through the 1970s, despite the occasional protest from foreign-owned firms.[22] Both EC rules and the GATT would eventually reduce some types of support, such as government purchases. For a time the policy was considered highly successful in the sense that the United Kingdom was one of the few countries in which a nationally-owned mainframe computer manufacturer retained a large share in competition with IBM. In the early 1980s, however, ICL had run into serious problems requiring substantial further government support through loan guarantees and leading it into a technical and marketing agreement with a major Japanese firm. Its circumstances improved subsequently, but in 1990 control of ICL was acquired by Fujitsu (*World Deal Review*, 1991, 406–7).

ICL was not the only UK effort to develop a presence in information technology. The Labour government of the 1970s planned to launch a number of small companies in this area under the aegis of the National Enterprise Board. It remained for its successor government to launch several of these in the early 1980s, not without much hesitation (*Financial Review*, 24 June 1981, 36).

Banking and finance consists of many sectors, some of which had been penetrated by foreign firms by the 1970s. However a series of informal understandings, as distinct from statutory instruments, prevented entry to some sectors. In 1977, for example, there were about 300 foreign banks in the United Kingdom which were authorized to deal in foreign exchange. Few of them had branches, however, and none were clearing banks. The attempt in 1981 by the Hong Kong and Shanghai Banking Corporation to secure control of the Royal Bank of Scotland, a clearing bank but not one of the four major ones, was turned away by the Monopolies and Mergers Commission. Opposition by the Bank of England was said to be an important factor in that decision. In 1982, faced with two bids (one foreign) for the same bank, the Bank of England indicated that it was opposed to foreign takeovers of the four major clearing banks. Both bids were turned down. In the Banking Bill of 1987 the government gave the Bank of England the power to block the purchase of over 15 per cent of a UK bank.[23] The Governor of the Bank of England has made it clear that he intended to use this power not only to assess whether a prospective investor is 'fit and proper', as the Act states, but also to ensure 'a strong and continuing British presence in the banking system'. Nevertheless some foreign-bank penetration of the clearing system was allowed in the late 1980s (*The Economist*, 1 December 1983, 80; 14 February 1987, 68; and 26 March 1988, 70; Bank of England, *Quarterly Bulletin*, November, 1987, 525–6).

The mid-1980s were critical in sweeping away a number of regulations which fixed minimum commission rates on securities trading, segregated financial markets, or limited access to them by foreign-owned firms. Such firms quickly extended their participation in the Stock Exchange, in stockbroking, the government bond market and insurance, in all of which their participation had been limited or prohibited in fact, if not in law. These trends were also becoming evident, more slowly, in other major European centres. It should be added that the UK Financial Services Act of 1986 allowed the government to divest foreign-owned firms or block foreign entry in certain financial service sectors on the ground of lack of reciprocity.

As in other countries, issues in petroleum attracted a great deal of government attention in the 1970s, including such questions as ensuring supply, increasing public revenue and domestic sourcing. The situation of the United Kingdom was somewhat different from that of some other countries in this study in that, along with the major foreign-controlled MNEs, there was a major Anglo-Dutch firm, a major UK firm with significant public ownership, and a number of smaller firms.[24]

The major changes in policy came as a result of the supply and price problems in petroleum in 1973–4. These coincided with the election of a Labour government in 1974, which moved quickly to deal with these problems. The British National Oil Corporation (BNOC) was established in 1975.[25] It was given a wide range of powers in exploration, transportation and production, and also took over the government's participation in UK licences. At the same time, the government's powers to control production of oil and gas, including the securing of information from licensees, were strengthened. Licences were granted on the basis that, with some exceptions, BNOC was entitled to a 51 per cent share in production. This was purchased by BNOC, then resold to the private firms, with a view to guaranteeing a more stable supply than was believed to be otherwise available. It appears that there was discussion in the government of securing partial ownership of the companies involved, in addition to the government stake in British Petroleum, but this was abandoned as expensive and perhaps ineffective.[26] The government also decided not to proceed with a plan to secure majority state participation in existing licences; such participation was to be 'voluntary', a somewhat elastic term, given the discretionary nature of the new awards available to the government. It is clear that the United Kingdom had moved to a more restrictive regime in a short time (Noreng, 1980, 51–3, 125; Grayson, 1981, 181–4).

The issuance of the licences at each round to national and multinational firms was the key to the state's influence. It involved consideration of the contribution the applicant had made to the UK economy, reciprocity in other countries, opportunity for local firms to compete for orders for goods and services, as well as cooperation in working out BNOC's share. The emphasis involved in the contributions made by the firms could vary; for example, in the early 1980s there was considerable emphasis on the development of new technologies. The potential leverage given by the licensing rounds was significant. Attempts to exercise that leverage involved significant monitoring. Perhaps particularly noteworthy was the scrutiny developed of industry purchases by the Offshore Supplies Office, along with assistance given UK firms so as to enable them to bid on offshore contracts. While there are data problems in such surveys, the share of UK firms in the offshore market was reported to have risen from 40 per cent in 1974 to 72 per cent in the five years to 1983 (Young *et al.*, 1988, 220–21; Noreng, 1980, 202).

In 1978 BNOC or British Gas were also given the first opportunity to negotiate for earlier licences which licence holders wished to yield.[27] All of this involved some tension between BNOC and the firms involved – both foreign and domestic – as did the state's attempt to secure a larger share of the rents.[28] The Conservative government elected in 1978 promptly indicated that major changes were in store for BNOC, including divestment of much of its offshore activity to the private sector and loss of its preferential position when existing licensing interests were assigned between firms or allocated in future rounds (Department of Energy, Press Release, 26 July 1979, number 130). In 1982 the offshore activities of BNOC were placed in a new firm, Britoil, 51 per cent of which was offered to the public. BNOC continued as a trader of the oil which other firms were required to sell to it. The resale of this oil on fixed-term contracts allowed it to influence pricing and other terms of sale in oil markets. In 1985, however, the government announced plans to end BNOC in view of the weakening in oil markets, a shift to short-term transactions and consequent losses incurred by BNOC. More gradually the monopoly of British Gas Corporation and its state ownership were also reduced.

Such changes did not mean that the Conservative government had given up all interest in intervention in the industry, particularly where foreign-owned firms were involved. There were clearly differences about foreign ownership within the Cabinet, as witnessed by the Westland affair, which is noted below, and there were also the views of opposition parties and segments of the public to take into account. The fate of Britoil in the late 1980s is instructive in this regard, both in terms of continuing doubts in some quarters about foreign ownership, and also of the problems of exercising state powers.[29]

In October 1987 the UK government sold its remaining 31.5 per cent stake in British Petroleum. The timing of this sale coincided with a crash on the stock markets. The sale was potentially very costly since the government had promised to buy back unsold shares from underwriters who were left with large holdings. The Kuwait Investment Office then proceeded to buy 22.5 per cent of British Petroleum shares, making it the largest single shareholder. In December 1988 British Petroleum launched a bid to acquire control of Britoil. The major competitor in the bidding which developed was a US firm which quit – not without a large profit – on the likelihood that the golden share would have been used to prevent foreign control of Britain's largest independent upstream producer, Britoil. The golden share was surrendered to British Petroleum, which agreed, among other things, to maintain Britoil as a separate subsidiary with headquarters in Scotland.

The UK government then asked the Monopolies and Mergers Commission to report whether the Kuwait Investment Office's holding was 'against the national interest'. The Commission ruled that it was, essentially on the grounds that the Kuwait government could use its holdings in British Petroleum to influence UK production. This could further the interests of Kuwait or of the Organization for Petroleum Economic Cooperation and conceivably lead to questions about British Petroleum's holdings in the United States.[30] The government then ordered Kuwait to reduce its shareholding to 9.9 per cent, which was accomplished by a sale to British Petroleum of 12 per cent of the Kuwait-held shares.

In concentrating on four sectors it should not be assumed that any United Kingdom government is immune from public pressure to prevent non-residents from acquiring key firms. In 1980 there was a storm of protest over the sale of Westland, a helicopter firm, to a US company. Two senior Cabinet ministers resigned when the government allowed the sale to go through. Security interests can be invoked in cases of this kind, but not in other cases noted in the next section.

Review of Inward Direct Investment

Some of the historical aspects of the review process have been noted above. It remains to describe briefly what was left of the review process, as distinct from restricted sector approaches, in the late 1970s before it was ended.[31]

The key once again was the Exchange Control Act of 1947, which gave wide powers to the Treasury with respect to inward FDI and other international transactions, including transactions involving non-residents which took place in the United Kingdom. Many of these powers were implemented by the Bank of England. Exchange control permission was needed for any change in control of a UK company passing to non-residents. In particular, setting up a new firm or acquisition of an existing firm would involve transactions which required approval, as would significant purchase of shares on the stock market by a non-resident. So far as inward direct investment was concerned, the Bank's objective was to ensure that it had a favourable reserve impact. The amount of foreign currency brought in to finance initial investment in fixed assets generally had to be proportionate to the interest of the foreign company in the subsidiary. Any further finance for fixed assets would require capital imports proportionate to the foreign stake. Inward direct investors from EC countries were given permission in 1972 to borrow sterling to finance investment in the United Kingdom, a privilege given in 1977 to all foreigners making direct investments in UK manufacturing. More generous treatment was accorded in some cases which promised special advantage to the United Kingdom, such as new investments in manufactures in depressed regions. The severity of conversion requirements had fluctuated with the balance of payments and repatriations, while regulated, appear to have been given liberal treatment in the 1970s (Bank of England, February 1977, 22–4; Steuer *et al.*, 1973, ch. 9).

The Bank's concern both on inward and outward direct investment centred on the balance of payments effects. But exchange controls serve as an early warning system and provide a reserve power which can be used by other agencies to screen and even deny particular direct investments. So far as one can determine, with a few exceptions that was not the way they were used in the late 1970s. Treasury and Industry, and also other departments when appropriate, reviewed all but the smaller cases, and even these latter when national interest was deemed to be involved. In the late 1970s such cases were treated quickly, informally and pragmatically, without stated criteria (beyond exchange control provisions) and most often without formal meetings. The conclusion of Steuer *et al.* (1973, 179–80) was noted earlier, to the effect that refusals were rare and no important case was declined by this review process so long as the financial conditions were met. The same can be said for the late 1970s. Undertakings were given by some firms which, while not subsequently involving sanctions or even systematic review, clearly carried some weight. These involved the maintenance of a majority of British directors and of minority shareholdings, and the maintenance or increase of domestic production, exports or development work. The latter types of undertakings were often, but not always, related to investment incentives.

This review process, it should be noted, was quite distinct from the approach adopted with some restricted sectors, such as petroleum, where undertakings from all firms on such matters as domestic purchases were monitored quite closely both before and after the general review process ended in 1979. Moreover the overlap of policy on foreign trade and foreign investment made it inevitable that government would be involved, despite the change in political colour in 1979. Two examples should suffice. In the second half of the 1970s, in the face of voluntary export restraints on television sets from Japan, several Japanese producers established plants in the EC, especially the United Kingdom. The UK government tried to persuade Hitachi to build its European plant there. The company apparently agreed to use at least 50 per cent British-made components and to export 50 per cent of its UK plant's output. That attempt ended because of opposition from UK manufacturers and unions, although a year later, in 1978, a joint venture was agreed to (*Financial Post,* 31 October 1977; *The Economist*, 16 December 1978, 120). Several years later a similar incident occurred under a Conservative government. The Japanese automobile industry faced stringent restrictions on imports to a number of European markets. To avoid these, Nissan announced early in 1981 that it was prepared to build a plant in the United Kingdom, and negotiations began on a sizeable package of incentives. These negotiations dragged on for several years owing to a variety of factors, including an economic recession and some indecision within Nissan about the investment. The opposition of the UK industry, facing recession and increased competition from a new UK producer, was also adamant. This opposition was a factor in the UK government's demand for 65 per cent local content by value, building up in a few years to 80 per cent. Nissan withdrew from the negotiations in 1982 but, late in 1983, renewed negotiations led to a deal involving less than 60 per cent local content (Young *et al.*, 1988, 224; *The Economist*, 10 July 1982, 14; 29 November 1983, 88).

It is important to add that the review process when it existed helped to ensure consistency with UK laws in general, such as those on competition, and also with such requirements as those of the City Panel on Takeovers and Mergers. Where these had not been cleared, the proposal was referred to the agencies involved and approval was denied until the requirements applicable to all firms, domestic and foreign, had been met.

These provisions continued to apply, of course, after the end of exchange controls. The Panel on Takeovers and Mergers is part of an industry self-regulating process involving rules designed to protect the interests of all equity holders. Among other provisions, an acquirer's identity must be revealed after 5 per cent or more of a company's equity has been purchased, and a full offer for all shares must be made once 30 per cent ownership is reached. Competition policy is of more interest for present purposes since it appears to have given weight on occasion to the nationality of the bidder. A proposal for merger or takeover is reviewed by the Fair Trade Office and can be referred by it or the Secretary of State for Trade to the Monopolies and

Merger Commission, which in turn makes a recommendation to the government. Transactions beyond a minimum size or market share must be considered for such referral. While several criteria dealing with competition effects are used for decision by the Commission, it is suggested occasionally that a particular takeover is rejected in part because of a desire to preserve domestic ownership. Multinationals as such are not singled out in the legislation, but broad phrases such as 'against the public interest' in the Fair Trading Act lend themselves to asking in particular cases just how foreign control could affect the public interest.[32]

Young *et al.* (1988, 210–17) have made a study of the ten references to the Monopolies and Mergers Commission from 1975 to 1986 which involved foreign firms. These accounted for less than 20 per cent of the references in that period. The criteria cited in the decisions do not suggest any systematic approach to the international aspects. Four of the ten cases were denied. In two of these cases the regional factor in Scotland appears to have been important, and in two others concerns about reduced UK purchasing were significant. Young *et al.* (217) note that it is difficult to use the Commission for screening FDI in any case, since only 3 per cent of proposed UK mergers and acquisitions are referred to it and 2 per cent (including those abandoned) are stopped. Nevertheless governments may find this a useful additional instrument in large or sensitive cases such as that noted above with regard to the Kuwait Investment Office. An even more striking example occurred in 1990. The Minister for Trade and Industry took the position that the degree of state ownership of foreign firms would be considered in deciding whether to refer proposed acquisitions to the Commission. This was necessary, he argued, in order to prevent 'nationalization by the back door'. He subsequently referred several such acquisitions, mainly by French state-owned firms, despite recommendations in some cases by the Office of Fair Trading that such referral was not warranted on competition grounds. The UK government subsequently abandoned this policy (*World Deal Review*, 1991, 717–18; Bailey *et al.*, 1991a, 36).

Finally, under the Industry Act of 1975, the government can prohibit the proposed takeover of a UK manufacturing firm by a non-resident, provided it decides the unit is of special importance to the United Kingdom or to a region and that the takeover would be contrary to the national interest. If the national interest cannot be otherwise protected, the government can acquire, with compensation, the property involved in such a proposed or completed transfer (OECD, 1982, 24). National interest was not defined. This provision of the Industry Act has not been used to date.

It is possible to put a stronger interpretation on the UK policy position and to conclude that the UK exercised 'hidden (screened) coordination' of policy (Boddewyn, 1974, 19–20). Whatever may have been the case or the intentions in the 1960s, it would be difficult to describe the actual utilization of these policy instruments in the late 1970s as a well coordinated screen, hidden or otherwise. What was still evident was concern, in a few strategic industries, to have domestic firms competing with foreign-controlled firms as well as efforts to achieve industrial restructuring in general. In October 1978, moreover, the remaining financing restrictions for direct investment, already much loosened, were removed as part of the termination of exchange controls. The Secretary of State for Industry subsequently declared:

> Since the lifting of exchange controls in 1979, non-residents have needed no official permission to invest in this country other than those, e.g. planning consent, which are required of all investors. Foreign investors are assured of receiving equal treatment with their UK counterparts and are eligible for the full range of incentives and benefits provided to investors generally.

He went on to note, however, that selective financial assistance would only be given, as with indigenous firms, in situations where the project benefited the UK in terms of prospects for exports, import substitution, job creation and the use of UK components (National Economic Development Council, 1982, 7).

This leads to our final topic, the fiscal and other incentives available to industry. Like other countries, the United Kingdom has relied on both general incentives which are received relatively automatically and others which are on a more discretionary basis. As a member of the EC and the OECD, these aids are available, in principle, to foreign-controlled firms on the same basis as domestic firms. Indeed the United Kingdom's overall and regional assistance is monitored by the EC. Nevertheless the discretionary grants allow for negotiating unique arrangements. It is worth noting that the system of attracting inward FDI is at four distinct levels which each have a degree of discretionary authority. The national coordinating body is the Invest in Britain Bureau of the Department of Industry, established in 1977. In 1980 the more important national and regional bodies were brought together in an informal group, the Committee on Overseas Promotion, which, however, has no monitoring function (Young *et al.*, 1988, 204–8).

As noted from the quotation above, the expected performance of the firm, whether it is domestic or foreign, is taken into account when support is considered. Indeed payment is phased with the accomplishment of the conditions involved. While such issues as regional development and upgrading of technology continue to be important, local content requirements have been particularly important in the 1980s. This is of particular interest throughout the EC, where there is no agreed standard among countries often competing for the same investment, and where explicit minimum local content as a condition of aid could be challenged. In the United Kingdom 60 per cent local content is often acceptable, while varying with the circumstances of each case. It should also be noted that, while there are not explicit incentives designed for inward FDI as such, investments which are believed to be highly mobile internationally will draw significant discretionary grants; the competition for a Nissan plant noted above, which might have been located in Europe, is a case in point (see also *Business International*, UK, 1986, 17–19).

Many of the fiscal incentives have been geared to attracting firms, whether from elsewhere in the United Kingdom or overseas, to the less industrially developed northern and western parts of the country. In overall terms MNEs accounted for about one-fifth of investment in manufactures and received 16 to 20 per cent of incentives under the two relevant sections of the Industry Act in 1978–9 (OECD, 1983, 225–6). On a regional basis MNE response to incentives appears to have been high and their impact on the industrial structure of assisted areas, which were losing older industries, has been assessed favourably by some writers. However, as in the case of Ireland, linkages with local firms and spinoffs of new enterprises have been weak. It is not clear just how much of this is because the firms are multinational (or, indeed, multi-plant UK-owned enterprises) and how much can be related to UK policy on industrial growth and competitiveness (Young *et al.*, 1988, ch. 4, especially 47–50). With the advent of the Conservative government of 1979 some attempts have been evident to downgrade the role of specific incentives to investment in favour of macro policies which were expected to stimulate investment. Nevertheless slower growth, strong competition within the EC for Japanese and other new investment, and divestment by some US firms have led to continued reliance on fiscal incentives to attract MNEs.

Conclusions

UK policies on both outward and inward FDI can be described as relatively liberal for most of the post-Second World War period. The key overall restriction for direct investment has been the regulation involved in an exchange control system, which, however, had become much less burdensome by the time it ended in 1979. The review which exchange controls allowed the Treasury and other Departments to undertake of the larger or more sensitive classes was highly informal and pragmatic, having more in common with those in Norway or Sweden than in France or Canada.

The reservations about inward FDI were expressed more directly through a significant number of restricted sector or key firm policies. These included the use of performance requirements on an ad hoc basis in industries such as automobiles and computers, and much more systematically and continuously in the petroleum sector. Fiscal and other incentives to attract FDI also included the use of performance conditions which involved more follow-through – as a condition of sequential payments – than did the ad hoc requirements.

In overall terms the policy approach appears to have been based on a perception of net benefit from inward FDI, qualified by concerns about the effects in some sectors and a desire to preserve a UK presence in certain industries, either because they were large (automobiles) or considered critical (information technology). In addition objectives such as international competitiveness have been associated with the presence of or attitudes to MNEs, although they are hardly limited to such firms. However it would be difficult to argue that any UK government before the 1980s had adopted a consistent policy towards MNEs in general and the associated elements of industrial policy. The Labour government of the late 1960s gave indications of a more systematic approach to MNEs but, in practice, hesitated to endorse the widespread discrimination to which some of its actions could have led. The Labour government of the late 1970s took a more welcoming line, in rhetoric as well as practice. The Conservative governments since 1979 have taken the route of deregulation and privatization – including opening up restricted sectors to FDI – without, however, avoiding the occasional discrimination against foreign owners in law or in policy. Even a government favouring private enterprise in general and international investment in particular cannot avoid the concerns of those who believe certain sectors are critical enough to be restricted and others important enough to warrant a domestic presence through significant subsidy or protection. The test of the consistency of policy which, in relative terms, the UK government has shown in the 1980s will be whether it will continue to surrender its golden shares in privatized firms after the five-year transition periods are up, and especially if that should lead to takeovers by foreign firms.

UNITED STATES

For a quarter of a century after the Second World War the outflows from the United States dominated global direct investment. Much of national policy elsewhere on MNEs was directed at firms from that country. In the United States the policy debate centred on how to minimize what were believed to be the adverse effects of the capital outflow on the *home* country. As the major home country, the United States was also trying to persuade host countries to minimize discrimination against foreign-controlled firms.

In the 1970s multinationals from the United States were increasingly challenged by those from other countries. The United States continued to be the major source of outward direct movement in the 1980s, but also became the major host country for MNE investments. While policy on inward investment has remained relatively liberal, the policy debate has increasingly reflected some of the concerns of a host country.

Outward FDI from the United States developed all through the nineteenth century, but notably in manufacturing after about 1875. It was highly concentrated by area. In 1914 about 70 per cent of total direct investment was in Canada, Mexico, the Caribbean and South America, and another 22 per cent in Europe.[33] The major expansion was in the 1950s and 1960s. It has been related to a wide range of factors, such as advances in communication and transportation, relative weakness in other home countries, the development of the European Common Market, and a relatively strong exchange rate. The United States was by a long way the most important home country through this period. In 1960 it accounted for 47 per cent of the global stock of direct investment and in 1975 it still had 44 per cent. This stock has become more concentrated in Western Europe and south east Asia, and less so in Canada and Latin America, during the 1970s and 1980s (Table 9.8).

The US position changed in the 1970s to a major host as well as home country. For example, the ratio of outward to inward stock of investment, which was as high as six to one in the late 1960s had fallen to four to one in the late 1970s and less than two to one in the 1980s. Outward direct investment flows (including retained earnings) had exceeded inward by wide margins during the 1960s and 1970s. This pattern of net outflows was reversed in the first half of the 1980s. The US share of the outward world stock of FDI fell from 44 per cent in 1975 to 40 and 35 per cent in 1980 and 1985. Meanwhile her share in the inward world stock of FDI rose from 11 per cent in 1975 to 29 per cent in 1985. In terms of flows, the United States had become in the 1980s by far the largest target for world MNE investment (Tables 3.1 to 3.3 and 9.9).

Inward FDI was prominent in some US industries in the late nineteenth century. Much of that was sold off or confiscated during the Second World War. Inflows accelerated in the 1960s after post-war reconstruction abroad, and speeded up in the 1970s. Many reasons have been advanced for the massive flows to the United States in the 1970s and later, including the rapid growth of the US market while production costs expanded relatively slowly in some periods; political tensions abroad; the relative increase in the income of major competitors and a degree of competitive catching up in the global market shares by their MNEs; the relative ease of acquiring US assets because of depreciation of the US dollar after the 1960s and especially in the 1980s; and, less certainly, trade protection.[34] Acquisitions rather than new establishments have been the dominant form of entry to the United States. In 1980–8 acquisitions averaged 80 per cent of the value of inward investment

Table 9.8 Area composition of US direct investment stock, inward and outward, 1970–86 (percentages)

Country (Area)	Inward Stock 1970	1980	1986	Outward Stock 1970	1980	1986
Western Europe	72.0	65.7	67.6	31.3	43.6	44.5
Japan	1.7	5.7	11.2	1.9	2.8	4.1
Canada	23.5	14.6	8.0	26.9	20.5	(1)
Other developed	(1)	1.4	3.8	7.9	9.8	27.1
Total developed	97.2	87.5	90.6	68.0	76.7	75.7
Latin America and Caribbean	1.9	10.8	6.1	18.8	14.8	13.2
South and south-east Asia	(1)	0.3	0.6	3.2	3.9	5.8
Other	0.9	1.4	2.7	5.5	2.8	3.6
Total developing	2.8	12.5	9.4	27.4	21.5	22.6
Total	100.0	100.0	100.0	95.4	98.2	98.3

Note:
Percentages for outward stock do not add to 100 because dollar totals include unspecified countries.
(1) Not separately available.

Source: UN (1988, 520, 526). Data exclude Netherlands Antilles. Canadian data inserted from other sources.

(Graham and Krugman, 1989, 19). This high rate of foreign acquisitions became at times part of the debate over policy on inward FDI.

US direct investment abroad has for some time been larger than inward in relation to domestic industry. In 1977, employment in US affiliates abroad was 7.8 per cent of domestic employment for all industry and 27.0 per cent for manufacturing alone. Inward FDI is still a small share of domestic industry compared with most other countries in this study, but that share has been rising; between 1977 and 1987 it rose from 1.7 per cent to 3.5 per cent for employment in all industry, and from 3.5 to 7.9 per cent in manufacturing. In sectoral terms, a wide range of industries show high ratios of sales and employment in affiliates located abroad as a percentage of domestic sales and employment; for example, employment shares were particularly high for chemicals (70 per cent), automobiles (58 per cent) and for mechanical engineering and electrical equipment (35 per cent each) in 1977. By contrast, only one manufacturing industry on the inward side exceeded 10

Table 9.9 US direct investment flows and stocks, 1960–90[a] ($US millions)

	Direct investment capital flows				*Stock of direct investment*	
	Inward (net)	*Of which retained earnings*	*Outward (net)*	*Of which retained earnings*	*Inward*	*Outward*
1960	315	174	2 941	1 266	6 910	31 865
1961	311	238	2 653	1 054	7 392	34 717
1962	346	214	2 852	1 198	7 612	37 276
1963	231	236	3 483	1 507	7 944	40 736
1964	322	327	3 759	1 431	8 363	44 480
1965	415	358	5 010	1 542	8 797	49 474
1966	425	339	5 416	1 791	9 054	51 792
1967	691	440	4 807	1 757	9 923	56 560
1968	807	488	5 295	2 440	10 815	61 907
1969	1 263	431	5 960	2 830	11 818	68 093
1970	1 464	434	7 589	3 176	13 270	75 480
1971	367	542	7 617	3 176	13 914	82 760
1972	949	569	7 746	4 532	14 868	89 878
1973	2 800	910	11 353	8 158	20 556	101 313
1974	4 760	1 065	9 052	7 777	25 144	110 078
1975	2 603	1 189	14 244	8 048	27 662	124 050
1976	4 346	1 659	11 949	7 696	30 770	136 809
1977	3 728	1 586	11 893	6 396	34 595	145 990
1978	7 897	2 583	16 056	11 343	42 471	162 727
1979	11 876	3 955	25 222	18 964	52 260	187 858
1980	16 918	5 177	19 222	17 017	83 046	215 375
1981	25 195	2 945	9 624	12 978	108 714	228 348
1982	13 792	-2 379	967	4 695	124 677	207 752
1983	11 946	89	6 695	13 462	137 061	207 203
1984	25 359	2 896	11 587	17 214	164 583	211 480
1985	19 022	-1 378	13 162	14 102	184 615	230 250
1986	34 091	-2 293	18 679	10 021	220 414	259 800
1987	58 119	-883	31 045	19 714	263 934	314 307
1988	59 424	2 816	17 879	13 327	314 754	335 893
1989	70 551	-3 844	33 388	22 370	373 763	370 091
1990	37 213	-14 008	33 437	22 250	403 735	421 494

Note:
[a]US Department of Commerce defines FDI as 10 per cent or more ownership of a firm by a single foreign investor.

Source: OECD (1987b, 172) up to 1980; *US Survey of Current Business*, August 1988 and August 1991 thereafter.

per cent in 1982, namely, chemicals and allied sectors at 36 per cent.[35] By 1987 foreign direct investment accounted for 12 per cent of manufacturing assets in the United States. In the banking sector foreign ownership of assets grew rapidly from 3.8 per cent in 1973 to 11.9 and 19.2 per cent in 1980 and 1988 (Dunning and Cantwell, 1987, 260–61; Graham and Krugman, 1989, 13, 21).

General Policy Position

The United States has for long taken the position that multinational investment should be largely unrestricted. In particular it has pressed for the right to establish, operate and expand firms on the same basis as domestic firms, with a few agreed exceptions. Such a position has reflected the interests of the major home country in protecting access to foreign markets by her firms. It also reflects a viewpoint which, more than that of many other countries in this study, has favoured relatively unrestricted private enterprise. And it reflects also a view that both home and host countries can gain from a significant MNE presence. This is witnessed by the still relatively easy access by foreign firms to the US market despite the growing investments in that market and the gradual introduction of some more restrictive policies.

US policy actions have fallen somewhat short of policy statements, as will be noted further below. For example, there is a significant list of industries which are partially or wholly closed to inward FDI, some of which would be hard to justify in national security terms. Nevertheless US governments have generally pressed for liberalization of host country policies and have recently largely contained congressional efforts to be more restrictive in this respect. Historically the USA accorded many countries national treatment on investment, except for some sectors, through a clause in bilateral treaties of friendship, navigation and commerce. When the Havana Charter for the International Trade Organization was being negotiated at the end of the Second World War, the United States proposed it apply to direct investment as well as trade. The proposal included provisions for compensation or retaliation where the guarantees of national treatment were violated, provisions whose dilution became a factor in the decision of the US Congress to deny approval of the Organization.[36] US governments also strongly supported the establishment of the OECD Code of Liberalization of Capital Movements (1961) and the OECD Declaration on International Investment and Multinational Enterprises (1976) and have pressed for improvement in the latter in particular. Much less enthusiasm has been shown for the proposed UN code on transnational enterprises, although in this case the reservations of the US government and business community are shared by some other home countries.

With the growth in FDI in the United States in the 1970s and congressional and other concerns becoming larger, the US executive announced in 1977 that the fundamental policy of the US government toward international investment is 'neither to promote nor to discourage inward or outward investment flows and activities' (Bale, 1984, 29). This neutral position was followed in 1983 by a stronger statement issued by President Reagan (US Government Statement by the President, 9 September 1983). It took the position that such flows were of benefit to international efficiency and to home and host countries. It expressed concern at the attempts by government to impede such flows, supported national treatment and announced a number of bilateral and multilateral steps to help liberalize international investment flows. The statement is significant in a number of ways. It makes a bow to congressional pressures calling for treatment of investment abroad equivalent to that given in the United States, and reserves the right to take action where that does not obtain. It takes aim at a number of specific measures, such as performance requirements as a condition of investment and restrictions on establishment of service industries, as well as underlining the US view of international law on expropriation. The statement also points to increased efforts to develop bilateral guarantees, improve OECD instruments and pursue other channels to assist FDI. We shall return to some of these below, but note here that trade-related performance requirements, increased protection for intellectual property and services trade have found themselves on the agenda for the Uruguay Round of the GATT, in part at US government insistence.

These positions have been qualified in practice, as with policy statements from other governments. In what follows some key aspects of outward FDI policies are first considered, then the debate and policy on the inward side.

Issues and Policies on Outward Direct Investment

While the attitude of the US government to outward FDI has been favourable over time, there have been exceptions to this stance within government and sharp differences of opinion among some groups. The underlying favourable position is evident in a wide variety of policies, including attempts from the 1950s to the 1980s to reduce impediments, whether domestic or foreign, to FDI abroad. An early example of such an approach was a requirement of the Mutual Security Act of 1951 that a study be made of impediments to private US direct investment abroad and of methods to reduce such impediments (US Department of Commerce, 1953–4). In the 1970s a programme was established to enter into a series of bilateral investment protection agreements. More recently the US government has given strong support in the Uruguay Round of the GATT for the inclusion of items related to FDI.

By contrast there have been attempts in the 1960s and 1970s to restrict FDI outflows because of a view that they affected the balance of payments and employment negatively. In addition there has been long-standing concern that US direct investment abroad had negative political consequences for the United States.

Full consideration of these economic and political effects of US direct investment abroad, whether real or perceived, whether in developed or developing countries, would take us far beyond the purposes of this study. In any case, literally scores of studies exist on this topic. Our purpose here is simply to highlight some of the more important debates in the United States in order to understand the basis for the policies which have been adopted or, in some cases, have come close to being put into effect.

The economic literature has long recognized the possibility of negative effects for the home country's income, employment or balance of payments from an unrestricted outflow of FDI. In terms of national welfare, for example, that literature has noted that FDI abroad can reduce the income of other foreign investors more than the return on the new investment. This result is more likely to be the case if the stock of investment abroad is large, and where the firms are in a more competitive industry. Moreover the tax laws and treaties of many countries allow a foreign tax credit on income from abroad so as to avoid double taxation. In such circumstances the taxes paid by a subsidiary to a host country can be credited in the home country up to the tax rate levied by that country on income earned abroad. Tax on the latter, moreover, is usually deferred until the income is actually paid to the parent. This can provide an incentive to reinvest subsidiary income so as to defer the tax payable in the home country. One effect of these policies has been that corporation tax rates in host countries have tended to converge in many cases with those of home countries, in order that the former can capture the tax revenues involved. This has become an issue in countries which have large investment income from abroad relative to that paid abroad. One estimate for United States FDI abroad concluded that close to 90 per cent of the tax was taken by host countries (Musgrave, 1975, 107–8).

Other arguments have been made reducing the value of direct investment from a home country viewpoint. Such investments can be lost to the home country through confiscation and other host country measures. Any dynamic benefits associated with capital investment, such as improvements in other inputs or industries, may accrue to the host country. Investment in raw materials can improve the terms of trade and stability of supply, but, in some circumstances, the development of competitors might worsen a home country's terms of trade. These and other arguments can be developed at length and also qualified in various ways. They have led to a series of proposals, such as an optimum tax to limit 'excessive' outward investment, an optimum tariff to improve the terms of trade and reduction of tax deferral.[37]

The first major effort to regulate outward FDI reflected various concerns about national welfare effects but concentrated more on the narrower goal of attempting to reduce deficits in the US balance of payments. In 1961–2 the Kennedy administration proposed that foreign tax credits and deferral be ended – strong proposals which did not get very far. In 1963 an interest equalization tax was applied, with some exceptions, to portfolio borrowing in the United States. In 1965 US firms were asked voluntarily to limit the outflow of capital to, and to increase the inflow of dividends from, their affiliates in the industrial countries. On 1 January 1968 this programme became mandatory. Direct investors, that is those owning 10 per cent or more of the equity of a foreign affiliate, were allowed to choose external investment quotas (termed 'allowables') from one of the following: (a) a worldwide 'minimum' allowable of $200 000, later raised to $1 million, then to $5 million; (b) 30 per cent of the annual earnings of affiliates in three country groupings in the preceding year; (c) a percentage of the average earnings in 1964–6 of the three country groupings, with the highest percentages for the developing countries and lowest for Western Europe. Annual, and in some cases quarterly, reports had to be filed by the firms. It is important to note that these limits were placed on sums transferred including retained earnings, not on the capital outlays, and that long-term capital borrowing abroad was an offset to such net transfer. Generally the foreign investor could continue or undertake any size of investment programme provided this could be met by foreign borrowing. Indeed the most obvious effect of the controls was to increase such borrowing and associated debt costs (Ellicott, 1969; US Presidential Commission, 1971, *Papers*, 113–38).

Strong opposition from US business interests and some doubts about the effectiveness of the controls led to their liberalization in 1969 and later. They were not fully removed until 1974, however, the same year in which the interest equalization tax was ended. The analytical point at issue was the effect of FDI abroad on the balance of payments of the home country. This issue was (and still is) often addressed in terms of a simple comparison of outflows of direct investment and inflows of income. This is a quite inadequate approach in view particularly of the direct and indirect links between FDI, exports and imports. Two comprehensive empirical analyses of this question were published in 1968, by Hufbauer and Adler for US firms and by Reddaway *et al.* for UK firms.[38] In both cases the critical question turned out to be whether FDI substituted for or supplemented investment in the home and host countries. Assume, from a home country perspective, that outward FDI is defensive; that is, FDI does displace home investment but it would have been matched abroad by host or third country investors before long in any case. In these circumstances, FDI abroad shows favourable effects for the home country within reasonably short periods. By contrast, if such host or third-country investors would not have appeared for some time, FDI has negative effects from a home country viewpoint. The second case, it may be added, is more likely to correspond to investment in some types of developing countries. On assumptions which seemed most likely regarding domestic investment and export substitution, these studies could be interpreted as concluding that FDI in manufacturing was helpful to the home country's balance of payments after a relatively short period or, alternatively, that continued controls on outward FDI were damaging.[39] These and other studies have implications for the debate on the employment effects of outward FDI which will be noted below.

A direct outcome of the controls on FDI abroad was the policies in a number of host countries limiting the borrowing by US and other foreign multinationals in their markets. It was noted earlier, for example, that both France and Australia took such steps in the last half of the 1960s. This was an inevitable result of the US decision to permit foreign borrowing to be offset against 'allowables' for transfers and reinvestments abroad. Such measures also contributed to an increasingly negative view in host countries of some other aspects of US direct investment. It is likely, however, that these other issues enjoyed a life of their own, as is evident from our earlier analysis of policy development in Canada. Along with the developing countries, Canada was exempted from the voluntary controls. In addition Canada was also exempted from the interest equalization tax and the mandatory controls programme. These exemptions were at Canada's insistence, and would have extended to the import taxes of the early 1970s if Canada had been able to persuade the US government.

The debate over the controls on the balance of payments was a prelude to the attempt to restrict outward FDI so as to preserve employment in the United States. Trade unions in particular saw the development of multinational production as exporting jobs and also as reducing unionized goods-producing jobs relative to non-unionized service jobs. These concerns are similar to those voiced by a number of unions in Sweden and other countries in Europe, as noted earlier. The American Federation of Labour and The Congress of Industrial Organizations developed, and pressed strongly for the adoption of, a set of proposals which became known as the Burke-Hartke bill, presented in 1972 in the US Congress. This bill proposed the following measures: (a) payment of taxes abroad by multinational firms would be treated as deductions from foreign income rather than as credits against US tax liabilities on that income; (b) elimination of the provision of deferral of taxation of foreign income until it was paid to the parent; (c) licensing by the President of exports of capital and of technology, with approval depending on the effect on US employment and other criteria; and (d) import quotas, along with termination of sections 807 and 806.30 of the Tariff Act, which allowed more favourable duty treatment for offshore assembly (Hood and Young, 1979, 704–5; Bergsten *et al.*, 1978, 111–12).

The provisions of the Burke-Hartke bill were not enacted but the bitter debate left its mark on US policies in a range of items. The Domestic International Sales Corporation Statute (DISC) which took effect in 1972, for example, provided a subsidy to exports by reducing taxes on earnings from exports for firms which qualified. This amounted to a form of tax deferral extended to export earnings. It has been criticized as inconsistent with GATT obligations, and was modified in the 1980s. A number of tax changes in 1975 and 1976, while retaining deferral, modified its effects in general or for particular industries, especially petroleum.[40] Transfer pricing practices of multinational firms, and the allocation of research and other costs among parent and subsidiary firms, can affect national tax collections. Such practices have been monitored more closely since the late 1970s.

Another outcome of these concerns was a series of studies assessing the domestic employment effects of outward FDI. Some of these studies are summarized in Table 9.10. It will be noted that the results are highly sensitive to the extent to which it is assumed that US firms retain foreign markets in the absence of foreign investment, that is, to the extent that such investment is defensive in nature.[41] The Tariff Commission made three different assumptions in this respect, giving US employment effects ranging from +488 000 to -1 297 000. The first of these figures was the one it considered most realistic.[42] Still other studies can be cited which bear on these results. Bergsten *et al.* (1978, ch. 3) conclude from their estimates that US investment is complementary with US exports up to a point, then displaces them. This is consistent with product cycle models of FDI. Studies by Lipsey and Weiss (1981, 1984) have underlined the complementarity of MNE exports and sales of subsidiaries. However these studies do not take account of general equilibrium effects. The investment substitution issue at an overall level, moreover, has not been resolved in empirical terms (Caves, 1982, 143–7). And those who might favour a sectoral approach agreed that the relevant industry studies were lacking.

While most measures of the net overall employment effects suggested that these were small in relation to the total changes in the labour force, they are significant in terms of the adjustment imposed on different groups of workers. The difficulties of the adjustment could be magnified if, as some studies suggested, the increases in jobs tend to be concentrated in more highly skilled workers, the decreases in less skilled (De la Torre *et al.*, 1973). The Trade Expansion Act of 1962 had introduced adjustment assistance to workers displaced by imports, including those from subsidiaries abroad. The

Table 9.10 The effects of international enterprises on US employment: summary of selected studies

			Employment effect (no. of jobs)			
Study	*Source of data*	*Estimate of % foreign markets retained by US firms in absence of foreign investment*	*US production displacement effect*	*Export stimulus effect*	*Home office and supporting firm employment effect*	*Net*
1. Ruttenberg AFL-CIO study (1971)	Aggregate official data	Inferred to be high	-500 000 jobs between 1966 and 1969 due to adverse trade movements, of which MNES account for an 'important part'	N/A	N/A	'Important part' of -500 000
2. Stobaugh & associates (1971)	9 case studies and aggregate data	Low or zero in the long run	(1)	+250 000	+350 000	+600 000
3. Emergency Committee for American Trade (1972)	Sample survey of 74 companies	Inferred to be low	N/A	+300 000	+250 000	Substantially positive
4. US Chamber of Commerce (1972)	Sample survey of 158 companies	Inferred to be low or zero	N/A	+311 345(2)	N/A	Positive
5. R.G. Hawkins (1972)	Aggregate data	Assumption 1 (5% of production of US affiliates retained in the US)	-190 000			+279 000
		Assumption 2 (10% of production retained)	-381 000	+260 000	+209 000	+89 000
		Assumption 3 (25% of production retained)	-791 000			-322 000
6. US Tariff Commission (1973)	Unpublished statistics on operations of US firms with foreign operations	Assumption 1 (average share of foreign markets actually held by US exports during 1960–61	-603 100	+286 000	+321 000	+488 000

Notes:
(1) Negligible.
(2) Based on net trade.

Source: Hood and Young (1979, 317) as taken from US Tariff Commission (1973) and Hawkins (1972).

Trade Act of 1974 extended this to assistance to communities, but not workers or firms, where the Secretary of Commerce decides that the transfer of firms or parts thereof abroad has contributed importantly to job layoffs. In addition firms locating abroad were asked on a voluntary basis to give at least 60 days' notice to the Secretary of Labour and Secretary of Commerce, and to make maximum use of adjustment assistance (Bergsten *et al.*, 1978, 24–30, 468–9).

The overvaluation of the US dollar which underlay many of the problems encountered in the balance of payments was reduced by a series of devaluations in the early 1970s. The controls on capital exports, as noted earlier, were ended in 1974. Attention was focused for a time on other international issues, notably the pressures brought about by oil price increases. When the issues surrounding outward FDI resurfaced, they focused on the treatment of such firms by host countries. This had arisen before, of course. A Presidential Commission which reported in 1971, for example, emphasized that trade negotiations should include investment issues, that the goal should be the reduction of 'artificial incentives and impediments to foreign direct investment in developed countries, whether they result from our own policies or from those of foreign governments. US policy in this regard should continue to be guided by the principles of freedom of entry, of the respect for property rights, and of national treatment' (p. 14). The US government was urged to strengthen OECD attempts to achieve these objectives, and also to not hesitate to use access to its own large market in the bargaining process when its interests were impaired by other countries (US Presidential Commission, 1971, *Report*, 12–14, 178–9).

By the early 1980s the US position on this range of issues had hardened considerably. This is best reflected in the hearings before the Senate Committee on Foreign Relations (US Senate, 1982). The incentives and disincentives to FDI which were criticized in those hearings will be examined more fully in Part III of this book. Here we note briefly some important policy developments. US business, labour, government officials and some researchers took strong exception to performance requirements (both in trade and in other respects) imposed as a condition of investment, as well as the often related incentives. Moreover people who were on record as preferring multilateral policy approaches were prepared at least to consider unilateral options. Hufbauer, for example, analysed ways, consistent with international commitments, to encourage private or public actions that would impose costs on host governments or derive compensation for injured parties in home countries. Bergsten, while also preferring other methods, has noted the possibilities under certain circumstances of a US response by way of emulation and retaliation (US Senate 1982, 143–59 and 1–18, respectively). Most of the other people giving evidence were less restrained in advocating unilateral approaches. The House of Representatives, meanwhile, was fully involved in the debate. One need note only the hearings on a bill to amend the Securities and Exchange Act of 1934 so that foreigners would be allowed to acquire US securities only to the extent to which their countries' laws offered reciprocity to US interests (US House of Representative, *Hearings*, 1981). Other versions of investment reciprocity bills abounded in the Congress.

The evidence submitted to such hearings, as will be noted later, suggested that Canada had fewer disincentives to investment than a number of other countries, both developed and developing. However Canadian policies became a primary target for the United States. This was partly because Canada is a developed country from which less policy deviation is expected and tolerated, partly because it is the single most important export market and investment location for the United States, but also because of concern that Canadian policies might influence developments in other major markets. The National Energy Program was announced in 1980 and implemented in 1981. At the same time there was some tightening of procedures in the Foreign Investment Review Agency and plans were announced for some potentially far-reaching new measures. The latter were not implemented, FIRA was eventually changed to Investment Canada, and the National Energy Program was largely dismantled after 1984 so far as the FDI aspects were concerned. Nevertheless there was a marked deterioration in relations between the two countries in 1981–2. A flurry of congressional hearings and bills concentrated on Canada's economic policies, extending well beyond FIRA and energy but propelled by these two in particular.

In the event, the storm blew over with relatively little bilateral wreckage in its wake. In part this was because the FIRA was not strengthened, and both it and the National Energy Program were made less restrictive – more, it is likely, because of the collapse of oil prices and the recession of the early 1980s than because of US threats.[43] The US administration was not prepared to take strong bilateral action against Canada on the investment issue. It did circulate a questionnaire to gather data on FIRA's practices and as noted in the section on Canada, launched a complaint against FIRA in the GATT, with partial success. A proposal to declare Canada a 'non-reciprocal nation' under the US Mineral Land Leasing Act of 1920 was declined after detailed investigation by the Department of the Interior and hearings before a subcommittee of the House Committee on Energy and Commerce; at the same time the Administration made clear its strong opposition to Canada's investment policies.[44] If such a declaration had been made, Canadian-owned firms would not have been allowed to obtain drilling or mining leases on federal lands.

While direct retaliation against Canada did not occur explicitly on any scale, and Canada's investment policies were modified, the policy debates on Canada in the early 1980s were influential for various reasons. First, as noted further below, they left their mark on the discussions in the United States on the need for more information and control on inward FDI, more reciprocity on trade and investment with other countries, and other issues. Second, US government and business interests gave a high priority to modifying Canada's policies on investment in the negotiations on a free trade area which began in the mid-1980s. As noted in the section on Canada, the US government succeeded in modifying Canada's investment policies in general, and in removing the restrictions on banking and some other finance areas in particular.

In addition 'reciprocity' was given more emphasis in US trade law. Reciprocity in the post-Second World War period had meant offering reductions of barriers to trade in goods, usually on a reciprocal basis through negotiation; these were then generalized to other trading partners in the GATT. In the 1970s it took on more and more the meaning of equivalent market access between the United States and particular trade partners, in terms of international investment and services trade as well as commodity trade. The term 'level playing field' began to be heard in this regard. The perception in this case was that other countries were using relatively greater investment controls, combined with investment subsidies and state ownership, to steer the investment and trade effects of multinationals in ways injurious to the United States. The specific action taken in 1984 was to revise section 301 of the Trade Act of 1974 to include investment practices; it had already been extended in 1979 to cover trade in services. Section 301 authorizes the President to suspend trade concessions and impose import restrictions where needed to eliminate any act or practice of a foreign government which is inconsistent with a trade agreement or unjustifiable, unreasonable or discriminatory. In this regard the President is required to report annually on steps taken to change objectionable foreign practices. A dispute with Brazil over some years on her restrictions on imports and investment in the informatics sector led in 1987 to US restrictions on imports of some Brazilian informatics products. In addition the Trade Act of 1988 put greater pressure on the President to retaliate against countries which were identified as engaging in unfair practice and which did not negotiate a solution of these with the United States. In the case of Japan, for example, talks held under the Structural Impediments Initiative in the late 1980s were aimed in part to reduce the alleged exclusionary practices of the *keiretsu* with respect to trade and investment (Bailey *et al.*, 1991c, 45).

Such unilateral measures appear quite inconsistent with the approach involved in the GATT. However the United States has also pressed for a new round of the GATT in which a variety of issues related to FDI would be given some emphasis: trade-related performance requirements, trade in services and more protection for intellectual property are cases in point. Progress in discussions on the first two items was evident in the mid-term review of this round, but lack of progress in other areas, notably agricultural subsidies, held up agreement.

The particular issues discussed to this point focus more on economic policies than on the broader political effects of a large outward MNE presence. Most of these effects have arisen from the concerns about US and other multinationals in the developing countries, host country policies designed to allay these concerns, and home country efforts to protect MNE interests. Lipson (1985) has analysed the efforts by home country governments such as the United States and United Kingdom to enforce a de facto set of rules on nationalizations in particular. These rules were challenged by a wave of expropriations and extensive national regulation of FDI in the 1960s. The sanctions against partial or full-scale default and other policies limiting MNE activities have been much weaker since then, ranging from legislation involving the termination of US foreign aid in some circumstances to writing public risk insurance for FDI or trying to influence international organizations.[45]

Of the various congressional committees in the 1970s which dealt with multinational firms, two received a good deal of attention. In the mid-1970s the subcommittee on multinational corporations held extensive hearings on the activities of a major US-controlled corporation in Chile and also on the effects on foreign policy of MNEs in petroleum (US Senate, 1973–5, 75). Hearings on corporate bribery of foreign officials dramatized several major cases and led to US legislation on the subject (US Senate, 1977). Those firms whose shares are quoted on the stock exchange are required by the Securities and Exchange Commission to disclose illegal or improper payments to government officials. Such legislation has not been widely imitated elsewhere, leading some US firms to argue they are at a competitive disadvantage as a consequence.

An issue which has attracted a great deal of attention at times is the extraterritorial application of home country law or policy to subsidiaries abroad through pressure on the parent companies.[46] This is an issue in many jurisdictions. For example, West German cartel law applies to firms located abroad if they affect German interests and there is an entity in Germany which can be reached. There are similar laws in Australia and the European Community, among others. UK requirements in the 1960s and 1970s that dividends be paid by subsidiaries located abroad resemble the US controls on external capital in the same period. However, it was the US policies which attracted the greatest protest. Canada, France and Argentina are among countries which have taken exception to the attempt by US authorities to block exports from US subsidiaries in the 1950s and 1960s to Cuba, North Korea, North Vietnam and China under the provisions of the US Trading with the Enemy Act of 1917. In addition efforts to coordinate controls on the export of technology to communist countries have led to disputes. A major controversy in this area was the attempt in 1982 by the US government to use the Export Administration Act to embargo the shipment to the USSR of pipeline equipment made under licence from US companies. This led to a bitter dispute with several West European governments before the United States lifted its sanctions in 1982.[47] A series of US anti-trust decisions over several decades which affected subsidiaries located abroad have also been contested by governments in Canada and Western Europe. These governments have also resisted the balance of payments controls of the United States as involving elements of extraterritoriality, the attempt by US courts to secure information located abroad, and some aspects of securities regulation.

The MNE is clearly caught in these cases in a conflict between sovereigns intent on preserving territorial jurisdiction. In effect the MNE cannot obey one authority without offending the other – a problem of 'conflicting requirements', to use the terminology of OECD reports. In other areas, such as taxation, such problems are settled by treaty. Reconciliation of the issues noted has proved impossible by such means. One result has been that the countries involved have reverted to national policies which do not resolve the underlying conflict. For example, a number of countries have enacted laws prohibiting local courts, executive authorities or companies from complying with orders issued abroad: Australia, Canada, France, the Netherlands and the United Kingdom are among these countries. The OECD has attempted a different approach. First, it stated a number of principles which should be considered when a country envisaged policies which might conflict with those of other member countries. Second, it arranged for early notification of such actions and, at the request of a member, consultations in the OECD.

Concerns about Inward FDI

US authorities were concerned about the impact of inward FDI in a number of sectors many decades ago, as the list of closed sectors in the next section will show. There was also a flurry of congressional bills, resolutions and investigations from the mid-1970s advocating controls on inward FDI. The timing and nature of the bills were clearly motivated by the fears, highly exaggerated as it turned out, of substantial numbers of takeovers of major US firms by the newly oil-rich countries. There was particular concern that some of these firms were in sensitive sectors involving national security issues. One might note particularly hearings of House Committees in 1980–

82 on the adequacy of the federal response to foreign (especially OPEC countries') investments in the United States. The majority views of these committees were highly critical of the data on inward FDI despite various new measures in the 1970s, believed that federal agencies were not monitoring such FDI effectively and urged Congress to consider a screening agency 'similar to the agencies in Canada, Mexico, and in many other countries'.[48] Direct investments by OPEC countries came under particular scrutiny, in part because they were believed to be more extensive than the reported one per cent of total FDI stock in the United States but also because some involved investments by state-owned firms and might also involve security issues. For example, the purchase of Sante Fe Petroleum by the Kuwait Petroleum Company provoked much investigation for the last two reasons.[49] In the early 1980s several congressional committees used the concept of reciprocity to attack investment restrictions abroad or to press for similar restrictions in the United States.

As it turned out, these and other congressional bills and hearings had a modest legislative impact, while laying the basis for stronger policies if those are generally agreed. Disclosure laws were strengthened in the 1970s and a somewhat more coordinated approach to FDI was taken at the executive level of government. Reciprocity in investment was added to section 301 of the Trade Act. The Committee on Foreign Investment became more active. Stronger initiatives were taken on the outward side, as noted earlier, with regard to tax policy, bilateral investment treaties and multinational institutions such as the OECD and the GATT. Potentially the most far-reaching measure, whose scope is still undefined, was the power given the President in the 1988 trade bill to stop foreign takeovers on grounds of national security.

The debates in Congress were paralleled by much public discussion and criticism of the economic and political effects of inward FDI, which are familiar from earlier chapters on host countries.[50] These criticisms have appeared at levels of foreign ownership of industry which are half or less of what one notes in most of the other countries considered here. Some of the strongest criticisms have been levelled at Japan, in part because of the perception that, despite liberalization, it remains relatively difficult to penetrate in both trade and investment.

The impact of such inflows to the United States has not received as much systematic study as has been the case for several other countries with a longer experience of significant foreign ownership. Graham and Krugman (1989, chs 3–4) have examined a number of the criticisms of inward FDI to the United States – that it will reduce employment or lead to less attractive jobs, worsen the trade deficit, reduce favourable externalities such as R&D and lead to outward redistribution of income through the economic and political presence of foreign-owned firms. In general they find such criticisms unfounded or unproved. They note, for example, that the average performance of foreign-owned firms in manufacturing is very similar to domestically-owned firms in such matters as compensation, value added and R&D. The former do have a higher propensity to import but this result could reflect measurement problems and the overall economic impact is considered to be small. These findings, while similar in some respects to those for several other countries studied earlier, need refining through finer industry breakdowns, allowance for size of firm and other possible determinants of the observed results. Graham and Krugman's main concerns about inward FDI are the possible effects on national security, as noted below.[51]

Reporting and Regulating Inward Investment

One issue which arose quickly was the lack of recent information on inward investment, in contrast with the considerable detail on the outward side. This lack is not surprising in view of the relatively low overall penetration of FDI into US industry in the 1960s. The US government was slow in responding to some of the congressional pressures on this point, perhaps in part because of a concern that the detailed types of company information demanded might have served as a prelude to monitoring of acquisitions. Nevertheless the concerns with OPEC investments in particular led to a number of bills improving information in the 1970s (Table 9.11).

The Foreign Investment Study Act of 1974 instructed the Secretaries of the Treasury and Commerce to survey and report on the extent and nature of both direct and portfolio investments in the United States. This was taken a step further in the International Investment Survey Act of 1976 which required a detailed benchmark survey every five years, as against the 'once-over' authority of the 1974 Act. The new law applied to foreign investors owning or controlling more than 10 per cent of the votes of a US business with sales, assets or income over $5 million and also where land holdings are over 200 acres. The Department of Commerce which conducts the survey also required, in 1979, a report on any foreign acquisition of a US business or real estate. This reporting system goes beyond those in effect earlier by including newly established firms and acquisitions of firms not publicly held. Also it was now possible to require disclosure of the beneficial owner, as distinct from the owner of record. In 1978 the Agricultural Foreign Investment Disclosure Act required foreign investors and US entities in which they had an interest of at least 5 per cent to report agricultural land holdings. The disclosure and ownership provisions of the Securities and Exchange Commission, dating back to 1934 and applying to all investors, were tightened up in 1977, partly with a view to getting more data on foreign investors. The Commission must be notified when any firm, whether owned in the USA or

Table 9.11 Policy development in the United States

Various sectoral restrictions dating from early in the nineteenth century, as outlined in text.
General policy stance, 1950s onwards, to reduce both domestic and foreign barriers to FDI.

1947	National Security Act denies security clearance to facilities under foreign ownership (some exceptions).
1965	Voluntary controls on MNE activities affecting the balance of payments.
1968	Mandatory controls on balance of payments, liberalized in 1969 and fully removed in 1974.
1975	Committee on Foreign Investment in the United States established at executive level.
1976	International Investment Survey Act.
Late 1970s	Tax changes to modify deferral of FDI income and monitor transfer prices more closely.
1984	Section 301 of Trade Act of 1974 revised to include investment practices. 'Super 301' in 1988 extends this power.
1988	Exon-Florio provision of 1988 Trade Act authorizes presidential review of foreign acquisition, merger or takeover of US firms on national security grounds.

abroad, intends to acquire more than 5 per cent of the equity of a publicly owned firm. Reporting is also required where beneficial ownership of more than 10 per cent of the equity is acquired. If part of the inward FDI is financed by certain US sources such as an offering of securities to the public, the issue must be registered. In 1980 an act required foreign investors to report annually on their US real property, both in order to enforce US capital gains tax more effectively and to secure better data on foreign property holdings. All of these acts, it may be noted, did not prevent congressional criticism of the information-gathering effort of the Administration and further attempts, as noted below, to secure disclosure. In 1975 the President established the Committee on Foreign Investment in the United States, also referred to as CFIUS.[52] It is composed of representatives, whose status is not below that of an Assistant Secretary, who are designated by the Secretaries of State, Treasury, Defence, Commerce, Justice, the Council of Economic Advisors, the Office of Management and Budget and the Office of the US Special Trade Representative, as well as representatives of other departments and agencies when their interests are affected. The Committee is chaired by

Treasury. This Committee has primary responsibility in the Executive Branch for monitoring the impact of foreign investment in the United States, both portfolio and direct. Its four functions are: to analyse trends in foreign investment in the United States; to consult in advance with foreign governments intending to make major investments in the United States, including those through firms in which their agencies have an interest; to review investments, whether by public agencies or private interests, which have major implications for the US national interest; and to consider proposals for new legislation or regulation of such investments. A special programme was established in the Department of Commerce to carry out the surveys noted above and also to support the reviews by CFIUS. Individual transactions with possible major implications for US national interests are referred to CFIUS, whose members may also raise particular cases.

CFIUS made it clear in 1975 that it expected to be consulted by foreign governments which were contemplating major direct investments in the United States. In particular agreement was reached on this with Middle Eastern OPEC countries, with one exception (US House of Representatives, 1980, 176). In 1978 the procedures and guidelines of the Committee were spelled out more fully. These made it clear that it was not a screening mechanism for new entrants, but rather a method for handling certain limited cases. Investment by governments or government-controlled entities were its focus, for a variety of reasons. These included a concern that foreign governments controlling resources such as oil might manage them in ways contrary to the US interest, for example, when the resource was in short supply; that foreign governments might avoid US laws and acquire military technology; and that such governments would operate the facilities in ways considered detrimental to the United States, through, for example, subsidization or regulation of trade (Bale, 1984, 38–9). However the door was left open in exceptional cases to review private investments. Notification could be made through diplomatic channels or in some other way chosen by the foreign government, and confidentiality could be requested. On being notified the Committee chairman can decide that a formal review is not needed and, provided other members concur when so informed, simply notify the government that further consultations are not needed. Where a meeting is convened it is up to the member(s) involved to demonstrate that there are major adverse implications for the national interest. The Committee avoided developing formal procedures; it did not develop criteria for evaluation of major adverse implication for the national interest, nor did it define the types of investments to be notified by governments or even the timing of the notification.

CFIUS itself has no legal power to modify or stop an investment. Until 1988 it could request these actions and resort to diplomatic negotiations. Its recommendations could also bring into action relevant US laws (not necessarily applying only to foreign-owned firms) which would have that effect – for example, on national security or on reciprocity in mineral exploration and development. The role of CFIUS expanded greatly in 1988 because of the Exon-Florio amendment, which is noted later in this section.

The Committee met formally only ten times during its first five years. In the next few years it met almost that many times annually, partly because of congressional pressure, but also because FDI in the United States involving government investment was rising. The types of cases before it during its first decade can be indicated by the following examples:[53]

1. In 1975–6 CFIUS had consultations with the government of Romania regarding an agreement for a joint venture with a subsidiary of Occidental Petroleum to open a new coal mine. The agreement was signed in 1978.
2. A plan by the government of Iran to acquire 9 per cent of the voting stock of Occidental Petroleum was discussed in 1976, with CFIUS concluding that there was no major adverse implication but deciding also that the plan should be reviewed elsewhere in the Executive Branch. The two parties failed to come to terms on a final agreement while the review was still in progress.
3. Consultations have run into some complications with the Government of France. In 1975 the target for a hostile takeover by Société Imetal appealed to the Committee on the grounds that the French government was involved as the half-owner of Imetal's nickel and copper subsidiary. The French government denied being involved in management of the French firm, and CFIUS concluded it had no basis for intervention. The French government declined the request of CFIUS to delay the takeover by Elf-Aquitaine of the interest of the Canada Development Corporation in Texasgulf in 1981, arguing that the acquisition was too far along to be delayed but also that Elf was run as a private firm and not entirely publicly owned. The French nationalizations of the early 1980s increased tensions significantly between the two governments for a time. Such nationalizations meant increased attention by CFIUS to French investments in the United States, albeit nothing like the attention which had been in effect for some time in the reverse direction.
4. Both defence and reciprocity on mineral leasing rights became issues in the case of Kuwait Petroleum Corporation which was engaged in several acquisitions in the United States in the early 1980s, notably that of Santa Fe International Corporation. These were considered by the relevant departments. Congressional hearings already noted gave a good deal of publicity to these acquisitions. For its part CFIUS, after several meetings, concluded that the investment did not have major negative implications for US national interests.

5. There have been a number of proposed acquisitions which were reviewed by CFIUS in large part for defence reasons. Since these are also covered by other laws and policies, they are considered further below.

Up to the mid-1980s there does not appear to have been a case where CFIUS recommended that an acquisition be stopped.[54] It is hard to conceive of it at that point as a screening agency, for reasons already noted: it had an ad hoc approach to investments, as distinct from some more or less systematic review; it concentrated almost entirely on government investments; the onus was on the Committee to show major adverse effects; it had no power to block an investment itself; and its procedures were highly informal. Like any such agency it could, of course, be operated in higher or lower gear if circumstances required this. Any government, moreover, even one where the tradition of law is strong, can invoke a variety of laws regulating all firms and also apply diplomatic pressure.

Statutory changes in the latter part of the 1980s have given potentially large powers to the President to deal with restrictive FDI policies of other countries and also to block takeovers of US firms by foreign interests. It is too early to say just how restrictive these changes will be in practice. The first change, already noted, was revision of the 1974 Trade Act in 1984 to include foreign investment practices. This requires the US Trade Representative to report annually on foreign barriers to US direct investment, especially those which affect US trade in goods and services. It also empowered the President to retaliate where progress was not made in removing restrictions considered to violate certain principles, including 'fair and equitable .... opportunities for the establishment of an enterprise'. The Omnibus Trade and Competitiveness Act of 1988 went further to set a time frame within which the President would identify those trading partners with broadly unfair practices, negotiate elimination of these practices, and either retaliate where this failed or explain why action was not taken.

On the inward side, the Trade Act of 1988 included a provision on national security which deserves emphasis. There already was some legislation on security. The National Security Act of 1947 requires defence contractors to have security clearance which, with some exceptions, is denied to facilities under foreign ownership. The President can also invoke his authority under the International Economic Powers Act to regulate or prohibit an acquisition or the use of property in which foreigners have an interest. This power can be invoked to deal with an extraordinary external threat to the United States, a circumstance which would severely limit its use for barring an acquisition. In fact, it has never been used. What appears to have led to further legislation was an agreement in 1987 to sell control of Fairchild Semiconductor Corporation, already controlled by French interests, to Fujitsu Ltd of Japan. This was met by a great deal of opposition, including that of the Departments of Commerce and Defense. A major concern was the role of Fairchild as an important supplier of microelectronic chips for defence industries, but anti-trust questions and the competition with Japan in this industry were also issues. In the face of the opposition, Fujitsu withdrew from the proposed acquisition. The national security issues, it may be noted, seem somewhat strained in this case in view of the fact that the US firm was already controlled abroad and its defence-related business was sold to another French firm in 1989 after the amendment to the Trade Bill, which is noted below, had come into effect.

During the debate on the Trade Act of 1988 two proposals which are relevant to FDI received detailed consideration. One, which was eventually dropped in the Senate-House Conference, would have required the disclosure of the identity of foreign direct investors beyond certain minimum investment sizes as well as disclosure of various financial data. Unlike information already collected, the details would have been available to government officials and researchers. Such bills have always been resisted by the executive branch and by major elements of business as breaching confidentiality, reducing inward FDI, and possibly leading to case-by-case review. The other proposal, known as the Exon-Florio amendment, survived the Conference and became law after some of the reservations of the executive branch were met, notably by dropping the proposed review of takeovers which threaten 'commerce essential to the national security'. What remained was the authority of the President to suspend or prohibit an acquisition, merger or takeover by foreign investors of a firm engaged in inter-state commerce where such action poses a threat to national security. A decision to suspend or prohibit requires an investigation within specified time limits to determine that there is credible evidence of such a threat, and a finding that other laws do not provide adequate protection, as well as a report to Congress. There is no requirement that firms report takeover proposals but divestment can be enforced if subsequent investigation reveals that the provisions of the Act are applicable. Under the draft regulations notification to CFIUS can be by any party directly involved in the transaction or by a member of CFIUS.

This amendment has caused much unease in some quarters. The draft regulations do not detail what is involved in national security and, indeed, appear to permit a wide interpretation – although administration officials have insisted that it will be narrowly construed in practice. Given the costs of not doing so, there has been a strong tendency for firms to take the safe route and submit proposals to CFIUS; about half the foreign firms involved in takeovers seek its formal approval. This has raised concern that the United States is backing into a form of investment review, or may be required to do so by congressional and public pressures.

The programme came into effect in August 1988. Up to about mid-1991 CFIUS had received 575 notifications, of which twelve went beyond the initial 30-day period within which CFIUS decides whether to review a case. It then has 45 days in which to decide whether to recommend acceptance or rejection to the President, or simply to summarize the arguments where the Committee is not unanimous. There has been one rejection, in the case of a Chinese aircraft technology business which was required to divest its interest in a firm which is a supplier to Boeing Corporation. In a few cases which have come to public attention a positive recommendation was conditional on various performance requirements to satisfy security concerns.[55]

Sectoral Limitations on Inward Direct Investment

There are a significant number of sectors, often called 'national interest' sectors, where federal or state laws limit or prohibit foreign investment. The precise impact of these laws varies a good deal, however. Some of them, for example, authorize restrictions which have been imposed on a limited scale, while others simply require US incorporation. These laws have varying definitions of foreign ownership and control, and of requirements for nationals as directors.

At the federal level these sectors can be classified under transport and trade, communications, energy and natural resources, banking and defence.[56]

(a) Transport and trade

Foreign-controlled firms cannot own vessels which engage in coastal or freshwater shipping, nor engage in dredging or salvage operations. Some exceptions are allowed, for example in the case of mining and manufacturing firms which can carry on a coastal trade incidental to their principal business. These laws go back to the period 1916–20. The Federal Aviation Act of 1958 provides that air transportation within the United States be restricted to domestically controlled firms and also restricts registration and use of foreign-owned aircraft. Increased ownership of US airlines by foreign airlines led the US government in 1989 to reaffirm its position that foreign firms not own more than 25 per cent of a US airline's equity nor be in a position substantially to influence its activities.[57]

(b) Communications

The Federal Acts prohibit aliens, foreign governments or foreign-controlled firms from acquiring licences for radio, television and telegraphs. Some exceptions exist, such as broadcasting which is ancillary to the firm's main activity. Ownership restrictions also apply to telephone companies with common carrier licences. In the case of cable-landing licences a partnership with a US firm would be required of a foreign-controlled firm. Unlike the situation in some other countries in this study, foreign investors can acquire control of magazines and newspapers.

(c) Energy and natural resources

Foreigners and foreign-controlled firms are barred from engaging in operations which produce or utilize atomic energy. Under the Mineral Leasing Act of 1920 a foreign-controlled firm is not allowed to acquire leases for mining coal, oil and some other minerals on federal lands, except where they are incorporated in the United States and where their home country affords reciprocity to US-owned firms. Up to the early 1980s only one country, not in the OECD, appears to have failed this test. Transfer of federally owned land must also meet a reciprocity test. As is the case elsewhere, there are some industries where foreigners may not invest through branches but can secure a lease by investment through a US subsidiary: these include deep seabed mining, deepwater ports, geothermal steam on federal lands, and electricity (OECD, 1987b, 65–6). Foreign-flag vessels are not allowed to fish in the US exclusive zone except by agreements negotiated between governments: in 1983 there were agreements with 12 countries and the EC (OECD, 1985a, 137).

(d) Banking

Foreign ownership of bank assets grew rapidly, from 3.8 per cent in 1973 to 11.9 per cent in 1980 and 19.2 per cent in 1988. Japanese firms own more than half of the foreign-owned assets (Graham and Krugman, 1989, 21). The International Banking Act of 1978 addressed some of the issues raised by this growth. For present purposes the main point is the anomalies created by the existence of both state and federal banks and laws. One major concern was the greater restrictions on domestic banks than on foreign banks. For example, a large domestic bank wishing to acquire another large bank in its home state might face more questions about competitive effects than was true of new entry by a foreign bank, and the domestic bank might not be allowed, until recently, to acquire a bank in another state.

The Act of 1978 was regarded by the government as removing some of the advantages enjoyed by foreign banks in such a system relative to domestic banks, rather than discriminating against the foreign banks. Various requirements of the Federal Reserve System were extended to foreign bank branches and agencies. The current branch-banking activities of foreign-owned banks across state lines were allowed to continue, but their future activities of this type were restricted, except when these were extended to all banks. Among the many changes in regulations affecting banking in the United States in the 1980s have been those on inter-state banking. By early 1986 there was legislation of varying kinds in 26 states allowing outsiders to buy banks within a state (*The Economist*, 22 March 1986, 23). The limitations on inter-state banking which continue make it impossible for the United States to offer effective reciprocity to some of its trading partners. The non-bank activities were ended for existing foreign banks by 1985, and prohibited for new foreign banks. However the Glass-Steagall Act does not allow commercial banks to underwrite and deal in securities, except for those foreign banks which already had securities affiliates before the 1978 Act. Foreign investment banks and brokers are treated in the same way as local firms and can operate in the securities business. Finally it should be noted that both the federal government and some states have citizenship requirements for bank directors, although the former's requirements were modified in 1978.

(e) Defence

In the OECD agreements and in other agreements limiting non-national treatment the defence sector is an allowed exception for reasons of maintaining public order or essential security interests. The United States and most other countries take advantage of this exclusion, not only for defence industry but for other less obvious sectors. In view of the considerable size of the US defence sector, the subsidies to it and the method of exception, a closer look at it is of interest.

Under the National Security Act of 1947 the Department of Defense has issued industrial security regulations which require defence contractors to obtain security clearances for facilities and personnel. Facilities under foreign ownership, control or influence are not eligible for such clearances. The reasoning is that, in such cases, classified information might be released by the management to the foreign owners or governments. Given the international involvement of many firms, one problem has been to decide the degree of foreign ownership, control or influence which would suggest that classified information might be released. This is determined by examining detailed data submitted by the firms involved, covering ownership, management and the degree of common business and technical interest of the US firm and its foreign affiliate. While a larger number of variables are reviewed, four receive special attention from the senior government officer involved: stock ownership or options over 20 per cent; foreign indebtedness of 15 per cent or more of the firm's assets, or where 20 per cent of the stock is pledged as collateral to a foreign interest; more than 5 per cent of income from communist countries; and where a voting trust or other agreement has been established in an effort to secure clearance. The last item refers to the possibility of isolating the US facility from foreign influence by having the foreign owners surrender both ownership and especially management prerogatives to US citizens who are not otherwise affiliated with the companies. In 1979 there were 11 000 contractors in the Department of Defense industrial security programme, of whom 1600 had some elements of foreign ownership, control or influence. Another 21 firms were operating under a trust agreement or a proxy agreement.[58]

It should be added that three countries – Canada, West Germany, and the United Kingdom – have bilateral agreements which allow them to secure security clearance for the individuals or companies seeking this. The clearances are limited in the sense that classified information which could not be released to the three governments is not released to the facilities involved.

This security programme does not directly prevent the acquisition of a defence production facility. Nevertheless several cases are on record where foreign acquisitions were deterred when the potential acquirer was informed that this would jeopardize the US firm's security clearance, and security clearance has been ended in some cases because of such acquisitions (US House of Representatives, 1981–2, part 2, 259–60).

Graham and Krugman (1989, 89–92, 120–25) suggest that this system is out of date, concentrating as it does on the possible leakage of US technology while playing down possible losses from the reduction of access to foreign technology via firms located in the United States. They take the position that it is not possible to build an exclusively domestically owned defence sector since many important technologies have both civilian and military uses and the former sometimes overwhelm the latter. They suggest the United States define as carefully as possible which technologies should be domestically owned for reasons of the presidential decision-making process on takeovers involving national security. One consequence could be attempts to assist financially weak firms which are domestically owned to develop a stronger base. Where the firm was foreign-owned, and especially if it was a monopoly (wherever owned) they suggest that it would be appropriate to have requirements such as compulsory licensing or local control for R&D or other critical inputs. In general their position in the defence sector is that broader access by foreign-owned firms is preferable to either the current rules or reliance on imports. Moran (1990) has suggested that the main risk from MNEs in defence is not the nationality of the firms as such but the high degree of concentration often involved in the international industry. He suggests that US policies on nationality, location of production sites and other variables be used to encourage the multiplication and diversification of suppliers, in an effort both to promote efficiency and to enhance national control in this critical sector.

(f) Agricultural land

There has been a great deal of interest in foreign ownership of land, fed in the 1970s by lack of data on the subject. The Foreign Investment Study Act of 1974 called for a study of the subject, completed a few years later (Wunderlich, 1976). The federal government's Agricultural Foreign Investment Disclosures Act of 1978 required all foreign owners of US agricultural land to report these holdings and various data on them to the Secretary of Agriculture, as of 1 February 1979, and to report acquisitions or disposition thereafter. The term 'agriculture' includes forestry and timber holdings. In 1980 another act, directed largely at tax purposes, required foreigners to report their real property in the United States.

While the federal government has resisted, with some exceptions already noted, proposals to restrict foreign ownership of agricultural land, the state governments have enacted a wide variety of laws on the subject. Many of these laws are of long standing, but eight states adopted new laws or tightened existing ones in the decade after 1977. By 1986 the number of states with some type of restriction on foreign ownership or use had risen to 30, with about 15 of these described as having significant restrictions (OECD, 1987b, 67–8). Many, though not all, of these laws are defined to apply to non-resident aliens. Graham and Krugman (1989, 24–5) note that the existing measures, while somewhat crude, indicate that in 1986–7 the overall foreign ownership of land remained at less than one per cent both of acreage and of real estate values. Its concentration in the centres of some major cities has attracted attention, however.

There are a number of things which are puzzling about this onslaught of laws at the state level. Not only were the foreign holdings small at the time the laws were passed, but the restrictions tend to be on non-resident aliens and on domestic farmland rather than real estate more generally. Laband (1984) has argued that the outcomes reflect what one would expect in a rent-seeking model where owners of small family farms believe lower prices favour their operations via expansion in acreage. His statistical tests suggest that the present restrictive state legislation is positively related to the proportion of legislators who are small farmers and to the ratio of farmers to property agents; that is, to those opposing restriction.[59] It should be added that depressed farm prices in the late 1980s may have led many farmers to take a more favourable view of foreign investment in agricultural land.

(g) Limitations and incentives by state governments

In addition to agricultural land, state governments limit access by foreign-owned firms to some other sectors, independently of the federal government and in conflict with its stated policy position. It is often difficult to ascertain the nature and especially the importance of these restrictions. In many cases they are not enforced, or would not be enforceable, given the federal power over inter-state trade. Sometimes, as in banking, there is a federal alternative. One must be especially careful to distinguish restrictions on out-of-state firms (often met simply by incorporation in the state) from restrictions on foreign-owned firms and aliens. One attempt to summarize state restrictions is shown in Table 9.12.[60]

It should be emphasized that economic development, rather than restricting foreign investment, is what all states emphasize in their relations with foreign firms. Direct support for inward FDI is limited at the federal level but the same cannot be said for the states.[61] Half of the states have development offices abroad (Little, 1986, 18). Almost all offer a wide range of financial assistance to manufacturing and related fields, including foreign-owned as well as domestic firms. These aids involve everything from hospitality and advice to substantial loans and tax incentives. The zeal with which many states compete for foreign investment has led to much questioning on, for example, the return involved on the subsidies paid and the effects on competing local firms (see Tolchin and Tolchin, 1988). None of this appears to have affected the enthusiasm of the states for such investment. In 1980, for example, 40 states competed for a Volkswagen assembly plant, with Pennsylvania winning with a substantial set of state and federally funded incentives (*The Economist*, 23 October 1980, 19). The federal government has at times expressed its concern over such competition, partly because it can carry limitations on inter-state trade and also because it weakens the US government's opposition to such measures in other countries. As noted for other countries also, such aid often carries at least implicit performance requirements.

One area where the federal government, along with many foreign governments and multinationals, has taken a strong stand is on the attempt by some states to impose worldwide unitary taxes. State governments find it difficult or impossible to define meaningfully for tax purposes the profits earned by an MNE in each state. One method used is to allocate countrywide profits to the state by means of shares of state sales, payrolls and assets. In 1960 California decided to allocate worldwide profits in this way, and was soon followed by a number of other states. While this method can help to deal with information problems or transfer pricing, and even yield more revenue, it also raises the possibility of double taxation and challenges some aspects of tax treaties. Under pressure from governments and multinationals California and some other states have allowed firms to elect either a country or world basis for allocating profits, but Alaska has held out with a world basis. The issue is still before the courts (Graham and Krugman, 1989, 106–7; Brean, 1984, 121–3).

Table 9.12 US state limitations on foreign direct investment, 1980–81

1. Limitation on land use and ownership
   There is little consistency between the states with respect to limitations of this kind. They are applied in just over 50 per cent of the states and include:
   - limitations on the duration of foreign ownership, 7 states;
   - quantitative limitations on foreign ownership, 6 states;
   - citizenship requirements for ownership, 11 states;
   - limitations to land essential for business, 2 states.

2. Limitations on corporations
   Virtually all states have special requirements for out-of-state corporations or individuals (this includes other US and foreign). For example, there are often additional reporting requirements applied to out-of-state corporations and preferences to local corporations in public purchasing. Some states discriminate against foreign-owned firms in their public procurement.

3. Limitations on economic sectors
   (a) Banking restrictions in this sector include:
   - special deposit requirements, 5 states;
   - US citizenship requirements for directors and incorporators, 16 states;
   - special certificate of authority for foreign banks, 5 states;
   - requirement of a reciprocal licensing relationship with the foreign country, 4 states;
   - limitations on breadth of financial banking activities, 4 states; and complete prohibitions against foreign banking in 2 states.

   (b) Insurance – restrictions in this sector include:
   - special deposit requirements, 12 states;
   - US citizenship requirements for incorporators and directors (beyond residency requirements), 17 states;
   - a bar against foreign firms in 5 states as distinct from 24 states which bar corporations which are controlled by any government.

   (c) Other – in addition:
   - in 4 states there is a US citizenship requirement for certain commercial fishing and maritime activities;
   - state restrictions are uncommon in the mining sector; however there are 6 states which restrict the granting of licences or leases for state-owned lands to US citizens;
   - the right of eminent domain is granted to US utilities but not to foreign firms in 11 states.

Source: Based on material in Raymond L. Waldmann, *Direct Investment and Development in the U.S.* (1980). It is important to note that many of the limitations referred to in the study are on out-of-state firms or individuals, other American as well as foreign. In what follows this has been distinguished from limitations on aliens, foreign firms or foreign-owned firms where possible. The implications of the two types of limitations are quite different.

Other Policies[62]

Returning to federal policies, there are a number of exceptions to national treatment in terms of access to federal aid and subsidies. Foreign-owned firms cannot obtain emergency agricultural loans, purchase government foreign investment insurance or guarantees for overseas investments, and are limited in various ways in access to aid for maritime transport and the Agency for International Development (OECD, 1985a, 136–8).

It should also be noted that a number of US laws and regulations, which are applicable to all firms in the United States, may at times seem very burdensome to foreign direct investors, partly because they are more stringent than requirements in their home markets. Perhaps best known are US antitrust legislation and securities legislation and regulations. The former in particular has caused considerable problems for some firms entering the US market by takeover or by joint ventures, and has thereby affected at least the form of investment.[63]

The main law involved is the Clayton Act, which prohibits mergers or acquisitions which may tend substantially to lessen competition or create a monopoly. As of 1976, pre-merger notification to the Department of Justice and the Federal Trade Commission is required for mergers above a certain size.[64] Inward FDI, whether by merger or new investment, can also be affected by the Sherman Act's provisions on monopolization and anti-competitive practices.

One example of the complications which can arise is the merger of Standard Oil Company of Ohio and British Petroleum in 1969–70. This was challenged by the Justice Department on the grounds that 30 per cent of the Ohio market was involved, which exceeded the 25 per cent test for permissible mergers contained in the department guidelines to business. The department's position was based on the view that merger could foreclose independent entry and the latter was more likely to increase competition or avoid monopolistic practices. There was an avalanche of transatlantic protest, including official involvement of the British Foreign Secretary, based on the concern that the merger was being blocked because British Petroleum was foreign and largely owned by the UK government. The case was settled by a consent decree which permitted the merger but provided also for Standard Oil to divest a given volume of sales capacity in Ohio (Penrose, 1969).

Many such challenges have arisen before and since. A variety of state laws can also be involved in any takeover, domestic or foreign. One extreme example is Maryland, where no firm can buy more than 10 per cent of the shares of a firm incorporated there unless the Board of the latter agrees. Many US firms faced by a takeover bid they do not welcome, or for which they wish to raise the price, will appeal not only to state and federal laws but also to congressional committees and various executive agencies, in a litigious fashion at variance with what most investors experience in their home countries. The opportunities to fight a bid exist because a number of notification requirements must be met before takeovers can proceed. These laws and related administrative practices, it should be emphasized, are generally couched in terms applicable to both domestic and foreign investors and hence cannot be treated as barriers to the latter unless one can demonstrate that they are used in that way. They are, in effect, one of many institutional differences which multinationals face when they go abroad. Nonetheless to foreign investors they must often appear as a barrier to FDI since the firms and some elements of state and federal governments do not hesitate to speculate on the negative social effects of a takeover by a foreign firm. Such effects may follow, of course; the arguments often made by or to a state government on the loss of local jobs or other negative local effects from a foreign takeover sound very much like the arguments often encountered in other countries. What may also be involved in some cases is a desire on the part of the target firm to secure a higher price for its owners and better terms for its managers, combined with a willingness to use tough tactics in the process. In other cases the issue may be 'greenmail', or acquisition of a stock not with the intent to secure control but rather to sell the stock back at a higher price as part of a deal to end the takeover effort.

Many foreign firms have gone through this process in the past decade as inward FDI has soared, especially in the form of acquisitions. For example, the hostile takeover bid in 1988 by Beazer PLC of the United Kingdom for Koppers Company was met by an extensive media campaign which involved some state and local officials in Pennsylvania, with part of the criticism directed against the US investment bank which acted with Beazer. Ohio passed an act in the same year allowing it to assess the economic effects of takeover bids, an act aimed at thwarting the hostile takeover bid by Campeau Corporation of Canada for Federated Department Stores. Many such state acts aimed at both domestic and foreign mergers have been successfully challenged on constitutional grounds (*Globe and Mail*, 13 February and 29 March 1988). During the merger wave of the 1980s in the United States, many firms developed a variety of devices to thwart hostile takeovers or to improve the terms of an offer. These devices have already been noted in the sections on Switzerland and West Germany, among other countries. The Securities and Exchange Commission has attempted to limit the extent to which firms can issue shares with reduced voting power but in the process has left a number of exemptions at the federal and state level (*Globe and Mail*, 8 July 1988).

Conclusions

Until the 1970s the United States was thought of as the major home country. It still remains the country with the largest outward stock of FDI, although its share of the world stock declined from almost half in 1960 to about one-third in 1985. In the meanwhile the United States also became the largest host country in absolute terms, although the proportion of US industry under foreign ownership remains one of the smaller ones in this study. In this process the United States has gone through a process of questioning of both outward and inward FDI.

The criticism of outward FDI in the 1960s centred on its balance of payments effects, in the 1970s on its employment and tax-loss effects, with concern throughout on some of the political consequences of a large MNE presence abroad. The 1973 and 1979 oil price increases triggered congressional concern on the inward side, while increased foreign acquisitions in the 1980s raised a host of concerns familiar in all host countries.

Several things have moderated the US policy response to these major changes. One is a belief in the benefits of such investment, one that is easier to understand from the perspective of the major home country but which has survived a massive inflow of FDI as well. The ability to intervene, in any case, is limited by the particular nature and ideology of the state–business relationship in the United States. The resistance of the executive branch to congressional efforts was emphasized earlier, a resistance born partly of a belief in the desirability of such FDI but also of the desire to avoid giving other countries any further justification for restrictions on US investments abroad. Vernon (1985) has noted the propensity of the US government to favour statutes of general applicability rather than more ad hoc measures aimed at particular firms, its aversion to state ownership, the tendency to check private power, and the problems in developing policy consistency at the bureaucratic level, given the turnover of many key positions as the presidency changes hands. All of this suggests that the US government, even if it wanted to do so, would have difficulty in imposing and especially in implementing some of the measures available in other countries, such as the more discretionary types of review mechanisms.

It is true, of course, that the stated policy stance of neutrality in 1977, and of more active encouragement of liberalization of policies in 1983, has not always been achieved by the United States. State governments have strongly encouraged inflows in some sectors while attempting to close off others. The federal government has sometimes pushed the interpretation of restricted sectors or particular cases beyond what seems reasonable in terms of the exceptions justified by public order or security. The limitations have been reviewed at some length above.

It is sometimes argued that the United States must be a very open economy with regard to inward FDI, as stressed by the flood of such investment. This is an unacceptable argument for the same reason that the absence of tariffs on (say) 90 per cent of imports cannot be taken to mean a low degree of protection. Prohibitory tariffs keep out imports, just as a restricted sector keeps out FDI. It is argued less frequently that the United States must be restrictive since there is a good deal of federal and state law on FDI, although much of that law is not enforced, or can be met by incorporation, or even applies to domestic as well as to foreign firms.[65]

The executive branch has been largely successful to date in warding off the more restrictive pressures from Congress and some private groups. Moreover, in examining the activities of CFIUS and the many qualifications to sectoral limitations, it is quite clear that the United States operates one of the more liberal policies on inward direct investment. The interesting issue is whether this relatively liberal policy will continue in the face of growing inward FDI and a significant body of public opinion favouring more controls. Some things could be done even without new laws. Some of the sectoral laws long in place could be enforced more vigorously, and both the Exon-Florio amendments and the reciprocity provisions of the Trade Acts contain the potential for much more restrictive policies. Whether such a move to investment protection occurs on any scale depends in good part on political responses in the United States to the concerns about Japanese investment in particular. It depends also on the response to the integrated initiative the US government and others took in the 1980s to freeing trade in goods, services and investment.

NOTES

1. See Table 9.1. However one should note that the FRG data on FDI are not very reliable for much of the period under review and, in particular, three sets of official data with varying definitions and methods exist along with private estimates. For a discussion, see Schlupp (1985). His estimates suggest outward and inward stocks had reached equality by 1970 and stayed roughly so until 1975, after which the outward side grew faster than the inward.
2. The FRG played a pioneering role with the conclusion of its first post-war bilateral investment treaty in 1959. See United Nations (1988, 332–7) for an outline of such treaties.
3. 25 per cent is also a blocking minority for some purposes.
4. *Globe and Mail*, 11 November 1988, G18; 19 June 1989; *The Economist*, 15 November 1988, 80; 7 December 1991, 91.
5. The Commerzbank, for example, identified temporary bank acquisitions of large holdings of equities, so as to fend off unwelcome foreign takeovers, as a desirable aspect of bank investments and an alternative to government intervention (Economics Department of Commerzbank, *Viewpoint*, report no. 3, 1987).
6. The holding company still held a 25.23 per cent minority blocking interest in 1991, in

addition to the 28 per cent Deutsche Bank interest noted earlier. See *The Economist,* 23 February 1991, 66–7.

7. For further details on these cases see *Business International*, FRG, September 1986, 8–11. See also Haggeney (1980) and Kartte (1976). The article by Kartte, President of the Federal Cartel Office, typifies much German official thinking on how to deal with multinationals. It emphasizes a strong competition policy, adequate tax (including transfer price) policies, disclosure of information and the need for multi-state cooperation in all of these.
8. We have selected one or two aspects of Switzerland which are of interest in terms of attitudes and policy on FDI. For an interpretation of that complex society emphasizing how domestic power relationships affect its international economic approach, see Katzenstein (1980).
9. Among the reasons suggested for this in interviews is the problems of measurement of stock data in particular and the fear of attracting taxation. The latter is also noted in Katzenstein (1980, 521). Union Bank of Switzerland constructs a (partial) series on flows which is reproduced in Dunning and Cantwell (1987, 210) but these are not consistent with the IMF series for the two years they overlap.
10. This included the major banks, which had many bearer shares, and which were now required to be demonstrably Swiss-controlled.
11. Dunning (1981, ch. 4) examines these issues in some detail, with conclusions which, up to that time, were fairly optimistic from a UK viewpoint.
12. For description of how these controls had evolved over the post-Second World War period, see Hood and Young (1979, 307–11). More detail is available in Bank of England (February 1977, 21–4).
13. A finer breakdown shows that foreign-owned firms' shares of employment in 1983 were highest at 63 per cent for vehicles, next highest at 39 per cent for office equipment, then 33 per cent for chemicals, 23 per cent for instrument engineering and 21 per cent for mechanical engineering (Young *et al.*, 1988, 81).
14. This was an outside research project sponsored by the Board of Trade (later, Department of Trade and Industry). It is of interest to note that the study for the Government of Canada, known as the Watkins Report, was begun at the same time, in 1967, as the report by Steuer *et al.* While the former was ultimately allowed about eight months to complete the work, the latter was allowed about four years.
15. The third category includes the UK production of UK-based multinationals.
16. See National Economic Development Council (1982, 11). For a statement of the attitudes of UK unions and their experience with MNEs, see Gennard (1972).
17. This account of the historical development of policy is based on Gillespie (1972), Graham (1982) and Hodges (1974).
18. A detailed analysis of the role of the Industrial Reorganization Corporation is given in Hague and Wilkinson (1983).
19. Interviewees in Industry and Treasury confirmed this, with the qualification that some firms would not apply to exchange control if preliminary talks indicated strong opposition to the investment, and a few withdrew during the application phase as such opposition became evident. However they went on to describe policy in the late 1970s as very liberal, one comparing it with that in Belgium and West Germany.
20. In the case of the Ford takeover the conditions involved more efforts to export, capital investment plans to be completed, high earnings retention as in the past, the board of directors to continue with a majority British membership, no change in employment or import policy (Hodges, 1974, 188). In the case of the Chrysler takeover in 1967, which had begun with a minority investment in 1964, similar conditions were involved for exports, the UK board and planned expansion, while a Rootes director was to act in each of the boards of Simca (English Chrysler) and Chrysler International and a minority UK holding was to be retained (Steuer *et al.*, 1973, 179–80). *The Economist* of 21 January 1967, 240 believes that these conditions were for face-saving reasons (in its language, 'a load of hogwash') except for participation in ownership by the Industrial Reorganization Corporation. Hodges (1974, 205–9) provides a more measured, though not more sanguine, review of these conditions.

21. See *The Economist* (25 February 1984, 49; 8 February 1986, 16; 29 March 1986, 14–15, 45). In 1989, however, Ford was able to acquire control of Jaguar when the UK government agreed to waive its 'golden share' power to veto such a purchase.
22. In 1976, for example, Honeywell Incorporated attacked the 'Buy British' policy in the media and in the courts, arguing that it had lost a contract to ICL although the latter's tender appeared to be the weakest of several and although Honeywell had been assured that this contract's tender process was to be genuine. The case was withdrawn when the courts appeared to be unsympathetic, *Globe and Mail*, 10 June 1976.
23. The government's intention in this regard was announced one day after the Australian ownership of a merchant bank was increased to 14 per cent. Foreign investors are major shareholders in a number of major British merchant banks (*Globe and Mail*, 13 February 1987).
24. British Petroleum differed from the state corporations described earlier for Canada and Norway. Government ownership had fallen to about 49 per cent by the mid-1970s and to 39 per cent in the early 1980s. The government appointed two directors with the right to veto board decisions. The veto had never been used and there appeared to be an understanding that it would not be used. The company was regarded in many respects as being similar to a private firm, a point which helped in its US acquisitions.
25. UK Department of Energy, Press Release, 4 April and 13 November 1985 (reference numbers 75 and 252) spell out the details of the Petroleum and Submarine Pipelines Act.
26. Based on an interview in 1982 with an official of the Department of Energy.
27. UK Department of Energy Press Releases, 5 April and 2 August 1978, reference numbers 109 and 255. Among the firms interviewed, some of the large foreign firms also claimed that new national entrants to the oil industry were favoured, while some Continental European firms believed US and UK firms were favoured.
28. The issue of the resale of BNOCs share to the firms was a matter of dispute at the beginning, for example (*The Economist*, 20 January 1976, 128–9). In 1978 the industry, despite its diversity, protested at the overall revenue taken by the state as well as some other policies. Two of the majors protested by refusing to participate in the sixth round of exploration licences.
29. The account which follows is based largely on reports in *The Economist* (6 February 1988, 79; 7 January 1989, 69) and *Globe and Mail* (24 August 1988; 7 November 1988).
30. Kuwait had attempted to ward off this type of criticism, in part by making a deed of covenant limiting its voting power to 14.9 per cent and stating it would not increase its shareholdings (*The Economist*, 17 July 1988, 66).
31. Some parts of this section are based on interviews with the Bank of England, the Treasury, and the Department of Industry in 1977 in connection with an earlier study, as well as repeat visits to the latter two and the Department of Energy in 1982.
32. According to a UK solicitor, where foreign control was involved the relevant Secretary could ask that the enquiry cover topics such as the balance of payments effects, export restrictions and increased imports, any transfer of UK operations abroad, the effects on UK technology and where the management is located – in addition to issues involved in domestic mergers (Sheldon, 1976, 205).
33. See Wilkins (1970) for an account of developments up to 1914.
34. See Caves and Mehra (1986) for a careful empirical test of the determinants of entry to the US market. Graham and Krugman (1989, ch. 1) assess the various reasons, favouring those which emphasize a relative decline in US technological and managerial strength.
35. These comparisons depend, of course, on the degree of disaggregation of industry used. Using a finer classification, Pugel (1985, 62) shows the following manufacturing sectors with inward FDI employment in 1980 exceeding 10 per cent of domestic employment: industrial chemicals, plastics and synthetics (17.0); drugs (24.9); soaps (14.1); agricultural chemicals (27.2); other chemicals (16.3); petroleum and oil products (38.8); special industry machinery (14.4); surgical, medical and related supplies (16.6); and watches and clocks (33.5).
36. Bale (1983, 5) reporting various accounts of the negotiations.

37. For a fuller statement of such arguments, and analysis of the evidence and proposed policies, see Bergsten *et al.* (1978), Caves (1982, ch. 8) and Hood and Young (1979, ch. 7). The taxation aspects are developed fully in Brean (1984). Some of these arguments are the reverse of those made in host countries, implying that both countries lose or that one set of arguments is wrong.
38. The differences between these studies were noted in the preceding section on the United Kingdom.
39. The results have been interpreted also as suggesting the reverse, partly on the basis of different assumptions and estimates on how long it takes for FDI to generate net inflows to the home country. See Behrman (1968). Note also Dunning (1970, ch. 2) who argues in some detail that while the Reddaway and other reports may suggest that short-term controls have an effect – whatever one thinks of their merit compared with other policies – the long-term effects are subject to many unsolved issues.
40. Bergsten *et al.* (1978, 175–6). The effects of repealing deferral and other tax measures are dealt with fully in the same source, ch. 6, and Horst (1977).
41. Put more fully, how far does FDI add to the foreign stock of capital and reduce the domestic stock, and how far do these changes in investment stocks affect foreign trade? These related ideas are the investment substitution and export substitution issues. See Caves (1982, 138) and Hufbauer and Adler (1968, ch. 1).
42. The Commission study covered a wide range of effects by MNEs, both globally and in terms of the US impact. See US Tariff Commission (1973, ch. 7).
43. See Clarkson (1982) for a detailed review of Canada–US issues in these years, with conclusions somewhat different from those noted here. US business and government attitudes and policies are discussed fully in Hufbauer and Samet (1982) and Bale (1983, 1984).
44. The Mineral Leasing Act of 1920 provided that foreign-owned firms can lease mineral rights on federal lands provided, among other things, that their home country offers reciprocal rights to US-owned corporations engaged in similar activities. In 1981 this was defined to mean that US firms can invest in the corporations of the other nation and also are not effectively excluded from access to the mineral resources of that nation. The investigation into Canada's status under this Act was launched as a result of a petition to the Secretary of the Interior by St. Joe Minerals, which was concerned about the possibility of a renewed takeover bid by a Canadian firm.
45. Lipson (1985, chs 6–7) analyses at some length the first two of these policies. See also Bergsten *et al.* (1978, ch. 2). The amendments requiring 'automatic' termination of US aid where expropriation was uncompensated were used only once and in 1973 the President was given power to waive them. They have been used to exert pressure on some occasions.
46. See United Nations (1988, 255–8, 346) for an overview, Thomas (1983) on US anti-trust law and Fazzone (1983) for US export control laws.
47. The issue is considered in Hufbauer and Schott (1985, ch. 11).
48. US House of Representatives (1980, 48, 55). As noted above, Canada's policies had fewer admirers in the next few years. However, as is evident from interviews during 1981–2, some elements of Congress remained favourable to screening while departmental representatives were uniformly hostile to the idea of formal screening in general and Canada's policies in particular.
49. See US House of Representatives (1980) and *Hearings* (1981, 1982), Subcommittee on Commerce, Consumer and Monetary Affairs. The one per cent figure is on p. 128 of the 1981 *Hearings*.
50. One poll conducted early in 1988 showed 78 per cent favoured a law limiting the extent of inward FDI and 89 per cent favoured requiring foreign investors to register with the US government. These proportions fell to 13 and 48 per cent in the case of public officials and business and media leaders (UN, 1988, 242).
51. Kudrle (1991) provides a critical assessment of several other studies.
52. US House of Representatives (1980, especially 162–84 and Appendix 2 reproducing the Executive Order establishing CFIUS). This Report contains a very critical account of

CFIUS. Apart from interviews, the account given here draws also on the statement by C. Fred Bergsten and Marc E. Leland of Treasury on 30 July 1979 and 20 October 1981, respectively, to US House of Representatives 1979 and 1981–2. See also Bale (1984).

53. See Bergsten and Leland in note 52.
54. CFIUS was involved in the Fujitsu case noted below, as were other agencies and departments.
55. The operation of the Exon-Florio provision is described in Graham and Krugman, 1988, 97–100; Theofilopoulou (1989); *Globe and Mail*, 9 February 1990, 30 July 1990; and *The Economist*, 29 June 1991, 25. One case involving conditional approval was the sale by Monsanto of its silicon wafer division to a West German firm, after the West German buyer agreed to retain production and R&D facilities in the United States (*Japan Times*, 26 January 1989, 9).
56. These are discussed in more detail in OECD (1985a, 1987b); Bale (1983); and Hufbauer and Samet (1982).
57. Such rules are obviously subject to interpretation, given the elasticity of the terms involved, including 'equity'. See *Globe and Mail*, 30 September 1989, B17 for some examples.
58. US House of Representatives (1981–2, Part 3, 206). The industrial security clearance programme is discussed in Part 2, 225–60, 387–406, and Part 3, 62–6.
59. Laband recognizes that a major inflation of land values would benefit farmers as landowners. He also argues that restrictions on land ownership by other Americans or resident aliens would be too costly.
60. A more recent summary, with slightly different emphasis, is in OECD (1987b, 66–9).
61. Direct federal support is outlined in US House of Representatives (1980, 184–92).
62. Some writers list the Buy American Act and similar state provisions as a restriction. With some exceptions that Act requires that government agencies acquire for use only products with at least 50 per cent American content by value. These laws discriminate in favour of local production, but not against foreign-owned firms in the United States.
63. For example, the officers of two large Japanese multinationals who were interviewed stated that they had decided to enter the United States by wholly-owned new subsidiaries because of concerns about the anti-trust implications of joint venture entry.
64. Notification is required when a firm with worldwide assets or net sales of over $100 million attempts to acquire 15 per cent or more of a firm with assets or net sales over $10 million.
65. Canada, FIRA (1982) is an example of a document which argues that the USA is not only well equipped to bar foreign investment but often operates this way in practice. To reach this conclusion it considers barriers to business investment in general, not just foreign-owned firms, and also political and cultural differences with other countries. The series of volumes issued by the UN Centre on Transnational Corporations, entitled *National Legislation and Regulations Relating to Transnational Corporations*, frequently fails to make it clear that many of the laws and regulations apply to domestically-owned firms also.

PART III

A Comparative Evaluation of Policies

10. Origins of Policies

As noted at the beginning of Chapter 5, the analysis in Part I suggested two broad expectations regarding policies towards MNEs. The first was with regard to the origins of the policies. National governments are interested in national wealth creation and distribution and in the preservation and distribution of power. MNEs may have an impact on any of these, or at least be caught up in the struggle over the distribution of wealth and power which goes on in any state. It is likely, therefore, that most governments will welcome such investments but also attempt to regulate them. The second expectation was that the effectiveness of that regulation was subject to two broad constraints, each of which also offered some opportunities. One of these is the degree of international involvement, the other the characteristics of the country. We assumed that there is a range for bargaining within which policies can bring national gain without reducing investment, but some policies could reduce national wealth while realizing more independence or a redistribution outcome. The bargaining outcome depends on country-, firm- and industry-specific characteristics, as noted in Chapter 4. Table 10.1 outlines the broad expectations which underlie the structure of Part III.

In Chapter 10 the origins of the policies are considered in two steps. This is done, firstly, through a comparative assessment of the country studies; for example, with regard to the effects of MNEs on wealth creation, and the particular circumstances in which the policies were adopted and changed. This material is supplemented, secondly, by an empirical test of the extent to which the degree of policy restrictiveness can be linked to measures of the four reasons which motivate government policies. In the next chapter the question of policy origins is pursued further by asking how far the nature of the policy instruments used reveals the reasons for the policies.

In Chapter 11 the effectiveness of the instruments is considered. If our expectations about policy are correct, what countries would be attempting is to increase their wealth and power while preserving or enhancing the inflow. In addition they should be adopting policies which reflect both the opportunities and the constraints in their country situations and in the types of MNEs they encounter. We will therefore review the types and effectiveness of the instruments with these in mind. In Chapter 12 we will consider the changes to a more liberal set of policies on inward FDI as such which

Table 10.1 Policies on FDI: origins and effectiveness

1. Origins of policy

Wealth production (micro, macro)	Wealth distribution (group, regional)	Preservation of power (external)	Distribution of power (internal)

lead to policies (disincentives, incentives) on FDI

2. Effectiveness of policies depends on:

(a) General country-specific assets (supply, demand, organization)

(b) Specific instrument choice and operation

Restricted sectors
Review mechanisms (includes exchange control)
Non-national treatment favouring local firms
Incentives and other fiscal–regulatory policies
Bilateral or multilateral policies

(c) Nature of firms or industries involved

(firm-specific assets)

characterized the 1980s, combined, however, with attempts to use trade and investment policies more selectively to reach MNEs more generally, whether domestic or foreign in origin. Chapter 13 draws together our conclusions.

In the present chapter two types of evidence are considered on the origins of the policies. One is the historical material on countries which was covered in Part II. The other is a statistical test of the determinants of the net degree of policy restrictiveness.

Before considering the evidence from the country studies, it is worth noting that theory gives somewhat mixed results on the welfare impact of MNEs. Economic theory tends to support the free movement of goods and factors of production on the grounds that these raise world economic welfare and are likely to raise national economic welfare. There have always been qualifications to such a position which have been used to justify government intervention on economic grounds. The assumptions underlying such a conclusion may not be met – assumptions such as competition, knowledge of the choices involved for consumers and producers, and a correspondence of private and social costs and benefits. Optimal tax (for capital) and tariff (for goods) arguments can be made. When MNEs are introduced, further welfare issues arise. As noted in Chapter 3, the standard theory of MNEs regards them as overcoming imperfections in the markets for certain kinds of transfers, but some have argued that such firms also add to market imperfections in order to enhance their private gains. Where MNEs enhance efficiency or secure rents, moreover, their international distribution is a matter of considerable interest to national governments. It has also been demonstrated that, in the presence of foreign-owned factors of production, trade liberalization which might otherwise have increased national welfare can have the reverse effect (Bhagwati and Brecher, 1980). Moreover Rodrik (1987) has argued that inward FDI in a protected sector can increase the welfare losses resulting from protection. Where a first-best policy of reduced protection is not possible, the host country's welfare may be improved by imposing an export requirement on foreign-owned firms. How MNEs influence the exercise of national power and group interest is also of concern to national governments.

This chapter on the origins of policies addresses some of these issues. Just how governments choose to deal with the problems is also of interest in terms of the welfare outcomes. The latter issue is dealt with in Chapter 11.

EVIDENCE FROM THE COUNTRY STUDIES: AN OVERVIEW

The policies introduced with respect to FDI in the period since 1945 were often triggered by particular incidents, such as the proposed acquisition by an MNE of an important firm, the election of a more interventionist government, or the exercise by home governments of some control over subsidiaries located abroad. Underlying these incidents, however, were concerns about the way in which MNEs might make an impact on, or appear to be associated with, wealth and power creation or distribution. At the risk of some simplification, we turn first, therefore, to a brief overview of the detailed country material on these concerns.

It is not difficult to find evidence for all four of the major determinants of policy and, indeed, for most of the sub-categories noted in Table 2.1 In most of the countries we noted the existence of substantial studies of the economic effects of FDI, both by private researchers and for governments. A number of microeconomic concerns were evident with regard to inward FDI, for example, that excessive reliance on it could reduce technological capacity and export development. Our assessment of the more rigorous of these studies is that they suggest that the domestic impact of MNE activities is neutral or positive in the main, particularly if considered relative to firms controlled locally. Studies outlined earlier for Australia, Canada, New Zealand, Sweden, Belgium, Ireland and the United Kingdom support such an overall conclusion, although not without qualification: for example, Dunning (1985a) had more reservations in the case of the United Kingdom than did Steuer *et al.* (1973) or Young *et al.* (1988). It is necessary to add that the impact of these microeconomic studies on the development of policy was limited. In part this was because the policy debates focused on all of the determinants noted above, not just the microeconomic. In part, also, writers who were often less rigorous but who addressed these other concerns, however imperfectly, attracted a good deal of public attention. The same can be said about the effects of outward FDI, although here the studies were fewer and perhaps more guarded in their conclusions. Nevertheless studies of the balance of payments and employment effects of outward FDI for the home country certainly do not point, in the main, to negative overall conclusions in the case of countries such as the United States, the United Kingdom, Sweden and Switzerland.

Two qualifications from such studies are worth noting here. First, on both the inward and outward sides there are significant income distribution effects from FDI, effects which governments are likely to heed.[1] Economic theory has given somewhat mixed results on this point. In his 1960 article MacDougall concluded that, assuming competitive conditions, an inflow of capital would raise real wages and lower returns to domestic capital. By distinguishing between capital and factors specific to MNEs and by making other assumptions it is possible to arrive at conclusions which differ (for example, Mutti and Gerking, 1983). On the outward side, studies for the United States discussed in Chapter 9 indicated that the overall employment effects of FDI were small but the group influences were significant. The second qualification is the evidence in some studies that the performance in R&D and some other respects by domestically owned MNEs is considered superior to that of foreign-owned subsidiaries, which in turn tend to outperform domestic firms which are not MNEs. We shall return to this latter point in Chapter 12 when noting the shift to strategic trade and investment promotion.

At the macroeconomic level governments have attempted to control FDI as part of foreign exchange control programmes intended to regulate the balance of payments. Also the importance of the natural resource sector in the economies of five countries led to particular policy measures designed to ensure that nationals shared in rising rents from natural resource development, as well as in developmental spinoffs from major resource projects. However it is important to add that most of the countries involved in this study have welcomed FDI, while attempting to regulate or steer it, because of a belief that it offered macro benefits in terms of economic growth in general and employment in particular. Almost all of the governments had significant incentives for investment, sometimes geared in part to FDI. While some of these incentives can be explained by a desire to offset the negative investment effects of restrictions on FDI – in effect achieving two objectives with two policies – others cannot. We note, for example, that some smaller economies, like Ireland and Belgium, with limited natural resources to exploit adopted very broad incentives aimed largely at MNEs and had very few restrictions.

Concerns about the effect of FDI on political independence have centred on extraterritorial extension of foreign law and policy through the subsidiaries, on the one hand, and the effects on the capability of governments to implement policy, on the other. On extraterritoriality, a long list of incidents from the late 1950s onwards strongly coloured Canadian views on the way US investments lessened independence. There were similar instances elsewhere, for example in the controversy over US government attempts in the early 1980s to prevent the export of gas pipeline technology to the USSR. We noted also the impetus given in the 1960s to foreign exchange and other controls on inward FDI in Australia, New Zealand and several other countries by the efforts of the UK and US governments to regulate the effects of outward FDI on their balances of payments.

The difficulties in dealing with firms which had multinational locations and headquarters abroad were evident in a number of interviews with government officials. Some Japanese officials, for example, believed subsidiaries were less likely to be amenable to 'administrative guidance', especially as the degree of foreign ownership increased in an industry. Some government officials in Canada also indicated that foreign firms were less likely to accommodate government views on implementing policy initiatives. It was difficult to pin down these issues in any systematic way. For example, some of the company officers believed they had to make a special effort to take on the protective colouring of their subsidiary's environment, if only because public officials and the media could so easily exert pressure on them because they were foreign-owned; and in several countries, notably the smaller resource-based economies such as New Zealand, the issues involved tended to overlap with concerns about the impact of large natural-resource-based corporations, not just those which were foreign-owned. Much larger countries also apparently felt vulnerable to excessive reliance on MNEs in some sectors. France used quotas from the mid-1920s onwards both to attract petroleum refinery capacity to France and also to discriminate in favour of French-owned firms so as to reduce its dependence on what it regarded as an Anglo-Saxon monopoly in this sector.

Many countries attempted to limit the participation by foreign-controlled banks in their domestic markets. No doubt this was for many reasons, such as attempts to secure better treatment for their own banks abroad and the desire by some local banks to limit competition. One motive frequently mentioned in interviews with bank officials was the belief that monetary controls would be more effective with nationally controlled banks. These expectations, if they were ever valid, lost much of their point with the internationalization of such national banks and of finance more generally, as well as the crumbling of the barriers between different kinds of financial activity.

Extraterritoriality and the effects on policy-making capability may not capture the concerns for political independence unless they are interpreted very broadly. National security issues were evident in all countries, as seen from the lists of restricted sectors in each chapter and in other national legislation. The long-standing aversion to foreign control of industry in Japan which was noted in Chapter 7 is inadequately captured by the phrases used here.

The third policy determinant was the distribution of income within the state. This is partly an extension of the point made in connection with the first policy determinant, the attempt to increase wealth subject to an equity constraint. MNEs can have an uneven impact not only on groups, as noted earlier, but also on regions. All countries, but particularly federal systems, have policies intended to achieve a more even distribution of income geographically, for both economic and non-economic reasons: hence the efforts to influence MNEs to locate in regions which are less economically developed.

What we also have in mind here, however, are efforts to influence policy on FDI so as to redistribute rents or income within a country, not simply to transfer rents to the country. Some of the objections to inward FDI come from groups having a vested interest in preserving or increasing rents, even though the overall level of investment and employment may be reduced in the process. Sectoral restrictions on inward FDI may protect vital non-economic interests and conceivably lead in time to efficient domestic firms through an infant industry learning process. Or they may lead to permanent protection of groups which will not become efficient because of insufficient competitive pressure. Performance requirements exacted by investment review agencies may help to develop local inputs on an efficient scale and ensure that the host country captures research or other critical developmental inputs. Or they may prove ineffective over time in so doing, while leading MNEs, whose initial costs are increased, to reduce investment or to try to evade the requirements. The fact that review agencies are an obstacle to acquisition of domestic firms can lead to transfer of rents to local owners from abroad. They may also reduce prices to domestic sellers *and* domestic buyers.

The distinction between the *effects* of MNE investments on groups or regions and how these *interests* may affect rent redistribution within a country is admittedly awkward to make in practice. The same can be said of the distinction between rent seeking in an economic sense and the attempt to affect the distribution of power within the state, encompassing in the latter the competition between different ideas of the appropriate relationship between firm and state. Issues with regard to FDI played an important role in elections in a number of countries (for example, Australia in 1972 and Canada in 1980) yet we know from Australian and New Zealand experience in the 1980s that identifying Labour parties with restrictive approaches oversimplifies the situation. How FDI issues are handled by politicians and bureaucracies can also greatly affect outcomes. We drew a contrast, in the design and experience of the review agencies, between the decision by Treasury officials in Australia to keep control of the process and to avoid strong intervention and the situation in Canada, where an apparently stronger set of policies was married to procedures which were difficult to implement. In part this difference in outcome reflected the opposition to the agency by some senior civil servants in Canada. In part also, however, the interviews in these and in other countries such as New Zealand and Norway suggested that the political processes involved attempted, as usual, to balance various interests. Specifically in this case the instruments were put in place in order to reassure significant sections of the public and to allow governments to address particular problems as needed, but were usually operated in a non-restrictive way in order to reassure foreign investors.

The views of ministries differed widely on MNEs, as we saw frequently, with those in a sector or for industry or science far more critical than those in finance or regional development. Federal systems, where competition between governments was possible, tended to weaken any proclivity by central governments towards more restrictive policies. More striking still were the differences of viewpoints between countries, reflecting in part different degrees of business–government linkage. In Japan and several of the European countries these links have been close, including attitudes to inward FDI, as is evident from the highly discretionary nature of the policies followed. One contrast was in the more critical views on MNEs of French business leaders and civil servants as compared with those in the United Kingdom, as revealed by surveys discussed in Chapter 9 in the section on the latter country. Even in countries whose economic and political structures were closer, these differences in attitudes to FDI in the senior civil service were striking. In the late 1970s and early 1980s it was difficult to find many such interviewees in the central government in Canada who did not believe that 'truncation' of industry and resulting economic dependency were due to foreign ownership. It was equally difficult to find many in Australia who did take this position.

Underlying the struggle over the distribution of power as it related to control of the MNE were striking differences in ideas of the appropriate degree of control over the large firm by the state. Again and again one is struck by the degree to which the debate over the MNE was part of a long-standing debate over control of large corporations, aggravated by the fact that the multinational enterprise is almost by definition in a stronger position to withstand pressure from any one national government. In some countries such as Canada the debate took the form of domestic firms versus foreign-owned multinationals, but countries such as Sweden and Switzerland had long had to face the fact of production dispersion abroad by their own firms. The Swedish Commission which reported in 1978 on the control of foreign investment split three ways, with the labour and social democratic group favouring controls on FDI at and after establishment, the conservative parties and some business groups favouring equality of treatment, and part of the centrist and liberal parties favouring episodic negotiations. Such differences go well beyond the economic issues noted earlier.

Table 10.2 sets out more systematically the proximate reasons for adopting review mechanisms on inward FDI. It is important to note that the table does not address systematically the other aspects of a restrictive policy on inward FDI, such as sectoral restrictions as noted in detail in Table 11.3. There is also the question of whether the gradual introduction of broader review procedures in the United States qualifies for inclusion. Formal review in the United Kingdom ended in 1979 when exchange control ended.

Despite these reservations some broad themes stand out. It was emphasized in Part II that exchange control in itself does not constitute a review of the broader economic impact of FDI. Yet such control did facilitate broader review. All the countries shown, except Canada, had exchange controls for part or all of the period covered in this study. The proposed foreign takeover of a firm in an industry considered sensitive often triggered a move to more general review mechanisms. A fuller list of such restricted sectors is given in Table 11.3, but the list in Table 10.2 clearly shows the broad range of sectors covered by the term 'sensitive'. Nevertheless natural resources, finance, media and defence stand out in such sectors. Almost all countries have had important policies in the natural resource sector. In the natural resource-producing countries this has involved a desire to secure rents for residents and also developmental spinoffs, while in other countries the desire to ensure supplies of petroleum in particular has led to discrimination against foreign-owned firms. Concerns about economic performance have been evident in a number of countries but were strong only in a few, if one judges by the way the review mechanisms were operated. However energy ministries, among

Table 10.2 Origins of inward review policies for FDI to 1980

Proximate reason	*Australia*	*Canada*	*NZ*	*Norway*	*Sweden*
Existence of exchange control	yes	no	yes	yes	yes
Takeover of a key firm	insurance 1968 uranium 1970 resources 1960s	bank 1963 uranium 1970 media 1960s	media 1964 resources 1960s	resources 1906–17	resources 1916 others 1970s
Concerns about performance	weak	strong	moderate or weak		moderate
Natural resource restrictions or rent participation	strong all resources late 1960s	strong energy 1970s	strong land & energy late 1960s	strong all resources 1906–17	strong all resources 1916
Policies abroad					
Balance of payments controls in US, UK	strong mid-1960s	strong mid-1960s	moderate or strong mid-1960s		
Extraterritoriality and independence		strong, from late 1950s		strong neutrality	strong neutrality

Proximate reason	*France*	*Japan*	*UK*	*USA*
Existence of exchange control	yes	yes	until 1979	1960s (partial)
Takeover of a key firm	computers 1964–6 some others	takeovers discouraged	motor cars banks	defence OPEC
Concerns about performance	strong (high-tech)	strong	weak	weak
Natural resource restrictions or rent participation	supply (petroleum)	supply (petroleum etc.)	moderate or strong energy	weak
Policies abroad				
Balance of payments controls in US, UK	strong mid-1960s			
Extraterritoriality and independence	Lack of EC policy military independence	strong general	weak	strong reciprocity

Note:
For further sectoral and other details not covered here, and for restricted sectors in particular, see Part II.

others, usually operated significant performance requirements. Balance of payments controls on direct investment outflows by home countries triggered a strong reaction in several countries, as did extraterritoriality and other issues related to political independence.

One point not noted in the tables is the relationship between the introduction of review mechanisms, including current or subsequent natural resource policies, and the political complexion of governments. The evidence on this from Part II is difficult to summarize and, in any case, is mixed. While it is possible to point to stronger policies being introduced in Australia or Canada in the 1970s, for example, because of the election of Labour-left governments or the influence of such parties, it is also possible to point to such policies under more conservative governments. We return to this issue in the next section.

A STATISTICAL TEST OF THE DETERMINANTS OF POLICY

Another approach to the origins of policy is to identify the factors which are statistically significant in determining the degree of government restrictiveness towards inward FDI. This approach has the virtue of requiring a more precise specification of some of the variables which were discussed in Parts I and II. It may also add some further light on the issue of policy determinants in general and those regarding inward FDI in particular. In brief an attempt is made to identify the relationship between a composite measure of the degree of restrictiveness of policy on inward FDI and a number of proxies for the determinants of policy which were discussed in Chapter 2. The regression used can be stated as follows:

DOR = f(GDP, GDPPC, UNEM, EXGDP, IMGDP, DI, PG, PRITOT, EPRITOT, TCIR, RD, GINI, FED, PEN, PROXA, PROXB, POL, GOV)
where the short forms have the following meanings:

DOR	Degree of restrictiveness of policy on inward FDI
GDP	Gross domestic product
GDPPC	GDP per capita
UNEM	Rate of unemployment of labour force
EXGDP	Exports of goods and service as a percentage of GDP
IMGDP	Imports of goods and services as a percentage of GDP
DI	Outward stock of FDI minus inward, as a percentage of the two stocks combined
PG	Share of primary commodities in total commodity exports
PRITOT	Share of primary sectors in total inward stock of FDI
EPRITOT	Share of primary sectors as a proportion of total employment
TCIR	Change in foreign exchange reserves
RD	Gross domestic expenditure on R&D as a percentage of GDP
GINI	Measure of income inequality
FED	Existence of a federal state
PEN	Foreign-owned firms' share of manufacturing employment
PROXA	Percentage of number of foreign-owned firms accounted for by firms from leading home country

PROXB	Same as PROXA for four leading home countries
POL	Percentage of time a Labour (left) government was in power or officially part of a ruling coalition
GOV	Government expenditures as a percentage of GDP

Plus a constant C

Part II covered the experience of 15 countries. Seven other OECD countries were added for these tests in order to give a larger sample. Various public sources were consulted to derive measures of the degree of restrictiveness, but the measures for the seven countries obviously lack the information derived from the interviews. While three of these countries (Austria, Denmark and Finland) show measured degrees of restrictiveness in Table 10.3 which fit well into the categories used to classify countries in Part II, as shown in Table 5.1, this is not so for the other four. Greece, Portugal, Spain and Turkey all show higher degrees of restrictiveness than the classification in Table 5.1 would suggest for smaller host countries lacking a major primary resource base.

Appendix IV spells out in more detail the nature and sources of the variables used. For some of the independent variables averages of several years were used to iron out year-to-year variation, a matter of some significance in the early 1980s especially. A brief summary of the variables is noted in the following sections, along with an analysis of the test results.

VARIABLES USED AND EXPECTED RELATIONSHIPS

The dependent variables, degree of policy restrictiveness or DOR, are composite measures of two or three of the following: the existence of exchange control (A), the existence of a review mechanism on establishment or subsequent merger (B), and the strength of such a review (C), offset by the existence of various incentives (D).[2] Depending on the existence and type of exchange control, a weight of 0 to 1.2 was used. The existence of a review mechanism on establishment received a weight of 1, while a weight of 0.5 was given for a reporting requirement, a partial screen, or the use of competition policy to police FDI, as discussed in Part II. The strength of a review mechanism was based on data in a variety of publications noted in Appendix IV and also on the author's interpretation of the interview material. Some of the issues which were considered with regard to the latter will be evident when review mechanisms are compared in the next chapter. A maximum weight of three was given for the strength of the review mechanism, in addition to the weight of one given for its existence.

Table 10.3 *Degree of restrictiveness of policy on FDI: comparative measures*

		1981				1985				1981[a]		
		ABCD	*BC*	*ABC*	*BCD*	*ABCD*	*BC*	*ABC*	*BCD*	*Rank of ABCD*	*Rank of BCD*	*Rank in Haner, 1979*[a]
1	Australia	3.18	3.00	3.80	2.38	2.67	2.50	2.90	2.27	11	10	11
2	Austria	0.62	0.50	0.90	0.22	0.22	0.50	0.90	-0.18	—	—	—
3	Belgium	0.39	0.50	0.90	-0.01	0.50	0.50	0.90	0.10	7	5–6	5–6
4	Canada	3.72	4.00	4.00	3.72	2.77	3.00	3.00	2.77	15	16–17	5–6
5	Denmark	1.07	0.50	1.30	0.27	1.13	0.50	1.30	0.33	8	8	9
6	Finland	3.12	3.00	3.40	2.72	3.29	3.00	3.40	2.89	—	—	—
7	France	4.52	4.00	4.80	3.72	3.69	3.00	3.80	2.89	17	16–17	14
8	FRG	0.10	0.50	0.50	0.10	0.16	0.50	0.50	0.16	6	7	3
9	Greece	3.59	2.50	3.70	2.39	3.08	2.50	3.70	1.88	14	11–12	15
10	Ireland	0.30	0.50	1.30	-0.50	0.30	0.50	1.30	-0.50	1	1	8
11	Italy	2.19	1.50	2.70	0.99	1.17	1.50	1.90	0.77	9	9	17
12	Japan	2.39	2.50	2.50	2.39	1.94	2.00	2.00	1.94	10	11–12	7
13	Neth	-0.40	0.00	0.00	-0.40	-0.51	0.00	0.00	-0.51	3	2	4
14	New Zealand	3.10	3.00	3.80	2.30	2.22	2.50	2.50	2.22	—	—	—
15	Norway	3.52	3.00	3.80	2.72	3.74	3.00	3.80	2.94	13	13	10
16	Portugal	5.03	4.00	5.20	3.83	3.80	3.00	4.20	2.60	18	18	19
17	Spain	4.23	4.00	4.80	3.43	3.29	3.00	3.80	2.49	16	15	16
18	Sweden	3.23	3.00	3.40	2.83	3.34	3.00	3.40	2.94	12	14	12
19	Switzerland	-0.17	0.00	0.00	-0.17	-0.23	0.00	0.00	-0.23	4	3	1
20	Turkey	5.20	4.00	5.20	4.00	4.52	4.00	5.20	3.32	19	19	18
21	UK	-0.01	0.50	0.50	-0.01	0.27	0.50	0.50	0.27	5	5–6	13
22	US	-0.11	0.50	0.50	-0.11	-0.16	0.50	0.50	-0.16	2	4	2

Note:
See Table 12.1 for some measures of the average changes from 1981 to 1985.
[a]The number 1 shows the least restrictive policies or, in Haner's case, least nationalistic country.

Source: Appendix IV and Haner (1980, 212–13). Haner does not give estimates for New Zealand, Austria and Finland. A refers to exchange controls, B to existence of review, C to strength of review, and D to incentives which are subtracted from the other three estimates.

The disincentives involved in a review mechanism can be partly offset by various incentives. In effect the authorities are aiming at two or more objectives and using two or more instruments. A maximum weight of one is given for incentives such as tax concessions and subsidies. This was deducted from the sum of the other items to give a measure of degree of policy restrictiveness.

What is most obviously missing in this measure is some allowance for restricted sectors. There were two problems here which proved insurmountable. First, a glance at Table 11.3 will show that all countries, even those without exchange controls or establishment review, have a variety of sectoral restrictions, making it difficult to distinguish between them on this basis. One way around this is to give different weights to the sectors, but once one gets beyond commodities, which are not the major part of output, sectoral breakdowns of output and other possible weights are highly aggregated. Nevertheless some broad weights might have been assigned by types of restrictions to the data in Table 11.3. Unfortunately there is a second problem. As noted below, we used measures which encompassed more than one year. The data on such restricted sectors for the two most recent available years, 1981 and 1985, clearly reflect a considerable increase in coverage over this period, thereby rendering them unreliable for a measure involving two years. The data are subject also to other problems of interpretation, such as how the natural resource restrictions are handled in Norway and Sweden (OECD, 1982, 1987b). Hence our data on DOR lack any measure for restricted sectors. The same problem arose with exceptions to national treatment, where definitions were clarified and coverage increased greatly in the second OECD study (OECD, 1985a, 7–8).

Some measures of degree of policy restrictiveness for 1981 and 1985 are summarized in Table 10.3. For comparison, the ranking in another study is also shown (Haner, 1980, Appendix A and C). Haner uses an index of business environment risk for different countries based on the judgement of staff associated with the preparation of the index. His sub-index on nationalism is what is referred to in Table 10.3. His measure differs from ours in content, and especially in weighting and methodology, but it is of interest to note that the ranking of the two sets of measures is very similar, except for four countries. Canada is ranked far lower (that is, less nationalistic) by Haner than the ranking given to FDI policies by our measures, while Ireland, Italy and the United Kingdom rank relatively higher or more nationalistic. The weights used by Haner go some way to explaining these differences: his sub-index on nationalism gives a weight of 32 per cent to attitude towards foreign investor and profit, 32 per cent to nationalization, 20 per cent to currency convertibility and 16 per cent to bureaucratic delays.

Turning to the independent variables, the relationship to the four broad determinants of policy noted in Chapter 2 is brought out below. In some cases a proxy is related to two of the determinants of policy.

Characteristic	*Proxy*
wealth increasing	GDP, GDPPC, UNEM, EXGDP, IMGDP, DI, PG, PRITOT, EPRITOT, TCIR, RD
wealth distributing	GINI, FED, UNEM
power increasing or maintaining	PEN, PROXA, PROXB, POL, PG PRITOT, EPRITOT
power distributing	PEN, PROXA, PROXB, POL, GOV

It will be noted that there are few proxies for wealth distribution in particular. This reflects the lack of data. It proved impossible, for example, to locate or derive measures of concentration of wealth or of industry for two years for the 22 countries involved, either of which might have served as a proxy for the influence of group or sectoral pressures.

In several cases a policy determinant is represented by several closely-related variables, partly in order to test different proxies for each policy determinant but also in order to capture somewhat different relationships. A large market, GDP, is not the same as a wealthy country, GDPPC.[3] It is useful to measure how DOR relates to dependence on primary product exports, PG, but some countries which are significant producers of such products may consume much of them, hence the use of PRITOT and EPRITOT. (Conversely the latter two alone would not be a good measure of the effects we are trying to capture, since countries like Sweden long ago blocked FDI in such sectors.) The experience of a country such as Canada, with substantial reliance on one other country for inward FDI, is captured by PROXA, but PROXB is more likely to reflect the experience of countries such as Australia.

Table 10.4 shows the expected relationship between DOR and various determinants of public policy, while Table 10.5 outlines the reasons for the expected signs in the regressions. These signs reflect our interpretation of ideas discussed at some length in Part I as well as in some sections of Part II. It is not difficult to think of exceptions to the signs noted, but the important point is whether these signs capture the general case. Sometimes they may not, partly because of problems in interpreting the available proxies. For example, POL is a weak proxy because minority governments may be supported *unofficially* by parties of the left or right, whereas POL takes account of official coalitions only. A large government presence through expenditure, GOV, could be interpreted as giving government sufficient levers to deal with FDI without requiring establishment review, but the sign used here implies that any such effect is overridden by the tendency of 'interventionist'

Table 10.4 Expected relationship between degree of restriction and various determinants of public policy

Proxy for policy determinant	*Expected relation to DOR*	*Determinants: expected relation to DOR*								*Relation of proxy to bargaining power (inward)*
		WI		*WD*		*PI*		*PD*		
		a	*b*	*a*	*b*	*a*	*b*	*a*	*b*	
GDP	+		+							+
GDPPC	+		+							+
UNEM	-		-		-					-
EXGDP	-		-							-
IMGDP	-		-							-
DI	-		-							-
PG	+		+			+				+
PRITOT	+		+			+				+
EPRITOT	+		+			+				+
TCIR	-		-							-
RD	-		-							-
GINI	+		(-)	+	-					+(?)
FED	-				-					-
PEN	+					+		+	+	-(?)
PROXA	+					+	+	+	+	-
PROXB	+					+		+	+	-
POL	+					+		+	+	+
GOV	+							+	+	+

Notes:
WI = wealth increasing
WD = wealth distributing
PI = political independence (external)
PD = power distributing (internal).

governments to favour investment review. A large government presence through public ownership would involve the same difficulties in interpreting the correct sign. Similarly, one could argue that a country with a weak exchange reserve position would be more open to inward FDI but, since there is then no guarantee that such firms would import the capital, we have taken the opposite position. It will be noted in Tables 10.4 and 10.5 that some proxies can be interpreted to explain more than one policy determinant. It is possible also to show opposite signs for a proxy so long as these appear in separate columns, as happens to be the case for GINI.

As noted in Part I, the desire to enact policies on FDI is not the same as the ability to bargain effectively with firms. The latter will be considered more fully in Chapter 11. The model used here integrates both the desire and the capacity to implement policy effectively, at least for some of the relevant bargaining variables. What is missing is the impact on investment flows, if we accept that the objective in many cases is to attract and steer investment rather than keep it out. For the time being it can be noted that, in terms of the degree of bargaining power, the expected relation of DOR to each policy determinant would probably also be that shown in Table 10.4. That is, large economies could exert more pressure on inward FDI if they wished to do so (GDP has a sign of +), those with a high proportion of exports could exert less (EXGDP is -), those with a high degree of government intervention could exert more (GOV sign is +). There are exceptions: the higher concentration of FDI from one or a few home countries might lead to more restriction (PROXA, PROXB expected to have a + relation to DOR) but this concentration might well lead to less leverage on MNEs because of possible retaliation from home governments. While the likely relation of the proxies to bargaining power issues is given in the last column of Table 10.4, this can be considered as re-enforcing the explanatory power of the four determinants of public policy rather than adding much by way of analysing bargaining power capacities.

ESTIMATION PROCEDURES

The ordinary least squares regression technique was used. Adjustment for heteroscedasticity showed only marginal improvements in parameter estimates and test statistics. Standard statistical measures of significance and variation were used as follows:

> t statistic tests the null hypothesis H_0: $\beta_i = 0$

If the computed t statistic turns out to be less than the critical value from the tables, one cannot reject the null hypothesis, namely that the respective parameter estimate is statistically different from zero. If one cannot reject the null, the proxy does not have a statistically significant impact on DOR.[4]

> F statistic tests the null hypothesis H_0; $\beta_1 = \beta_2 = \ldots = \beta_k = 0$

If the computed F statistic is less than the critical value from the tables, one cannot reject the hypothesis that all the parameter estimates taken together are statistically different from zero. In effect this statistic indicates whether the model underlying the particular regression has any significance.

> $\bar{R}^2$ (adjusted) is a measure of the proportion of total variation in the dependent variable which is explained by the independent variables.

Table 10.5 Reasons for expected signs in regressions

Variable and sign	*Reasons*
GDP +	Larger markets allow bargaining for better terms of access: not as dependent internationally
GDPPC +	Wealthier countries can afford to be more restrictive: higher resource rents, if available, attract more restrictions
UNEM –	Higher unemployment rate encourages import of FDI to create jobs, nationally and especially regionally if some regions have very high rates
EXGDP –	International involvement increases desire to preserve open system and also increases fear of retaliation
IMGDP –	Same as EXGDP. Also desire to encourage local production through FDI if IMGDP high
DI –	Home countries take non-restrictive position to protect outward FDI stock
PG +	Countries with large natural resources (export share) can and will attempt to capture rents. Resources less mobile than manufactures. Independence concerns for a key sector
PRITOT +	Same as PG
EPRITOT +	Same as PG
TCIR –	Weak reserve position involves restrictions on FDI to ensure positive contribution to balance of payments; but weakens bargaining position
RD –	Countries with relatively low research performance ('technology gaps') will use review mechanisms and other methods to favour own firms or capture MNE research
GINI +	More unequal income distribution means group or sectoral interests are likely to prevail in reducing competition from FDI or securing quasi-rents from FDI through review mechanisms and other policies (can also argue government will be less restrictive so as to reduce regional inequalities)
FED –	Existence of federal state reduces restrictiveness as more emphasis on wealth distribution and also as more voices in policy
PEN +	Higher foreign ownership increases concerns on independence, exacerbates ideological debate, limits bureaucratic power – all leading to more restrictiveness. Bargaining power stronger in some ways (existing firms are hostages) but weaker as high degree of international involvement
PROXA +	Concentration of FDI in one home country increases concerns about exercise of power, external and internal
PROXB +	Same as PROXA
POL +	Labour–left governments are more restrictive for reasons of ideology, maintenance of capacity of government to intervene (this could be extended across other categories to encompass economic concerns)
GOV +	Restrictions on FDI as an aspect of a larger government presence in general

Source: Part I.

Table 10.6 Test results, determinants of policy on FDI, 1981

	C	*DI1*	*POL1*	*GDPPC1*	*UNEM1*	*GOV1*	*PG1*	*EXGDP1*	*IMGDP1*	*TCIR1*	*EPRIT1*	*RD1*
1. ABC	-3.1206	-0.0013	-0.06925	0.00027	-0.27985	0.16781	-0.05707	0.8896	-0.82357	0.00161	0.222	-1.276
	(-0.339)	(-0.0757)	(-3.691)	(1.889)	(-3.2015)	(3.4058)	(-0.9996)	(3.0108)	(-2.878)	(4.2827)	(3.2683)	(-2.6779)
2. BC	-2.7302	0.00191	-0.0677	0.000245	-0.26463	0.15463	-0.0582	0.88144	-0.81784	0.001685	0.19724	-1.0642
	(-0.30171)	(0.11322)	(-3.5872)	(1.7468)	(-3.0735)	(3.1864)	(-1.035)	(3.0281)	(-2.9025)	(4.529)	(2.9483)	(-2.2675)
3. BCD	-4.9003	-0.0062	-0.08057	0.00029	-0.29403	0.15577	-0.09377	0.8786	-0.80262	.0.00201	0.19487	-1.1592
	(-0.43186)	(-0.2944)	(-3.4023)	(1.696)	(-2.7237)	(2.5598)	(-1.329)	(2.4077)	(-2.2717)	(4.3263)	(2.323)	(-1.9699)
4. ABC	—	—	-0.07827	0.00021	-0.25932	0.19216	-0.05992	0.88455	-0.81674	0.00161	0.20905	-1.5901
			(-5.353)	(1.7045)	(-3.0158)	(4.6841)	(-3.145)	(4.2902)	(-4.5522)	(4.7604)	(3.6516)	(-4.9525)
5. BC	—	—	-0.078	0.0002107	-0.25255	0.17207	-0.06248	0.85783	-0.79005	0.0017109	0.18274	-1.3146
			(-5.6198)	(1.8018)	(-3.0938)	(4.4183)	(-3.7639)	(4.3827)	(-4.6386)	(5.3239)	(3.3624)	(-4.3128)
6. BCD	—	—	-0.0815	0.00025	-0.27651	0.17785	-0.07304	0.95577	-0.88187	0.00195	0.20223	-1.4464
			(-5.6925)	(2.0962)	(-3.2842)	(4.4275)	(-4.2665)	(4.7343)	(-5.0199)	(5.884)	(3.6076)	(-4.6007)
7. ABC	—	—	-0.072	—	-0.287	0.1952	-0.0593	0.77723	-0.7287	0.001502	0.15713	-1.4171
			(-4.58)	—	(-3.05)	(4.2810)	(-3.0856)	(3.5577)	(-3.8108)	(4.0622)	(2.9132)	(-4.1809)
8. BC	—	—	-0.072	—	-0.28039	0.17515	-0.06688	0.75014	-0.70127	0.00160	0.13064	-1.1409
			(-4.7315)	—	(-3.0910)	(3.9778)	(-3.599)	(3.5563)	(-3.8006)	(4.484)	(2.5084)	(-3.4863)
9. BCD	—	—	-0.074	—	-0.3099	0.18156	-0.07833	0.82654	-0.77533	0.001819	0.13971	-1.238
			(-4.493)	—	(-3.1412)	(3.791)	(-3.875)	(3.6027)	(-3.8633)	(4.6832)	(2.6466)	(-3.4781)
10. ABC	—	—	-0.0603	0.00028	—	0.15534	-0.03763	0.75315	-0.71254	0.00132	0.21434	-1.4526
			(-3.1843)	(1.6338)	—	(2.7964)	(-1.6069)	(2.6349)	(-2.853)	(2.876)	(2.6407)	(-3.222)
11. BC	—	—	-0.0605	0.000279	—	0.13621	-0.0455	0.72987	-0.6885	0.00143	0.18789	-1.1806
			(-3.3168)	(1.6894)	—	(2.5454)	(-2.0201)	(2.6507)	(-2.8623)	(3.2266)	(2.4031)	(-2.7188)
12. BCD	—	—	-0.0635	0.000327	—	0.13860	-0.05453	0.81566	-0.77068	0.00164	0.20787	-1.2997
			(-3.1981)	(1.8565)	—	(2.4239)	(-2.2629)	(2.7723)	(-2.9984)	(3.4687)	(2.4881)	(-2.8011)
Signs for ABC, BC, BCD[a]	x	x	-	+	-	+	-	+	-	+	+	-

Data limitations meant we could secure only the sign, not the magnitude, of the impact of any given proxy on DOR. An overall significance level of 90 per cent was used, since data limitations did not allow use of preferred higher levels. The method used was somewhat heuristic in that a 'build down' approach was used. Regressions were run using all the independent variables, then some were eliminated using *t* statistics while ensuring that the *F* statistic was large enough to ensure joint significance of the parameter estimates.

GDP, GDPPC and UNEM are the only independent variables which pose a multicollinearity problem; that is, which are highly correlated and hence distort the statistics used to interpret the regressions.

PEN	*PROXA*	*PROXB*	*FED*	*PRITOT*	*GINI*	$\bar{R}^2$	*F*	*Degrees of freedom*	*Critical values*
0.03582	0.13832	-0.28492	-1.8012	-0.10927	0.65969	0.83	7.04	17	
(0.60327)	(1.5033)	(-1.6032)	(-2.1105)	(-1.5733)	(5.4718)			3	
0.0399	0.13554	-0.26744	-1.7602	-0.10175	0.61013	0.77	5.2	17	$F_3^{*17} = 5.2$
(0.6829)	(1.4957)	(-1.528)	(-2.0941)	(-1.487)	(5.1383)			3	$t_4^* = 1.53$
-0.000326	0.11390	-0.2358	-1.9568	-0.0862	0.67587	0.69	3.8	17	
(-0.00445)	(1.0024)	(-1.0744)	(-1.8565)	(-1.0055)	(4.5394)			3	
—	0.13310	-0.28697	-1.0122	-0.11144	0.59437	0.82	7.6	14	
	(3.1602)	(-3.9607)	(-1.8374)	(-3.5997)	(6.0115)			7	
—	0.126888	-0.26437	-1.1204	-0.0977	0.55523	0.77	6.0	14	$F_7^{*14} = 2.7$
	(3.1733)	(-3.8436)	(-2.1424)	(-3.3272)	(5.9154)			7	$t_7^* = 1.4$
—	0.14115	-0.29598	-1.3444	-0.11022	0.61651	0.78	6.6	14	
	(3.4228)	(-4.1721)	(-2.4924)	(-3.6359)	(6.3682)			7	
—	0.0856	-0.20824	-0.90714	-0.0846	0.52811	0.77	6.5	13	
	(2.435)	(-3.3524)	(-1.4892)	(-2.8493)	(5.2206)			8	
—	0.07925	-0.18537	-1.0150	-0.07267	0.488	0.71	4.9	13	$F_8^{*13} = 2.5$
	(2.3343)	(-3.0908)	(-1.7257)	(-2.48)	(5.003)			8	$t_8^* = 1.4$
—	0.0840	-0.20118	-1.2179	-0.0800	0.53672	0.70	4.7	13	
	(2.2749)	(-3.0841)	(-1.9039)	(-2.514)	(5.0523)			8	
—	0.12327	-0.25049	-0.728	-0.1092	0.45815	0.63	3.7	13	
	(2.069)	(-2.4721)	(-0.945)	(-2.487)	(3.6725)			8	
—	0.1173	-0.22885	-0.84363	-0.09559	0.42256	0.53	2.8	13	$F_8^{*13} = 2.5$
	(2.0446)	(-2.344)	(-1.1376)	(-2.2606)	(3.5164)			8	$t_8^* = 1.4$
—	0.13067	-0.25709	-1.0414	-0.10782	0.47126	0.53	2.8	13	
	(2.1315)	(-2.465)	(-1.3142)	(-2.3862)	(3.6701)			8	
x	+	-	-	-	+				

Notes:
Regressions 7, 8, 9 drop GDPPC, and 10, 11, 12 drop UNEM.
[a] x means variable excluded.

TEST RESULTS

1981 Table 10.6

Regressions 1, 2, 3 relate all three measures of DOR to all the independent variables in the data set. Parameter estimates are given on the first line in each case, *t* statistics on the second.

Critical values: $t^*_4 = 1.5$ $F^*(17,3) = 5.2$.

Table 10.7 Test results, determinants of policy on FDI, 1985

	C	*DI2*	*POL2*	*GDPPC2*	*UNEM2*	*GOV2*	*PG2*	*EXGDP2*	*IMGDP2*	*TCIR2*	*EPRIT2*	*RD2*
1. ABC	3.0378	0.0209	0.0036	-0.00027	-0.18125	0.03768	0.00407	0.3046	-0.32096	-0.00027	0.0691	-0.4592
	0.246	0.929	0.202	-0.748	-1.218	0.471	0.116	1.60	-1.833	-0.51	0.61	-0.49
2. BC	-3.4404	0.0192	0.00127	-0.00032	-0.1978	0.0334	-0.1286	0.31766	-0.3221	-0.00037	0.0875	-0.088
	-0.315	0.967	0.0807	-0.977	-1.50	0.471	-0.415	1.888	-2.07	-0.788	0.875	-0.106
3. BCD	-4.043	0.0224	-0.00134	-0.00029	-0.234	0.0320	-0.0111	0.334	-0.3419	-0.00027	0.1001	-0.1009
	-0.31818	0.966	-0.0728	-0.756	-1.5303	0.3887	-0.30918	1.7094	-1.889	-0.497	0.860	-0.104
				GDP								
4. ABC	—	—	—	-0.0014	—	—	—	0.095	-0.1417	-0.0004	0.0686	—
				-3.77				1.561	-2.168	-1.772	1.834	
5. BC	—	—	—	-0.0011	—	—	—	0.0891	-0.13261	-0.00036	0.0565	—
				-3.327				1.6048	-2.228	-1.684	1.6598	
6. BCD	—	—	—	-0.00132	—	—	—	0.1158	-0.1656	-0.0004	0.0548	—
				-3.316				1.825	-2.439	-1.643	1.410	
7. ABC	—	—	—	-0.00108	—	—	—	0.1885	-0.216	-0.000412	0.128	—
				-2.594				2.250	-2.640	-1.673	2.914	
8. BC	—	—	—	-0.000904	—	—	—	0.1541	-0.18494	-0.000356	0.098	—
				-2.413				2.0471	-2.504	-1.6106	2.4928	
9. BCD	—	—	—	-0.00104	—	—	—	0.18417	-0.2207	-0.000397	0.0935	—
				-2.4618				2.1492	-2.6267	-1.575	2.206	
Signs for ABC, BC, BCD[a]	x	x	x	-	x	x	x	+	-	-	+	x

Some of the *t* statistics computed from the regression have values less than the required critical value. These were dropped.

Regressions 4, 5, 6 delete C, DI1, PEN.

Critical values: $t^*_7 = 1.4$ $F^*(14,7) = 2.7$.

All computed *t*s are now greater than the critical value, as are the computed *F* statistics. There is now a significant relationship between all three measures of DOR and all remaining proxies. Adjusted R^2 are in the high 70s and low 80s, implying that most of the variation is explained by the regression.

Because of multicollinearity, we reran the regressions, first without GDPPC (regressions 7, 8, 9) and then without UNEM (regressions 10, 11, 12).

Critical values: $t^*_8 = 1.4$ $F^*(13,8) = 2.5$.

PEN	*PROXA*	*PROXB*	*FED*	*PRITOT*	*GINI*	$\bar{R}^2$	*F*	*Degrees of freedom*	*Critical values*
0.1083	-0.00025	-0.079	-1.3936	-0.02814	0.23428	0.02	1.0	17	
1.45	-0.0035	-0.609	-1.144	-0.397	1.324			4	
0.0969	-0.0320	-0.0042	-1.143	0.0025	0.28306	0.05	0.94	17	$F_4^{*17} = 5.8$
1.47	-0.499	-0.036	-1.05	0.040	1.8052			4	$t_4^* = 1.5$
0.11036	-0.0327	-0.0105	-1.3791	-0.00038	0.30506	0.23	0.76	17	
1.44	-0.437	-0.078	-1.097	-0.0052	1.6704			4	
—	—	—	-1.102	—	0.1255	0.64	7.3	6	
			-2.286		6.324			15	
—	—	—	-0.79	—	0.107	0.59	6.1	6	$F_{15}^{*6} = 2.8$
			-1.808		5.933			15	$t_{15}^* = 1.3$
—	—	—	-0.846	—	0.10506	0.54	5.1	6	
			-1.687		5.0923			15	
—	—	-0.0372	—	—	0.170	0.61	6.4	6	
		-1.836			4.349			15	
—	—	-0.0259	—	—	0.13794	0.57	5.5	6	$F_{15}^{*6} = 2.8$
		-1.426			3.9225			15	$t_{15}^* = 1.3$
—	—	-0.0273	—	—	0.137	0.51	4.7	6	
		-1.320			3.431			15	
x	x	-	x	x	+				

Notes:
Regressions 4 to 9 substitute GDP for GDPPC. In 4, 5, 6 FED is included but not PROXB, while the reverse is the case for 7, 8, 9.
[a] x means variable excluded.

All the computed *F* statistics are still significant and, for the most part, the signs on the parameters are both still significant and unchanged from the previous regressions.

In regressions 10, 11, 12 FED gives statistics which are all less than the critical values, meaning that in these regressions FED had no statistically significant impact on DOR.

Based on adjusted R^2, the amount of variation explained, UNEM turns out to be very important in the determination of government policy towards MNEs. Adjusted R^2 falls far more when UNEM is dropped in equations 10, 11 and 12 than when GDPPC is dropped in equations 7, 8 and 9. If one takes into account that they are adjusted for multicollinearity, the best regressions are 7, 8, 9, where the percentage of total variation explained ranges from 70 to 77 per cent. In terms of the signs of the variables, there is no contradictory evidence among the various regressions.

Table 10.8 Test results, determinants of policy on FDI, 1985 on 1981

	C	*DI1*	*POL1*	*GDPPC1*	*UNEM1*	*GOV1*	*PG1*	*EXGDP1*	*IMGDP1*	*TCIR1*	*EPRIT1*	*RD1*
1. ABC	5.3485	-0.01197	-0.06512	0.00039	-0.2308	0.1329	-0.0457	0.80705	-0.73811	0.00156	0.19410	-1.1928
	0.6295	-0.7547	-3.673	2.968	-2.855	2.9178	-0.866	2.953	-2.7902	4.4771	3.0904	-2.707
2. BC	-0.1763	-0.00529	-0.0575	0.000276	-0.2395	0.11827	-0.0517	0.7687	-0.7028	0.01545	0.17351	-0.88002
	-0.0228	-0.3663	-3.566	2.299	-3.257	2.852	-1.076	3.092	-2.919	4.8628	3.0361	-2.195
3. BCD	-2.1868	-0.00669	-0.0628	0.00036	-0.294	0.1203	-0.0632	0.852	-0.775	0.00176	0.1943	-0.9051
	-0.229	-0.375	-3.154	2.45	-3.24	2.35	-1.066	2.77	-2.609	4.499	2.75	-1.82
4. ABC	12.70	—	-0.0627	0.000281	-0.1677	0.1754	—	0.86116	-0.80583	0.001211	0.20305	-1.6972
	2.672		-4.311	2.248	-1.924	4.275		3.8072	-4.055	4.0238	3.4782	-4.68
5. BC	9.2659	—	-0.0532	0.000240	-0.1775	0.14175	—	0.7932	-0.7387	0.001103	0.19235	-1.2589
	1.9009		-3.569	1.8744	-1.985	3.3671		3.4186	-3.623	3.5719	3.2121	-3.3839
6. BCD	9.494	—	-0.0575	0.00031	-0.22085	0.1505	—	0.88544	-0.8237	0.00122	0.21768	-1.378
	1.5976		-3.1654	2.0396	-2.025	2.9334		3.13	-3.314	3.2473	2.9815	-3.0387
7. ABC	11.917	—	-0.0509	—	-0.195	0.169	—	0.698	-0.670	0.0010	0.1353	-1.35
	2.0877		-3.116		-1.879	3.43		2.7060	-2.94	2.907	2.24	-3.417
8. BC	8.595	—	-0.0431	—	-0.201	0.1368	—	0.654	-0.623	0.000925	0.1345	-0.967
	1.563		-2.743		-2.008	2.879		2.630	-2.835	2.783	2.317	-2.53
9. BCD	8.6054	—	-0.0442	—	-0.252	0.144	—	0.70104	-0.6707	0.000986	0.1409	-0.991
	1.2491		-2.242		-2.0096	2.4191		2.2500	-2.4353	2.3686	1.9379	-2.0698
10. ABC	10.268	—	-0.0521	0.000315	—	0.15151	—	0.75548	-0.71793	0.00109	0.19847	-1.5681
	1.966		-3.395	2.232		3.397		3.019	-3.255	3.254	2.984	-3.858
11. BC	6.6921	—	-0.0420	0.00027	—	0.11641	—	0.6813	-0.6456	0.00097	0.1875	-1.122
	1.236		-2.64	1.888		2.519		2.628	-2.825	2.809	2.720	-2.664
12. BCD	6.2928	—	-0.0436	0.00036	—	0.1190	—	0.7463	-0.7080	0.00106	0.2116	-1.208
	0.9473		-2.23	2.0251		2.0989		2.345	-2.524	2.498	2.50	-2.337
Signs of ABC, BC, BCD[a]	x	-	+	-	+	x	+	-	+	+	-	-

1985 Table 10.7

The analysis for 1985 was not nearly as fruitful as that for 1981. Regressions 1, 2 and 3 with all variables gave very poor results. Again we eliminated non-significant variables in various tests. The only set of independent variables to yield satisfactory results were those shown as regressions 4 to 9.

Critical values: $t^{*}_{15} = 1.3$ $F^{*}(6,15) = 2.8$.

Regressions 4 to 9 include GDP instead of GDPPC. The latter, like many other variables, was not significant in the initial runs for 1985. While GDP

PEN	PROXA	PROXB	FED	PRITOT	GINI	$\bar{R}^2$	F	Degrees of freedom	Critical values
0.00476	0.1707	-0.35869	-1.7515	-0.11715	0.5133	0.79	5.7	17	
0.08671	2.0065	-2.1828	-2.2195	-1.824	4.6047			4	
0.010452	0.13171	-0.26326	-1.7390	-0.0890	0.525	0.77	5.0	17	$F_4^{*17} = 3.9$
0.20918	1.7014	-1.76	-2.421	-1.523	5.178			4	$t_4^* = 1.5$
0.00961	0.14125	-0.2803	-2.158	-0.08912	0.6064	0.69	3.8	17	
0.15587	1.477	-1.518	-2.43	-1.23	4.84			4	
—	0.20079	-0.43174	—	-0.1492	0.368	0.72	5.0	13	
	3.8072	-4.216		-4.0343	3.950			8	
—	0.17406	-0.3682	—	-0.11669	0.35416	0.59	3.3	13	$F_8^{*13} = 2.5$
	3.2175	-3.5056		-3.0753	3.7065			8	$t_8^* = 1.4$
—	0.1947	-0.4129	—	-0.12421	0.39915	0.47	2.5	13	
	2.953	-3.224		-2.685	3.426			8	
—	0.1325	-0.3123	—	-0.111	0.268	0.58	3.5	12	
	2.551	-2.961		-2.809	2.72			9	
—	0.11572	-0.2662	—	-0.0845	0.2693	0.47	2.6	12	$F_9^{*12} = 2.4$
	2.312	-2.619		-2.208	2.829			9	$t_9^* = 1.4$
—	0.1173	-0.2775	—	-0.0816	0.2866	0.29	1.7	12	
	1.8717	-2.1801		-1.7009	2.4035			9	
—	0.17889	-0.37301	—	-0.14038	0.30763	0.63	4.0	12	
	3.046	-3.346		-3.3542	3.0762			9	
—	0.15089	-0.30610	—	-0.1073	0.290	0.46	2.5	12	$F_9^{*12} = 2.4$
	2.479	-2.650		-2.4747	2.80010			9	$t_9^* = 1.4$
—	0.1659	-0.335	—	-0.1125	0.31967	0.29	1.7	12	
	2.22	-2.36		-2.11	2.513			9	
x	+	-	x	-	+				

Notes:
Regressions 7, 8, 9 drop GDPPC, and 10, 11, 12 drop UNEM.
[a] x means variable excluded.

was significant in these runs and also in regressions 4 to 9, its sign was negative as against an expected positive sign. There was a tradeoff between FED and PROXB in that inclusion of one of these gave the most significant results. Regressions 4, 5, 6 include FED but not PROXB, while the reverse is the case for 7, 8, 9. The adjusted R^2 was better for regressions 4, 5, 6 than for 7, 8, 9, though not nearly as good as in 1981. Again there was no contradictory evidence about signs in the various sets of regressions.

Comparing 1981 with 1985 we note that there is no contradictory evidence on the signs of the parameter estimates, although as noted many proxies had to be excluded in 1985. The one setback here was the problem regarding GDP and GDPPC for 1985. The relatively poor tests of significance for 1985 may result from the need to use some data from or near 1981 for 1985. PEN for some countries goes as far back as 1975 for both 1981 and 1985, for example. PROXA and PROXB are available for a single year only, 1983. GINI and PRITOT present similar problems. Some of these data problems may be solved with time, but some other variables did not work out well either for 1985.

1985 on 1981 Table 10.8

One experiment was to regress the 1985 dependent variables on the 1981 independent variables. The idea here was that the independent variables would affect policy with a significant lag. Regressions 1, 2, 3 relate DOR from 1985 on all the independent variables from 1981. After eliminating those independent variables not having a significant impact on DOR, (DI1,PG1,PEN,FED)[5] we have regressions 4, 5, 6.

Critical values: $t^*_8 = 1.4$ $F^*(13,8) = 2.5$.

Regressions 4, 5, and 6 have computed t and F statistics that are significant. The signs on the regressors all coincide with the first two sets of regressions shown in Tables 10.6 and 10.7, and GDPPC has the same sign as in the 1981 set of regressions. As before, there is strong evidence in support of the direction of impact that each proxy has on the DOR measures.

One experiment was to run the regressions without GDPPC (7, 8, 9) and without UNEM (10, 11, 12). However, when we drop GDPPC there is only a marginal change in adjusted R^2 relative to when we drop UNEM. In the 1981 experiment, adjusted R^2 was considerably higher when UNEM was included. Considering data for 1981 and 1985 on 1981, it appears that both GDPPC and UNEM have a significant effect through time, but the impact of UNEM may be more important at a particular point of time.

Summary on Signs (Table 10.9)

It was noted above that the signs of the variables remain very largely the same across years and in the different equations. Table 10.9 summarizes this information for the three preceding tables: except for the problems already noted for GDP and GDPPC, only TCIR has a change in sign in the various tests. Table 10.9 also compares the signs from the regressions with those expected from our earlier analysis. The actual signs differ from the expected in the case of EXGDP, PG, PRITOT, PROXB and POL. Our reasoning for the expected signs is shown in Tables 10.4 and 10.5 and discussed more fully in various sections of Parts I and II. We must leave it to the reader to judge how far the theoretical and historical arguments contained therein override the statistical evidence presented here. As noted in discussing Table 10.4 and 10.5, what is at issue in part is whether the expected signs correctly interpret the general case, rather than any exceptions, and also some problems in interpreting the available proxies. It would have been of more concern if PROXA's actual and expected signs had differed, for example. POL, moreover, is a weak proxy since it takes account of official coalitions only, while, as we saw for Canada and some other countries, unofficial support of minority governments by parties of the left or right can significantly affect policy in this area. It is more difficult to know what to make of the differences of actual and expected signs for both PRITOT and PROXB. Along with EPRITOT, these were expected to have positive signs in the regressions, reflecting the reasons noted in Chapter 6 and Table 10.5 for

Table 10.9 Expected and actual signs, test results for determinants of policy on FDI

	Expected[a]	*1981*	*1985*	*1985 on 1981*
		Actual Signs		
GDP	+	N/A	–	N/A
GDPPC	+	+	–	+
UNEM	–	–	x	–
EXGDP	–	+	+	+
IMGDP	–	–	–	–
DI	–	x	x	x
PG	+	–	x	x
PRITOT	+	–	x	–
EPRITOT	+	+	+	+
TCIR	–	+	–	+
RD	–	–	x	–
GINI	+	+	+	+
FED	–	–	x	x
PEN	+	x	x	x
PROXA	+	+	x	+
PROXB	+	–	–	–
POL	+	–	x	–
GOV	+	+	x	+

Notes:
[a] From Table 10.4.
x means excluded as not significant.
N/A means not included in regressions. See text under *Test results*.

believing natural resource host countries would be relatively restrictive towards inward FDI.

We are not yet in a position to draw together the conclusions on policy beyond noting that the country studies and the statistical tests yield some support for the view that all four determinants of policy, and some of the sub-categories, have played significant roles. More light is thrown on the origins by an examination of the effectiveness of the actual policies used, and the fact that other policies which sometimes look superior were avoided. Effectiveness of policy is considered on a cross-country basis in the next chapter.

NOTES

1. Such group income distribution effects due to FDI could be placed in the third category of policy determinants, along with regional effects.
2. Combining exchange control with both review and incentives did not work well in some earlier statistical tests, perhaps because of aggregation of quite different policies. Exchange control does complement review, however, and incentives often go with review, as noted in Part II and Chapter 11. Hence the measures for DOR in Table 10.3 which were used in the regressions were ABC, BC, and BCD.
3. There are statistical problems when similar variables are used, problems whose treatment is described below.
4. It is not necessary explicitly to create confidence intervals using these parameter estimates in order to determine whether the sign is indeed positive or negative for any given parameter. If a t statistic is significant, this implies that zero would not enter into the confidence interval.
5. FED was significant, but its elimination improved the significance of other variables.

11. Effectiveness of Policies

It has been argued in Part II that what the countries in this study will generally attempt is to increase their wealth and power while preserving or enhancing capital inflow. The policies adopted for these ends should reflect both the opportunities and the constraints in their country situations and the types of MNEs they face. In this chapter the nature and effectiveness of policies intended to affect performance of firms and those directed to ownership are considered at some length, with occasional reference to some related policies. As with the country studies, we neglect framework policies directed at all firms, and bilateral or multilateral policies directed particularly at MNEs. These latter two sets of policies are not unimportant in terms of their actual or probable investment effects.

In the 1980s many industrial countries made significant changes in the tax treatment of corporation income. While these changes generally applied to all firms, part of the reasoning behind them was to create a more attractive investment climate. Multilateral investment can also be significantly affected by treaties increasing the size of market and easing restrictions on investment, such as the Canada–United States Free Trade Area. While in the next chapter we will comment more fully on the reasons for and effects of the apparent easing of restrictions on FDI in the late 1980s, this chapter concentrates on the regimes in effect up to about the mid-1980s.

POLICIES ON PERFORMANCE

One of the more important policies designed to influence the behaviour of foreign-owned firms is review on establishment and subsequent merger or acquisition. In Table 11.1 some characteristics of the review mechanisms covered in this study are noted as of the early 1980s. Some of these agencies were undergoing, or about to undergo, a significant liberalization of their policies. The United Kingdom does not fit well with the others. It abandoned exchange control and general review in 1979, and its system of general review always had more to do with exchange control and sectoral policies than was the case for the other systems. The table is not designed to cover exchange control or restricted sector policies, including the separate evalua-

Table 11.1 Characteristics of general review systems for inward FDI, early 1980s

	Australia	*Canada*	*NZ*	*Norway*	*Sweden*	*France*	*Japan*	*UK*
Year Established	1975 (1972)	1974-75	1973 (1964)	1906–17 1961-63	1916 (1983 general)	1966	1949–50 (1980)	(to 1979)
EXPLICITNESS								
significant legal definition[1]	yes for takeovers	yes	yes	some (resources)	yes	no	yes (1980)	no
defined agency	yes	yes	yes	no	no	no	no	no
explicit criteria for assessment	yes	yes	yes	yes (1963)	no (informal & broad)	no (informal & broad)	no (formal & broad)	no
major decision criteria clear	yes	no	yes (resources)	no	no	yes (varies re plan)	no	no (beyond sectoral)
standardized and known procedures	yes	yes	yes	some	some	some	some	some
data publication significant	yes	yes	yes	no	no	no	some	no
MAJOR OBJECTIVES								
performance	no	yes	no	no except petrol	no except structural	yes	yes	sectoral
ownership:								
resources	yes	yes (energy)	yes	yes	yes	yes (energy)	yes	yes (energy)
other	yes	yes	no	no	some	yes	sectors	sectors
COVERAGE[2]								
new	yes	yes	yes	yes	no	yes	yes	yes
takeover	yes	yes	yes	yes	yes	yes	yes	yes
indirect	yes	yes	yes (pro forma)	yes (pro forma)	?	yes	no	?
expansion new lines	yes	yes	yes	yes	?	yes	yes	no
expansion old lines	no	no	no	yes (pro forma)	no	yes (finance)	no	no

MAJOR CHANGES in system, 1960–early 1980s (exclude resources)	yes	yes	some	some	yes	yes	yes	some
PERCENTAGE foreign ownership which triggers review	15 (40 if 2+ associates)	5 (25 or 40 if 2+ associates)	25	10	10 (20, 40, 50)	20 exEC	10 (exceptions)	N/A
BARGAINING PROCESS for increased benefits[3]	no	yes	no	no	no	some sectors	pre-1980	some sectors
frequent search for domestic alternative[4]	no (some)	no	no	no (some)	no (some)	yes	no (takeovers difficult)	no (some)
sectoral distinctions:								
natural resource	yes	yes	yes	yes	yes	yes	yes	yes
high technology	yes	yes	yes	some	some	yes	yes	yes
maximum time to process (days)	30+100	60 or up	42	90 or up	?	60 or up	30+120	N/A
regular monitoring[5] of commitments	no	yes	no	short term	no	short term	not clear	no
REJECTION RATE (FORMAL)[6]								
new firms	2.7[7]	7.1	5.4 (70–85)	rare	rare	rare	rare	rare
acquisitions	(76–84)	6.9 (75–84)	7.1 (65–85)					

Notes:
Derived from Part II. The table refers to establishment and merger or acquisition review rather than policy more generally, such as that on restricted sectors or exchange controls. In interpreting the necessarily brief summary given here, the reader should consult Part II for fuller details and qualifications. Years in parentheses indicate important precedents for general review systems (Australia and New Zealand), major clarification of review (Norway and Sweden), and ending of formal review (Japan and UK).

1. Apart from exchange control, which existed in all countries except Canada.
2. France and Japan also approved licenses and similar property rights, although in the former case this did not involve a general review.
3. All review systems ensure net benefits or the national interest. Those specified attempted to increase net benefits.
4. Excludes restricted sectors, including natural resources, where such a search is sometimes implied.
5. Apart from major resource projects and those related to fiscal incentives.
6. OECD (1979, Part III) gives data on number of rejections for three years in the late 1970s for the countries shown here as rarely rejecting formal applications. The totals for three years ranged from none for the UK to four for Norway.
7. Includes acquisitions.

tion often given to major projects wherever they are owned. A case could be made for including the United States by the late 1980s. More generally any such summary table of a complex set of institutions is likely to be over-simplified, if not misleading, in some respects. The country studies should be consulted for fuller details.

The discussion of review systems will be organized around four issues: (a) the organization and policy stance of the systems; (b) other aspects of the bargaining process; (c) some of the economic effects; and (d) some related policy issues.

Organization and Procedures

Review systems can be classified in a variety of ways. That which is emphasized here is the explicitness or transparency of the systems, on the one hand, and the way in which the procedures (especially the bargaining process) were carried out, on the other.

The Australian, Canadian and New Zealand systems were clearly more explicit than the rest. This is partly because they were more fully defined in law to begin with and involved a defined agency rather than an interdepartmental committee or an even less formal organization. These three agencies were established (in New Zealand's case, redefined) in the early 1970s, while the other systems had earlier origins.[1] The three also had more explicit criteria for assessment, and more standardized and known procedures. They also published far more information on their decisions than any of the others. Australia and New Zealand also had indicated their major decision criteria, particularly the tradeoff between ownership and performance in favour of the former, as noted more fully in Chapter 6. Japan changed to a more defined structure in the early 1980s but it still remained less explicit than those involved in these three countries.

Indeed, in terms of major objectives, only Canada, France and Japan before 1980 appeared to place major emphasis on performance in the general review process. If one goes beyond the review process, of course, performance objectives loom much larger – for example, in major projects and in petroleum, or where discretionary incentives were important. All countries pursued ownership objectives where resources (in some cases, only energy) were involved. In other sectors the pursuit of ownership objectives through the general review process was mixed.

The policy position on control of the firms, as distinct from ownership, is not easily summarized so far as the review process is concerned. All of the systems tended to operate broadly on the principle that, if foreign ownership was already high in a sector, further foreign acquisitions might be blocked or, if allowed, more gains would be expected in terms of performance. But this is still an approach which is based on ownership. Canada, France and Japan before 1980 put the more consistent emphasis on the broader issues involved in effective control, as distinct from ownership of voting stock. Thus the Canadian legislation involved a much lower trigger point for review than did the others, while the French and Japanese authorities registered licences and the latter reviewed them. These three countries also tended to look at control concepts across all sectors, while in some of the others these received particular attention in particular sectors such as resources. The three countries also put more emphasis on reviewing purchasing and marketing ties with parents, a potential source of control of the subsidiary. Nevertheless one is struck by the fact that, pre-1980s Japan apart, so little attention was given to the many ways in which control can be exercised apart from ownership.

It is worth noting that the systems which offered more clarity of policies did not necessarily offer more continuity. The country studies clearly point to major changes in both the more explicit and the more discretionary systems. Neither type of system requires legislation in order to change significantly. In Canada, for example, the formal rejection rate rose rapidly in the late 1970s, then fell to zero for part of the early 1980s with no change in law, much as happened in a more dramatic way in France in the 1960s. Our reading of the evidence suggests that none of the systems were stable in the two decades before the early 1980s, even if one excludes natural resource policy. Those of New Zealand, Norway and the United Kingdom probably underwent less change than the others. As noted in the next chapter, several of the systems also underwent major changes in the 1980s.

The coverage of the review systems was very similar. All eight countries, except for Sweden, reviewed entry through new investments up to the early 1980s. All of the countries reviewed direct takeovers from abroad as well as subsequent acquisitions, while some also reviewed indirect takeovers where the ownership of the subsidiary changed because ownership of the foreign parent changed. Most reviewed expansion into new lines of business. Only France has been listed as reviewing expansion in old lines, but only because of the financial approval involved in expansion of investment at that time. In the late 1970s Canada seriously considered monitoring the performance of the larger established foreign-owned firms, but did not do so in the wake of the controversy over the National Energy Program and the recession of the early 1980s.

Performance Requirements and Other Aspects of the Bargaining Process

If one turns to other issues that influence the bargaining process, at first glance the Canadian agency stands out in Table 11.1. It bargained fairly generally for increased benefits, rather than simply reviewing applications with some norm in mind; it was involved in far more systematic monitoring of undertakings given by firms; and its rejection rate for formal applications was both published and higher than those of the others. We argued in the country studies, however, that both France and Japan achieved similar objectives with their more discretionary systems of review, for example by deferring decisions rather than formally rejecting an application. They also went much further in controlling FDI in some industrial sectors, given their greater capacities to influence business decisions.

These three countries and the others in this study would need to take account of regional income differences when making decisions on FDI, but federal states such as Canada faced further regional pressures. Provincial and state governments have constitutional powers in their own right and often pursue distinctive industrial policies, including those on FDI. The problems Canada had in implementing energy policies are a case in point. All cases before its review agency must be referred to the relevant province for an opinion. Australia faced similar issues in the natural resource field. The Australian federal government had considerable influence on natural resource projects through its power to approve export prices, to supply federal funding and control external state borrowing, as well as to require Australian participation in ownership. Nevertheless it was the state governments which negotiated the deals, including infrastructure cost sharing, royalties and other matters, and it was often difficult for the federal government to attempt to change significant subsidy and other elements of the package. The one unitary state with a review agency which faced constraints similar to those on federal states was France. As a member of the EC, France was subject to its policies on the freedom of capital in the EC, overall control on subsidies and other matters. It was noted that, up to the early 1980s, France was able to find ways to exert some policy independence with regard to establishment of FDI even from countries in the EC.

One significant difference in the bargaining process relative to Canada's was that in France a search could be made for a domestic alternative to a foreign acquisition, while such acquisitions were subject to both private and public restrictions in Japan. Australia also occasionally instituted such a search. The Canadian government's plans to search for and subsidize such alternatives were set aside around 1980.

An important aspect of the review process was the 'performance requirements' which firms undertook to meet as a condition of entry and merger, or of receiving fiscal and other incentives where these were involved. Governments often prefer terms such as 'voluntary undertakings'. They argue that these are not required as a condition of entry or merger, particularly in any bargaining sense. There is something to be said for such a view, given the lax enforcement of these undertakings as noted below. Even the undertakings given as fiscal incentives are often difficult to monitor and enforce, although the financial accountability required by law imposes some constraints in these cases. In any event, the firms involved understood quite clearly that approval of the investment or of the incentives could be denied if the undertakings did not satisfy the authorities. Such performance requirements go well beyond the review process to encompass defence contracting and the fuller assessment often given to major projects; in such cases governments are often more likely to attempt to extract and monitor performance requirements in some quantitative way, if only because of the substantial fiscal costs and developmental effects.

Satisfactory measures of the overall incidence of such performance requirements do not exist. In part this is because such a wide range of regulatory devices is involved, reflecting administrative processes with varying degrees of explicitness all the way to quite informal understandings. As was noted in the country studies, some governments are inclined to underreport such measures to international organizations while others put the least restrictive interpretations on them – they may, after all, be involved in negotiating these with firms or even other governments. The firms, in turn, are sometimes reluctant to report on them fully, partly so as not to appear critical of those who wield fiscal and regulatory power. What are often opaque measures at best are also opaquely reported at most.

Quite another problem is that some of the most comprehensive sources of data are not suited to issues relevant here; that is, how prominently the various performance requirements have figured in entry or acquisition cases by country. The most comprehensive sources are the benchmark surveys of US direct investment abroad. That for 1977 showed that 14 per cent of the entire population of 23 641 US non-bank affiliates abroad were subject to one or more performance requirements. Only 1.5 per cent of the firms reported a minimum export requirement, 2.5 per cent a maximum import limit, 2.5 per cent a minimum local content requirement, 8 per cent a local labour requirement and 5.7 per cent had to limit the parent's equity in the affiliate. The survey for 1982 reported on a population of 17 213 firms. The percentages for various performance requirements, in the same order, were 1.6, 1.5, 1.1, 7.6 and 4.3 per cent. The 1982 survey also reported that 3.6 per cent of the firms were required to transfer technology to the host country and 1.4 per cent to maintain a specified ratio of exports to imports or of foreign exchange receipts to payments. It may be noted that, excluding the requirement on parent's equity, 27 per cent of the requirements in 1977 and 15 per cent in 1982 were reported to be for foreign-owned firms only. In both years the ratios for performance requirements were much higher for less developed countries than for more developed. The incidence of requirements was particularly heavy in industries where foreign-owned firms are heavily represented, such as electrical, transportation equipment, chemicals, non-electrical machinery and primary industries such as mining and petroleum. The automobile industry is particularly liable to attract such measures, both in terms of local content and export regulations as well as related incentives.

While of interest for some purposes, these studies clearly differ sharply from the data on the incidence of review requirements as noted in the country studies. The reasons are straightforward. A census of the entire stock of companies which have gone abroad over many decades will diminish the incidence of requirements largely imposed in the 1960s or 1970s. Also requirements are typically imposed when a firm enters the country or expands by merger. If it expands in its traditional lines and avoids mergers or acquisitions it will escape review systems. Firms are more likely to encounter various incentives, even long after establishment: as we will see, the incidence of incentives was far larger in the 1977 and 1982 surveys.[2]

While some of the country studies document more fully on a current basis the types of undertakings given by firms (see Table 6.7 on Australia) they do not take us very far in assessing the extent to which the performance of the firms was actually changed to conform to the preferences of the authorities. The reasons are evident if one refers to Canada's Foreign Investment Review Agency, which was more fully defined than any of the others, with the possible exception of Australia. Each year it published, for individual proposals which were approved, a list of expected benefits as indicated by the firms and assessed by the agency. In addition in many cases the detail of the actual undertakings given is available in letters sent to the firms by the Minister (see Appendix III for some of the more detailed examples). Many of these expected benefits are related to foreign trade; about one-third showed 'additional exports' and close to two-thirds indicated expected benefits by way of 'increased resource processing or use of Canadian parts and services'.

A reading of the available cases suggests that many of the undertakings made by the firms to support their proposals were very general statements of intentions to which they could be held with difficulty, if at all. Other more specific undertakings are so hedged by standard conditions, such as purchases from Canadian manufacturers 'subject to availability, competitive prices, quality and suitability' that they suggest a best-efforts approach, at most. It is also not difficult to find unqualified and specific undertakings, both in the more important cases where details are public and from interviews and other sources. The conditions involved in the Australian review process applied to only one-third of the approved applications and did not refer in the main to economic performance. They covered such matters as tax issues where restructuring or financing were involved, local equity participation and related reporting or follow-through. In most of the other review systems such undertakings were not well reported, but our interviews suggested that they were pursued in a less systematic and more flexible manner. Some of the European countries, for example, concentrated on relatively few requirements and measurable shorter-term effects, such as those on investment or employment.

The effectiveness of the performance requirements depends in good part on the extent to which the undertakings given by firms are enforced. Some are relatively easy to monitor and can be fairly strictly enforced: nationality of the officers and, less certainly, ownership of the firm are cases in point. Others are not easily enforced. Undertakings given by firms are often no more than general statements of what they hope to achieve if conditions warrant. An intention to export is a conditional statement which any number of unforeseen (and arguable) developments can change. FIRA monitored commitments more thoroughly than other review systems, including measurable items such as company accounts, investments and employment as well as seeking explanations where other commitments were not met. That is a long way from saying that the detailed list of undertakings was met or enforced. Very few cases went to court, or required reordering and stricter adherence to commitments, from the thousands of legally binding undertakings involved. None of the other agencies appear to have had as systematic a monitoring process as FIRA. Indeed most had no such formal process, relying on subsequent contacts the firms had with government authorities to act as a form of monitoring.

Still another problem in assessing the impact of the review systems is that it is the *increase* in firm activity which is relevant, not what the firm would have done in any case. Review systems attempted to measure the former in the bargaining process – that is, to secure increases in exports or employment or productivity – but it is not clear whether and how far that was achieved. The firms would hardly overshoot in their proposals, for they would then run the risk of having the agency ask for more or being unable to meet undertakings. If anything, the bargaining process would suggest that they submit minimum feasible proposals.[3] Governments, in turn, have various devices to check such gamesmanship, such as looking at data on average industrial performance. However it is hard to believe in the general case that governments would be better informed than firms on such matters within the usual time and resource constraints.

Thus, while it is correct in principle to argue that performance requirements tend to raise net costs to firms or increase uncertainty, it is not at all clear how far these happened in practice. As noted in the section on Canada, no really satisfactory empirical test exists of the effects of an instrument such as FIRA, much less the other, less transparent systems. Some theoretical work on performance requirements will be referred to in the last section of this chapter.

Investment Incentives

It would be a mistake to suggest that policy on international direct investment focuses simply on restricting entry or expansion by MNEs. Where review mechanisms exist, the object, except for certain sectors, is generally not to keep out direct investment but to ensure or increase the net industrial benefit from a national viewpoint. In addition, however, there is a wide range of incentives to attract such investment or to keep it by increasing the profit or reducing the risk associated with the investment. In principle these incentives are available to all firms, regardless of ownership. In practice some governments have gone to great lengths to make them attractive to MNEs. These incentives are heavily concentrated at the level of national governments in most countries, but in some countries such as Canada and West Germany the regional governments also play an important role and in the United States they play the major role (OECD, 1989b, 18–21).

The US Department of Commerce benchmark study for 1977 published in 1981 showed 26 per cent of the entire population of 23 641 US non-bank affiliates abroad received one or more such incentives, with little variation between developed and developing countries but a good deal by industry and country. Twenty per cent received tax concessions, 8 per cent tariff concessions, 9 per cent subsidies and 5 per cent other incentives. About one-fifth of those receiving these four types of concessions in each case believed the incentives were available to foreign-owned firms only. The US Department of Commerce benchmark study for 1982 published in 1985 reported on a population of 17 213 firms. The percentages receiving various types of incentives, in the same order as above, had risen to 24, 10, 14 and 7 per cent. Closer to 10 per cent now believed the incentives received were available to foreign-owned firms only. The size of these incentives in relation to investment costs was frequently substantial: in regional aid programmes, for example, the maxima tended to be about 25 per cent of investment costs in OECD member countries, rising to 60 per cent or more for some countries. Foreign-owned firms received substantial portions of the investment incentives: for example, 20 per cent and 16 per cent respectively of all investment assisted under sections 7 and 8 of the UK Industry Act in 1978–9, two-thirds of Export Sales Relief capital grant programme awards in Ireland in 1977, and 53 per cent of investment incentives in Belgium in 1977 (OECD, 1983, 23–4).

For present purposes three questions need to be asked: why such incentives and performance requirements exist at the same time and often for the same investment; whether they were directed in some cases to FDI only; and to what extent MNE decisions on location could be influenced by them. On the first point, it might seem odd to be applying at the same time disincentives to investment through the review process and various types of incentives. This can be understood in part as the result of incentives granted automatically to all firms which met certain requirements, wherever owned: some tax and tariff incentives would meet these criteria. Many incentives are given on a discretionary basis, however. It should be recalled that most of the countries in the period covered were not interested in keeping FDI out, except for certain sectors, but in attracting it and influencing its decisions. Thus a combination of a performance requirement on (say) research or exports plus a directed incentive would both indicate the objective desired and offset any net cost the firm might meet from the former.

One might well ask, in that case, why the government should not cancel out both the possible disincentive to the firm (the performance requirement) and the actual incentive which is likely to involve a cost to government. The answer could lie in many directions, beginning with reservations about other ways to obtain the desired influence on firm policies such as by general tax or expenditure policy. It might also be difficult to cancel the disincentive, in effect to cease the review process, because it is serving other objectives than improving the performance of FDI. These other objectives could include, among other reasons, giving an advantage to domestically owned firms in the market for mergers, giving government officials a lever in dealing with MNEs on a range of policies, meeting the demands of some sectors of the population for strong policies on MNEs, and so on.[4] In the models of competition for FDI developed by Guisinger *et al.* (1985), moreover, incentives offer particular advantages in dealing with MNEs which differ in their market orientation and in other respects. For example, if the country is attempting to secure import-substituting investment by tariffs and is not prepared to use quotas for treaty or other reasons, a performance requirement on local content helps to ensure that any resulting FDI will act in an import-substituting way. Finally some type of grants can be made in ways which are more assured of securing the desired performance than a performance requirement as such – where the grant is paid in instalments, for example, which are closely related to performance, or focused on a very limited objective. There are problems in enforcing performance requirements linked to financial incentives, but governments may be more inclined to enforce some of these than those involved in review mechanisms, given Treasury and legislative controls on the former. There are clearly opportunities to use a combination of performance requirements and various types of incentives to attempt to ensure multiple policy objectives and to fine-tune the resulting net effects on firm decisions. All of this assumes, of course, that better ways to achieve the objectives are not feasible and that the information and other problems of such an approach can be overcome.

It is not clear whether incentives are, in general, sufficient to offset disincentives in terms of their impact on investment decisions. The estimates of degree of restrictiveness given in Table 10.3 imply that the disincentives were more important except for a few countries, but this is partly a reflection of the weighting used in constructing the measures. One would expect that the existence of a screening process would normally have a broader effect, given the potential impact on a range of strategic issues such as the ease of subsequent mergers and acquisitions (OECD, 1989b, 60–62).

The second question noted above is how far incentives are directed to international investment as such. In a detailed study by the OECD (1983), all of the governments covered in the present study reported that they did not distinguish between foreign-owned and domestically owned firms either in the award of investment incentives or in the preconditions and performance requirements which accompany such awards. A subsequent study by the OECD (1989b, 26) takes the same position, with very few exceptions. It also argues that OECD countries do not generally have incentive programmes geared to attract FDI, although noting that in some countries such as Ireland the incentive schemes were partly designed with FDI in mind. In our view governments are far more discriminating in this respect than such studies suggest. In every country in this study some of those who influence government policy are prepared to discriminate in favour of domestically owned firms because they believe the outcomes are more favourable in terms of the creation or distribution of wealth and power. Sometimes the only applicants are foreign-owned MNEs, and officials may find that what they bring to a project by way of skills and in other respects differs a good deal.

The evidence on this is not as firm as one would like but it suggests at least some caution in accepting the view that governments do not discriminate significantly on the incentives side. The evidence in Guisinger *et al.* (1985) suggests that governments tailor their overall strategies even by types of MNEs, especially market orientation, and that some of the methods used are clearly directed to MNE strategies. US Commerce (1981) shows that one-fifth of those receiving incentives abroad in 1977 believed that they were available only to foreign-owned firms. In the similar study for 1982 the figure was one-tenth. Such studies are subjective, of course, since they do not test whether 'identical' domestically owned firms would be denied the incentive. In the country studies we concluded that some countries such as Ireland and Belgium in certain periods geared their entire programmes to attracting FDI, to the point where they evoked considerable criticism within the EC and from those noting the inadequacy of the programmes for domestic industry. More convincing still were the examples given of incentives provided to particular domestically owned firms in order to preserve or develop a domestic presence in that sector. The loans and government purchasing preferences extended to computer firms in France, the UK and Japan, for example, were certainly not extended to all foreign-owned firms, even those located in such countries. The very concept of exceptions to national treatment, whether allowable under various instruments or not, refers to discrimination by nationality of ownership among established firms. In Chapter 12 we will note that such discriminatory support has become more common as countries attempt to develop nationally owned firms in new or growing sectors.

The third question is how far such incentives have actually affected investment location. A considerable number of empirical studies suggest that investment incentives are far less important as determinants of FDI location than are the attractions of the particular market, various cost and supply factors, and the investment climate more broadly (such as regulations directed to, and government attitudes regarding, MNEs). One can cite, for example, a study by Reuber *et al.* (1973) for developing countries which found that firms were unwilling to undertake investments which were heavily dependent on incentives for acceptable rates of return. Root and Ahmed (1978), in a study of developing countries, found the corporate tax rate affected investment flows but not tax incentives as such. A survey of the literature on investment determinants, based in part on a review of more empirical studies in the 1960s and 1970s, concluded that incentives had a limited effect on the decision to undertake foreign investment, although two of the studies suggested that financial incentives could be significant determinants in Scotland and Ireland (OECD, 1983, especially 41).

The reasons for the doubts expressed in these earlier studies are straightforward. A short-term incentive in itself (apart from other determinants of investment) is unlikely to attract a long-term investment, unless it is large enough to make a significant continuing difference to the rate of return. Unless the incentive is concentrated in a large early payment, there is often no guarantee it will continue. Competition between governments can cancel out the effects on investment for any one country, or on the overall flow of investment. One could go on to list other reservations, many of which are familiar from literature questioning the effects of regional development incentives within a country.

Along with this overall conclusion, the studies suggest some significant qualification or supplementary points. Incentives can have an effect between countries or regions of countries which are geographically close and have other similarities – between Canada and the United States, for example, or within the EC. The studies referred to above were largely written before the 1980s. In periods of increased unemployment and increased uncertainty the incentives could play a larger role, partly because governments will use them more often but also because firms become more conscious of cost considerations. Also incentives can be more important in certain types of industry situations, such as those where low transport costs and other factors make it possible to locate plants in one country to serve much of the world market. In industries such as electronics and motor cars evidence of organization on that scale became increasingly evident in the 1970s, as did the practice of 'subsidy shopping' by firms. Many more sectors exhibited such tendencies in the 1980s, as will be evident below.

In addition it should be emphasized that investment incentives go together with the various policies towards MNEs noted earlier. It is one thing to talk of performance requirements related directly to the investment incentives, quite another to take into account also that there is scope for discretionary treatment in authorization or review procedures, in national treatment, and even in the designation of restricted sectors. One study which has taken an integrated approach is that by Guisinger *et al.* (1985). It concentrated on four industries (motor cars, computers, food products and petrochemicals) in ten countries, including seven developing countries. The approach taken is to define three separate 'markets' for FDI: the first where it is oriented to the domestic market of one country; the second where it serves a common market; and the third where it produces for a worldwide export market. The existence and direction of various incentives and disincentives are noted in some detail, but it proved impossible to measure average net incentives by country. The authors argue that countries compete for FDI in each of the three 'markets' with varying intensity – most severely in the second and least in the first. Competitive strategies of countries are examined in the context of Porter's model of firm strategies, with the behaviour of other countries as the most important factor.

Guisinger *et al.* concluded that net incentives do affect the supply of FDI, at least for the industries and countries examined, and that countries compete for FDI in differentiated markets. The effect of incentives is uneven and can be overwhelmed by other factors. Nevertheless, in two-thirds of the 74 specific projects they examined, policies in host countries influenced the location decision of MNEs. This figure is much higher than those for earlier studies. Wells (1986) has suggested that the differing results can be explained by the inclusion of both commodity incentives and factor incentives in Guisinger *et al.*, whereas the earlier studies referred largely to the latter. In the case of FDI directed to supplying a local market, commodity incentives such as tariffs and other forms of import protection are likely to have some effect on the decision to locate there rather than to export to that market. However both the Guisinger study and earlier ones found that *factor* incentives had little impact on such investment decisions. Where a large part of the production is destined for export, or is in a common market setting, such factor incentives are much more likely to have an influence on the choice of location.

Finally it will be recalled that Ireland and Belgium developed major incentive programmes geared in large part to MNEs, which responded significantly to such incentives in the EC context. Apart from some questions of policy design – such broad incentives are expensive and some were geared too heavily to capital-intensive firms – two problems stand out. Linkages to domestic industry were slow to develop and the incentive programmes were not well suited to older indigenous industry. The programmes were significantly changed from the late 1970s on, for example, so as to aim at particular sectors and to secure more linkage effects.

POLICIES ON OWNERSHIP

Policies on performance overlap with those on ownership in many ways. The review systems have to trade off ownership and performance in several respects, as when a firm offers to export if it is allowed full ownership of a subsidiary or when a government presses for such an outcome.

In addition review systems usually also monitor the sectoral restrictions on foreign ownership. These can be grouped in four categories. The first is discrimination against a foreign-owned firm after it is established in a country. The second is the attempt to introduce ownership and performance policies with respect to natural resources, on the one hand, and high-technology sectors, on the other, particularly in the 1960s and later. The third is the set of sectoral restrictions, largely in services and defence, usually dating back even earlier and emphasizing ownership objectives. Finally certain firms are considered so important that governments will intervene to prevent or limit foreign ownership in them.

National Treatment

At various points throughout the country studies it was noted that, even after establishment or subsequent merger, the foreign-owned firm encounters something less than national treatment. This phrase refers to 'treatment under their laws, regulations and administrative practices, consistent with international law and no less favourable than that accorded in like situations to domestic enterprises' (OECD, 1976, 8). The OECD agreements allow a variety of exceptions to national treatment, apart from those involved in establishment review and subsequent merger. These exceptions include measures needed to maintain public order, to protect essential security interests and to fulfil commitments relating to international peace and security.

Table 11.2 lists the types of measures and the OECD countries involved as reported in an OECD study covering the year 1983. It is not possible to make comparisons with an earlier study (OECD, 1978) since the later study reflected much larger coverage and greater clarity on the meaning of the various exceptions to national treatment. In the interest of transparency, the study for 1983 included the three types of allowable exceptions to national treatment, along with some other measures favouring domestically owned

Table 11.2 National treatment in selected OECD countries, 1983

	Official aids and subsidies		*Access to financing*		*Tax obligations*		*Government purchasing*	
	E	*T*	*E*	*T*	*E*	*T*	*E*	*T*
Australia	yes	yes	no	—	no	yes	yes	—
Belgium	no	—	no	—	no	yes	no	—
Canada	yes	yes	—	—	yes	—	yes	—
France	no	—	no	—	no	—	yes	yes
FRG	no	yes	no	—	no	—	yes	—
Ireland	no	—	yes	—	no	—	no	—
Italy	yes	—	yes	—	no	—	yes	—
Japan	no	—	no	—	no	—	no	—
Netherlands	no	—	no	—	no	—	yes	—
New Zealand	yes	—	yes	—	yes	—	yes	—
Norway	no	yes	no	—	no	—	no	—
Sweden	no	—	yes	—	no	yes	no	—
Switzerland	yes	—	no	—	no	—	yes	—
UK	no	yes	no	—	no	—	yes	—
USA	yes	yes	no	—	no	—	yes	yes

Notes:
Yes: one or more listed.
No: reply was none.
—: nothing was shown in this category.
E: an exception to national treatment is involved.
T: an allowable exception and some other measures favouring locally owned firms, reported for reasons of transparency.
The data reported here may not agree with those in the country studies for Part II, which should be consulted for further details.

Source: OECD (1985a) as reported by member governments. See publication for details on sub-categories not shown here.

firms which governments might not consider to be exceptions to national treatment.

The great variety of these measures can be indicated briefly.[5] The first column of the table, official aids and subsidies, covers such items as preferential grants to domestically owned firms for oil exploration or production in Canada, financial assistance for tourism by locally owned firms in New Zealand, and subsidies for film production in various countries. It is difficult to specify some of these aids. Limitations on access to local financing are often associated with exchange control requirements regarding, for example, the import of capital for new investment or mergers. One can argue that these are based on residency rather than nationality and hence not an exception to national treatment. They may have more impact on MNEs, whether controlled at home or abroad. Tax obligations can encompass such matters as higher taxes on the transfer of real estate to non-residents or foreigners, as levied by two Canadian provinces, and the less favourable tax treatment of unincorporated branches of foreign firms in several countries. Bilateral treaties tend to limit the differences in tax treatment accorded to foreign-owned firms. The most important of the four categories listed in Table 11.2 is likely to be government purchasing and public contracts, covering such matters as preferential treatment for locally owned firms in the defence sector and requirements that government employees use national airlines (OECD, 1985a, 48–53).

While the study published in 1985 and discussions in the GATT on similar issues have clarified the concept of national treatment, much remains to be done in defining their scope and importance. For example, for reasons of definition and in other respects, the data reported by governments as noted in Table 11.2 remain incomplete. To take just one example, the data in Table 11.2 on Japan are not consistent with the discussion of national treatment in Chapter 7, which is based on interviews and other sources as well as OECD material. In the late 1980s the OECD proceeded not only to clarify and extend its reporting system for such measures, but also, subject to some qualifications, to introduce a standstill provision with regard to them and also an undertaking to begin to roll them back.

Non-national treatment might seem inconsistent with the desire to attract foreign-owned firms for possible economic gains, but the apparent conflict is readily explained. Many of the exceptions to national treatment are sector-specific and are intended to meet particular concerns such as maintenance of a domestically owned defence sector or certain cultural activities. More generally, once a country has decided, for whatever reasons, to preserve domestically owned firms in a given sector it may have to resort to discrimination against the foreign-owned firms which are already in that sector. In the following sections the policy of sectoral restrictions is considered more directly.

Natural Resources and High-Technology Sectors

In Table 11.1 it was noted that *all* of the countries with review systems followed special policies in the natural resources and high-technology sectors, as did most of the others in this study. At the same time, MNE strategies as outlined in Chapter 3 suggest that natural resources and high-technology sectors are among those which lead to internalization of activity within the firm. The large sunk costs in such industries lead to efforts by the firm to reduce uncertainty (Vernon, 1983). In raw materials, the attempt to stabilize demand and to minimize problems in supply often leads to vertical integration. Ownership may be shared with local investors or other firms but control is likely to be maintained. In addition, in the high-technology sector, the firm must try to realize a return on its investment in knowledge in the face of host-country policies favouring local production and often favouring locally owned firms as well. Minimizing risk from governments and competitors in such circumstances leads to FDI or perhaps to joint ventures controlled by the MNE. Also internalization suggests that MNEs are more likely to accommodate government demands for decentralization of production than for decentralization of headquarters functions such as research, some aspects of finance and global marketing. In developing special policies with regard to its natural resource industries a country may have several motives: for example, to take advantage of a country-specific asset in the bargaining process with MNEs, to secure rents or to meet a strongly-held view that natural resources are a special case for conservation and other reasons. The outcomes can only be described as mixed.

Both the objectives of the policies and the elements affecting bargaining power varied a good deal. Australia's main policy was the relatively modest one of sharing ownership of new natural resource projects while leaving intact control both of such projects and of existing firms. Norway had the good fortune to have a rich energy resource as well as long experience with a concession system. These were used in a discretionary way to encourage a significant degree of ownership and operational participation by local firms, as well as major tax collection. Both the late timing and the form of Canada's major energy policies were affected by difficult jurisdictional and regional pressures. They also involved higher risks than in other developed countries for potentially higher rewards – more domestic control of firms (including repatriation) as well as ownership, significant increases in rent collection in a short period and more federal control of the industry in other respects. The price declines in the early 1980s effectively led to the end of most of these policies. One might note that it is not common among the set of countries considered here to tackle so directly the control of existing firms in an industry, even where foreign ownership is high, as it was in Canada. Japan managed to reduce foreign ownership in refining over time. The United Kingdom considered and rejected the idea of securing more domestic ownership of existing petroleum firms, settling instead for other policies to secure control of supply, rents and development effects. France nationalized significant sectors of industry in the early 1980s, including some MNE activities, but the latter were not the sole or major objective of the programme. Other countries not listed in Table 11.1 also had special policies directed at natural resources. The Netherlands, for example, secured agreement to use local supplies when awarding concessions for inland gas exploration and also negotiated 'gentlemen's agreements' with two large firms to reinvest 'excess profits'.

Sectoral incentives and disincentives aimed at MNEs were also evident in the high-technology sector, where considerations of defence mingled with the expectation of positive externalities and also developmental linkages. Sometimes the tariffs, fiscal incentives and government purchasing contracts were designed to secure local production regardless of ownership; often these or other policies heavily favoured domestically owned firms. The computer industry is a case in point, where various forms of discrimination in favour of locally owned firms or joint ventures were largely ineffective in France and the United Kingdom and highly effective in Japan. Other sectoral policies in less research-intensive sectors are evident, again with mixed success – some can be claimed for electronics in Ireland, little for repeated attempts to maintain an efficient and partly locally owned motor sector in the United Kingdom. In a number of ways the review systems showed considerable appreciation for the firm- and industry-specific characteristics of high-technology firms, even if the policies up to the early 1980s were not yet fully considered or developed. Australia's agency, for example, explicitly allowed 100 per cent foreign ownership of firms in manufacturing where proprietary knowledge or high technology more generally was involved. The Canadian authorities had begun to favour 'world product mandates' where not only was specialized production located in Canada for export but where research, marketing and other related functions and authority were also decentralized. As we will note in the next chapter, some theory and much practice has moved to favouring industry-specific policies in the 1980s.

Other Restricted Sectors

All of the countries in this study have restricted FDI in a number of sectors, sometimes exempting those firms already in the sector. In some countries

Table 11.3 *Position of OECD countries regarding sectoral controls and impediments to inward direct investment (August 1986)*

Countries	*1*	*2*	*3*	*4*	*5*	*6*	*7*	*8*	*9*	*10*	*11*	*12*	*13*	*14*	*15*	*16*	*17*	*18*	*19*	*20*	*21*	*22*	*23*	*24*	*25*	*26*	*27*	*28*	*29*	*30*	*31*	*32*	*33*	*34*	*35*
Australia	RI	R			RI	R	M				MR	MR	R	R	R	R	R	R	R		M	M				MR									
Austria	RI	I	R	I		M	M			M	R	R	R		R	R	R					R				M	R				M	M			
Belgium				I		M	M				M	M	MR									M													
Canada	RI	R		MR	R	R	M					R			R	R	R				M									R					
Denmark				RI																			I												
Finland	RI	RI		MR		MR	MR		M	M	MR	R	R		R	R		R	R			R	R	R	R	M				MR					
France	RI	RI	R	RI	I	MR	M	RI	R		MRI	MR	R			MRI	MRI	RI		MRI	RI	M	M		RI	R	R	R	I		M				M
FRG	I					M	M				M	MRI	R													M									
Greece	RI			I		M	M				M	M	MI		I	I	M					M				M									
Ireland	RI	I		RI		M	M				M	R	RI	R				R																	
Italy	RI			RI		MR	M				M	R	R			I	R			M	M	M				M									
Japan	I	I				I	MI					I	I	R		R	R	R	R												M	M			
Luxembourg				MI		M	M															M													
Netherlands	RI	I				M	M				M	R	R									M	I												
New Zealand				MR			R	M			M	M	R		R	R						M													
Norway	RI	R		RI		M	M				M	R	R	MR	R	R		M			R	M			R	M				M			M		
Portugal	R			RI			M	R			M	M	MR				M					M	M		R									M	I
Spain		I		MI		MR	M				M	R					M			M	I					R					M				
Sweden	R	R		I		M	M			M	M	R	R		R								I			M				M			M		
Switzerland	RI	I				M	M	R			M	MI	MI		R		M			I	I	I	M							M					
Turkey	RI	I		RI		M	M			R	M	M			R	R	R					M	M			M				M	M				
United Kingdom	I	I		I		MR	M				M	R	R									M													
United States	I			I		MR	MR				R	R	R	R	R	R	R			R	R														

Notes:

R = Sectors in which some or all activities are subject to controls or impediments to inward direct investment that are regarded as restrictions in the sense of the Code of Liberalization of Capital Movements.

I = Sectors in which some or all activities are restricted by other impediments.

M = Sectors in which some or all activities are closed to investment due to public, private or mixed monopolies.

This table shows on a country-by-country basis those sectors which, to a greater or lesser degree, are restricted to foreign investment either because of *obstacles* which apply specifically or more severely to non-resident investors, or because of the presence of public, private or mixed *monopolies*. Where obstacles are considered as restrictions in the sense of the Code they are marked with an R. In other cases, an I (for Impediments) is used. Monopolies are indicated with an M. As a result of space limitations, some sectors include a number of specific activities (see for example maritime transportation); the presence of an obstacle or monopoly in any activity of that sector results, as far as this table is concerned, in a mark being entered against the entire sector. In some instances, an activity of a specific sector may be restricted in the sense of the Code and an R appears in the column, while in another activity of the same subject a monopoly may exist, which is reflected by an M. Thus, for the same sector, two letters may appear. Detailed information is not available for Iceland which maintains a general derogation from the obligations of the Code of Liberalisation of Capital Movements.

Key

Banking	1	Agriculture, agricultural products	18
Other financial services (including stockbroking)	2	Forestry	19
Auditing	3	Nuclear industries	20
Insurance	4	Exploitation of water resources, water power	21
Press, publishing, printing	5	Overall energy production and public utilities (including water, gas, electricity)	22
Broadcasting (radio, television, cable)	6	Armaments, explosives, gunpowder	23
Post, telephone, telecommunications	7	Security guard and private detective services	24
Audiovisual works, film distribution	8	Tourism, travel services	25
Health and social security	9	Gaming, casinos, lottos, lotteries, etc.	26
Employment agencies and services	10	Jurisprudence, legal profession	27
Land transport (includes railways, buses, road construction and maintenance)	11	Teaching, education	28
Air transport (includes airport construction and operation in some cases)	12	Merchants and craftsmen	29
Maritime transportation (includes shipping, ship brokerage, forwarding, inland waterways, operation of seaports, cabotage, offshore supply, salvaging and dredging, ownership of fishing vessels)	13	Import, export and distribution of alcoholic beverages	30
		Tobacco, matches	31
		Salt	32
Fishing	14	Pharmaceuticals, medicines, narcotics	33
Real estate	15	Steel	34
Mining, minerals	16	Public works and services	35
Petroleum	17		

Source: OECD (1987b) *Controls and Impediments Affecting Inward Direct Investment*.

such sectors are fairly well defined in law: Canada, the United States, Switzerland, Norway and Sweden are examples. Many other states rely also on review mechanisms and other methods to define such restricted sectors, sometimes in an ad hoc manner. It is important to note that public ownership of industry, while not necessarily directed at foreign ownership, can restrict access by both foreign and domestic private firms. There may be a monopoly for publicly owned firms in some cases and, where this is not so, private firms are often unwilling to compete against what may be favoured public firms.

It is difficult to summarize the situation with regard to such restricted sectors for all of the reasons noted earlier – their uneven definition in law, the many devices used to restrict FDI in such sectors, the varying degrees of restriction, and the uneven reporting. The reader is urged to refer to the country studies for fuller detail. The most complete listing is that by the OECD (1987b), which was one of the sources for Part II. Some comments on its derivation will help interpret Table 11.3, summarizing both public monopolies and sectoral restrictions directed to MNE investments (see OECD, 1987b, Ch. 1).

In 1961 the OECD adopted a Code of Liberalization of Capital Movements which included, among other things, an obligation by member countries to authorize automatically the transactions involving FDI, including any liquidations. Members could lodge a reservation if this obligation was not met. In 1984 the obligation was extended beyond the formal right of entry and the related financial transfers to effective operational access. Members now had to revise any reservations they had notified to the Code to reflect obstacles to MNEs which were not equally applied to domestically owned firms. It is important to note that the liberalization provisions of the Code do not encompass agreed restrictions based on essential security interests, public order, and cases where an investment could have an exceptionally detrimental effect on the member country's interests.

Table 11.3 summarizes the sectoral restrictions. These are *apart from* general restrictions on FDI, such as those covered by the screening mechanisms discussed in the previous sections of this chapter. The sectoral restrictions are classified in three categories. One lists restrictions in the sense of the Code of Liberalization. A second category lists other kinds of sectoral restrictions not covered by reservations to the Code, such as sectoral reciprocity measures. The third shows sectors closed to FDI and also to private domestic investors because of public, private or mixed monopolies.

The first two categories are heavily concentrated in a number of service sectors and in natural resources including energy (Table 11.4). It will be evident that a range of devices are used to restrict MNE activities and that, in many cases, the restrictions do not completely bar such activities (OECD,

1987b, 12–14). In some cases, such as domestic air transport and maritime transport, the sector or related activities are largely closed to foreigners in most countries. In a number of countries foreign investment is not allowed in some types of banking, media or communication, or armaments, among others. In many countries a special authorization or concession is needed to take part in certain activities, a procedure usually involving a case-by-case review. Frequently, as in banking and insurance in many countries, access to the sector depends on reciprocity requirements or an agreement limiting access to that granted by the investor's home country. Some of the measures shade over into exceptions to national treatment for established firms. The third category in Table 11.3 is activities closed to private investors, both foreign and domestic, because of public monopolies or publicly sanctioned private or mixed monopolies. These are particularly prevalent in the sectors shown in Table 11.4. There are many other sectors for particular countries.

Table 11.4 Industry concentration of sectoral controls and state monopolies

Out of 23 countries	*Sectoral controls*	*Public, private or mixed monopolies*
6 or more	Real estate, mining & minerals, petroleum, agriculture products, water resources	Air transport, games
12 or more	Other financial services Air transport & facilities	Broadcasting Land transport Energy & related utilities
18 or more	Banking, insurance Maritime transport & related facilities	Post, telephone, telecommunications

The decision to close a sector or activity to FDI and to buy out, or otherwise press into leaving, any existing foreign-owned firms is the strongest position which a country can take. In recent decades such actions have not been frequent in the countries in this study, but they have occurred. Some examples are publishing and petroleum in Canada, and several important firms during the French nationalizations of the early 1980s. In many other sectors, however, entry is blocked to new foreign firms or obstacles set up which can raise costs to both new and established foreign firms. While overt divestment may not be the outcome, slower expansion in that market and reduced competitive power can well result in some cases.

Closing a sector to FDI is at one extreme of the spectrum of policies which a country can adopt. It achieves fully the objective of domestic ownership, with whatever exceptions the government may make for existing firms or occasional entry by new ones. If taken to the limit it is equivalent to recognizing no tradeoff between the benefits from domestic ownership, on the one hand, and possible economic gains from foreign investment, on the other. In terms of foreign trade policy that would be equivalent to a zero quota on imports of final goods and services; that is, subject to the possibility of intermediate product imports. In the case of a non-tradeable service, full restriction to domestic firms would remove competition from both foreign-owned firms and imports.

The expectation in some cases noted in Part II is that there are gains from restrictions on FDI which offset any loss and that other techniques to secure the gains are not feasible. Petroleum was a case in point, where governments believed they could capture rents via private domestic or public ownership, as well as by taxation measures, and also believed they had more leverage over domestic firms in ensuring domestic sourcing and other developmental spillovers. It is certainly tempting to think of the restricted sectors as such key or strategic sectors where these considerations of national capture of rents and other positive externalities prevailed. The efforts to preserve a national presence in high-technology sectors also point in these directions. The attempts in the 1960s to preserve domestic control of media and similar sectors associated with national identity also support such a position for non-economic reasons (Table 10.2).

At least three things suggest that one needs to go much further to account for these restrictions. First, many of the sectors were restricted through public ownership or monopoly provisions long before the concerns with FDI which appeared in the 1960s, although in some cases the private firms which were affected were owned abroad. Many were clearly in sectors where public ownership or regulation were considered necessary because private ownership or unfettered private activity was considered undesirable: 'natural monopolies' in some types of communication and transport are examples. These regulations would often be administered by government departments or special agencies rather than the review mechanisms which were developed in the 1960s and later. Privatization and deregulation during the 1980s has begun to open many of these sectors not only to competition from domestic private investment but, with varying conditions attached, to foreign owners as well. The great expansion in FDI in services during the 1980s is one aspect of these changes, including particularly the multinational spread of various financial services.

Second, after a certain point it is difficult to find any common criteria for sectoral restrictions. One is hard pressed to know why insurance should be a key sector while motor cars are not – both have had an international dimension for some time. An important consideration here may be the costs of reserving a sector or developing a substitute for foreign MNEs in some industries. It is noteworthy that, apart from Japan, *none* of the developed countries in this study has attempted to keep MNEs out of the sectors in manufacturing where they concentrate most heavily, namely, chemicals, electrical machinery, non-electrical machinery and some more specific sectors such as motor cars. Italy can be thought of also as an exception in some ways, given its large state ownership in some of these sectors, but it did not attempt to keep out foreign-owned firms. Other exceptions to this statement exist in some sectors, as in the British and French computer industries, but again they have tended to be partial exclusions or supported by subsidies to domestic firms. It may well be that the costs of developing domestic substitutes are higher for some of these sectors, and that markets and cooperative modes such as joint ventures are imperfect substitutes for firms in these industries, as internalization theory suggests.[6] Once again we note some changes in this regard in recent years, at least in the sense that governments appear more willing to promote domestically owned MNEs in more of these sectors.

Finally we emphasize that in most cases governments did not fully prohibit FDI in a sector even when there were strong reservations about such investment or a strong desire to support domestically owned firms. The costs of forcing out foreign-owned firms could be high, in terms not only of net compensation but also of potential retaliation. Often it was simpler to favour the local firm or handicap the foreign, or to allow collaborative arrangements through licensing or joint ventures, so as to encourage local firms while not losing some of the gains from FDI. Many of the sectoral restrictions are, in fact, quite porous, suggesting that terms such as 'strategic' are too strong for many of them.

Despite these reservations on the origins and meaning of many of the restricted sectors, it bears repeating that most governments were concerned to preserve or develop domestically owned firms in some of these research-intensive sectors both for national security reasons and because of their concerns that they would otherwise lose out on any special gains from such industries. The nationalizations of various manufacturing industries in the period just after the Second World War in countries such as the United Kingdom, France and Italy were inspired by many concerns: for example, to preserve employment in some sectors such as steel and coal, to preserve a military capability in others such as aviation, or to ensure government control of a variety of sectors. Another motive was to prevent some of these sectors from becoming foreign-owned. In the 1960s and later, as was evident from the country studies, a number of governments were prepared to go further with public ownership and various incentives in order to preserve a domestic presence in selected sectors of industry.[7] National security concerns have led to a number of restrictions on FDI in the United States, including the loosely defined Exon-Florio amendment which has led many firms entering the United States to submit to a notification process.

The concept of restricted sectors merges at some points with the concept of 'key' firms. All of the countries in this study have found a way to prevent, or at least to review, the effects of a foreign takeover of such firms. That was the case whether or not such governments had a general review policy or a declared restriction on foreign takeovers in that sector. As indicated in Part II and Table 10.2, in fact, the proposed takeover of firms which were not protected by such policies sometimes influenced governments to adopt general or sectoral restrictions. As reported in interviews, several large Swedish firms which requested the removal of the alien's clause from their charters were refused, although in one of these the government later agreed to a modified proposal which kept effective control in Sweden. More broadly the US and West German governments, among others, instituted notification requirements informally when takeovers of some major firms by OPEC governments seemed possible, and the former established a committee whose scope for review has been expanded.

The definition of key firms, beyond restricted sectors, is nowhere spelled out. The treaties which limit discrimination against foreign-owned firms usually put the allowable exceptions in quite broad terms, such as public order and essential security interests, as determined by the country involved. The UK Industry Act of 1975, which gives the government power to block a foreign takeover, specifies only that such a takeover be contrary to the national interest. The Netherlands has a similar Act. Neither of these Acts has been invoked in practice. In speaking of foreign acquisitions, Boddewyn (1974, 73) notes that 'The acquisition of "national-flag" companies (e.g. Belgium's only petroleum firm), of firms in industries which the government is trying to "restructure" (e.g. heavy electrical equipment in France) or of "last-straw" situations (e.g. one more Italian pharmaceutical concern) are particularly resented or resisted in this context.'

Such key firms in the private sector overlap, in turn, with the attempts by governments to promote state-owned firms, partly in order to counter the effects of foreign-owned firms. The petroleum and computer sectors were among those noted in Part II, while Airbus and other joint efforts by European countries have been developed to counter MNEs from the United States and Japan. At times governments looked on such firms as simply recapturing domestic market share from foreign MNEs – French policy in the early

1980s had strong elements of such an approach – but this gave way quickly to supporting domestically owned MNEs.

FOREIGN TAKEOVERS: EXPLICIT AND IMPLICIT CONSTRAINTS

Up to this point the emphasis has been on policies which restrict foreign ownership on establishment or discriminate against it subsequently, including review of subsequent mergers and acquisitions by foreign-owned firms. Two further points on foreign takeovers need comment: they are generally regarded more negatively than greenfields investment; and a country's policies on mergers and acquisitions in general can reinforce its stance on foreign takeovers.

In discussing Table 11.1 it was noted that virtually all of the countries with review systems consider both greenfields investment and takeovers. What was clear from the country studies was the generally strong preference for the former.[8] The stronger stance against takeovers has been defended on a number of economic grounds. There may be a more competitive effect in the first case, for example, since the number of domestic sellers is increased, and the employment and development effects of greenfields investment are more evident.

It is not difficult to see the problems of such reasoning, since it is easy to construct counter-cases in welfare terms. For example, a foreign firm which uses a greenfields investment to push out of production a sole domestic competitor, or even one of several, may not make the domestic market more competitive. By contrast, a foreign firm which rejuvenates a failing domestic firm or improves a continuing one may have made the domestic market more competitive. Everything depends on the other assumptions about company activities one makes in such cases. These types of issues would be considered by competition authorities in countries where competition policy is active or, in some cases, by other regulatory authorities.

It is even more difficult to see a distinction between greenfields and takeover investments from abroad on macroeconomic grounds. The argument frequently heard from government officials that the former leads to a net increase in real investment while the latter does no do so appears to depend on unspecified assumptions regarding the intentions of the *sellers* of the acquired firms.[9] MacDougall (1960) noted a particular possibility where inward FDI was largely by way of foreign takeovers and local sellers of assets acted in ways which did not raise capital stock. The outcome could be a decline in locally owned capital stock. One test of this proposition was for Canada in the period 1951–62, when every $1.00 of FDI from abroad was associated with $2.00 of additional domestic investment (Caves and Reuber, 1971, ch. 4).

Ultimately the economic case for or against takeovers from abroad will rest on the case made for or against them apart from their nationality; that is, whether they improve the productivity, international competitiveness and other welfare aspects of the firms involved. Such issues were certainly considered by review agencies in a general way, and a more careful review of such questions was undertaken in the more sensitive cases. There was little evidence that this was done in a systematic way based on models related to the business or economic literature. There generally was not time in most cases, given the number of cases and the timing and resource constraints, for even elementary cost–benefit analyses at a macro level, much less the strategic international analysis of firm and industry behaviour which would have been necessary to assess the viability of particular takeovers.[10] In the more important cases the review systems relied on the studies and experience of other departments of government. If a significant grant was involved, for example, the impact of the investment would be studied more closely and monitored. In brief what becomes relevant is the capacity of governments to deliver an integrated and supportive set of industrial policies, including those associated with foreign investment. This issue is taken up at the end of this chapter. What was apparent in the review systems was the use of more limited and partial attempts to deal with the generality of cases. For example, the Australian agency took the position that a loss in ownership was involved in a takeover so that other benefits had to offset this. Where such benefits were low, maintaining some Australian ownership would be proposed; otherwise a 100 per cent takeover might be approved. If foreign ownership was high in the sector even larger benefits were needed. That foreign takeovers brought such benefits by way of increased employment, improved management, scale economies, new products and so on seemed to be implied by the way in which review agencies kept reporting these (for example, Australia, FIRB Report, 1982, 87, and Canada FIRA Report, 1982–3, Appendix B).

The negative view of takeovers as against greenfields investment in review agencies is by no means the only obstacle to foreign acquisitions of domestic firms. The degree of state ownership, the extent to which shares are closely held, and the scope for protection against hostile takeovers are also important and may overshadow any review process. Such obstacles to takeover may limit both domestic and foreign investors in principle. However public authorities and private domestic investors have cooperated at times to turn the obstacles against unwanted foreign investors. It is worth noting that such obstacles, which are difficult to measure and not necessarily directed against

FDI, play no part in the measures of degree of restrictiveness of policy noted in Chapter 10.

The strength of competition policy was noted as one factor which differed among countries and which, as a consequence, some foreign investors might regard as discriminatory towards FDI. We were unable to uncover systematic discrimination, however burdensome such policy might appear to firms accustomed to different procedures in their home market. US firms, for example, will use federal and state laws to attempt to block unwanted foreign takeovers, but they use such laws to block domestic takeovers also. Young *et al.* (1988, 210–17) failed to find much evidence that the Monopolies and Mergers Commission in the United Kingdom was screening FDI as such. Again in the FRG the competition authority takes into account the effects of MNEs while not discriminating against them. On occasion, however, governments appear to have used competition policy to at least delay foreign takeovers in sensitive sectors or where the foreign acquirer is state-owned.

What is of more importance to FDI is the obstacles to hostile mergers or acquisitions in terms of limited shareholders' rights and related issues, on the one hand, and close public or private ownership, on the other. Close state or private holdings of many firms' shares in countries such as Italy, France, West Germany and Japan make it far more difficult for hostile takeovers from any source to succeed.[11] It is relatively easy in such circumstances for public authorities and private owners to discuss the implications of significant takeovers, including those from abroad, and to find ways to thwart them if this is desired. The ways in which the FRG and the United States reacted to the fear of major takeovers by OPEC governments in the 1970s is instructive in this regard. The former established gentlemen's agreements with the governments and relied on the banks to monitor these, while the latter set up a committee at the executive level which has gradually found its mandate broadened by congressional pressure.

Close holdings of shares were not the only obstacle facing hostile takeover. In some countries there was an explicit limitation in law on takeover by foreign firms as such. This was so for many firms in natural resources and 'real estate' in Norway and Sweden from the early decades of the century. In Japan it became possible to acquire majority or 100 per cent foreign control in most industries only in the 1970s, and until 1980 there was a requirement that the consent of the acquired firm was needed in any takeover, domestic or foreign. It has continued to be virtually impossible to acquire larger firms except with the agreement of the various stakeholders involved, particularly in the bank-centred industrial groups. There are also other obstacles, varying from the Japanese aversion to foreign control to the high price to earnings ratio of Japanese firms. Even in the late 1980s, when Japanese acquisitions of firms abroad had increased rapidly, there were still relatively few acquisitions of Japanese firms by foreign interests (*The Economist* , 17 September 1988, 87).

In Part II it was noted that in some countries in the 1960s and 1970s many laws were introduced to allow firms additional protection against hostile takeovers, in some cases specifically because of fears about foreign takeovers. As a result, in countries such as Switzerland, the FRG and the Netherlands, a plethora of devices were introduced by firms to make hostile acquisitions more difficult or impossible. There is a major difference of opinion on the justification for such laws and the more general issue of the ease or difficulty of effecting business takeovers. Some have argued that the relative ease of hostile takeovers in some countries leads managers to take an excessively short-term view of their responsibilities in order to show quick financial returns and avoid takeovers. Another view argues that excessive protection against takeovers leads managers to avoid necessary decisions which would enhance the long-term interests of the firm or at least those of the other stakeholders. Whatever one's views on this very complex issue, two points are relevant for present purposes. Takeover defences are hardly unknown outside the countries noted above. In countries such as Canada, the United Kingdom and especially the United States, however, the major spread of such defences came in the 1980s and they have not prevented a very considerable number of hostile takeovers among the larger firms.[12] Moreover one critical aspect of this process, the protection of shareholders' rights, has lagged significantly in the former group of countries. A recent study on shareholders' rights ranked countries on four matters – disclosure of corporate information, voting rights, shareholder rights to introduce resolutions, and notification to shareholders of meetings and proxy rights. This is obviously a limited set of issues which does not touch on some larger matters raised above, but the differences between countries are striking. If one places the United States at 100, Canada ranks at 80, the United Kingdom and Australia at 73 and 65, three countries (FRG, France, Japan) at 48, Italy and Holland at 40, and Switzerland at only 18 (Table 11.5).

During the late 1980s these types of implicit constraints on cross-border mergers and acquisitions began to receive a great deal of attention. This was in the context of a situation where most governments had liberalized inward review of FDI but were attempting to encourage the trade and investment of their own MNEs. We return to this topic in the next chapter.

Table 11.5 Shareholders' rights in selected countries

	Disclosure	*Voting rights*	*Resolution procedures*	*Shareholder notification*	*Average*
Canada	80	70	80	90	80
UK	80	70	60	80	73
Australia	70	70	60	60	65
FRG	40	40	40	70	48
France	60	40	50	40	48
Japan	40	50	40	60	48
Italy	50	50	30	30	40
Netherlands	70	40	30	30	40
Switzerland	30	10	10	20	18

Note:
Scores are calculated using American measures as 100.

Source: Investor Responsibility Research Centre, as reported in *The Economist*, 29 April 1989, 76.

FURTHER CONSEQUENCES: MNE REACTIONS, RENT SEEKING, INTERNATIONAL EFFECTS

Policies such as those described above have many consequences, some of which have already been touched on. Three deserve particular attention. First, how did the firms react to the policies noted? Second, how extensive and how successful was rent transference to nationals? Third, what were the other international consequences?

In Chapter 4 it was noted that firms had a variety of ways of reacting to policies which reduced net incentives to investment in a particular location.[13] These were labelled accommodation, voice, cope, avoid and (in the medium or longer term) insulate and exit. The company interviews noted in Appendix I cannot be considered as a test of the reactions of the firms to policy. They were designed more as a cross-check on the information received from government and other sources, and were also not comprehensive enough for such a test. They did, however, reveal examples of each of the above reactions, in some cases in some depth.

Accommodation involves acceptance of a policy and, in some cases, active cooperation with it as a strategic move by the MNE. For example, MNEs in many countries have been prepared to move beyond wholly-owned or even majority-owned subsidiaries as ways of transferring their knowledge. Many of the officers interviewed insisted they preferred wholly-owned or controlled subsidiaries in many contexts as an aspect of the desire to preserve standards, more effectively transfer techniques, more fully secure a return on their investment in knowledge and other reasons familiar from internalization theory. (Some of those in Japanese firms preferred exports to FDI, largely because of their preferred supplier and labour arrangements at home.) Consistent with that theory, they were prepared to use joint ventures, licences and other organizational forms in smaller markets, with more mature products or processes, where risks were particularly large or (in natural resources) capital costs and risk exceptionally high. Two things appear to have happened in the last few decades. One is that increased competition from many more MNEs and the partly-related increased uncertainty in economic activity have led firms to more cooperative arrangements. These arrangements allow risk reduction, knowledge sharing and other advantages. They are not usually taken so far as to threaten the core activities of firms, however, and are less likely at some stages or types of production where there may be more need to protect proprietary rights. The other is an increased responsiveness to government preferences for joint venture and other cooperative arrangements. These two points occurred repeatedly in the interviews. They are clearly related, but we have no way of separating the influence of each.

One striking example of accommodation becoming active cooperation with public policy as a strategic move by the MNE was seen in the willingness of some of the less dominant computer firms to enter joint ventures with local firms, partly as a way of countering the competitive power of the dominant firm. This has been evident in countries as different as France and Mexico. Some major firms have decentralized decision making to a very large degree, partly because it was considered the appropriate business strategy but also, in some cases, in an attempt to accommodate government preferences in what are considered politically sensitive sectors of industry.

Voice, or persuading a government to change its position or at least its method, is not as easy as it seems for an MNE. To act publicly and alone, especially for a US multinational or one in a sensitive sector, can easily be turned against the firm by host governments or domestically owned firms. Action through an industry association is likely to be more effective, provided the firm can carry along not only other MNEs but domestic firms and perhaps state-owned firms. Companies can work through multinational organizations such as the OECD or EC, go to court, or even appeal to the home government, but there are clearly risks in all cases, especially the last of these, for firms which need host government cooperation on a variety of ongoing matters. Much depends on institutions and traditions in the country involved. The US Congressional Committee system, for example, leaves room for more explicit lobbying than elsewhere. And much depends on whether one is speaking of a well-established and well-connected firm which has been careful to cultivate a good image, or a firm which is trying to secure entry to the country.

Some of the firms which were well established were quite certain of their ability to *cope*, and also preferred it to the other methods. Coping means to keep a low profile, try to deal with the disincentive effects of the policies and wait for a better policy. It may be that the options elsewhere are no more attractive, in the sense that everyone regulates the sector heavily. Some writers have argued that the stakes are low in such cases, but this is not clear: having a large stake and not being able to exercise other options effectively could lead to this outcome. We shall return to this in discussing strategies below.

Still another strategy is to attempt to *avoid* the effects of a policy. If a minority joint venture is all that a multinational is allowed, for example, it is possible in some countries to make arrangements with passive investors which leaves the multinational with effective control. Some types of transfer pricing arrangements can undermine, or at least complicate, a government's objectives.

Over the medium or longer term two other strategies are feasible. One is to *insulate* the firm to some degree from government pressures. Rapid change in products or processes may have this effect, at least if other variables, such as the firm's reputation, are also favourable. This can also serve to limit imitation and other competitive pressures. Having key processes or components located in more than one country can provide a degree of protection. Some firms have gradually moved to parts of a vertically integrated production process, or even to quite different product lines, which are subject to less intervention.

At some point this leads to *exit* from the country. Divesting part or all of a firm's operations is a continuing and significant phenomenon, for a wide variety of reasons reflecting the changing comparative advantage of countries and of firms. Such divestments have been studied in detail for Europe (Van Den Bulcke *et al.*, 1979) and for US multinationals (Bonin, 1984, 180–81). What is of interest here is exit because of policies which reduce net incentives for firms in a given location, and specifically those policies which are directed at established MNEs. Exit is an extreme reaction even over time, for a variety of reasons. It may be very difficult to leave a large market or one where significant resource holdings are involved, given overall MNE strategy. Worker layoff costs are substantial in some countries, and for this and other reasons any loss in public confidence could affect the firm's reputation elsewhere. A decision subsequently to re-enter could be very costly, for example in recapturing market share or securing necessary government approvals. Hence it is much more common for a firm to use other tactics if divestment is considered necessary: to reduce the scale of the operation over time in favour of other locations, for example, or to sell off part of the operation.

Nevertheless some of the firms interviewed in this study had divested all or a substantial part of their operations from several of the countries in this study, as well as from a larger number of less developed countries. In the case of the former, the prime example was in the petroleum sector, where divestment from Canada, Italy and Norway had occurred in good part in response to policies which the firms considered had had a more negative impact on foreign MNEs than on domestic firms, or which explicitly discriminated in favour of the latter. The loss of incentives of various kinds had also led some firms to divest, although here it was not clear that these policies were directed at MNEs as such. Increased public support and other regulations favouring state-owned firms had also led to some divestments.

At a more aggregative level we have noted in the country studies the impact of policy on FDI flows in certain short periods when policy changed sharply, such as Canada with the National Energy Program and France with nationalization in the early 1980s. The changing pattern of flows and stocks, standardized to US dollars, is brought out in Tables 3.1 to 3.3. These changes over longer periods, which are dramatic for some countries, clearly reflect far more than the impact of policy on FDI; factors such as changing country advantages, for example, and changing sources of FDI.

The second policy effect noted above was that of rent transference to nationally owned firms and governments. Several possibilities for improving national welfare through rent transfers from foreign firms were noted throughout this study. For example, if one assumes there is a range within which firms will bargain on entry or subsequent merger – the minimum return they require given options elsewhere, and the maximum they can expect given market and cost opportunities as determined by competition and available resources – then governments may be able to secure part of this range. If governments calculate incorrectly and raise net costs to the firm sufficiently, they risk losing the investment. They also risk sending the wrong signals to other potential entrants. The same can be said about an established foreign-owned firm which finds its profits sharply increased by exogenous factors: a sharp increase in natural resource prices, for example, because of a successful international producers' cartel. Governments may once again be tempted to capture such profits rather than let them accrue to foreign owners, and once again run risks such as overshooting rents or running into resistance from the firms or home governments. However it is not only policies which discriminate against foreign-owned firms which allow such potential gains. In general any policy which brings benefits to some residents, such as consumers, while imposing costs on other residents, such as foreign owners, may bring net national benefits. Trade liberalization in a largely foreign-owned industry is one example, assuming that losses to other domestic factors of production are small or transitional.

It is likely that, where rent transfers through such policies are from foreign to domestic resource owners, there is an incentive for nationals to invest in rent-seeking activities. This investment could reduce real national wealth if the competition was with other nationals (Krueger, 1974). What is being discussed here, however, is rent seeking at the expense of foreign owners, hence the potential for national gain remains. One situation often noted in Part II is that where the review process results in a price to domestic sellers which is lower than what they would receive if they had the unrestricted right to sell to foreign investors. Assuming there is some competition in the market for acquisitions, government intervention against foreign investors in such cases would benefit competing domestic bidders at the expense of domestic sellers.[14]

Many of the governments in this study were clearly attempting to shift rents to nationals by one means or another, as well as to secure other economic gains.[15] In terms of bargaining models, for example, all of the review agencies attached some conditions to some approved investments and the different incentive mechanisms also involved performance conditions. We have already commented on the difficulties met by some of the more ambitious review mechanisms in identifying and implementing such bargaining opportunities, notably in the case of following through on performance requirements. The practice in some agencies of seeking alternative bids could raise prices to sellers if bid competition was lacking, or could simply shift any rents from sellers to domestic buyers by blocking the foreign investor. In France, for example, the authorities frequently consulted the French firms in an industry where a foreign takeover was proposed, and also at times actively attempted to find a French bidder. They do not appear to have been unduly influenced by the fact that the French seller might receive less – merely raising the price would not be convincing if it was believed that some important other benefits were involved in domestic ownership (Carlson, 1980, 43–4). The problem of maintaining confidentiality and other issues in such a policy were discussed at some length in the case of Australia, where there were often problems of getting competing Australian bids. The authorities exercised their powers to bring forth such bids only occasionally and through the medium of asking the foreign investor to announce the bid. This 'opportunities test' was abolished in 1986.[16] Both in Norway and Sweden where local governments or firms or unions were consulted, a competing bid would sometimes emerge to a foreign investment proposal, a fact confirmed by several firms which were interviewed. In Canada a plan to require announcement of foreign bids and to subsidize Canadian bidders was dropped. Nevertheless news of a foreign bid was often reported by the private parties involved or ferreted out by the financial community, with competing bids sometimes developing.

In all of the major natural resource-producing countries in this study efforts were made to capture more of the rents accruing from natural resource booms. The methods differed widely, as did the degree of success. The Australian approach secured 50 per cent Australian ownership in new projects and avoided some of the risks involved in large-scale repatriation of existing firms. Non-controlling local partners or widespread local ownership are not ideal ways to collect rent, especially if the foreign firm is also given some leeway in timing so as to price the shares to secure such rent. The Canadian policy in petroleum and gas was far better designed to secure both control and rent but also ran much bigger risks, most of which were realized. Norway was in a stronger position, given the demand for her resource and her experience with concessions. Allocation of the better blocks to the public and private Norwegian firms clearly internalized much rent which would otherwise have accrued to foreign MNEs, although one must note that one of the major private firms had significant foreign ownership.

All of these countries, along with others such as the United Kingdom, also developed various taxes designed to collect rents or excess profits. The question arises why they did not use various taxes more fully to collect rent, thus not only capturing it nationally but also for government. The same argument obtains for private foreign and domestic owners: in theory, rent can be extracted without affecting their decisions on production and investment. The same practical problems of implementation apply in both cases. Of course domestic owners would object to such tax policies, as was very evident in the case of the National Energy Program in Canada. There are also problems in some federal states in designing policies which achieve these ends, given the separation of powers over taxation and control of resource development. Governments would not rely only on such tax policies since they also had other objectives in mind, such as increasing local sourcing, which might require more domestic or governmental control of industry.

It is difficult to generalize across such different experiences, particularly since the available data and our coverage have been uneven. One thing which does stand out is the very large information costs of measuring rents, including the large risks involved in errors. For example, while measurement is very complex, Chapter 6 lent some support to the view that Canada's review agency probably imposed net costs on Canada – that any rent transfer and other economic gains were exceeded by losses on investment. It appears far more likely that, in the circumstances of the 1980s, Canada's National Energy Program reduced real national wealth. Another point which stands out is the differential group impact of policies on FDI. Rent transfers and other aspects of policy clearly benefited some groups but sometimes harmed others.

One question that arises is why those who are in the latter group fail to resist such policies. Sometimes the answer may lie in the costs of organization. Sellers of firms, for example, are in a large number of industries, which militates against organization. By contrast, domestic bidders who may wish to protest the entrance of a foreign competitor, or who may wish to bid against the latter, are *more likely* to be in the industry of the seller or one closely associated with it. There are important qualifications to this, given financial intermediation in merger and acquisition markets, but the ultimate domestic bidders may be much more concentrated than ultimate domestic sellers. Other factors are also involved. It is easy to see domestic bidders arguing publicly the benefits of keeping domestic control, and hard to imagine sellers receiving as sympathetic a public hearing for securing a higher price in a 'sell-out' to foreign interests. It is true that Japan before the mid-1970s succeeded in following a policy which largely prohibited acquisitions of local firms by foreign interests. We noted, however, that it was easier to secure a consensus among politicians, bureaucrats and officers of larger Japanese firms – indeed the three overlapped to a significant degree over time – while the interests of consumers, smaller firms and other potential losers from such policies were not as effectively represented.

The third effect noted above was the international consequences of the policies, apart from rent transference from foreign owners to nationals or governments of the host country. In particular the policies noted in this chapter are intended to increase exports or reduce imports and may succeed in doing so. Sometimes the effects on trade are at one or more removes, as when a firm's investment location and future trade are affected by such policies. The welter of policies used is well illustrated by the following quotation reflecting the experience of the motor industry:

> These performance requirements generally occur in combination with other government policies that limit imports of similar products into the host country. Such import limiting policies might include high – often prohibitive – tariffs, various types of tax and other non-tariff barriers that discriminate against imports, limitations on foreign exchange available for imports, or other forms of restrictions such as quotas. In order to stimulate domestic production of the import-limited product, tariff concessions which often reduce or waive the high rates imposed on selected imports are given to firms that make the desired investments in local production. Other industrial policies may provide for tax rebates applicable variously to local sales, or to export sales of items produced in the host country, or to the investment required to accomplish local production. Additional forms of industrial policy may include modifications or waiver of limitations on foreign ownership, more liberal terms for remittance of dividends, concessionary credit facilities, duty free importations of machinery and equipment, etc. Moreover, many of these national policies can be informal or shaped to fit the circumstances of individual investment programs approved by the host government.[17]

The incidence of performance requirements was noted earlier in this chapter, including the fact that many were intended directly to increase exports, reduce imports, raise domestic content and so on as a condition for approval of the investment. In addition the review agencies were usually careful to reject investment applications which appeared to be largely or wholly an import mechanism, as distinct from engaging to some degree in local production. The performance requirements were not always binding in practice, as already noted, but to the extent that they were effective other countries could be expected to protest. Some of the export requirements could have effects abroad which were similar to those resulting from export subsidies, for example, while some import requirements resembled quotas on trade.

In those situations where investment incentives – alone or with reinforcing adjustments in restrictive policies – actually affect the location of international investment, the issues which arise are similar.[18] Investment tends to be shifted from countries which do not have such programmes or are unable to match them. If these other countries do match the incentives, the effect on investment shifting cancels out, but the competing countries find themselves paying higher public subsidies for private investment, perhaps to the benefit of the treasuries of the firms' home countries. In effect any potential rents are passed back to non-resident owners, in the hope of attracting an investment or steering it regionally and in other ways. At one remove, such policies can affect trade when the investment is in place, perhaps accompanied by trade-related performance requirements as a condition of the incentive or because of the foreign investment review process. Once the investment is in place, moreover, it becomes harder for other countries to take action.

Similar issues have arisen with regard to state-owned firms. Vernon (1979) has suggested that there is on-going bargaining between such firms and the government officials to whom they respond, with the latter offering benefits such as subsidies, protection against imports and reduced taxes, in return for services such as taking on high-risk projects, retaining labour which is redundant, or holding down prices. He suggests also that such officials would tend to urge the firms to purchase domestic products or even those made by firms owned by nationals, and to export. Foreign governments will often take exception to such tactics because of the effects on trade and investment. Most governments also look more closely at inward FDI from state-owned firms, because of potential concerns about foreign government influence in general and security issues in particular.

Finally the restriction of certain sectors to locally owned firms has similar effects when governments are tempted to use such sectors as channels for trade restrictions.Where the products are tradeable internationally, the temptation to protect the sector may be strong. Otherwise the government may find itself prohibiting foreign ownership of a sector whose domestic content is swamped by imports. As noted in Part II, questions of reciprocal access frequently arise when firms in such sectors attempt to invest abroad.

The problems created by such potentially trade-distorting techniques became increasingly evident in the 1980s. Most governments see the possibilities for improving national wealth through a more efficient distribution of capital and techniques, including FDI. This is evident from the fact that, except for Japan until recently, and except for certain sectors, none of those in this study has tried to block FDI or to reduce substantially the presence of MNEs. At the same time all governments have intervened with FDI in one way or another, for wealth-increasing and for other reasons. Some governments, for example, have argued that performance requirements are needed to correct for intra-MNE restrictions on trade and technology which harm their national interests, and all governments protect some sectors which are considered strategic. One result of such regulation is to raise questions about reciprocal access to one another's markets for trade and investment. Another and related issue is the increased risk of emulation or retaliation by other countries, thus increasing the likelihood of zero-sum or negative-sum outcomes for the countries involved.

Such problems have long since led to attempts at bilateral resolution, such as investment protection treaties, or multilateral agreements. With respect to the latter, reference was made earlier to attempts in the EC to constrain subsidy competition and to promote the freedom of intra-EC direct investment. The OECD declaration on multinationals is an example at a broader level. More specifically the GATT decision on the use of trade-related performance requirements by Canada's FIRA was only the beginning of an attempt to deal with this range of issues. In the Uruguay Round of GATT the issues noted above have become far more prominent. Trade in services, for example, often requires that establishment rights for FDI be increased. Trade-related investment measures are on the agenda, as are export subsidies again. In the meantime the United States has moved ahead with reciprocity provisions in its Trade Bills which promise retaliatory measures if other countries' investment and other measures appear to be more restrictive than those in the United States. The EC, among other regions, has devised new ways of applying import controls in order to force larger domestic content for Japanese FDI in particular. In the next chapter it will be made clear that the resort by many countries to more selective trade and investment policies poses a major challenge to such multilateral policies aimed at liberalization or standardization of policy in these areas. We defer our conclusions on policy effectiveness until these new policies have been reviewed.

NOTES

1. Encarnation and Wells (1985) suggest, on the basis of study of projects in four less-developed countries, that more centralized systems for dealing with FDI involve a major internal political cost because of the implied reduction of departmental powers. They go on to suggest that centralized systems are likely to reflect a more liberal approach to FDI, negotiations with individual departments a more restrictive approach, and interdepartmental committees and the like an in-between stance. Guisinger *et al.* (1985) identified three approaches to government organization in dealing with FDI: decentralization, coordination and delegation to a single agency. Two of the countries in their sample used a single agency, while five used a mixture of coordination through a board or committee combined with decentralization. The single agency model indicated that the government was attempting to emphasize FDI issues, whether in order to attract the firms or to screen them.
2. The figures given here are underestimates also because of non-responses to these questions. For the reasons noted, the incidence by country of the performance requirements, measured as a ratio of the stock, would give a misleading measure of the relative incidence of review systems *in the 1960s and 1970s*. Hence they were not used for the derivation of degree of restrictiveness of review systems which is noted in Appendix IV.
3. Several lawyers interviewed said quite bluntly that they advised their clients to consider these and other tactics.
4. If the disincentives cannot be ended, offsetting them by incentives might improve economic welfare where the incentives themselves did not lead to negative welfare effects.
5. For fuller information see OECD (1985a) and also Part II above.
6. It is evident that many developing countries did not accept this argument or favoured domestic ownership and control for other reasons, since more of them limited FDI in such sectors.
7. Holland (1974) has argued that the desire to prevent foreign, especially US, ownership is the key to the expansion of public ownership in Europe in the post-Second World War period.
8. It is of interest to note that the data for Canada in Table 6.14 do not show a systematic difference in disallowance rates for new businesses and acquisitions, although interviews with officers of FIRA generally showed the same reservations on takeovers as those with officers of other agencies.
9. We assume here that the capital inflow effects, and any consequent exchange rate or interest rate effects, are similar for new and takeover investments.
10. Encarnation and Wells (1985, 69–74) found that no government explicitly performed a single socioeconomic cost–benefit analysis for four countries – Singapore, the Philippines, Indonesia and India – in greenfields investments in four industries from 1978 to 1982 inclusive.
11. The most detailed comparisons of mergers and acquisitions among countries are on the numbers of firms, rather than by firm size. These are not useful for present purposes. For example, a country such as Japan can have an active market for smaller firms and a largely inactive one for larger firms.
12. We do not have a measure of hostile takeovers, but other figures make the point. As late as 1989, for example, buy-outs by existing management and buy-ins by outside management totalled \$23 billion in the United States. In Western Europe they totalled \$17 billion, two-thirds of which was in the United Kingdom (*The Economist*, 11 November 1990, 93–4).
13. A full analysis of the effects of reduced net incentives would include the reactions of firms not already established in the country.
14. If there is no other bid except that from a foreign investor, government intervention could have the positive effect of securing other bids, as noted in some of the country references below.

15. Shifting rents from foreign to domestic owners is not the same thing as attempting to secure positive externalities believed to be associated with certain kinds of activities. Both were being attempted by governments, along with securing more linkage, which differs from either of the other two benefits.
16. This is not the same thing as the 50 per cent Australian ownership test in natural resources.
17. Statement of the Motor Vehicle Manufacturers Association of the United States, Inc., to the US Senate Subcommittee on International Economic Policy (1982, 588).
18. Whether a particular measure is an incentive or a disincentive to investment depends on the circumstances. A local content requirement might persuade an outside firm not to invest in the country, while an established firm might decide it had no option but to increase investment. In the latter case any negative effects on the costs and investment of other firms would need to be considered.

12. The New Policies: Managed Internationalism in the 1980s[1]

Policies on direct investment underwent a major change in the 1980s. Many restricted sectors were opened up to FDI to some degree, investment review mechanisms were ended or liberalized, and some of the incentives to MNEs were increased. All of this led to some convergence of policies towards MNEs. Such convergence, however, is not necessarily in the direction of non-intervention. Generalized intervention directed at foreign-owned MNEs has often given way to selective intervention in an international context. Policy on foreign-owned MNEs has tended to converge with international industrial policy, involving trade and investment policies aimed at both domestic and foreign MNEs. In this chapter the origins of the changes in policy towards foreign MNEs are examined, the new policies are considered, and some probable outcomes are indicated.

ORIGINS OF POLICY CHANGES

One reason for the changed policies was the slower and less stable rate of economic growth. World output increased at an annual rate of 5.5 per cent during 1961–73, 3.6 per cent during 1974–80, and 2.7 per cent during 1981–6; in the developed market economies the figures were 5.0, 2.5, and 2.2 (UN, 1988, 17). Supply shocks, exchange rate instability and erratic macro policy responses have all contributed to general instability. The collapse of resource prices in Australia and Canada at the onset of the recession of the early 1980s, for example, triggered some of the easing in their policies on inward FDI. Most countries in recessionary periods attempt to encourage investment through a reduction in net disincentives.

This by itself could hardly be an explanation for the changes in policy on inward FDI. The recession, while sharp, soon gave way to a prolonged upswing in the industrial countries. One must note also a move in many countries to deregulation of some sectors of industry and finance and to privatization, that is, the selling of state-owned firms to private buyers. In the process a number of privately owned service sectors in particular were opened further to FDI, notably in finance and especially in banking. In addition a number of service sectors which were public, or mixed public and private monopolies were opened to private investment, often with some limitation on the degree of foreign ownership. All of this was one reason why FDI flows in services accounted for half of all FDI flows in the 1980s.

A few examples of the privatization process are worth noting (UN, 1988, 256–7). In the United Kingdom a significant number of major state-owned firms have been privatized in part or whole. In many of these the government retained a golden share, which can be used to prevent any investor, domestic or foreign, from acquiring more than a certain percentage of the equity, usually 15 per cent, and also to insist on UK directors for the company. The change to a non-socialist government in France in the mid-1980s spurred a drive to privatize many firms, including especially those nationalized a few years earlier. Foreign participation has most often been restricted to 20 per cent, and the government has kept a golden share in order to prevent foreign takeovers where this was considered desirable. In 1985 Japan opened the telecommunications markets to new domestic and foreign investors, with a limit of one-third of capital in the latter case for some types of services.

A third and related reason for the changed policies on FDI was the rapid pace of technological change in some sectors, notably in information technologies.[2] The impact of such changes on services has led to a major expansion in service MNEs, especially in the finance sector. The compartmentalization of financial services in most countries, both in law and in commercial practice, has increasingly broken down, allowing firms to diversify across financial service sectors. Diversification across countries has been allowed increasingly, indeed often forced by the pace of technological change in financial markets. More generally a substantial amount of structural adjustment in both the commodity and service sectors has been necessary in the past two decades in response to such technological change, economic slowdown, the increasing competitiveness of some newly industrialized countries and for other reasons. The MNE has been seen as partly the carrier of such changes and partly an ally in responding to such changes.

In managing the decline of older sectors and attempting to capture nationally some of the newer ones, governments have utilized a wide array of selective trade and investment policies which will be examined below. For the moment, it can be noted that studies of the ways in which MNEs have responded to such changes have concerned governments but also led them to try to work with MNEs, both domestic and foreign. No government likes to see plant closures and especially loss of higher-skill facilities as part of a globalization process in part beyond its control. All will go to great lengths to capture a share of these newer or restructured industries in particular. Yet the more favourable attitude to MNEs, including those controlled abroad, may have something to do also with the evidence that such firms can assist structural change. Some, at least, of the detailed studies of MNE performance in Part II point in this direction. One can note, for example, the conclusion of an OECD study after reviewing the evidence for a number of countries, to the effect that plant closure and employment data do not in general show much difference for MNEs and domestic enterprises in their responses to structural changes. If anything, the MNE record in employment is somewhat better than that for domestic enterprises, and MNEs have sometimes shown more capacity to anticipate changes before problems become serious. The study goes on to note some areas where performance may differ, and to note also that both organized labour and governments are likely to want a say in the outcomes (OECD, 1985c, 8, 41–2, Annex I and II).

Other reasons can also be suggested for more liberal approaches to FDI. Many host countries found themselves both home and host to MNEs. Such firms not only came from more countries, but appeared to be more flexible in the organizational forms used to exploit their knowledge. Pressure from other countries and from international agencies may have led some countries to speed up modifications in restrictions – US government pressure on Japan and other countries through its Trade Acts is one example. Finally, as argued in Chapter 11, the restrictions on FDI had been difficult to implement in practice and, by the early 1980s, had become highly porous.

Before turning to the new policies, it is useful to look briefly at MNE responses to this new environment. Both increased internationalization and increased globalization have occurred. Many more countries have MNEs, they have become highly significant in a variety of service sectors, and small as well as large firms are now well represented. Moreover more firms are following global competitive strategies for at least a significant range of their outputs. Indeed one of the reasons suggested for the heavy investment in the United States by European and other firms has been an attempt to catch up with US competitors which earlier had increased their global market shares (for example, Caves and Mehra, 1986, 73).

A second reaction by MNEs has been to try to reduce the uncertainty involved in the kind of world noted, where several of the major environmental changes have increased it. There are many ways for an MNE to manage uncertainty, ranging from the choice of a particular global competitive strategy to the hedging of exchange rate risk. From the point of view of national policies, three outcomes related to attempts to reduce uncertainty can be noted. First, FDI has become heavily concentrated in a relatively small range of countries – especially in the United States among the developed countries, and the newly-industrializing countries among the developing countries. Second, while data here are inadequate, there is some evidence that mergers and acquisitions have played a larger role in foreign entry, at least in the major target for foreign investors, the United States, and perhaps in some other markets. In terms of *numbers*, for example, newly-formed subsidiaries were 44 per cent of all subsidiaries formed by non-US-based parent systems during 1946–58. They fell for each subsequent three-year period to a figure of only 30 per cent by 1968–70. In the case of US-based parent systems the comparable percentages were 55 per cent in 1946–58, and 38 per cent in 1965–7 (Vaupel and Curhan, 1973, 347–8). In 1980–88 acquisitions averaged 80 per cent of the *value* of inward FDI to the United States (Graham and Krugman, 1989, 19). Such mergers and acquisitions have speeded up for a variety of reasons, including a reduction in uncertainty when compared with a greenfields investment (Caves, 1982, 82). Finally there is more cooperation between firms in licensing, joint ventures, research consortia, management contracts, international subcontracting, strategic alliances and other organizational forms. Again the reasons are mixed, but government policy preferences, the desire to secure access to the technology of others, and the reduction of risk have all been factors.[3]

What emerged from Part II was a clear trend to liberalize many policies which affected MNEs, directly or indirectly. Deregulation and privatization together have opened up a number of sectors for private investors, including foreign-owned firms. Most of the developed countries which had establishment review have substantially eased the disincentive aspects or discarded systematic review in favour of notification with occasional challenges. Exchange control has largely faded out. The picture on other aspects of national treatment is not clear-cut, both because such policies tend to be hard to define and because some types of selective industrial support have increased. Finally there has been an increase in some types of fiscal and other incentives designed to attract MNEs, to increase local content or to affect MNE activities in other ways. This is particularly the case if one considers both factor protection and commodity protection, with the latter encompassing a variety of tariff and especially non-tariff barriers, including more active use of countervail and anti-dumping practices (Guisinger *et al.*, 1985, 9).[4]

The overall trend in the first half of the 1980s can be summarized by noting the degree of restrictiveness of policy shown in Table 12.1. Both the arithmetic mean and standard deviation fell from 1981 to 1985, although the range did not change much. Partial information for the last half of the 1980s suggests that this tendency towards less restrictive policies continued.

Some convergence of national policies on MNEs is evident, especially on the inward side.[5] It is important to note that this convergence is basically towards domestic industrial policies on trade and investment designed to attract and steer investment, on the one hand, and to develop domestically controlled MNEs on the other. Many more countries are now involved as both home and host countries on a significant scale. That phenomenon alone over longer periods would lead both to more convergence of different countries' policies and to a tendency to merge domestic policy with that on MNEs – that is, to try to reach all international firms, wherever owned. In addition, for reasons which are easily explained within the set of policy determinants noted in Chapter 2, the major emphasis in both old and new policies has been on regulatory and discretionary approaches. The old policies tended to be restrictive on the inward side, but also offered incentives to get steering effects, while on the outward side they were exchange control-oriented or non-existent. The new policies rely more heavily on the steering effects of selective incentives, often backed up by various forms of non-tariff barriers, while also selectively promoting domestic MNEs as well as exports. A regional and, at times, global strategy of production by MNEs is being gradually met by a regional and, at times, global strategy of *national* policies on trade and investment. We turn now to look at these new policies in more detail.

Table 12.1 Changes in degree of restrictiveness of policy, 1981–5

	1981				*1985*			
	ABCD	*ABC*	*BC*	*BCD*	*ABCD*	*ABC*	*BC*	*BCD*
Arithmetic mean	2.22	2.59	2.05	1.67	1.87	2.25	1.80	1.42
Standard deviation	1.88	1.80	1.53	1.62	1.61	1.55	1.29	1.38
Minimum	-0.40	0.00	0.00	-0.50	-0.51	0.00	0.00	-0.51
Maximum	5.20	5.20	4.00	4.00	4.52	5.20	4.00	3.32

Source: Derived from Table 10.3.

THE NEW POLICIES

The new policies can be discussed under three headings – incentives (including those for research), trade and multinationals. In the 1980s there have been attempts to integrate these and some other policies in order to increase the domestic capacity for successful innovation, particularly in newer industrial sectors.[6] While a case can be made that there has been reduced selectivity and increased liberalization for some aspects of each of these policies, a case can also be made for exactly the opposite tendencies.

Fiscal Incentives

Fiscal incentives to investment changed in the 1980s. A study by the OECD (1989b, ch. 1) noted that there is now more reliance on promoting structural adjustment and on enhancing some newer industries, as against the defensive support for declining sectors earlier in the decade. The administrative framework has been simplified and, in some cases, general tax reductions have been enacted in place of incentive programmes. Yet some things have not changed. Such support has always been conditional on economic performance in some degree, broadly so where it was given automatically in response to general criteria, quite specifically so where the support involved a high degree of discretion on the part of the authorities. Almost all governments will claim that almost all of the incentives are given to firms regardless of the nationality of the ownership of the firm (see, for example, OECD 1983, 16–17; 1989b, 26). Some doubts were expressed about such claims in the preceding chapter. Not only is the scope for discretion large but incentives are frequently integrated with the screening policy on FDI in order to achieve particular objectives. Governments are sensitive to the fact that MNE strategies may differ among themselves and from those of local firms, and they react accordingly in the way they offer incentives (see Guisinger *et al.*, 1985 for evidence on these points). In the case of restricted sectors and even key firms which are partially or wholly protected from foreign control, governments have supplied fiscal incentives for many years which were not available to foreign-controlled firms. In some entire countries such as Belgium and Ireland the major emphasis in incentive programmes has been for long periods on MNE investment, as noted in some detail in Chapter 8.

Bond and Guisinger (1985) have argued that reductions in tariff protection can be offset by increases in factor-based incentives, such as capital grants or tax holidays, so as to maintain the same effective rate of protection to an industry. They note that such incentives can be directed more narrowly by sectors or by ownership of the firm, and the level can be changed more easily, than is the case for tariffs. Moreover factor-based incentives can be used to promote net exports in circumstances where treaties or other constraints inhibit taxes and subsidies closely related to foreign trade. What needs to be emphasized is that the performance conditions associated with fiscal incentives are often similar in nature to those required by foreign investment screening mechanisms – for example, export- or import-substitution effects, employment guarantees and R&D increases. The effects on welfare are not necessarily the same, however, given the budgetary aspect and the way such incentives affect prices and output.

It is difficult to find comparative measures of the extent and the changes over time of the various types of fiscal incentives for non-agricultural production. A number of measures suggest that they are important and some indicate a significant growth over time. Table 12.2 shows subsidies (excluding tax concessions) for seven major economies as a percentage of gross domestic product from 1952 to 1985. The measures show a rising trend over time for all countries except the United Kingdom, even if one stops before the recession of the early 1980s. Also Winters (1988, 1485) quotes other studies suggesting West German subsidies of over DM 1 billion to each of nuclear fuels and chemicals, steel, mechanical engineering and electrical engineering industries; subsidies in France (including EC disbursements) of 6 per cent of value added in industry in 1981; and national subsidies of between 2 per cent and 15 per cent of industrial output in other member states in 1981. In countries such as the United States the federal government's contribution to industrial subsidies through the defence budget is well known. What has also become evident since the 1970s is the very extensive role of state governments in subsidizing mobile investments (Waldmann, 1980).

Studies also suggest that many of the fiscal incentives noted above have increasingly been sectoral and oriented especially to high-technology uses. This includes the application of advanced technologies to older industries, but the emphasis has been shifting particularly to sectoral policies for newer industries (OECD, 1989b, 33–5). Such policies are hardly new. Concern in the 1960s with gaps in technology internationally led to intervention in support of domestic firms in many countries. What is more evident in the 1980s is an attempt to integrate fiscal incentives for research-intensive sectors with policy on trade, mergers and other areas so as to develop their own MNEs and to support the underlying innovations. This set of policies in turn reflects a desire to structure industry and employment more towards knowledge-intensive sectors combined with a view that domestically owned MNEs are more likely to preserve such sectors, at least for a time. There is evidence to suggest that domestic MNEs are more research-intensive in the home market than are foreign-owned subsidiaries, which are in turn more R&D-intensive than national firms. There is also evidence to suggest that these differences decrease with time, as MNEs spread some research more evenly to take advantage of favourable research settings or to secure access to other firm's research.[7]

Trade Policy

Such subsidies and other fiscal incentives are only one part of the policies directed to securing or influencing local production, whether by foreign or domestic firms. Extensive factor protection has been accompanied by innovations in and more intensive use of commodity protection. Several types of commodity protection have been developed very extensively in the 1980s, at the same time that tariffs have declined. For example, from July 1980 to June 1988 a total of 1174 anti-dumping cases and 452 countervail cases were initiated under the GATT codes on these instruments (Anderson and Rugman, 1990, 5–10). Fully 57 per cent of the former and 31 per cent of the

Table 12.2 Subsidies as percentage of GDP

Country[1,2]	*1952*	*1956*	*1960*	*1964*	*1968*	*1972*	*1976*	*1980*	*1982*	*1983*	*1984*	*1985*
Italy	0.89	1.30	1.51	1.23	1.67	2.29	2.60	3.02	3.69	3.33	3.49	3.43
France	1.71	2.71	1.62	2.03	2.62	1.99	2.68	2.51	2.71	2.80	3.00	3.01
Canada	0.41	0.39	0.81	0.85	0.87	0.83	1.87	2.68	2.50	2.49	2.80	2.48
United Kingdom	2.68	1.76	1.93	1.56	2.06	1.82	2.72	2.50	2.15	2.13	2.44	2.22
Germany, Fed. Rep. of	0.65	0.20	0.79	0.99	1.44	1.48	1.97	2.06	1.84	1.90	2.07	2.01
Japan	0.79	0.26	0.34	0.65	1.11	1.12	1.31	1.50	1.40	1.42	1.28	1.15
United States	0.11	0.20	0.25	0.44	0.50	0.59	0.33	0.40	0.49	0.66	0.61	0.58

Notes:
1. Countries listed in order of amount of subsidies as a percentage of GDP in 1985.
2. The data do not include subsidies such as tax concessions. In Germany total tax concessions to enterprises averaged about 1.8 per cent of GDP a year in 1975–85, while in the United States federal tax concessions to industry were about 1.5 per cent of GDP a year during 1975–87; similar data are not available for other countries.

Source: Kelly *et al.*, (1988) Issues and Developments in International Trade Policy, IMF Occasional Paper 63, December, Table A11.

latter led to some form of restriction of trade. Virtually all of the anti-dumping cases were initiated by four countries or regions, namely the United States (30 per cent of the cases), Australia (27 per cent), Canada (22 per cent) and the EC (19 per cent). Such cases are initiated by the European Community rather than by member countries. Fully 58 per cent of countervail cases have been initiated by the United States. This figure rises to 92 per cent if one eliminates the 31 per cent of the cases initiated by Chile, which abandoned all but one of them. By contrast, before the GATT codes were adopted in 1980, the United States initiated only 11 countervail cases in 1970–74 and 104 in 1975–9 (Nam, 1987, Table 2). The relative ease with which private parties can begin the process of administrative review of particular imports under current US trade law has been an important factor in the considerable expansion of US countervail cases during the 1980s (Rugman and Anderson, 1987).

The close relationship between trade policy and MNEs can be underlined by noting that a substantial part of world trade is undertaken by the MNEs, much of it being intra-firm.[8] As a particular example, it is of interest to note the ways in which the EC and member countries have reacted to imports and investment from Japan and several other countries in South East Asia. In the absence of Community-wide rules on local content, or because of rights antedating the Treaty of Rome, EC member states set very different import quotas and local content rules for some firms from outside the Community. Differences of view on these matters have threatened at times to lead to intra-EC protection on a significant scale. EC anti-dumping duties have been applied to a range of consumer electronic goods and office equipment imported from South East Asia. The efforts by such producers to avoid such duties by setting up European assembly operations led in 1987 to an EC regulation on such 'screwdriver' plants. In effect anti-dumping continued to apply until at least 40 per cent of the parts were from countries other than the home country. An attempt to import photocopiers from Japanese plants in the United States was dubbed by the EC as an import from Japan. The 1987 regulation has been appealed by Japan to the GATT.

It may be noted that problems have arisen also in the differing domestic content regulations of EC countries with respect to Japanese motor car plants, with consequent threats to ban intra-EC trade. Such intra-EC barriers could not be enforced with the ending of border regulations in 1992. The European Commission proposed in 1989 that quotas and local content regulations be replaced by voluntary export restraints on car exports from Japan to Europe, restraints which would include Japanese-owned factories in the EC. In effect Japan's market share of the EC would be allowed to rise through the 1990s on a controlled basis, notably in Italy, Spain and France, where pre-Treaty restrictions are in effect (*The Economist*, 9 September 1989, 82–5; 1 December 1989, 15).

Many of the anti-dumping and countervail measures have been directed at imports into older industries undergoing major structural change, such as iron and steel and textiles, but a significant proportion of the anti-dumping cases in both the United States and the EC have been in chemicals, metals manufactures, and electrical and non-electrical machinery, which are among the most research-intensive industries (Messerlin, 1989, 94–6).

A further example of the new trade and investment policies is the development of reciprocity as a unilateral and often protectionist device. The meaning of reciprocity in trade policy has changed substantially. As a central concept of the GATT it meant the pairing of mutual concessions which were then generalized to all members; in effect it was used synonymously with unconditional most-favoured nation treatment. It has now often come to mean that imports and foreign-controlled firms will be given the same treatment domestically as your exports and multinationals receive in the originating country. Reciprocity in this latter sense has been used by many countries for some time as evident in the many sectors such as banking where entry to a country was partly dependent on reciprocal access to the home country. In the country studies the US use of this technique was highlighted since it has been used aggressively and broadly in recent years. The 1974 Trade Act gave the President the power to seek 'substantially equivalent competitive opportunities' on a sector-by-sector or product-by-product basis, failing which the President could take unilateral action to restore such equivalence. Later trade acts broadened this power to include investment opportunities and to address structural impediments in the countries involved which could hamper trade and investment.

It is important to note that reciprocity in the unilateral sense usually addresses only situations where the United States believes that foreign impediments exceed those in the United States, rather than the reverse cases.[9] If both possibilities were addressed, some net impediment would be the target – for example, a net subsidy for import countervail purposes after taking account of the subsidies on the production in the United States. But the main point is the problems raised by unilateral reciprocity for the multilateral trading system developed in good part as a result of US leadership, and still heavily dependent on that leadership. Bhagwati (1990, 1312–16) notes that the policy of aggressive and discriminatory unilateralism is clearly in violation of the GATT obligation on most-favoured nation treatment. When exercised by a major power it can lead those acceding to its demands to divert trade from other countries. Bhagwati examines but largely discounts the rationale that such policies exist for benign reasons, such as forcing adherence to agreed concessions. Such unilateral extraction of concessions by the major power may, on the contrary, cast doubt on the fairness of the entire trade process. The other trade policies noted above have raised similar problems, as will be evident below when we explore the way trade and investment policy have been combined with industrial policy to give new arguments for selective protection.

Multinationals and Strategic Trade and Investment Policies

Much of the factor protection and commodity protection now used is directly aimed at export promotion and the creation or encouragement of domestic MNEs. Strategic MNE promotion has had a considerably history in Europe and elsewhere. What has changed is the context, with internationalization and globalization pressures forcing governments and firms to be more aware of trade and investment pressures and of opportunities on both outward and inward sides. Where global competition is involved, actually or potentially, the efficiency problems of concentrating simply on import substitution are many, even for a large domestic market.[10] That is particularly likely to be the case when the large market is a set of independent countries which realize only to an imperfect degree the elements of an economic union. In what follows, therefore, it will be assumed not only that strategic export and domestic MNE promotion is the aim, but also that policies promoting import substitution and inward FDI often have an objective of at least regional, if not international, export promotion.

Modifications of traditional trade theory have led to new arguments for protection in recent years. The assumption of imperfect competition and of economies of scale have led to the proposal that governments can use subsidies to capture an export market for their producers and thereby take a larger portion of the rents associated with imperfect competition. Activist trade policies are also advocated in the case of external economies; that is, where technological or other spillovers to the rest of the economy are used to justify protection or export subsidies to a particular sector. Brander and Spencer pioneered systematic models spelling out the circumstances in which rent shifting between countries could be promoted by trade policy under duopoly situations.[11] It is critical in such cases that the government understand the structure of the industry and make a credible commitment by way of export subsidy, so that the domestic duopolist plays its leadership role in competition with the foreign duopolist. Brander and Spencer consider also the case where, rather than shifting profits between the duopolists, joint optimization through export taxes increases even further the total profit taken from the export market, at the expense of a third country. Profit shifting is critical also to Krugman's (1984) restatement of the case for infant-industry protection, given international duopoly and economies of scale. Protecting the home market reduces the marginal cost of the domestic firm and raises that of the foreign firm. The domestic firm will then move to expand its sales in unprotected markets while the foreign firm's changed cost situation leads to the opposite effect. Once again, government intervention induces under duopoly an expansion in profitable exports of the domestic firm at the expense of the foreign firm.

Subsequent analysis has severely qualified the case for using such ideas as the basis for trade policy. Eaton and Grossman (1986) have shown that the desirable policy varies with the nature of oligopolistic competition involved: an export subsidy is the appropriate instrument for profit shifting, for example, if each duopolist assumes that the other's output does not change as its output changes, but an export tax becomes appropriate if each conjectures that the other's price does not change. Dixit and Grossman (1986) noted that the general equilibrium effects could destroy the conclusions which might be valid in a partial equilibrium framework. If the oligopolistic industries employ a common resource for which the supply is inelastic, such as highly-skilled technical personnel, policies encouraging expansion in one sector lead to contraction in others. Beyond the theoretical issues there are major problems of implementation – preventing other firms from entering the market given the excess profits earned, restricting the policy to the favoured one or few firms, discriminating against the foreign-owned firms already in the industry, collecting accurate information on the structure of the global industry from suppliers who have an interest in the outcome, possible intervention from other governments, the usual problems of measuring externalities, timely removal of the subsidy or tax, and so on. Both the critics and some of the pioneers of work in this area recognize that demonstrating that national welfare can be increased by profit shifting or externalities is one thing, devising and implementing appropriate policies is a much more imposing task.

What needs more emphasis in this debate is the ways in which foreign ownership of a country's industry, on the one hand, and the existence of its own MNEs, on the other, complicate the policy problem. Harris (1991) shows that the home government has no interest in subsidizing or taxing exports if the home exporter is fully foreign-owned and the government's objective is to capture rents. If the objective is to increase employment in an export sector which is imperfectly competitive, it may help to subsidize local firms regardless of ownership. If the product is not tradeable, rent shifting to a domestic firm or the government could be justified unless any cost differential in favour of the foreign firm is large.[12]

In the country studies we noted the complications faced by governments which attempted to develop a set of key firms or sectors at least partially limited to locally owned firms. Sometimes the objectives were to capture rents or developmental spinoffs (oil), sometimes to capture industries with economic or military externalities (computers), and sometimes to maintain sectors which were large employers or politically sensitive in other ways (motor cars). The results of these and similar efforts are difficult to measure, but our work and that of most observers suggest they were mixed at best.

Strategic trade and investment policy must also take account of the strategies of a country's own MNEs. Such firms will choose from among a range of ways for transferring their knowledge abroad, the choices depending, for example, on the appropriability of rents on firm-specific assets, the need to share risk while protecting the core business of the firm, the desire to secure access to the technology of competitors, and the need to cope with the preferences of host governments for non-equity forms of investment (see, for example, Bertin 1987). The possible range of modes of transfer of technology is quite wide, including not only exports and fully-owned subsidiaries but various types of cooperative arrangements, as noted earlier. Home governments may well have preferences among these, probably beginning with exports or some combination of exports and domestic MNEs. We noted earlier that in the 1960s and 1970s no government tried systematically to review outward FDI for the impact on national welfare, in part because of the inability to determine when an investment abroad was necessary in order to retain a given market for exports. The information issue becomes more complex when different modes of investing abroad are introduced. In sum, governments must contend not only with all of the implementation problems of strategic trade policy described above, but also with assessing the information supplied by its domestic firms on the best methods for exploiting its products abroad.

All of this is with regard to new investment abroad through MNEs or otherwise. The situation becomes even more complex for home governments when they are dealing with MNEs already established abroad, which must then take some account of the private and public pressures of the host country environments. One particularly difficult aspect of this is the role played by key or strategic firms which have a degree of public ownership or substantial subsidy and which become multinational. They may then run into difficulties at both ends – from home country governments which may prefer to capture any externalities at home rather than see these go abroad, for example, and host country governments suspicious of subsidized investments and of the possible interference of home governments. The fine-tuning required for strategic trade and investment policy may have difficulties coping with both firms and host country governments in such circumstances.

The analysis in Part II on country experience with outward FDI helps to clarify some of these points. Attempts by EC countries and others to develop national champions in competition with foreign MNEs meant matching or exceeding the very intangible assets which led the latter to predominate in the first place. Host governments often bargained with foreign MNEs in order to leave room for their own MNEs, whether independently or in cooperative modes of activity. The characteristics of some of the high-technology firms involved – technology intensity, product differentiation, significant international exchange – are among those which are likely to make bargaining more difficult. Once the country's MNE was established abroad, trying to influence its activities so as to benefit the home country raised new issues. Such countries may prefer exports and cooperative modes such as licences to the subsidiary form in the belief that it is easier to capture taxes and spillover benefits. If exports and FDI abroad are complements, there may be less to worry about. They may be substitutes to a degree, however, particularly for final products, and judgements about this require much information which is likely to come in part from the firm.

All of this is likely to make the screening of outward FDI even more difficult than that on the inward side. How the developed countries have approached policy on the outward side in the past can be recalled briefly. Efforts have been made in many countries through exchange control devices to improve their balance of payments, efforts which were largely abandoned in the 1980s, if not earlier. In any case, apart from exchange control considerations, no developed country inaugurated a system of review on the outward side comparable with the review mechanisms on the inward, despite many concerns and investigations in the 1970s on the domestic impact of such outward investment. Firms in countries where unions have some input into management decisions have occasionally experienced some pressure to reduce or postpone outward FDI or the expansion of subsidiaries abroad. Particular issues have attracted attention as home governments tried to secure benefits in particular areas (taxation) or to enforce security issues (export controls). Sweden in particular came close to outward review but abandoned that effort in the early 1980s. Japan also went well beyond policy for balance of payments reasons in order to attempt to integrate outward FDI with industrial policy more generally. In most cases, however, such efforts have been overwhelmed by policies designed to protect and promote domestic MNEs, most notably in the major home countries.

Trends towards globalization and privatization in the 1980s increased the problems of monitoring outward FDI. Nevertheless it is clear that countries continue to place a high value on domestic ownership, although the tactics for achieving this have changed. A more selective sectoral approach is likely to be adopted, including that involved in developing domestic MNEs with precisely directed protection and subsidy measures. Techniques such as the golden share, while often applied generally, help control the foreign ownership aspects as well.

The above discussion highlights once again an issue noted in Chapter 11 and several country studies, namely the existence of a set of *implicit* cross-border 'restrictions' on mergers and acquisitions. Many of these restrictions may reflect differences in the ways firms and governments organize or regulate economic activity rather than simply ways of keeping out foreign firms. Yet their uneven development by country had led to major policy questions by the late 1980s. Four points might be noted. First, the measurement and analysis of cross-border mergers have lagged considerably behind those on FDI, although the former probably now forms the major component of the latter. There is little agreement on the impact of such cross-border mergers. Some writers emphasize improvements in the allocation of resources, for example, while others point to monopolization issues or differential gains for various interests associated with the firms involved. Much more work remains to be done on the measurement of such effects. Second, it is the differences in country situations which give rise to the difficulties firms encounter – differences in private concentration of control, state ownership and merger law, for example. However it is not self-evident just how far countries should go in tackling these differences by demanding reciprocity of treatment. To rely entirely on this approach would probably mean that the situation in the largest market would tend to become the standard, whatever its justification on other grounds. More transparent national policies and more effective enforcement, along with national treatment, could be part of the solution to such problems.

Third, a number of these issues are already being dealt with unilaterally or regionally, but not as yet in broader groupings such as the GATT. We noted in Chapter 9 that the United States had used section 301 of the Trade Act to engage Japan in negotiations on 'structural impediments' to trade and investment. The new competition law which came into effect in 1990 allows the European Commission to deal with the larger mergers and acquisitions. Fourth, the issue of state-owned firms engaging in cross–border mergers has raised many awkward questions – for example, concerns about subsidized competition, the influence of their home governments and the 'renationalization' of domestic firms which are being privatized. For example, Investment Canada has given very close scrutiny and required detailed commitments before allowing some of the acquisitions by state-owned firms, and the Committee on Foreign Investment in the United States also gives close attention to such cases. Finally, where review no longer exists, governments may try to invoke other instruments, particularly competition policy, to deal with a number of these issues. For example, in 1990 the UK government referred several proposed acquisitions involving mainly French state-owned firms to the Monopolies and Mergers Commission. This was partly on the grounds that they were backed by government finance, could not themselves be acquired and hence could limit competition. Problems of this kind are likely to be exacerbated as both globalization of firms and strategic policy intervention by governments increase.

STRATEGIC INDUSTRIAL POLICY APPROACHES

Strategic industrial policy approaches are already popular, albeit not in the sophisticated way their proponents would prefer. That such approaches are popular is hardly surprising, given the possibility in some sectors of significant national economic and non-economic gains and the attractiveness of sectoral support policies to many of the private and bureaucratic interest groups involved. In this section we note some of the MNE policy issues involved for the countries or groups in this study.

The attempt to reduce further or to eliminate by 1992 the remaining barriers to goods, services and factors in the EC has already led to some restructuring of European industry. The drive for greater internal integration has also raised some familiar issues on the relations of the EC with other countries and regions. The process is well understood from the earlier effects of the Treaty of Rome and other common market studies. Expansion of the EC market would lead to increases in both trade *and* cross-border mergers and investment within Europe, if the past is any guide (Franko, 1977; Robson 1984, 182). Internal market expansion and reorganization, even with external barriers given, would attract more FDI from outside the EC as foreign MNEs attempt to maintain global and regional market shares. In fact the number and value of cross-border mergers and acquisitions in the EC rose rapidly in the late 1980s. At the same time, non-EC based firms, particularly those from the United States and Japan, increased their direct investment in the EC, including their EC cross-border takeovers. Between 1981–3 and 1984–7, for example, five EC members raised their EC share of their total direct investment outflows from 22 per cent to 30 per cent, while Canada, Japan and the United States raised their comparable shares from 16 per cent to 35 per cent (United Nations, 1989; Gittelman, 1990).

One difference from the experience of the 1960s is the more varied sources of non-EC multinationals, with countries such as Japan and Sweden playing a significant role along with the United States. Another difference is that European governments are more determined than before, in part because of the existence now of an influential bureaucracy in Brussels, that European-based firms and especially European-owned MNEs will take more advantage of the potential gains from the enlarged market. The strategies of the EC firms will play the major role in meeting competition from non-EC multinationals, through mergers, rationalization of production, joint ventures, research consortia and similar methods. Nevertheless governments have been active in aiding such strategies in order to encourage the development of stronger EC-based firms in at least some high-technology sectors, capable of competing with non-EC multinationals. Dunning and Robson (1988b) have spelled out the rationale and methods for such government support and noted also that it is likely to involve more favourable treatment of EC than non-EC firms through subsidies and other measures.

The outcome of such efforts in the EC, as elsewhere, will not be known for some time. In terms of the present study, three issues are critical: the EC decision on national trade and investment subsidies, the position on non-EC firms, and the further development of competition policies. In terms of the first point, Winters (1988) argues that reduced border measures in a completed EC will be replaced by increased national subsidies unless the latter are also limited.[13] The studies by Guisinger *et al.* (1985) amply support this point. It was noted in the previous section that strategic trade promotion in several oligopolistic industries which are using a common inelastic resource could lead to expansion of some sectors at the expense of others. Governments must then be able to distinguish and subsidize firms with more than the average ability to capture rents. Winters shows that if the inelastic input is mobile across borders, as in an economic association, countries can still gain by attracting the inputs. Retaliation and subsidy wars are likely in such cases.

This issue extends well beyond the question of competition with non-EC multinationals. The larger question is how far national governments will be allowed to continue support for national firms after 1992, to that extent offsetting the concept of a single EC market. Such support can be offered in a variety of ways, such as public procurement and national or sectoral industrial standards, which are being limited after 1992. The great array of fiscal subsidies appears to be the major challenge facing the Community. A study for the EC for 1981–6, for example, showed average annual support at 85 billion écus ($78 billion) or 3 per cent of gross domestic product in the EC. About 12 per cent was for agriculture and 45 per cent for manufacturing. In 1986–8 the support averaged 82 billion écus. The EC Commission has power to curtail competition-distorting subsidies but until 1990 had used these only with regard to new aids and appears to lack the machinery to monitor this support effectively.[14]

Second, reduced border measures could lead to increased use of incentives to attract non-EC investments. Moreover the scope for restrictive policies on inward FDI is reduced, since intra-Community trade cannot be blocked as readily. The EC has had a chequered history on policy towards non-EC investment. There has been no uniform set of rules on rights of establishment from third countries, and non-EC firms established in a particular country are not necessarily treated as firms based in the Community when intra-EC investment occurs.

The position of France serves to illustrate the issues. France attempted in the early 1960s, unsuccessfully, to secure a common policy towards direct investment from outside the Community. In succeeding years, despite various compromises with her Community partners, French governments did not hesitate to review inward FDI from EC partners, even those headquartered in the EC, if their economic plans required this (Bertin, 1977, 94–5). In 1980 France agreed to prior notification rather than a general review in the case of acquisitions by firms headquartered in the EC, but with exceptions that appear to go beyond those allowed by EC rules on public order, health and security (OECD, 1982, 21). Other EC countries, when making rules on takeovers, have also distinguished between firms according to the ultimate location of the parent.

It is obviously going to be more difficult to carry out EC trade and investment initiatives if EC countries follow different policies towards inward FDI from outside the EC and even towards intra-EC investment. This issue has already risen sharply in the different views taken towards acceptable local content for Japanese direct investments. It has also arisen in terms of suggestions that subsidiaries of non-EC firms might not be accorded access to the enlarged market on the same terms as Community-owned firms, or perhaps only if reciprocity exists in the formers' home markets. Many countries still have such reciprocity provisions with regard to FDI in particular sectors, and the United States has incorporated such a provision into its trade legislation. Both the United States and the EC now have large hostage populations of each other's subsidiaries which could be used to counter one another's retaliatory moves.

Third, if the view expressed above, that FDI policies are tending to converge into domestic industrial policies, is correct then competition policy in general and merger and acquisition policies in particular become more important. Depending on how broadly the criteria are defined and now actively the policies are followed, some significant parts of what is done in an external review mechanism can be done by merger policies. Such policies apply to domestic or European firms as well as MNEs, so that two questions arise: just how far EC competition policy affects the market penetration strategies of non-EC investors, and how it reacts to the regrouping of EC firms in the face of such competition. What may be of equal importance, there are quite different notification and other requirements for mergers and acquisitions in EC member countries, and quite different constraints at the private level because of the degree to which stocks are closely held and cooperation exists among private interests. It would be difficult to envisage in West Germany and most other European countries the same degree of hostile takeover of publicly listed companies as one has witnessed in the United States in recent years. The process of regrouping firms is also more likely to be structured by government in the EC since state holdings are still common in some of the sectors involved.

Late in 1990 a new EC competition law came into effect on many of these issues (*The Economist*, 22 September 1990, 81). The European Commission was henceforth to rule on the larger mergers and acquisitions: that is, those with worldwide annual sales of more than 5 billion écus and EC sales for each party of 250 million écus or more. National governments can block decisions of the Commission only where 'public security, plurality of the media and prudential rules' are involved, unless the Commission agrees to further exceptions. There are at least two provisions which could cause difficulties with national governments. One is the need to consider 'technical and economic progress', not just competition effects, when evaluating a merger. The other is that a national competition authority can intervene if a dominant position in a 'distinct' market in its own territory is likely.

Various countries in the EC have had experience with sectoral or firm policies designed in part to meet competition from non-EC multinationals, but it is going to be difficult to secure the coordination necessary to secure overall economic gain from Community or country strategic trade and investment policy. In Part II, for example, we noted the attempts by countries such as France and the United Kingdom to establish nationally owned or controlled computer firms. In the late 1980s these efforts turned in various industries to establishing European-based firms, through subsidy and other public support for a variety of cooperative technology projects. As in the United States, a primary objective of such consortia is to cope with competition from Japanese firms.

Mytelka and Delapierre (1988) note that such consortia are partly a response to a number of developments in the 1970s and 1980s which have reduced the effectiveness of protective policies designed to give a particular firm either a leading position or a monopoly in a well-defined segment of the national market. One is the development of knowledge-based oligopolies attempting to develop a more flexible technological base which aims at product development for a variety of markets. Competition has also increased, given rising R&D costs and shortened product life cycles. Mytelka and Delapierre go on to note that, whatever governments may prefer, European firms had gone decidedly outward by the early 1980s in searching for alliances. For example, they note two studies showing that European firms in such industries as aerospace, information technology, biotechnology, materials science and pharmaceuticals had made most of their agreements with firms outside the EC, notably with US firms (p. 129).

Similar problems have appeared in computers, from the perspective of those interested in developing pan-European firms (*The Economist*, 6 October 1990, 16–79, 79). The four European firms supplying complete computer systems have less than 10 per cent of world markets and 25 per cent of European sales. Japan's Fujitsu has bought 80 per cent of the largest UK computer maker, ICL. France's Groupe Bull has accepted small ownership stakes from Japanese and US firms as well as significant commercial and technical ties. IBM has been admitted to the European consortium on information technology, ESPRIT.

In turning to consider these MNE issues as they relate to industrial policies in other countries, one should note briefly the 'intangible assets' some states possess in their capacity to cope with major economic changes. There is a considerable literature on this (for example, Olson, 1982; Katzenstein, 1985). The essence is the ability of governments, business organizations, trade unions and other institutions to cooperate in resolving what are often issues of income distribution. These issues arise from economic and other problems or opportunities, including those associated with MNEs and strategic trade and investment policies. Our analysis in Part II suggested that some states, such as Japan and several European countries, appear to have such intangible assets in abundance, while others do not.

The United States has the advantage that it can avoid some of the inter-country coordination problems noted above. Directed technological efforts are not unknown, notably in defence, with some significant (if costly) industrial spinoffs. Nevertheless recent history is not encouraging when one considers the requirements for a successful strategic trade and investment policy. If one excludes defence and some still regulated sectors, fiscal subsidies directed to manufacturing are mainly at the state level and thus risk the very dissipation that Winters has noted for the EC. The main developments in trade policy in recent years are hardly inspiring. Voluntary export restraints required of various trading partners have allowed substantial rents to be collected by such exporters while not stopping the flood of imports. The system of countervail and anti-dumping now in place appears, as in some other countries, to provide shelter without allowing the discrimination between sectors which a more strategic approach would require (Rugman and Verbeke, 1990, 74–7). The reciprocity provisions of trade acts in the 1980s involve a unilateral assertion of pressure on other countries, a policy which is fraught with political and, in some cases, economic costs that are difficult even for a hegemon to impose – much less a hegemon which is beginning to look like a troika.

Nowhere is the US incapacity to mount the elements of a strategic industrial policy more evident than with respect to policy on FDI. In the 1960s the United States did attempt to stem the effect on its balance of payments of the large outflow of FDI, a move which had some negative economic and political consequences, as noted in Chapter 9. It also tightened up on tax revenue losses in the 1970s and later. However for some time the United States experienced on the outward side a situation which some proponents of strategic industrial policy are likely to consider unsatisfactory in terms of national welfare. During 1957–77 the share of world exports of manufactures which was accounted for by US multinationals rose, while the share of US exports of manufactures fell sharply. This suggests that the overall technological and competitive capacity of US firms had not declined in this period, as distinct from the competitiveness of the US economy (Lipsey and Kravis, 1985). The point has been developed further by Julius (1990, ch. 4), who argues that comparative advantage as a territorial concept is quite different from firm or ownership-related competitiveness in a world of mobile factors. One outcome is to measure competitiveness not simply by territorial exports and imports but through FDI-related trade and production.

If one turns to the inward side it is equally clear that systematic review of FDI has not developed in the United States except for security reasons. This is the case despite the existence of a number of closed sectors, occasional pressure by the Committee on Foreign Investment in the United States and other agencies at the executive level, and the extension of trade reciprocity provisions to investment. It is true that congressional committees threaten from time to time to translate into stronger policies the concerns over growing penetration of foreign MNEs and the frustration over other countries' investment policies. To date the executive arm has largely resisted such policies, while putting pressure on international organizations and particular countries to limit restrictions on MNEs. It has allowed an unprecedented degree of merger activity to proceed throughout the 1980s without invoking a full review process.

Nevertheless, as indicated in Chapter 9, the 1980s did witness more emphasis on newer forms of protection and on bilateral policies, as well as some extension of inward FDI policies. It remains to be seen whether the United States, with its division of government powers and traditional opposition to direct state intervention, can develop the policy integration and selectivity needed for a strategic trade and investment approach on any scale. In particular, if it does undertake to review inward FDI in the next few years, it will be interesting to see if it can do a better job of such review in the more volatile context of the 1990s than more consensus-oriented and less legalistic developed countries did in the 1960s and 1970s.

Japan can be dealt with more briefly, if only because of doubts as to how much its considerable past achievement is relevant to today's efforts to develop industrial strategy. Our reading of past policies on inward FDI is that no other industrial country felt motivated or able to grow on the basis of technology import largely divorced from the foreign MNE.[15] At the same time it is not clear how far strategic trade and investment policy, as distinct from other policies and private-sector organization, was responsible for Japan's remarkable performance. For example, macro policies involving low real interest rates and high savings rates must have had a great deal to do with Japanese economic growth. Rather than give yet another series of anecdotes about MITI's earlier successes and failures, perhaps some of the current circumstances need to be noted. Japan stripped away most of her controls on inward FDI through the 1970s and early 1980s, with notification and occasional review taking the place of highly protective policies. But hostile takeover of larger firms remains almost impossible, and takeovers accepted by major owners of such firms would usually require agreement from other private and public interests. The penetration of foreign firms into an economy is a function of many variables, of course. Yet both theory and statistical evidence, as cited in Chapter 3, suggest that oligopolistic MNEs attempt to catch up on market shares by acquisitions and otherwise when competitive circumstances permit. The unusually small increase in foreign control of Japanese industry during the 1980s suggests that such oligopolistic catch-up is going to be less influential in the case of Japan.

On the other side, Japan is unlikely to maintain its remarkable capacity for consensus in the face of greatly enlarged FDI abroad, deregulation in some sectors and the adjustments imposed by such shocks as the appreciation of the yen and the fluctuations in financial markets. It certainly has not been able to count on global growth plus protection to carry it along as it did before (Yamamura, 1986). Nevertheless one might conjecture that social and political changes will come more slowly to Japan than they have elsewhere, so that experiments in industrial strategy will continue to have a higher pay-off than in most other industrial countries. That involves a judgement that the other countries will not put still more pressure on Japan or that Japan will continue to appease them with concessions which do not cripple her fundamental competitive strengths. Such judgements are risky, but no more so than those involved in predicting success from strategic policies in less homogenous states.

With respect to the remaining smaller countries in this study, which are not in the EC, three points are of interest here. First, strategic trade and investment policy would appear to be of less interest in principle. Such countries do not have the large domestic markets within which protection will allow growth of firms to an efficient scale in a range of industries. Nor are they as likely as the major economic powers to have a large enough part of the international market to secure oligopoly rents through government-supported strategic policies. There are some exceptions to these points. In some natural resources they may have a significant part of the regional supply or a resource which is of such quality as to yield rents or other national benefits for inward review. Oil in Norway in the 1970s was one example we noted. Some of the markets are clearly large enough to allow some firms to develop to an efficient scale, given sufficient protection by inward review, close private holdings of equity, and public subsidy or regulatory requirements in various forms. It is not difficult to cite examples from countries as different as Canada, Sweden and Switzerland in terms of the relations between business and governments.

The second and related point, however, is that the likelihood that many such firms will develop into successful MNEs depends in good part on the type of economic policies followed. It is quite striking that two of these smaller countries, Sweden and Switzerland, developed quite early a high degree of industrial specialization on a world level, particularly in terms of successful domestically controlled MNEs. The remaining smaller countries – Australia, Canada, New Zealand and Norway – developed a significant set of domestic MNEs only in the 1980s, although some, such as Canada, had some important MNEs before then. In all cases primary resources and the processing industries based on them played an important role among their MNEs.

There are obviously many roads to successful involvement in the global economy and important setbacks can occur along the way. Yet Sweden and Switzerland, different as they are in many other ways, had at least two things in common: an early focus on allowing and encouraging outward FDI, combined with relatively low import protection in many sectors. Australia, Canada and New Zealand each followed more protectionist policies, in Canada's case at least until the GATT reductions of the 1970s and in the other two countries until the 1980s. Some directed sectoral policies were pursued, but their efforts to build manufacturing industry on a broad front could not but hinder the development of domestic manufacturing MNEs.[16] The inward focus of much opinion in Canada so far as FDI is concerned was clearly evident in the debate on a Canada–United States free trade agreement in the late 1980s. Many Canadians appeared to be preoccupied with foreign control of Canadian industry, which had fallen significantly since 1970, and unwilling to consider the implications for policy of what had by then become a significant Canadian MNE presence in the United States especially (see, for example, Safarian, 1991b).

Third, it is also clear that all of these countries have moved in various ways to reduce their market uncertainty under the regional and global pressures of the 1980s. Canada moved to secure more certain access for her exports and FDI in the United States through a free trade agreement which came into effect at the beginning of 1988. The agreement provides that negotiations must take place on subsidies, countervail and anti-dumping measures within a given period. There is clearly some scope still for a Canadian or US government to engage in strategic trade or investment policies, given the lack of agreement on trade-distorting subsidies and, particularly on the Canadian side, the power retained to review larger acquisitions by foreign-owned firms. That scope will be reduced should agreement be reached on a subsidies and anti-dumping code. It might be still further reduced if decentralization of federal government powers in Canada were to increase the costs of reaching federal–provincial agreement on international industrial policies.[17]

Similar trends are evident in the other smaller countries. Australia and New Zealand have not only reduced protection generally and deregulated in some sectors, but reached a free trade agreement. The governments of Sweden and Switzerland have had to consider a closer association with the EC in view of the greater economic integration of the Community, and the former has decided to apply for membership. Their MNEs, particularly Sweden's, have already moved quickly to increase their stake inside the Community. All of this will reduce the scope for any strategic subsidies on the export side or restrictions, either formal or informal, on EC investment into those countries.

We shall return to some of the international issues raised by strategic trade and investment policies in the next and final chapter, after reviewing the origins and effectiveness of the policies covered in this study.

NOTES

1. An earlier version of this chapter appeared in the author's article, 'Firm and Government Strategies', in B. Bürgenmeier and J.L. Mucchielli (eds), (1991) *Multinationals and Europe 1992*, London and New York: Routledge.
2. Eden (1991) examines how changes in manufacturing technology and trade policies are affecting MNE strategies on organization and location.
3. The incidence of and reasons for these forms were noted in Chapter 3. See also Safarian (1991a).
4. The range of items covered here clearly includes both incentives and disincentives to FDI, depending on whether one is thinking of new firms or established ones, for example.
5. While noting some convergence on FDI policies, for reasons evident in Part II we would differ with the view of Graham and Krugman (1989, 107–8) to the effect that the industrial countries do not differ greatly among themselves and from the United States in their policies on FDI as such. One of the sources they cite to support their position argues that authorization procedures for FDI vary 'extensively' in OECD countries and that the overall position on FDI 'differs considerably' among countries (OECD, 1987b, 3 and 11). The authors do go on to point out the great differences in the investment incentives and associated performance requirements, a point included below in our discussion of new policies.
6. Ostry (1990, chs 2 and 3) develops the issues in trade and subsidy policies directed to MNEs, emphasizing innovation policies.
7. Pearce (1989) examines in detail the decentralization of R&D in MNEs, emphasizing the diversity of experience and the policy implications. See also Caves (1982, 198–200)

and Cantwell (1991). The Swedish experience is outlined in Vahlne (1983) and Part I of Hörnell and Vahlne (1986).

8. Hipple (1990, 500) indicates that 40 per cent of the US trade in manufactures and 35 per cent of total US trade in 1982 were accounted for by US multinationals plus foreign-based multinationals in the United States. Julius (1990, 74) estimates that 55 per cent of US exports and 52 per cent of imports were FDI-related in 1986, while the comparable figures for Japan in 1983 were 41 per cent and 57 per cent, respectively. US data in detail over time are available in UN (1991, 70).
9. In the structural impediments talks with Japan, however, such impediments in the United States also came under scrutiny.
10. This argument is weakened to the extent that new technologies reduce the scope for economies of scale in both the short and long run. The extent to which this will occur is not clear.
11. For a full statement of the origins, content and criticisms of these arguments, see Stegemann (1989). The following draws in part on this account. Brander and Spencer (1985) give a detailed account of their position, while Brander (1984) is a more accessible statement. Krugman (1984) states the case for import protection as a means of export promotion.
12. See Waverman (1991, 66–8) for some similar arguments.
13. For those who like analogies with Japan, it can be noted that subsidy competition directed at foreign MNEs was not a factor in that country and the major fiscal subsidies and other support given industry were often not available to foreign-owned firms – indeed the whole point was to create and encourage domestic firms in competition with the latter.
14. The above account of national subsidies in the EC is based on *The Economist*, 18 November 1989, 85 and 17 November 1990, 83–4.
15. A few smaller countries, such as Sweden, did manage to develop an impressive array of domestic MNEs while keeping foreign ownership of industry relatively low.
16. Rugman and Verbeke (1990, ch. 8) develop the idea that, given a small open economy and a propensity for direct government intervention, the appropriate industrial policy would include free trade with selective differentiation or 'niched' sectoral policy, among other proposals.
17. Canadian federalism is already sufficiently decentralized to allow strategic trade and investment policy to be considered by provincial governments, which are likely to run into at least as many problems as efforts by the federal government. The recommendations of the Ontario Premier's Council, for example, include fiscal incentives to medium-sized export-oriented, Ontario-controlled firms, and creation of a 'core-group of major technology-driven multinationals', headquartered in Ontario, by use of R&D incentives, the purchasing power of the government and its agencies, and financial support. See Ontario (1988, I, 11–34).

13. Conclusions

In this study the origins, nature and effectiveness of the policies regarding FDI and MNEs have been examined in some detail up to about the mid-1980s. We have also considered the so-called liberalization of policies thereafter. In this chapter the findings on origins and effectiveness are summarized. The study concludes with some observations on governments and multinationals in an increasingly internationalized setting.

SUMMARY OF POLICY EXPERIENCE

We began in Part I with a review of the determinants of public policy and of the strategies of different kinds of firms and governments. Our expectations from this review were summarized at the start of Chapter 5. At first sight the data and analysis presented in Parts II and III suggest that the major policies gave mixed results at best and were surprisingly weak in a number of critical aspects. Further reflection suggests that evaluation depends on the model of public policy one has in mind.

Consider, first, some of the findings on the review mechanisms. First, only Canada, France, and also Japan before 1980, placed major emphasis on performance requirements in the general review process, although most other countries did for some major or sensitive projects. Many such requirements were general and qualified undertakings, however, which were not monitored very effectively and may not have raised net costs for the firms. Second, these and other countries also shared an interest in securing domestic control in certain sectors, in part through the operation of review mechanisms. However only Japan's policies, before 1980 in particular, gave close attention to the many ways apart from ownership in which firms can exercise control. Third, all of the systems of review went through significant change prior to the 1980s, even apart from the natural resource sector, and almost all went through major change in the 1980s. Fourth, except for the early years of FDI in a country, the major expansion of the stock of direct investment occurs through growth of existing firms which reinvest retained earnings in their existing lines of business. Yet no country even monitored this, much less reviewed it, although parts of this growth were affected by review where subsequent acquisition was involved, where government policies favoured domestically owned competitors, and where exchange controls existed. Finally, investment incentives offset to some extent any negative effects which performance requirements had on FDI, although such incentives served steering and other purposes. In any case the effects on investment location of such incentives were far outweighed by market attractiveness, cost of operation and supply availability, and the policy climate for investment more generally.

To operate such a review successfully from the point of view of a bargaining model requires certain prior decisions by government. First, there has to be some idea of the priorities involved in the goals being pursued so that tradeoffs are possible where conflicts exist – for example, between requiring some domestic ownership and demanding significant export volume. We dealt with this issue at some length in the case of FIRA in Canada, which, in some respects, was the most fully defined of the review agencies. Second, there should be some way of determining the macroeconomic effects of such firm- or industry-level review. It is probably too much to expect a general equilibrium analysis, given the state of theory on the macroeconomic effects of microeconomic developments. Some type of social cost–benefit analysis of projects can allow consideration of some of these general effects. In our experience, such analyses were usually reserved for major resource projects and a few sensitive cases. One reason for this is the third requirement for a successful system – sufficient skilled personnel and time to analyse and, where desired, to negotiate. In fact the personnel directly involved were often quite few and large numbers of proposals of varying importance had to be dealt with in very short periods of time. A fourth requirement is that the objectives and procedures be defined in ways which minimize conflict with home countries who believe their interests are harmed by investment review. Agencies which are more explicit and more ambitious are likely to be the primary targets for protest and retaliation, but the others have not escaped attention, as the inclusion of trade-related investment measures in the Uruguay Round of the GATT suggests. A fifth requirement is for enough political support for review to ensure reasonably stable policies when governments change. Finally, close attention to agency design is needed so that departmental functions can be satisfied without crippling the agency, on the one hand, or giving an excessively restrictive or open impression of the government's stance, on the other. Even countries with a high level of administrative skills and with private markets which usually work have trouble implementing all or even much of this, as the country studies have spelled out.

Policies directed to securing domestic ownership have some advantages, such as ensuring that economic rents accrue to domestic owners and giving governments more leverage on firms. Just how significant the economic costs will be depends on what contribution MNEs may bring to the sector and how quickly and efficiently domestic enterprises can fill any such gap. Governments will also view some sectors, such as defence and some cultural industries, as involving objectives which are so critical that they are prepared to overlook any economic losses resulting from keeping out foreign firms and imports. In fact in most sectors such access was limited rather than prohibited, partly so as to minimize such losses.

Some important policy problems arise with such ownership approaches. First, the economic argument is similar to the infant industry argument, but the protection is for domestic ownership rather than for domestic production. The economic argument for such protection runs up against a whole set of problems in practice, as is evident from tariff history. Particularly in smaller economies, for example, there may be a lack of incentives to achieve efficient production and hence pressures to maintain protection indefinitely. Second, where a sector is reserved or MNEs are required to share ownership, large rents can be created for domestic owners. Governments can attempt to tax these rents from both sets of owners. Third, achieving ownership is not the same thing as achieving control. Where reliance on imports, techniques and markets continues, considerable dependence can result, even where equity is fully held locally. Finally, when firms in the restricted and subsidized sectors do go abroad, questions arise about subsidized exports and reciprocal access.

One must be careful in assessing the results of policies on ownership, given the very different kinds of sectors and firms involved, ranging from natural monopolies and state ownership in the period before and just after the Second World War to many policies in the natural resource and high-technology sector dating from the 1960s or 1970s. The policy outcomes can best be described as mixed. Natural resource rents and other gains were increased through trial and error. Royalties were increased and also supplemented with increased taxes, domestic private or public equity, and local sourcing and other developmental commitments. But rents may have been reflected in the prices charged domestic owners for shares (Australia in the 1970s) or dissipated by poor timing of policy (Canada in the early 1980s). The attempt to develop a major domestically owned presence in computers went awry in France and the United Kingdom, but succeeded in Japan. The idea of key firms or 'national champions' ran into many difficulties. Even the state-owned firms tended to develop strong private sector drives of their own, such as a desire to go multinational, and to become less responsive to national government directives. It is probably necessary to maintain a broad definition of key firms, as in the phrase 'public order and essential security interests', in order to deal with future contingencies. Yet such phrasing permits full play to a wide variety of interest groups, private and public, which are only too willing to secure the protection and subsidies involved.

Many MNEs were prepared to accommodate government preferences for other than fully-owned subsidiaries, and few appear to have actually divested from these countries because of discriminatory policies. Yet it was also clear that where core business and proprietary knowledge were involved the firms were unwilling to share ownership and especially control. Government screening authorities in countries such as France, Australia and Canada often showed some appreciation for and acceptance of these company strategies.

POLICY IN TERMS OF A BARGAINING MODEL

It was emphasized throughout Chapter 3 that the standard theory of MNEs regards them as overcoming market imperfections. It was also noted that some writers and governments have argued that MNEs add to or exploit such imperfections. Moreover the international distribution of any economic gains from MNE activities is a key issue for national governments. The effects of MNEs on the exercise of power by governments, and on group interests, are also likely to preoccupy national governments.

Economists have tended to argue that welfare concerns are best addressed by policies directed to the underlying causes of the discrepancy between private and social costs and benefits. Such policies may need to be at an international level when country policies conflict or where they would be ineffective in reaching MNEs. Competition policy and tax policy are cases in point. In addition economic theory has tended to favour a tax or a subsidy to correct for differences in output between what is considered socially desirable and what is forthcoming from private activity (see, for example, Casson, 1979, ch. 5). The policies discussed in this study are quite different from these types of actions, involving attempts to influence directly the behaviour of firms or to restrict their entry in various degrees. While tax and subsidy policies attempt to influence prices and hence the profits, production and other activities of firms, regulatory policies directly control such activities. This is true even of the many incentive policies, which carry specific activity commitments with them. In addition a tax–subsidy approach is often applied generally to all firms which meet given criteria, if only because they tend to be more transparent policies, while direct controls on the behaviour of firms can often be applied more selectively.

It is not difficult to note some advantages which a policy of direct controls might have over a tax–subsidy approach. It avoids windfall gains to some firms which would take the desired actions without such incentives. It also ensures specified outcomes in situations where such assurance is considered critical, as distinct from giving firms price incentives to move in desirable ways. Where discretionary policies are involved, governments can often discriminate between firms so as to maximize domestic rent capture or other objectives. Such opaque policies may also reduce the risk of foreign retaliation. Discretionary techniques may also make it more difficult, both at home and abroad, to assess the costs of such intervention.

The problem with such approaches is in part the monitoring costs involved in ensuring that the outcomes specified in direct controls are realized. More broadly, information costs are substantial when discriminating between different firms. Even if information is complete on given cases, optimization may not be the outcome as firms surmise from such decisions how policy will be made in the future. There is a strong case in such circumstances for a rules-oriented approach and one where the rules are known.[1]

In terms of policy on FDI, the literature on direct control of trade performance requirements suggests that improvements in domestic welfare are possible but difficult to achieve. Grossman (1981) has noted that the requirement that the final product include a given percentage of domestic value added or of components involves elements of a tariff on intermediate products and a subsidy to final goods producers. He also emphasized that the degree of protection is variable and difficult to predict, and can therefore lead to the opposite of what is intended. Davidson *et al.* (1985, 876–90) use a duopolistic model to examine the effects of local content rules and minimum export requirements designed to raise the production costs of foreign-owned firms and to increase the profits of locally owned firms. They conclude that world welfare falls as world output is reduced, and the home country's welfare also falls, since monopoly rents are shifted from its firms to locally owned firms. The host country's welfare also falls as consumer surplus is reduced more than monopoly rent is increased. These results also hold for oligopoly except that, in the case of the host country, welfare declines only if the sales by its firms are less than the sales by foreign-owned subsidiaries. It is important to add that minimum content legislation can increase domestic employment, provided that the content ratios do not rise above certain limits (ibid., pp. 888–9).

How well do the direct control policies discussed in Part II and this chapter fit the bargaining model developed in Chapter 4? It was suggested there that country strategies, to be effective, would vary with the country-specific assets which they could offer to MNEs, on the one hand, and the particular types of MNEs they were dealing with, on the other. Broadly the country assets can be categorized under market and supply characteristics and the organizational effectiveness of governments. Similarly firms (and, less convincingly, industries) have certain market, supply, and organizational characteristics.

There is certainly evidence from the country studies, as summarized at the beginning of this chapter, to indicate that the governments in this study took account of these determinants of bargaining power in devising policies on FDI. The fact that some exacted undertakings as the price of entry to the local market reflected in part their recognized right under international treaties to intervene at this point. It was also the point at which leverage over the firms was large. Moreover those with screens extended this power to mergers after establishment, despite some conflict with the principle of national treatment.

Where countries had to be careful was to recognize that their bargaining power varied with the marketing focus of the firm: that it was large if the firm aimed mainly to supply the local market and smaller once an export market and particularly a common market was involved. In the case of the last of these, for example, it is more difficult for a country to follow restrictive policies since the firms can locate in another part of the common market. Indeed such countries may have to compete with subsidies to attract investment since their use of import barriers is constrained. Some countries clearly kept such strategies in mind even though they were modified by other factors. France, for example, was the only country in the EC to have formal review of inward FDI beyond purely exchange control requirements, although the United Kingdom intermittently exercised some elements of a screen prior to 1979. Outside such trading areas, tariff and other forms of import protection were often sufficient to induce domestic production, the extent depending on the size and growth of the market. Exports of manufactures often required further support, however, such as a fiscal incentive, or a restructuring of the entire operation with government support if the country hoped to act as a major supplier of the product and to secure some research and other 'headquarters' functions.

Supply-side issues reinforced these findings. Most of the countries with a relatively high natural resource content in production had review of inward FDI, as well as some ownership restrictions in this sector. All countries had some policies favouring domestic firms in selected high-technology sectors, sometimes related to security interests. Most were also anxious to attract or retain research-intensive firms, as is evident from the benefits criteria used in screening, in the willingness to allow full foreign ownership of a firm where proprietary technology was involved, in the availability of special fiscal and other benefits for such firms, and in the restrictions designed to retain research facilities when such firms were acquired by non-residents.

Strategic concerns are also evident if one looks at policies restricting sectoral access by FDI. Few sectors were wholly closed, particularly in research-intensive manufacturing where substitution for any benefits of MNEs might be more difficult.

The most striking difference between countries was in the organizational capability to deliver an integrated and consistent set of policies on FDI. In part this difference was due to the inability or unwillingness to develop industrial policy in general, while attempting also to develop what is a subset of such policies, namely an industrial policy on FDI. The term 'industrial policy' can refer to policies available to all industries equally, such as measures to increase productivity, training and research. Here we use the term in a strategic sense for policies directed at and giving priority to certain sectors, firms or products. While many types of policies may be used to implement strategic industrial policy, those involving a high degree of administrative discretion are likely to be important.

The normative motives for sectoral policies can vary a good deal, ranging from a desire to keep domestic control of defence sectors or those involving high-technology rents or other positive externalities to efforts to preserve or adjust declining sectors. Along with the market and supply issues noted earlier, the traditions and institutions of a country appear to have a great deal to do with the effectiveness of sectoral policies. The size of the domestic economy has certainly been used effectively by countries such as Japan to bargain effectively with foreign MNEs, but small countries such as Sweden have also achieved a high degree of industrial performance for significant periods of time. Public ownership of a significant portion of the economy has given French governments some leverage in dealing with MNEs, yet Japan has dealt effectively with foreign MNEs and strategic industrial policy with very little public ownership of industry. The interventionist role of the Japanese government in helping to restructure industry contrasts with the more passive industrial policies of a country such as Switzerland.

What seems to matter for successful policy is not so much these particular national characteristics or methods but what Katzenstein (1985, 32) has described as 'the voluntary, cooperative regulation of conflicts over economic and social issues through highly structured and interpenetrating political relationships between business, trade unions and the state,' one result of which is 'low-voltage politics'.[2] Katzenstein applies this to the analysis of the success of several smaller European states but, as we have seen in Chapter 7, some variants of it can be applied to a larger and relatively homogenous state such as Japan. Such states would have less trouble in coping with the information and other transaction costs involved in satisfying the five conditions for a successful review mechanism, as outlined at the beginning of this section. What that suggests is that countries which lack such cohesiveness may have difficulty in mounting particular types of sectoral policy. One country's successful industrial strategy can be another country's recipe for failure, most particularly in the distributional adjustments which sectoral policies involve.

The country studies suggest that Japan clearly stands out from all of the others in its ability to deliver a consistent and integrated set of FDI policies as an aspect of industrial policy. It is the only country where entry was largely limited to licences and majority Japanese-controlled joint ventures. When liberalization began in 1967 it was done slowly and deliberately over a decade and a half, beginning with the stronger sectors. Some controls remained even after the 1980 law which codified the liberalization process: notification of FDI is in effect, with review possible though apparently infrequent; a number of restricted sectors remain; and review of technological borrowing is possible in larger contracts in some sectors. Most importantly, acquisitions by foreigners of the larger Japanese firms in particular remain almost impossible because of extensive cross-holdings and a continuing aversion to foreign control. Throughout the post-war period Japan has shown an ability both to pursue growth-oriented policies at a macro level, including quick adjustment to substantial international economic change, and to pinpoint growth sectors with considerable success.

France was less successful in delivering a cohesive and continuing industrial policy or a related set of FDI policies, but not for want of trying. Changes in the political complexion of government, unlike the situation in Japan, might be considered partly responsible for this instability. However one should note that changes in the way screening was implemented occurred under continuing governments, as did changes in some related sets of policies. Restrictive FDI policy was constrained also by France's presence in a common market.

The Labour government in the United Kingdom during 1964–70 took some strong initiatives to restructure industry, both overall and in sectors such as motor cars and computers, but hesitated to discriminate widely against FDI. The Labour government of 1974–9 had a much less interventionist stance. Both Labour and Conservative governments used screening on a very intermittent basis. While the inward screening process lost its base once exchange controls ended in 1979, performance requirements have been set on Japanese FDI in particular.

One can certainly point to a number of strong sectoral policies in these and other countries. The petroleum and gas sectors involved significant policy directed at FDI in both consuming and producing countries. High-technology sectors attracted attention, with policies both subsidizing FDI in some respects and regulating it in others. A whole range of declining sectors attracted support, regardless of ownership. Yet the experiments with strategic industrial policy and related aspects of FDI policy are neither notable nor notably consistent in many countries in this study. Some countries, such as Canada, can hardly be said to have had a strong and consistent set of industrial policies, in part because of the constraints imposed by a decentralized federal state, while undertaking relatively ambitious policies on inward FDI. The United States has been caught for 15 years in a struggle between elements in Congress which desire a more restrictive policy on inward FDI and on trade and administrations which tend to favour a more open position, while a broader debate continues on the extent to which a strategic industrial policy is either desirable or feasible in US circumstances. Belgium and Ireland consistently followed a policy of subsidizing inward FDI geared to exports in the EC in particular, but switched to a more selective approach in the late 1970s designed in part to favour newer or higher-technology sectors and to restructure older and often locally owned sectors. Sweden enjoyed considerable success for a time in developing her own MNEs and a high per capita income. Sharply differing views in the 1970s and later on industrial policy in general and policy on FDI in particular marred her success, as did some failures in macro policy.

Our reading of the evidence in Part II is that it has been generally difficult to develop a consistent policy on FDI within a consistent set of industrial policies. However this conclusion assumes that the main objective of policy was to set up a process whereby, in dealing with MNEs, national real income gains would be realized. An alternative explanation is that the policies were designed mainly to achieve other objectives of public policy. There is evidence in the country studies for this interpretation also.

A POLITICAL ECONOMY VIEW OF POLICY

In Chapter 2 it was suggested that the determinants of policy can be broadly subsumed under wealth increasing and distributing and power increasing and distributing. A bargaining power model directed to increasing national wealth and power can certainly be used to describe some of what was achieved, or at least attempted, with policies on FDI. Under optimum conditions in terms of information on the reactions of firms and other countries it is possible to increase real national wealth by securing more rents domestically and by improving the economic performance of firms. Both direct and indirect methods of influencing firms require information and both can, in principle, yield net national benefits. It is also possible to gear screening and incentive programmes in part towards regional or sectoral development. Finally it is possible by use of key sector policies and laws forbidding particular behaviour to deal with issues involving sovereignty or independence – reserving defence sectors or those related to national identity, countering extraterritorial extension of home country law and policy through the MNE, and similar measures. Table 10.2 indicates in summary form how the origins of host country review policies were affected by concerns about the proposed takeover of key firms in security-related areas and media and by home country policies, as well as by economic concerns.

Let us extend this analysis to include issues involving domestic power distribution and domestic wealth distribution, in each case leaving national power and wealth unchanged. Once again there is clear evidence in these studies of the role such determinants played in the origin and nature of the policies. The MNE attracted ideological criticism from parties of the left in particular, although some of them began to change their perspectives in the 1980s. Such firms did not escape the attention of parties on the right, however, partly because of the influence of those of their supporters who wished to protect domestic entrepreneurial capacity. The review process in most countries offered opportunities, in some cases explicitly, for competing domestic firms to benefit from the bidding by foreign firms. The resulting investment in rent-seeking activity could be nationally beneficial or not, depending on the assumptions made. There were possibilities for national gain where the bids induced from domestic firms by the review process led MNEs to raise the price paid or the undertakings given. There were possibilities for transfers from sellers to domestic buyers where the review process blocked out a foreign owner on non-economic grounds. And there were possibilities for bargains for domestic purchasers, cessation of activity by sellers, or extensive public subsidy when foreign ownership was prohibited or severely restricted in a sector deemed strategic. It is possible to cite examples of each of these from the country studies, but impossible to weigh them in the overall decision-making process.[3]

All of this points to a process where a balance is struck between the costs and benefits of policy on FDI as between the different policy objectives and interests, a balance which is adjusted as the underlying market and other determinants change.[4] The precise nature of the balance will depend on the influence of the different interests involved in policy making. Presumably the politician will ensure that electoral issues are kept clearly in mind. Bureaucratic and private interest groups which are well organized will not go unheard. However, as we have seen repeatedly, ideology in the sense of strongly held values, along with media exposure will ensure that the other factors involved in the increase or distribution of wealth and power are not forgotten.

If one accepts such a view of policy formation, implementation and change, some further clarification is possible of issues which were discussed earlier. First, it becomes clearer why direct intervention and discretionary policies of the kinds studied here may be preferred to generalized policies, tax subsidy approaches and clearly defined rules. Direct intervention carries a clearer message to voters that something is being done, when compared with policies expected to work indirectly through price and profit effects. At the same time, selective or discretionary applications of direct intervention allow more scope for balancing of costs and benefits to different interest groups, including the preferences of those politicians and civil servants who develop, apply and modify the policies. These and related points have been developed at some length in studies of regulation (for example, Trebilcock *et al.*, 1982, ch. 3).

Second, the need to balance costs and benefits among different groups and to deal with different perceptions of the effects of FDI helps explain the weaknesses of an explanatory model based on increasing national wealth and power. The political process will give some emphasis to the latter objectives because there is serious debate about them inside and outside government, but in practice it will yield less than optimal solutions in these respects precisely because the internal distribution of wealth and power is important and may dominate at critical points of decision. There is one view of this process of political conciliation which adheres to what might be called the placebo effect. It argues that policies appearing to restrict FDI and MNEs are put in place because there is a demand for them, but such policies are limited in application because those with public power or private influence are not seriously concerned about FDI or perhaps even concerned that strong FDI policies could ultimately damage their interests as well. One need not adopt such a view in order to acknowledge that a need to balance the different objectives and interests outlined above would yield policies which lacked clarity and consistency from any one perspective. Moreover the information and other transacting costs of a rational public choice optimizing model involving all of the policy determinants noted above are far more complex than a rational economic or power optimizing model.

We have cited various kinds of evidence for this broader model in Chapter 10, including a summary of our detailed country studies and some statistical tests. At various points in the country studies, for example, we cited the views of a range of interviewees who believed the birth and operation of review mechanisms and of some types of restricted sectors reflected just such balancing of welfare objectives and interest groups. In Norway, Canada and New Zealand, for example, a number of interviewees made the point that once the review was in place it was possible to take a more relaxed view of MNEs and to deal with specific issues in a pragmatic way – at least until some other major new question demanded political attention. One might even suggest that the apparently weak design and implementation of the review processes – the small size of staffs, lack of enforcement of undertakings, lack of applicability to the major on-going operations of MNEs – might reflect such a balancing of interests, although the information and other problems of more ambitious approaches also account for these apparent weaknesses. And one can cite a variety of other studies on FDI which emphasize the balancing principle. In his detailed study of Colombian policies toward FDI, for example, Lombard (1978) gives some support to the view that tough policies and language were combined with permissive screening in order to placate domestic opposition to FDI while continuing to secure it. Hedlund and Otterbeck (1977, 110–11) found evidence in their study of Swedish policy that senior public officials were the interviewees who saw the greatest need to regulate FDI but also intermediated between other groups by devising apparently restrictive policies which could be operated liberally.

We began this section with a model of policy determinants emphasizing national economic welfare and political independence, on the one hand, and internal distribution of rents and power, on the other. Implementing either of these approaches involves major information and other transaction costs, while realizing both increases such costs significantly. Yet both can find some support in what governments have been attempting to do regarding FDI and MNEs. And both complicate what governments, firms and others are attempting to do in reaching an accommodation among themselves and with each other in an increasingly international world.

NEW POLICIES AND NEW CHOICES?

Policies on MNEs have tended to converge into industrial policy more generally in the rapidly changing technological and globalizing world of the late 1980s and early 1990s. In one sense this can be described as liberalization, in that some restricted sectors have been deregulated and privatized and exchange controls and review mechanisms have been eased or ended. The new policies, however, continue to protect and promote national firms, but in more selective ways, as governments attempt to capture some of the newer technology-intensive sectors and to aid adjustment in the older ones. Fiscal incentives have not only grown but have been directed more narrowly by sector. They have been accompanied by newer forms of import protection, as reflected in the great expansion of measures involving countervail, anti-dumping, reciprocity and local content. Factor and commodity protection on the inward side have been accompanied by selective trade and investment promotion on the outward, often designed to develop domestically owned MNEs.

In many respects the new policies are an accentuation of trends which were evident in the decades before the 1980s. They pose issues which are also familiar from choices governments have had to make in much of the period since 1945. Those choices involve policies based on nationality of the firm, on the degree of selectivity and the degree of internationalism of policy. The issue of nationality has usually been put in terms of a choice between foreign or domestic ownership and control of industry. Various welfare conclusions are drawn, depending on what one thinks of the evidence on the economic and political consequences of each type of ownership. The issue was never posed in that way by those in home countries who were concerned about the effects of *domestic* MNEs on employment and other issues. It has become harder to pose such a choice in host countries which have increasingly become home countries also for MNEs. As globalization increases, moreover, the production, licensing and other decisions of firms which have no ownership affiliations abroad are seen as having similar impacts on interest groups.

We often found in the country studies that the alleged disadvantages of foreign-owned firms did not stand up to careful examination. Moreover the alleged advantages of domestic MNEs, while apparent relative to foreign-owned subsidiaries, looked less convincing in the longer term as domestic MNEs put more of their assets and sourcing abroad, even in the case of some headquarters functions, and home governments began to lose their leverage. Whatever one's position on this, it is difficult to see why the welfare effects for various interests are any less important simply because the source of the decision is a domestic firm, a domestic MNE or a foreign MNE. Substantial layoffs of workers who lack alternatives can hardly be dismissed because these derive from one source rather than another. If it is believed that one of these three types of firms generally tends more to a particular form of behaviour, the issue is capable of testing. Even then the question of dealing with particular cases arises, whatever the average differences between such firms suggest. One does not have to believe that nationality is of no significance to argue that similar consequences should be similarly treated.

If one decides to aim at consequences rather than ownership, there remains a second critical question. There is often a choice between general policy approaches, including those which improve private sector performance, and those favouring specific interventions in specific circumstances. The strategic trade and investment approach falls into the second group, in the sense of favouring direct intervention to support some types of domestically owned and domestically located firms operating at a global level. Many governments have converted their trade and investment policies to such efforts, encouraging mergers or research consortia to capture high technology sectors.

It is one thing to show that countries can benefit from selective intervention in particular cases, quite another to demonstrate that the outcomes will be favourable, given all of the implementation problems. The evidence from this study suggests that most governments have had great difficulty in surmounting the information problems on everything from firm reactions to appropriate timing. They have had even greater problems in reconciling the various objectives of policy and the group interests involved. All of this is with regard to policies on the inward side: none really attempted anything like review on the outward side, which is likely to be more difficult still. The capacity to organize such policies differed widely among the countries in this study, and does not appear to be a quality which is easily imitated in some of the more pluralist countries or in regional trading areas.

The third choice posed above is the degree of internationalism of policy. Many of the policies noted in this study, whether by home or host countries, influenced negatively other countries. The idea that the policies were intended to correct for negative effects of MNEs received short shrift from both sets of countries – whatever their validity. Few countries, if any, were prepared to accept unilateral decisions and policies on such matters of mutual interest. The effects in many cases were similar to trade distortion, but sometimes even more damaging; there is a contradiction, for example, in allowing a foreign firm to establish itself and expecting (or even enjoining) it to perform in a beneficial way, then handicapping it with special merger provisions and other forms of treatment not extended to domestically owned firms.

The new policies seem destined to repeat the errors of the old – to do considerable damage to the multilateral trading system while failing clearly to advance national welfare. They are causing more confrontation than the old policies because, being more narrowly directed, they are more likely to invite retaliation. Governments often appear to be doing two contradictory things: developing their own MNEs through subsidies, protected national markets, concentrated ownership and the like, while insisting they must have access to other countries' markets through acquisitions of firms and through trade. It is not difficult to see why other countries would counter subsidized trade and investment entry, either by blocking it or by offering equivalent subsidies to local groups. Nor is it difficult to envisage the damage to foreign trade and investment which such policies can bring – indeed have already brought – through a welter of new or extended trade and investment-distorting measures.

The usual method for dealing with such problems is through mutually restraining international agreements. In principle it is not difficult to see what would be involved in such agreements, apart from the fact that freeing trade helps complementary investments. Much of this has been under discussion in the Uruguay Round of the GATT: for example, establishment rights in the services sectors, rules on trade-related investment measures and intellectual property rights as they relate to high-technology and other trade, and a subsidies and countervail code. Other parts are evident in the OECD instruments requiring notification of, and at least a moratorium and consultation on, such matters as barriers to entry based on nationality, non-national treatment and conflicting governmental requirements. The Canada–USA Trade Agreement and the greater integration envisaged in the EC have tackled or are tackling such issues.

A few deserve to be highlighted because they will involve special problems. All such agreements involve security or other public interest provisions which call for sectoral exemptions. The international problem is in defining these so that they do not become a means of escaping the agreed constraints on other policies or sectors. There are also difficult national problems, as we saw in discussing US experience of how best to protect security, for example, while maintaining efficiency and technological dynamism. Dealing with these sets of issues will undoubtedly raise the problem of extraterritorial extension of law, or of conflicting requirements, since defence issues are often linked to these. Governments find it hard to yield on the sovereignty issues involved, even when their own MNEs' position abroad is greatly eroded in the process. This is the type of issue where the OECD process, as has already begun, may be better suited for initial consideration. The process of decision making should be eased by the changing attitudes to some of the formerly restricted sectors, as witnessed by deregulation and privatization in some areas. It should also be eased to the extent that there is agreement on the point made above, that nationality of ownership is not the key to economic performance.

A second complex issue is the different national approaches to mergers, acquisitions and shareholders' rights, given that these are deeply embedded in national institutions and traditions. It seems unlikely that these differences can be removed and, in some respects, this may not be desirable. While they do restrict the flow of capital, they may also impart more stability for company investment planning. What one can strive for is national treatment; that is, ensuring that exclusion on the basis of nationality is not involved. One must recognize that such treatment, in itself, may not allow entry where shares are closely held, for example. If other countries believe that such close holdings convey competitive advantages, they are in a position to develop them in their own ways. One need not develop a Japanese *keiretsu* system or a German universal banking system in order to encourage closer holdings of shares by parties who have a direct interest in the operations of the firm. Changes in tax laws and in regulations so as to encourage management and employee ownership can give similar results, assuming the country is prepared to live with the other consequences of such changes.

It is clear from the experience of the EC as it moves to closer integration that some standardization of merger, acquisition and shareholder laws becomes necessary, if only to ensure that the gains from trade and investment which are possible from such integration are realized. Even outside such formal trading areas, highly asymmetrical law or custom on mergers and related areas can lead to considerable resentment, as is evident in US government attempts to secure reciprocity of treatment from Japan. There is yet another reason to develop international policy in this area. Much FDI today is by merger or acquisition, where governments are more sceptical of gains than with new investment. Much is in concentrated sectors where governments believe firms may add to market imperfections. We have noted earlier some doubts about these positions but one cannot doubt that they are widely held. International rules on some aspects of competition policy would be one way to address these questions, a way which recommends itself for other reasons, as will be evident shortly.

This is not the place to try to develop in detail an international policy approach towards FDI and MNEs. Rather we need to consider one final point which comes out of this study. We have argued that government policy making is driven partly by a desire to maintain or increase national wealth and independence, but also (and, often, mainly) by struggles over internal wealth and power distribution. We have also argued that MNEs offer the potential for wealth increases – not without some problems – but may reduce national independence or at least complicate its exercise. People may, with reason, regard both imperfect governments and imperfect firms with a jaundiced eye at times. Yet both governments and multinationals serve valid purposes and, in any case, neither is going to wither away. How to secure the best balance between them becomes the issue, recognizing not only what each offers but also how each can go astray.

Posing the issue in this way points up an obvious problem: how does one go about achieving welfare-improving agreements when the principal parties make the rules or are expected to live by them? Why would one not expect, as with the national policies on FDI described earlier, that a balance of all the different objectives and interests would be struck? It is not unthinkable that one frequent outcome would be that governments and firms would collaborate to suppress markets, thereby favouring particular groups at the expense of others and perhaps of international wealth creation. Such outcomes are not unknown in both domestic and foreign trade, and are one view of what is going on with many strategic trade and investment policies.

There is no clear answer to this question of how reform of institutions proceeds when those involved in making the reforms are themselves affected by them. At the national level one can only leave this to each country to work out in its own way. There will be a great deal left for national governments to do with regard to international competition, regardless of the rules eventually developed on the latter. Even if the focus is on general policies directed to improving the competitiveness of all firms located in or attracted to a country, no government is likely to leave the fate of large or critical projects entirely to a market dominated by MNEs. But at the international level one can point to the overriding need to have enforceable rules on the way in which both governments and firms compete and how they collaborate. It is the re-establishment or preservation of an open system which provides the best guarantee that such competition and collaboration ultimately serves more than a parochial interest.

NOTES

1. This argument has been made by Kydland and Prescott (1976). Unlike earlier arguments for rules it does not depend on ignorance of the timing and magnitude of the effects of policy or on the policy maker's preferences for other ends. We shall have more to say on the latter below.
2. The word 'voluntary' must be interpreted in a situation where one of the parties, the state, has a considerable but not unlimited power to exercise coercion in many circumstances, should it so desire.
3. The death of a highly respected Canadian publishing firm, Lester and Orpen Dennys, in 1991, was ascribed in part to a policy which generally required 51 per cent Canadian ownership of such firms and hence limited the bidding interest from foreign firms. However the importance of this particular policy has been disputed. See the articles in the *Globe and Mail*, 19 January 1991, D1.
4. Peltzman (1976) develops such a model as a generalization of Stigler (1971).

Appendix I List of Interviews[1]

CHAPTER 6 THE NATURAL RESOURCE-BASED ECONOMIES

Australia

Foreign Investment Review Board; Departments of the *Treasury, Trade* and *Resources*, Business and Consumer Affairs, Attorney General, Foreign Affairs; Reserve Bank of Australia; New South Wales Departments of Industrial Development, Mineral Resources.

Canada

Foreign Investment Review Agency; Investment Canada; Departments of Finance; External Affairs; Consumer and Corporate Affairs; Industry, Trade and Commerce; Privy Council Office.

New Zealand

Overseas Investment Commission; Ministries of the *Treasury, Energy*; Reserve Bank of New Zealand.

Norway

Department of *Industry*; Norges Bank.

Sweden

Ministry of Industry; Sveriges Riksbank.

CHAPTER 7 OTHER COUNTRIES WITH REVIEW

France

Ministries of Industry, Economy and *Finance*; *DATAR* (Délegation de l'Aménagement du Territoire et à l'Action Régionale); Commissariat du Plan.

Japan

Ministries of *International Trade and Industry* (MITI), *Finance*; Bank of Japan; Fair Trade Commission.

CHAPTER 8 HOST COUNTRIES LACKING REVIEW

Belgium

Ministries of Economic Affairs, Finance.

Ireland

Industrial Development Authority, Industrial Training Authority.

Italy

Treasury, Bank of Italy.

CHAPTER 9 HOME COUNTRIES LACKING REVIEW

Federal Republic of Germany

Ministry of Economics.

The Netherlands

Ministry of Economic Affairs.

Switzerland

Departments of *Public Economy*, Justice, Finance.

United Kingdom

Departments of *Trade and Industry*, Energy; *Her Majesty's Treasury*; Bank of England.

United States of America

Departments of *Commerce*, *Treasury*; Office of the Trade Representative; Securities and Exchange Commission.

OTHER INTERVIEWS

Parent firms 23 (of which seven in Japan, nine in EC and five in USA);
Affiliates 27 (of which 17 in EC);[2]
University researchers 24, other researchers 18;
Other (industry associations, lawyers, trade unions, staff of legislative committees) 21.

NOTES

1. Federal government only, except where otherwise specified. The country interviews include those listed under *Other Interviews*. For example, parent company officials were interviewed about experience in particular host countries. Agencies which were relied on most heavily are italicized.
2. Put differently, there were 31 distinct corporate groups represented, five of which were state-owned firms. Six were in the petroleum sector, five in electrical products, four in finance and two each in fibres and textiles, automobiles, chemicals, computers and mining, one in services and the others in a variety of manufactures.

Appendix II Letters to Interviewees

LETTER TO GOVERNMENT DEPARTMENTS, AGENCIES AND CENTRAL BANKS

I am writing to ask for your assistance with a study I have undertaken regarding government policies towards multinational enterprises.

The study is outlined on the attached, including the types of issues I would like to examine with officers of relevant government departments and agencies. Briefly, my questions are intended to identify the types of policies in effect, the circumstances in which they were developed, and how far they have realized their objectives.

One point I should emphasize is that my project is an independent academic study. It is funded by the Social Sciences and Humanities Research Council of Canada and by the University of Toronto, but is entirely my responsibility. The interviews are conducted on a confidential basis, both with regard to the identity of individual participants and any material supplied which is not already public.

Yours sincerely,

A.E. Safarian
Professor of Economics

AES/lt
Encls.

LETTER TO MULTINATIONAL ENTERPRISES

I am writing to ask for your assistance with a study I have undertaken regarding government policies towards multinational enterprises.

The study is outlined on the attached. Briefly, I am attempting to identify the types of policies followed by the developed industrial countries and to analyze the effects of the policies, including ways in which companies have responded to them.

I have already conducted interviews with officers of the relevant government departments or agencies in a number of countries. The issues I wish to examine with the officers of the parent companies are noted in broad terms on the attached. What particulary interests me is the experience your company has had in the 'seventies with those developed countries which have significantly restricted or regulated the activities of companies owned abroad, whether at the point of establishment or subsequently. I appreciate that some of this may need to be discussed with division heads and/or with officers of subsidiaries abroad, particulary specific examples noted in item 4 of the attached sheet. I am prepared to follow up on these in more detail, if necessary at a later stage, and will be visiting a number of countries overseas.

One point I should emphasize is that my project is an independent academic study. It is funded by the Social Sciences and Humanities Research Council of Canada and by the University of Toronto, but is entirely my responsibility. The interviews are conducted on a confidential basis, both with respect to the identity of participating companies and any material supplied which is not already public.

Yours sincerely,

A.E. Safarian
Professor of Economics

AES/lt
Encls.

POLICY ON MULTINATIONAL ENTERPRISES IN DEVELOPED COUNTRIES

Interviews with Officials of Government Departments and Agencies and Central Banks

These questions indicate the major points to be raised in the interviews. The questions are intended as a general guide covering several related topics rather than a reflection of any particular country's approach. The countries to be studied are those in Western Europe (excluding Spain, Portugal and Greece), Canada, the United States, Japan, Australia and New Zealand. Please note that the study focuses on policies which distinguish companies controlled by non-residents, not policies which affect all companies regardless of country of ownership.

Where documents have been prepared and are available, copies would be appreciated.

1. **Objectives**
What is the general legal and policy position of the government towards inward direct investment? Please comment on the circumstances in which the major present policies were developed and reasons for the policies.

2. **Type of policies in effect towards direct investment**
(a) Government review on establishment or subsequent expansion, sectors closed to foreign-owned enterprises, treatment after entry which differs from that accorded to companies owned by nationals of the country. Details on the implementation procedures for the policies would be appreciated.
(b) Particulars of performance requirements directed towards foreign-owned firms, such as sources of financing and of senior personnel, income payments abroad, and trade or technology performance.
(c) Preferences for particular organizational forms for transfer of foreign technology (licenses, joint ventures, etc.) and procedures for monitoring technology sectors.
(d) Requirements, if different, in the natural resource industries, finance or service sectors.

3. **Policies towards outward direct investment**
Nature of such policies, criteria and process for approval, circumstances in which the policies were developed.

POLICY ON MULTINATIONAL ENTERPRISES IN DEVELOPED COUNTRIES

Interviews with Officers of Enterprises

These questions indicate the major points to be raised in the interviews. As noted in point 4, it would be useful to consider in more detail a few of your company's more important experiences in the 'seventies with policy changes (including administrative processes) directed particularly to foreign-owned companies. The countries to be studied are those in Western Europe (excluding Spain, Portugal and Greece), Canada, the United States, Japan, Australia and New Zealand. Please note that the study focuses on policies which distinguish companies owned by non-residents, not policies which affect all companies regardless of country of ownership.

1. *Information about the company*, such as number of subsidiaries/branches abroad and in countries listed above, their weight in the overall enterprise, reporting relationship to parent company.

2. *Foreign government policies towards your company's subsidiaries abroad*
- (a) Types of policies: government review on establishment or subsequent expansion, sectors closed to your business, treatment after establishment which is less favourable than that accorded companies owned by nationals of country.
- (b) Particulars of performance requirements, local ownership and other conditions set by governments, and of grants and other concessions to attract or retain investment.

3. *Origins of policies and effects on company's operations:*
- (a) Circumstances in which the major policies were established.
- (b) Options available to the firm in responding to policy changes.
- (c) Effects on your company's operations, such as the level of your investment in the country, nature of your industrial activity, competitive capacity of the subsidiary, and organizational forms used in international business.

4. *Specific cases*
Given the complexity of major multinational enterprises and of these policy issues, I would be interested in pursuing these issues with regard to several of the more important specific instances where a change in policy or a new policy affected your company in any of the above countries during the past decade.

POLICY ON MULTINATIONAL ENTERPRISES IN DEVELOPED COUNTRIES

Background of the Study

This study is concerned with the objectives, methods and consequences of government control of multinational enterprises, with reference particularly to the experience of the more developed countries. The expansion of such controls in recent years has had major effects on the relations between government, business and other groups, and on relations between governments.

One serious obstacle to research in this field has been the lack of information on what various governments have done (particularly by way of administrative processes) and why they have chosen some instruments rather than others. Another question has been the relative effectiveness of various forms of technology transfer such as wholly-owned subsidiaries, licences and joint ventures.

Several sources of information will be used for this study. One source is interviews with government officials who are involved in decisions on entry of multinationals, on policy towards them after entry, and on policy on direct investment abroad. Moreover interviews with officers of multinational enterprises will give further insights into the public policy process and also yield some of the data on alternative ways of transferring knowledge. I plan to interview academics and others working in the field and to utilize various public sources of information.

I have already conducted a number of interviews in Western Europe, Canada and the United States in order to test the feasibility of this approach and to derive some preliminary results. This preliminary work encourages me to think that this study will help to further our knowledge of decision making both in multinational enterprises and in government agencies, and to understand the relevant welfare effects at the group, national and international level. In the early months of 1981 I shall move my base to Europe in order to conduct interviews in a number of West European countries.

The Social Sciences and Humanities Research Council of Canada has agreed to underwrite planned research costs for this study over a three-year period. I have arranged research leave for 1981–2 in order to devote full time to the study.

September 1981–August 1982
Faculté de Droit
et des Sciences Economiques
Université de Nice
Avenue Robert Schuman
06000 NICE – FRANCE
Tel.: (93) 98.08.00
Res.: (93) 55.57.30

Professor of Economics
Institute for Policy Analysis
University of Toronto
150 St. George Street
Toronto, Ontario
Canada M5S 1A1

Appendix III Selected Decisions on Investment Proposals

STATEMENTS BY THE TREASURER OF AUSTRALIA, THE HON. JOHN HOWARD, MP

1 Foreign Investment Proposal
Bowater Australia Pty Ltd./Escor Ltd.

The Government has determined that a proposal by Bowater Australia Pty Ltd., a wholly owned subsidiary of The Bowater Corporation Ltd. of the UK, to increase its shareholding in Escor Ltd. from 46 per cent to 100 per cent is inconsistent with foreign investment policy.

The proposal is examinable under foreign investment policy because it involves an increase in a substantial foreign shareholding in an Australian company. For approval to be granted, the government would have to be satisfied that there are sufficient national benefits to offset the loss of Australian ownership.

Escor is based in Melbourne and operates throughout Australia. It has substantial involvement in transport and construction equipment, engineering products, paper and textiles. Escor is a diversified company and the main benefit claimed for the proposal related to the progressive rationalisation of the company's activities, consequential gains in efficiency and the position of Australian shareholders.

The Government is not satisfied that rationalisation of Escor cannot be achieved without loss of Australian ownership.

In reaching its decision the Government took careful account of whether Australian shareholders should be allowed to decide if they wished to accept the Bowater offer or to retain their interests in the company. The Government also took account of an offer by Bowater to readmit 25 per cent Australian equity to Escor in the future.

However, the Government concluded that the potential national benefits which might result from the acquisitions would not be sufficient to offset the substantial loss of Australian ownership and that approval was not warranted.

Canberra Act
7 May 1981

2 Development of Oaky Creek Coaking Coal Project

In my statements of 24 September and 5 December 1980, I indicated that the participants in the Oaky Creek project had been advised that the Government would be prepared to give consideration to approval for the project's development if they provided suitable joint and unequivocal undertakings that Australian equity would be introduced to a level of at least 50 per cent by the time first shipments of coal take place. I also stated that it would be necessary for the parties to inform Government of how they would adjust their equity shares to admit the necessary level of Australian equity and that the Government would wish to see the Australian equity in place as soon as possible.

The participants in the project have now provided undertakings that 50 per cent Australian equity will be introduced into the project prior to the commencement of the shipments of coal. In addition, MIM has advised the Foreign Investment Review Board that it accepts sole responsibility for taking the necessary steps to increase Australian equity in the project to 50 per cent and has undertaken to fulfil this commitment in a way acceptable to the Government in terms of its foreign investment policy. MIM has advised the government of a number of alternative methods it has under detailed consideration by which 50 per cent Australian equity may be achieved.

The Government welcomes this commitment by the parties and, on this basis, has advised them that it has no objections to the undertakings of construction of the mine facilities and infrastructure commitments in order that coal production may be possible by mid-1983.

At that time, prior to first shipments, when the parties have met their commitment and the Australian equity guidelines are satisfied the Government would be in a position to grant final approval to allow commercial production at Oaky Creek to commence.

Canberra Act
30 April 1981

PRESS RELEASES BY THE FOREIGN INVESTMENT REVIEW AGENCY, OTTAWA

1 16 October 1980

A proposal by Aalco Limited of London, England, which is a wholly-owned subsidiary of Amari Limited, in turn owned by Selection Trust Limited, both of England, to acquire control of the business carried on by Kaiser Aluminum & Chemical of Canada Limited consisting of the *service centre operation* (the Centre) of its Kaiser Aluminum Division, at Scarborough, Ontario. Kaiser Aluminum & Chemical of Canada Limited, is a wholly-owned subsidiary of Kaiser Aluminum & Chemical corporation, of Oakland, California, USA.

In announcing the Government's decision to allow this transaction, the Minister noted that it will result in increased employment, significant import replacement, increased exports, and greater participation by Canadians in the affairs of the business. More specifically, the applicant has undertaken, in support of its proposals:

- to offer employment to all employees of the Centre other than to those to be retained by the vendor on terms and conditions no less favourable than those currently enjoyed;
- to employ a total of 18 employees within two years;
- to employ only Canadians subject to availability of qualified personnel and to provide training at no cost;
- to cause the Centre to expand processing activities and to this end to install processing equipment costing approximately $190,000 within 2 years, and purchase such equipment from Canadian manufacturers subject to availability, competitive price, quality and suitability;
- not to engage in importing or trading in carbon steel products;
- to cause the Centre to source all its metal products in Canada including aluminum, stainless steel and copper, subject to availability and competitive prices;
- to cause the Centre to purchase all other materials, supplies, components and parts in Canada subject to availability and competitive prices;
- to cause the Centre to act as the applicant's purchasing agent for Canadian produced metals for export to the UK and the European Economic Community;
- to cause the Centre to actively promote the export of Canadian-made products to the USA;
- to cause the Centre to annually seek the advice of federal and provincial departments to determine whether there are additional processing activities which the Centre might perform which could lead to reducing Canada's imports of finished metal products;
- to immediately appoint Canadians to all officer and director positions; and
- to provide key employees with the opportunity to acquire an equity interest in the business within 5 years.

2 4 March 1982

A proposal by Unilever of London, England and Unilever N.V. of the Netherlands, to acquire control of Nacan Products Limited (Nacan) of Toronto, Ontario, Lepage's Limited (Lepage's) of Bramalea, Ontario, Foodpro National Inc. (Foodpro) of Lachine, Quebec and Lawry's Foods Limited (Lawry's) of Toronto, Ontario. Nacan is engaged in the production of adhesives and resins for industrial use and specialty starch products which are used by the food, paper and textile industries and in packaging. Lepage's is engaged in the manufacture and distribution of adhesives and allied home care, plaster and wallboard fillers and other decorator aid products, coatings for concrete, wood stains and other wood and metal finishes. Foodpro is engaged in the production of various food additives and in the importation and sale of stabilizers, emulsifiers, natural smoke extracts and soya proteins. Lawry's is engaged in the manufacture and distribution of a specialty line of high-quality seasonings, sauce mixes, packaged soups, Mexican foods and salad dressing mixes.

In announcing the Government's decision, Mr Gray noted this was the third proposal by Unilever Limited and Unilever NV (Unilever), as ultimate controllers, to acquire Nacan, Lepage's and Foodpro and their second attempt to acquire Lawry's. The previous applications were disallowed by Orders in council in 1979 and 1980.

Since the previous application, Unilever has made several improvements and additions to its undertakings which the government considers demonstrate significant benefit to Canada. Among its major commitments, Unilever has undertaken that within three years it will restructure its business in Canada by creating a new Unilever company incorporated in Canada (Unilever Canada) which will be a subsidiary of Unilever. Unilever Canada will acquire control of all present and future Unilever operating companies in Canada. The Board of Directors of Unilever Canada will be responsible directly to the Board of Directors of Unilever for all policy and investment decisions of the operating companies.

Within five years of the incorporation of Unilever Canada, its Board of Directors will give consideration to the offering of a significant portion of its equity capital with full voting rights to the Canadian public. Unilever has also undertaken to create, through Nacan, a new Canadian research facility in Ontario which will be the centre of Nacan's R&D and will be the focal point for research within Unilever in certain areas of particular interest to Canada. The new facility will be completed by 1985.

Unilever has also committed itself to a major investment program in Canada over the next five years, which includes modernization and expansion of the Lever Detergents Limited plant at Toronto, Ontario, and investment in manufacturing and related facilities at Nacan's plants at Toronto and Boucherville, Quebec, and also at Lepage's and Foodpro. In sum this program will involve an investment of between $30 and $60 million.

The Minister noted that Unilever will take a number of measures to increase exports, including a program for the development of sales of specialty fats, the allocation to Hart Chemicals Limited, located at Guelph, Ontario, of a mandate which will make it the prime centre of Unilever's North American operations for the manufacture of certain specialty chemicals, and the conduct of test marketing of certain of Lawry's products in Japan and Hong Kong with a view of increasing its exports to those countries.

Finally, Mr Gray pointed out that Unilever will encourage Unilever Canada to actively search for appropriate opportunities for the independent development of each of its operating companies with the objective of becoming, whenever appropriate, a prime full product cycle (design, development, manufacturing, marketing) centre.

3 21 September 1981

A proposal by Apple Computer Inc. (Apple), of Cupertine, California, USA, to establish a new business at Toronto, Ontario, to import, distribute and possibly manufacture computers and related products.

In announcing the Government's decision, Mr Gray drew attention to the following undertakings given by Apple in support of its proposal:

- to cause all officers, excepting the chairman of the board and the secretary, all management, including the president, and all permanent employees to be resident Canadians; any appointments of individuals who are not permanent residents for the purpose of discharging specific training or other extraordinary functions will not exceed one year;
- to cause the new business to maintain a policy of selling at least 80 per cent of its product through independent Canadian retailers but, should market conditions dictate the use of highly trained company personnel to handle certain sales directly, the new business will do so to maintain its competitive position;
- to cause the new business, both directly and through its Canadian dealer organization, to perform at least 80 per cent of all repair and maintenance service for products manufactured by the applicant or the new business and sold in Canada;
- to cause the new business to actively seek and recommend to its customers Canadian sources of compatible peripherals and materials for use with the Apple product line, subjective to availability in sufficient quantities;

- to commence manufacturing in Canada when sales of any of the applicant's products justify the establishment of a manufacturing 'module' employing approximately 100 people (anticipated within 3 years) and to review its progress toward this goal with Department of Industry, Trade and Commerce twice a year. If several products meet the criterion of a manufacturing 'module', the applicant will implement their manufacturing sequentially no later than six months from each other;
- to cause the new business to vigorously carry out the provisions of the agreement of 1 May 1981 between Norpak Limited, the applicant, and the new business, for the use of Telidon Interface Kit (TIK) in Apple II computer and for the dedication of Apple and its subsidiaries to the creation of a world market for TIKs. Inasmuch as Telidon remains a major graphics communications technology, and subject to its successful implementation of the Apple II computer, the applicant will continue to promote Telidon as a technology, particularly by using Telidon preferentially in its current and future products and will continue to support Telidon as a standard in the standards committee in which the applicant participates;
- to actively seek out and develop, in cooperation with the new business and the Department of Industry, Trade and Commerce, Canadian sources for Canadian-made goods that could be incorporated into products made either by the applicant or the new business and to purchase such goods, if competitively available. Specifically, the applicant will actively seek to develop Canadian sources for power supply units and semiconductor memories. In the event that power supply units or any other components can be sourced in Canada at competitive prices, quality, reliability, and in quantities sufficiently large to meet the needs of the applicant and of the new business, the applicant will purchase such products and components. For such purposes, complete information will be provided to Canadian suppliers regarding future worldwide requirements of the applicant, industry prices, and technology which the applicant is not restricted from communicating by previous agreements with third parties and which, in the judgement of the applicant, is required by such suppliers. A corporate purchasing task force will be established with the specific mandate of identifying and developing Canadian sources of supply for the worldwide requirements of the applicant;
- to recommend to its worldwide dealers in its periodic communications to them, Canadian-made peripheral equipment, providing such products are competitive in price, performance and availability;
- to ensure that at the end of the first year following allowance, Canadian value added (CVA), calculated in accordance with the specified

formula, will not be less than 30 per cent of the cost of goods sold in Canada. Thereafter, the applicant will exercise its reasonable best efforts to achieve the highest levels of CVA in accordance with the schedule submitted to the Agency by the applicant in this regard. To the maximum extent possible, the new business will emphasize the purchase of components and products in Canada that involve high technological content;

- to cause the new business, within one year, to complete the establishment of a Software Research and Development Group, whose activities will be concerned mainly with software development for new products rather than the maintenance of existing products and the new business will incur additional expenditures for the latter activity;
- to cause the new business, within three years, to use its reasonable best efforts to initiate R&D projects related to hardware, providing there is an adequate availability in Canada of Canadian manufactured advanced microelectronic products of the type used by the applicant. The applicant will use its reasonable best efforts to stay abreast of semiconductor and microelectronic component development in Canada from the standpoint of their application to products of the applicant, and with the view to reaching R&D expenditures in Canada comparable to the level in the USA.

INVESTMENT CANADA, OTTAWA, 13 DECEMBER 1989: SUMMARY OF KEY UNDERTAKINGS BY INSTITUT MÉRIEUX S.A.

The undertakings of Institut Mérieux S.A. with respect to the proposed takeover of Connaught BioSciences are divided between those binding Mérieux for a period of 10 years and those binding Mérieux indefinitely.

I Undertakings Binding Mérieux for 10 years

R&D

- Fifteen per cent of the consolidated sales revenues of the combined enterprise will be spent on R&D activities. These expenditures will be exclusive of government contributions.
- Connaught's share of the total R&D budget of the combined enterprise will not be less than its existing 36 per cent share.
- Connaught will spend an aggregate of not less than $160 million (in 1988 Canadian dollars) on R&D in Canada during the five calendar years following the implementation of the investment; the pace of expenditures

within the 5 years is subject to approval by the US Food and Drug administration (FDA) of Mérieux's pending applications for certain vaccines.

- Connaught's annual spending on R&D in Canada will be at least 65 per cent of its total spent in North America.
- Mérieux undertakes to allocate at least an average of 25 per cent of total R&D spending in Canada, during the first five calendar years following implementation of the investment, on basic research and will ensure that an aggregate of at least $39 million (in 1988 Canadian dollars) will be spent on basic research in that period; subject to FDA approval of the vaccines.
- Mérieux will consult on an annual basis with selected federal government departments and agencies and with interested provincial governments to seek their advice and input in the development of biotechnology at Connaught and will report annually to Investment Canada on these consultations. As an integral part of these considerations, Mérieux will submit within six months a medium-term operating plan and longer-term strategic plan for government advice and input.
- Connaught will commit to a higher level of contracted out R&D projects and joint research projects with Canadian academic, institutional and industrial centres than is currently contracted out by Connaught (refer also to agreement dated 24 October 1989 with the University of Toronto).

Capital expenditures

- Mérieux will build a Biotechnology Centre at Connaught's Willowdale site over a three-phase process to become fully operational within a period of five to seven years following the implementation of the investment. Capital expenditures to complete the centre are estimated to be C$30 to C$40 million and will be made by Connaught. The centre will employ approximately 125 people when completed and create a total of approximately 30 to 50 new, permanent positions. Connaught will enter into a meaningful cooperation agreement with the University of Toronto with respect to the operations of the centre, as provided in Mérieux's agreement dated 24 October 1989 with the University of Toronto.
- Mérieux will assess the feasibility of establishing in Canada a blood fractionation plant based on Institut Mérieux's state-of-the-art technology.

II Undertakings Binding Mérieux Indefinitely

Canadian control/participation and identity

- A majority of the 10 members of Connaught's Board of Directors must be 'resident Canadians' and five of the resident Canadian directors will be independent of Mérieux; the other five, including the Chairman, with an additional casting vote, will be nominated by Mérieux. The Canadian directors will be chosen in consultation with the governments of Canada and Ontario.

- Any fundamental decisions affecting the essential Canadian identity of Connaught would require two-thirds of the votes of the Board of Directors.
- Not later than six months after the implementation of the investment, Mérieux will offer to Canadian investors those voting shares of Connaught BioSciences Inc. then owned by Institut Mérieux and its affiliates which exceed 50 per cent of the voting shares then outstanding on a fully diluted basis at a price equal to their cost of such shares and that such offer for sale will remain outstanding for a period of at least one year.
- Mérieux will offer for sale up to 49 per cent of its voting shares, in a manner reasonably expected to provide the opportunity for their acquisition by Canadian investors without affecting the majority ownership of Institut Mérieux International S.A.
- Mérieux will appoint 'resident Canadians' to the Board of directors of Institut Mérieux to ensure Canadian representation on the Board of Directors of Institut Mérieux that is proportionate to the amount of Canadian participation in the voting equity of Institut Mérieux. In anticipation of such participation Institut Mérieux is prepared as soon as practicable after implementation of the investment to appoint to the Board of Directors of Institut Mérieux S.A. at least two of the 'resident Canadians' elected to the board of Connaught.
- Connaught will retain its name, a strong Canadian identity, its headquarters, all key corporate functions and a full range of activities in Canada.
- Connaught will enjoy autonomy and decision-making authority in setting its own direction, priorities, plans and budgets and will have operational authority in managing its international operations, including the continued reporting of Connaught's US subsidiaries to Canadian headquarters.

Company development and growth

- Connaught will be maintained and developed as a world-class company in the vaccine, biotechnology and health care products industries, with the mandate and resources to vie for the position of a leading worldwide vaccine producer.
- The employment level of Connaught will not be reduced from that attained in 1988.
- Connaught's current production activity will not be reduced or moved from Canada, nor will the level of employment in its production operations fall below that attained in 1988.

- Mérieux will transfer to Connaught in Canada production of certain Mérieux-developed products for the North American market.
- Connaught's products will be marketed and distributed worldwide, employing Connaught's existing distribution system in North America and that of Institut Mérieux in Europe in particular. Institut Mérieux will afford Connaught every opportunity to play a leading role in developing new and expanded export markets in such areas as the Caribbean, Commonwealth, Pacific Rim, and Central and Latin America and will cause Connaught to have the resources to exploit these opportunities (with the exception of sales to international relief agencies such as UNICEF and WHO for which Connaught and Institut Mérieux will continue to bid separately, as they have in the past).
- Connaught will have a world product mandate for every new and existing product and their derivatives developed by Connaught and will have proportionally equal, fair and full opportunity to develop new products.

Divestitures

- Mérieux will recommend to the Board of Connaught the disposal of Connaught's interest in BioResearch Inc. with priority given to any competitive bid at fair market value by a Canadian purchaser or purchasers.
- Mérieux will also recommend that preference be given to any competitive bid at fair market value by a Canadian purchaser or purchasers if Connaught's Board decides to sell its interest in Nordic Laboratories Inc.

R&D and technology transfers

- Mérieux will appoint an R&D Committee to conduct an extensive review of R&D projects currently under way at Mérieux and Connaught, the Committee being composed of an equal number of Mérieux and Connaught employees.
- Connaught's management will retain a substantial measure of control over the company's R&D direction.
- Connaught's annual R&D spending in Canada will not fall below the amount of R&D spending attained in 1988 (expressed in constant dollars).
- There will be no reduction in the level of employment in Connaught's R&D in Canada from the 1988 level.
- Connaught's industrial process development skills and capabilities will be enhanced.
- Mérieux will make available to Connaught its proprietary production technology, including its microcarrier culture techniques and purification processes.

Security of supply/self-sufficiency

- Connaught will continue to supply vaccines to the Department of National Defence.
- Connaught will provide at least six months' notice to Health and Welfare Canada and to Investment Canada of any plans to discontinue Canadian production of any vaccine or commence production abroad of any new or improved vaccine which would render obsolete a product made by Connaught in Canada.
- Connaught will develop, within six months of the implementation of investment, a satisfactory contingency plan to supply Canada, whether alone, or in collaboration with other vaccine makers, with vaccines of strategic importance.
- Both Mérieux and Connaught will ensure that Canada receives a fair and appropriate share of the supply of new products which may be in high demand in the initial stages of production and distribution.
- The availability and price of insulin in Canada sold by Connaught will not be adversely affected by the investment and Connaught will continue its support of diabetes education and research programs in Canada.
- The prices of vaccines and other products currently produced and/or marketed by Connaught in Canada will not increase as a result of the investment.
- Connaught will not take any action that would have the effect of impairing or hindering Connaught's ability to meet its past liabilities for vaccine injury.

Collaboration with Canadian universities, research centres and biotechnology firms

- Connaught's outreach programs to universities and other research institutions in Canada to assist in basic and applied research, particularly biotechnology, will be expanded substantially. Collaboration with commercial/business partners in Canada will be increased.
- In particular, in accordance with the agreement dated 24 October 1989 with the University of Toronto, Mérieux undertakes to make:
- a total minimum expenditure of $9 million (in 1989 dollars), to be distributed in instalments during the calendar years 1990 to 1999 inclusive, for fundamental, leading-edge research on vaccines and related immunological topics at the University of Toronto; and
- an additional total minimum expenditure of $6 million (in 1989 dollars), to be distributed in instalments during the calendar years 1990 to 1999 inclusive, to be spent on research in Canada at Canadian universities (including the University of Toronto if merited), institutes and granting councils. Connaught will have the exclusive right to exploit and develop

any intellectual results deriving from research projects at the University of Toronto funded by Mérieux, subject only to royalty arrangements. It is anticipated that similar arrangements would apply at other Canadian universities, institutes and granting councils.

- Connaught will enter into commercial contracts with other Canadian biotechnology firms to develop scale-up and purification processes for new biotechnology products.

STANDARD CONDITIONS REQUIRED FOR A CONCESSION IN NORWAY

The concession conditions applicable to wholly owned or partially foreign-owned industrial enterprises have, in practice, the following pattern:

I. A/S ... is to be an independent Norwegian corporation with its main place of business in Norway. The majority of the directors are to be Norwegian citizens. The company's articles of incorporation and amendments to these are to be submitted to the Ministry for approval.

II. Up to ... per cent of the ordinary stock may be owned by ... Any transfer of stock to foreign legal entities must be approved by the Ministry. The share register of the company shall contain information as to citizenship and domicile of all shareholders.

III. The firm is to be managed in accordance with sound business practice. The corporation may not, without the Ministry's approval, engage in activity other than the production and sale of ... and related activities.

IV. The business connection with ... [parent firm] and such companies affiliated with it is to be based upon realistic pricing and best possible conditions for the Norwegian company.

In this connection the following is stipulated:

(a) There may be no export of the firm's products at prices below normal market prices without the Ministry's approval.

(b) There may be no import of machinery, raw materials, semi-manufactures, etc. at prices in excess of normal market prices, except with the Ministry's approval.

(c) The Ministry must approve agreements related to compensation paid for economic, technical, mercantile or other assistance.

V. The company is required to submit to such supervision as the Ministry deems necessary to control that the terms of the concession are observed. The company can be ordered to pay the cost of such supervision.

VI. The Ministry may impose a fine of Kr. 500 to Kr. 2000 per day for violation of the concession conditions. Repeated or continued violation may result in revocation of the concession.

Source: Christiana Bank, 14.

Appendix IV Variables Used to Measure the Determinants of Policy on FDI in Chapter 10

THE DEPENDENT VARIABLE: DEGREE OF RESTRICTIVENESS (DOR)

In order to derive a measure of the degree of restrictiveness of government policy towards multinationals, four instruments of government are measured for each of 22 countries (Table AIV.1). It should be noted that combining exchange control with both review and incentives did not work well statistically, perhaps because of aggregation of quite different policies. Exchange control complements review, and incentives often go with review, as noted in Part II and Chapter 11. Hence the measures for DOR in Table 10.3 which were used in the regressions were ABC, BC and BCD, but not ABCD. The instruments, and the corresponding weights, follow:

(A) exchange controls (min = 0, max = 1.2)
weight: 0 if no exchange control; 0.4 for each of the following:
(1) controls on current transactions,
(2) controls on capital transactions,
(3) surrender of export proceeds required.

Source: IMF Annual Report on Exchange Arrangements and Exchange Restrictions, Washington, DC, various issues.

(B) Existence of review (min = 0, max = 1)
weight: 0 if no review; 0.5 if a reporting requirement or partial screen or use competition policy on FDI; 1 if screen.

Source: OECD, 1982, 1987b.

(C) Strength of review (min = 0, max = 3)
Estimates by the author based on material in Part II, including particularly interviews; OECD (1982, 1985a, 1987b); Bale (1983); and UN,

Table AIV.1 Summary of components of DOR, 1981, 1985

		1981				1985			
		A	*B*	*C*	*D*	*A*	*B*	*C*	*D*
1	Australia	0.8	1.0	2.0	0.62	0.40	1.00	1.50	0.23
2	Austria	0.4	0.5	0.0	0.28	0.40	0.50	0.00	0.68
3	Belgium	0.4	0.5	0.0	0.51	0.40	0.50	0.00	0.40
4	Canada	0.0	1.0	3.0	0.28	0.00	1.00	2.00	0.23
5	Denmark	0.8	0.5	0.0	0.23	0.80	0.50	0.00	0.17
6	Finland	0.4	1.0	2.0	0.28	0.40	1.00	2.00	0.11
7	France	0.8	1.0	3.0	0.28	0.80	1.00	2.00	0.11
8	FRG	0.0	0.5	0.0	0.40	0.00	0.50	0.00	0.34
9	Greece	1.2	1.0	1.5	0.11	1.20	1.00	1.50	0.62
10	Ireland	0.8	0.5	0.0	1.00	0.80	0.50	0.00	1.00
11	Italy	1.2	0.5	1.0	0.51	0.40	0.50	1.00	0.73
12	Japan	0.0	0.5	2.0	0.11	0.00	0.50	1.50	0.06
13	Netherlands	0.0	0.0	0.0	0.40	0.00	0.00	0.00	0.51
14	New Zealand	0.8	1.0	2.0	0.70	0.00	1.00	1.50	0.28
15	Norway	0.8	1.0	2.0	0.28	0.80	1.00	2.00	0.06
16	Portugal	1.2	1.0	3.0	0.17	1.20	1.00	2.00	0.40
17	Spain	0.8	1.0	3.0	0.57	0.80	1.00	2.00	0.51
18	Sweden	0.4	1.0	2.0	0.17	0.40	1.00	2.00	0.06
19	Switzerland	0.0	0.0	0.0	0.17	0.00	0.00	0.00	0.23
20	Turkey	1.2	1.0	3.0	0.00	1.20	1.00	3.00	0.68
21	UK	0.0	0.5	0.0	0.51	0.00	0.50	0.00	0.23
22	US	0.0	0.5	0.0	0.61	0.00	0.50	0.00	0.66

Notes:
A: exchange controls.
B: existence of review.
C: strength of review.
D: incentives (subtract).

National Legislation and Regulations Relating to Transnational Corporations, various years. See also Table 10.6. The tables of performance requirements in the US Commerce Benchmark Surveys for 1977 and 1982 were not used, for reasons noted in the second section of Chapter 11.

(D) Incentives (min = 0, max = 1)
Note: this enters as a negative in the calculation of DOR. It was derived by taking the total number of incentives received by foreign-owned companies which were available to foreign-owned companies only, as a proportion of the number of affiliates in that country. This value was then scaled to obtain a maximum value of 1.

Source: (1) US Commerce 1981, 1985 Benchmark Surveys; (2) US Subcommittee on International Economic Policy.

Note: using the study for 1977 the US Subcommittee on International Economic Policy computed the percentage of US firms abroad which received *at least one* of the following incentives: tax concessions, tariff concessions, subsidies, all other incentives.

It was not possible to derive the same data from the study for 1982, so data which were common to both the studies for 1977 and 1982 were used. These consisted of the number of incentives received by foreign-owned companies which were available to foreign-owned companies only, as a proportion of total number of affiliates in that country.

INDEPENDENT VARIABLES

There are significant year-to-year variations in some variables for cyclical and other reasons. In some cases below averages of several years are used to offset these variations.

$$DI = \frac{OUT - IN}{OUT + IN}$$

OUT = outward stock of FDI
IN = inward stock of FDI

Averages for 1975–80, 1981–5.

Sources: OECD, 1987b; IMF, *Balance of Payments Yearbooks*; and United Nations, *Salient Features and Trends in Foreign Direct Investment*, 1983. Data for Greece, Ireland and Turkey inferred from data on flows and comparisons with some other countries:

PROXA, PROXB
Percentage of number of affiliates accounted for by corporations from leading home country (PROXA) four leading home countries (PROXB) This variable is reported for 1980 only.

Source: United Nations, *Transnational Corporations in World Development*, Third Survey, 1983, pp. 336–48.

PEN
Employment in foreign affiliates as a percentage of all employment in manufacturing. This variable is reported for various years.

Source: Dunning and Cantwell (1987).

PRITOT

Derived from the sectoral distribution of inward foreign direct investment capital stock,where PRITOT is the percentage of investment in the primary sector as a proportion of all foreign investment. This variable is reported for 1982.

Source: Dunning and Cantwell (1987). Switzerland set to zero because of negligible inward FDI in primary sector.

GDP, GDPPC

Gross domestic product, and gross domestic product per capita, in $US and exchange rates of 1980. Averages for 1975–80, 1981–5.

Source: OECD, *National Accounts, 1960–80*, Main Aggregates, vol. 1, 1988.

UNEM

Unemployment rate. Averages for 1975–80, 1981–5.

Source: OECD, *Labour Force Statistics, 1965–85*, Paris, 1987.

EXGDP, IMGDP

Exports (imports) of goods and services as a percentage of GDP. Averages for 1975–80, 1981–5.

Source: OECD, *Historical Statistics, 1960–85*, 1987.

TCIR

Total change in foreign exchange reserves. Averages for 1975–80, 1981–5.

Source: IMF, *International Financial Statistics*, 1987.

RD

Gross domestic expenditure on R&D as a proportion of GDP.

Source: OECD, *Science and Technology Indicators (1) Report (1986), R&D, Inventions and Competitiveness. (2) Report (1989), R&D, Productivity and Diffusion of Technology.*

PG

Share of primary commodities in total commodity exports. Averages for 1975–80, 1981–5.

Source: OECD, *Historical Statistics, 1960–80*, 1987. New Zealand and Turkey from Government Financial Statistics, 1987.

POL
Percentage of time a Labour (left) government was either in power or officially a member of a ruling coalition. Periods 1960–80, and 1981–5.

Source: A.S. Banks (ed.), *Political Handbook of the World, 1987*, Binghamton, NY: SA Publications, 1987.

GOV
Government expenditures (including provincial-state) as percentage of GDP.

Source: OECD, *Historical Statistics 1960–85*, 1987.

FED
A dummy variable taking a value of 1 if the country is a federal state and 0 otherwise.

EPRITOT
Employment in the primary sectors as a proportion of total employment (agriculture, hunting, fishing, forestry, oil, and gas). Averages for 1975–80, 1981–5

Source: OECD, *Industrial Structure Statistics*, various issues.

GINI
Kuznet's measure of inequality, calculated as follows from quintile shares:

$$\frac{1}{1.6} \times \text{SUM [Absolute value (S(1)} - 0.2)]$$

S(1) = share of income accruing to the *i*th quintile of the population.

Notes
1. Complete equality implies GINI = 0; complete inequality implies GINI = 1.
2. Austria was assigned same value as Germany and Greece was assigned the same value as Spain.

Source: World Bank, *World Development Report 1987* (1987). Kuznet's measure as cited in Sawyer (1976).

Bibliography

ABECOR (Associated Banks of Europe) (1976), *Foreign Investment in Europe*.

Acocella, N. (1979), 'Multinational Corporations and National Capital in Italy', *La Spettatore Internazionale*, **14**, (3), 191–222.

Agmon, T. and C.P. Kindleberger (eds) (1977), *Multinationals from Small Countries*, Cambridge, Mass: MIT Press.

Aitken, H.J.G. (1961), *American Capital and Canadian Resources*, Cambridge: Harvard University Press.

Allen, G.C. (1968), *Japan's Place in Trade Strategy: Larger Role in Pacific Region*, London: Atlantic Trade Study.

Allison, G.T. (1971), *The Essence of Decision: Explaining the Cuban Missile Crisis*, Boston: Little, Brown and Company.

American Chamber of Commerce in Japan (1979), 'United States Manufacturing Investment in Japan', report prepared by A.T. Kearney International, Inc., Tokyo.

—— (1982), 'Report on 1981–82 Trade/Investment Barriers: Membership Survey', mimeo, March.

Anderson, A. and A.M. Rugman (1990), 'Country Factor Bias in the Administration of Anti-Dumping and Countervailing Duty Cases', Working Paper 30, Ontario Centre for International Business, mimeo.

Anderson, F.L. (1984), *Foreign Investment Control in the Canadian Mineral Sector: Lessons from the Australian Experience* Kingston: Queen's University, Centre for Resource Studies.

Anderson, P.A. (1983), 'Decision Making by Objection and the Cuban Missile Crisis', *Administrative Science Quarterly*, **28**, 201–22.

Arndt, H.W. (1977), 'Foreign Investment', in J.P. Nieuwenhuysen and P.J. Drake (eds), *Australian Economic Policies*, Melbourne: The University Press.

Arndt, H.W. and D.R. Sherk (1959), 'Export Franchises of Australian Companies with Overseas Affiliations', *Economic Record*, **35**, 239–42.

Arrow, K.J. (1951), *Social Choice and Individual Values*, New York: John Wiley and Sons.

Australia (1965), *Report of the Committee of Economic Enquiry*, vols I and II, Canberra: Commonwealth Government Printer (Vernon Report).

—— (1977), *White Paper on Manufacturing Industry*, Canberra.

—— (1979), 'Report of the Study Group on Structural Adjustment', (Chairman Sir John Crawford), *Journal of Industry and Commerce*, no. 19 (Supplement).

—— (1984), 'Outline of a "Greenfields" resource rent tax in the petroleum sector', mimeo.

Australia, Department of the Treasury (1972), *Overseas Investment in Australia*, Treasury Economic Paper No. 1, Canberra.

Australia, Department of the Treasury (1979–80, 1982, 1987) *Australia's Foreign Investment Policy: A Guide for Investors*.

Australia, Foreign Investment Review Board, *Reports* 1977 to 1987–8 inclusive, Canberra: Government Publishing Service.

Australian Bureau of Investment (1983), *Foreign Investment 1981–2*, Canberra: Australian Government Publishing Service.

Australian Bureau of Statistics, *Foreign Ownership and Control of Manufactures*, various years.

Bailey, D., G. Harte, R. Sugden (1991a), 'A Description of Recent French Policy Towards Transnational Corporations', Research Centre for Industrial Strategy, University of Birmingham, mimeo.

—— (1991b), 'Dirigisme at the Core of French Approach to Inward Investment', *Multinational Business*, **2**, 34–43.

—— (1991c), 'A Description of Recent Japanese Policy Towards Transnational Corporations', Research Centre for Industrial Strategy, University of Birmingham, mimeo.

Baker, J.C. and T. Kondo (1970), 'Japanese Policy Concerning Foreign Investment in Japan', *University of Washington Business Review*, Autumn.

Baldwin, A. and P. Gorecki (1983), 'Trade, Tariffs, Product Diversity and Length of Production Run in Canadian Manufacturing Industries 1970–79', Discussion Paper 247, Ottawa: Economic Council of Canada.

Baldwin, R. and P. Krugman (1988), 'Market Access and International Trade: A Simulation Study of 16K Random Access Memories', in R. Feenstra (ed.), *Empirical Methods For International Trade*, Cambridge: MIT Press.

Bale, H.E., Jr. (1983), 'Trade Policy Aspects of International Direct Investment Policies', presented to a Conference on Recent Issues and Initiatives in US Trade Policy, NBER, Cambridge: Mass., 1983, mimeo.

—— (1984), 'The US Federal Government's Policy Toward Foreign Direct Investment', in E.H. Fry and L.H. Radebaugh (eds), *Regulation of Foreign Direct Investment in Canada and the United States*, pp. 29–46, Brigham Young University.

Bank of England (February 1977), *A Guide to United Kingdom Exchange Control*.

Bank of Japan (1981), *Outline of Foreign Exchange Control in Japan*, March.

Banks, A.S. (ed.) (1987), *Political Handbook of the World, 1987*, Binghampton, NY: SA Publications.

Batra, R.N. and J. Hadar (1979), 'Theory of Multinational Firm: Fixed Versus Floating Exchange Rates', *Oxford Economic Papers*, **31**, 258–9.

Behrman, J.N. (1968), *Direct Manufacturing Investment, Exports and the Balance of Payments*, New York: National Foreign Trade Council, Inc.

Bell, H.F. (1975), 'Australian Government Policy in Relation to Foreign Investment', *The Australian Quarterly*, March, 44–58.

Bergsten, G.F., T. Horst and T.H. Moran (1978), *American Multinationals and American Interests*, Washington: Brookings Institution.

Bertin, G.Y. (ed.) (1973) *La Croissance de la Grande Firme Multinationale*, Paris, Centre Nationale de la Recherche Scientifique.

—— (1975), *L'Industrie Française Face Aux Multinationals*, Paris: La Documentation Française.

—— (1977), 'France as Host to Small Country Foreign Investment', in T. Agmon and C. Kindleberger (eds), *Multinationals from Small Countries*, Cambridge, MA and London, England: MIT Press.

—— (1987), 'Multinational Enterprise, Transfer Partners and Transfer Policies', in Safarian and Bertin (eds), *Multinationals, Governments, and International Technology Transfer.*

Bhagwati, J. (1990), 'Departures from Multilateralism: Regionalism and Aggressive Unilateralism', *Economic Journal*, **100**, 1304–17.

Bhagwati, J.N. and R.A. Brecher (1980), 'National Welfare in an Open Economy in The Presence of Foreign-owned Factors of Production', *Journal of International Economics*, **10**, 103–15.

Bierstecker, T.J. (1980), 'The Illusion of State Power: Transnational Corporations and the Neutralization of Host-Country Legislation', *Journal of Peace Research*, vol. 17, (3), 207–21.

Birembaum, D. and S.K. Zackula (1988), 'Foreign Investment in Japan: Current Limits and Restrictions', *East Asia Executive Reports*, October.

Bloomfield, G. (1978), *The World Auto Industry*, London: David and Charles.

Boddewyn, J.J. (1972), 'Issues Between the Multinational Corporation and Host Governments: the European Case', in A. Kapoor and P.D. Grub (eds), *The Multinational Enterprise in Transition*, Princeton, NJ: Darwin Press.

—— (1974), 'Western European Policies Towards U.S. Investors', *The Bulletin*, Institute of Finance, New York University, March, 7–95.

Boddewyn, J.J., M.B. Halbrich and A.C. Perry (1986), 'Service Multinationals: Conceptualization, Measurement and Theory', *Journal of International Business Studies*, Fall.

Bond, E.W. and S.E. Guisinger (1985), 'Investment Incentives as Tariff

Substitutes: a Comprehensive Measure of Protection', *Review of Economics and Statistics*, **67**, (1), 91–9.
Bonin, B. (1984), *L'entreprise multinationale et l'Etat*, Montréal: Editions Etudes Vivantes.
Bonnaud, J.J. et A. Bosser (1973), 'La politique économique des pouvoirs publics et les grandes firmes internationales en France', in G.Y. Bertin (ed.), *La Croissance de la Grande Firme Multinationale*.
Borner, S. *et al.* (1985), 'Global Structural Change and International Competition Among Industrial Firms: The Case of Switzerland', *Kyklos*, **38**, (1), 77–103.
Brander, J.A. (1984), 'Rationales for Strategic Trade and Industrial Policy', in P.R. Krugman (ed.), *Strategic Trade Policy and the New International Economics*, Cambridge, Mass.: MIT Press.
Brander, J.A. and B.J. Spencer (1985), 'Export Subsidies and International Market Share Rivalry', *Journal of International Economics*, **18**, February, 83–100.
Brash, D.T. (1966), *American Investment in Australian Industry*, Canberra: Australian National University Press.
—— (1975), 'Foreign Investment in New Zealand', in R.H. Carey (ed.), *Foreign Investment Policy in New Zealand*, 90–107, Wellington: New Zealand Institute of Public Administration.
Brean, D.J.S. (1984), *International Issues in Taxation: The Canadian Perspective*, Toronto: Canadian Tax Foundation.
Breton, A. (1964), 'The Economics of Nationalism', *Journal of Political Economy*, **72**, (4), 376–86.
Briner, H. (1976), 'Switzerland', *International Business Lawyer*, **4**, (1), 67–74.
Britton, J.N.H. and J.M. Gilmour (1978), *The Weakest Link*, Ottawa: Science Council of Canada, Background Study 43.
Brooke, M.Z. and H.L. Remmers (1970), *The Strategy of Multinational Enterprise: Organization and Finance*, New York: American Elsevier.
Buchanan, J. and G. Tullock (1962), *The Calculus of Consent*, Ann Arbor: University of Michigan Press.
Buckley, P.J. (1981), 'A Critical Review of Theories of the Multinational Enterprise', *Aussenwirtschaft*, **36**, (1), 70–87.
—— (1983), 'New Forms of International Industrial Co-operation: a Survey of the Literature with Special Reference to North–South Technology Transfer', *Aussenwirtschaft*, **38**, 195–222.
—— (1988), 'The Limits of Explanation: Testing the International Theory of The Multinational Enterprise', *Journal of International Business Studies*, **19**, (2), 181–93.
Buckley, P.J. and M. Casson (1976), *The Future of the Multinational Enterprise*, London: Macmillan.

Bürgenmeier, B. (1991), 'Swiss Foreign Direct Investment', in B. Bürgenmeier and J.-L. Mucchielli (eds), *Multinationals and Europe 1992*.

Bürgenmeier, B. and J.-L. Mucchielli (eds) (1991), *Multinationals and Europe 1992*, London and New York: Routledge.

Business International (various dates and countries) 'Investing, Licensing and Trading Conditions Abroad' (ILT), New York: Business International Corporation.

Cairns, R. (1980), 'Rationales for Regulation', Ottawa: Economic Council of Canada, Technical Report 2.

Canada (1956), *Preliminary Report of the Royal Commission on Canada's Economic Prospects*, Ottawa (Gordon Report).

—— (1968), *Foreign Ownership and the Structure of Canadian Industry*, Ottawa: Privy Council Office (Watkins Report).

—— (1972), *Foreign Direct Investment in Canada*, Ottawa: Information Canada (Gray Report).

Canada, Energy Mines and Resources (1980), *The National Energy Program*, Ottawa.

Canada, Foreign Investment Review Act (1974–5 to 1984–5 inclusive), *Annual Report*, Ottawa: Ministry of Supply and Services.

Canada, FIRA (Foreign Investment Review Agency, 1977, 1978), *Selected Readings in Canadian Legislation Affecting Foreign Investment in Canada. Part I: Federal Laws and Regulations as of October 1977. Part II: Provincial Laws and Regulations as of November 1977*, Ottawa: Foreign Investment Review Agency.

—— (1979), *A Comparison of Foreign Investment Controls in Canada and Australia*, Ottawa: FIRA papers No. 5, April.

—— (1982), 'Barriers to Foreign Investment in the United States', mimeo.

Cantwell, J. (1991), 'The Theory of Technological Competence and its Application to International Production', in McFetridge (ed.), *Foreign Investment, Technology and Economic Growth*.

Carey, R.H. (1975) (ed.), *Foreign Investment Policy in New Zealand*, Wellington, New Zealand: Institute of Public Administration.

Carlson, S. (1980), 'Fransk Kontrol Av Internationella Direktinvesteringar: Bakgrund, syften och arbetssätt', Upsalla, 1980, mimeo ('French Control of International Direct Investments: Background, Aims and Implementation', a report prepared for the Swedish Committee on Direct Investment (unofficial translation into English with S. Carlson's permission).

Carr, D.W. (1978), *Foreign Investment and Development in the South-West Pacific, with special reference to Australia and Indonesia*, New York: Praeger Publishers.

Casson, M. (1979), *Alternatives to the Multinational Enterprise* London: Macmillan.

—— (1991), 'Modelling the Multinational Enterprise: A Research Agenda', *Millenium Journal of International Studies*, **20**, (2), 271–85.

Caves, R.E. (1971), 'International Corporations: The Industrial Economics of Foreign Investment', *Economica*, **38**, February 1–27.

—— (1980), 'Industrial Organization, Corporate Strategy and Structure', *Journal of Economic Literature*, **18**, (1), 64–92.

—— (1982), *Multinational Enterprise and Economic Analysis*, Cambridge: Cambridge University Press.

Caves, R.E. and S.K. Mehra (1986), 'Entry of Foreign Multinationals into U.S. Manufacturing Industries', in M.E. Porter (ed.), *Competition in Global Industries*, ch. 14, pp. 449–481, Boston: Harvard Business School Press.

Caves, R.E. and G.L. Reuber (1971), *Capital Transfers and Economic Policy 1951–1962*, Cambridge, Mass.: Harvard University Press.

Chopra, T., J.T. Boddewyn and R.L. Torneden (1978), 'U.S. Foreign Divestment: a 1972–1975 Updating', *Columbia Journal of World Business*, Spring.

Christiana Bank og Kreditkasse (no date), *Establishing a Business in Norway*, Oslo.

Cibbora, C. (1991), 'Alliances as Learning Experiences: Cooperation, Competition and Change in High Tech Industries', in Mytelka (ed.), *Strategic Partnerships*.

Clark, R. (1979), *The Japanese Company*, New Haven: Yale University Press.

Clarkson, S. (1982), *Canada and the Reagan Challenge*, Ottawa: Canadian Institute for Economic Policy.

Coase, R.H. (1937), 'The Nature of the Firm', *Economica*, **4**, November, 386–405.

Crough, G.J. and E.L. Wheelwright, (1981), *Australia, The Client State: A Study of the Effects of Transnational Corporations*, Sydney: University of Sydney, Transnational Corporations Research Project, Working Paper No. 9.

Curzon, G. and V. Curzon (eds) (1977), *The Multinational Enterprise in a Hostile World*, London: Macmillan.

Davidson, C., S.J. Matusz and M.E. Kreinin (1985), 'Analysis of Performance Standards for Direct Foreign Investments', *Canadian Journal of Economics*, XVIII, (4), 876–90.

Davidson, W.H. and D.G. McFetridge (1984), 'International Technology Transactions and the Theory of the Firm', *Journal of Industrial Economics*, March, pp. 253–64.

—— (1985), 'Key Characteristics in the Choice of International Technology Transfer Mode', *Journal of International Business Studies*, Summer.

Deane, R.S. (1970), *Foreign Investment in New Zealand Manufacturing*, Wellington, New Zealand: Sweet and Maxwell.

—— (1975), 'An Economic Policy Dilemma: The Case of Foreign Investment in New Zealand', in R.H. Carey (ed.), *Foreign Investment Policy in New Zealand*.

De Jong, H.W. (1973), 'Multinational Enterprise in the "Low Countries"', in G.Y. Bertin (ed.), *La Croissance de la Grande Firme Multinationale*.

Delapierre, M. et C-A Michalet (1976), *Les Implantations Etrangères en France: Stratégies et Structures*, Paris: Calmann-Lévy.

De la Torre, J., R.B. Stobaugh and P. Telesio (1973), 'U.S. Multinational Enterprise and Changes in the Skill Composition of U.S. Employment', in D. Kujawa (ed.), *American Labor and the Multinational Corporation*, New York: Praeger Publishers.

de Meirleir, M.J. (1976), *A Comparative Analysis of the Incentives Offered to Industry in the Common Market Countries*, Brussels: Plant Location International.

Dickie, R.B. (1970), *Foreign Investment: France, A Case Study*, Leyden: A.W. Sijthoff.

Dixit, A.K. and G.M. Grossman (1986), 'Targeted Export Promotion with Several Oligopolistic Industries', *Journal of International Economics*, **21**, November, 233–49.

Dosi, G., C. Freeman, R. Nelson, G. Silverberg and L. Soete (eds) (1988), *Technical Change and Economic Theory*, London: Pinter Publishers.

Downs, A. (1957), *An Economic Theory of Democracy*, New York: Harper.

Doyle, A.L. (1983), 'The French Nationalizations: Mitterrand Challenges the Multinationals', in B.S. Fisher and J. Turner (eds), *Regulating the Multinational Enterprise*, New York: Praeger Publishers.

Doz, Y.L. (1980), 'Strategic Management in Multinational Companies', *Sloan Management Review*, **21**, 27–46.

Doz, Y.L. and C.K. Pralahad (1980), 'How MNEs Cope with Host Government Intervention', *Harvard Business Review*, **58**, March–April, 51–7.

Dunning, J.H. (1958), *American Investment in British Manufacturing Industry*, London: Allen and Unwin.

—— (1970), *Studies in International Investment*, London: George Allen and Unwin.

—— (1973), 'The Determinants of International Production', *Oxford Economic Papers*, 25, November, 289–336.

—— (1977), 'Trade, Location of Economic Activity, and the MNE: A Search For an Eclectic Approach', in B. Ohlin *et al.* (eds), *The International Allocation of Economic Activity*, New York: Holmes and Meier.

—— (1979), 'Explaining Changing Patterns of International Production: In Defence of the Eclectic Theory', *Oxford Bulletin of Economics and Statistics*, **41**, 269–95.

—— (1981), *International Production and the Multinational Enterprise*, London: George Allen and Unwin.
—— (1983), 'Changes in the Level and Structure of International Production: The Last One Hundred Years', in M. Casson (ed.), *The Growth of International Business*, 84–134, London: George Allen and Unwin.
—— (ed.) (1985a), *Multinational Enterprises, Economic Structure and International Competitiveness*, Chichester: John Wiley and Sons.
—— (1985b), 'The United Kingdom', in J.H. Dunning (ed.), *Multinational Enterprises, Economic Structure and International Competitiveness*.
—— (1988), 'The Eclectic Paradigm of International Production: A Restatement and Some Possible Extensions', *Journal of International Business Studies*, **19**, (1), 1–31.
—— (1990), 'Dunning on Porter: Reshaping the Diamond of Competitive Advantage', paper to the annual meeting of the Academy of International Business, Toronto, October.
Dunning, J.H. and J. Cantwell (1987), *IRM Directory of Statistics of International Investment and Production*, London: Macmillan.
Dunning, J.H. and M. Gilman (1977), 'Alternative Policy Prescriptions and the Multinational Enterprise', in Curzon and Curzon (eds), *The Multinational Enterprise in a Hostile World*.
Dunning, J.H. and P. Robson (eds) (1988a), *Multinationals and the European Community*, Oxford: Basil Blackwell.
—— (1988b), 'Multinational Corporate Integration and Regional Economic Integration', in Dunning and Robson (eds), *Multinationals and the European Community*, 1–23.
Dye, T.R. (1972), *Understanding Public Policy*, Englewood Cliffs, NJ: Prentice Hall.
Eastman, H.C. and S. Stykolt (1967), *The Tariff and Competition in Canada*, Toronto: Macmillan.
Eaton, J. and G.M. Grossman (1986), 'Optimal Trade Policy and Industrial Policy Under Oligopoly', *Quarterly Journal of Economics*, May, 383–406.
Eckerberg, P. (1978), *Kontroll av utländsk Företagsetablering i Sverige m.m.* (Control of the Establishment of Foreign Companies in Sweden, with an English Summary), 45–68, Stockholm: Statens offentliga utredningar, Justitiedepartementet.
Economic Council of Canada (1983), *The Bottom Line: Technology, Trade and Income Growth*, Ottawa: Minister of Supply and Services Canada.
Eden, L., (1990), New Directions in International Business Research', *Research in Global Business Management*, 163–75, Greenwich Conn.: JAI Press.
—— (1991), 'Multinational Responses to Trade and Technology Changes:

Implications for Canada', in McFetridge (ed.), *Foreign Investment, Technology and Economic Growth.*

Ehrman, C.M. and M. Hamburg (1986), 'Information Search for Foreign Direct Investment Using Two-Stage Country Selection Procedures: a New Procedure', *Journal of International Business Studies*, Summer, (42), 93–106.

Einarsen, J. (1970), 'Foreign Investment in Norway', in Litvak and Maule (eds), *Foreign Investment: the Experience of Host Countries.*

Ellicott, J. (1969), 'United States Controls on Foreign Direct Investment: the 1969 Program', *Law and Contemporary Problems*, School of Law, Duke University, Winter, **34**, (1), 47–63.

Encarnation, D.J. and L.T. Wells, Jr. (1985), 'Sovereignty En Garde: Negotiating with Foreign Investors', *International Organization*, **39**, (1), Winter, 47–78.

Fagre, N. and L.T. Wells, Jr. (1982), 'Bargaining Power of Multinationals and Host Governments', *Journal of International Business Studies*, Fall, 9–23.

Fayerweather, John (1973), *Foreign Investment in Canada – Prospects for National Policy*, New York: International Arts and Sciences Press.

—— (1974), *The Mercantile Bank Affair*, New York: New York University Press.

Fazzone, P.B. (1983), 'Business Effects of the Extraterritorial Reach of the U.S. Export Control Laws', New York University, *Journal of International Law and Politics*, Spring, 545–84.

Federal Reserve Bank of New York (1979–80), 'National Policies Toward Foreign Direct Investment', *Quarterly Review*, Winter.

Forbes, M.J. (1979), 'Ireland: The New Scheme of Industrial Tax Incentives', *Intertax*, **9**, 352–58.

France, Conseil Economique et Social (1981), 'Les Investissements Français à l'Etranger et les Investissements Etranger en France, Avis, et Rapport par M. Jacques Ehrsam', *Journal Officiel de la République Française*, 25 February.

France, DATAR (1974), *Investissements Etrangers et Aménagement du Territoire*, Paris: Livre Blanc.

Frank, I. and R. Hirono (eds) (1974), *How the United States and Japan See Each Other's Economy*, New York: Committee for Economic Development.

Franko, L.G. (1976), *The European Multinationals*, London: Harper and Row.

—— (1977), 'European Multinational Enterprises in the Integration Process', in Curzon and Curzon (eds), *The Multinational Enterprise in a Hostile World.*

—— (1989), 'Use of Minority and 50–50 Joint Ventures by United States Multinationals During the 1970s: The Interaction of Host Country Policies and Corporate Strategies', *Journal of International Business Studies*, Spring.

Fuss, M. and L. Waverman (1987), 'The Japanese Productivity Advantage in Automobile Production: Can it be Transferred to North America?' in Safarian and Bertin (eds), *Multinationals, Governments and International Technology Transfer.*

Garnaut, R. and A.C. Ross (1978), 'Alternative Approach to the Taxation of Natural Resource Projects', in Sir John Crawford and S. Okita (ed.), *Raw Materials and Pacific Economic Integration*, Canberra: Australian National University Press.

—— (1983), *Taxation of Mineral Rents*, Oxford: Clarendon Press.

Gates, S.R. and W.G. Egelhoff (1986) 'Centralization in Headquarters – Subsidiary Relationships', *Journal of International Business Studies*, Summer.

Gennard, J. (1972), *British Labour and Multinational Corporations: a Review of Responses and Attitudes*, London: British North American Research Committee.

Giddy, D.H. and S. Young (1982), 'Conventional Theory and Unconventional Multinationals: Do New Forms of Multinational Enterprise Require New Theories?', in Rugman, *New Theories of the Multinational Enterprise.*

Gillespie, R.W. (1972), 'The Policies of England, France and Germany as Recipients of Foreign Direct Investment', in F. Machlup *et al.* (eds), *International Mobility and Movement of Capital*, New York: Columbia University Press.

Gilpin, R. (1968), *France in The Age of The Scientific State*, Princeton: University Press.

Gittelman, M. (1990), 'Transnational Corporations in Europe 1992: Implications for Developing Countries', *UN–CTC Reporter*, Spring, 35–42.

Gladwin, N.T. and J. Walter (1983), 'How Multinationals Can Manage Social Conflict', in W.H. Goldberg (ed.), *Governments and Multinationals.*

Globerman, S. (1979), *U.S. Ownership of Firms in Canada*, Montreal: C.D. Howe Research Institute.

—— (1984a), 'The Consistency of Canada's Foreign Investment Review Agency: a Temporal Analysis', *Journal of International Business Studies*, Spring/Summer, 119–29.

—— (1984b), 'Canada's Foreign Investment Review Agency and the Direct Investment Process in Canada', *Canadian Public Administration*, **27**, (3), 313–28.

Goldberg, R.M. and C.P. Kindleberger (1970), 'Towards a GATT for Investment: A Proposal for Supervision of the International Corporation', *Law and Policy in International Business*, **2**, (2), 295–325.

Goldberg, W.H. (ed.) with A.P. Negandhi (1983), *Governments and Multinationals: The Policy of Controls vs. Autonomy*, Cambridge, Mass.: Oelgeschlager, Gunnand Hain.

Goldsbrough, D.J. (1979), 'The Role of Foreign Direct Investment in the External Adjustment Process', *IMF Staff Paper*, 26, 725–54.

—— (1981), 'International Trade of MNEs and its Responsiveness to Changes in Aggregate Demand and Relative Prices', IMF Staff Papers, **28**, (3), 573–99.

Gomes-Casseres, B. (1990), 'Firm Ownership Preferences and Host Government Restrictions: an Integrated Approach', *Journal of International Business Studies*, **21**, (1), 1–22.

Gotlieb, C.C. and Z.P. Zeman (1980), 'Towards a National Computer and Communications Policy: Seven National Approaches', Toronto, May, Report for the Department of Communications, mimeo.

Graham, E.M. (1978), 'Transatlantic Investment by Multinational Firms: A Rivalistic Phenomenon?', *Journal of Post Keynesian Economics*, **1**, (1), 82–99.

Graham, E.M. and P.R. Krugman (1989), *Foreign Direct Investment in the United States*, Washington, DC: Institute for International Economics.

Graham, N. (1982), 'Developed Countries and Multinational Corporations: Threat, Perceptions and Policy Response in France and the U.K.', in J. Fayerweather (ed.), *Host National Attitudes Towards Multinational Corporations*, New York: Praeger Publishers.

Gray, H.P. (ed.) (1986), *Uncle Sam as Host*, Research in International Business and Finance, vol. 5, Greenwich, Conn.: JAI Press.

Gray Report (1972), *Foreign Direct Investment in Canada*, Ottawa: Report to the Honourable Herb Gray, prepared for the Government of Canada.

Grayson, L.E. (1981), *National Oil Companies*, New York: John Wiley.

Grosse, R.E. (1980), *Foreign Investment Codes and Location of Direct Investment*, New York: Praeger Publishers.

Grossman, G.M. (1981), 'The Theory of Domestic Content Protection and Content Preference', *Quarterly Journal of Economics*, **96**, 583–603.

Guisinger, S. and associates (ed.) (1985), *Investment Incentives and Performance Requirements*, New York: Praeger Publishers.

Hagedoorn, J. (1990), 'Organizational Modes of Inter-Firm Cooperation and Technology Transfer', *Technovation*, **10**, (1), 17–30.

Hagedoorn, J., and J. Schackenraad (1990), 'Technology Co-operation, Strategic Alliances and Their Motives: Brother Can You Spare a Dime or Do You Have a Light?', paper for SMS Conference, Stockholm, September, Maastricht Institute on Innovation and Technology.

Haggeney, B. (1976), 'Restrictions on Foreign Investments: Germany', *International Business Lawyer*, **4**, (1), 59–67.

—— (1980), 'Germany', *International Business Lawyer*, **8**, (5), 141–5.

Hague, D. and G. Wilkinson (1983), *The IRC: an Experiment in Industrial Intervention*, London: Allen and Unwin.

Haner, F.T. (1980), *Global Business Strategy for the 1980s*, New York: Praeger Publishers.

Hannequart, A. (1974), 'Aspects de la Politique Industrielle en Belgique', *Etudes Economiques*, Mons, no. 1.

Harris, R.G. (1991), 'Strategic Trade Policy, Technology, Spillovers and Foreign Investment', in McFetridge (ed.), *Foreign Investment, Technology and Economic Growth*.

Harris, Richard G. with David Cox (1983), *Trade, Industrial Policy and Canadian Manufacturing*, Toronto: Ontario Economic Council.

Hartle, D.G. (1976), *A Theory of the Expenditure Budgetary Process*, Toronto: Ontario Economic Council.

Harvey, I. (1981), 'Host Country Review of Foreign Direct Investment: a Comparative Study of Canadian and Australian Regulation', Master of Laws thesis, Toronto: York University, Osgoode Hall Law School.

Hawkins, R.G. (1972), 'Job Displacement and the Multinational Firm: a Methodological Review', Washington: Center for Multinational Studies, Occasional Paper 3.

Hay, K.A. (1971), *Japan: Challenge and Opportunity for Canadian Industry*, Montreal: Canadian Economic Policy Committee.

Hedlund, G. and L. Otterbeck (1977), *The Multinational Corporation, the Nation State, and the Trade Unions: a European Perspective*, Kent, Ohio: Kent State University Press.

Helliwell, J.F., M.E. MacGregor and A. Plourde (1984), 'Changes in Canadian Energy Demand, Supply and Policies, 1974–86,' *Natural Resources Journal*, **24**, Special Issue April 1984, 297–324.

Helpman, E. (1984), 'A Simple Theory of International Trade with Multinational Corporations', *Journal of Political Economy*, **92**, (3), 451–71.

Helpman, S.H. and P.R. Krugman (1985), *Market Structure and Foreign Trade: Increasing Returns, Imperfect Competition and the Market Economy*, Cambridge, Mass.: MIT Press.

Henderson, D.F. (1975), *Foreign Enterprise in Japan: Laws and Policies*, Rutland, Vermont and Tokyo, Japan: Charles E. Tuttle Company Inc.

Hernes, G. (1982), *Maktutredningen: Sluttrapport*, Oslo: Universitetsförlaget (*The Power Evaluation: Final Report*), of a Royal Commission chaired by G. Hernes, Oslo: University Publishing Company.

Heum, P.A. (1979), 'Foreigners as Domestic Citizens: Multinational Corporations and the Nation State', *Cooperation and Conflict*, **XII**, 35–47.

—— (1982), 'Multinational Companies: International Decision-Units in the Norwegian Economy', ch. 6 of G. Hernes, *The Power Evaluation*.

Hipple, F.S. (1990), 'Multinational Companies and International Trade: The Impact of Intrafirm Shipments on U.S. Foreign Trade 1977–1982', *Journal of International Business Studies*, **21**, (3), 495–504.

Hirschman, A.O. (1970), *Exit, Voice and Loyalty*, Cambridge, Mass.: Harvard University Press.

Hodges, M. (1974), *Multinational Corporations and National Government*, London: Saxon House.

Holland, S. (1974), 'Europe's New State Enterprises', in R. Vernon (ed.), *Big Business and the State*, Cambridge, Mass.: Harvard University Press.

Hood, N. and S. Young (1979), *The Economics of Multinational Enterprise*, New York: Longman Inc.

Hörnell, E. and Vahlne, J.-E. (1986), *Multinationals: The Swedish Case*, London: Croom Helm.

Horst, T. (1972) 'The Industrial Composition of U.S. Exports and Subsidiary Sales to the Canadian Market', *American Economic Review*, **62**, March, 37–45.

—— (1977), 'American Taxation of Multinational Firms', *American Economic Review*, **67**, (3), 376–89.

Hufbauer, G.C. and F.M. Adler (1968), *Overseas Manufacturing Investment and the Balance of Payments*, Washington, DC: US Treasury, Tax Policy Research Study no. 1.

Hufbauer, G.C. and A.J. Samet (1982), 'Canadian–American Investment Relations', in W. Armstrong, L. Armstrong and F. Wilcox (eds), *Canada and the United States: Dependence and Divergence*, Cambridge, Mass.: Ballinger.

Hufbauer G.C. and J.J. Schott (1985), 'The Soviet–European Gas Pipeline: a Case of Failed Sanction', in T. Moran (ed.), *Multinational Corporations: The Political Economy of Foreign Direct Investment*, Lexington: D.C. Heath.

Hymer, S.H. (1960) 'The International Operations of National Firms: A Study of Direct Foreign Investment', PhD. dissertation, MIT (published by MIT Press, 1976).

InterData Pty. Ltd. (1988), *Business Destinations Australia*, 3rd ed.

International Labour Office (1981), *Employment Effects of Multinational Enterprises in Industrialized Countries*, Geneva: ILO.

International Monetary Fund (various years), *Balance of Payments Yearbook*, Washington, DC: IMF.

—— (various years), *International Financial Statistics*, Washington, DC: IMF.

Ireland (1984), *White Paper on Industrial Policy*, Dublin: The Stationery Office.

Ishimine, T. (1978), 'Fiscal Incentives for Japan's Exports and Direct Foreign Investment', *Bulletin of Intenational Fiscal Documentation*.

Itagaki, T. (1981), 'The Theory of the Multinational Firm Under Exchange Rate Uncertainty', *Canadian Journal of Economics*, **14**, 276–97.

Itaki, M. (1991), 'A Critical Assessment of the Eclectic Theory of the Multinational Enterprise', *Journal of International Business Studies*, **22**, (3,) 445–60.

Japan, Fair Trade Commission (1968), 'Antimonopoly Act Guidelines for International Licensing Agreements', mimeo.

—— (1979), *Annual Report* (unofficial translation).

Japan, Ministry of Finance (1974), *Manual of Foreign Investment in Japan*, Tokyo: Ministry of Finance and Bank of Japan, January.

—— (1980a), 'Foreign Exchange and Foreign Control Law As Amended by Law No. 15' dated 19 December 1979.

—— (1980b), 'Commentary on the Amendment of the Foreign Exchange Control Law'.

—— (1981), 'Foreign Exchange and Control Order and Cabinet Order Concerning Direct Domestic Investments etc.'

Japan, MITI (1974), 'Japan's Overseas Investments: Background Information', September.

—— (1980), 'Foreign Investment in Japan', *Japan Reporting*, April.

—— (1981), 'Outline of Existing Measures Concerning Direct Overseas Investment', mimeo.

—— (1983), 'Questions and Answers Concerning Direct Investment in Japan', mimeo.

Japan, Science Technology Agency (1981), *Annual Report on Introduction of Foreign Technology*, Prime Minister's Office, Tokyo: Government Printing Office (unofficial translation).

Jenkins, G.P. (1979), 'Taxes and Tariffs and the Evaluation of the Benefit from Foreign Investment', *Canadian Journal of Economics*, **12**, August, 410–25.

Johnson, C. (1977), 'MITI and Japanese International Economic Policy', in R.A. Scalapino (ed.), *The Foreign Policy of Modern Japan*, Berkeley: University of California Press.

Johnson, H.G. (1965), 'A Theoretical Model of Economic Nationalism in New and Developing States', *Political Science Quarterly*, June.

—— (1970), 'The Efficiency and Welfare Implications of the Multinational Corporation', in C.P. Kindleberger (ed.), *The International Corporation: A Symposium*; ch. 2, Cambridge, Mass.: MIT Press.

Johnstone, A.W. (1965), *United States Direct Investment in France: an Investigation of the French Charges*, Cambridge, Mass.: MIT Press.

Julius, D. (1990), *Global Companies and Public Policy: The Growing Challenge of Foreign Direct Investment*, London, Pinter Publishers, for Royal Institute of International Affairs.

Kartte, W. (1976), 'Are New Instruments Needed for Government Control of the Decision-Making Process in Multinational Firms?', *German Economic Review*, **14**, (2), 93–111.

Katzenstein, P.J. (1980), 'Capitalism in One Country: Switzerland in the International Economy', *International Organization*, **34**, (4), 507–40.

—— (1985), *Small States in World Markets*, Ithaca: Cornell University Press.

Kelly, M., N. Kirmani, M. Xafa, C. Bounekamp and P. Winglee (1988), 'Issues and Developments in International Trade Policy', Occasional Paper 63, Washington, DC: International Monetary Fund.

Kemper, N.J. and M. De Smidt (1980), 'Foreign Manufacturing Establishments in The Netherlands', *Tijdschrift voor Econ. en Soc. Geografie*, **71**, (1), 21–40.

Kester, W.C. (1988), 'Capital and Ownership Structure: A Comparison of U.S. and Japanese Manufacturing Corporations', in A.M. Spence and H.A. Hazard (eds), *International Competitiveness*, Cambridge, Mass.: Ballinger Publishing Company.

Kim, E. and J.R. Peters (1975), 'Guide to International Trade Law in Japan', *Journal of World Trade Law*, **5**, October.

Kindleberger, C.P. (1969), *American Business Abroad*, New Haven: Yale University Press.

—— (1984), *Multinational Excursions*, Cambridge, Mass.: MIT Press.

Knickerbocker, F.T. (1973), *Oligopolistic Reaction and Multinational Enterprise*, Boston: Division of Research, Graduate School of Business Administration, Harvard University.

Knudsen, O. (1980), 'Foreign Investment and Multinational Companies in the Nordic Countries', *Cooperation and Conflict*, **XV**, 209–15.

Knudsen, O. and E.A. Landmark (1980), 'Multinasjonale selskapers rolle i de nordiske lands okonomi', *(The Role of Multinational Companies in the Economies of the Nordic Nations*, a report by the Nordic Ministerial Council's Contact Group on Multinational Companies), Stockholm: GOTAB.

Kobayashi, N. (1970), 'Foreign Investment in Japan', in Litvak and Maule (eds), *Foreign Investment: The Experience of Host Countries*.

Kobrin, S.J. (1980), 'Foreign Enterprise and Forced Divestment in LDCs', *International Organization*, **34**, (1), Winter, 65–88.

Kojima, J. and T. Ozawa (1985), 'Toward a Theory of Industrial Restructuring and Dynamic Comparative Advantage', *Hitotsubashi Journal of Economics*, **26**, 2.

Kojima, K. (1978), *Japanese Direct Foreign Investment: a Model of Multinational Business Operations*, Tokyo: Charles E. Tuttle Company.

—— (1982), 'Macroeconomic Versus International Business Approach to Direct Foreign Investment', *Hitotsubashi Journal of Economics*, **23**, 1–19.

Komiya, R. (1972), 'Direct Foreign Investment in Post War Japan', in P. Drysdale (ed.), *Direct Foreign Investment in Asia and the Pacific*, 137–68, Canberra: Australian National University Press.

—— (1988), 'Japan's Foreign Direct Investment: Facts and Theoretical Considerations', in Silvio Borner (ed.), *International Finance and Trade in a Polycentric World*, 241–89, London: Macmillan.

Kresl, P.K. (1976), *The Concession Process and Foreign Capital in Norway*, Scriftserie no. 4, Oslo: Norges Bank.

Krueger, A.O. (1974), 'The Political Economy of the Rent-Seeking Society', *American Economic Review*, **64**, (June), 291–303.

Krugman, P.R. (1984), 'The U.S. Response to Foreign Industrial Targeting', *Brookings Papers on Economic Activity*, **1**, 77–121.

Kudrle, R.T. (1991), 'Good for the Gander? Foreign Direct Investment in the United States', *International Organisation*, **45**, (3), 397–424.

Kydland, F.E. and E.C. Prescott (1976), 'Rules Rather than Discretion: The Inconsistency of Optimal Plans', *Journal of Political Economy*, **85**, (3), 1173–91.

Laband, D.N. (1984), 'Restriction of Farm Ownership as Rent-Seeking Behavior', *American Journal of Economics and Sociology*, **43**, (2), 179–89.

Lall, S. and P. Streeten (1977), *Foreign Investment, Transnationals and Developing Countries*, London: Macmillan.

LeCraw, D.L. (1984), 'Bargaining Power, Ownership and Profitability of Transnational Corporation in Developing Countries', *Journal of International Business Studies*, Spring/Summer, 27–43.

Levitt, K. (1970), *Silent Surrender: the Multinational Corporation in Canada*, Toronto: Macmillan of Canada.

Leyton-Brown, D. (1974), 'The Multinational Enterprise and Conflict in Canadian–American Relations', *International Organization*, **28**, (4), 733–53.

Lindberger, L. (1975), *Internationella Koncerner i industriländer*, Stockholm: Statens offentliga utredningar, Industridepartementet (Summary in English, 297–324).

Lipsey R.E. and I.B. Kravis (1985), 'The Competitive Position of US Manufacturing Firms', Working Paper 1557, Cambridge, MA: National Bureau of Economic Research.

Lipsey, R.E. and M.Y. Weiss (1981), 'Foreign Production and Exports in Manufacturing Industries', *Review of Economics and Statistics*, **63**, 488–94.

—— (1984), 'Foreign Production and Exports of Individual Firms', *Review of Economics and Statistics*, **66**, 304–8.

Lipson, C. (1985), *Standing Guard: Protecting Foreign Capital in the Nineteenth and Twentieth Centuries*, Berkeley: University of California Press.

Little, J.S. (1986), 'Recent Trends in Foreign Direct Investment in the United States: An Overview', in H.P. Gray (ed.), *Uncle Sam as Host*.

Litvak, J.A. and C.J. Maule (eds) (1970), *Foreign Investment: The Experience of Host Countries*, New York: Praeger Publishers.

Lockwood, W.W. (1968), *The Economic Development of Japan*, Princeton, NJ: Princeton University Press.

Lombard, F.J. (1978), 'Screening Foreign Direct Investment in LDCs: Empirical Findings of the Colombian Case (1967–1975)', *Journal of International Business Studies*, **9**, (3), 66–80.

Lowi, T. (1972), 'Four Systems of Policy, Politics and Choice', *Public Administration Review*, 32.

MacCharles, D.C. (1987), *Trade Among Multinationals: Intra-Industry Trade and National Competitiveness*, London: Croom Helm.

MacDougall, G.D.A. (1960), 'The Benefits and Costs of Direct Investment from Abroad: A Theoretical Approach', *Economic Record*, 36.

MacDowell, D. (1984), *A Fit Place for Investment?*, Ottawa: Conference Board of Canada, Study 81.

Madeuf, B. (1987), 'Trends in Technological Competitiveness within the OECD, 1970–1980', in Safarian and Bertin (eds).

Mansfield, E., and A. Romeo (1980), 'Technology Transfer to Overseas Subsidiaries by U.S.-Based Firms', *Quarterly Journal of Economics*, **95** 737–50.

Manuali, L. (1967) *La France face à l'implantation étrangère*, Paris: Editions S.E.F.

Mariotti, S. (1988), 'Italian Inward and Outward Direct Investment: a Comparison', in F. Chida and G. Viesti (eds), *The Italian Multinationals*, London: Croom Helm, 133–49.

Markusen, J.R. (1984), 'Multinationals, Multi-Plant Economies, and the Gains from Trade', *Journal of International Economics*, **16**, 205–26.

Marshall, H., F.A. Southard, Jr. and K.W. Taylor (1936), *Canadian–American Industry*, New Haven: Yale University Press.

Maxcy, G. (1981), *The Multinational Motor Industry*, London: Croom Helm.

McAleese, D. (1977), *A Profile of Grant-Aided Industry in Ireland*, Dublin: Industrial Development Authority.

—— (1978), 'Outward Looking Policies, Manufactured Exports and Economic Growth: The Irish Experience', in K.J. Artis and A.R. Nobay (eds), *Contemporary Economic Analysis: Proceedings of the 1977 ACUTE Conference*, Oxford: Basil Blackwell.

McArthur, G.H. and B.R. Scott (1969), *Industrial Planning in France*, Boston Mass.: Harvard University Press.

McFarlane, C.D. (1977), 'Laws Restrict Foreign Banks', *Euromoney*, March.

McFetridge, D.G. (1987), 'The Timing, Mode and Terms of Technology Transfer: Some Recent Findings', in Safarian and Bertin (eds), *Multinationals, Governments and International Technology Transfer.*

—— (ed.) (1991), *Foreign Investment, Technology and Economic Growth*, University of Calgary Press, in cooperation with Investment Canada.

McKeon, J. (1980), 'Economic Appraisal of Industrial Projects in Ireland', paper read before the Statistical and Social Enquiry Society of Ireland, mimeo.

McKern, R.B. (1976), *Multinational Enterprise and Natural Resources*, Sydney: McGraw-Hill.

Messerlin, P. (1987), 'International Investment, Protection and Technical Transfer: A Preliminary Examination of the Franco-Japanese Case', in Safarian and Bertin (eds), *Multinationals, Governments and International Technology Transfer.*

—— (1989), 'The Uruguay Negotiations on Subsidies and Countervailing Measures: Past and Future Constraints', in B. Balassa (ed.), *Subsidies and Countervailing Measures: Critical Issues for the Uruguay Round*, Washington, DC: World Bank.

Michalet, C.-A. (1991), 'Strategic Partnerships and the Changing Internationalization Process', in Mytelka, *Strategic Partnerships.*

Michalet, C.-A. and T. Chevallier (1985), 'France', in Dunning (ed.), *Multinational Enterprises, Economic Structure and International Competitiveness.*

Michalet, C.-A. and M. Delapierre (1973), *La multinationalisation des entreprises françaises*, Paris: Gauthier-Villars (published in English as *The Multinationalization of French Firms*, Chicago: Academy of International Business, 1975, Translated by David Ashton).

Mikesell, R.F. (eds) (1971a), *Foreign Investment in the Petroleum and Mineral Industries: Case Studies of Investor–Host Country Relations*, Baltimore: Johns Hopkins Press, for Resources for the Future.

—— (1971b), 'Conflict in Foreign Investor–Host Country Relations: a Preliminary Analysis', in Mikesell (ed.), *Foreign Investment in the Petroleum and Mineral Industries.*

Moran, T.H. (1973), 'Transnational Strategies of Protection and Defense by Multinational Corporations: Spreading the Risk and Raising the Cost for Nationalization in Natural Resources', *International Organization*, June, 273–87.

—— (1990), 'The Globalization of America's Defense Industries', *International Security*, Summer, **15**, (1), 57–99.

Mowery, D.C. (1988), 'Collaborative Ventures Between U.S. and Foreign Manufacturing Firms: An Overview', in D.C. Mowery (ed.), *International Collaborative Ventures in U.S. Manufacturing*, Cambridge, MA: Ballinger.

Mucchielli, J.-L. (1985), 'Les firmes multinationales fraçaises et la hierarchisation des nations', *Revue d'Economie Politique*, no. 5, 611–636.

Musgrave, P.B. (1975), *Direct Investment Abroad and the Multinationals: Effects on the United States Economy*, Subcommittee on Multinational Corporations, Committee on Foreign Relations, US Senate, Washington, DC: Government Printing Office.

Mutti, J.H. and S.D. Gerking (1983), 'Multinational Corporations and Discriminatory Investment Controls', Welwirtschaftliches Archiv Bd **CXIX**, 649–62.

Mytelka, L.K. (1986), 'The State and Foreign Capital in the Advanced Industrial Capitalist Countries', in A. Blais (ed.), *Industrial Policy*, Toronto: University of Toronto Press.

Mytelka, L. (ed.) (1991), *Strategic Partnerships: States, Firms, and International Competition*, London: Pinter Publishers.

Mytelka, L.K. and M. Delapierre (1988), 'The Alliance Strategies of European Firms in the Information Technology Industry and the Role of ESPRIT', in J.H. Dunning and P. Robson (eds), *Multinationals and the European Community*.

Nam, C.H. (1987), 'Export-Promoting Subsidies, Countervailing Threats and The General Agreement on Tariffs and Trade', *World Bank Economic Review*, **1**, (4), 727–43.

National Economic Development Council (UK) (1982), 'Overseas Investment: Memorandum by the TUC (11)', mimeo; 'Direct Inward Investment: Memorandum by the Secretary of State (7)', mimeo.

Neilson, W.A. (1973), *The Australian Regulation of Foreign Direct Investment: Recent Experience Relevant to Canadian Policies*, Report for the Ontario Select Committee on Economic and Cultural Nationalism, Toronto: Queen's Printer for Ontario.

Nelson, R.N. and S.G. Winter (1982), 'The Schumpeterian Tradeoff Revisited', *American Economic Review*, March, **72**, (1), 114–32.

Netherlands, Ministry of Economic Affairs (no date, probably 1979), *Business Entities and Company Law in the Netherlands*.

New Zealand, Overseas Investment Commission (1980), *A Guide for Investors*, Wellington.

New Zealand, Reserve Bank (May 1980), 'New Zealand Economy Information', mimeo.

—— (1981), *Foreign Investment in New Zealand*, Supplement to Reserve Bank of New Zealand Bulletin, November.

—— (1987a), 'Overseas Investment in New Zealand', April, mimeo.

—— (1987b), 'Foreign Investment in New Zealand', June, mimeo.

Niehans, J. (1977), 'Benefits of Multinational Firms for a Small Parent

Economy: The Case of Switzerland', in T. Agmon and C.P. Kindleberger (eds), *Multinationals from Small Countries*, 1–47.

Noreng, O. (1980), *The Oil Industry and Government Strategy in the North Sea*, London: Croom Helm.

Norway, Industry Department (1974–5), *Utenlandske eierinteressen i norsk naeringsliv*, St. prp. nr. 1 *(Foreign Ownership Interests in the Norwegian Economy)*, pp. 14-20 especially, Oslo.

O'Farrell, P.N. (1980), 'Multinational Enterprises and Regional Development: Irish Evidence', *Regional Studies*, **14**, (2), 141–50.

O'Farrell, P.N. and B. O'Loughlin (1980), 'Risk Analysis of New Industry Linkages in Ireland', Dublin: Industrial Development Authority.

O'Hagan, J.W. and K.Y. McStay (1981), *The Evolution of Manufacturing Industry in Ireland*, Dublin: Helicon Limited, Confederation of Irish Industry.

O'Loughlin, B. and P.N. O'Farrell (1980), 'Foreign Direct Investment in Ireland: Empirical Evidence and Theoretical Implications', *The Economic and Social Review*, **11**, (3), 155–85.

O'Malley, E.J. (1980), *Industrial Policy and Development: A Survey of Literature from the Early 1960s*, Dublin: National Economic and Social Council.

Okimoto, D.I. (1987), 'Outsider Trading: Coping with Japanese Industrial Organization', in K.B. Pyle (ed.), *The Trade Crisis: How Will Japan Respond?*, Seattle, Washington: Society for Japanese Studies.

Okita, S. and T. Miki (1967), 'Treatment of Foreign Control: A Case Study for Japan', in J.H. Adler (ed.), *Capital Movements*, London: Macmillan.

Olson, M. (1965), *The Logic of Collective Action*, Cambridge, Mass.: Harvard University Press.

—— (1982), *The Rise and Decline of Nations*, New Haven: Yale University Press.

Oman, C. (1984), *New Forms of International Investment in Developing Countries*, Paris: OECD.

Onida, F. and G. Viesti (eds) (1988), *The Italian Multinationals*, London: Croom Helm.

Ontario (1988), *Competing in the New Global Economy*, vol. 1, Toronto: Report of the Premier's Council.

Organization for Economic Co-operation and Development (OECD) (1961), *Code of Liberalization of Capital Movements*, Paris.

—— (1976), *Declaration on International Investment and Multinational Enterprises*, Paris.

—— (1978), *National Treatment for Foreign-Controlled Enterprises Established in OECD Countries*, Paris.

—— (1979), *International Direct Investment: Policies, Procedures and Practices in OECD Member Countries*, Paris.
—— (1981), *Recent International Direct Investment Trends*, Paris.
—— (1982), *Controls and Impediments Affecting Inward Direct Investment in OECD Member Countries*, Paris.
—— (1983), *Investment Incentives and Disincentives and the International Investment Process*, Paris.
—— (1985a), *National Treatment for Foreign-Controlled Enterprises*, Paris.
—— (1985b), *OECD Economic Surveys: Ireland*, Paris.
—— (1985c), *Structural Adjustment and Multinational Enterprises*, Paris.
—— (1987a), *Recent Trends in International Direct Investment*, Paris.
—— (1987b), *Controls and Impediments Affecting Inward Direct Investment in OECD Member Countries*, Paris.
—— (1987c), *OECD Economic Surveys: Ireland*, Paris.
—— (1989a), *Industrial Policies in OECD Countries: Annual Review 1989*, Paris.
—— (1989b), *Investment Incentives and Disincentives: Effects on International Direct Investment*, Paris.
—— (1990), *The 1990 Review of the OECD 1976 Declaration and Decisions on International Investments and Multinational Enterprises*, Paris.
Orr, D. (1975), 'The Industrial Composition of U.S. Exports and Subsidiary Sales to the Canadian Market: Comment', *American Economic Review*, **65**, 230–34.
Ostry, S. (1990), *Governments and Corporations in a Shrinking World: Trade and Innovation Policies in the United States, Europe and Japan*, New York: Council on Foreign Relations.
Ozawa, T. (1979), *Multinationalism, Japanese Style: The Political Economy of Outward Dependence*, Princeton: University Press.
—— (1981), 'Technology Transfer and Japanese Economic Growth in the Post-War Period', in R. Hawkins and A.J. Prasad (eds), *Technology Transfer and Economic Development*, Greenwich, Conn.: JAI Press.
—— (1985), 'Japan', in J. Dunning (ed.), *Multinational Enterprises, Economic Structure and International Competitiveness*.
Parry, T.G. (1983), 'Arguments For and Against Foreign Investment in Australia', Canberra: Parliament of the Commonwealth of Australia, Legislative Research Service, Report No. 6.
Parry, T.G. and J.F. Watson (1979), 'Technology Flows and Foreign Investment in the Australian Manufacturing Sector', *Australian Economic Papers*, June, 103–17 and Appendix.
Paterson, R.K. (1975a), 'Legal Controls on Foreign Investment in New Zealand', *Australian Business Law Review*, March, **3**, (1), 76–86.

—— (1975b), 'Legal Restrictions on Foreign Investment in New Zealand', *Journal of World Trade Law*, March/April, **9**, 177–205.

Pearce, R.D. (1989), *The Internationalisation of Research and Development by Multinational Enterprises*, London: Macmillan.

Pearl, A. (1972), 'Liberalization of Capital in Japan', Parts I and II, *Harvard International Law Review*, 13.

Peltzman, S. (1976), 'Toward a More General Theory of Regulation', *Journal of Law and Economics*, **19**, 211–40.

Penrose, E. (1956), 'Foreign Investment and the Growth of the Firm', *Economic Journal*, **66**, 220–35.

—— (1969), 'BP and the Yankee Market', *New Statesman*, 21 November, 720.

Pettersson, E. (1983), *Naringspolitiska effekter av internationella investeringar* (Effects of International Investments on Economic Policies, English Summary pp. 19–28), Stockholm: Statens offentliga utrednigar, Industridepartementet.

Porter, M.E. (1980), *Competitive Strategy*, New York: Free Press.

—— (1990), *The Competitive Advantage of Nations*, New York: Free Press.

Poynter, T.A. (1985), *Multinational Enterprises and Government Intervention*, London: Croom Helm.

Pugel, T.A. (1985), 'The United States', in J.H. Dunning (ed.), *Multinational Enterprises, Economic Structure and International Competitiveness*, ch. 2.

Rainelli, M. (1984), 'Pouvoirs Publics et Firmes Multinationales: l'Exemple Français', *Revue d'Economie Politique*, **4**, 491–502.

Reddaway, W.B. in collaboration with S.J. Potter and C.T. Taylor (1968), *Effects of U.K. Direct Investment Overseas: Final Report*, Cambridge: Cambridge University Press.

Reserve Bank of Australia (1980), *Exchange Control*, Sydney.

Reuber, G. *et al.* (1973), *Private Foreign Investment in Development*, Oxford: Clarendon Press.

Robinson, R. (1976), *National Control of Foreign Business Entry*, New York: Praeger Publishers.

Robson, P. (1984), *The Economics of International Integration*, London: George Allen and Unwin.

Rodrik, D. (1987), 'The Economics of Export-Performance Requirements', *Journal of Economics*, **102**, 633–50.

Root, F.R. and A.A. Ahmed (1978), 'The Influence of Policy Instruments on Manufacturing Direct Foreign Investment in Developing Countries', *Journal of International Business Studies*, Winter, 81–93.

Rowling, W.E. (1975), 'The Aims and Operation of Foreign Investment Policy', in Carey (ed.), *Foreign Investment Policy in New Zealand*.

Ruane, F. (1979), 'Project Analysis and Industrial Employment in Ireland',

Quarterly Economic Commentary, Dublin: Economic and Social Research Institute, June.
—— (1980), 'Optimal Labour Subsidies and Industrial Development in Ireland', *Economic and Social Review*, **11**, (2), 77–98.
Ruane, F.P. and A.A. John (1984), 'Government Intervention and the Cost of Capital in Irish Industry', *Economic and Social Review*, October.
Rugman, A.M. (1981a), *Inside the Multinationals: The Economics of Internal Markets*, New York: Columbia University Press.
—— (1981b), 'Research and Development by Multinational and Domestic Firms in Canada', *Canadian Public Policy*, Autumn, 604–16.
—— (1982), *New Theories of the Multinational Enterprise*, London: Croom Helm.
—— (1987a), 'Canadian Foreign Direct Investment', in Safarian and Bertin (eds), *Multinationals, Governments and International Technology Transfer*.
—— (1987b), *Outward Bound: Canadian Direct Investment in the United States*, Toronto and Washington: Canadian–American Committee.
—— (1991), 'Diamond in the Rough', *Business Quarterly*, **55**, (3), 61–4.
Rugman, A.M. and A.O. Anderson (1987), *Administered Protection in America*, London and New York: Routledge/Croom Helm.
Rugman, A.M. and A. Verbeke (1990), *Global Corporate Strategy and Trade Policy*, London and New York: Routledge.
Safarian, A.E. (1964), 'The Exports of American-Owned Enterprises in Canada', *Papers and Proceedings of American Economic Association*, May.
—— (1966), *Foreign Ownership of Canadian Industry*, Toronto: McGraw-Hill.
—— (1978), 'Policy on Multinational Enterprises in Developed Countries', *Canadian Journal of Economics*, November, 114.
—— (1979), 'Foreign Ownership and Industrial Behaviour: A Comment on J.N.H. Britton and J.M. Gilmour "The Weakest Link"', *Canadian Public Policy*.
—— (1983a), *Governments and Multinationals: Policies in the Developed Countries*, Washington, DC: British-North American Committee.
—— (1983b), 'Trade-Related Investment Issues', in W.R. Cline (ed.), *Trade Policy in the 1980s*, Washington, DC: Institute for International Economics.
—— (1985a), *Foreign Direct Investment: A Survey of Canadian Research*, Montreal: The Institute for Research on Public Policy.
—— (1985b), 'Government Control of Foreign Business Investment', in J. Whalley (ed.), *Domestic Policies in the International Economic Environment*, Toronto: University of Toronto Press.
—— (1985c), 'FIRA and FIRB: Canadian and Australian Policies on For-

eign Direct Investment', Toronto: Ontario Economic Council, Discussion Paper Series.

—— (1988), 'The Canada-U.S. Free Trade Agreement and Foreign Direct Investment', Toronto: C.D. Howe Institute, Trade Monitor.

—— (1991a), 'Foreign Direct Investment and International Cooperative Agreements: Trends and Issues', paper to a Canada–Germany Symposium, *Competitive Policy in an Interdependent World Economy*, Institut für Wirtschaftsforschung, Hamburg, mimeo.

—— (1991b), 'Direct Investment Strategies and the Canada–U.S. Free Trade Agreement', in C.W. Reynolds, L. Waverman and G. Bueno (eds), *The Dynamics of North American Trade and Investment*, Stanford, California: Stanford University Press, 147–65.

—— (1991c), 'Firm and Government Strategies in the Context of Economic Integration', in B. Bürgenmeier and J.-L. Mucchielli (eds), *Multinationals and Europe 1992*.

Safarian, A.E. and G.Y. Bertin (eds) (1987), *Multinationals, Governments and International Technology Transfer*, London: Croom Helm.

Sakamoto, H. (1989), 'Japan's Outward and Inward FDI', UN Centre on Transnational Corporations, *The CTC Reporter*, Spring.

Savary, J. (1984), *French Multinationals*, Geneva: Institute for Research and Information on Multinationals (first published as *Les Multinationales Françaises*, Paris: IRM, 1981).

Sawyer, M. (1976), 'Income Distribution in OECD Countries', Occasional Study, Paris: OECD Department of Economics and Statistics.

Scherer, F.M., A. Beckenstein, K. Kaufer and R.D. Murphy, with F. Bougeon-Maassen (1975), *The Economics of Multiplant Operation: An International Comparisons Study*, Harvard Economic Studies, no. 145, Cambridge, Mass.: Harvard University Press.

Schlupp, F. (1985), 'Macroeconomic Data on Foreign Direct Investment', *CTC Reporter*, **20**, Autumn, 52–5.

Schultz, R. (1979), *Federalism and the Regulatory Process*, Ottawa: Institute for Research on Public Policy.

Schultz, R., F. Swedlove and K. Swinton (1980), 'The Cabinet as a Regulating Body: The Case of the Foreign Investment Review Act', Ottawa: Economic Council of Canada, Regulatory Reference Working Paper 6.

Schultze, C.L. (1983), 'Industrial Policy: A Dissent', *The Brookings Review*, Fall, (2), 1, 3–12.

Sekiguchi, S. and K. Matsuba (1975), 'Direct Foreign Investment in Japan', *Japanese Economic Studies*, **4**, (1).

Servan-Schreiber, J.J. (1968), *The American Challenge*, New York: Atheneum.

Sexton, M. (1974), 'Regulation of Direct Foreign Investment: A Case of

Delayed Reaction in Australia and Canada', *Australian Business Law Review*, **2**, (4), 241–69.

—— (1979), 'Regulation of Transnational Corporations in Australia and New Zealand', University of New South Wales, mimeo.

Sexton, M. and A. Adamovich (1981), *The Regulation of Foreign Investment in Australia*, Sydney: C.C.H. Australia Limited.

Sharp, Mitchell (1972), 'Canada-U.S. Relations: Options for the Future', *International Perspective*, Special Issue, Autumn, Ottawa: External Affairs Canada.

Sheldon, M.H. (1976), 'United Kingdom', *International Business Lawyer*, **4**, 11.

Sheridan, K. (1975), 'Business Performance of American and British Affiliated Firms in Australia', *Economic Record*, **51**, (136), 549–63.

Sleuwaegen, L. (1988), 'Multinationals, The European Community and Belgium: Recent Developments', in J. Dunning and P. Robson (eds), *Multinationals and the European Community.*

Smith, K. (1981), Review of Noreng, O. (1980), 'The Oil Industry and Government Strategy in the North Sea', *Economic Journal*, **91**, (363), September, 765–7.

Smith, Malcolm (1983), 'The Internationalization of the Japanese Economy: The Legal Framework', paper to a Conference of the Institute of International Relations and the Institute for Research on Public Policy, Vancouver: June, mimeo.

Statistics Canada, *System of National Accounts, Quarterly Estimates of the Canadian Balance of International Payments*, cat. no. 67–001, various issues.

——, *System of National Accounts, Canada's International Investment Position*, cat. no. 67-203, various issues.

——, (1991), *Canada's Balance of International Payments, Historical Statistics 1926 to 1990*, cat. no. 67–508.

Stegemann, K. (1989), 'Policy Rivalry Among Industrial States: What Can We Learn From Models of Strategic Trade Policy?' *International Organization*, **43**, (1), Winter, 73–100.

Steuer, M.D. *et al.* (1973), *The Impact of Foreign Direct Investment on the United Kingdom*, London: HM Stationary Office, for Department of Trade and Industry.

Stevenson, G. (1976), *The Control of Foreign Direct Investment in a Federation: Canadian and Australian Experience*, Sydney: University of Sydney, Transnational Corporations Research Project.

Stewart, J. (1985), 'Aspects of the Financial Behaviour of Multinational Companies in Ireland', in J. Fitzpatrick and J. Kelly (eds), *Perspectives on Irish Industry*, Dublin: Irish Management Institute.

Stigler, G.J. (1971), 'The Theory of Economic Regulation', *Journal of Economics and Management Science*, **2**, (1), 3–21.

Stonehill, A. (1965), *Foreign Ownership in Norwegian Enterprises*, Oslo: Central Bureau of Statistics.

Stopford, J.M. and L. Turner (1985), *Britain and the Multinationals*, Chichester: John Wiley.

Stopford, J.M. and J.H. Dunning (1983), *Multinationals: Company Performance and Global Trends*, London: Macmillan.

Stopford, J.M. and L.T. Wells, Jr. (1972), *Managing the Multinational Enterprise: Organization of the Firm and Ownership of the Subsidiaries*, New York: Basic Books.

Stykolt, S. and H.C. Eastman (1960), 'A Model for the Study of Protected Oligopolies', *Economic Journal*, **70**, 336–47.

Sutch, W.B. (1972), *Takeover New Zealand*, Wellington: A.H. and A.W. Reed.

Sweden (1975), 'Internationella koncerner: industrialänder' (Commission chaired by Lars Lindberger), Stockholm: SOU 1975, 50.

—— (1978), 'Kontrol av Ütländsk företagsetablering: i Sverige m.m.' ('Control of the Establishment of Foreign Companies in Sweden', Commission chaired by Per Ekkerberg), Stockholm: SOU 1978: 73 (Chapter 2 is a summary in English).

—— (1983), 'Näringspolitiska effecter av internationella investeringar', (vol. 6, 'Effects of International Investments on Economic Policies', deliberations of the Committee on Direct Investment, chaired by Eric Petterssen), Stockholm: SOU 1983: 17, pp. 19–28, summary in English.

Swedenborg, B. (1979), *The Multinational Operations of Swedish Firms: An Analysis of Determinants and Effects*, Stockholm: Industrial Institute for Economic and Social Research.

—— (1985), 'Sweden', in J.H. Dunning (ed.), *Multinational Enterprises, Economic Structure and International Competitiveness*.

Teece, D.J. (1977), 'Technology Transfer by Multinational Firms: The Resource Cost of Transferring Technological Know-How', *Economic Journal*, **87**, 242–61.

—— (1981), 'The Market for Know-How and Efficient International Transfer of Technology', Annals of the American Academy of Political and Social Science, 458.

Telesio, P. (1979), *Technology Licensing and Multinational Enterprises*, New York: Praeger Publishers.

Theofilopoulou, A. (1989), 'Disclosure of Information on FDI on the United States', *The CTC Reporter*, **27**, 54–6.

Thomas, J.C. (1983), 'Conflict over Extraterritorial Application of United States Antitrust Law: A Canadian Perspective', paper to a conference of the UBC Institute for International Relations and the Institute for Research on Public Policy, Vancouver, mimeo.

Tolchin, M. and S. Tolchin (1988), *Buying into America: How Foreign Money is Changing the Face of our Nation*, New York: Time Books.

Trebilcock, M.J., J.R.S. Prichard, D.G. Hartle and D.W. Dewees (1982), *The Choice of Governing Instrument*, Ottawa: Economic Council of Canada.

United Nations (1978), *Transnational Corporations in World Development: a Re-Examination*, New York: UN.

—— (various years), *National Legislation and Regulations Relating to Transnational Corporations*, New York: Centre on Transnational Corporations.

—— (1983), *Salient Features and Trends in Foreign Direct Investment*, New York: Centre on Transnational Corporations.

—— (1988), *Transnational Corporations in World Development: Trends and Prospects*, New York: UN Centre on Transnational Corporations.

—— (1989), 'The Impact of 1992', *CTC Reporter*, Spring, 21–4.

—— (1991), *World Investment Report: The Triad in Foreign Direct Investment*, New York, UN Centre on Transnational Corporations.

US Department of Commerce (1953–4), *Factors Limiting U.S. Investment Abroad*, Part I, Survey of Factors in Foreign Countries; Part II, Business Views on the U.S. Government's Role.

—— (1978), 'Incentives and Performance Requirements for Foreign Direct Investments in Selected Countries'. Staff Economic Report, Bureau of International Economic Policy and Research, mimeo.

—— (1981), *US Direct Investment Abroad, 1977*, Washington, DC: US Department of Commerce.

—— (1985), *US Direct Investment Abroad, 1982*, Washington, DC: US Department of Commerce.

US Department of the Treasury (1978), 'Trade Between Japan and the United States: The Setting, the Current U.S. Position and U.S. Prospects. A Report by the Boston Consulting Group K.K.', Tokyo, mimeo.

US House of Representatives (1979), (1981–2), *Federal Response to OPEC Country Investments in the United States*, Hearings before the Subcommittee on Commerce, Consumer, and Monetary Affairs of the Committee on Government Operations. July 30, 1979; October 20 and 22, November 24, and December 9, 1981; and April 6, 1982, 97th Congress, Washington, DC: US Government Printing Office.

—— (1980), *The Adequacy of the Federal Response to Foreign Investment in the United States*, Twentieth Report by the Committee on Government Operations, 96th Congress, 2nd Session Report No. 96-1216, Washington, DC: US Government Printing Office.

—— (1981), *Reciprocity in Investment*, Hearings before the Subcommittee on Consumer Protection and Finance of the Committee on Interstate and Foreign Commerce, August 19 and September 9, 1980, 96th Congress, 2nd Session, Washington, DC: US Government Printing Office.

US Presidential Commission on International Trade and Investment Policy (1971), *Report, Papers I and Papers II*, Washington, DC.

US Senate (1973–5), Hearings before the Subcommittee on Multinational Corporations of the Committee on Foreign Relations, Parts I–II of 93rd and 94th Congress.

—— (1975), Hearings Before the Subcommittee on Securities of the Committee on Banking, Housing and Urban Affairs, 94th Congress, *The Regulation of Direct Investment in Australia, Canada, France, Japan and Mexico*, Washington, DC: US Government Printing Office.

—— (1977), Report of the Committee on Banking, Housing and Urban Affairs, 95th Congress, *Foreign Corrupt Practices and Domestic and Foreign Investment Improved Disclosure Acts of 1977*, Washington, DC: US Government Printing Office.

—— (1982), Hearings before the Subcommittee on International Economic Policy of the Committee on Foreign Relations, 97th Congress, *U.S. Policy Toward International Investment*, July 30, September 28, and October 28, 1981, Washington, DC: US Government Printing Office.

US Tariff Commission (1973), *Implications of Multinational Firms for World Trade and Investment and for U.S. Trade and Labor*, Report to the Committee on Finance, US Senate, Washington, DC: Government Printing Office.

Vahlne, J.-E. (1983), 'Foreign Direct Investments: A Swedish Problem', in Goldberg (ed.), *Governments and Multinationals*, 207-17.

Vaitsos, C.V. (1970), 'Bargaining and the Distribution of Returns in the Purchase of Technology by the Developing Countries', *Bulletin of the Institute of Development Studies*, **3**, 16–23.

Van Den Bulcke, D. (1983), 'Belgian Industrial Policy and Foreign Multinational Corporations: Objectives versus Performance', in Goldberg (ed.), *Governments and Multinationals*.

—— (1985), 'Belgium', in J.H. Dunning (ed.) *Multinational Enterprises, Economic Structure and International Competitiveness*.

Van Den Bulcke, D. and E. Halsberghe (1976), *Employment Effects of Multinational Enterprises. A Belgian Case Study*, Geneva: International Labour Office.

Van Den Bulcke, D., J.J. Boddewyn, B. Martens and P. Klenmmer (1979), *Politiques d'investissement, réductions ou cessations d'activités de multinationales en Europe*, Paris: Presses Universitaires de France.

Vaupel, J.W. and J.P. Curhan (1973), *The World's Multinational Enterprises: a Sourcebook of Tables*, Boston: Harvard University Graduate School of Business Administration.

Vernon, R. (1971), *Sovereignty at Bay: The Multinational Spread of U.S. Enterprises*, New York: Basic Books.

—— (1977), *Storm over the Multinationals*, Cambridge, Mass.: Harvard University Press.

—— (1979), 'The Product Cycle Hypothesis in a New International Environment', *Oxford Bulletin of Economics and Statistics*, **41**, 255–6.

—— (1983), 'Organizational and Institutional Responses to International Risk', in R.J. Herring (ed.), *Managing International Risk*, Cambridge: Cambridge University Press.

—— (1985), 'Government Control Over Its Multinational Enterprises: the U.S. Case', Harvard University, Center for Business and Government, June, mimeo.

Viesti, G. (1988), 'Size and Trends of Italian Direct Investment Abroad: A Quantitative Assessment', in F. Onida and G. Viesti (eds), *The Italian Multinationals*, 30–48.

Vogel, E.F. (1979), *Japan as Number One*, Tokyo: Charles E. Tuttle.

Waldmann, R.J. (1980), *Direct Investment and Development in the U.S.: Guide to Incentive Programs, Laws and Restrictions 1980–81*, Washington, DC: Transnational Investments Ltd.

Waverman, L. (1991), 'Strategic Trade Policy and 1992', in B. Bürgenmeier and J.L. Mucchielli (eds), *Multinationals and Europe 1992*.

Weil, F.A. and H.D. Glick (1979), 'Japan: Is the Market Open? A View of the Japanese Market Drawn from U.S. Corporate Experience', *Law and Policy in International Business*, **11**, 3.

Wells, J. Jr. (1986), 'Investment Incentives: an Unnecessary Debate', *UN, CTC Reporter*, **22**, Autumn.

Wilkins, M. (1970), *The Emergence of Multinational Enterprise: American Business Abroad from the Colonial Era to 1941*, Cambridge, Mass.: Harvard University Press.

Williams, G. (1986), *Not for Export: Toward a Political Economy of Canada's Arrested Industrialization*, Toronto: McClelland and Stewart.

Williamson, O.E. (1975), *Markets and Hierarchies: Analysis and Antitrust Implications*, New York: Free Press/Macmillan.

Winters, A. (1988), 'Completing the European Internal Market. Some Notes on Trade Policy', *European Economic Review*, **32**, (7), September, 1477–1500.

World Deal Review (1991), New York: Dixon and Company.

Wunderlich, G. (1976), 'Summary of the Report: Foreign Investment in U.S.

Real Estate', Washington, DC: US Department of Agriculture, Bulletin No. 400.

Yamamura, K. (1986), 'Caveat Emptor: The Industrial Policy of Japan', in P. Krugman (ed.), *Strategic Trade Policy and the New International Economics*, Cambridge, Mass.: MIT Press.

Yanagihara, W. (1976), 'Japanese Enterprises in the Multinational Era', *Economics and Business Review*, May, Kyoto: Sanyo University.

Yoshino, M.Y. (1975), 'Japan as Host to the International Corporation', in I. Frank (ed.), *The Japanese Economy in International Perspective*, 273–90, Baltimore: Johns Hopkins University Press.

Young, S., N. Hood and J. Hamill (1988), *Foreign Multinationals and the British Economy*, London: Croom Helm.

Name Index

Subject Index